MANAGEMENT GUIDE FOR ENGINEERS AND TECHNICAL ADMINISTRATORS

Nicholas P. Chironis
Senior Associate Editor, *Product Engineering* Magazine

McGRAW-HILL BOOK COMPANY   New York   St. Louis   San Francisco
London   Sydney   Toronto   Mexico   Panama

MANAGEMENT GUIDE FOR ENGINEERS AND TECHNICAL
  ADMINISTRATORS

Library of Congress Catalog Card Number 68–8661

10794

1234567890   HDBP   754321069

PREFACE

Sooner or later almost everyone in industry gets caught up in the world of management, becomes enmeshed in its methods of operation, its intricate, almost intangible problems, and its seemingly ruthless games. Engineers, for example, often find themselves thrust almost unwillingly into this world.

Early in his career, the engineer may be simply one of the "troops," doing his often difficult technical job while studiously trying to avoid the interdepartmental politics that invariably arise within an organization, no matter how small. Later on, though, he may find himself serving as a group leader, a department supervisor, or even an upper-echelon executive. That's when he discovers that it pays to know the multitude of management concepts and rules of thumb for working with people and persuading them to carry out tasks.

This book is offered as a guide, counselor, and aid to people in all facets of industry—not only to engineers and their managers but also to plant administrators, production supervisors, designers, draftsmen, and researchers.

A reader who is not already in management will not become a manager just by reading this book. But no one is too young or too old to start learning the management way of life. And engineers in jobs that carry management responsibility enjoy much higher salaries than those confined to technical functions.

This volume is intended to spark ideas that go beyond the daily routine of a technical job. It seeks to give both inspiration and help, to show a reader how to do his work better, more easily, and more enjoyably. It contains a compilation of ideas, proven techniques, and "inside facts" on a wide range of topics, by more than 80 experts—top managers, corporate executives, chief engineers, and others—many of whom are well known in management circles.

Included is information on how to succeed as an administrator, on the factors that lead to satisfaction or dissatisfaction in a department, on how to develop key men, and on how to forge ahead in an organization. There are chapters on engineering organization and relationships, on when and how to develop new products, on techniques for making better decisions, on ways of estimating engineering and product-development costs, on systems for scheduling and controlling projects, on methods of speeding up drafting and reproducing operations, and on procedures for releasing and controlling drawings. Chapters also cover creativity, inventiveness, and patent law; market research; the use of consultants and outside services;

improvement of writing, speaking, and reading abilities; and the area of salaries, ethics, and job satisfaction.

Much of the material comes from *Product Engineering*, but articles have also been drawn selectively from other publications. Acknowledgment is gratefully made to *Industrial Management, American Machinist, Business Week, Chemical Engineering, Design Engineering, Dun's Review, Factory Management and Maintenance, Graphic Science,* and *The SAE Journal*.

Nicholas P. Chironis

CONTENTS

1.

How to Succeed as an Adminstrator

Let's take a new look at the
Engineer as executive

Are "design engineer" and "test engineer" careers? The author contends that they should be merely steps in progress

R. G. MURDICK, *Professor, State University of New York, Albany*

ENGINEERS are expected to perform (often they insist on performing) many kinds of tasks. We see some directing the work of other engineers, technicians, analysts, and clerks. Some perform highly abstract analysis. Some hand-assemble test equipment or perhaps solder circuits on a breadboard. Others work at drafting boards. Many make repetitive calculations with a slide rule or desk calculator. I recently observed a $12,000-per-year engineer set up a heat-balance problem, then spend two days with a slide rule on routine calculations to complete a table of values.

There certainly appears to be a contrast between the nature of engineering work as educators, management, and engineers say it should be, and the nature of engineering work in practice. Engineering has been recognized as a profession and certainly fits the most stringent criteria, as given

1. THE PROMOTION LADDER IN THREE PROFESSIONS

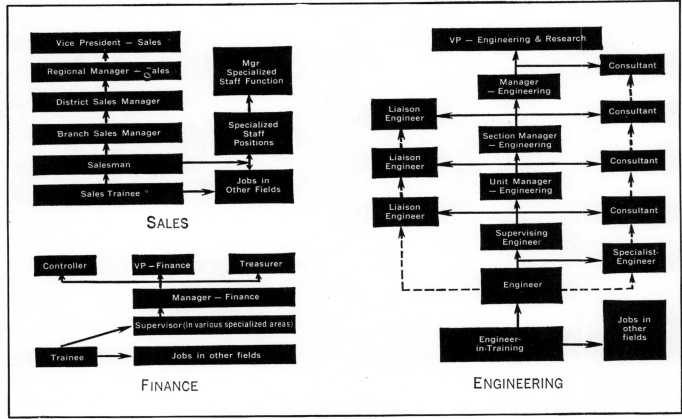

SALES

FINANCE

ENGINEERING

in Fig 3, "Criteria for a Profession." Most importantly, engineering, in common with other recognized professions, requires long, intensive, and specialized training. Consequently, engineering should be in actual practice "predominantly mental" work.

Engineers and employers agree to this concept, yet both accept a contrary situation in practice. What is the source of this paradox? Basically, it seems that careers for engineers have not been defined in the minds of people who hire them. Thus engineers are treated like interchangeable units of labor applied to solve technical problems on a short-term basis. (Short-term may be as long as several years, but this is short-term from a career viewpoint.)

What are the legitimate careers for engineers? Three basic roads "up" for engineers are to the positions of:
1. Manager of engineering
2. Consulting engineer
3. Liaison engineer

A few comments are in order with regard to the roads. First, we are not concerned with goals outside of true engineering. Thus the president may be an engineer, but he is many other things as well. Related or service work requiring an engineering background is not strictly engineering, either. Sales engineer, technical-information specialist, and technical writer or editor are examples, and people in these fields must develop other talents progressively greater than their engineering talents.

When is a career a career?

Note that "design engineer" and "test engineer" are not listed as career goals. When the work a man does at the end of his lifetime employment is much the same as when he started, such a job should not be considered a career goal. It is the failure of many business leaders and educators to recognize this fact which leads them to bewail the shortage of engineering graduates. There is actually a surplus of people with engineering degrees, as is evidenced by the many who are performing clerical and hack technical tasks.

College students have apparently become more sophisticated than employers of engineers, because they discriminate between true career prospects in engineering and potential waste of their talents in a field for which they are not outstandingly suited. The student recognizes that unless he is highly gifted to fit into one of the three careers mentioned above, he would be better off to take his chances elsewhere, despite the lure of high starting salaries.

The engineering career which most closely corresponds to that of the majority of doctors and lawyers is that of the self-employed consulting engineer. But because most engineers are employed by industry, comparison with positions in other business functions is more appropriate (Fig 1). The consulting engineer here is the highly competent specialist who appears at various levels in the engineering organization. He may be the heat-transfer consultant, or, perhaps, materials-application consultant to a section manager, or he may be a high-level consultant such as Glenn Warren, former vice-president of the Turbine Division of General Electric.

The career engineer is an executive regardless of which of the three careers he pursues. It is not his function to spend his time doing repetitive calculations, filing, transcribing data, drafting, drawing graphs, or even performing analyses that lesser-trained technicians can do. The function of the engineer is to conceive, evaluate, and interpret the design of products, to perform complex analyses required

2. THE ENGINEER'S "HANDS"

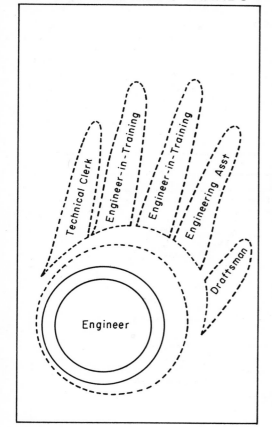

Technical Clerk
Engineer-in-Training
Engineer-in-Training
Engineering Asst
Draftsman
Engineer

3. CRITERIA FOR A PROFESSION

1. Professional work requires application of knowledge obtained in a prolonged formal course of specialized study as distinguished from general academic education and from an apprenticeship.
2. Professional work requires regular exercise of discretion, judgment, and personal responsibility.
3. A member of a profession must be regulated by a national-level association of its members which: a. Establishes minimum levels of skill and knowledge. b. Establishes standards of ethical practice. c. Standardizes terminology. d. Sets policies and procedures. e. Publishes the official journal for the profession. f. Promotes the advancement of the profession.
4. An in-training or internship period (in additional to formal educational requirements) is required before professional status is achieved.
5. Practitioners are expected to extend the knowledge upon which the profession is based.
6. Practitioners make their knowledge and contributions freely available to others in the profession and assume responsibility for assisting and developing the newer members of the profession.
7. Members are required by law to be licensed to practice the profession.
8. The professional man maintains at all times an attitude towards his work and society characterized by:
   a. A social consciousness, a desire to contribute to rather than simply benefit from civilization; a resolve to place the public welfare above other considerations.
   b. Continued acquisition of special skills on a high intellectual plane, generally evaluated by means of self-imposed standards of excellence.
   c. A sense of trusteeship—personal responsibility to protect the employer's interest.
   d. Individual initiative and acceptance of individual responsibility, both of the highest order.
   e. A right to expect and receive adequate financial recognition appropriate to the work performed.

for product development, or to plan and direct test work. In carrying out his function, he requires trained people to act as extensions of his thinking and execution. Instead of having five engineers, say, limited by their own physical ability to do a certain amount of work, one engineer could be doing the creative work which is implemented largely by other people at his direction (Fig 2). Furthermore, when the engineer is given people to assist him, it should be because the work assigned is great enough to keep everyone working at full capacity.

The new engineering graduate would not normally step into the position of executive. Rather, he serves as an engineer-in-training for a period of six months to two years. (This corresponds to the licensing concepts in most States.) He is then given more responsible jobs and provided with the assistance required to implement his ideas. Fig 4 shows how his function grows by stages. Only enough engineers are needed, and hired, to fill executive positions. Gone would be the all-too-common sight of engineers 50 to 60 years old sitting in a corner refining the design of the same products they designed 30 years before at a salary which has remained about the same. Individuals not suited for advancement from engineer-in-training are advised promptly to try some other career. The proper concept of engineering as complex mental work would be maintained.

The three basic engineering careers may be expressed in terms of this concept of the engineer as an executive. The engineer who climbs the managerial ladder is really an engineer-business-executive. He must be concerned with the quality and the economics of the engineering work in terms of company business objectives. At the same time, he must provide some technical leadership; he cannot be said to have "laid down his slide rule" regardless of his level in the organization.

By redefining the engineer as an executive, we have established the position of "engineer" as a career. Whereas, in present practice, "design engineer" refers to the lifetime lone operator doing everything himself, the new concept presents "design engineer" as the individual who grows in expertness and ability in his field because he has technical/clerical support and can devote himself to his work at its highest level. In this new concept, it is not implied that the individual must climb high in one of the three avenues of endeavor, but merely that he reach the level where he is doing professional work.

The consultant-executive

The engineer who elects to follow the career of consultant is actually a consultant-technical executive. He will always be a solver of technical problems, yet if he is to grow in his ability to solve larger and more complex problems, he must have technical assistance. He may need an engineer-in-training to set up his mathematical formulations for solution by electronic computers. He may use a technical clerk to prepare graphs and make routine calculations. If he is engaged in the preparation of general specifica-

tions for new processes and materials, he may need considerable secretarial help. These services should be made available when he needs them. He should not have to spend his time searching for this assistance, begging some manager to lend him people when they have a little free time. It is just as logical to schedule the assignment of personnel to consultants as it is to schedule their assignment to a project manager.

The liaison engineer

The liaison engineer faces the same problem as the consultant, but to a much lesser degree. The liaison engineer is likely to have varying and sometimes heavy loads of correspondence to conduct and files to maintain. The liaison engineer is the engineer-business staff executive. He assists line management with the function of co-ordination, either entirely between two engineering groups or between an engineering organization and some other organization such as production, sales, customer, vendor, or Government agency.

It is simply economic common sense for employers of engineers to seek and retain only those people who are suited for careers in engineering. The technical knowledge and creativity of the engineer can only be exploited fully if he is given the extensions required to implement his ideas. Rather than hiring large number of engineers to solve problems by trampling them to death, employers should be seeking to develop more skilled technical people of all kinds to assist the engineer in his work. ■

4. HOW THE ENGINEER MAY DEVELOP

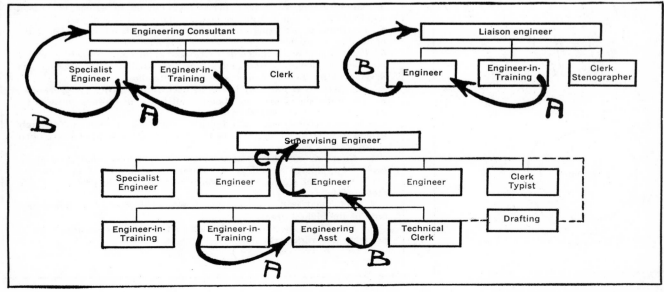

You'll need new skills, viewpoints
What it is to be a boss

Most engineers think sooner or later of switching from technical work to a managerial position. Are you? If so, here's what you can expect.

ROGER K CRANE, chief engineer, American Technical Co

ABOUT THE AUTHOR

Our question to Roger Crane about his career brought this cogent statement: "I'm a graduate engineer with an ME degree who has worked in product engineering, power plants, hydraulic systems, etc. About five years ago I got into management and went through much of the experience described in the article. Since then things have been easier. For the last several years I've done management consulting for a variety of technically oriented firms."

YOU, and only you, can answer the question: Should I switch from engineering to management? To answer it accurately you must know yourself. You must know what you want in life, where you want to go, how much effort you're willing to put into your career.

Suppose you do change to management. What new problems will you meet? What new skills must you develop? How will your rewards compare with those for a job well done in engineering? Let's see:

Specific to general

In engineering you work with specifics—weight, length, height, pressure, force. In management you work with generalities—supervision, arbitra-

tion, sales, delegation, negotiation. Engineering has its neat slide rule, graph paper, handbooks, laboratory tests, and formulas. After a few years you become a specialist in one or two areas. These become comfortable, well-defined boundaries which give you satisfaction and a livelihood, and allow you to contribute to technology. You always know where you stand because you can measure results accurately. And you can be as exact as you wish. Your tools are known; your theories can be tested and proved by accepted methods.

Management, too, has its tools. But they are crude compared to the precise tools of engineering. Why? Because the problems of management are affected by so many unpredictable variables, human, economic, and political.

So the first difference you'll find between engineering and management is one of specifics vs generalities. In engineering there is almost always an equation you can use or develop. In management there is hardly ever an equation you can apply.

During your first few months in management you'll find yourself trying to plot curves for or to tabulate non-measurable data. After several attempts you'll give up. And then you may say to yourself, as one new engineering manager did, "Everything here is gray; there's no right answer."

That's just it. There isn't any "right" answer. There's only a workable answer that may be right today and wrong tomorrow. Once you real-

ize that, you'll throw away your graphs and tables. You'll mentally balance yourself like a boxer on his toes, ready to change with external conditions. For your world is no longer neatly bounded by slide rules, formulas, and handbooks. Instead it has no real boundary and its elements are constantly changing.

People, people everywhere

In engineering you figured a beam, designed a new machine, or wrote a specification. In management you delegate work, settle disputes, approve expenditures for projects whose outcome is a gamble. But always there are people.

Some engineers work on a project for weeks and have little or no contact with other people. As part of a management team you can hardly work five minutes without dealing with other people. And the people are all kinds: happy, angry, disappointed, engaging, healthy, sick.

You must deal with them in hundreds of ways. You will delegate work, settle disputes, reprimand, explain, answer questions, decide between alternatives. In management you may spend as much as 80% of your time talking with people. It isn't always easy, particularly when you're trying to convince, sway, or influence them.

Probably the most difficult part of changing from engineering to management is learning to cope with the irrational verbal and written demands of outside people. Your first reaction

5

as an engineer will be to search for a logical, factual answer to complaints or insistent demands of someone who has little knowledge of your business. After a few attempts you'll find that a completely logical and factual answer is seldom satisfactory. Why? Because you're dealing with human beings. You'll push your engineering books to the corner of the bookshelf and replace them with a few books on psychology and human relations. Once you do this you're well on your way to becoming an educated manager.

Even some of your managerial associates may puzzle you at first. For instead of operating in accordance with equations, theorems or physical laws, they seem to operate by means of some strange, unseen waves. Actually, there's nothing strange about their ways. These experienced managers are constantly analyzing, judging and evaluating business situations. And they're rapidly altering their opinions, concepts and theories as they meet new situations.

You, too, must learn to think faster. Many of your quick decisions may be wrong. But instead of fretting, as many engineers are inclined to do, you must rectify your decision and go on to your next problem. For in dealing with people instead of facts you seldom have time to spend days and days analyzing a situation. People are often hurried; there's always a phone ringing; someone is impatiently waiting in the lobby to see you.

Your reading will change

Today, as an experienced and skilled engineer, you probably read a dozen or more technical magazines every month. You study all kinds of good articles—design procedures, maintenance operations, new equipment, etc. You're looking for new ways to do a better engineering job. Specific procedures, exact details, and proven values are of greatest importance to you. These are data you need ways to do a better engineering job.

Change to management and you'll alter your reading habits. You'll still read the same magazines, plus a few more, but your attitude toward the subjects will change. Instead of trying to understand every step in a process or procedure, you'll look for the results. Your eye will seek out hourly production rates, costs, manpower needs. You'll mark an article for the assistant chief engineer with: "Jim, please check this process; it might save us some money on the new design." And Jim will check the details while you present the idea to upper-level management.

Personnel columns will mean more to you in management than they did in engineering. You'll seek out the news of promotions, retirements, transfers. Because once again, your main concern is with people and their effect on your firm's business.

You'll read different books. Texts on finance, production, sales, speech-making, patents, inventions, human relations, and publicity will nudge your engineering handbooks and texts aside. You'll seek general methods—not specific procedures. You will begin to operate by "feel" instead of by fixed formulas or rules. The generalist aspects of your character will emerge to take over and push the specialist training of your engineering career into the background.

You'll make speeches

Management solves many of its problems in meetings, conferences, and panels. You'll be called on to speak. In a company meeting you'll be expected to explain, defend, propose, excuse, or present ideas of all kinds. Much of your future will depend on how well you act at these gatherings. For higher-level management will not only be judging your business decisions—they'll also be evaluating you as an individual. So to succeed you'll have to learn how to talk and think on your feet.

The company meeting is not the place for nervousness, slips of the tongue, or immature self-centeredness. So get to know yourself better. Remember that your engineering training is a priceless asset. As an ex-engineer you'll be respected by non-engineering management. They'll look to you for technical opinions, for judgments involving production, design and maintenance. So forget your nervousness; concentrate on what you're saying. But don't try to impress them with your personal intelligence and special education. Slice your opinion to the bone; give results, costs, advantages.

Omit long-winded step-by-step procedures. These take up valuable time. Remember: you are now a generalist, not a specialist. Use these hints and you'll soon see a new you emerging— a valuable and respected you, a real asset on any management team.

You'll also speak in public to audiences of all sizes. And you'll be frightened at first—everyone is. But stick to it. Prepare your speech early; practice long. Get yourself several good books on public speaking. If these don't give you what you want, seek professional advice. Today there are speech-training classes in almost every large city.

Your success as a manager will depend, to a large extent, on your ability to motivate other people. So learning how to speak well before others is one of your most valuable tools. Start developing your speaking skill today.

Your thinking will change

As part of the management team you'll think differently. Instead of being confined to a single engineering project, your viewpoint will be company-wide. Over-all profits and losses will be of extreme importance. Also, the financial performance of your own department will be a daily concern. You'll begin to see how your efforts affect the entire company. To many ex-engineers there is nothing as challenging as guiding a group of people along the path to high profits.

Your methods of thinking will change too. You'll find that you must:
Think of others first
Think ahead of your present problems
Think of many alternatives
Think in terms of selling
Think of new-business sources
Think while listening to others
Think to get to the core of problems quickly
Much depends on your firm, its products, and your new job. But you must realize now that, in many ways,

Do you really want

Management is a treadmill. If you choose to get on, you can't get off until you fall off or reach the end. It means longer hours, a constant condition of overwork, social engagements that are actually business contacts, community committees and boards, **endless details and meetings, dull work like budgets and reports instead of engineering. You'll read and hear much more and enjoy it less, much of it in fields in which you're not now interested. Your loyalties will be fixed—the company comes first—so,**

your thinking must change if you are to succeed in management.

Don't resist these new thinking patterns when they are introduced to you. If you do, you'll be inefficient and the change from engineering to management will be a painful process. Remember—you must wholeheartedly accept your new environment. If you do not put all your energy and skill into the new tasks you face, your road will be rough and full of disappointment. So you must learn to think as a manager.

You'll train people

As part of the management team you'll have the problem of training people for new or different jobs. At first your training duties may be no more than instructing a secretary about her job. But as time passes you may be called on to train people for more responsible positions. When faced with this task you'll begin to realize the importance of right thinking, ability to handle people, and good speaking habits.

Training others can be one of the most gratifying aspects of management. It gives you a chance to pass your experience along to others for their ultimate benefit and the benefit of the company. And the questions and discussions that arise during training sessions will open new vistas of self-knowledge and job skills to you. You will see, more clearly than ever before, that the human factor is the most important single element managers must handle—every day of the year.

Human relations

Many firms now have clinics in human relations for all new management personnel—particularly ex-engineers. The need for these clinics is widely recognized. And there isn't one progressive firm today that overlooks the importance of human relations. Why? Once again, management is primarily

the function of getting the best from people with the least effort and friction. Here are six rules of human relations that will help smooth your switch to management. Start using them today—they'll save you much misery and wasted effort in any job and in your private life.

1. Express and show interest in people and their problems
2. Be as impartial as you can in all dealings with people
3. Treat everyone as an individual
4. Show appreciation whenever it is deserved
5. Be firm and fair in dealing with others
6. Look for what others can do, not for what *you* want

In dealing with people at work, keep their needs foremost in your mind. What do men and women want at work? Studies show that almost all of us want recognition, fair pay, security, good working conditions, agreeable supervisors, a chance to advance, important duties, and treatment as individuals. Keep these needs in view when dealing with other people. They are often the key to vague complaints, poor work, absenteeism, and other problems. As long as you are in management your dealings with people will never end. Cultivate good human relations and you'll solve more problems faster.

Learn how to delegate

To the new manager, the biggest problems of his day are those related to giving orders to others. Orders must be given. But to be effective, your orders must be delivered clearly, concisely and pleasantly. The secret of giving effective orders is to build enthusiasm in the person receiving them. You can't build enthusiasm by giving a lecture, threatening, or shouting. You build job pleasure and willingness in others in two ways: (1) by genuinely feeling this way yourself, and (2) by being friendly and courteous to your

associates at *all* times—not just when giving orders.

Watch the successful managers around you. Most of them are well-liked and happy people. They have a ready grin; they tackle their work with enthusiasm and gusto. Their spirit infects their associates; theirs is a happy "shop". And when they give an order it is carried out quickly and efficiently. So learn now to delegate successfully—you'll find that it will be the most valuable tool in your management kit.

A new creativity for you

In engineering you cracked your mental whip to develop a new machine, solve a knotty vibration problem, or design a new process. The more creative your ideas, the greater your success as an engineer.

Much the same is true in management. But your creativity will run in different channels. Your ingenuity will help you search out the motives of other people; it will take the pulse of economic and political situations. As an engineer you may have neglected financial and business news. As a manager you will be sensitive to the many complex factors that affect your business. And the creative efforts you give to your job will include these complex elements, in addition to any technical factors you must consider. The challenge of management will open a whole new field to your mind. It will stimulate and exhilarate you much like a challenging engineering problem.

Morale will mean more

Morale on engineering projects varies considerably. In some firms the morale is high at the start of a new project. As work progresses, there may be a loss of interest; sometimes there is a tedious atmosphere about the whole effort.

This may not occur in management. Here there is a steady push, a constant grappling with new and changing problems. So your morale may stay on a higher plane. And to get the best from your associates you'll try to build their morale. In doing this your own enthusiasm will increase. The atmosphere will continuously stimulate you to better effort, higher efficiency, and greater skills. ■

to be a big shot ?

in providing your wife and children with a "better life," you'll be subtracting an increasing amount of yourself for travel and officer overtime. Your neck is always out and the competitive axe is sharp—from above, below, and both sides. You can't be affable or

likable to your employes. You'll be constantly insecure because of politics, have to take sides in obscure situations, have to be restless and bullheadedly persistent. If these things, the money and the status attract you, go ahead—and luck! —ED

What makes a good manager?

by Dr. F. Couey, management consultant

The manager is one who gets work done through other people. But in moving from the status of employee to that of a manager, one of the most important and difficult things to do is to stop doing the work yourself. It is necessary to find ways to get others to do it, and to get them interested in doing it. Since the supervisor must work through other people, it follows that he must have their support and interest.

There are eight major activities in the role of the manager:

Staffing

The manager needs to select people who can do the work assigned to his unit, and he needs to select people who will fit into the work group. If he gets people who are unable to do the work, for any reason, the unit will not be able to produce. If he gets people who are not appropriate to the group, he will have adjustment problems which he may or may not be able to resolve.

Organization

The manager must schedule work and work flow so that lost time is minimized and so that production fits in with the requirements of other organizational units in the business. He must use his own time so that he can devote attention to developing controls over production, and to creating a good work organization.

Personnel development

The manager identifies possibilities for employees in his unit to improve their present skills and status, and to be promoted when eligible. He observes and studies his group, and confers with employees to develop plans for their growth.

Planning

The manager plans the work of his unit carefully. He understands and applies the basic principles of management — unity of command, span of control, co-ordination, and delegation of authority. He interprets policies and makes decisions. He recognizes both upward and downward needs for this kind of information, and is able to transmit information to his superior, as well as to employees in his unit.

Communicating

The manager not only understands the principles of good communication, and applies them in his day-to-day work, but also knows the relation of communication to change, and to resistance to change. He uses communications skills in giving orders and in developing a work unit in which employees and manager work together.

Standards

The manager knows how to simplify work procedures without sacrificing performance standards, and how to get the work group to meet higher standards. He is able to judge performance of individual employees, and to conduct performance appraisal interviews with them.

Training

In line with personnel development, the manager conducts training sessions for employees. For the new employee, he directs training toward the survival level, so that they will be able to survive the probationary period. For longer service employees, he develops supplementary and cross training, so they will know more about the work.

Counselling

The manager acts as friend and adviser to employees in his unit. Through good supervisory methods, he minimizes the development of problems, and helps employees in their adjustment to the company and to the unit. He is able to talk to them about their personal problems, without getting involved too deeply. ■

Attributes

Tolerance

Since all people have faults and shortcomings, it is not good for a supervisor to be a perfectionist. A good leader must be tolerant of a person's shortcomings in the same way that he must respect and recognize each person's strong points.

Ability to Reason

Many managers believe that an argument can be decided on facts alone. However, when a subordinate really believes that he is right, and you know that he is wrong, it may not be adequate to use logical reasoning. In cases like this, it may be necessary to cater to emotions, to "bring people around".

Empathy

The narrow definition of empathy is the capacity to feel what others feel. Empathy should be a spontaneous thing, not something that is consciously turned on and off. One important facet of empathy is saving face for the other fellow, which ties in with the previous point about using emotionally oriented arguments. Few people like to be proved wrong, even when the facts show they are wrong. Hence, some form of face-saving for the subordinate is extremely important to his emotional wellbeing.

Good Emotional Control

The leader who is always losing his temper or showing irritation with people will rarely command the respect of his subordinates. This doesn't mean that the boss can't get mad occasionally and blow off steam. This is only human. But when there is an underlying current of emotionalism between the supervisor and

good managers should possess

by Gerald A. Lessells,
U.S. Industrial Chemicals Company

his people, it quickly undermines any confidence his subordinates may have in him.

Readiness to Give Others Credit

The manager who appears to be always right (even if he **is** always right) generally has difficulty motivating his subordinates to work creatively. So it is well to meet people more than half way in handing out credit for various successes.

Willingness to Listen

Many executives feel that because they are the boss they should do most of the talking. When they do this, subordinates naturally stop speaking up, with the result that the sources of information from down the line dry up and the supervisor becomes ill-informed on important happenings in his area.

Quick to Praise

A good manager will praise his men for a job well done and will blame them by constructive criticism for jobs poorly done. A supervisor should not deliver off-the-cuff criticism that can degrade dignity.

Quickness to See Good in Others

If a manager does not have this trait, he owes it to himself to develop it by being more optimistic—looking for good points first, not the bad ones.

Recognition of Differences

If the executive recognizes that some of his people are self-confident and optimistic, he should approach them differently than he does others who may lack self-confidence and need to be assured more often. The good super-visor will also try to help these people help themselves to strengthen their weak points; this kind of coaching usually improves work efficiency.

Lack of Suspicion

Mutual trust is extremely necessary to generate confidence in the subordinate. If the supervisor is a cynic and does not believe in people, this will be reflected in poor morale, poor work and a corresponding cynical attitude on the part of his subordinates.

Confidence and Self-assurance

If the leader does not display too much of these traits, they will rub off on his people. The reverse is also true; if a leader does not have self-confidence, his attitude will pervade the group and will be reflected in poor work output.

Flexibility

A good supervisor cannot afford to be inflexible, because he is dealing primarily with people rather than things, ideas or facts. Since people exhibit varying behaviour under different circumstances, flexibility is a must to cope with these changing situations.

Fairness

Interestingly, a manager who is fair a great majority of the time can *occasionally* be extremely unfair and yet be forgiven by his subordinates. The same act committed by a manager who is usually arbitrary and capricious would be met by great resentment. The author can state from experience that the sincere and fair supervisor can even occasionally commit the cardinal sin of bawling someone out in public without arousing undue hostility.

Recognition of Differing Views

The executive must recognize not only that two or more points of view can exist; on occasion, more than one may also be correct. This attribute of a mature supervisor can earn him a great deal of respect from his people.

Good Sense of Humour

Probably the most important part of a good sense of humour is the ability to laugh at oneself. This single attribute can earn mountains of respect for the supervisor in situations where more "scientific" techniques would be to no avail.

Freedom from Prejudice

The antonym of the word "prejudice" is "judgment". Hence, prejudice can be equated with lack of judgment. Certainly the good executive must be free of minority-group prejudice to be fair and effective with a worker from a minority group. Even if this work situation does not exist, it is probable that a supervisor with narrow racial prejudices would have prejudices carrying over into other areas. We *all* have prejudices, but we should continually strive to subjugate them.

Ability for Self-evaluation

A manager can attain a fairly objective view of himself by seeking criticism from others such as his boss, his colleagues, his subordinates. Reading books and taking college courses in the social sciences will also help. If the supervisor can identify his faults and work on them, his value will go up tremendously.

By doing your difficult work when you feel your best—during your peak energy periods—you have time to recover when mental fatigue strikes

How to work more efficiently

Researchers have found that business executives who claim they are fatigued are often only emotionally exhausted not physically tired. A simple formula is available that will help managers solve this

ONE PUZZLING ASPECT about fatigue, which makes it difficult to overcome, is that its causes are not clearly understood.

In investigating fatigue, scientists have explored two main areas. The physiologist is apt to view fatigue in terms of consumption of chemical energy and the production of chemical waste (a pair of tired feet are twin problems in body chemistry). The psychologist is more concerned with discovering the causes and consequences of the *feeling* of tiredness.

Unfortunately, the relation between muscular fatigue and the feeling of tiredness is not obvious. We can become emotionally weary with some jobs after a minimum of physical effort. Conversely, a man may be exhausted—in the physical sense —but watch him run if pursued by a tiger!

Present theories indicate that fatigue is both physical and emotional, the product of a number of factors that operate on the individual at the same time. This nebulous con-

by Auren Uris,
Research Institute of America

clusion unfortunately doesn't give the researcher much to go on in formulating remedies for fatigue.

However, as in many other instances, where theory falters, empirical approaches can yield practical results. There are several things that can be done to minimize the effect of fatigue.

Energy levels—Perhaps you have noticed that some people seem to be able to put out a steady amount of work each day, while others seem to get bogged down at just the point where they need the most energy.

Some clues on how to maximize your personal efficiency is provided by research conducted by Professor Norman R. F. Maier, who has studied the productivity of people at various times of the day. His studies show how the efficiency of the average person in industry and commerce varies during a work day.

Two characteristics should be

noted. First is the warm up period in the morning. Most people seem to require about an hour to build up a full head of steam.

After lunch, however, no warm up period is necessary.

Second characteristic is the fatigue drop—the lowering of working efficiency during the fourth hour of work during both the morning and afternoon. The efficiency curves of some people show a third trend, the end-spurt. This is indicated by an increase in efficiency as a particular goal (usually the end of the day) is approached.

In addition to this daily cycle, research suggests that our over-all efficiency also varies on a longer-term cycle of days, weeks or even months. Various investigators have believed these longer-range cycles are caused by atmospheric conditions, the position of the planets, cosmic rays.

It has also been proposed that men have an internal biological cycle similar to the menstrual cycle of

women that can cause alternating periods of energy and depression. Whatever the basis for these longer cycles, so little is known about them that it is difficult to anticipate them and plan accordingly. Therefore the stress in this article is on the daily cycle, which can be anticipated with greater certainty.

Chart your course—It can pay you to chart your own ups and downs of daily efficiency. Keep a brief record of the times when you have the most physical energy; when fatigue catches up with you; when you feel most mentally alert; when you find it difficult to work.

Over a period of time, you can pinpoint your strong and weak periods. Then arrange your daily routine around your chart. Save the difficult jobs for your high-energy periods, routine tasks for the low points. In this way, you will still be able to compensate for your mental doldrums by filling these times in with assignments that almost do themselves or require little mental effort.

Proper scheduling can also ease the *feeling* of fatigue during various periods. Know which tasks can be set aside temporarily and which ones you should stick with. Nothing can be so fatiguing as the nagging feeling of an unpleasant half-finished task that is hanging over your head. Better get it over with immediately.

In other cases, where there is not a single large unpleasant job to contend with, it may pay to start one assignment, carry it through to a convenient stopping point, and then go on to something else. When you return to the first job, your energy and interest may be renewed. Weariness and boredom are often closely allied.

Common misconceptions—There is a current belief that some people are human dynamos who can keep up a terrific work pace without taking any rest.

That idea is false. Research has shown that all people take rest periods—one way or another. According to industrial psychologists, the choice is not whether you should rest or not, but rather what form your rest will take. The human dynamo type, for example, generally rests by slowing down a bit on routine tasks, taking a little longer than is actually necessary, so that he is resting in a fashion, although no break is apparent in his work pattern.

Generally, you are better off to completely interrupt your regular work activity. Whether you do this by taking a coffee break or by completely relaxing in your chair for a few minutes makes little difference. What is important is to dovetail these rest periods with your overall work schedule so that you take your rest

at the point where your energy has started to drop off.

Research conducted in a munitions plant showed this statement— the longer the work week, the bigger volume of work you are able to turn out—is largely false.

When the work week in the plant began to be cut back from 70 hours, worker productivity began to rise so that the increase in output per hour just about balanced the decrease in total hours worked.

The most effective work week in terms of a worker's output per hour seems to be about 40 hours. The most effective work week in terms of total output appears to be 48-54 hours.

Work conditions—This statement —stale air causes headaches, irritation and fatigue—was proved false in experiments conducted by the New York State Ventilation Commission. A number of people were confined in an airtight chamber filled with stale air. They complained of lassitude, headaches and similar symptoms. But when allowed to breathe fresh air from the outside through tubes, they still complained of the same symptoms. On the other hand, people outside the chamber who breathed the stale air piped to them from inside the chamber showed no ill effects.

Conclusion: stale air is harmful only when it is not circulating and interfers with the regulation of body temperature. Fatigue and other ill effects caused by stale air disappear when the same air is circulated by fans.

The major cause of eye fatigue is not over-use of the eyes. Misuse of the eyes is the chief cause of eye weariness, say the lighting engineers. They stress these points:

Aim at uniform illumination. Uneven lighting on your desk, either glare or shadow, lessens appreciably the time that you can use your eyes without noticing fatigue.

Consider your whole visual field Your eyes have to adjust not only to your work, but to nearby walls and windows. The lighter the colour of your walls, the greater the light reflection and the less unevenness of lighting you get.

Watch the intensity of your light. Several studies show that efficiency improves with greater light intensity —up to the glare point. ■

How to work with others

By E. J. Tangerman

YEARS AGO, I knew a consulting "efficiency expert". He'd study a plant and give pep talks to its foremen. Productivity would increase and management would be pleased with his innovations and pay his high fees. But, a few months later, productivity would drop back into its same old rut. **It wasn't his innovations, but his personality, the breath of fresh air he brought with him, that got my friend results.**

Western Electric discovered the same thing in the famous Hawthorne experiment. Essentially, the company found that improvement in working conditions is fine, but not as important as change. **A major deterrent to productivity is monotony. A little excitement occasionally, even of the wrong sort, is better than constant calm.**

This is a hard lesson to learn, because the usual manager seeks a smooth-running organization with no upsets. He frowns on troublemakers. He is impressed by serious-minded steadiness, by diligence, by apparent attention to the job.

He couldn't be more wrong, unless he's a martinet and his men vent their feelings by hating him. That's the old-fashioned way to run a business—be tough and get yourself cordially hated. **Hatred makes some men work.** I remember two of my old bosses who got me to do outstanding work—just to try to show them up. I also remember best, after all these years, those college professors, who bore down on me hardest. They literally **made** me learn.

In modern business, however, there is no place for the martinet. He is passé even in the military. Today we are expected to arrive at management by sweet reason, and the fewer upsets the better. We're expected to listen to the workers' opinions and be guided by them.

Strangely enough, **there's plenty of evidence to support the statement that the boss who listens—and really hears—is a better boss.**

As a simple example, take the recent test at a farm-machinery company. Supervisors were asked to write their conception of the workers' opinion of them as supervisors, and workers were asked to describe the supervisor. Comparison of results showed that in high-productivity departments, the supervisors had described their workers' opinions quite accurately; in low-productivity departments, they hadn't.

The old concept of a gang leader was that he was admired, respected, even loved, and that's why men did his bidding. But many gang leaders are brutes, feared and hated; the gang just doesn't have the energy to break away. So it is in management, particularly when jobs are scarce—then anybody can hold a group together, even get them to work after a fashion. The problem is to get the work done and done right, fair weather or foul.

The first step in being a leader is to realize that the differences between leader and led are very small. Studies won't show them clearly. One study, for example, compared the accuracy of decisions of leaders and led and found only a percentage point or two of difference. **Thus, have confidence in yourself,** but don't assume you're better or different.

Next, plan what you're doing, and follow through. You've got to know what you're doing or nobody else will. Implement and detail it in your own mind. And don't assume the plan will work out without a hitch. Figure out where difficulties can arise and provide alternatives to handle them. With the solid planning, you can act decisively.

To get things done, you must have two more characteristics: an inquiring mind and stick-to-it-iveness. Never take anything for granted. Give your men responsibility and authority, but discreetly check to see how things are going—at least until you're sure of your men. Don't wait until due date and be caught short if the delegated job isn't done—or is done wrong. Check, just a little, as you go, and remind where necessary. You'll be called an agitator on occasion, but that can't be helped.

Many a good plan or idea fails just because its proponent gives up too easily. Be sure you're right, then go ahead at full speed. If you yield to apparent criticism, lose confidence because someone above you or below you does, anticipate trouble, how can the job be done? **Don't give up easily!**

There are ways to make all this easier. The first is to have some sort of call-up system or inventory so you can work out priorities for jobs, know which to do first, which must be done first, when to check on whom, and so on. A pocket notebook will serve, if you remember to write things in on the proper days, and to read it each morning. **You'll find that some things you're doing can be postponed, some can be forgotten, some change priority because the situation changes.** It's no excuse to be busy if you're busy with the wrong things.

Establish deadlines, not only for total jobs but for each step. Don't delegate a job to an assistant and forget it—put down a note in your little black book that if you haven't the answer or sure knowledge that the job is done by some deadline date, you'll ask about it.

In between times, do your homework. Be sure your plans are made, that you know what steps you'll take in case various possibilities occur. You can get a reputation for being a fast thinker by being a thorough one who remembers the Boy Scout motto to be prepared.

Communication is vital in follow-through. Don't leave it to chance. Decide whether you want to telephone, write, or talk face to face, and think out in advance what you're going to say and how you'll say it, depending on the man. Be sure he gets the message—even if you have to ask him to repeat it as they do in the army.

Lastly, **remember to thank everybody concerned when the job is done.** A pat on the back never hurt anybody, and it makes the next job look better. It isn't enough to hand out perfunctory thanks to the actual worker; remember, too, the others who contributed. And remember longer than an hour or two; some mention of a good job done, weeks or months later, re-establishes the good feeling. ■

Ask yourself this: Have I the human touch?

How you treat people can be all important. Here are some guides

By Auren Uris, Research Institute of America

see questionnaire, next page

PEOPLE are the mind, heart and muscle of the corporation. They can work together in harmony and with effectiveness. Or, disturbed by dissatisfaction and low morale, they can work ineffectively.

The factor that decides how effectively the people in a company function depends largely on their relationships. This fact can be stated in a number of different ways. Some authorities say leadership is the determining factor. Others say it is management's human relations policies and practices that is a key element.

Regardless of which view is taken, there is no doubt that the quality of contacts among the people in an organization can be crucial to its effectiveness and success.

Human relations training for managers, accordingly, has always been high on the list of management development programmes. The fact is, effective human relations practices must exist at every level of management—from the front line up to the very top.

You, as a member of top management, must from time to time assess this area of your executive responsibility. How good are you as a practitioner of the science or art of human relations?

Your capability in this area is crucial because it influences attitudes through all levels of organizational activity.

In general, observers have noted a wide variation in the human relations know-how of top executives. Some company heads definitely have the human touch. Others with outstanding intelligence and an understanding of the technical aspects of their business fail in their human relationships.

This failure almost invariably has a destructive result. Instead of adding to corporate capability, their leadership tends to limit the effectiveness of their companies. Low morale and dissatisfaction among their subordinates tends to filter down to the lower echelons.

Easy Solutions that Fail—Some executives seek to solve their human relations problem by over-simplification. Consider the "charm school approach." Some executives think that as long as they are pleasant and considerate to subordinates, they are doing all that is necessary.

The executive who says good-morning pleasantly to his secretary, asks after the health of his assistant's wife, and inquires as to the weekend golf score of one of his department heads, mistakenly thinks he has solved the problem. His reasoning is not illogical, but it is misguided. He feels he creates an attractive image by spreading his charm and attentiveness among his people. This approach is likely to fail, however, because it is patronizing and paternalistic. Essentially it insults both the intelligence and the integrity of the people who work with him.

"My door is always open."—Other executives solve the problem by assuring their subordinates that they may come in at any time to discuss a problem or a grievance.

But executives who adopt this approach have discovered two things. First that their offer is seldom accepted and, second, when it is, it tends to be for such extreme emergency reasons, that the basic objective of cordial and open communications is usually defeated. As

one subordinate put it bitterly, "Sure, my boss's door is open. That's so he can kick me out when I go in."

A satisfactory human relations approach for the top executive must be based on a realistic appreciation of the psychology and the values that people bring into a working relationship. For example, here are some of the expectations that people bring to their jobs, whether they are vice presidents or truck drivers:

● **Recognition as a person.** A man wants to be treated as an individual, not as a cog in a machine.

● **Fair treatment.** Everybody wants fair treatment. Bias, or the playing of favourites, is always damaging to the executive's reputation for good human relationships.

● **A chance to be heard.** Every employee, regardless of where he stands on the organizational ladder, wants to feel that what he has to say deserves a hearing. This is true whether he has a complaint or wants to make suggestions.

● **The worthiness of his work.** A man wants to feel that he's doing something useful, that his work has value which is appreciated by his superiors.

● **A sense of belonging.** An employee wants to feel that he's accepted by his group and by his superior.

● **The help of leadership.** Everybody wants leadership, the reassurance that an individual with wisdom and impartiality can guide him in his daily and long-range efforts.

The executive whose approach to human relations takes these expectations into consideration is much more likely to be successful than the man who oversimplifies and tries to work out simple and sure-fire formulas.

How are you doing?—It is possible to make an appraisal of one's capability in human relations. The self-rating quiz below is neither a precise nor scientific instrument. But it can shed considerable light on the degree to which one possesses this important ability.

Accordingly, go through the questions below, answering each as accurately as possible. The more closely your answers correspond with the facts, the more useful your score. Directions for rating will be found following the quizes.

The questions are given under three major headings: Man Building, Communications, and Leadership. ■

QUESTIONNAIRE: Have You Got the Human Touch?

Man building

	True	False
1. In building your organization you feel it is desirable for your key people to be generally of the same type, to minimize feuding and conflict.	☐	☐
2. You feel it is desirable that at least your immediate subordinates should have the same values and think as you do.	☐	☐
3. When hiring, it is advisable to pay at least as much attention to a man's ultimate capabilities as to his ability to fill the immediate job at hand.	☐	☐
4. You feel that when you hire a man, you hire his entire family.	☐	☐
5. A good man-building policy may be stated this way: "Hire a good man; turn the job over to him; and leave him alone."	☐	☐
6. It is unwise to help your lieutenants solve their personal problems.	☐	☐
7. You can help people grow by delegating challenging assignments.	☐	☐
8. You delegate a task to a subordinate and he fails. Shortly after, you delegate a similar assignment based on the principle that, "If at first he doesn't succeed, let him try, try again." This is good practice.	☐	☐
9. A subordinate who can "think on his feet" is likely to be your most dependable and creative person.	☐	☐
10. Generally, it is good policy to encourage your lieutenants to develop subordinates who can step into their shoes.	☐	☐

Communications

This category includes the contacts you have with people and your awareness and responsiveness to their needs.

	Yes	No
1. When an employee starts a conversation, do you tend to interrupt, either to correct what he says or to tell him your views?	☐	☐
2. Do you brush aside a subordinate's arguments because you are sure you are right?	☐	☐
3. Are you quick to label a speaker misinformed?	☐	☐
4. Do you prefer talking to listening?	☐	☐
5. Do you go out of your way to establish mutual interests with subordinates—stressing, for example, a sincere interest in his career objectives, an unaffected interest in his personal interests, hopes, and so on?	☐	☐
6. Do you try to keep the communication lines sufficiently open and used so that the times you seek out contacts with subordinates are not something special and ominous?	☐	☐
7. Is it clear to your secretary that whenever a subordinate wants to contact you, he should be given the same consideration as a customer or other person of importance?	☐	☐
8. In the interviews that you have with subordinates, do you try to create a relaxed, unhurried air that helps the man feel at ease and emphasizes your receptivity?	☐	☐

Leadership

The third area of your human relations contacts has to do with the guidance and motivation you supply to your people. Answer each question carefully.

	Yes.	No
1. Do you build mutual respect and liking among your subordinates by avoiding criticism of one individual in another's hearing?	☐	☐
2. Do you help build group morale by: Stressing that each man's job links up with others in the company?	☐	☐
Informing employees of colleagues' needs with which they may be able to help?	☐	☐
Encouraging and praising efforts that show team spirit and a desire to help a colleague?	☐	☐
3. To emphasize the respect you have for a subordinate's capabilities, do you occasionally use *reverse* consultation—that is, consult him on decisions *you* have to make?	☐	☐
4. Do you encourage initiative by praising the performance of the man who displays it?	☐	☐
5. Do you give your people full credit for ideas and suggestions they pass along to you—and do you make the reward tangible where possible?	☐	☐
6. Do you try to encourage your people to make decisions within the area of their responsibility—and possibly, even more difficult, back them up even when a decision may not have worked out perfectly?	☐	☐
7. Do you agree that encouragement can inspire people to perform even beyond their own expectations?	☐	☐

Have you got the human touch? *Continued*

Recommended answers

Man building—Give yourself 10 points for each correct answer. Then rate yourself on the scale that follows answer No. 10.

1. **False.** Such thinking tends to "thin the blood" of an organization. Most companies feel that it is only through cross pollination that new attitudes, new values, and new ideas can be generated.

2. **False.** The top executive surrounded by a group of assenters or "yes" men misses the value of having checks and balances and stimulation to his own thinking.

3. **True.** In these days of rapidly accelerating technology, skills and experience are obsolescing rapidly. When hiring isn't future-minded, its success is often short-lived.

4. **Either answer is correct.** If you are aware of the problem, that is probably enough. Some companies insist on interviewing a wife before hiring her husband for a top position. Other companies feel this to be an invasion of the individual's personal and private life. Whichever view you take on this question, it is advisable that you do so knowingly.

5. **False.** Of course, you should hire a good man and his job should be clearly defined, but it is also essential that he be given at least some broad guidelines and that he keep you informed of how the work is progressing in general. An executive always retains the responsibility for a subordinate's handling of an assignment, no matter how much freedom of action he is given.

6. **Again, either way your answer may be considered correct.** There are certain considerations to keep in mind, however. First, you shouldn't offer help when the individual intends to shift a personal responsibility on to your shoulders. Second, you shouldn't offer advice in a professional area. If a subordinate needs medical or psychiatric or legal counsel, the most you should do is suggest sources for such professional guidance. Third, from time to time in a man's career, the help of a respected superior can be of crucial importance. If your experience and your perspective can help an individual make a constructive career decision, chances are you will be doing both your subordinate and yourself a good turn.

7. **True.** Personnel experts agree that learning by doing is still one of the most effective means of developing a man.

8. **False.** Before the second delegation takes place, it is highly desirable that the reasons for the failure be pinpointed. Unless these can be found and eliminated, a second failure is likely.

9. **False.** It may be obvious to most executives that the statement is untrue. But the fact is many businessmen have a strong bias in favour of the quick-thinking, quick-talking man. However, the wise executive knows that the slow-thinker is often the profound thinker and he gives his less speedy people the time they need in order to produce their ideas, comments, opinions, criticisms and so on.

10. **True.** Even though it's a cliche of management, it is actually a somewhat touchy process. It sometimes suggests to a subordinate that you want to have a ready replacement on hand in case he falls into disfavour. Nevertheless, it is also an obvious requirement for advancement. Where an executive balks at developing a second-in-command for himself, you may have to have a heart-to-heart talk with him to find out the reasons for his insecurity.

90-100: You're an outstanding man-builder.

70-80: Your man-building talents are quite good.

Below 70: Your man-building could use some strengthening.

Communications—**No** is the preferred answer for questions 1-4, **Yes** for 5-8. Give yourself 10 points for each question answered correctly. Then rate yourself on the following scale:

70-80: You're an outstanding communicator.

50-60: You're performing satisfactorily in this difficult area.

Below 50: Your communications are suffering from one or more blocks and inadequacies.

Leadership—Give yourself 10 points for each **Yes**. Then check your score according to the following scale:

80-90: Your leadership is excellent.

70-80: You are a good leader.

Below 70: There is quite a lot of room for improvement. ∎

Knowing how to delegate

Can't be in three places at once? Delegate's the magic word. Take it from a top consultant. He'll save your sanity, make you a better plant executive.

CAPACITY   RESPONSIBILITY

HERE'S A PICTURE of you at work: No matter how good an executive you are, your responsibilities will always be greater than your capacity to carry them out.

That's not a criticism. It's an accepted fact. No one expects the company president personally to produce, package, and sell his product. No one, that is, except an occasional overburdened company president himself.

The encircled man above shows the situation graphically.

Outer circle represents the limit of your responsibility; inner circle, the boundary of your capacity. White area represents work you must delegate to others—your secretary, assistants, subordinates.

Occasionally you'll find a man who refuses to accept this simple fact of executive life. He won't delegate. He'll strive with all his might to push the inner ring outward in an attempt to make the two circles coincide. And he'll complain:

...*"I have to be in three places at once."*

...*"I don't dare take a day off."*

...*"I've got ulcers."*

You'll also find executives who head for trouble in the opposite direction. They over-delegate. You've heard their cry:

"Why doesn't somebody tell me these things!"

By AUREN URIS
Research Institute of America, New York

Adapted from a chapter of author's newest book, "Developing Your Executive Skills." McGraw-Hill Book Company, New York.

The trick of delegation is to concentrate the most important matters within the circle of things you handle yourself. The less important details can be left to others while you give the weightier problems the attention they deserve.

Delegation is a sanity saver for several reasons. It gives you freedom of action, allows you to turn your attention to the areas of your job that need it most. It gives you more time to spend on important long-range planning.

HOW DELEGATION BUILDS A TEAM

But greater efficiency isn't the only motive for delegating a part of your job. Enlargement of a subordinate's job can produce three other important results for him:

...*Develop his sense of responsibility.* You may want to make an assignment purely in the interest of increasing his ability and value to your activity as a whole.

...*Enlarge his general understanding.* For instance, the best way to stress the importance of customer relations for one of your assistants might be to ask him to take over customers' complaints.

...*Increase his job satisfaction.* Some subordinates thrive on varied assignments. Their interest in the job increases along with its responsibility. Delegation of small projects helps maintain their effectiveness as team members.

Used in these ways, delegation is another means of getting employee cooperation.

Properly handled, delegation guarantees that your over-all job will remain in control and that the people working under you will keep moving in the right direction. But there are hazards.

You'd be wrong for example, to assume that delegation is a one-shot affair. You can't delegate and forget. Chief reason is that your responsibilities change. New problems come up, make fresh demands

on your time. You must be ready to review past delegations. You may have to make corresponding changes in tasks you've assigned to others.

WHEN TO DELEGATE

There are specific occasions in the course of your work when delegation is called for. Here, for example, are three instances:

...*When you're overburdened.* It's a safe general rule that you simply can't handle all your responsibilities and still do a good job on the important ones.

...*In emergencies.* Your first thought may be to let everything else drop. Yet the temporary suspension of even a routine matter may leave you with too big a backlog when the crisis is over.

...*In your absence.* It might be a two-week vacation—or a series of conferences. But someone will have to provide minimum authority while you're gone.

As a starter, check up on the time you spend now in: (a) filling out routine reports, requisitions, etc.; (b) making calculations and entries; (c) checking materials and supplies; (d) running your own errands; (e) engaging repeatedly in certain simple, mechanical tasks.

If you can reduce any of these tasks to a matter of final O.K., a signature, or dispatch of a messenger, consider handing them over to some subordinate.

WHEN NOT TO DELEGATE

There's another side to the delegation coin. Just as there are situations for which delegation is a solution, there are circumstances that make it inadvisable.

Delegation can cause trouble if you hand over the wrong duties. Some of your responsibilities are yours for keeps:

...*Power to discipline.* It's the backbone of executive authority.

...*Responsibility for maintaining morale.* You may call upon others to help carry out assignments that will improve morale. You cannot ask anybody else to maintain it.

...*Over-all control.* No matter how extensive the delegations, responsibility for final performance rests on your shoulders.

...*The hot potato.* Don't ever make the mistake of passing one along just to take yourself off the spot.

You must retain some jobs. It's best to hang on to them, if . . .

...*They are too technical.* Computing a floor load or projecting a cost estimate may be routine for you—but may be completely beyond a subordinate's skill.

...*The duty involves a trust or confidence.* For instance, handling confidential cost data, dealing with the personal affairs of one of your people.

To keep things moving at full blast, you may find it necessary at times to delegate duties involving initiative, judgment, and decision. But consider these factors: (a) the duty to be delegated, (b) the ability of the person it will go to, (c) your ability to keep control—that is, to keep posted on progress.

HOW TO DELEGATE

To get the most from delegation, tell your delegate . . .

...*The facts.* Give him a clear picture of what he's to do, how to do it, and how much authority he has with which to get it done. "You never told me" is the sorry epitaph on many a well-meant delegation.

...*The relative importance of the job.* You know how important a job is because you see it in the setting of your whole responsibility. Your delegate can't make the necessary adjustments when he runs into trouble unless you have given him the complete background.

...*Whom he must deal with.* If the assignment will bring him into contact with new people—for instance, men in other departments—introduce him in these places yourself. And be sure you let everybody involved know that they're to deal with your subordinate.

...*Why you picked him.* In other words, prepare him psychologically. He may feel an excessive weight of responsibility. Lessen the tension by removing his sense of crisis. Show your confidence in his ability—that's why you picked him. Reassure him from time to time.

And emphasize your availability whenever he's in doubt.

Get others to cooperate—Often the responsibility you assign does require a certain amount of authority over others. It may be minor, but even a clerk—trying to collect figures for a report you want to make—is likely to find people with their backs up, slow to cooperate.

To avoid conflict, follow these simple rules:

...*Define scope.* Specify the exact nature of the duties and authority you are delegating. That's essential to keep your delegate on the right track. He may think you're handing over your job unless you tell him what's what.

...*Tell the others.* Define clearly and publicly the limits of the authority you delegate. And take care of complaints about overstepped boundaries promptly.

Set harmony as a goal—Reserve the right to discipline. Don't let your delegate try to enforce cooperation. Impress him with the importance of working harmoniously with other members of your team. Sell your people on the need for delegating the job.

Keep control—When you delegate, you don't really get rid of responsibility. You must still keep control. You'll need it in order to get coordination—to make sure the assigned task ties in with other objectives you have in view.

Your instructions must include a standard operating procedure—actual rules by which the subordinate can handle the situations that constantly recur. Examination of the results is the easiest kind of control you can exercise. You simply look at the completed performance.

It's a sort of "hands off, men working" policy, used where your assistant is highly capable or where the task is largely mechanical.

...*Follow-up.* Often it isn't wise to wait until performance is complete. Errors may be too expensive, too hard to correct. You may want to check progress by inspecting, sampling, spot-checking. This is especially good where responsibility is new, large, or hard to handle.

...*Progress reports.* For a variety of reasons—time element, location, etc.—you may prefer to have your subordinate report on how he is making out. Such a report may be frequent or infrequent, written

or oral, in person or by telephone. You must decide what will be adequate under the circumstances involved in each case.

CHECKLIST FOR DELEGATION

Occasionally you may find yourself too wound up in controls, too badly snarled in red tape. Ask yourself these questions:

...*Have I delegated duties* I can more efficiently handle myself? When you have to follow up with constant observation, the game of delegation isn't worth the candle.

...*Are my delegations boomeranging?* When you pass a sizable task to a worker, you may have to give him an understudy. Otherwise, when he's absent, the delegated duty comes home to roost.

...*Have I set up the right controls?* Ability to make controls work effectively—is the real test of executive leadership. Measure any questionable control by these tests:

Duplication. Is this control necessary? Do you get the same information elsewhere?

Reports. Are you getting long, rambling, time-consuming reports?

Delayed control. Are you relying on "control by result" in a delegation where damage can be done before you can act?

Frequency. Are you checking too often on unimportant matters? Facing a pile of progress reports you just can't read?

BE PREPARED FOR TROUBLE

Delegation is no bed of roses. So prepare yourself for trouble. It'll range from the trouble that makes you shrug to the trouble that makes you shudder.

If a man buys an article for $7.75 and sells it for $9.25, does he gain or lose? You remember the schoolboy's answer to this question: "He loses on the cents, but gains on the dollars." Frequently, with delegation, you face a similar situation. You lose on the cents (short-range) but the gain on the dollars (long-range) makes it worthwhile.

Face it. The man you delegate won't do the job the way you would. Even if you've given complete instructions, don't be surprised if many a delegated assignment ends up in unexpected fashion. If you're inclined to throw up your hands, don't. It's probably time for you to reassess your delegation procedures. ■

10 WAYS TO RELIEVE TENSIONS

Often oriented toward introversion, the engineer
more than others is prone to tensions, the author says.
To alleviate them, some do-it-yourself ways are suggested.

A. A. Klautsch, associate professor of psychology, General Motors Institute.

Ten ways are available to engineers to reduce the tensions spawned by worry, anxiety, and other forms of fear. Because his temperament and personality incline him to take pressures seriously, these tension-reducing processes are especially applicable to the engineer. You can use all 10 for yourself:

1. Realize what hostility or escape patterns are hindering rather than helping you in your daily life.
2. Be moderate. (Don't eat, drink, relax, enjoy recreation, or react too much.)
3. Apportion your time better among the work, family, and recreational areas of your life.
4. Develop interests and hobbies apart from your work.
5. Learn to counter failure or loss with examples of success and gain.
6. Develop the capacity to laugh at yourself.
7. Live each day for what it is.
8. Re-examine and readjust your value systems from time to time.
9. Orient your life toward unselfishness in regard to others.
10. Pray unselfishly – and with trust in the goodness and wisdom of God.

Realize what hostility or escape patterns are hindering rather than helping you. No one can handle his problems well or reduce his tensions who frequently explodes in anger or resentment; who sulks or withdraws; or who uses escape mechanisms indiscriminately. The beginning of tension-control is to eliminate or reduce these reactions.

Be moderate. Don't eat, drink, relax, or enjoy recreation too much. Don't over-react to situations in your daily life. Moderation is a key to a balanced life pattern. Bouncing from excessively heavy work to unrestricted pleasure or recreation only results in greater tensions and expanded inadequacies.

Apportion your time better. Your work must always require a large share of your time. But your family and your social life should get attention too. Job-generated tensions often can be relieved in enjoyment of one's family or of social-recreational activities.

Develop interests and hobbies apart from your work. These can help offset the one-sidedness that complete absorption in work tends to produce. Of course, the hobby or outside interest must be absorbing, truly satisfying. It must be powerful enough to take your complete attention; not just remain a side issue. A hobby that is just another escape mechanism is no good.

(An engineer's wife might well help, not hinder, her husband to develop sound hobbies – as long as they don't create worse problems and lead to over-emphasis in other-than-work interests.)

About the author

Dr. A. A. Klautsch, has, through his GM teaching activities become deeply involved not only with engineering courses, but also with engineers.

As an associate professor at GM Institute he teaches psychology courses to GMI engineering students. His major efforts, however, are devoted to covering the psychological areas associated with the special, intensive training courses held at the Institute for GM administrative personnel. For this group he plans and conducts sessions on human relations aspects of the management functions. In the areas of methods, standards, and materials handling, he deals with physiological psychology and human capabilities. In courses on value analysis, he discusses problem solving techniques. His work also takes him to various GM plants to set up discussion courses for supervisory personnel and executives.

Queried as to the moralistic tone of his article, he writes: "I have done a great deal of counseling with people who have deep and heavy problems. I keep coming back to the basic fact that a living faith in God and a consequent living of that faith toward our fellow man is about the only effective defense that man has to offset the problems, frustrations, and woes which drive him to maladjustment."

COMMON TO ENGINEERS

Learn to counter failure or loss with success and gain. Everyone tends to exaggerate the significance of his failures, and lose sight of his successes. Severe depression can overtake the individual who concentrates on his frustrations and failures; fails to count his blessings. When depression strikes, make a more realistic appraisal of your whole situation. Also, it is important to try to see your successes as well as your failures in realistic perspective.

Develop capacity to laugh at yourself. The man who can accept, without damage to his self-esteem, that he is sometimes ridiculous can be sure he is developing a workable frustration tolerance. His self-esteem uninjured, he no longer strikes out blindly to defend it. Tension no longer builds up to make adjustment even more impossible.

Live each day for what it is. Regretting what's past and worrying endlessly over a vague future is a futile and tension-producing habit. When a day has been disappointing or annoying, why add the problems of past and future to an already heavy load? Bitter regret can never undo the unhappy past. Nor can endless worry avert what may be threatening in the future. Don't downgrade the present in frantic or useless concentration on either past or future.

Each day has its own place in your life. Each day has its own importance, successes, failures. Learn to appreciate each day. Learn to appreciate its little changes, the surprise and adventure which may be a part of it. See each day as an opportunity to live. Then, almost surely, your tensions will be less.

Re-examine and readjust your value systems from time to time. Many are working with an outmoded set of values, established years ago. Tensions haunt such individuals because they don't realize their goals are unattainable or have greatly changed in value.

Periodic review of goals and realistic appraisal of their attainability may well reduce a useless load of tension.

Orient your life toward unselfishness in regard to others. As tensions mount, one becomes ever more absorbed in himself. Then relations with others deteriorate rapidly. The more energetically one seeks to realize selfish goals, the more he comes into conflict with others . . . and the greater are the tensions within him.

Those who orient their lives on a more unselfish basis have fewer tensions — and suffer less from the tensions they have. Also, unselfishly oriented people are more capable of adjusting to setbacks.

Sincere and generous interest in others can be of great help in allowing you to change your goals . . . and then to move toward the new goals without increasing tensions.

Pray unselfishly — and with trust in the goodness and wisdom of God. Religious faith achieves no benefit to the individual who uses it as a super-tranquillizer, a convenient escape mechanism, or a means of reaching arbitrary decisions of no benefit to themselves or others. Nor is it fruitful when dipped in self-righteousness and garnished with self-centered selfishness.

Trust in the goodness as well as the wisdom of God makes logical prayer which truly asks "Thy will be done." When this point is reached, tensions can only temporarily disorganize an individual's life. When this point is reached, he will experience a peace and contentment forever denied lives distraught and disturbed as tensions penetrate deeply and become constant burdens. ■

INCOME AND PROSPECTS ?

VINCE COOGAN

How to get an increase in salary

The decisive factor that governs almost all top executives' income is how much impact their decisions have on profits. The 'up and coming' executive however, often finds that his salary is more dependent upon personal strategy

AS ANY YOUNG EXECUTIVE on his first job finds out, doing an excellent job does not automatically mean the boss will rain money on your bright young head.

Assuming your work is satisfactory, the frequency and size of your raises still is at least partly in your hands. Like any business proposition, you have to plan your long-range strategy and then think out your tactics.

You will want to go into a salary interview armed with enough facts to support your case, instead of relying on refutable generalities. Yet you must be flexible enough to change a setback like a "business is bad" plea to work to your advantage.

These tips may help you get that raise faster. But don't expect any radically new system to hypnotize your boss. He has probably used it himself. Here's how you can plan your campaign.

Get under a microscope

Find out what you're worth, both inside and outside your office. Compare your salary with that of your associates. Chances are they won't tell you what they're earning. But there are clues. What kind of cars do they drive, how big a mortgage are they carrying on their homes and what is their standard of living? This kind of information will let you know how strong your bargaining point is.

It's easier to find what you're worth outside. Check "situations wanted" advertisements; see how much is offered for your skills. However, the better paid jobs may not be listed—so calculate accordingly. Visit a management recruiting firm. A specialist like this will let you know if your salary aspirations are out of line.

Don't divulge your salary

Above all, don't enter into any confidences. If anyone else wants to talk about his salary, listen. But keep your own secret. If the superior gets word that your salary is an open book, you'll have a difficult time convincing him that you need a raise. And the misfortune is that you'll never know why he turned your application down.

You will also gain a psychological advantage by keeping quiet about any outside income. There's no point in giving the boss the idea that you don't really need the money or that you aren't devoting full time to your job.

Talk about the future

Draw your boss out on the subject of where you will be financially five and ten years from now. If possible make him commit himself on a specific figure. You can always remind him of what he said if your raises are behind schedule—that is, provided your work continues above average.

Rate your rating

If your job is evaluated annually, make sure the rating sheet is available to you. Concentrate on heavy point markers. Usually the most points are scored for creative thinking, how many subordinates you have, and how much responsibility you have for fiscal decisions. So, do your best to expand your job in these areas. As far as performance is concerned, Robert F. Moore, Robert F. Moore Associates, New York, points out that most companies rate managerial attributes in the following order:

1. Leadership.
2. Skill and ability.
3. Professional competence.
4. Relationship with your subordinates, peers, and superiors.
5. Health and dependability.
6. Office neatness (rated near the bottom, so don't worry if you keep a sloppy desk).

Avoid status symbols

Don't let the boss side-track salary demands by offering status symbols—a private secretary, panelled office, etc. You'll get them anyway if your position calls for them. Remember, a carpeted office doesn't help your income at all.

Don't curry favour

Want to lose friends and alienate your contemporaries? It's easy. Continuously going into the boss's office to fawn over him accomplishes nothing. Even if he likes flattery you'll hurt yourself. Nothing goes through the office faster than antagonism toward the man who tried too hard to please. A remark by his secretary or the tone of your co-manager's voice can alert the boss that he has a disruptive force in the company.

Don't be timid or shy

Establish a rapport that is on a manager-to-manager, rather than an employee-to-employer basis during salary discussions. This will give you more room to discuss or even to argue points. If you persist in talking up to the boss, he can cut the conversation whenever it is to his advantage.

Support your staff

Try hard to get raises for your subordinates—the efficient ones. In this way you establish an atmosphere of giving rewards for good performance. It also helps you in an indirect way. As the salaries of your top men rise, it narrows the gap between your salary and theirs. And the narrowed gap is a very good bargaining point when it comes time to make the effort for yourself.

Don't stress personal needs

By all means let the boss know if you get married, your wife has a baby, or you buy a new house. But not in a salary discussion. Your boss can rightly come back at you with "We're running a business,

not a charity." You'll gain a better psychological advantage by letting him know these personal facts in an offhand way.

Keep up with the ledger sheet

Familiarize yourself with the company's financial position—the long-range picture, not just the current situation. You'll be in good position to refute any "poor house" story your boss might tell you.

Counterattack

Always acknowledge your mistakes, but don't be too defensive. Talk up your accomplishments. Show him the steps you've taken to correct your error. Endeavour to direct the conversation to how much more valuable you'll be with the improvements he suggests.

Timing is important

Have some valuable other managers quit? Is an important project on the boards? Have you just got that big order out on time? These are the times to approach the boss for a raise. Size him up. His moods may not be obvious, so interpret the signs—over-talkativeness, pacing more than usual, twiddling a coin or pencil.

Above all, never raise the question of your salary anywhere but in the office. There are few things that can antagonize a superior faster than to be approached about such matters outside the office or after business hours.

Know your organization

Familiarize yourself with the worth of each of your associates. Then, if one lazy man leaves to take a high paying job elsewhere, you have a subtle argument for a salary increase for yourself.

Be an ingrate

All right, your boss calls you into his office and raises your salary 10 per cent. Thank him briefly, leaving the impression that after all, "this was coming to me". Then use the raise as a point of departure. Ask him what you can do to raise your salary still higher. Emphasize your expanding job. Make one salary raise a base for the next. If done successfully you've seized the offensive.

Document your worth

Keep a record of actual cost savings you've instituted. But don't be smug if your operation saved the company a great deal of money in the past year. Remember that you had an entire organization to help you. In fact, it's a good idea to bring up cost savings only if you have saved the company more than ten times your annual salary. But don't let your boss forget the less obvious savings: sharing a secretary with someone or getting along with less clerical help than the other managers do.

Always look for work

Forget the old dictum about never volunteering. Look for new assignments and expand your own job whenever possible. If there's a vacuum, fill it. There's no more irrefutable argument for a raise than pointing out that you're doing more than your job specification calls for. ■

How Authoritative is Your Organization?—A Questionnaire

Here's a questionnaire that gives a quick view of your organization's management attitudes. According to Dr. Rensis Lickert, Director of the Institute for Social Research at the University of Michigan, who considered a study of organization systems, engineering groups which fall under the structure of participative management (the column at the extreme right) are more productive than those that lean toward the authoritarian type of management.

Profile of an Organization

Operating characteristics	Exploitive	Benevolent	Consultative	Participative
How much confidence do superiors have in subordinates?	None	Condescending, like master and servant	Substantial, but still control decisions	Complete
Does superior get ideas from subordinates to help solve job problems?	Seldom	Sometimes gets ideas	Usually	Always
What attitudes are developed toward organization and its goals?	Usually hostile	Sometimes hostile	Usually favorable	Very favorable
Are communications accepted by subordinates?	No; viewed with great suspicion	Some accepted, some viewed with suspicion	Often; if not, may/may not be openly questioned	Generally; if not, then openly questioned
How much cooperative teamwork?	None	Relatively little	Moderate	Very substantial throughout organization
What is character of employee interaction?	Little; always fear and distrust	Little; condescension by superiors, fear by subordinates	Moderate; fair amount of trust	Extensive; friendly, high degree of trust
At what level are decisions made?	Bulk at top	Policy at top, specific decisions lower down	Policy at top, many at lower levels, checked with top	Throughout organization
Are decision-makers aware of problems, esp. at lower levels?	Often unaware	Of some, not others	Moderately	Well aware
Does decision-making process motivate those carrying out decisions?	Little or not at all	Relatively little	To some extent	Substantially
Are subordinates involved in decisions regarding jobs?	Not at all	Never; sometimes consulted	Not generally, but usually consulted	Fully
How are goals set or ordered?	Orders issued	Orders issued with or without chance to comment	Goals set, orders issued after discussion with subordinates	Goals set usually by group participation
How are cost, productivity, (etc.) data used? For self-guidance, or	Punitively for policing	Policing (reward and punishment), sometimes punitively	Policing (reward, some punishment); guidance in accord with orders	Self-guidance coordinated problem-solving

2.

Engineering Organization Charts of 25 Modern Companies

Engineering Organization

Present-day demands are altering the organization diagrams in Design and R & D almost as fast as they are drawn. Here is a study based on personal interviews with heads *of some 50 organizations, coast to coast, showing their latest setups, with notes on reasoⁿ for changes, budgeting, titles and ratios of engineers*

E. J. TANGERMAN

methods of organization . . .

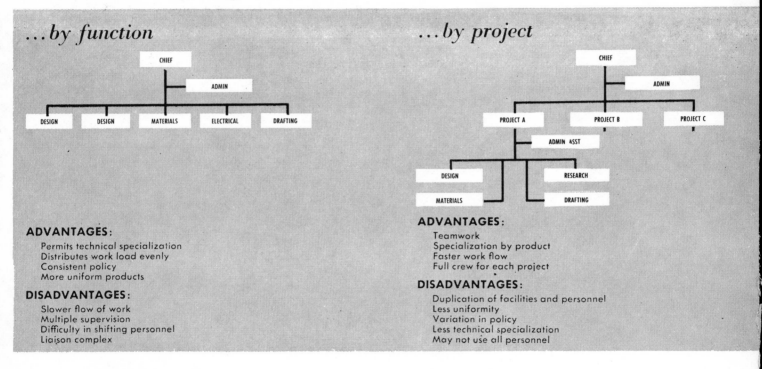

...by function

ADVANTAGES:
- Permits technical specialization
- Distributes work load evenly
- Consistent policy
- More uniform products

DISADVANTAGES:
- Slower flow of work
- Multiple supervision
- Difficulty in shifting personnel
- Liaison complex

...by project

ADVANTAGES:
- Teamwork
- Specialization by product
- Faster work flow
- Full crew for each project

DISADVANTAGES:
- Duplication of facilities and personnel
- Less uniformity
- Variation in policy
- Less technical specialization
- May not use all personnel

basic relationships in organization . . .

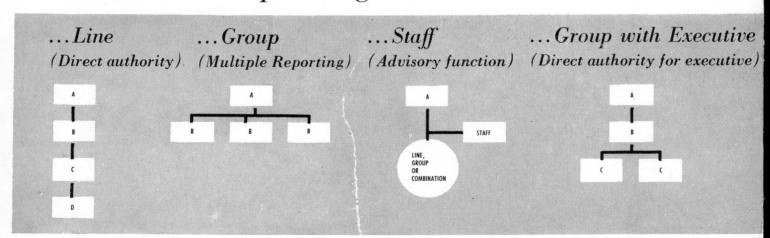

...Line (Direct authority) **...Group** (Multiple Reporting) **...Staff** (Advisory function) **...Group with Executive** (Direct authority for executive)

Charts of 25 Modern Companies

The familiar functional organization has been largely succeeded by project organization, and this in turn by a combination that includes both functional and project elements in line, group and staff relationships. Large companies and research groups tend to favor organization by function, small and medium companies favor organization by project. Companies with many short-term jobs tend to favor project structure, those with mostly long-term ones tend to favor functional. Aircraft companies tend toward a task-force variant of the combination structure, (functional organizations with projects). But there is no constant, or even common, pattern; as would be expected, each organization has been varied to suit conditions peculiar to the company, its locations, products, and the skills and personalities of its particular personnel. In some cases, the organization diagram is a company secret; in others, it is broadcast; in a few, there is no diagram extant.

An old rule has it that one man should boss no more than five others, but this is currently widely disregarded. In 100 large companies studied recently, the range was one to 24, with the median eight or nine. But 24 of the 100 companies had one executive handling 13 or more men. ∎

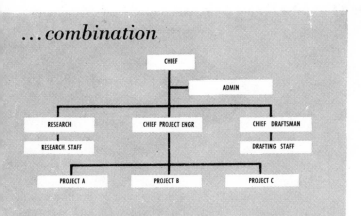

...combination

Has most advantages of the other two types, but requires more complex planning and supervision

FUNCTIONS OF THE ENGINEERING DEPARTMENT

(including R & D, design, analysis & drafting)

ADMINISTRATIVE AND EXECUTIVE
Policies and objectives
Personnel-selection, training
  wage reviews, promotion
Duty assignments
Planning, scheduling, work control
Progress reports
Budgets, pricing, charges
Procurement
Security
Space, office equipment

RESEARCH
Search for new data, principles, laws
Solution of broad, basic problems
Test & evaluation
Control of model making
Patent search
Literature search
Technical services, counsel

PRODUCT DEVELOPMENT
Search for new products
Design of new products
Redesign & improvement
Standardization of parts, materials
Preparation of proposals
Analysis of proposals & quotations

DRAFTING
Layout
Detailing
Checking
Illustrations
Drawing & part numbers

ANALYSIS
Calculation, computing
Statistics
Analytical services
Operations research

LIAISON
With other depts
With customers
With vendors
With consultants

SERVICES
Prints
Release of drawings, prints, charts
Publications
Library
Steno, typing, filing,
  supplies, files & records
Model shop
Laboratories
Legal (patent, trademark, copyright)
Test facilities

...Combination
(Line & Group together)

...Group with Staff
(Staff advises executive)

...Typical
(A complex combination)

ORGANIZATION

WHY HAVE AN ORGANIZATION DIAGRAM?

1. Shows basic relationships and authority
2. Framework for scheduling, budgeting
3. Assigns responsibility
4. Basis for procedures, directives
5. Spots weak or indefinite control
6. Provides sense of security
7. Basis for crash programming

of the engineering department

It is difficult to generalize in discussing engineering organizations; they must vary with size and product of the company, skills and personalities of the personnel, policy and preferences of executives. Our intent here, therefore, is to picture a number of organizations, most of them in simplified form, and to discuss their characteristics individually. Thus it is possible for you to evaluate various forms and select the portions or entire plans that best suit your particular needs. These picture, in the main, large plants or divisions, but they also picture in enlarged form the essential functions. A small plant can utilize the ideas by combining functions—as long as the essential functions are not neglected.

Interviews with engineer-executives bring out again and again that the primary problem is people. Personalities and seniority are both factors that should not affect a basic diagram—but do. Further, there are no average engineers. Skills—disciplined knowledge combined with the ability and imagination to apply it effectively, based on sound technical planning—are scarce. Interest in scientific and engineering skills lagged for a time, it takes longer to acquire them, military service delays and disrupts careers, and complexity of modern products requires much higher concentration of talent. Hence engineering costs are higher, and the good engineer comes high—one engineering vice-president says 80% of his costs are salaries and wages.

Skill problems have resulted in group or functional organization in some companies which would prefer to follow the project plan, because the group can be specialized and trained, headed by the best talent, designed for as good communication as is possible. It also avoids duplication of effort in the frequent recourse to science that is now mandatory.

Science and engineering must be integrated to work smoothly together, but science cannot replace sound engineering and good engineering research, any more than management training can replace the sound judgment of experienced men. Linearized theory and management theory are neither one reliable without experimental verification.

Another looming problem is the necessity of integrating engineering design, tool design and production capability. Costs, materials, processes are all now so complex that designing in an ivory tower is suicidal. Thus many engineering organizations include elaborate liaison or even closer integration with tool engineering and production planning. One device is manufacturing research (call it that, manufacturing capability, producibility, value analysis, or what you will).

Variation in organization is also created by the method of selling a product. Annual redesign, as in automobiles, appliances and other products sold to consumers, requires a different approach than design of longer-lived capital goods; civilian design differs from military. To design an ultrasonic washer for industry is much more practical, for example, than to design one for the housewife, because the marketing problems are not nearly so great. Thus a radical change in design can be made to pay off quicker. The military looks for the out-of-the-blue design and can pay for it; the civilian tends to resist change and certainly resists paying a cost premium for it. Thus the civilian-goods producer must have a more-conservative, more-style-conscious engineering staff. Further, it need not incorporate elements to match the liaison men of its customers as the military contractor or subcontractor must. And its design usually follows an orderly, step-by-step procedure, while that for the military may have preliminary design, design, prototype, and tooling-up all under way at the same time. Thus, even in stylized and simplified form, the organization diagram for an aircraft plant is complex (see chart).

For contrast, take the engineering setup of a large

Stylized line organization for an aircraft plant

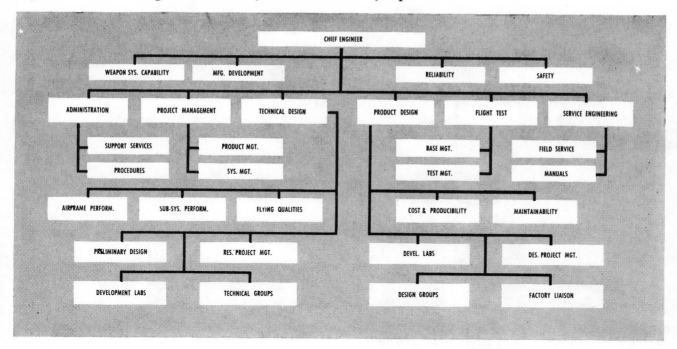

producer of capital and consumer goods. It has some 70 engineering groups at various locations, each headed by a manager. To him reports either a sub-manager (if the department is large) or a series of section managers. Section managers of large sections have supervising engineers reporting to them; in small ones the engineers report direct. Engineers do all R & D and design work, so their assignments from day to day may vary from one to the other. All groups have essentially the same organization.

More and more commonly, the top exectuive of an engineering organization is provided with a direct Number 2 man who can function for him in his absence, and often with an assistant or staff for paper work. This reflects the increasing frequency of executive field trips and visits, as well as the burgeoning volume of paper work to be handled. Complexity of modern products often makes the engineering executive also a technical assistant to the company president or division executive, which makes a staff the more advisable. In several such cases, the staff includes such assistants as these: administration, general projects, development services, field service, research (if it is not a separate function), product design, test, and analysis.

Contract shops show some interesting variations, particularly if they also have some products of their own. Let's detail one such case: Two entirely distinct engineering departments are maintained, one a group organization, the other project. But, paradoxically, the project setup is for the company's own product, the group for customers. Some groups or services are common: administration (50 or 60 people) and technical services (130 people) of a total of 320 (half engineers). Technical services sells time to projects and groups—thus exists almost as a separate subcontractor, although it reports to the chief engineer as the other departments do.

In this case, administrative engineering includes release and change control, publications and accounting sections. The group plan has three sections, research (65 people), components (20), and systems (3). The project setup includes a technical engineering section (design, drafting & checking, experimental, analysis, and test) as well as two project sections: developmental (10 project engineers) and production (3 project engineers), each with its own chief project engineer.

In other plants, a special department is set up to act as expediter on a project basis. Unusual is the fact that its members can order other groups to expedite, at *both* exectuive and engineering levels in Engineering. One such function is called "program engineer", to distinguish the person from "project engineer," whose responsibilities are technical only.

PRESENT-DAY GROUP TITLES IN AIRCRAFT ENGINEERING SHOW ORGANIZATION COMPLEXITY

ANALYTICAL
Fluid dynamics
Reliability
Aerothermodynamics
Performance
Dynamics
Loads
Weights
Structures
Strengths
Aerodynamics
Boundary Layer Research
Digital Computing
Analog Computing
Computing & Data Handling
Computing Equipment
Wind Tunnel

DEVELOPMENT
Systems integration
Astronautics
Avionics
Armament
Ground Operations
Air Defense Systems
Weapons Systems
Strategic Systems
Automatic Controls
Metallurgy
Physics
Processes
Propulsion

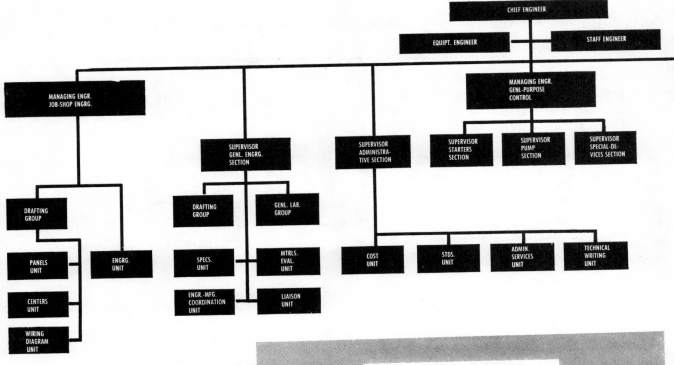

Traditional heavy-machinery setup adds R&D . . .

This 100-man engineering department handles its own R & D, but under a separate budget from service engineering for each product. Each product has a project engineer. Production liaison is, however, handled by the Production Department, not by Engineering.

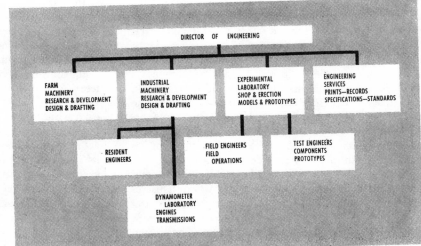

RESPONSIBILITIES OF A PROJECT ENGINEER

1. Technical and administrative execution of projects
2. Testing of prototypes
3. Monitoring engineering assignments to assure all necessary work is done
4. Scheduling to meet target dates
5. Assigning engineering work on his project
6. Supplying sufficient information with each assignment
7. Coordinating original preparation and subsequent changes to project estimates, schedules and budgets
8. Conducting periodic review of manpower and material expenditures
9. Maintaining adequate liaison with other departments and groups
10. Maintaining adequate liaison with vendors and customers

The two plants of this company build the same general types of products, although they vary considerably in principle. Thus there is no reason to subdivide Engineering by products. Three division chief engineers split the tasks. The Product Division handles all orders, design of installations, and service. The Technical Division provides technical services to all other divisions and to Sales. It also handles field testing such as torsiographing, vibration analysis, etc., as well as stresses and stress measurements for the Development Division. Designs are made as near to production units as possible, so R & D and design people are thrown into daily contact with field problems and each other. Present manpower is 270 (engineers) with 25% in Development, 10% in Technical. Engineering is 7% of total employment. Costs are 4% of sales.

Organization diagram shows levels of authority . . .

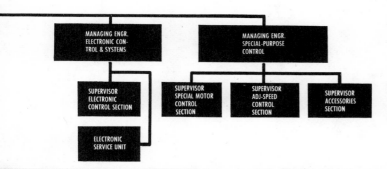

Electrical and electronic controls for industrial use are produced in this 164-man engineering setup. The three departments at right do R & D of components, as well as design, while that at left combines them into systems. The two sections at left are service units. Of the staff, 47% are engineers, 13% technicians, 29% draftsmen, 2.5% technical clerks, 8.5% non-technical clerks, secretaries and blueprint operators. Unusual is the system of titling, with units forming groups which in turn form sections. Sections are headed by supervisors, while managing engineers head departments. Engineering reports to a division head, who in turn reports to the executive vice president.

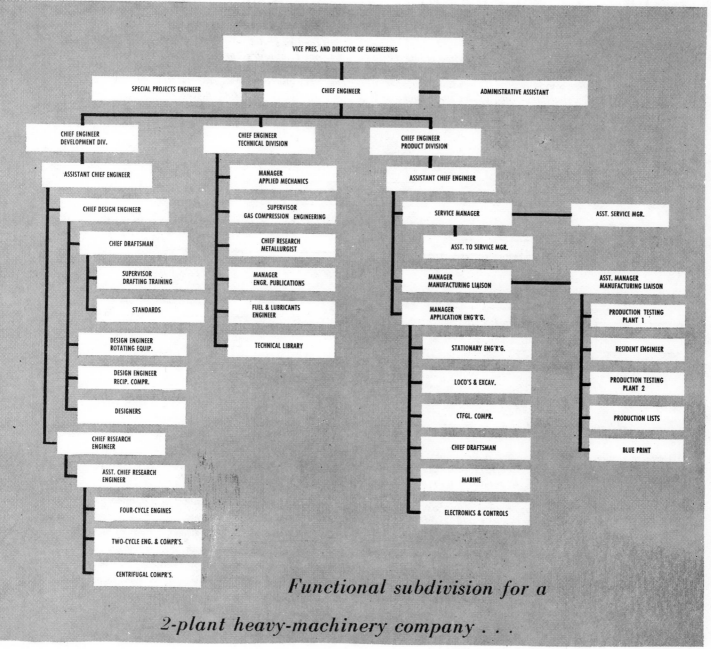

Functional subdivision for a 2-plant heavy-machinery company . . .

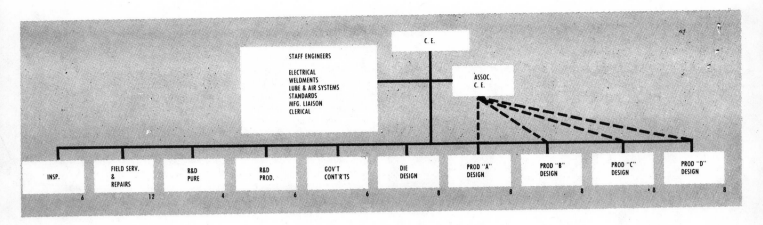

Products subdivision, twin R&D, inspection included in engineering . . .

Engineering of this heavy-machinery division is by products, with separate R & D. The latter is in two groups, the first long-range (10-20 years), the second immediate (0-10 years), with a 50% larger budget, although both are flexible. (There is also a company R & D available for special problems.) R & D departments are in the same room with other departments, so there is free liaison. There are 75 engineers (5% of division total), broken down thus: 8 supervisors, 10 senior designers, 20 designers, 18 junior engineers, 5 layout men, 14 detailers. Large projects are assigned to senior designers, smaller ones to designers, who become temporary "project engineers" for project duration. Staff engineers and the associate chief engineer have only advisory functions and staff relationship to product designers. Blueprint operators, clerks, etc, are not shown. Unusual is the inclusion of Inspection; the chief inspector rarely consults the chief engineer, and has a salvage department which deals with manufacturing.

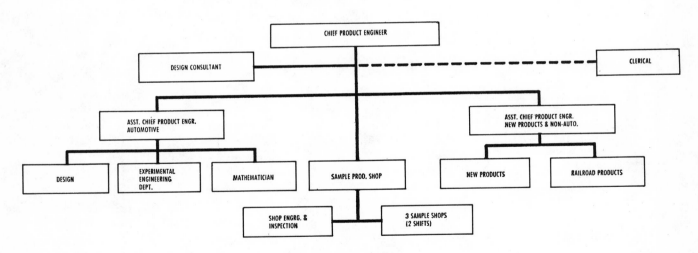

Line department in a corporate division . . .

Decentralization of this company a year ago separated very diverse products into divisions, more or less by type of customer. A central R & D department serves all on basic problems, but research technical services and product development are done by each division as well. In this division, Engineering has about 110 employees, includes an experimental laboratory and a sample shop that work two shifts. Emphasis is on automotive products. The non-automotive product engineer has only six people, so subdivision is simple. The corporation has a VP-Engineering, but his responsibilities are quality control, industrial engineering, plant and equipment engineering, and material and process control. He does check all redesigns by divisions, however, but authority is vested in the line organization.

RESPONSIBILITIES OF A SUPERVISOR OF PROJECT ENGINEERS . . .

1. General administration of all operations
2. Schedule manpower
3. Maintain liaison between groups as required
4. Maintain liaison with other groups as required
5. Monitor direct-labor overhead charges
6. Assign and schedule work to meet target dates
7. Establish and maintain technical standards
8. Monitor work for compliance to customer, safety and company requirements

Line organization of divisions with engineering staff . . .

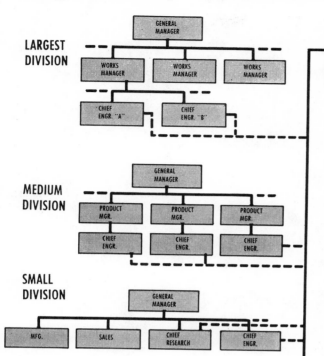

Five plants of this heavy-equipment company each has its own engineering function, under line control. Thus, the VP-Engineering works in staff relationship with the various chief engineers, and has line responsibility for Patent Department, R & D and a central staff.

The largest division has four chief engineers reporting through works managers of three plants. Two other large divisions, each in single locations, have chief engineers reporting through product managers, four in one case, six in the other. None of these divisions has an administrative head of engineering. In small divisions, chief engineers report directly to the general manager, as do other operating heads. One has his own research department, as shown.

Responsibilities: R & D Station for conception and development of product additions to existing lines. Can also work on promising improvements to *existing* lines. Division Engineering Departments for *customer* acceptance of their products. Can also introduce additions, but this is not their prime responsibility.

Line organization with central engineering staff & laboratories . . .

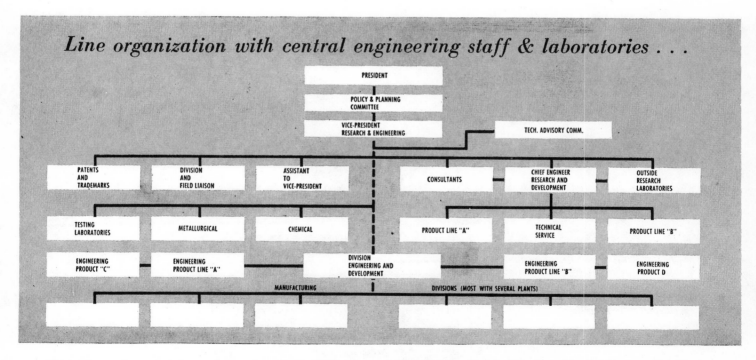

This company has more than a dozen plants in the US and Canada, set up in four divisions. Each has its own engineering department reporting to its general manager. Monthly engineering reports are made through division to the vice-president, R & E, and all major projects must be cleared by the Policy & Planning Committee before development and again before manufacture. Thus, headquarters engineering has a "dotted-line" or staff relationship to division engineering, plus an advisory relationship on general engineering and a regulatory one on engineering and patent-standard procedures. Next to bottom line of blocks identified by "Product Line," represent divisional product-development sections, each with its own engineering manager who has final responsibility for all engineering on his division's product line. Sales and field liaison is also done here. These groups are superior to Engineering only on products—functional management is directly from the division general manager. There is a central research department at the headquarters location which handles all of the long-term projects and new-product development activity, but takes on little basic product research (upper right in diagram).

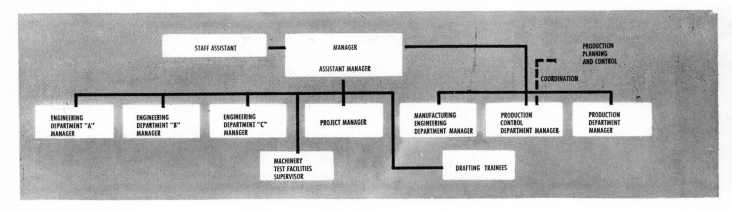

Multi-product management organization . . .

Several kinds of products, similar in production, but differing in principle, are produced in this division. There are three separate engineering departments under the assistant manager, who is an engineer (the manager is not). This amounts to project organization at the top-management level.

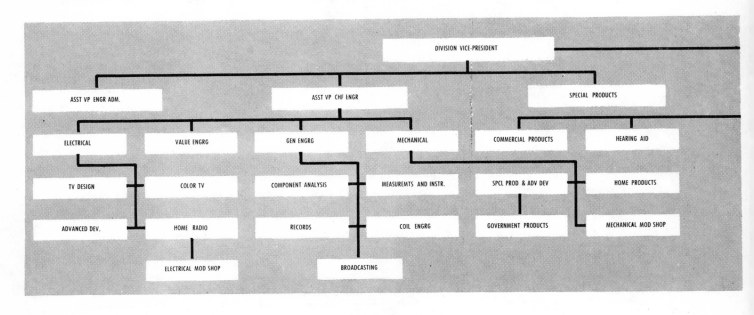

Engineering of controls includes process . . .

Many types of small regulatory units are included in products of this company, involving a variety of problems. Unusual is addition of such functions as machine controls and process engineering (including tool design). Only executives and specialists are shown.

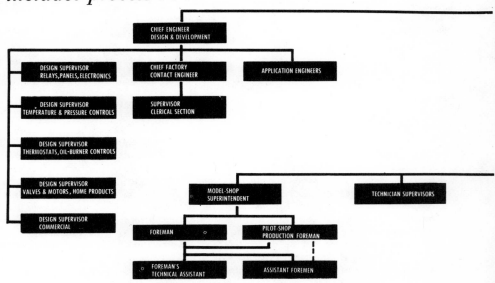

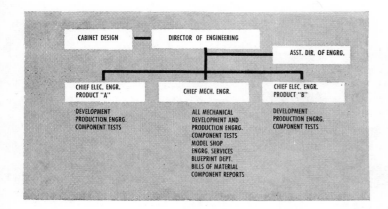

Subdivision by product (modified) . . .

This organization makes two major lines of electrical products sold to consumers through retail stores and dealers. It has, in effect, a project engineer for each product, plus a service and administrative group combined with mechanical-element design, which plays a small part in the products. A good example of balancing work loads and controlling design directly, with an assistant to relieve the head of detail.

Group organization has research, no R&D . . .

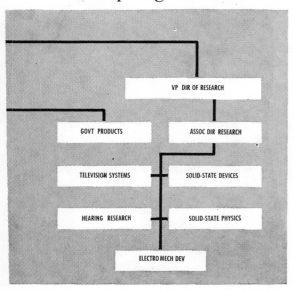

R & D is present in both the design and research portions of this engineering organization. Engineering (2nd block) is concerned with design and development of products to be manufactured, Research with investigations and projects which have no scheduled commercial application.
Within Engineering, a given individual or group normally handles prototype design and design for production. There are roughly 300 people in Engineering, 100 in Research. There is no fixed relationship between gross sales and the budget of either department. Products are electronic, both defense and civilian.

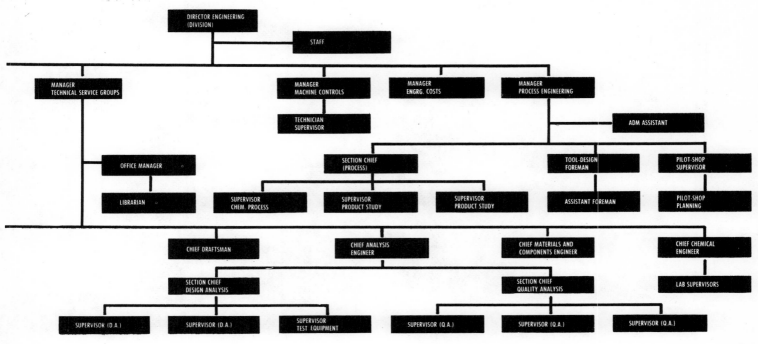

25 product lines in one department of 60 people . . .

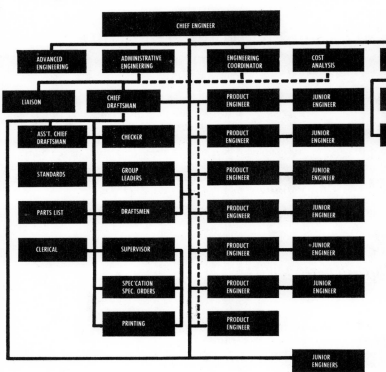

This 100-year-old maker of pumps, compressors, mining and construction machinery has evolved this organization for one of its plants. It operates on a project system, under "product engineers," each with several projects and a junior engineer to handle follow-up and details. They handle not only design, but also operation and are actively concerned with manufacturing costs. "Coordination" concerns itself with standardizing basic relationships between various sizes of a product line—important when it is considered that items vary from 100 to 70,000 lb and in value from $100 to $60,000. It and "Cost Analysis" work with all members of Engineering. "Liaison" covers production shops, is staffed by old-timers mostly from Inspection rather than Engineering. Group leaders handle only one product line at a time, but may be loaned out temporarily. New ideas may come from anywhere, go either to "Advanced" or "Research," and the basic design is followed through by the original engineer up to the point of production design. Work force is about 1700 people, so engineering ratic is 1:29, annual sales $40-million.

Group system applied to aircraft & missile design . . .

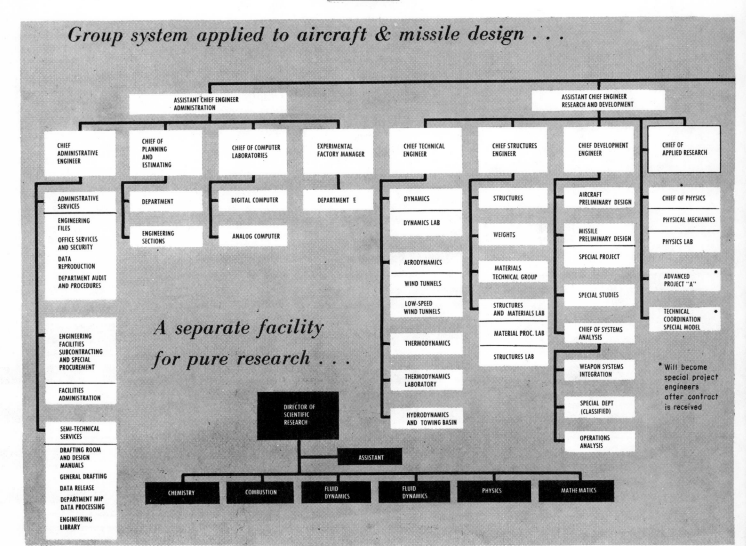

34

Research division set up as group-staff combination . . .

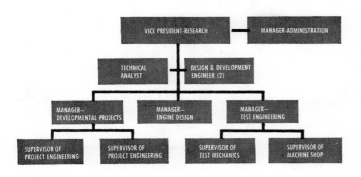

This 107-man organization serves a 4000-man company (2.7%), handles all research and development through production design. Included are design and development engineers (3), design engineers (6), draftsmen (7), test engineers (21), instrumentation engineer, machinists (12), technicians (9), test mechanics (27), field-test engineers (2), clerical (4). **The separate engineering division has 109 people. Research budgets have averaged 1.21% of sales for five years, (and about one person per $1-million of sales).**

This complex diagram reflects the tremendous variety of problems encountered in design for space and speed. Estimates are that there is over 100 times as much engineering effort in a missile as in an airplane of World War II. Less than a year old, the diagram is already out of date, although some corrections have been entered. For example, the electronics section is new (and larger than shown), having recently emerged from an organizational position as a division of R & D. Faced with limited availability of skilled specialists, this plant (one division of a 4-division company) uses a group system to make its specialists broadly available. Some 20% of its employees are in product engineering. There is a separate basic-science research facility (shown), which permits engineers to pursue, temporarily, promising study in pure research with the advice of scientists. In this group are 51 people, 34 of them professionals, half PhD's. Preliminary design is handled on a project basis, necessary specialists being assigned as needed, although they remain physically and organizationally under the control of their technical group leader, who can thus apply his superior knowledge to all projects.

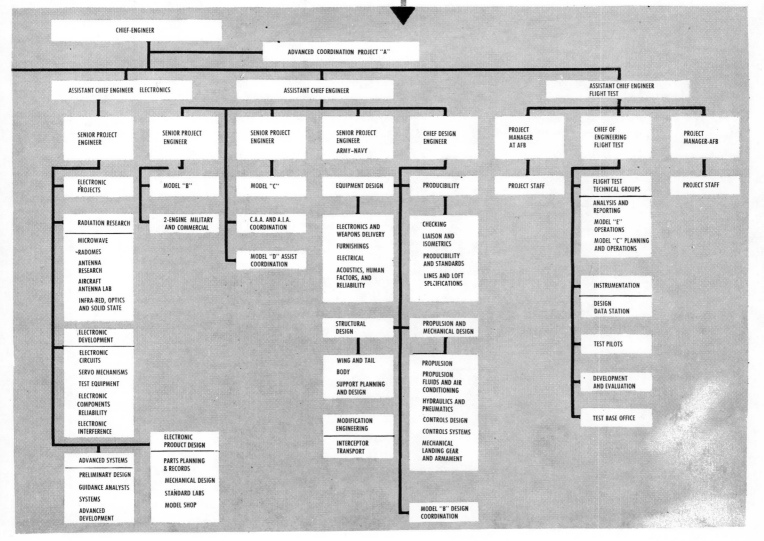

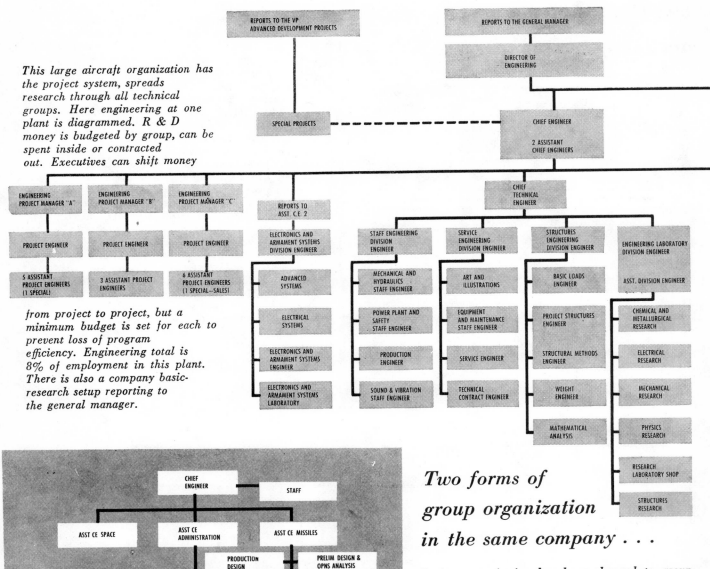

REPORTS TO THE GENERAL MANAGER

DIRECTOR OF ENGINEERING

This large aircraft organization has the project system, spreads research through all technical groups. Here engineering at one plant is diagrammed. R & D money is budgeted by group, can be spent inside or contracted out. Executives can shift money

SPECIAL PROJECTS

CHIEF ENGINEER — 2 ASSISTANT CHIEF ENGINEERS

ENGINEERING PROJECT MANAGER "A" | ENGINEERING PROJECT MANAGER "B" | ENGINEERING PROJECT MANAGER "C" | REPORTS TO ASST. C.E. 2 | CHIEF TECHNICAL ENGINEER

PROJECT ENGINEER | PROJECT ENGINEER | PROJECT ENGINEER

5 ASSISTANT PROJECT ENGINEERS (1 SPECIAL) | 3 ASSISTANT PROJECT ENGINEERS | 6 ASSISTANT PROJECT ENGINEERS (1 SPECIAL—SALES)

ELECTRONICS AND ARMAMENT SYSTEMS DIVISION ENGINEER
- ADVANCED SYSTEMS
- ELECTRICAL SYSTEMS
- ELECTRONICS AND ARMAMENT SYSTEMS ENGINEER
- ELECTRONICS AND ARMAMENT SYSTEMS LABORATORY

STAFF ENGINEERING DIVISION ENGINEER
- MECHANICAL AND HYDRAULICS STAFF ENGINEER
- POWER PLANT AND SAFETY STAFF ENGINEER
- PRODUCTION ENGINEER
- SOUND & VIBRATION STAFF ENGINEER

SERVICE ENGINEERING DIVISION ENGINEER
- ART AND ILLUSTRATIONS
- EQUIPMENT AND MAINTENANCE STAFF ENGINEER
- SERVICE ENGINEER
- TECHNICAL CONTRACT ENGINEER

STRUCTURES ENGINEERING DIVISION ENGINEER
- BASIC LOADS ENGINEER
- PROJECT STRUCTURES ENGINEER
- STRUCTURAL METHODS ENGINEER
- WEIGHT ENGINEER
- MATHEMATICAL ANALYSIS

ENGINEERING LABORATORY DIVISION ENGINEER
- ASST. DIVISION ENGINEER
- CHEMICAL AND METALLURGICAL RESEARCH
- ELECTRICAL RESEARCH
- MECHANICAL RESEARCH
- PHYSICS RESEARCH
- RESEARCH LABORATORY SHOP
- STRUCTURES RESEARCH

from project to project, but a minimum budget is set for each to prevent loss of program efficiency. Engineering total is 8% of employment in this plant. There is also a company basic-research setup reporting to the general manager.

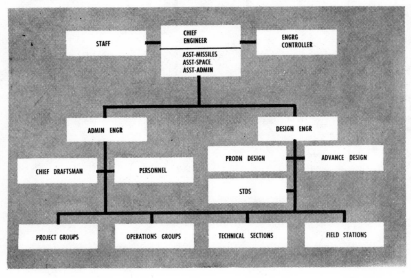

CHIEF ENGINEER — STAFF

ASST CE SPACE | ASST CE ADMINISTRATION | ASST CE MISSILES

PRODUCTION DESIGN | PRELIM DESIGN & OPNS ANALYSIS

PROJECT GROUPS | OPERATIONS GROUPS | TECHNICAL SECTIONS | FIELD STATIONS

8   3   15

STAFF — CHIEF ENGINEER — ENGRG CONTROLLER

ASST-MISSILES ASST-SPACE ASST-ADMIN

ADMIN ENGR | DESIGN ENGR

CHIEF DRAFTSMAN | PERSONNEL | PRODN DESIGN | ADVANCE DESIGN

STDS

PROJECT GROUPS | OPERATIONS GROUPS | TECHNICAL SECTIONS | FIELD STATIONS

Two forms of group organization in the same company . . .

Project organization has been changed to group organization in divisions of this company, but in two separate patterns. In each, there is provision for space craft. Also, administrative matters are reported to one executive, technical ones to another. The upper diagram (for the largest plant) includes eight project groups, 15 technical sections. Each unit does its own research. Design responsibility is in the assistant chief engineers, hence variation in contracts results in variation of number of assistant chief engineers. Project engineers now are really coordinators of work done in technical groups and contacts. Included in technical sections are: aerodynamics, armament, automatic controls, checking, data & computing, equipment, ground equipment, hydraulics, power plant, production liaison, reliability, research, strength, structures, weight. Ratio of engineers and draftsmen to technicians is 2:1; about 50% of the work is on the board. Total engineering employment is 10,000—about 14% of the company total.

Project system applied to aircraft design . . .

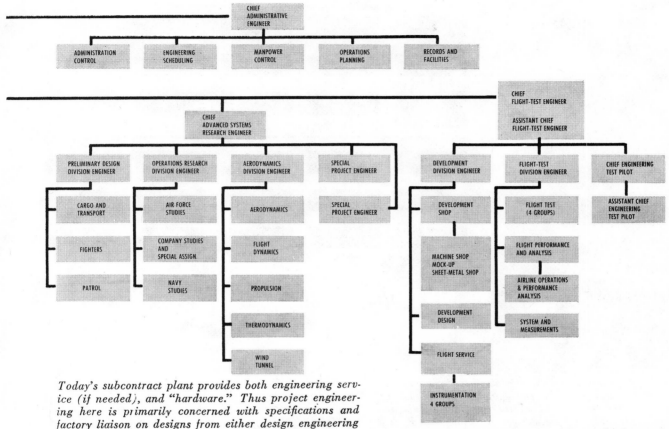

Today's subcontract plant provides both engineering service (if needed), and "hardware." Thus project engineering here is primarily concerned with specifications and factory liaison on designs from either design engineering or outside. Costing is extremely important, because "minor" design changes can—and usually do—surpass any contract contingency provision.

The large loft is in two groups, one for design support, the other for tooling, yet the "paper" (drawings) and "metal" (actual tooling) are kept together for close co-ordination. These personnel totals emphasize preceding points: general engineering 23, blueprint control 118, engineering standards 18, engineering design 114, stresses & weights 13, engineering liaison 117, engineering release 90, laboratories 40, lofting 153, contracting 22. Engineering is 4.5% of total employment.

Subcontractor provides optional design service . . .

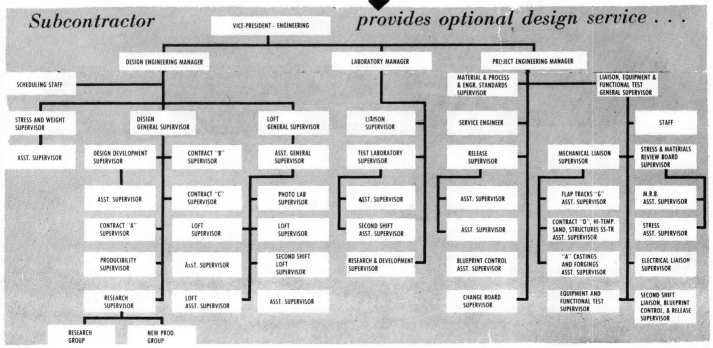

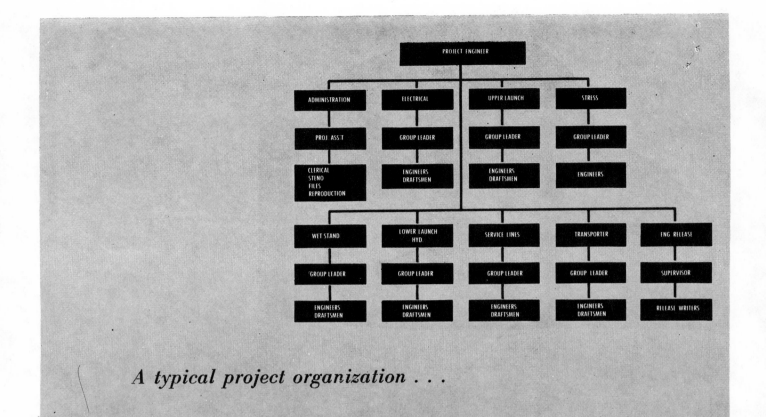

A typical project organization . . .

About 75% of the personnel of this 425-man department is on R & D, because of the frequency and magnitude of almost-constant redesign of military products. This also makes it advisable to have one group handle both R & D and design. The two are distinguished by the contracts themselves at any given time, but knowledge and experience are carried over from one phase to the next. Engineering design includes four steps: (1) producibility check to

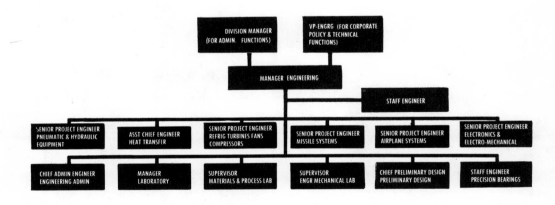

Division setup includes services to
parent corporation . . .

Here is a contracting division of a larger corporation, organized on a project basis. Engineering includes 650 people, 400 in design and development, 250 in clerical and administrative. Note dual reporting of the executive and use of unusual titles. The senior groups handle all development, design, and ultimately production of "hardware" items. The chief administrative engineer also handles personnel advising for the parent corporation, and controls such services as drafting, blueprinting and release. Specifications, proposals and the technical library are under the chief of preliminary design; this group also advises project engineers on current problems. The bearings engineer has analysts and engineers who handle bearing problems of all divisions.

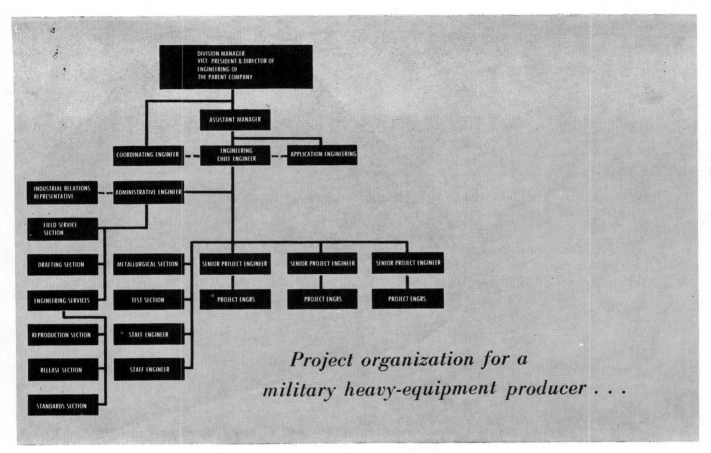

standardize and cut cost of R & D design while maintaining performance and durability requirements, (2) detail drawings, (3) maintaining engineering-release records, (4) product-improvement design. The department has its

own experimental shop for prototypes and test equipment, proving grounds and a special R & D procurement group (none shown). The department is 13% of total employment, has 73% engineering draftsmen.

THE MATTER OF MONEY

In only a few cases are companies willing to report the percentage of sales income expended in engineering, and available figures are not directly comparable because of differences in accounting practices and policies. The minimum annual cost of engineering appears, however, to be 2 to 3% of sales for an established company in a relatively static field, 4 to 5% in heavy capital-goods manufacturing, 9% for a large company involved in an aggressive marketing campaign, 2½% for an electrical-control manufacturer.

These figures in general cover both design and R & D, but the practice in budgeting is not consistent. In aircraft companies, where R & D is frequently done all through engineering, it is impossible to isolate the R & D figure. Likewise in a company in electronics or missile technology in which most of the work is in research anyway. In older fields, where the rate of development—or at least the emphasis—is lower, budgets are tied percentage-wise to company sales. A diesel maker shows an R & D budget of 1.21% of sales, for example. Sometimes, all

engineering of whatever type is lumped together. Case in point: a company with a diverse line of products and many divisions spent 3.5% of its sales dollar in engineering last year, 40% of it on R & D, 16% on design, 15% on tool, and 29% on general engineering.

However, where R & D is a separate organization, there seems to be a trend toward considering it without relation to sales or income. One company making a diverse line of capital and consumer goods, for example, considers R & D a company-wide capital expense, handles this budget just as it does one for new buildings, while engineering is paid for by divisions in their separate budgets. Another company, just as large, handles its R & D as a series of capital investments, authorizing projects individually and billing its divisions for their share. In still another, divisions carry the cost of a general engineering laboratory and a general research lab, the first financed 85% by payments for specific projects assigned by divisions, the second only 15% that way. The remainders are charged to divisions. ∎

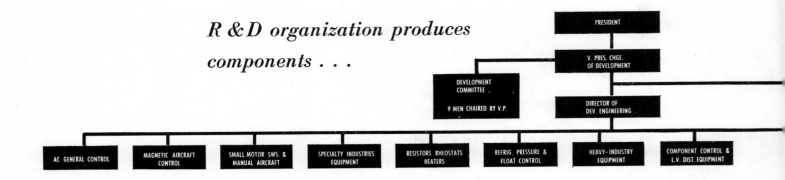

R & D organization produces

components . . .

Organization chart boxes: PRESIDENT — V. PRES. CHGE. OF DEVELOPMENT — DEVELOPMENT COMMITTEE (9 MEN CHAIRED BY V.P.) — DIRECTOR OF DEV. ENGINEERING — AC GENERAL CONTROL — MAGNETIC AIRCRAFT CONTROL — SMALL MOTOR SWS. & MANUAL AIRCRAFT — SPECIALTY INDUSTRIES EQUIPMENT — RESISTORS RHEOSTATS HEATERS — REFRIG. PRESSURE & FLOAT CONTROL — HEAVY-INDUSTRY EQUIPMENT — COMPONENT CONTROL & L.V. DIST. EQUIPMENT

the research and development
ORGANIZATION

Major among the factors causing flux in engineering organizations is research & development, familiar to every engineer as "R & D." This was once just another function of the engineering department and was handled by the usual functional or project groups, however designated, with an occasional special project group or "committee" set up for some radically different study or idea.

With increasing complexity of materials and designs, however, special research setups began to appear, at first primarily materials labs or testing stations, associated with Engineering, but later sometimes divorced both physically and organizationally. As the rate of change in some types of products began to accelerate, R & D assumed more importance, became even a separate division in some instances. Studies of creativity and the "atmosphere for research," economic surveys of the importance of new products to a company's life, and the dictates of fashion in organization all contributed to the burgeoning emphasis on R & D. Major corporations established large research centers, particularly in the vicinity of suburban research-oriented universities such as MIT, Princeton, Chicago, Stanford, UC (Berkeley), etc. Smaller companies followed suit. In many companies today, the R & D budget is larger than that for Engineering.

There still remains in many minds, however, the outmoded idea that R & D is "just a laboratory or an ivory tower." Nothing could be further from the truth. While some R & D installations are primarily sales showcases or merely the departments handling next-year's design, the great majority are major installations determining both the form and engineering content of future products, hence of basic importance in selecting materials, components, processes of manufacture—in fact the sales course of the company itself.

Several strictly R & D organizations are, therefore, diagrammed here in addition to those shown previously as integral parts of engineering diagrams.

Some general notes may be in order. One form of organization has separate executives for research and engineering, another a general engineering executive who has direct charge of R & D and only staff or advisory relationships to engineering departments which are incorporated in the line management of divisions or product departments. There are often product-planning committees, composed of various engineering executives, sales manufacturing and policy heads, which meet regularly or on call to review development, determine direction, initiate programs, set policy and the like. One company, for example, has such a committee meeting monthly for each product, another has an over-all "senior engineering committee" with three engineering executives as permanent members and three from other functions as rotating members.

Budgets are set by varied means also. If R & D is a part of Engineering, it of course will be part of that budget, shown separately or not. But where it is a separate department, it may have a budget related to anticipated sales like those of other operating departments, or it may have one based on individual projects or even on capital investment as if it were a new building or new equipment. Depending upon individual company definition, the emphasis may be either on "research" or on "development." If it is the former, the tendency is to charge R & D as a capital expense; if the latter, the tendency is to budget by project, or even to bill sponsoring other departments.

Interesting in any analysis of R & D is the fact that relatively few aircraft companies have R & D setups as such. Popularly, they are supposed to be the strongholds of R & D and the recipients of most R & D funds. Both concepts are true, but R & D is so large a portion of present aircraft and missile work that it is distributed all through engineering groups, rather than being concentrated in an identifiable place.

One diagram shows half the home-plant R & D organi-

This electrical-control manufacturer has the R & D oriented to produce components or building blocks for systems. A separate organization solves problems in systems, most of them for one-time use.

With high reliability the key problem, the emphasis must be on developments that will have a long sales life, rather than short-term "spectaculars." New product plans are administered by a committee.

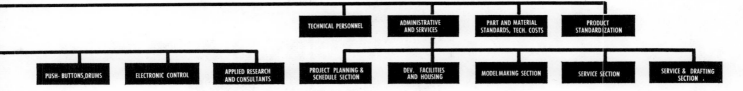

Corporate R & D organization for a complex product line . . .

Both basic and applied research are handled by this department, subdivided by areas rather than time. Also handled are technical service and new-product development, the former being charged at an hourly rate. Some 200 people here may even make the prototype. Individual labs are expected to spend 10-15% on "blue-sky" projects; an "exploratory research" project is budgeted to provide funds for blue-sky work even in general departments. Design engineering, by contrast, is decentralized in product groups.

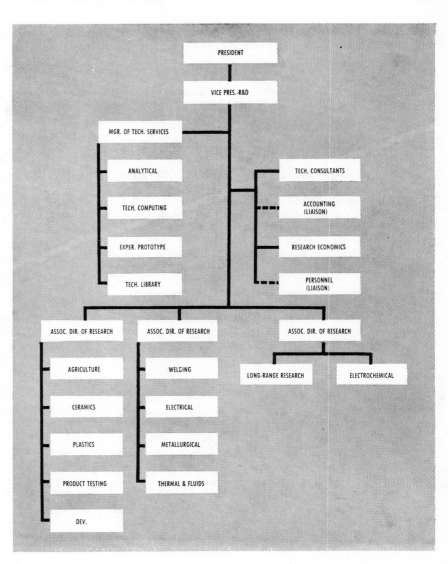

zation of a large radio company. It is unique in that, for the past 2½ years, dual supervision has been used at both division and department levels, to attain both skilled technical direction and better business management. The department head is an engineer or scientist, the manager is also, but the head concentrates on technology, the manager on administration. They are partners, and can act for each other when necessary, so the head can travel much more than formerly. The manager, who normally is in the office, has a non-technical assistant. He supervises draftsmen, technicians, clerks and secretaries, monitors costs, administers salaries and personnel, prepares routine proposals. The head roughs out proposals on brand-new types, decides whether or not to bid, handles customer liaison. The head selects his own manager—usually from among his own department heads. (The same procedure is followed in design engineering, incidentally.)

This is in sharp contrast to the relatively common practice of having an administrative assistant (often nontechnical) for details to relieve the department head—or even the occasional one of having a non-technical

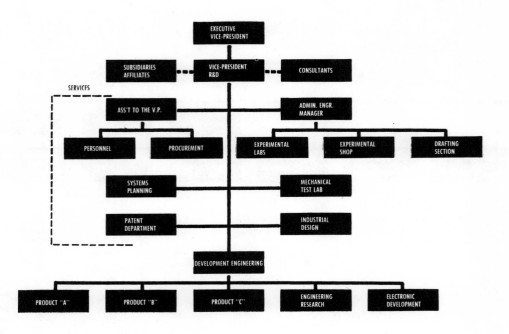

R & D setup with emphasis on product development . . .

Product development is the major assignment of this R & D division for a 9000-man company. Total R & D personnel is 225, of which 125 are engineers and draftsmen, 70 technicians and shop people, 30 clerical and administrative. The asst to the vp and the administrative engineering manager have broad responsibilities for project administration separate from, or in addition to, the line responsibilities charted. General management approves product-development projects and completed products as acceptable for production, but R & D has complete and final responsibility for both functional and appearance design and operation. There is a headquarters product-planning group to prepare requirements for products, as well as a production-engineering department to review R & D-developed products for producibility. Professional personnel in R & D are ranked from junior engineer, engineer, staff engineer, project engineer, senior staff engineer and senior project engineer, based on training, ability and inclination to staff or project work. When assigned a project or group of projects, they take the temporary title of supervisor, so maximum flexibility is possible. A small applied-research department at one plant handles military work, and small teams attack basic research.

("business man") head of the department with a technical second in command. In these cases, there is usually strong tie-in with financial and administrative structures of the parent company and often some danger of divided allegiance.

This company has line organization throughout. With the emphasis heavily electrical and electronic, it would be normal to have a single concentrated mechanical-design department. Here, however, each department has its own mechanical-design section for close cooperation. This has proved an advantage particularly where mechanical-design requirements become more severe and complex than the electrical ones—as in aircraft instruments, where vibration, shock, heat transfer, aerodynamics and material considerations now loom as most important.

With so much emphasis on R & D, these divisions become operating units rather than a subsidiary of general or engineering management. In fact, in this case product design and basic research are both also handled by the "R & D organization" rather than by the "engineering department"—in the minds of company officials.

One company supplying aircraft service equipment has two R & D labs at opposite ends of the country, each complete and under its own technical director. Projects are under control of "project engineers," as distinct from "project managers" in the product-engineering department. The R & D units, in contrast to the preceding one, never design the product. They carry on applied research through the report or breadboard stage, do state-of-the-art improvements on present products, handle prime R & D contracts or sub-contracts in areas associated with the company's proposed direction, and act as consultants for the engineering department. Such consulting services are charged direct to the particular project. R & D utilizes 3% of company personnel, about half graduate engineers, scientists or mathematicians, and 5% of sales income, not counting special R & D contracts undertaken, which are charged direct.

Studies of R & D to overcome some of the problems of semantics on what to include and how to evaluate government participation have been made by the Bureau of Labor Statistics, National Science Foundation, Industrial Research Institute, and various colleges. (For example, Prof. A. H. Rubenstein, School of Industrial Management, MIT, is surveying R & D in large decentralized companies, and Harvard studied percentages of sales income spent on R & D.) However, very little comprehensive material has been published. ∎

Central research division of an electronic complex . . .

Eight technical divisions of this company, which employs 38,000 people (11% engineers and scientists), each has its own engineering and R & D groups, the latter called "advanced development." A chief engineer heads each. This central department has its own vice-president, reporting directly to the president's office. The corporation has a
vice-president of engineering & research (not shown) who has over-all functional cognizance of research, development and engineering. Annual budget in 1959 for these activities is 18% of sales, but includes some directly funded by the government—which is hardly comparable to companies doing only their own R & D.

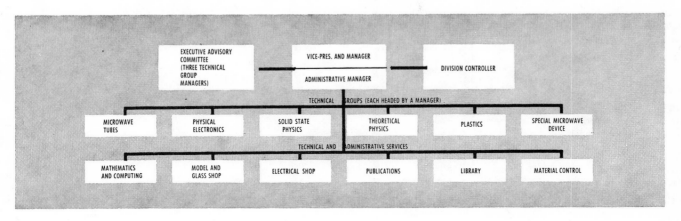

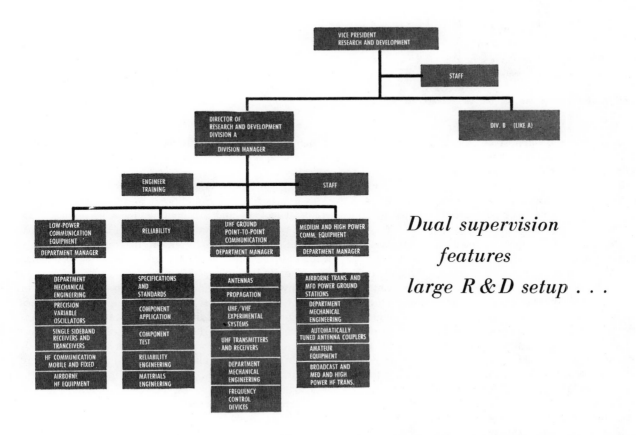

Dual supervision features large R & D setup . . .

Half of the organization of one of three R & D structures for a 7500-man company with 4/5 of its $122-million sales to the military. Some 2000 people (27%) are on R & D, including 700 engineers. Division B (not shown) includes five more R & D departments ("Reliability" is not duplicated). Not shown are service departments such as publications, model shop (fabricated parts only), pilot assem-
bly, drafting, engineering stores and facilities, lab-assistant administration. Unique is the dual supervision—a director and division manager, and a department head and department manager at that level, providing both technical direction and administrative supervision. Also, each department has its own mechanical design section, significant here since products are basically electronic.

What do their titles really mean?

This basic structure of an engineering organization calls for only four job functions—no matter what the title—and titles vary widely among different organizations. Can you find these functions in your setup?

TOP MANAGEMENT ENGINEER	MIDDLE MANAGEMENT ENGINEER	EXPERIENCED ENGINEER	ENGINEER IN TRAINING
Chief engineer	Project engineer	Designer	Mechanical engineer
Director of engineering	Works engineer	Design engineer	Engineer
Technical director	Industrial engineer	Product designer	Electrical engineer
Vice-president, engineering	Group leader	Research engineer	Junior engineer
Research director	Senior engineer	Development engineer	Laboratory engineer
Engineering manager	Section engineer	Product engineer	Assistant engineer
	Supervisory engineer	Tool engineer	
		Structural engineer	
		Machine designer	
		Methods engineer	

The question of titles . . . .

Titles in the Old World and titles in the New are different, but the importance is the same. Politics, personalities and incomes are all affected by titles—and affect them in turn. Our study turned up some interesting embellishments of the endless tide of title changes.

Titles in engineering are almost as diverse as companies or products. They tend to grow like Topsy, both for individuals and for groups, as the organization expands. Periodically, there is a shakeup, and simplified, "standardized" titles are introduced. Then the cycle is repeated. A good example is illustrated here of just such an occurrence in one plant.

There are, for example, vice-presidents of engineering who have nothing to do with design engineering, but only with plant and production engineering. Sometimes the chief engineer is a division or plant executive, sometimes head of an advisory group, sometimes the chief over a series of "engineering managers" in various plants. Sometimes, either the chief engineer or the engineering vice-president has charge of production as well, sometimes of tool engineering, process control or some other phase.

The same situation exists within engineering departments, so no standard titles exist, nor any standard definition of functions. As one chief engineer said, "Titles are often the result of a particular personality problem." One of these is obviously the older engineer who has become a narrow specialist, is out-dated in some areas of technology, or cannot or will not supervise other men. He becomes, quite commonly nowadays, a "staff engineer" or "consultant," attached to the office of the engineering executive. He is given assignments and is available for consulting by younger men. His knowledge

is there when needed, but neither he nor the younger man is committed to its cooperative use under ordinary conditions.

Endless variations hinge on this problem of particular skills and peculiar personalities. Many engineering diagrams reflect it—and are continually being changed because of it—as men retire or leave. Also, there is no "typical engineer," so the ideal diagram is inevitably warped to suit the particular group and the particular size of organization.

Subdivisions of engineering departments are also in constant flux. Changes in product emphasis, sales records, company reorganizations, and other factors are involved, plus the effort to maintain precise designation of functions as some grow and others shrink. This is most noticeable in the aircraft and missiles plants as they move into the "Age of Space" (and as they find it necessary to match men, rank for rank, with contract liaison men from the armed services, or prime contractors). As one aircraft executive said: "Functions that once were part of the job of one man may now be handled by a 50-man group. We are concerned, for example, with thermodynamics as well as aerodynamics, fatigue at temperatures at both ends of the scale, stresses that require new materials and new structural forms almost constantly. Each must be specialized in by a group with the knowledge and capacity to keep us uptodate."

—AND THE MAN

One non-aircraft company has engineering groups for physical electronics, theoretical electronics, solid-state physics, theoretical physics, plastics, special microwave devices, standard microwave devices, and so on. Another is concerned with three phases in development: immediate, 1 to 5 years, and 5 to 10 years; arranges sub-groups and titles to suit.

The general advice of engineering executives who have been through the cycle a few times is: "Stick with simple, standard titles for people and groups. Show specialization in functional diagrams or departmental memos, but keep them out of the basic pattern, or you'll end up in impossible complications. It may even be advisable to follow a company standard for all departments, using a manager-supervisor-foreman system even in Engineering—except for the odd-ball engineer who works alone. His title can be whatever he demands—within reason—because it influences no one else."

Case in point: a company with almost a hundred individual engineering departments. Each is headed by an engineering manager who may have sub-managers (in large setups) or just section managers. Large sections are broken into groups headed by supervising engineers; in smaller groups, the engineers report direct. Thus there are only four supervisory titles. Non-supervisory men are classified in rank from lowest to highest as: junior, intermediate engineer, senior engineer, fellow engineer. ■

HOW TITLES HAVE RECENTLY BEEN STANDARDIZED IN ONE AIRCRAFT COMPANY

Former Classification	Replaced by
Aerodynamicist "A"	Engineer
Aerodynamicist "B"	Associate Engineer
Aerodynamics Engineer	Senior Engineer
Computer Development Engineer	Engineer
Computer Research Engineer	Engineer
Computing Equipment Specialist	Senior Engineer
Computing Specialist "A"	Engineering Specialist
Design Specialist "A"	Engineering Specialist
Design Weight Engineer	Senior Engineer
Dynamacist "A"	Engineer
Dynamacist "B"	Associate Engineer
Dynamics Engineer	Senior Engineer
Engineering Designer "A"	Senior Engineer
Instrumentation Engineer	Engineer
Preliminary Designer "A"	Engineering Specialist
Preliminary Design Engineer "A"	Engineering Specialist
Research Analyst "A"	Engineer
Research Engineer "A"	Senior Engineer
Staff Engineer "A"	Engineering Specialist
Stress Analyst "A"	Engineering Specialist
Stress Engineer "A"	Engineer
Structures Engineer "A"	Senior Engineer
Thermodynamacist "A"	Engineer
Thermodynamics Analyst "A"	Engineer
Thermodynamics Engineer "A"	Senior Engineer
Weight Control Engineer "A"	Engineer

How many engineers?
How many degrees?

Some companies are so concerned with engineering degrees that the degree becomes a sales argument, almost a fetish; others lump degree holders and non-graduates with engineering experience indiscriminately. But most draw sharp distinctions between engineers and supporting personnel such as administrative, clerical, specialist and technician classifications. The typical engineering departments seems to work out at 40 to 50% engineers. R & D departments are somewhat more heavily populated by engineers and scientists, apparently.

R & D may be well over half the total in engineering, particularly where the company is expanding. The most noteworthy example of this is a company with 75% of its engineering personnel (74% engineers) in R & D, and engineering representing 14.2% of total employment. Military development contracts account for this high proportion, as they do in an aircraft subcontractor which has 18.3% of its employees in design, 25% in R & D, with 45% and 50% degree holders respectively. Another similar contractor has only 7½% of its employment in engineering, half being degree holders.

Major aircraft producers provide some interesting statistics. One has 8% engineering personnel. Among the 1700 people represented here are 968 BS degrees, 300 in ME, 238 in Aero E, 180 in EE. There are also 155 advanced degrees. Designers (half the total) show 12½ years median experience. 58% of the personnel have over 8 years experience; the median is 9.9 years. In another company, 10.4% of the payroll are engineers, 15.8% of the payroll are in the engineering department, 53.8% of engineering-department people are engineers. For two plants, the comparable figures are 11.5 and 7.3% of payroll engineers, 17 and 12.4% in engineering, 55.5 and 47.1% engineers. The larger percentages are in the home plant, where designing is centered. In still another, the ratio of engineers and technicians in the company has risen from the 1:15 of World War II to 1:5 today. Average experience of its executive group is 21 years.

Another aircraft company has ⅔ of its engineering personnel in engineers, design specialists, draftsmen and checking personnel to technicians and other assistants. Board work is about 50% of the job. Engineering employment is one in seven of the company total. One subcontractor has 5% engineers in the main plant, 2% in a subsidiary, to average 4.6%. Another has about five chief project or group engineers, each of these in turn having five or six lead engineers or leadmen, each again with six or seven designers and draftsmen. This company has 5% engineering personnel (70% engineers), and even lead engineers have budgets.

Among non-military capital-goods companies, the figures vary similarly. One electrical manufacturer has 14% of its total in engineering, 40% of them degree holders. A control manufacturer has 8% in design, 47% of them engineers. 40% of this department is on R & D—which went up last year while total engineering employment dropped 20%! One diesel maker has 2.5% of its employees in engineering, 2.7% in R & D, another has a total of 3¾%, a third has 7% (30% degree holders) divided 25% on development, 10% on technical design, and 65% on product design.

One electronics company has 11% scientists and engineers, another 14% (⅔ degree holders), a heavy-equipment maker has 10%, another only 3% (but 69% degree holders). A holding company shows 2½% in R & D alone, 55% of them engineering-degree holders. A large company with diverse product lines totals 5% design-engineering personnel in its various product departments, a third as many on central R & D.

There is some recognition also of the problem of the expert designer or specialist who has no management ambitions or abilities. He is promoted to the post of "consultant" or some equivalent title, may upon occasion be paid more than the department manager, and usually reports directly to the highest-ranking engineering executive. He is available for consultation by anyone.

A similar organizational setup may be established in plants where specified specialist problems are frequently encountered. The chief engineer of one division of a large press builder has, for example, six specialist staff engineers as advisers. One division of a large corporation has a bearing specialist in the engineering dept; he is a consultant on bearings for the whole corporation. ■

RATIO OF TECHNICIANS TO ENGINEERS & SCIENTISTS IN VARIOUS INDUSTRIES

	All Activities	R&D Only
All Industries	0.8	0.7
Food	0.8	0.3
Chemicals	0.4	0.6
Petroleum	0.5	0.7
Rubber	0.5	0.6
Primary Metal	0.7	0.6
Fabricated Metal	1.2	0.5
Machinery	1.1	0.8
Elec Equipt	1.0	0.8
Aircraft & Parts	0.6	0.6
Instruments	1.0	0.7
Other Mfg	1.1	1.1
Non-mfg	0.7	0.5

3.

How to Develop Key Men in Your Organization

How old should an executive be

by Vance Packard

The people who size-up executive performance and potential increasingly feel that age is the decisive factor in the final analysis. As more and more companies become conscious of the vital necessity of providing for the development of a strong line of succession, fewer executives can reasonably expect to hold high office and responsibility after age 55.

THE PEOPLE WHO size up candidates for executive openings are likely to say the candidate should be a "good age," and let it go at that. Some laws make it illegal to discriminate on the basis of age (i.e., being "too old"). In actual practice the managements of a great many companies—and their recruiting consultants—take age very much into consideration in filling openings and weighing a man's future prospects.

Management people talk about "age-position relationships," "back-up policies," and "successor-planning policies," all with age factors in mind.

They also agree ruefully that, so far as age is concerned, the choice tends to be relatively small today in the age bracket where they normally prefer to look for candidates for top-level jobs: the group now between 45 and 55 years of age.

A U-shaped curve depicts how, over the years, the number of candidates coming into management-training programmes has varied. Our present prime prospects for presidencies in the 45 to 55-year-old group came into management at the bottom of the U. This is particularly likely to be true if they are in an older company. Younger companies tend to have younger top executives.

In general, however, it can be said that the prime prospects for top jobs in this age group are in a wonderful seller's market for their talent. To turn the coin over, it might also be suggested that the survival-of-the-fittest law has not worked too rigorously with this group. Quite a few of them are sad excuses for executives by any standard. Today's young men, especially those under 35, face a much tighter competitive situation. In some ways this is a hopeful development—or could be in a situation where the criteria for success are ethically and socially sound ones that challenge the young men to become outstanding leaders, and not just to win on the basis of blandness, adaptability, and political skill.

Most of the serious candidates for corporate presidencies in the US today are in their early fifties. They will, on the average, be selected for such positions by the age of 55. In Great Britain they are chosen somewhat earlier.

Two sides of the coin—Patterns vary drastically by companies, of course. The executive suites of a number of successful companies—usually fairly new electronics or prefabricated-home companies—are manned almost entirely by men under 40. An ambitious, talented man may hesitate to join such a company because, barring upheavals and premature deaths, he might have to wait at least two decades to get a chance at the top. On the other hand, in many other companies, particularly in the utility field, the executive suites are occupied almost entirely by men over 60 who are apt to feel strongly that a man is incapable of assuming serious responsibility unless he is near their age. In one utility company, all but two of the company's top 16 men are in their sixties or late fifties.

In any company a man at any level may well conclude that his future progress is likely to be slower if men his own age move into the important positions immediately above him. Such a man, who feels he is blocked or has been by-passed because of age factors, is "movable". The executive recruiters are constantly searching for "movable"—or secretly discontented—men (and women). They can often look at the age pattern of the top six or eight men in a company and then say, "Here is your movable man."

Succession planning—The president of a $500 million (£178m.) company modestly attributed his achievement in attaining such high office by the age of 40 to poor planning. The founder of the company, he said, had "expected to live forever" and had given little thought to providing for the development of a strong line of succession.

Few major corporations today are guilty of such neglect. A company recruiting officer told a presidents' forum of the American Management Association in 1960 that proper *timing* belongs in every executive development programme. He was re-

ferring to the effect of age and its relationship to the problem of executive retention. A second-level team often finds itself behind a top team which still has years to go before retirement. This second team often contains outstanding men who are fully developed and ready but, because of bad timing, are frustrated and "stymied" and consequently receptive to offers from other companies.

In some instances the larger, older companies reportedly slow down the progress of a highly promotable young man simply because they fear that the spectacle of such a young man making prodigious strides might create more anxiety among other managers in the hierarchy than his services at the top would be worth at that point. Similarly, I came across instructions in an appraisal manual which specified that a man over 50 should not be considered for the job of manager of field sales—regardless of his qualifications—because this post should be reserved for a younger "backup man" who could ultimately replace the general sales manager. It was felt that a man over 50 could never attain the position of general sales manager, and so shouldn't be moved into the backup position.

Appraising potential — John Handy, a management consultant, suggests that "the appraisal of a man's growth potential cannot be determined by simply plotting an extension of his earlier progress. Every man has a ceiling to which he progresses easily and without serious check, but when he reaches this he commences going sideways. . ."

The younger a man is when he reaches any point in a hierarchy the better he is likely to look on the form charts. He should never get into a position where he is competing with younger men, because everyone would rather have younger than older. If a man is 52 and hopes to be a department head it is possible that he is being compared to men who are department heads at the age of 45. Up in general management, however, he can be 60 and not be considered too old.

A career counsellor once explained the hazard in these words: "If the man is at the same spot at 40 that another man is at by the age of 35 he is not going to get the same consideration. Other things being equal, they will look for the younger man

because of the desire for continuity of management. They prefer a man of 15 years' potential rather than one of ten."

Dangers of relegation—A man who falls significantly behind his age group faces the danger of being classified—formally or informally—as a competitor who has already reached his optimum. One of the questions that interviewers of candidates for the Diamond Alkali Company's sales force are expected to answer is: "Is he past his peak?" Some suggest that there is a need in corporations today for more approved and honoured ways that men who are not ambitious to reach high levels can win recognition at their present levels.

It should be noted that impressive recoveries have been made by men presumed to be over-age. Arch Patton, another management consultant, relates: "Executives who have fallen behind those in their age group on the organizational ladder frequently do outstanding work when given encouraging leadership. For example, a man who had been a divisional plant superintendent for ten years, suddenly, at the age of 52, started a meteoric rise that lifted him to the executive vice-presidency of the company at 59." It seems that the man, by nature uncompetitive, belatedly realized that his contemporaries were moving ahead of him and he opened up with a brilliant burst of effort that made him stand out from the others.

Similarly there are many occasions when a seemingly over-age man is sought for an important job. An executive of one company reported that his organization was looking for a man approaching 60 for an executive vice-president's job that would pay $125,000 (£44,643) a year. The very promising younger men coming along were not ready and the company did not want to block their way by bringing in someone of their own age. This company, he said, had not reasonably phased out its development of leaders. He cited another instance of a company that hoped to find a good man of about 62 who could serve as financial vice-president of a $100 million company for about three years until a young man the company was grooming was ready to take over.

A good deal of thought has been given to assessing what Mr. Handy calls the "Age-Position Relationship" as one variable factor in establishing a man's potential. Where should the man be on the success scale at each age level and what action should he be taking to further his career prospects?

Age to earnings ratio — On Handy's scale, for example, anyone over 33 should be making more than $15,000 (£5,357). Or as he put it to me: "Any man 33 years old and making $15,000 a year I would like to see. On the other hand if you have a man of 40 making only $18,000 (£6,429) a year you wonder if perhaps he has started going sideways." To put the relationship in terms of job title, he said that it looks fine if a man is a chief industrial engineer at the age of 34, but if he holds the same position at the age of 44 one begins to wonder how much more potential he has.

An American recruiting officer, Martin Flesher, had drawn up an "Age to Earnings Ratio" that involves five checkpoints. To separate the "doers" from the "dreamers" he has posed these minimum earnings:

By age	Earnings	
25	$5-6,000	£1,786-2,143
30	$10,000	£3,571
33-35	$15,000	£5,375
40	$25,000	£8,929
45	$25-35,000	£8,929-12,499

Hergenrather Associates advises me it has arrived at a slightly different age-earnings relationship for "top-drawer" men:

Age	Earnings	
27-30	$9-12,000	£3,214-4,285
30-35	$12-18,000	£4,285-6,429
36-40	$18-25,000	£6,429-8,929
40-45	$20-30,000	£7,143-10,714
46-50	$23-35,000	£8,214-12,500
Over 50	$28-50,000	£10,000-17,857

Some other recruiters questioned whether any age-salary table could have much meaning nationally because of all the variables.

Age to ambition ratio — How should a man of high ambition comport himself at each level? Ideally, in the years between 25 and 35 the ambitious man should be running hard to get himself out in front of the herd. One executive counsellor suggests that "a man should be pretty well up into middle management by 35. If he is not well advanced by that age he won't develop enough momentum in the next seven or eight years to carry him into a top spot."

Mr. Handy offers the thought that "it is a blessing if he does not meet the right girl until he is 28, because he should hold himself free to move from one company or industry to another, and to any area of the country, where his best opportunity for experience and growth lies. He should try to avoid during these years finding himself in a spot where he must consider any other factor in the selection of a job than the prospect that it will develop him, and presents a logical advancement in his career as planned." Mr. Handy considers it wise for the man under 35 to broaden his experience by taking three or four different jobs—provided that he stays at least two years on each and confines his area of operations to the same industry or line of work.

By the age of 36, however, "your gambling years are over," Mr. Handy states sternly. By then the man should have a pretty good and realistic concept of his potential and his goals.

Restless aspirants—It is in this next period—35 to 45—that many aspiring managers become profoundly restless. One survey found that more than half of all executives in this age group wanted to move. Some suggest this restlessness is due to "career menopause". Perhaps another explanation is that many men who in their early years have had a number of easy and fairly rapid advances find themselves bumping up against ceilings.

When a man reaches 38, Mr. Handy contends, he should consider settling down, watch carefully his percentage of successes, try to get into organizations that are well managed, and work toward a position in general management.

The youth among the men who have passed beyond functional responsibilities up into the area of general management is 40 to 45, he says. "Companies are looking for the fellow age 42 who has a proven record of success and has proven while on management committees that he has good judgment. One of the biggest steps in growth is to go from being a departmental head into general management. The head of the sales department, for example, may well know more about the department than anyone under him. But if he gets into general management he will have people under him who know their jobs better than he knows their jobs."

Personality changes — Another way to view the stages of executive life is the psychodynamic one. Dr. W. E. Henry, social behaviourist now at Michigan State University, studied the personalities of three groups of executives that had mean ages of 30, 40, and 50. He subjected them to projective tests in which they were invited to interpret pictures.

The 30-year-olds. For them life seems "amazingly simple". They see the world in which they work as demanding achievement and are convinced that "assertively following the leads provided them by that world will result in success. This younger group is thus oriented to the organization, to what they understand to be the expectations of others."

The 40-year-olds. These executives, in contrast, are starting to see the world as far more complicated. "They are by no means as certain that the objectives of the organization are inevitably correct, and they begin to wonder if wholehearted devotion to achievement and accomplishment in the business world is indeed the one true life," Dr. Henry noted. Along with a more questioning attitude these men are also beginning "to re-examine their own inner lives and personal desires. This frequently takes the form of wondering if they should not have chosen some other occupation, one they propose as more attuned to human values, to the rewards of interpersonal relations." Although more questioning, they hold to their earlier goals in business but see the goals in broader perspective.

The 50-year-olds. The concerns over conflict of values continue, yet tend to be resolved on more internal and personal terms. More than either of the younger groups, the 50-year-olds become "contemplative and philosophic". Their concern is more with "integrative schemes than with the earlier direct action". They seek to derive a rationale and a meaning from their previous experience as guidelines for the future. Some, Dr. Henry pointed out, work out sound, analytic rationales; others simply fall into patterns of "nostalgic reconstruction of their successes" and must seem like repetitious "windbags" to the juniors who must work under them. ■

Probing that urge to achieve

Find Execs with High-Ach Scores

AS ANY businessman knows, most people can be divided, psychologically, into two broad groups: a minority that is challenged by opportunity and willing to work hard to achieve something, and the majority that really does not care all that much.

For 20 years, psychologists have been trying to penetrate the mystery of this curious division. Their studies have sought answers to questions like these:

• Is the need to achieve an accident, is it hereditary, or the result of environment?

• Is this need a single, isolatable human motive, or a combination of motives—the desire for wealth, power, fame?

• Most important of all, is there some technique that could give this urge to achieve to people, even whole societies, that do not now have it?

The research is far from complete, and there are still no definitive answers. But the psychologists now believe they have partial answers to most of these questions, and insights into all of them.

Writing in a recent issue of the IBM magazine *Think*, David C. McClelland, a professor of psychology at Harvard University in the US, reports on the progress of the studies.

The most significant finding is that there is, in fact, a distinct human motive for achievement, which can be found, and even tested for, in any individual or group.

Further, this motive can be acquired, with varying degrees of success, by groups that do not possess it.

In the psychologists' jargon, this elusive motive is called *n* Ach for an individual's "need for Achievement." People who possess high *n* Ach generally display certain marked personality characteristics.

Such individuals, Professor McClelland writes, "are always setting challenges for themselves, tasks to make them stretch themselves a little."

But, he adds, "they behave like this only if *they* can influence the outcome by performing the work themselves. They prefer not to gamble at all."

Give an individual with high *n* Ach a choice between rolling dice with a one-in-three chance of winning and working on a problem with a one-in-three chance of solution and he will choose the work even though the odds of winning are the same.

Professor McClelland says this is because individuals who score high in *n* Ach are "concerned with personal achievement rather than with the rewards of success per se."

He adds that people with a strong *n* Ach motive also show "a strong preference for work situations in which they get concrete feedback on how well they are doing."

Why do certain men develop this way? On one level, says Professor McClelland, the answer is simple: "because they habitually spend their time thinking about doing things better."

Objective test—The psychologists, in fact, generally measure the strength of a man's *n* Ach drive by taking samples of his spontaneous thoughts (such as making up a story about a picture he has been shown) and counting the frequency with which he mentions doing things better. The count is objective and can even be made these days with the help of a computer programme for content analysis.

But the simple answer begs the crucial question—why some people and not others continually think about doing things better.

The evidence to date, reports Professor McClelland, suggests "it is not because they are born that way, but because of special training they get in the home from parents who set moderately high achievement goals but who are warm, encouraging and nonauthoritarian in helping their children reach these goals."

What has been learned, McClelland continues, helps to correct a lot of so-called common sense ideas about human motivation. For example, much business policy is based on the notion that people will work harder "if they have to." At best, McClelland says, this is only a half truth.

Or again, it is frequently assumed that any strong motive will lead to doing things better. But the new, detailed knowledge of human motivation shows that each motive leads people to behave in different ways.

One of the researchers' experiments makes this point neatly. Subjects were told they could choose as a working partner either a close friend or a stranger who was known to be an expert on the problem to be solved.

Individuals with high *n* Ach chose experts over friends.

As Professor McClelland notes, those who chose friends were not unmotivated: "their desire to be with someone they liked was simply a stronger motive than their desire to excel at the task."

Active seekers—But whatever the profession, says Professor McClelland, when people begin to think often in *n* Ach terms, "things begin to move. Men with high *n* Ach get more raises and are promoted more rapidly, because they keep actively seeking ways to do a better job."

Companies with many such men grow faster. In one study of two Mexican firms it was discovered that all except one of the top executives in the faster growing company had higher *n* Ach scores than the highest scoring executives in the equally large but slower growing of the two firms. The same principle seems to apply to countries. Correlations have regularly been found, McClelland reports, between the *n* Ach content in popular literature and rates of national economic growth.

But even if psychologists can detect and analyse *n* Ach levels in individuals and nations, the crucial question remains whether this trait can be imparted to those who do not have it.

Training for achievement—Since 1960, psychologists in Professor McClelland's research unit at Harvard have been seeking to answer this question by running "total push" training courses of a week to 10 days to help individuals increase their *n* Ach level.

The courses had four broad goals: to teach the participants how to think, talk and act like a person with high *n* Ach; to stimulate them to set higher but realistic work goals for themselves over the next two years; to give them greater knowledge about themselves; and to create an *esprit de corps* among the group.

In every experiment except one, Professor McClelland reports, "it was possible to demonstrate statistically, some two years later, that the men who took the course had done better (made more money, got promoted faster, expanded their businesses faster) than comparable men who did not take the course or who took some other management course." ∎

Use staff meetings to discover and develop executive potential

When you next hold a staff meeting, plan to give participants plenty of opportunity to discuss, argue and put forward ideas. Because it's here you'll most likely find your executive personnel of the future

by B. Y. Auger
Minnesota Mining & Manufacturing Co.

A MANAGER IS ONLY as good as his staff—and his staff is only as capable as he makes it.

Every executive admits to this fact, but few put it into practice. Young staff members capable of doing outstanding work aren't born professionals. They have to be developed by men who are—managers with ability and courage who challenge every newcomer to aim for the top. They're also astute enough to know a first-class staff is their own guarantee of success.

The two key elements in this talent hunt for good people is to know where to look and how to bring individual talents to the fore. Many times, a capable young staff member is lost to a company because not enough emphasis was placed on looking for managers in the corporate organization. The grass always seems to be greener in a competitor's pasture or the ivy-covered confines of a university campus.

Testing grounds—You add to an effective staff by constantly testing and retesting young executives—putting them in situations where they must display the type of talent vital to future management function. One of the best corporate testing grounds is the business meeting. For example:
• The business meeting gives managers a chance to see their entire staff in action.
• A meeting is the acid test of management capability. If a man can't hold his temper when his ideas are challenged, sway opinion, move to definite conclusions at a meeting, there's little chance he will do so at other times.
• The meeting is an invaluable barometer of staff morale and attitudes.
• A meeting is often spontaneous, and an excellent test of a young executive's ability to think quickly. Impromptu reactions are hard to come by when holding conversations with individual members of the staff.
• A meeting is excellent for discovery of "problem-solvers". The man who comes to the meeting to find answers to problems—rather than report on what a sterling job he's doing—is the greatest find a manager can hope to uncover. Any company thrives on the man interested in getting the job done today, not bragging about what he accomplished yesterday.
• Most important, the meeting is a guarantee managers won't overlook talented executives developing under their noses. Corporations literally spend millions on training new employees—but can lose out on the investment if this talent isn't recognized or applied correctly.

To gain maximum value from a meeting in light of executive development, it is critical that managers create a meeting climate which stimulates, rather than dulls participation. Everything from the physical layout of the meeting room to orchestrating the agenda must receive your careful consideration.

There are common sense rules which managers can put into operation which will help them find talented young executives.

Stimulate interest—First, create a positive attitude towards the value of meetings both to the individual and the company. Many executives consider meetings a waste of time—dull and uninformative and an "anchor around their necks" keeping them from getting the job done and moving ahead.

In many cases, criticism of meetings is warranted. The average executive spends almost 60 per cent of every working day in meetings of one type or another. It's also a fact many of these meetings are unnecessary, time wasting and accomplish very little.

The only proven method of making meetings mean anything to your staff is by example. Nothing gives more encouragement than a well-run meeting which gets things done. Everyone wants to associate with success. Show your staff that you call a meeting only when it's necessary for achieving a set goal. They'll catch the spirit.

As soon as you can, educate young executives to the fact that active participation in meetings pays handsome dividends for them. In brief, make sure they know the meeting is one of the best management courses they can attend—and a locale where you hunt for future top executives.

Gaining perspective—Point out how the meeting gives a man the opportunity to exchange ideas with other men in their own department—an excellent way of learning the total function of the department. Explain how an inter-departmental meeting will enable him to tie together all of the functional aspects of running a business, to see the other man's point of view, and most important, to learn the overall company view.

The business meeting also offers him an opportunity to sharpen his own knowledge and skills. A meeting forces him to think actively. He must prepare well, think about goals, viewpoints of others, resources and technical problems. And he has a roomful of critics who will review his thinking and help advance it to the next stage of accomplishment.

It is impossible to stress too highly the importance of spotlighting the subjective value of meetings for each member of your staff.

If the executive feels the meeting is an "unfriendly" atmosphere or that an occasional useless idea will bring ridicule, no amount of prodding will get him to volunteer anything or to assume an active role. And he will do

everything possible to avoid future company meetings.

Most of us are familiar with the admonition, "Show me the man who never makes a mistake, and I'll show you a man who never gets anything done." If your audience is made aware that you know this—and that you believe in it—they will be encouraged to voice their own ideas.

Fear of mistakes and of the penalties that go with them breeds inertia. If you can convince your audience that there are no penalties for bad ideas or for trying something new, they will overcome what is probably a natural hesitancy to strike out alone.

Control the group—Another cardinal rule is involvement. A manager must be able to direct a meeting so that of those attending, each has his turn on the meeting stage. This means not letting the direction of the meeting drift, not letting one man play too great a part, and not permitting intolerance with an individual's ideas, no matter how far-fetched they may seem. Respect a man who thinks. His next idea could be worth millions to the company.

Keep an open mind. Every one of us has a subconscious tendency to think our ideas are the only answer. Where would the giants of industry stand today if they had been forced to depend on just one man? Stimulate ideas from everyone at the meeting. But don't allow brain-storming to turn into personality feuds.

Put your men into situations where they must think and act. Ask questions, prod, occasionally switch ideas quickly. I don't mean to harass a man excessively, but rather test his ability to deal with new ideas. A valuable asset for any management-calibre executive is his ability to piece together unfamiliar facts and circumstances into a cohesive plan of action.

Be alert to the man who can separate the essentials from the non-essentials and bore in to the core of a problem. But solution is as important as discovery. Urge him to advance a conclusion. Anyone who can master this pattern of decision-making is worth watching.

It is very important to stimulate interaction between the meeting participants. The brightest, most determined young executive, will never function effectively as a manager unless he's able to gain the respect of his colleagues. This doesn't mean they will love him or even agree with his ideas. But he should be capable of stimulating reaction without alienating or provoking others.

Anticipate participation—This interaction can be planned in advance. When you prepare your meeting agenda and circulate it to those invited to the meeting, you know in advance who will champion which viewpoint. Make sure both sides have a chance to present their views.

Don't embarrass participants by putting them in positions they can't defend. Each man at a meeting was invited because of a specific body of facts he can contribute to the overall problem. Use your men to this end. Direct them in channels which will best utilize their knowledge in the light of their responsibilities.

Use visual aids—Add colour to the meeting with visual aids—overhead projectors, slides, film, chalkboards, visual control boards, etc. Your staff is less likely to remember facts and figures they hear and which are not illustrated.

This is especially true, for example, if an accountant is reviewing profit and loss figures with non-financial men such as field salesmen. People remember and understand better when they become involved by hearing, seeing and participating.

Don't allow disruptive stimuli to throw the meeting off its course. Once continuity is broken, it rarely can be pieced together again. Have telephone operators withhold all calls, discourage secretaries from slipping into the meeting with so-called "urgent" notes. These can just as easily be delivered during a pause in the meeting. Also make sure everything you need for the meeting is ready before the meeting so people aren't rushing back and forth during the meeting.

Examining performance — Fix accountability for action. One of the best methods for testing the timbre of an executive at the next meeting is how well he followed through on decisions and actions decided at this meeting. Talk is cheap. Performance is priceless. ∎

HOW YOU CAN MEASURE

Advancement in executive circles often depends on how well you can measure the ability of superiors and subordinates. And an important part of rating other executives is their reaction to power

by Auren Uris, **Research Institute of America**

HAVING DIFFICULTY in assessing your superior or subordinates? Well, fortunately you don't have to be a psychoanalyst to get them into perspective. While there's no sure way to anticipate how they will act in any situation there are vital clues to their patterns of action.

Here's an approach, simple and lucid, that offers you the opportunity to gain insight into the character of your superior or of those who work under you. And, as a result, improve relationships with them.

Watch managers at work and you'll note that their behaviour usually falls into two distinct patterns. And the key is their reaction to power.

The **power lover** gets pleasure out of being in a position of authority. And precisely because he relishes power, he sometimes unknowingly abuses it.

These are his trademarks:

1. Competition and pressure stimulate him. The harder the push, the harder he pushes himself. He enjoys the combat of the assembly line arena.

2. He accepts responsibility, but bears it lightly. He is not afraid of changing the production line even though he may have to account to his boss and the chairman of the board of directors.

3. He is neither surprised nor repelled that some of his subordinates develop a certain amount of dependency towards him. They consult him about breakdowns, personnel problems, and even about the social matters. He enjoys the "big father" role.

4. Most executives say they want challenge. The power lover really means it. He is encouraged by such phrases as, "It's impossible to meet that delivery schedule," or, "We can't hold it to that close a tolerance."

On the other hand, the manager stricken with **power phobia** is apt to be tense and anxious. This doesn't mean his accomplishments or abilities are less than the power lover. But he worries more. Here's how you can recognize him:

1. His job is a 24-hour-a-day proposition. If you meet him outside working hours he will be talking about work problems rather than the soccer team performance.

2. He's a perfectionist and, what's worse, expects no less from his subordinates.

3. He can probably stand a lot of tension, but it bothers him. So he blows off steam at his nearest target —often you. But it doesn't mean a thing.

4. His power of concentration is superior. Since he strongly fears failure, he will undertake the job with an involvement that can be astounding.

With these characteristics you can decide with fair accuracy in what category a person belongs. However, most managers are a mixture, with a tendency towards one or the other type. For a more exact appraisement use the test at the end of this article.

If the object of your study is a power lover, his sins are usually those of omission and unawareness. Since he plunges head-first into any task, he is liable to disregard others', as well as his own, limitations. Some things he should avoid but can't are:

Blind faith: "If I can do so, so can he," says this manager of his assistant. He's too quick to attribute his own feelings and capabilities to others. He can't understand why everybody isn't completely absorbed in his objectives or the plant's welfare. He is puzzled by a fellow manager who hesitates to pull up roots to take a position in the corporation's new plant, even though it is many miles away.

Insensitivity: He gets so excited over a new product, that he tends to run roughshod over the protests of those about him—even though justified. "We will worry about that later," is his aggravating pet slogan. The "that" may be possible production, quality control, or delivery problems.

The interesting thing is that he often gets away with his power tactics. But in many cases slight consideration or caution might have

EXECUTIVE TALENTS

doubled his accomplishment while halving his headaches.

Blueprint hater: "We'll play it by ear," is another battle cry of this manager. He loves the sometimes dubious feeling of being able to show his flexibility to meet developing events.

In certain situations this flexibility is fine. But occasionally he tries to charge through a situation that requires precise preparation. And the disaster can be stupendous.

You can swing these weaknesses to your advantage. Since the power lover doesn't want to be bothered with the details of planning, he must delegate the job. At the very least he will avail himself of the services of a subordinate. Here is where you come in. Your caution must temper his exuberance. You don't disagree with him, but you do try to spell out your modifications of his ideas tactfully.

Generally, you won't get anywhere trying to counter his moves. If he's a bull in a given situation, don't try to play bear. But suggest modifications while praising him: "That sounds a good idea. But just on the off-chance that production can't hold that tolerance, let's . . ." Give him concrete examples only. He will be the first to thank you if it gets him out of trouble later.

Your power lover tends to be an easy mark for your pet projects. Generally, he'll allow you as much initiative as you're willing to take, but he doesn't mind your bringing headaches to him. Make sure you do this if you have a maintenance problem that's sure to go wrong. If you consult him, then the job is a success, you're both doing good work. But if you should fail, he's then willing to share the blame.

On the other hand, if you have trouble with a project that you haven't alerted him to in advance, you won't rate very high in his eyes. He doesn't like failures, and working with them makes the power lover feel vaguely uncomfortable.

If your man is a power hater, he will more than likely be handicapped by the following characteristics.

Overcaution: He's a poor decision maker, waiting till the last moment to make a move. This aggravates his susceptibility to worry, because when he does move it's with a deadline staring him in the face.

Rigidity: He tends to overplan. This means depending on comprehensiveness rather than on flexibility to take care of the unexpected.

Failure to delegate: It goes against his grain to trust subordinates, and his suspicions are based on exaggerated memories of past failures.

Your biggest job in getting along with a power fearing superior is to subtly gain his confidence. Volunteer for a small assignment—where failure would not be fatal. When you succeed at this, he will be less cautious about giving you important tasks.

Strive to show him concrete results. Vagueness leaves him suspicious or cold. In making a proposal, describe your objective, how you intend to achieve it, what it will cost, and when you expect to complete it. When you report to him on progress, restate these objectives. Then spell out progress to date.

In your final report, pin down what's been done, costs, benefits, lessons learned, and possible advantages to be followed up. You will never make him angry by acknowledging the role that he has played. This is a quality he shares with every kind of manager. ■

How to rate executive reaction to power

Answer the questions as accurately as possible, selecting the alternative that comes closest to describing his normal type of behaviour:

1. *You tell your boss, "Mr. Smith, I have a good idea for improving our quality control procedure on the new line." He says—*
   a. "That's fine. Try it, and then let me know how it works out."
   b. "That's fine. Give it to me in a report and I'll consider it."

2. *At the end of the day—*
   a. He settles in for overtime work.
   b. He frequently is off for his club, a social event in town, or a sports contest.

3. *As far as taking you into his confidence about problems at hand is concerned—*
   a. He has surprised you by his openness in discussing his thoughts and concerns about the work.
   b. He seems to feel that his business is his business, and he isn't likely to lower the invisible barrier he uses to screen off his problems.

4. *He seems to be—*
   a. Philosophical about his subordinate's failures.
   b. Viewing subordinates' failures or failings with concern. Makes visible efforts to offset them.

5. *About his general manner, you'd say—*
   a. He's extroverted, an optimist, and brims over with enthusiasm for his work.
   b. He's introverted, pessimistic, serious-minded, an ultrarealist.

6. *As far as delegation is concerned—*
   a. He uses it freely; indeed, sometimes appears to over-use it.
   b. He uses it cautiously; and seems to under-delegate.

Probably for the large majority, the score will be mixed—3 a's, 3 b's, or 4 and 2, in one combination or the other. This is pretty much what one would expect just on the basis of normal distribution. Nevertheless, even if your man seems to be sitting on the fence, give a moment's thought to other areas of activity or signs not included in the brief quiz above to evaluate the manager's style. It will help you deal with him successfully.

How to motivate key men

Individual incentive to succeed is closely associated with high job performance. Here are seven motivators that never fail—which you can apply to your employees to help them realize their top potential

by Paul J. Meyer
Success Motivation Institute

PEOPLE ARE the same the world over. Consider any key employee. However great his talent or ambition, he still needs inspiration and psychological support from his superior if he is to perform at the peak of his ability.

Repeated study proves that the employee who is spurred by a self-motivating attitude is from two to 10 times more efficient and productive than his inadequately motivated counterpart.

This holds specially true for the employee who operates abroad on a full time or periodic basis. His business and personal problems are more complicated. His hours are often long and unpredictable. His responsibilities are greater.

Since an extra effort is expected of him, a compensating extra effort in job satisfaction and recognition must be offered to him, in his support, by his superiors.

Many managers don't spend enough of their time motivating people. They are too busy with procedures and solving day-to-day operational problems. This is where they defeat themselves. Without realizing it, they stifle potential when they should be releasing it.

Seven motivators—Here are seven motivators you and your departmental managers can apply to help you tap the latent productive power of employees:

1. *Uncover tools of self-motivation that work best for each employee.*

A New York exporter's vice-president was shocked when a key product manager resigned to go to work for a competitor. The vice-president honestly believed that he had shown the manager every consideration.

Whenever a personal emergency arose, he claimed, he always gave the matter his fullest attention and concern. This was true. But a deeper probe showed that only rarely did he take the time to investigate problems and needs that were not called to his attention by others.

In this case, the product manager felt frustrated. He believed that his talents were not being adequately used, and that his career was stuck in a rut. The fact that his feelings were largely groundless is not significant. What matters most is that his boss was too busy to either recognize the feelings or take the appropiate steps to set them straight.

The importance of applying the so-called "personal touch"—rallying to the aid of people in trouble; getting to know the employee, his family and his hobbies—cannot be overstressed.

The effectiveness of each motivational tool varies from person to person. The trick is to really get to know your people—to see them as they see themselves. It's not hard to do. All it takes is a little time; and no investment is more worthwhile.

Talk to your key people. Ask questions. Study their reactions. Identify their frustrations, whether they are groundless or not.

Differentiate between those factors that fuel enthusiasm and those that sap interest and initiative.

Only then will you be able to discover and apply the particular self-motivational tools that work best for each employee.

2. *Get your key people personally involved in the goal-setting act.*

The truly inspired employee possesses a burning desire to achieve and surpass his stated goals. Before such inspiration can be generated, the employee must be convinced that his goals are realistic and attainable. Then, by getting him to commit himself openly to the goal's fulfilment in front of other people, his desire to achieve will be multiplied to the point of peak performance.

How can you inspire both total conviction and total commitment? There's one sure way.

Encourage the employee to formulate his own goals as completely as possible. He will need your judgement and guidance to set a goal that neither exceeds the mark, nor falls short of it. But if you can get him to spell out the final specifics for himself, and couple this statement with open commitment, his determination to succeed will know no bounds.

Studies prove beyond doubt that the self-imposed challenge boosts performance by sparking job interest and adding a stimulating dash of excitement to normal routine.

Moreover, shooting for a goal that he truly believes in, and played a key role in creating, satisfies an important psychological need for the employee. It makes for a harmonious meshing of company and individual objectives.

3. *Kindle employee fires with enthusiastic leadership.*

A Brussels-based assistant branch manager was assigned the job of tracking down distributors for a new product line of solvents. The assistant was handed a few brochures. He was briefed in routine fashion about the line. And he was given two weeks to accomplish his mission.

When he returned to the office he had nine contracts in his briefcase.

Vital spark—Unhappy with results, headquarters sent a key executive to check into the situation. This man was completely different from the assistant's boss. His eyes sparkled. There was an edge of excitement in his voice when he talked.

When the executive discussed the new product line, the air virtually crackled with electricity. He punched the table to punctuate his words. The intensity in his voice was contagious. Before the session was through, the assistant was convinced that the new line was one of the biggest things ever to happen to his company.

The opportunities, he was convinced were unlimited. The size of the branch —and with it, the importance of his job—could double in six months as a result of this special effort.

Subsequently, next morning, the assistant went out for another two-week trip. This time, he came back more fully charged than when he left. He felt completely fulfilled, having more than tripled the performance of his first trip.

It never fails. Enthusiasm is one of the most potent self-motivators known. Enthusiasm triggers action and inspires cooperation. It is capable of converting a "blah" attitude into a compelling, rip-roaring GO-GO-GO.

4. *Flatter employees by consulting them on important matters.*

Any action that boosts an employee's feeling of importance and personal worth has a motivational impact that inspires peak performance.

Test this for yourself on one of your key people. Ask his opinion about a thorny problem. Solicit his views on an important decision. Or invite him to sit in on a high level meeting. Then watch his reaction.

Possibly his face will light up with pleasure. And don't be surprised if his action response exceeds your estimate of his ability. In one company, a data processing manager, invited to sit in on a sales meeting, came up with a brilliant new incentive plan that increased his company's sales by a spectacular 20 per cent.

When you invite an employee to participate above his normal level, he will interpret your action as a sign that you respect his judgement and appreciate his value.

By appreciation, Voltaire said, we make excellence in others our own property. It is a motivational investment that is worth making because it pays a handsome return.

5. *Shoot for total understanding of policies and objectives.*

Ask any executive to state his most pressing problem, and more often than not his answer will be "communications". On an international basis, this problem takes on added complications.

The best motivated employees are those who work with their superiors in a climate of mutual trust and respect. When minds do not meet effectively, such a climate is virtually impossible to achieve.

Problem analysed—What makes communications such a problem is chiefly the lack of adequate communications about the art of communications itself.

A sales manager in a multinational oil company was asked to give a percentage estimate of how well he got through to his people. His opinion was that he communicated effectively 90 per cent of the time.

About the author

Paul J. Meyer was a millionaire insurance salesman at the age of 27. Then, five years ago, he established Success Motivation Institute, which has its headquarters in Waco, Texas. Meyer has made a success out of making other people successful, and he claims: "With a self-motivating attitude, any individual can reach any goal he sets his mind on."

Then his people were asked the same question. In their view, he got through only 50 per cent of the time.

Obviously, somewhere the gears weren't meshing. Do you share this problem? If so, there's a way to solve it. Guarantee your communications effectiveness by testing your people's information output while you are in the act of communicating.

You can do this by feeding information on a "controlled flow and response" basis. Communicate one measured portion of information at a time. Then, before proceeding, test the response in these three ways:

1. Pay close attention to the employee's reaction. If the message isn't getting through, the expression on his face will often tip you off.
2. Ask pertinent questions to check his understanding.
3. Get the employee to repeat your meaning in his own words.

The longer you communicate without testing, the more likely you will be to experience information lapse. And information lapse undermines the motivational effort.

6. *Combat job tedium by challenging the employee to surpass himself.*

A machine tool company's engineer was sent out to a customer on a sensitive trouble-shooting assignment. The man was petrified. He was strictly a desk man who had never left the office before, and he didn't altogether relish the idea of doing so now.

The boss brushed aside his fears. "You're the best man we have for this job. I just can't risk jeopardizing the account by sending another man with less ability."

Despite his doubts, the engineer followed through on the assignment. He not only solved the problem, but received a special commendation from the customer for his effort.

Untapped potential—It's a proven fact. Nothing thrills an employee more than the discovery that he is better than he thought, or that he can convince others he is a better man than they thought.

Every individual, short of the mentally incapable, possesses a remarkable depth of untapped potential awaiting little more than a well-timed prod to be profitably released.

All that it takes to drive this latent talent to the surface through self-motivation is the provision of an honest and stimulating challenge.

It is not always easy to apply. First, the challenge must be backed by your honest belief in the individual's ability to succeed. Then, your belief must be backed by willingness to shift large chunks of responsibility on to the back of the untried employee.

7. *Set performance standards high but within grasp. Then give your people free rein to make the grade on their own momentum.*

A business machines salesman wrote $100,000 (£35,714) of business a year out of one branch office. He ranked fifth among eight salesmen. Then he was transferred to another branch where performance standards were higher. Here, he wrote almost $150,000 (£53,570) worth of business and ranked sixth among 10 salesmen.

It is a much repeated pattern. An employee will respond to the excellence of his group by motivating himself to meet or surpass his peers. Individual incentive to succeed is closely associated with high performance, no matter what the job may be.

In short, set high but attainable standards for your people to shoot for. Then surround them with competent associates in an atmosphere of shared mutual respect.

Finally, allow them a free measure of self-achievement unrestricted by direct pressures to produce. You will have one of the most powerful motivational tools known to man, working in your behalf. ■

"Snodgrass, I just wanted to let you know how you stand on our team."

Executive Coaching Catches On

Many companies are turning to tete-a-tetes between a manager and his assistant to let subordinate know where he stands in company and discuss how he can become more effective in his job.

IN OFFICES all over the U.S. today, a manager and the man immediately under him self-consciously face each other in a soul-searching discussion of the subordinate's performance. For many of these men, it will be the most awkward situation of the whole year. Yet the practice is spreading as more top management men see it as a help in coaching junior executives.

• **Wide Interest**—American Management Assn. reports that applicants come in through the windows whenever it announces a seminar on appraisal reviews. And management consultants, a sure barometer of management interests, are jumping into the field. Dozens of companies already are subjecting their executives to these personal evaluation sessions. Among some of the big ones now doing it are Monsanto Chemical Co., Boeing Airplane Co., Atlantic Refining Co., Procter & Gamble Co., General Foods Corp., Food Machinery & Chemical Corp., General Mills, Inc. Hundreds of others are getting set to give executive coaching a try.

• **What It Is**—In theory, the appraisal review works this way. The boss closets himself with his subordinate and there ensues a comprehensive give-and-take discussion of the subordinate's performance on the job, relations with fellow workers, standing with his superiors, all his strengths and weaknesses. The wind-up is a heart-to-heart talk on how the junior manager can improve himself. Most frequently, before this interview takes place, the boss talks with his own superior or a committee of higher executives to make the initial appraisal.

Many companies are now turning to the appraisal review because it gives the boss a chance to tell his next-in-line just where he stands and possibly where he is going. It also provides a means for "improving" a man, mold him to fit in with the company team.

Some companies, however, will have nothing to do with appraisal reviews at all on the grounds that "the personnel function is already much too formalized."

• **Conventional Method**—A large number of companies, of course, already do have superiors fill out written appraisals or merit forms on the people who work under them. These reports make their way up the line to higher executives and then into the files. The difficulty with this system: The people being judged wonder and worry about the results. One member of a large consumer goods company voiced a popular complaint when he confided: "They never fire anybody. They never tell you how you are doing. You don't know, so pretty soon you get awfully restless."

• **Management Questions**—Just how well do face-to-face appraisal programs work out in practice: Is there any resistance on the part of the people who are expected to participate? Do the parties really let their hair down and freely express their thoughts during the interviews, is there a true give-and-take exchange? Do the subordinate employees actually improve or develop? Are the programs worth the thousands of dollars that companies are sinking into them? These are the questions a lot of management people are asking themselves.

• **General Findings**—BUSINESS WEEK reporters visited consultants, top executives, and middle management men across the country to get a glimmer of some of the answers. They found different systems among the companies they called on, got different reactions at various levels of management within the companies. In general, this is the picture:

• The appraisal review is pretty largely a middle management affair. The senior executives who sanction the procedure, rarely prescribe it for themselves. Most are willing, even anxious, to get reports and establish rapport with the men below them. Middle management men voice some doubts about the system, have some strong complaints about it, but also some kind words.

• Really open, two-way talks seldom occur. Usually the superior does the giving and his assistant the taking, with few letting their hair all the way down.

• Most executives seem to doubt that tete-a-tete appraisals effect any deep changes in their juniors, or in themselves.

• Appraisal interviews are extremely hard to conduct—especially when they get away from job performance and move into attitudes or personal habits. And when handled ineptly by the senior manager, they can cause some flare-ups.

• **The Interview**—What goes on in an appraisal interview varies with the company, the men, and the jobs involved, but there is a discernible pattern.

Normally, the interview starts with a review of the subordinate's strong points. "They can't keep a chip on their shoulders while they're taking a bow," explains one personnel man.

Then the senior executive gradually moves into areas where the assistant could stand improvement. "Let the subordinate do all the talking. He'll tell you what's wrong with himself, and all you have to do is agree," says one manager.

From this point, in some companies, the interview progresses to a man's attitudes or even to his personal habits. He may be told, "This is why you don't get along with fellow workers," or "You're not trying very hard." The senior executive may expound his concept of what top management expects in the way of employee decorum. The subordinate may get gentle hints to put away his loud ties, to drop certain

of his luncheon companions.

Before the interview is concluded, the two men are supposed to have agreed on what areas of performance are poor and how they will be worked on. At the next appraisal, or perhaps sooner, they will meet again to see how the improvement program is coming along.

"The process is a gentle form of whip, combined with a friendly arm around the shoulder," thinks one executive.

But applying the technique raises some special problems.

• **Question of Authority**—One manager interviewed by BUSINESS WEEK brought up another problem. "What comes of these reviews?" he asks. "If I tell a man he is doing well but can't give him a raise, does that make him feel better or worse? If I tell a man he is doing poorly but can't fire him, then what?" Most managers are in the same position. They can make recommendations, but the actual power of giving out raises, firing a person, even directing his work often rests two or three levels higher. Actually, many companies deliberately schedule the appraisal sessions far apart from the salary review period, so employees won't expect raises after a favorable review.

In some respects an appraisal review is like calling in your wife, telling her you've had an eye on her performance for the past year, are generally pleased, but would like to make a few suggestions for improvement. Everyone admits the situation could be handled better on a day-to-day basis.

• **The Advantages**—But most executives seem to agree that the appraisal review draws attention to the job and brings it into sharper focus. They also cite these other reasons in favor of the system.

• It forces them to analyze their men—and this must be done in a fairly objective manner, since they must justify their appraisals to the men personally.

• It brings into the open problems that might otherwise be overlooked. At one interview, a subordinate blurted out that his work was being ignored. This turned out to be true—but it isn't anymore.

• It can prevent a good man from getting lost in the shuffle. One interviewee, given a low rating in initiative by his chief two years ago, complained at that time that he never got a chance to show any. Taken at his word, he was tossed some tough assignments, did well, and recently moved up a rung when his boss got promoted.

• "It reassures the nervous Nellys you find in every department, and if you get along well with your men it

gives them a chance for a quiet hour in which to get things off their chests or have that chat you've all been too busy for," says one executive.

• **Interviewees' Reaction**—Interviewees generally find the appraisal interviews uncomfortable, but say they do like the idea of knowing where they stand with the boss and what's going on record.

How effective an interview is depends largely on the interviewers. "If your boss is relaxed, and confident about his own position, you usually get a pretty good interview," says one Pittsburgh veteran. Quite a few men think that going through an interview themselves with their own chiefs, helps them give a better one in turn.

• **Picking Up Tips**—Recent college graduates take to reviews quite easily. They are accustomed to being told how they stand and are eager for any tips on how to adjust, says a personnel man. The same, he says, holds true for the "hot shots," rising young men pretty sure they are doing a good job but anxious for any extra tips they can pick up on how to please the top brass.

Those apt to dread the reviews are usually men who know they are doing poorly.

Most men seem to look on reviews as handy reference guides for external behavior on the job. They only balk when the reviews become too much of a pressure session or degenerate into a layman's form of psychology.

• **Injured Feelings**—One engineer, affronted at his superiors' comments on his private life, left for another job. They "eliminated a man who didn't fit the pattern, but they also lost one of their most creative designers," says a consultant.

• **Committee Approach**—Appraisal review systems vary from company to company. But as management becomes more familiar and experienced with the method in general, one particular system seems to be coming to the fore. That's the committee approach.

Under this setup, a committee of seniors, including a man's immediate supervisor, hold an appraising session. Then, the supervisor closets himself with his assistant and presents the group findings and suggestions. From there, the two men discuss in what ways improvements can be made.

This system offers several advantages. Since the appraisal committee usually represents an important segment of hierarchial authority, its pronouncements generally carry a good deal of weight. The committee approach also eliminates any tendencies for personal prejudice. And it takes a great load off the supervisor. Instead of saying "I think . . . ," he can say, "We believe. . . ." ∎

EXECUTIVES, WIVES—AND TROUBLE

There are troubles galore when the ladies mix with business.

—W. R. ROBERTS

Most Americans, says famed psychoanalyst Erich Fromm, conceive of the ideal relationship between a man and his wife as that of a "smoothly functioning team." They believe, Fromm says, that the partnership works because both parties are cooperative and tolerant with each other even as they are exhibiting such "get ahead" qualities as ambition and aggressiveness.

Nowhere is this concept of the team marriage followed more closely—and in no area has it become more of a problem—than in American industry today. With the rise of business entertainment, wives have become intertwined in business affairs to a marked degree. They appear at conventions, at company cocktail parties, at industrial dinners. And they act as hostesses or guests, of course, when executives entertain each other.

But what, exactly, should the role of a wife be in business? Indeed, should she be considered as playing a part in business at all? In other words, if the executive is considered as being part of a husband-wife team, it would seem to follow that his wife's qualities should be considered when the man himself comes up for promotion, no matter how capable he personally may be.

These questions only hint at the full range of problems that can arise from the mere existence of the executive wife. Should she, for example, be allowed to accompany her executive husband on a business trip? If she should, then at what management level does this particular form of corporate togetherness begin? And when she does go on a business trip or attend a convention, how much should she be expected to do?

It is unlikely that more controversial questions than these have ever been presented to the nearly 300 top-ranking executives who make up the DUN'S REVIEW Presidents' Panel. This is pointed up by the fact that an unusually high number of the panelists requested that their names not be used with their answers. In all, some 60% agreed to tell what they thought about executive wives—but only if they could do it anonymously.

And from their answers there would seem to be no doubt that wives can cause trouble both in a man's career and in the fortunes of even the largest corporation. Consider the reaction of the panelists when they were asked what characteristics made for an unsatisfactory executive wife. Only one panelist could think of none. All the other executives had no trouble in being specific. Repeatedly, in fact, they cited three characteristics that must be among the most common sins of the executive wife:

• "A shrew that makes a man unhappy at home."
• "Putting on the dog with other wives."
• "Insisting that her husband should move along faster than his ability warrants."

The nature of the corporation today is also contributing to the importance of the wife. The modern multidivision corporation means increased movement for today's executives, both travel of the day-to-day variety and major moves of home and children from one city to another as positions

FULLER

change. If the executive wife rebels, if she is unable to adjust to such changes, the husband—and his company—will suffer.

And even that only hints at the headaches that can come from the executive wife. An equally thorny problem, and one that can cause friction among executives themselves, is the problem of travel; specifically, the extent to which a wife should accompany her husband on a business trip. That industry has adopted no hard-and-fast rules here either is indicated by the widely varying answers of the panelists to the question "Do you feel that wives should be included in their husband's business travels?" The wide range of answers:

- "Yes"—15%.
- "No"—13%.
- "Occasionally"—28%.
- "Rarely"—7%.
- "Not as a rule"—2%.
- "Depending on purpose of the trip" —4%.
- "Not unless they want to"—2%.
- "Only when necessary"—7%.
- "To an extent"—4%.

When the wife goes along, the panelists seem to say, particularly on an international trip, it is the corporation's intent that she provide the husband with companionship and good cheer. On an overseas journey, from the company standpoint, the wife's "job" is primarily on the personal level. The social aspects, "mixing" with other executive wives and attendance at evening affairs, becomes relatively more important on shorter trips.

In this regard, some panel members take a hard line. Says President M.W. Townsend of Handy & Harman: "A wife should be included on a business trip only when there is a planned program for wives, such as at a convention."

Other panelists, however, have a quite different approach. President Charles W. Perelle of American Bosch Arma Corp. feels that the executive wife should accompany her husband "as often as she can be persuaded to go." Perelle is particularly in favor of her going along on longer trips.

The personal touch

But choosing the events that she should attend is only one part of the problem of the traveling executive wife. There is another, equally perilous question that must be faced by top management: At what level on the management totem pole should an executive be allowed to take his wife on a business trip? This problem, of course, touches on the always delicate problem of the executive and his ego.

Here, too, the nation's corporations do not seem to have worked out any clear policy, possibly because some companies are more entertainment-minded than others. Some 38.2% of the panelists say that wives should be taken along on trips only by top management; that is, president, chairman and those executives who are listed as officers in the articles of corporation.

Another 32.4%, however, broaden out the executive group. As they see it,

wives should be taken along by what might be called senior management, such as executive vice presidents, comptrollers, group vice presidents and, particularly in the larger companies, division managers.

The remaining 29.4% of the panelists would allow men much further down the management ladder to take their wives on trips. They would include department heads, assistant vice presidents, sales managers and other such members of middle management.

When the wives do go along on a business trip, however, the corporation is taking one very perilous fact for granted. It is assuming that she can help her husband close a business deal and enhance the reputation of the company. More importantly, it is also making the tacit assumption that she will not hinder or hurt whatever business may be transacted.

All of which leads to the inevitable question: What kind of woman makes the perfect executive wife? What are the qualities that she needs most? To the head of one of the nation's largest manufacturing companies, there are just three qualities to look for. The perfect executive wife, he argues, is "well-mannered, gracious and even-tempered."

As the wives might be the first to complain, a man tends to expect many things of a woman. No exceptions, the panelists mention still other qualities they seek in an executive wife. Among them: "a good dresser," "a patient sounding board for her husband," "acceptable in the community," "someone who entertains well" and—somewhat racily—"a good looker."

What about the other side of the coin? Just as any number of qualities make up a satisfactory executive wife, there are any number of other qualities that can make a wife unsatisfactory. And as the panelists' remarks quoted earlier in this article indicate, this is one area in which management has compiled a lot of experience.

President Richard J. Stockham of Stockham Valves and Fittings reflects the views of many panelists in summing up the qualities of the unsatisfactory wife. By and large, he says, she is a woman who tends to "dismiss the importance of the success of the organization," who is "spoiled and overly ambitious, constantly attempting to be 'upstage.'" Stockham warns against "wives with dominant characters" who tend to

"throw their weight around," thereby creating problems "within the organization as well as with customers."

Other panel members criticize wives who get "too involved in company matters" or who exert "too much influence on their husbands' relationships with others in the company." And several panelists mention wives who control their husbands' recommendations as to actual personnel policies, including promotions and salary increases.

Corporate "togetherness"

The desire for some degree of business socializing seems almost universal among the panelists, but it is nearly matched by concern over too much company "togetherness" on the social level. Several presidents feel that "togetherness" of any kind can only lead to friction. Reports of interference by company wives in the operations of the firm are particularly prevalent for family-owned organizations.

The recognition of the importance of the executive wife, both positively and negatively, run throughout the replies of the Presidents' Panel. Even those panelists who shy away from too lengthy a discussion of the subject agree to its importance. And this attitude is quite accurately reflected in replies to one of the more controversial inquiries posed in the questionnaire: "Do you feel it is necessary for top management to meet a man's wife before he is appointed to a high executive position?" More than two-thirds feel that a meeting is either necessary or, at the very least, highly desirable.

An interview with the wife is also considered useful in determining whether she would be a liability to her husband. The company, many panelists agree, should know about disagreeable social habits or other factors that might hamper an executive's career.

Thus, though many respondents were plainly unhappy about discussing the role of the executive wife, most voted for the "meeting" with an appointee's wife as being in the mainstream of modern corporate practice. Lest this be construed, however, as blanket approval of the social role of the wife as opposed to the more personal role, one panel member quoted Euripides to indicate where he placed the greatest importance. "Man's best possession," said that ancient worthy, "is a sympathetic wife." ∎

A Way to Produce Group Leaders

Businessmen will be hearing a lot about "group dynamics" in the next year or two. This concept—actually a method of high-level training—may be one of the keys to supervisory and executive development that industry has long needed, and never found.

If you attend many company conferences—and what executive does not?—you will appreciate that a prime need is for (1) a way to make group meetings much more productive than they are, and (2) a way to develop group leaders (executives) who can take charge of meetings and guide them to effective results. Good leadership and responsive participation are in great demand.

Group dynamics may furnish the answer—a teaching method that relies on student participation in practical exercises, and probes the basic elements of the group leader's role, the group member's role, and the function of the group as a whole.

The idea was developed in the U.S.A. by members of the National Training Laboratories, which is a branch of the National Education Association of America. (The writer attended a six-weeks spe-

cial course at the Gould Academy in Bethel, Maine, U.S.A., conducted by the NTL. He was one of three British members on a 22-person mission to America, sponsored by the European Productivity Agency, Paris.)

The form of training is called "T-Group" (Training Group). The purpose is to allow a person to see himself at work as others see him —an experience which can be both exhilarating and humbling. This is the method:

Fifteen or 16 trainees sit around a large table together with a man designated as trainer. The trainer is originally looked to by all members as the person who will give guidance on how the sessions will be run. After a time, members realize that this man is giving no guidance at all. Some become irritated at his lack of leadership; others may suggest topics for discussion, and these proposals may or may not be accepted by the group. Periodically the trainer will intervene to suggest what is in fact taking place in the group. He may point out that various members have tried to take the lead in guiding the group; some having a degree of success, others not.

The trainer is something like the chorus in a Greek play. He describes what is happening within the group—but without helping resolve the tensions that may be apparent to the members.

Members may talk about whatever they wish. Once this is realized—and further, that the sanction for continuing with a topic lies with the members and not the trainer—the trainer is no longer a threatening figure. It usually takes several hours of discussion before most members see the trainer in this light.

It is gradually realized that the insights into the working of the group can in some ways be generalized, and applied to other work groups. Sometimes these observations are made by members, sometimes by the trainer. For instance, is voting by a show of hands the best method of gaining assent? Does silence indicate agreement? Under what conditions will a person disagree?

Gradually, course members begin to see the importance of emotion, and realize that in every meeting there is the inter-play of two levels of reality. On the surface is the task, the immediate problem; below the surface are the social and emotional needs facing the group and the individuals within the group. These emotions can help, or hinder, the making of sound decisions.

Certain aspects of running meetings take on new significance for the trainee. How much does a person have to give up—of his own feelings and beliefs—to belong effectively to a work group? What is the real meaning of consensus of opinion? What must be done to deal with problems rationally, not emotionally? Is it possible to arrive at decisions so as not to give rise to a jubilant majority and a resentful minority? This form of training permits a person to ask himself and others these very searching questions—and to attain reasonable answers.

Running simultaneously with the T-Group are three other forms of training which are part of group dynamics. These, too, give insight into human behaviour:

• Theory sessions—where lecturers illustrate and explain the great power of group standards and what happens when people try to push a group too fast, or try to dominate a group.

• A-Groups—informal afternoon gatherings, practice sessions where novice group leaders are shown how difficult it is sometimes to institute social change and reconcile genuine differences.

• C-Groups—community groups, very much like what the British Army calls "grouse-sessions." The purpose is to allow people to come together and talk "off the cuff"—informally and candidly—about aspects of the course which bother or frustrate them.

These exercises reveal the power, resilience, and heart-warming solidarity that can be maintained in work groups. This dormant productivity cannot be harnessed through inspired leadership alone. It depends on each member helping to create an atmosphere of mutual confidence in which the gifted can contribute to the benefit of all, and the silent feel encouraged to speak. The best chairman is a moderator, not a dominator. This is the type which industry needs so urgently. More than anything else, the chairman's job is one of coordination. ∎

How to displace executives

WHEN a top executive is removed from his job, the move must be calculated to avoid damaging company morale, public relations and the company's prospects.

According to Frank L. Bird, a manufacturing manager of a large US industrial company, there are five ways to displace an executive, depending on the reasons for the move. These are familiar to everyone in business. But in Michigan State University's 'Business Topics' Bird lays them out in systematic order around the points of the compass. In dry, analytical language he describes them this way:

• *Moving the job, not the man:* Accomplished through retention of office and title and the movement of a subgroup out from under the individual. This is a difficult exercise and is used where it is important that the displacement be concealed from the public. The dangers lie in the maintenance of morale and productivity within a subgroup that is suddenly forced to break communication and loyalty ties and construct a similar relationship with another group and its manager. Communications from outside sources to this office are often difficult to handle without an announcement that "he isn't responsible for that any more."

• *West and Out:* Obviously the most simple procedure and one that is final in most cases. Although it is often the most humane, this direction is being used less and less because fewer managers have the moral fibre to confront a subordinate; it creates a possible deteriorating effect on the morale of that part of the organization that thinks the action unfair; there is the possibility of publicity and adverse effects on sales contacts and investors who may assume there is instability within the company.

This direction can be softened, of course, by the possibility of early retirement or disability leave of absence if the age and health of the individual provide an excuse for the action.

• *North and Up:* Often used because it is easiest, this step may be disguised to the public and the organization and even the affected individual

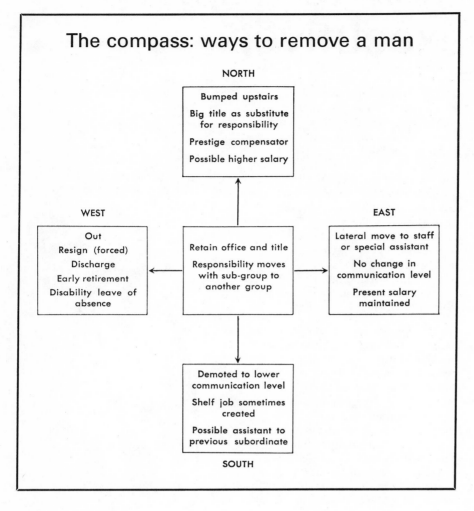

The compass: ways to remove a man

NORTH

Bumped upstairs

Big title as substitute for responsibility

Prestige compensator

Possible higher salary

WEST

Out

Resign (forced)

Discharge

Early retirement

Disability leave of absence

Retain office and title

Responsibility moves with sub-group to another group

EAST

Lateral move to staff or special assistant

No change in communication level

Present salary maintained

Demoted to lower communication level

Shelf job sometimes created

Possible assistant to previous subordinate

SOUTH

The publicity risk is minimal.

Reason number five has perhaps the most important advantage, since the individual, maintaining his organizational level and status, may be assigned work of real value designed to broaden, train and utilize his particular talents to the fullest.

As reason number six suggests, if a mistake has been made or the atmosphere changes, the individual can be salvaged and the company investment in the person is protected.

● *South and Down:* The application of this method should be restricted to those individuals who are old enough, or sick enough, and willing enough to go down, and take it well. It is not likely that a younger manager can accept the humiliation of a demotion and reduction in salary and still maintain an attitude of loyalty to the company. Far more serious than his own low productivity would be the effect on the morale of other members of his sub-group.

This move should be made down even to a non-managerial job instead of the next lower level, to reduce the pressure and embarrassment to the individual and to sever all psychological ties and commitments to his previous associates.

A manoeuvre sometimes used is moving the individual North, East or South in the hope that he will move West and Out of his own accord. This action is indefensible and carries implications of weakness and cowardice on the part of the top managers. Worse than the cruelty to the individual is its effect on the attitude and morale of the people in the organization, who must see this obvious action taken by their superiors in its true light.

Depending on the circumstances and reasons for displacing an executive, any move within the company should provide an opportunity to start a new project or to conduct a new study that would not be possible without the availability of the man. If the company is really interested in the conservation of a human resource, a programme of rehabilitation and development should be initiated. Too often, Bird notes, this phase of the operation is totally neglected. ∎

as a promotion. Morale of both the executive and his group may be maintained. This direction is particularly useful when the individual has developed strong loyalty ties to customers, dealers and public. Through his position, communications with these contacts may be kept. But it should be remembered that this technique is the most expensive since salaries are generally maintained and in some cases even increased.

If the move has been made unwillingly, there is an element of risk if the individual occupies a special place with his subordinates and illegally uses this advantage to exert influence and control on groups no longer under his jurisdiction. If these situations cannot be controlled by the erection of communications "fences" and other organizational barriers, it may be necessary to move the executive in a westerly direction.

● *Laterally East:* There are seven good reasons for using this method, which involves moving the executive to a staff or special assistant position. (1) It may be used to satisfy almost every situation previously mentioned. (2) It is relatively easy to effect. (3) The salary may be maintained at the same level. (4) The individual is frequently agreeable. (5) Job assignments of greater value may be made to the individual with expectation of higher productivity. (6) If conditions change, the individual may move back to the same or equal level without loss of prestige or inconsistency of policy. (7)

HOW GOOD

ARE ENGINEERING

APTITUDE TESTS?

We put this question to several testing agencies and personnel departments of large corporations. Here's a distillation of their experience, what the tests are like, and some warnings to the unwary.

C J Lynch

■ One way to put all personnel managers out of work is to develop the perfect pre-employment test.

They're not worried—quite the contrary, personnel managers are the most enthusiastic patrons of psychological tests. Constantly hopeful, usually disappointed, they encourage the psychologists to try and try again, and progress **is** being made.

While still far from a strictly mechanical filtration procedure, the science of mental measurement has come a long way in the last few years. A complete spectrum of tests has been developed—interest, personality, ability— and aptitude tests evaluate only a part of a man's personality. Job suitability, for the man as well as his employer, is made up of so many disparate factors that only the complete battery of tests, supplemented with job histories and personal interviews, can do a significant job of discriminating among applicants.

What they measure

Aptitude, achievement and IQ tests are commonly lumped together as "ability" tests. There is really little distinction between an aptitude test and an achievement test—the name depends largely on how it is applied. A test intended to measure achievement in algebra could be an excellent predictor of success in trigonometry. Ability tests can accurately measure what a man knows and how well he is able to apply it.

Interest and personality inventories are usually less accurate. Interest tests try to find how a man prefers to spend his time by asking such questions as, "Would you rather design a computer or give a speech on how computers are changing business operations?" Results are usually tabulated to show comparative interest in mechanical, computational, artistic, persuasive areas. Two popular interest inventories are the Kuder Preference Record and the Strong Vocational Interest Blank. Per-

sonality tests are intended to measure such traits as objectivity, agreeableness, energy level, social leadership, cheerfulness, emotional stability. They ask you to give an honest accounting of yourself: "Have you enjoyed reading books as much as having company in?" or "Do you prefer short men to tall men?" These tests, to a certain extent, measure how well a man will fit in with the organization. Two well-known examples are the Bernreuter Personality Inventory and the Thurstone Temperament Schedule.

For engineers, among the most common ability tests are the Revised Minnesota Paper Form Board (a test of spatial visualization), the Bennett Test of Mechanical Comprehension, and Minnesota Engineering Analogies Test. (Some examples are shown on page 66.) The problem is that ability tests alone are not sufficient to pick suitable new employes:

"Engineers as a group are a pretty bright bunch of guys and will do pretty well on almost any ability test you throw at them," says the director of one NY testing center. Engineers represent a preselected group, and their scores on most ability tests will cluster close to the top of the scale with very little spread. Such tests are statistically difficult to analyze and generally more useful in rejecting a poor applicant than identifying an outstanding one.

And what if a man has the ability, but not the interest or motivation for the work? What an employe **can** do and what he **will** do may be very different. Some differences may be uncovered with the personality and interest tests; others come out in interviews or by inspection of the man's biographical record. Most companies put a great deal of weight on the interviews. Keith R. Jewell, consulting psychologist for management consultants George Fry & Associates, in Chicago says, "We don't throw the test results out, certainly, but we always

Typical aptitude-test problems

Sample Problems

X. Through which quarter turn is the most power applied to the flywheel?
(If no difference, mark E.)

Y Which shelf will hold the heaviest weight?
(If no difference, mark E.)

Reprinted, courtesy The Psychological Corp, N Y

temper them with good penetrating interviews. Testing of engineers can be oversold—sometimes it is mostly guesswork or statistics, and people aren't numbers."

Who uses tests and for what?

It is estimated that over 70% of industrial concerns, both small and large, use psychological tests in some phase of their personnel work. Small firms may have their testing done by an outside agency or college testing center. Large outfits ordinarily have their own personnel office and a resident psychologist. Six large corporations—American Telephone and Telegraph, Detroit Edison, B F Goodrich, IBM, Sandia Corporation, Westinghouse Electric—in cooperation with Educational Testing Service, Princeton, NJ, have recently begun a research program to develop tests that discriminate between engineers that are likely to be successful in certain phases of engineering work and those that are not. To date, findings indicate that interest tests are most effective discriminators for engineers with 4 to 7 years' experience. Aptitude tests rank second and are particularly helpful in spotting ability in abstract reasoning.

In addition to tests for employe selection, industry uses them to upgrade present employes, appraise executives and evaluate would-be executives. The engineer often finds the tests valuable in planning his own future or selecting new job opportunities. Some job-hunters take aptitude tests at their own expense and have the results sent from the testing center to prospective employers.

Can they reduce "break-in" time?

In almost all instances, yes. With tests, the number of potential misfits is reduced—those accepted are less expensive to train and more likely to stay with the job. Of course, this must be balanced against the testing costs—if requirements are strict, too many men may have to be tested to get the desired number of employes. ∎

Mechanical comprehension test

Several forms are available, representing varying levels of complexity. They measure a person's ability to understand physical and mechanical relationships. Samples below are from a 60-question test written by psychologists Owen and Bennett, published by The Psychological Corp.

Although sometimes given to graduate engineers, the test is intended for candidates for engineering school and adult men of similar ability.

Engineering analogies

One of the most difficult and zealously guarded aptitude tests for engineers is the Minnesota Engineering Analogies Test (MEAT). To protect integrity of this test, it is distributed, through a licensing agreement, only to authorized testing agencies. In some places even the test administrators are barred from seeing what's inside the test booklet. All scores are reported to and kept on file by The Psychological Corp, publisher of the test.

Typical "ratio" problems are:
1. Add : subtract : : multiply : (a) integrate, (b) divide, (c) magnify, (d) differentiate
2. In a triode,
    Spectators : turnstile : : plate current : (a) cathode, (b) plate, (c) anode, (d) grid
3. Rate of fluid flow : electric current : : pipe friction : (a) electromotive force, (b) electrical resistance, (c) electrical conductance, (d) resistivity

The test measures the engineer's knowledge of subject matter and reasoning ability. MEAT therefore shows not only what he knows, but how well he is able to apply it. It is sensitive enough to discriminate between proficiency differences of high-ability graduate engineers.

Verbal reasoning

A number of intelligence tests require the subject to draw conclusions from a series of stated facts. The example below was taken from a sample problem in a 10-part battery of employment tests published by Psychological Services Inc, Los Angeles. This part of the battery includes six such problems to be worked in five minutes.

FACTS Chris is a widow
   Jane works for Co B
   Chris' only child is a girl
   Co A makes spark plugs
   Co A employs no women
CONCLUSIONS (true, false or unknown?)
  1. Chris does not work for Co A
  2. Chris' son is ill
  3. Chris works for Co C
  4. Chris has never been married
  5. Chris inspects spark plugs

4.

Steps in Developing New Products

How new products can increase profits

A realistic planning programme is the only way to ensure that your new products have a better than average chance of survival

by Clarence F. Manning,
Vice President,
Reynolds Metals Company

DESPITE CLEAR EVIDENCE that corporate growth is largely dependent on new product development, new product planning appears to be a weak spot in the management of many companies.

On one hand, we have the fear of change—which does strange things to some corporations. It closes their eyes, ties their hands, stops them from thinking or questioning. It stops growth.

Opposed to this fear of change, we have some companies which, without the benefit of a formal product development programme based on planned marketing strategy, pour out new products at a staggering rate. For their efforts they have an almost unbelievable rate of failures.

It has been estimated that more than 98 per cent of products in the US, for example, fail to survive the first two years. I suspect the rate is closer to four failures for every five new products introduced. But this is still an extremely bad record. A record that indicates hundreds of millions of dollars are being spent on research, engineering, production, marketing and sales—without reaping the hoped-for end result: profit.

Product effectiveness—Profit is the one common denominator of effective performance shared by all corporate functions. A new product programme is no exception. There are a number of ways—directly and indirectly—that a new product can add to a company's profit.

They include:

1. By filling out an existing product line and thus reducing over-all selling costs. Competition in all business is becoming more fierce. This means adequate sales budgets are increasingly important. By adding new products, the sales cost can be reduced while maintaining or even increasing the strength of the sales organization. However, where this approach is used, the new products must be products that the existing sales force can sell effectively without disrupting their present business.

2. By having a basic material accepted by a market or industry now using another material. For example, in many cases we have had to develop and produce end products to prove aluminium's advantages. Aluminium cans are a recent example.

3. By advancing the technological knowledge and possible applications of a basic material. For example, the design of the recently launched Aluminaut, the world's first all-aluminium submarine represents a substantial breakthrough in pressure hull design. Its construction has resulted in significant advancements in the state of the metalworking and forming arts.

4. By increasing the saleability of an existing product. For example, peanut butter sells more peanuts—cake mix more flour—automatic burners more fuel oil to homes.

5. By using the material generated or left over in the manufacture of one product in the manufacture of another product. The petroleum industry has been particularly successful developing "by-products".

6. By increasing public knowledge of a company's basic product. This was one of the basic reasons for the development and marketing of Reynolds Wrap.

Finally a new product can contribute to a company's profit by replacing a product which has become tired or unprofitable.

There are, of course, more than seven ways a new product can contribute to profit. But I believe I've made my point.

First considerations — Naturally not all of these examples apply to every company. To determine which ones do apply, a company must first consider its marketing, research and management experience and capabilities; its production facilities and material resources; and where the company stands in relation to its competition and customers.

For example, a company well versed in manufacturing and selling heavy industrial equipment is not usually in a position to effectively market consumer products. Or a new product may require an investment in new plant facilities beyond a company's financial capabilities

But so far we have only discussed the basic approach to new product strategy. If we go no further, we can expect a good percentage of new product failures.

What are some of the causes of new product failures?

1. The marketing and selling programmes are not planned carefully enough.

2. The price range is wrong. The price range needs to be geared to the market and to the value expected by the buyer. And there must also be a sufficient margin between the cost and the selling price to cover a sustained selling and advertising effort.

3. Not enough care is given to design or engineering details.

4. The quality of manufacture is not good enough.

5. The product is introduced at the wrong time.

6. Impatience — underestimating the time and money needed for orderly market development and growth.

Except under very exceptional circumstances, a new product should be handled as a seed is planted in a garden. It should be allowed to grow and form a good root system. In this way, miscalculations and errors can be corrected before commitment has become too big or final.

By the same reasoning when a new product is launched, it must not be forgotten that this new product is, in effect, a new baby in the family of the corporation. It needs to be treated as a baby—nurtured and allowed to grow, not only during the development period but also after its introduction and until it has been successfully established. If a new product has been soundly conceived and its future carefully planned, it will grow.

Product confidence — Another cause for the failure of a new product is that the people who have to sell it, including salesmen and dealers, are not given sufficient training and indoctrination. People cannot become enthusiastic about something they don't understand. As a matter of fact, they are usually afraid of anything new until they acquire enough knowledge to give them the necessary selling confidence.

Finally, a new product can fail if giveaway offers or low prices are used as a substitute for selling effort. I believe most people are interested in the quality, reliability and convenience of a product. And let's not forget that many people measure quality by price.

What is the answer? How can you have a high average of success in introducing new products?

In my opinion it is to have sales, research, manufacturing and finance work as a team from the very beginning of the new product development, realistically and objectively facing up to the basic problems involved. Among other things:

There should be a feasibility study by research. A market research study by sales.

A feasibility study by manufacturing.

Styling and design guidance.

Economic and profitability study by finance.

There should almost always be a restricted market sales test. However, before this is undertaken, there should be a complete long range marketing, selling, and advertising programme developed—with sales volume and sales costs projected to give the company a satisfactory volume and profit.

Planning objectives—The objective of the sales test should be to determine: whether or not a new product can be sold in the required volume at the prices and the selling cost contemplated in the long range sales programme; whether or not the marketing and advertising strategy designed for the long range programme produces desired results. Otherwise a market sales test can be meaningless if not misleading.

This all requires hard, tedious, detailed thinking and planning. But in my opinion it means the difference between planned success and unplanned failure. It is the difference between successfully reaching your goal by careful, sound strategy and just trying to get there with luck or chance. There are not many successes made in business with only pure chance.

Since my own company's Reynolds Wrap is generally considered to be a particularly successful product, perhaps it would be interesting to review just a few of the basic strategic principles we used in the development and marketing of this product—a product so new that consumers did not know what it was and how or why they should use it.

Few people knew that aluminium foil was actually a thin sheet of metal—aluminium. Too few packaging engineers knew or understood its properties—moisture proof, unusual thermal qualities, mouldability, and strength, to mention a few.

Reynolds Metals Company was not widely known 17 years ago. Institutional advertising had proved largely ineffective in getting the story across. Therefore, our idea was to develop and market a consumer product which would demonstrate aluminium's distinctive properties.

Into the kitchen—The kitchen was selected as the focal point of our attention. A competent home economist was installed in a kitchen where she spent full time for weeks using aluminium foil in every conceivable way.

Experiments were made using aluminium foil for cooking and kitchen packaging of lunches and leftovers. Many practical uses were discovered, and our home economist determined the thickness, width, and temper suitable for most uses.

Our styling and design department developed a package using colours appealing to the ladies. Manufacturing devised ways of producing, spooling and packaging the foil under very rigid quality control conditions.

At this point the key decision in the development of the product was made—to promote it as a basic household item, and sell it through the big mass-outlet market—grocery stores.

Selection of a name was perhaps the most difficult decision. We insisted it should be a short name—include the name of the company and be descriptive of the product. You wouldn't believe how long it took to come up with the simple name "Reynolds Wrap" which met our conditions.

A complete marketing programme was developed in detail, including the number of cases to be sold in each of more than 100 cities, the number of retail salesmen required to produce that volume in each city, the amount to be spent on advertising in each as well as advertising copy to be used during the introductory period.

Test site—One medium sized city was selected for the market test. According to the long-range marketing plan, this city was entitled to one salesman. In 1947, after suitable training, this one salesman went to work with the guidance of the new consumer sales manager.

The home economist moved out of the kitchen into public relations. She lectured, visited women's editors, restaurant operators, radio stations, and did a thorough public relations job in this test city.

The salesman was required to spend one day each week demonstrating in some retail grocery store. We did not use the "blast" method. The advertising department contracted for the amount of advertising support which had been predetermined was allowable to that particular city according to the plan.

It took a year to bring the sales volume in this first test city up to the required volume.

We then selected a larger city which we had been told was a difficult place to successfully introduce a new product. That's the very reason we selected it. It was difficult. But we succeeded there, again using the same master plan.

We then opened one city at a time until we had 30 markets functioning according to our master plan before we went to a national scale.

At the end of about five years, we achieved the goals in volume, cost and manpower set down in our original master long-range plan and had achieved our other basic objectives. ∎

A MATHEMATICAL TECHNIQUE FOR CHOOSING THE RIGHT NEW-PRODUCT IDEA

Among all the candidates, how do you choose the "right" one? This technique cuts guesswork—analyzes a number of promising ideas throughout their development, then methodically eliminates the weaklings that can't meet predetermined standards.

CLARENCE HUETTEN, *director, Electrophysical Laboratories, and*
LOUIS SWEANY, *senior engineer*
PR Mallory & Co Inc

Choosing a new product for development is an important decision. But too often it's an all-or-nothing gamble. You're forced to decide on the basis of guess and hope, and then carry on—no matter how bad the guess was, or how the engineering or market situation changes.

There is a more realistic approach. It recognizes that many starting ideas will never get to production—perhaps 99 out of 100 will drop along the wayside. And it helps you spot the nonprofitable candidates early in the elimination contest—less time and money wasted on ideas that won't pan out.

This method starts all ideas through the development mill on an equal basis. But at seven distinct stages you force a formal reevaluation of the idea in terms of the company's criteria of acceptability. If it passes, fine. Send it on to the next stage. If it doesn't, file the idea for future reference—times change and the candidate might look altogether different in five or ten years.

Note that this system adds hours and dollars to product-development budgets, but it reduces risks—so much so that successful products pay for all their own development, and for all the drop-outs as well.

DECISION CRITERIA

At each stage the basic question asked of a new product is: "Will it make money?" Various tests can be applied—the significance of each depends on the type of company and its policies. Three factors that always interest prospective investors are:

Ratio of gain to risk. Will profit exceed expense by enough to make the risk worthwhile? The company must set a minimum ratio (generally about 2.5:1) for proposed new products. This ratio then becomes one of the criteria applied at each step.

Estimated annual dollar volume. Will over-all volume be a satisfactory proportion of the company's annual business? Again the company must set a minimum limit. The new product may be acceptable by other criteria, yet represent too small a percentage of the over-all goals set by the company.

Break-even time. How long will money be tied up before a return can be expected? The company must set a limit on how much time its money can be unavailable for other use.

These are not the only criteria that can or should be used as a measure of acceptability of a new product. Other decision factors generally considered during the idea-screening process should be applied at each of the seven distinct stages of reevaluation (see "Seven Steps of Analysis," at right).

At the end of each stage the criteria are applied in the light of the new information made available, and a decision is reached—does the product justify further development? Note that the gain-to-risk ratio for each individual product does not include expenses incurred by all other products under evaluation. This ratio must be adjusted

Text continued on page 72.

SEVEN STEPS OF ANALYSIS

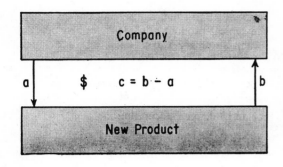

BASIC BUSINESS CONCEPT (left): company spends a dollars on new product, expecting return of b dollars for a gain of c dollars over life of product ($c = b - a$). Basic concept is broken down below into 7 steps.

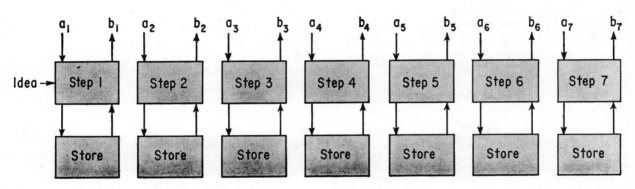

1. **Is an idea worth considering at all?** Past experience, a brief literature search, and an informal market analysis will tell you. Select a descriptive name and define the scope of the idea. Write general requirements, which should be rather brief and not too restrictive for later method or approach. Estimate and calculate a's and b's. On this basis the idea is either accepted, or rejected and stored for future review. Recording the information and making the calculations necessary to complete the analysis should take less than half an hour and give the answer —is it still a good idea?

2. **Next, make a detailed study of technical requirements.** Is the idea feasible? Obtain opinion from experts in marketing, production, and engineering; and make a literature search. Now you can make a basic proposal. Each idea analyzed here may cost several times that of a Step 1 analysis. Should you go on?

3. **Now test basic technical features** and make a formal, but brief, market analysis. This is the critical step in the technical life of the new idea— which idea has come this far on the strength of a number of "ifs", both in technical features and market aspects. Conduct sufficient laboratory exploratory work to assure feasibility of the approach. If possible, make a demonstration model. What will it cost to make? How much can it be sold for? At that price, what market can be expected? Have a preliminary patent search made. Are there any infringements? With all this information reestimate the a's and b's and the acceptance criteria. Are you ready to proceed with a formal proposal to management for a full-scale R & D program?

4. **Set up a comprehensive technical development program and make a thorough market analysis.** Review technical requirements to make sure nothing has been omitted and that they are in keeping with the expected performance of the product. At the end of this stage recalculate a's and b's. Is the product worth further effort?

5. **Here you design and tool up for production, purchase material for initial production, and train production personnel.** The sum of all costs up to and including this step determines maximum financial risk in the product. Acceptance criteria should be periodically reviewed during this phase, using the latest information available from the manufacturing unit, market research, and other sources.

6. **Analysis here determines the breakeven point in the financial history of the new product.** The breakeven point reflects all costs to date. During this phase, costs and income should be periodically reviewed. The acceptance criteria are then applied to the latest analysis. Significant changes may indicate advisable corrective measures.

7. **Adjust production levels to suit the market.** Continue until profits decline.

	ESTIMATE	REMARKS
p	$1.50	Selling price
V_m	1,300,000	Unit volume per year (max)
f_m	1,950,000	Dollar volume per year (max)
t_a	2	Acceleration time, years
a_1	COSTS 50	Preliminary analysis
a_2	250	Analysis and paper approach
a_3	2,500	Analysis and exploratory
a_4	35,000	Research and development
a_5	108,916	Tooling, pre-production, interest, etc.
a_6	1,891,169	Expenses during breakeven period
a_7	9,963,429	Expenses during remaining production time
a	12,001,314	Total Expenses (sum of a_1 thru a_7)
b_1	INCOME 0	None expected
b_2	0	None expected
b_3	0	None expected
b_4	0	None expected
b_5	0	None expected
b_6	2,037,885	To break even
b_7	10,736,454	During remaining production time
b	12,774,339	Total Income (sum of b_1 thru b_7)
t_1	TIME	Analysis
t_2	0.2	Analysis and paper-approach
t_3		Analysis and exploratory
t_4	1.0	Research and development
t_5	0.5	Tooling and product engineering
t_6	1.9	To break even
t_7	6.4	Remaining production time
t	10.0	Total Time (sum of t_1 thru t_7)

Subject: PRODUCT X   No.   Date:

$c = 773,025$ (net gain) | $d = 146,716$ (risk) | $c/d = 5:1$ (gain/risk)

SAMPLE SUMMARY SHEET, containing all information necessary for making decisions. Data shown is for typical product X at stage. 1. Here, the a's, b's, c and d are in $; t's are in years. Similar sheet is used for each stage, providing complete history of product.

upward so that when expenses of all drop-outs are added, the ratio will still be within company requirements.

SUMMARY SHEETS

The system is simple to use when the analysis is summarized for permanent record. The single summary sheet shown above collects the many lists of information necessary and organizes them so that acceptance criteria can be applied at a glance. It contains estimated selling price; annual unit and dollar volumes; acceleration time; a, b, and t factors; gain, risk, and gain-to-risk ratio. It should also include any other factors you require as acceptance criteria. This sample sheet includes data for a mythical product X, which will be described later. For now, let's consider the form itself.

The a's represent expenses at each step; b's represent expected income at each step; and t's are the time the product spends in each phase. The sum of a_1 through a_5 is the maximum risk, called d. Net gain, c, is calculated by subtracting the sum of a_1 through a_7 from the total of all b's. Gain-to-risk ratio, c/d, is gain divided by risk.

Selling price must be estimated directly or developed through costing and profit calculations. Assuming something is known about the potential market for the product from published market figures, an estimate can be made as to what portion of this market your company might expect to capture at the estimated selling price. Because most products have a growth period, a relatively stable period of production, and then a period of decline, an estimate can be made of maximum expected yearly volume, V_m. Selling price times maximum unit volume gives maximum dollar volume.

Because of the number of assumptions necessary for calculation of acceleration time, t_a, the explanation is incorporated in the typical product analysis described below.

Behind each summary sheet lies a lot of detailed information which should be available for examination if questions arise as to how certain estimates were made, etc. The supporting sheets should contain raw data, methods of calculating, and a log of thoughts concerning the product and market information.

COLLECTING INFORMATION

Information for the analysis is mainly dependent upon estimates guided by factual information that can be had economically. Obviously, full-scale market researches and detailed product-cost analyses on hundreds of new-product ideas should not be made in the earlier steps. You can estimate product-cost information from the cost of known items already being produced by the company. In time, a reference file of material, labor, and overhead costs can be accumulated. Market information on a wide variety of products is available in a number of current publications. This information is generally in terms of yearly unit or dollar volume sales or factory shipments. Other publications not specifically related to marketing often have articles on product trends and estimates on future product sales that are helpful in making unit or dollar-volume estimates for the analysis.

At the completion of Step 4 or during Step 5, you must accurately determine product costs, using a detailed study of manufacturing processes and material costs. A comprehensive market survey can be conducted through the company operation or by hiring a market-survey.

Success of the new-product analysis program will be measured by management in terms of the dollars income resulting from the program and the cost of operating it. The 7-step analysis system is somewhat like the Seven Falls tourist attraction at Colorado Springs; a lot of water had to come from the little spring above before the first drop fell into pool below. The system is greedy for new ideas; this sparks the search for new ways of coming up with them. The uniform method of handling such analyses is inherently economical and the quality of the new-product ideas is maintained by considering its whole life in each step analysis. This type of analysis speaks management's language—in dollars and time. Result is an aura of clarity and understanding in the discussion of new products with management.

TYPICAL PRODUCT ANALYSIS

Analysis of a new product based upon this technique requires certain factors to be estimated and others to be calculated. Accuracy of the estimates depends on the experience of the estimators and the amount of supporting information available.

The summary sheet shows an analysis for product X that follows the a and b concept, with additional information required to complete the analysis. Selling price, p, is estimated to be $1.50. Maximum expected volume, V_m, is estimated to be 1,300,000 units per year. Maximum yearly dollar volume, f_m, is then $1.50 x 1,300,000, or $1,950,000.

Acceleration time, t_a, then completes this segment of the analysis by telling how long it will take to reach maximum production. For product X, it was estimated that maximum production would be realized two years after start of production. To simplify calculations the rate of production increase might be considered linear; or you could use a more representative curve of actual rate increase based on past experience.

For this analysis, the curves shown here

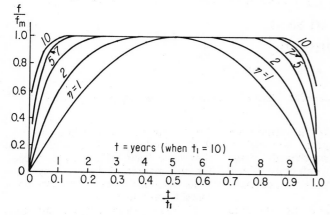

were derived from the expression:

$$\frac{f}{f_m} = 1 - \left(1 - \frac{2t}{t_1}\right)^{2n}$$

where: f = Dollars at any time t
f_m = Maximum estimated dollars income
t_1 = 10 years
n = 2

As n is varied, a family of curves is produced; f_m occurs at the midpoint of the curve in all cases and acceleration time based on f_m is always $t_1/2$. Because the slope of the curve increases as n is increased, acceleration time should be estimated on the basis of reaching some percentage of f_m. Using 90%, this point occurs at $t = 2.3$ years on the $n = 2$ curve, which is nearest the 2-year acceleration time estimate for product X. When using a family of curves, estimates of acceleration time are determined independently of the curves. Then a curve is selected which is closest to the 90% f_m value at the estimated acceleration time.

The next segment of information is product expense a throughout product life. For product X it was estimated that $50 should cover the step-1 preliminary analysis; $250, the cost of developing a "paper approach" and preparing a step-2 analysis; and that $2500 would be enough to cover cost of laboratory exploratory work—to verify

the "paper approach" and make a step-3 analysis. Based upon past experience with similar products, the research-and-development cost a_4 was estimated at $35,000.

The $108,916 shown in a_5 is broken down on another sheet of the analysis and consists of tooling costs, preproduction costs, formal market-survey cost, and interest on risk. The sum of a_1 through a_5 is the maximum risk and is $146,716. This amount is entered as d on the bottom line of the analysis summary sheet.

The expense during the breakeven period is a_6. It is calculated to be $1,891,169 when related to the risk and the anticipated net profit. In the case of product X, a 15% net profit before taxes was used with a 52% tax rate. The percent net profit after taxes is then 48% of 15% or 7.2%. At this rate, $a_6 = 12.89d$ or $1,891,169. The amount for a_7 was calculated from b_7 as $9,963,429 and is the expense during the remaining production time. The sum of a_1 through a_7 is the total expense and is equal to $12,001,314.

Income dollars from product X are listed in the b section of the analysis summary sheet. Since this product will be supported only by the company, no income is expected until production begins and the amounts for b_1, b_2, b_3, b_4, and b_5 are zero. (Income before b_6 is possible in the case of government contracts or other external support.) Income dollars required to break even were calculated to be $2,037,885 and were entered for b_6. This amount is the sum of a_6 and d. Income during remaining production time after the breakeven point was then calculated to be $10,736,454; this amount was entered as b_7. The sum of b_6 and b_7 is then the total income b of $12,774,339. The difference between a and b is $773,025—entered on the bottom line of the analysis sheet as the net gain c. The net gain-to-risk ratio, or c/d, is 5:1.

The times associated with each phase of the product are listed in the t section of the analysis summary sheet. t_1, t_2, and t_3 have been lumped together and estimated at 0.2 year. The R & D program was estimated to take 1 year; tooling and product engineering time, 0.5 years. Product life was estimated at 10 years. Breakeven time t_6 was calculated from the breakeven dollars b_6 and found to be 1.9 years. This leaves a remaining production time t_7 of 6.4 years. The exact method of calculating a_7, b_7, and t_6 has been purposely omitted because of their dependence upon the type of production curve that might be used.

Analysis of product X as summarized on the sample form is based upon estimates guided by economically available information and past experience, with certain assumptions made to simplify calculations. It states that if you start now on this product, you can expect a net financial gain of $773,025 in 10 years at a risk of $146,716 and a gain-to-risk ratio of 5:1. Now apply the acceptance criteria: gain-to-risk ratio required, estimated dollar volume limit, and breakeven time limit. Should product X be advanced to the next step? ■

A workable approach to

New-product planning

How can gestation from idea to product
be controlled? Engineering and sales
must work together. Here's one way

JOHN W. PETERSEN, Manager of Marketing Services, Racine Hydraulics & Machinery Inc, Racine, Wis

As expenditures in research and development for new products skyrocket, it becomes essential for the company to plan effectively every step of the way. On one hand there is the incentive of new products that will help capture the larger share of the market, but on the other there is the danger of excessive expenditures on products with no profit potential.

A recent study, conducted by the National Industrial Conference Board, cited three primary causes of new-product failure:

1) Inaccurate appraisal of the need for a product, the extent of its market, and the competition it is likely to face.

2) Introduction of products before they have been sufficiently developed for the market or before they have been adequately tested under actual market conditions.

3) Poorly planned or inadequate introductory marketing campaigns.

THE FLOW OF NEW PRODUCT PLANNING ⇨

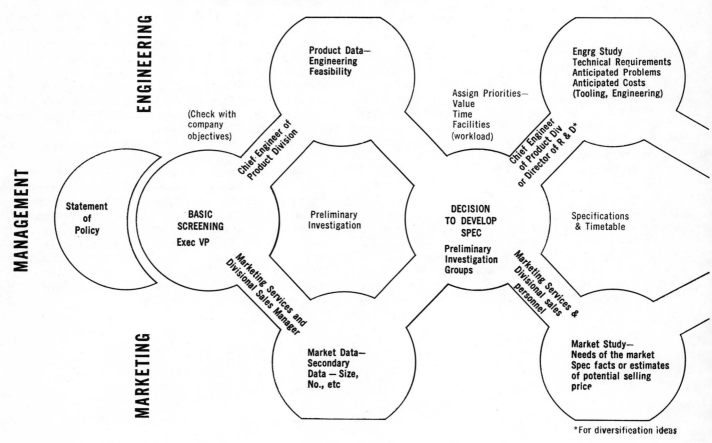

*For diversification ideas

To guard against these dangers, we have developed a new-products planning manual to improve communications and to provide frequent decision points. The actual procedure consists of four basic steps, separated by decision points. Because each step represents increasingly large expenditures in money and manpower, the earlier a losing or marginal idea can be eliminated, the more effective the over-all product development program. The situation is very much like that in poker. Each round the ante becomes larger. To win you have to stay in until the end, but it's a waste of money to stay in on a losing hand.

Decision Point I

Our planning procedure is diagrammed. Note that it begins with a statement of policy. This sets up the broad framework for preliminary screening of new-product ideas, and it helps stimulate ideas by offering some direction and guidance for people who generate them. The first decision point is a basic or preliminary screening. It is designed to eliminate obviously bad ideas, those that are not within the scope of the company program and those that are not in the direction in which the company plans to move.

This screening is done in our case by the executive vice president, who must OK the next step: a preliminary market and engineering check.

Preliminary investigation

This is a quick study area for new product ideas that may have merit. We are seeking only general information to decide whether a formal detailed study should be undertaken and to estimate the relative value of the idea to the company so that proper emphasis can be placed on the project in succeeding stages. The latter decision is, of course, subject to change at each decision point. Engineering feasibility is investigated by the chief engineer of the division concerned and market aspects are investigated by the sales manager of the division and by the corporate marketing services group. It is at this stage that the marketing division decides whether or not a formal market study is needed, and if so whether consultants should be called in, how much the study will cost, and the like. Engineering makes a similar evaluation and estimates the probability of engineering success if the product is actually developed. Engineering must also decide whether the product will fit into the existing line,

whether it will obsolete existing products, how broad a line will be required (size and types), whether the product is compatible with our engineering, manufacturing and marketing experience, and the competition.

Decision Point II

This brings us to a second decision point, that involving specifications. This is probably the most difficult of all decision points because information is still general, but a large number of ideas should be eliminated at this stage. Remaining ones should be assigned priorities. The decision is made by the executive vice-president and the people who undertook the preliminary investigation. It results in a new-product control sheet and timetable for the accepted products, and selection of either R&D or division engineering for further study and development of specifications. Participants should complete the status portion of the control sheet to calculate a rating. This rating is recalculated as conditions and subsequent estimates change.

Specifications stage

We now enter the specifications stage with a formal study of the new product that shows promise. The ob-

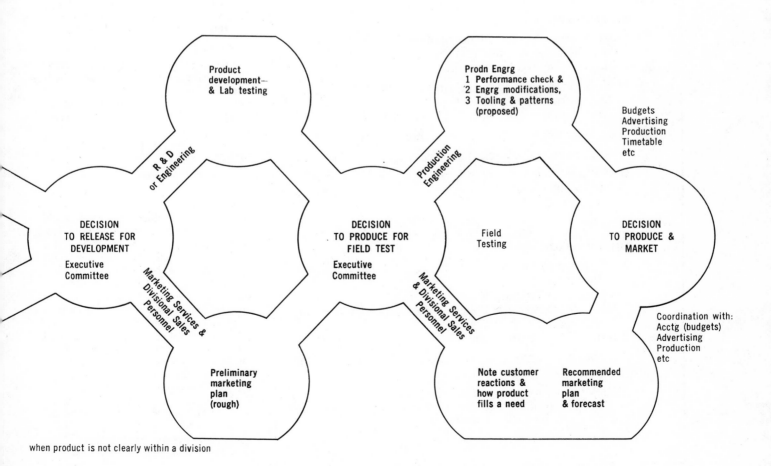

when product is not clearly within a division

MARKETING CHECK LIST ...
Marketing
Sales
Advertising
Finance

THE MARKET OPPORTUNITY

☐ Who are the potential customers for this product?
—By **industry** classification
—By **types**—OEM and user
—Specific **names** if possible

☐ **How many** potential customers?

☐ Where are the customers **located?**
—By **region**
—By **state**
—By trading **areas**

☐ What is the potential sales volume of this product? (Dollar volume and units)
—**What share** of the market can we expect to sell?

☐ **Why would customers buy** this product?
—**What features** are important to them?
—How much is it **needed?**
—What are their **buying habits?**

☐ Is this a **growth market?** What future?
—Product obsolescence characteristics

☐ What is the **price range** for this product?

DISTRIBUTION

☐ What are the **channels of distribution** for this product?
—What **policies** are important to these channels?
—How do they conduct their business?

☐ What is our "company image" in this industry?
—Are we known or not?
—What do they think of us? Of our products?

☐ What advertising is likely to be required? How much?

☐ What promotional effort is indicated?

☐ Does the product fit our established channels? Which ones?
—Can it be handled without neglecting our present products?

COMPETITION

☐ What **competition** can we expect? (Companies and Products)
—What is their **"image"?**
—How do they sell? Policies, distribution, etc? (Any soft spots?)
—Is the field overcrowded?

☐ Can we expect to compete successfully with existing products?
—Why?

☐ Can present products be quickly improved or can our products be easily copied?

jective here is to determine what marketing and engineering facts are needed to make the next decision. Marketing must provide information about requirements, market size, location and structure, potential customers, buying motives, and channels of distribution and must present an estimate of sales potential based on the checklist reproduced at left. R&D or Engineering should decide what is required to develop and produce the product. This includes an estimate of the problems and the various costs in accordance with the engineering checklist reproduced at right. Extremely close coordination between Marketing and Engineering is essential for success at this stage. In spite of screening, more products are likely to enter this stage than can possibly be processed. Thus a backlog will result and priorities must be determined and constantly adjusted against a timetable. It is possible for good but low-payout ideas to remain in this stage indefinitely, held up by a low priority.

The marketing or engineering study may develop information that suggests very radical changes in priority rating. In this case the product idea should be returned to the preceding decision point for approval of the change rating. Both Marketing and Engineering should end up with written reports at the end of this stage.

Decision Point III

The third decision point is release for development. In our case it is handled by the company executive committee because it involves investment of R&D creative talent, one of our most important assets. The executive committee determines whether the idea is worth the investment.

Product development stages

Following this decision we enter the longest and least predictable stage in new-product planning—product development. Creativity cannot be scheduled and future progress of the idea must wait until development problems are identified and resolved. During this stage, Marketing Services should prepare a preliminary marketing plan in cooperation with divisional sales personnel. This is a blueprint or road map of method and sequence of steps, and a timetable for launching. It should include recommendations of marketing steps such as lists of industries and types of customers that should be included in the test. Close coordination with R&D is necessary because the development of design features may have strong marketing implications. Conversely, certain planned features may not be practical or may be too expensive. And their absence will reduce or eliminate certain segments of the planned customer group.

This stage may take months or years, so the timetable changes emphasis according to company marketing requirements. It does not become a practical timetable until the later stages of product development, when the remaining time schedule can be estimated. It is in this stage that detailed studies of costs, capital investment, estimated return, and manufacturing problems must be studied. Also of importance at this time is potential patent protection.

Decision Point IV

Fourth of the decision points is that concerning the field test. A decision to field test a new product means that the product has been developed and that there appears to be a good market potential for it. Again, this decision is made by the executive committee. It is at this point also that the rough marketing plan is examined and the responsible division or sales executive designated. From the engineering point of view this is important as well, because it is the decision that precedes field testing.

Field Test

Many products work well in the laboratory but develop serious problems under actual operating conditions. Field testing is necessary to uncover these problems. At this time outstanding sales features can be identified and sales weaknesses corrected. At this stage also, a complete marketing plan must be worked out. Usually, moreover, this marks the transfer from R&D or Engineering to Production Engineering. Final drawings are made, manufacturing problems resolved, and costs checked out, so exact price may be set. Plans for tooling and facilities are completed.

Decision Point V

The final decision point is whether to produce and market the product. This occurs at the end of the formal testing period and marks the coordination of all marketing functions and a decided reduction in engineering operations. Henceforth the product is a Manufacturing and Sales problem, with Engineering concerned only to the extent of improvements, correction of faults, and development of the next generation of products. This is followed by the production and marketing stage. The new product is now the responsibility of an operating division. A marketing target date is set, and other production and marketing decisions are made. ■

TECHNICAL CHECK LIST

1. . Patent problems or advantages
2. . Number of sizes and types
3. . Time to develop
4. . Cost to develop
5. . Problems in development
6. . Availability of enginering equipment and personnel
7. . Problems in manufacturing
8. . Problems of materials
9. . Rough estimate of capital required to put into production, including tooling and facilities
10. . Rough estimates of costs and selling prices
11. . Profit generation
12. . Time to reach break-even
13. . Time to absorb development costs
14. . Return on investment
15. . Long-term profit outlook
16. . Profit margin in relation to development costs and capital requirements
17. . Long-range prospects
18. . Possibility of establishing foothold on new technology

NEW PRODUCT CONTROL SHEET   Date_____

NEW PRODUCT IDEA

STATUS
Preliminary Stage   Specification Stage
High Med Low
3 2 1 Probability of Development - - - - - - - - - - - - - - - - _____ %
3 2 1 Probability of Marketing - - - - - - - - - - - - - - - - _____ %
4 2 0 Size of Market   Estimated Volume - - - - - - _____ Units (x)
         & Competition
4 2 0 Estimated profit   Est. Profit Contr. - - - - - $_____ (x)
1 2 3 Time Required   Selling Price _____
                                  Cost _____
1 2 3 Development Costs (Future) - - - - - - - - - - - - - $_____ (÷)

+ _____   Rating   _____
        (Date)   (Date)

STEPS: Things to be done   Comments   Estimated Time Estimated Expense

Preliminary Investigation:_____

Specifications:_____

Development:_____

Field Testing:_____

PROGRESS REPORT:

    DATE   COMMENTS

- 9 -

12-phase program speeds new products through development stages

Ingenuity must replace money in many
small companies. Here is a 12-phase program
for finding and developing new ideas

M. L. CLEVETT, JR, *Director, Product Research, Irving Air Chute Co Inc, Lexington, Ky*

Dr Charles Kettering once observed that the two most important things necessary for a successful new-product development are money and ingenuity; if you are seriously short of one ingredient, you must have a lot of the other.

Many of us have very little money for new-product development, so we must cultivate ingenuity. I have developed during the past 20 years some practical, though somewhat unorthodox, techniques and systems for putting new ideas to work.

This is a detailed description of the various steps and factors that have been found helpful in converting a crude idea into a refined, profit-making product. All the phases will not be applicable to every conceivable product, but could apply to most.

Phase 1. Definition of the problem or goal—It has been said that a goal or problem well defined is a problem half solved. In this first phase, we search for worthwhile objectives, and try to match these with our own interests and capabilities. It is important to keep a project log book or product diary, in which to record the objectives of the experimental program. Writing down one's thoughts tends to crystallize the problem, and possible solutions almost immediately begin to form in the subconscious mind. The human mind is capable of simultaneous study of many problems, which is why most professional inventors "program" their minds with several new-product problems at once.

Phase 2. Literature search—Once the new-product category has been established, start scanning a wide variety of literature with the problem or possible product in mind. Success in coming up with new ideas is almost in direct proportion to the variety and quantity of elementary ideas which can be recombined to form an invention. I regularly search through the *Official US Patent Gazette* and nearly 50 other periodicals each month in an effort to keep my mind well stocked with fresh, new idea-building elements. Through practice, this literature search phase can be efficiently accomplished in from one to two hours each day.

Phase 3. Conception of ideas—With the simultaneous activation of phases 1 and 2, new ideas automatically start to form. For the most part, these ideas will be discarded shortly after inception by logical reasoning under the harsh light of preliminary objective scrutiny. In this all-important phase, it is best to record ideas that seem to stand up under preliminary examination.

Strive for as many different ideas as possible in the early stages rather than for one big idea. In case of doubt, record all ideas that can be reasonably described. Frequent review of your idea file will help you achieve a more realistic perspective of each individual concept. It is best to have your new-idea records signed by a witness to establish some legal authenticity. This is the "crazy" phase; don't hesitate to record ideas which seem ridiculous. Nearly every good current product appeared crazy to most people when it was first conceived. (Thousands of pages have been written on the art of producing new ideas, but it is assumed here that the reader is already well versed in creative thinking.)

Phase 4. Models and initial experiments—Having roughly described your ideas in writing, you must reduce them to practice to determine their true potential. Too many people go to great expense to prepare elaborate drawings, descriptions, and models before determining if the idea works. Absolute simplicity should be the guiding light. Accordingly, precious time and money can be saved by resorting to simple models, calculations, and sketches. Plenty of courage is required in exposing crude handmade experimental models to the light of realistic laboratory and field testing. But only through this painful process can you gain a true functional perspective. Mr Irvin's first free-fall parachute jump was an excellent example of the importance of realistic testing.

In many cases, the first experimental model can be designed to have a certain degree of aesthetic appeal, so it may also serve as a photogenic publicity model. In this one aspect alone, considerable time and money can be saved through careful design of a combination experimental test model and publicity model.

Phase 5. Preliminary patent search—At this stage, if the idea still looks good, a competent patent attorney should initiate a preliminary search to determine just how much of your "new" idea is really new. Before beginning his search, the patent attorney should be given good sketches, descriptions, a working model, and any other information that will help define the limitations of the invention. Abstracts of all US patents are contained in the *Official Gazette*, published weekly. More than three million patents are in its volumes (cost $30/yr).

Phase 6. Prototype design and mock production—Sometimes it's fun to pretend. With this technique of new-product development, pretending production is a necessary prelude to the first press releases. We pretend that mass production is scheduled to begin in a few days and we tool-up in our minds to produce our new product. While in this production state of mind, we formulate a "final" design and establish a firm selling price which can eventually assure a reasonable profit when full-scale production begins. Mock production may involve some actual temporary tooling and crude product samples. The primary objectives of this phase are an intelligent initial selling price, and a workable, photogenic, engineering prototype. (You can also carry out destruction testing of the engineering prototype, *after* good photographs have been made of the product in simulated use.)

Considerable savings of time and money can be brought about by pretending that each minute and dollar spent is coming out of your own personal account. I have found that the best way to achieve this "pretense" is to practice this method privately, at my own expense. In this mock-production phase you actually begin the necessary design compromises to insure successful mass production.

Phase 7. Initial press releases—It is at this point that we begin to depart rather boldly from accepted new-product procedure. Industrial firms are understandably fearful of bad public images and so at this early stage most companies fear publicity, to say nothing of seeking it. The advantages of violating convention, in this case, far outweigh the disadvantages.

The essential, irreplaceable ingredient called "public opinion" is often added into the new-product program too late under conventional procedures. As a result, warehouses throughout the world contain neatly stacked products that no one will buy. The seemingly premature exposure of a new product to the people, through the medium of the press, can have many advantages, if you do it right. For one thing, it's important that your initial press releases should be nearly *works of creative art* and *not* simply the usual, run-of-the-mill "hacked-out blurbs" found all too often in technical periodicals. Accompanying product-in-use photographs of first-rate quality are absolutely essential.

A successful news editor once took the trouble to explain that people want drama, romance, and excitement in their news stories. This is often extremely difficult to achieve when, for example, we are writing a news story about new types of door knobs, toilet paper, or cotter keys. However difficult to achieve, it is essential that good news coverage be obtained at this stage, so that realistic, firm market reactions and criticism can be forthcoming. To protect the company image, it is frequently recommended that the product first be promoted under its own trade name with separate post office box address.

The selling price and source address should be included in all publicity. This again deviates somewhat from traditional practice. Many companies believe it unwise to let people know the price, but news editors will tell you that public response is much greater from news releases that contain such pertinent information. [*True. The alert new-product editor also asks sources, particularly if he suspects this technique is being used, to provide a firm delivery date. Readers are understandably irritated if they order something that is not available*—Editor]

Phase 8. Analysis of public reaction—History has shown that the general public is sometimes wrong. But, right or wrong, the reactions of the buying public should be carefully analyzed as soon as possible. By blending public reaction with your own intuition, experience, and calculations, you can now decide what course to take. This might mean discontinuing the project completely or revising the design to suit the desires of the public. Whatever decision is made at this point, it can be made with the obliging, free advice from the responding potential customers who read your news stories.

Phase 9. Redesign and patent application—Armed with the various suggestions submitted by the people who have responded to your new-product press stories, you can now approach a final production design. Formal drawings prepared in this phase may also be sent to the patent attorney, so that a patent application can be prepared. In this phase, close coordination should be maintained with the appropriate engineering, production, and sales departments. The revised designs should again be translated into three-dimensional models to be thoroughly tested.

Phase 10. Pilot production—With luck, at this phase the initial orders will start to materialize. Therefore, it is important that pilot production be started to fill these first orders and to evolve the necessary tooling for eventual mass production. The lapse of time from pilot to mass production varies widely, depending upon sales inertia.

Pilot production usually involves considerable handwork, temporary tools, and compromises in material selection. Hopefully, the major production "bugs" can be eliminated in pilot production.

Phase 11. Initial sales and customer testing—Once the buying public has spent hard-earned cash for your product, you quickly begin to get very valuable "feedback" from customers who now know what is right or wrong with it. In many instances it is necessary to give free samples to potential customers in order to gain their valuable testing and evaluation response. In filling initial orders, it is wise to ask the customer for ideas on how the product can be improved. It is amazing how cooperative the average customer will be when you let him know that he is helping to pioneer a new product. Beware of the "phony" customer who is a competitor in disguise.

Phase 12. Final design and mass production and sales—Final design drawings can now be prepared, or previous drawings revised, and given to the production department with some confidence that what they make will be sold. In this final design phase, the inventor and production engineers should view with surgical objectivity the possibility of making the product simpler and better before final tooling. Before, during, and after production begins, an aggressive sales campaign should be conducted.

Success of a sales program may also be contingent upon the amount of creative thinking expended on sales ideas. Big companies expend millions of dollars each week to stimulate sales. For smaller companies, highly creative sales ideas can produce comparable results. Once more the gentlemen of the press can be of great assistance. Good, exciting news releases (with excellent photos) should be prepared and distributed with the aid and guidance of the top company executives, professional news writers, and the new-product research staff. [*Here again, the alert new-product editor will trip you up. He publishes information on each new product once, so if he published the Phase 7 release, he won't use this one, unless major changes have been made*—Editor.]

The success of any new-product program is highly contingent upon the flexibility and mobility of the executive philosophy. If, for example, a company rigidly confines its new-product thinking to one or two product "lines," then it cannot take advantage of opportunities beyond these limits. In recent months, several large companies have indicated that their success depends to a large extent upon flexibility, which enables them to make money on *any* good new product. ∎

The Project Engineer's Role in Product Development

LOUIS SCHEIB

The Project Engineer will have occasion to require the performance of all or many of the following functions: customer liaison, field investigation, specification writing, design, experimental jury rig testing, prototype testing, periodical and patent research, fabrication and assembly, and manual writing. To assist him in these functions the Project Engineer may establish groups to supply the services required. The Project Engineer's relationship to these groups can best be illustrated by a wheel in which the Project Engineer acts as the hub and the various contributing groups are the spokes.

Functions not covered by the contributing groups would be handled by the Project Engineer. Expediting or specification writing would be handled by his immediate staff. If the operation is a small scale one, other functions may be undertaken by the Project Engineer such as testing, investigations, etc. The number of groups assisting the Project Engineer will vary with the size of the organization and the number of projects in process at one time. The Project Engineer is in no way tied down to his own company facilities, but he may, and indeed it is his perogative, to use whatever outside services will most expeditiously obtain the information he requires.

In his central position in the project organization the project engineer can properly direct, coordinate, anticipate future needs, and apply extraordinary effort where it is required.

With full responsibility for the success or failure of the project, the Project Engineer must have complete authority. Within the framework of the project he should be boss and his word should be final.

Project Procedure

Project procedures employing stages and sub-stages can be so arranged that the necessary information can be speedily acted upon. One such stage system described here divides the project into nine stages and fifty-four sub-stages. It is possible to pursue several stages at once and it is often feasible to finish a later stage before a preceding stage is completed. However, complications and rework are avoided if the proper chronological order is maintained.

The use of the stage chart permits the selection of arbitrary intermediate goals, and it may be described as a detailed sub-division of the job. Without sub-division, attempts at control of the many work components could lead to confusion. The stages start with the first concepts and step by step proceed through acceptability, design, working drawings and a fabricated prototype.

Stage I concerns the interpretation of the problem. One of the most difficult tasks of the Project Engineer is to condense the nebulous ideas concerning the equipment or process into definite and exact specifications. The importance of Stage I cannot be overestimated, for here is provided the foundation upon which all future action will build. Specifications should be written so that the required operations and conditions may be listed; so that the project team working with them have a common understanding of the goal; and finally, so that those paying for the project know the exact nature and extent of the proposed effort. This does not mean, of course, that the specifications are unchangeable but it does supply the common foundation upon which to start full scale operations.

To further assist the Project Engineer it is necessary to establish a committee to whom the Project Engineer is responsible, consisting of individuals whose opinions are highly valued by management. The Project Engineer will meet with the committee from time to time to report progress and to obtain approval for succeeding stages. The composition of the committee may vary with the type of machine concerned. It should have a representative of a sales division, the manager of engi-

I PROBLEM ANALYSIS

1) Preliminary discussion of problem with initiating individuals and management.
2) Formation of committee consisting of design, management, customer contact and consultant groups hereinafter to be called the committee.
3) Draw-up of initial performance and basic design specifications.
4) Draw up initial financial picture including cost and profit estimates.
5) Hold meeting with committee for initial approval to proceed.

II INITIAL INVESTIGATION

6) Outline technical problems and coordinate necessary engineering effort.
7) Investigate utilization, adaptation or conversion of existing machines or equipment.
8) Institute search of patents and periodicals.
9) Prepare initial layouts of possible machines and sub-unit devices.
10) Review layouts with committee.
11) Revise preliminary performance and design specifications to conform with new findings and committee recommendations.
12) Plan experimental program required to coordinate activities and complete development of machine.
13) Make cost estimates of experimental program.
14) Review experimental program with committee.
15) Design necessary jury rigs and experimental test equipment.

III MECHANISM AND CONCEPT PROOF

16) Order fabrication of jury rigs and experimental equipment and expedite delivery of same.
17) Write test specifications and prepare data charts.
18) Run tests and record data.
19) Review test data and alter design and/or performance specifications to guide design.
20) Demonstrate jury rig to committee, discuss revised specifications and obtain permission to proceed to Stage IV.

IV REVISED ENGINEERING ESTIMATES

21) Prepare revised estimates of development, tooling and fabrication costs.
22) Prepare revised estimates of manpower and facility requirement.
23) Draw up revised project stage completion program.

V DETAILED LAYOUTS

24) Plan machine and prepare overall layout.
25) Make detailed design layouts of basic machine and unit mechanisms.
26) Review design layouts with committee.
27) Revise layouts where required.
28) Obtain committee approval and signatures on revised layouts.

VI COMPLETE DETAILS AND ASSEMBLY DRAWINGS

29) Prepare drawing schedule.
30) Prepare details and sub-assembly drawings.
31) Check details and sub-assemblies.
32) Prepare main and unit assembly drawings.
33) Prepare Bill of Material.
34) Check assembly drawings and Bill of Materials.
35) Review all drawings with committee and obtain approval for prototype construction.

VII PROTOTYPE FABRICATION

36) Place fabrication order for machine.
37) Prepare fabrication schedule.
38) Follow receipt of equipment and expedite delivery of bottleneck items.
39) Assemble components and keep log of fabrication alterations. Check workmanship, inspection report, and adherence to specifications.

VIII PROTOTYPE TESTING

40) Make initial adjustment and run-in on machine.
41) Prepare test specifications and data charts based on performance specifications.
42) Run tests and record data.
43) Make whatever modifications are found necessary one machine to meet performance specifications.
44) Analyze test data and record machine modifications in log.
45) Report and review results of tests with committee.
46) Demonstrate machine operation to committee.
47) Analyze alterations which demonstration and committee may require. Start with Stage IV on these and again take through Stage VIII.
48) Obtain committee approval of machine.

IX FINALIZING DRAWINGS AND PREPARATION FOR MANUFACTURE

49) Alter drawings to conform with prototype fabrication and testing changes.
50) Secure signatures of committee on drawings.
51) Prepare operating and instruction manual.
52) Prepare maintenance manual including lubrication charts, gasket charts, spare parts lists, and installation procedure.
53) Prepare history of machine.
54) Maintain liaison with production engineering to expedite manufacture and to facilitate installation of mass manufacture methods.

---

neering, and possibly heads of other departments closely affected by the project.

Stage V is primarily design effort. Detailed layouts of all components are made based upon last specifications. Commercial items with long delivery dates may be ordered prior to completion.

Stage II starts the basic work on the machine itself. Initial sketches and layouts based upon specifications drawn up in Stage I are prepared. Simultaneously, investigations into available equipment or portions of equipment are made. Use of commercially available equipment sometimes eliminates the need for a new design or parts of the design. Competitive machines should be investigated or bought for study. Current literature, periodicals and patents may supply ideas.

Changes in specifications during the initial stages are to be expected. If during the latter stages, major changes in specifications are indicated it is wise to consider such variance as a change in scope and to return to Stage I, II, III, or IV, treating that portion of the project as a completely new project.

The Project Engineer does many jobs: he starts the ball rolling; sparks its development; anticipates difficulties, and eliminates bottlenecks; he maintains a complete record of schedules, cost and progress at his fingertips; and he makes all information available to management. The Project Engineer has established his niche in the machinery industry. He has become a necessity in a complex industrial world where new developments are uncertain quantities. ∎

Designer's Checklist for New Products

Lest you forget—here's a set of
reminders pointing to the little things
that breed waste and inefficiency.

WALTER R. SCHERB, Western Electric Co, Kearny Works, Kearny, NJ

GENERAL

☐ *1..* Is this a proposal or an actual design project?

☐ *2..* To what extent should we consider annual requirements?

☐ *3..* Is the new design necessary, or would a simple modification of an existing one suffice?

☐ *4..* If the new design supersedes an existing one, are the economies sound with respect to tool and machine investment, etc?

☐ *5..* Are the engineering requirements, limits, and tolerances specified necessary or are they unnecessarily strict and likely to result in excessive manufacturing cost?

☐ *6..* Are the requirements consistent with those for similar equipment so that gages and test facilities can be used?

☐ *7..* Can the engineering requirements be interpreted in only one way so costly discussions do not result?

☐ *8..* Are those dimensions of component parts which affect their assembly properly related to a common base point?

☐ *9..* Are additional drawings introduced when information could just as effectively be added to existing drawings?

☐ *10..* Are new parts called for where existing parts could be used, either with or without modification?

☐ *11..* Has the minimum number of parts been used to reduce assembly effort?

☐ *12..* Are assemblies in the most practical stage for economical and safe shipping?

☐ *13..* Is wiring style correct—local cable, surface wiring, direct wiring?

☐ *14..* Can length, diameter, number of threads, material, and finish of screws, bolts, nuts, washers, etc, be simplified to reduce the number of parts?

☐ *15..* If stamping is to be performed after assembly, is the location convenient?

☐ *16..* If cost estimates are required, are they accurate enough for their intended purpose? Do they reflect the uncertainties?

RAW MATERIAL

☐ *1..* Have standard raw materials been specified so they are obtainable without special order?

☐ *2..* Can a cheaper, thinner, or more workable material be used?

☐ *3..* Can grained or ground surfaces be eliminated by obtaining a prepared surface or a better-grade material?

☐ **4 . .** Can plated or prepared surface on steel be used where more costly solid material is specified?

☐ **5 . .** If a high-grade fiber is specified, will the electrical requirements allow the use of a lower and less expensive grade?

☐ **6 . .** Can specially rolled or formed stock, supplied directly from the mill, be used advantageously?

☐ **7 . .** Where sheet is specified, can strip stock be used to reduce manufacturing cost?

☐ **8 . .** Would a standard width of sheet be more economical than a special width?

MANUFACTURING

☐ **1 . .** Is there an application for any of the highly productive molding processes such as forging, die casting or powdered metal?

☐ **2 . .** Can formed punching replace castings, etc, or would a casting eliminate the assembly of a number of parts?

☐ **3 . .** Do castings have surfaces suitable for easy clamping for machine operations or should these be specially provided?

☐ **4 . .** Are holes too close to edges or shoulders, causing difficulty in die design or maintenance?

☐ **5 . .** Can the number of sizes of holes, taps, or screws be reduced? Can the sizes themselves be larger to facilitate manufacture?

☐ **6 . .** Do hole sizes correspond to standard drill sizes?

☐ **7 . .** Have blind tapped holes been specified where through holes would be satisfactory?

☐ **8 . .** Have standard threads been specified for screws and tapped holes and are they preferred sizes?

☐ **9 . .** Are screws, bolts, or other fasteners accessible without special wrenches, screwdrivers, etc?

☐ **10 . .** Are countersunk screws used where others would be satisfactory?

☐ **11 . .** Are screws adaptable to power-driven assembly methods?

☐ **12 . .** If an irregular hole is shown, which would necessitate filing or broaching, can it be changed so milling or drilling can be performed?

☐ **13 . .** Can engraved characters be replaced by depressed stamped characters or rubber-stamped inked characters protected with shellac?

☐ **14 . .** Will the requirements justify or permit metal etching instead of engraving or stamping?

☐ **15 . .** Can arc or spot welding be used to replace riveting or other more costly fastening methods?

☐ **16 . .** Can weld nuts replace embossed tapped holes, or similar threaded studs replace riveted ones?

☐ **17 . .** Can deburring be replaced by tumbling?

☐ **18 . .** Are jigs and fixtures designed so both left and right hands can be used to advantage?

FINISHING

☐ **1 . .** Can specified finishes be eliminated?

☐ **2 . .** Can a less expensive finish be used?

☐ **3 . .** Can the surface preparation for a subsequent finish be eliminated or simplified?

☐ **4 . .** Does the design permit finishing as specified?

☐ **5 . .** Is the required finish specified at the proper stage of completion to avoid damage to the finish in subsequent handling?

☐ **6 . .** Will an electrochemical finish penetrate all recesses?

☐ **7 . .** Can the finish specified be applied economically in the lots anticipated?

☐ **8 . .** Has an electrochemical finish been specified on a partial assembly where purging at joints will occur?

Value analysis: myth or a practical reality?

A relatively new concept for keeping costs down is being used by a number of firms. But the idea isn't altogether accepted by many top companies

A COMPANY IN THE US was having difficulty designing a cheap and effective rectangular reflector for a bathroom light fixture. Then a VE —for Value Engineering—expert noticed that the prototype reflector looked like a cake pan. The company bought a large consignment of cake pans and found it had the answer to its problems.

A simple case of human resourcefulness? Perhaps. But the fact is that a new breed of men in industry, the VEs (value engineers) and VAs (value analysts), are coming up with perhaps more than their share of bright ideas.

The reason is that they are concerned with finding what a product costs in terms of what it does. Their minds are oriented to the need for systematic cost cutting and the eradication of production waste.

In the opinion of A. B. Kight, president of Borg-Warner's Norge Division, value analysis is "as important as mother love". But Walter C. Loeman, vice-president of Parker-Hannifin Corp., another U.S. firm, sees no need for value analysis or value engineering. "When you put a VE committee on the job," he said, "you just duplicate the work the regular engineering section is doing—or ought to be doing".

Pros and cons—Who is right, Kight or Loeman? The spectrum of opinion is wide.

Value engineers are a relatively new type of specialist. They claim that their organised approach is ten times worth the effort in terms of cash savings. And they are unimpressed by the critical view that the savings are in costs that never should have crept in at all.

What is more, the VE engineers say, their art is not merely a way to detect unneeded costs. It is also a way to anticipate unnecessary costs by instituting value engineering at the design stage. In the words of one VE expert: "You don't want to let the horse out of the barn and then give yourself a medal for bringing it back."

Value analysis and value engineering aren't precisely identical, although many companies use the terms interchangeably. Generally, VA means a systematic review, often periodically, of products and parts to see if cost-saving changes in design can be made. VE is usually associated with the original design stage, making its systematic review of design before production starts.

Close relations—Both VE and VA are close relatives of conventional cost reduction, but they differ from it in at least two ways:

1. Their heavy stress on precisely expressing the function of a product in terms of dollars and cents.

2. Their use of a highly organized, company-wide approach.

Value engineering has cut $20 (£7.1) off the retail price of Hoover vacuum cleaners in the past four years. Says a Hoover official: "One of the big advantages of the value engineering programme is its organized approach to cost reduction. Every proposed change goes through step by step, and each department has a chance to comment."

The system avoids the making of changes that would give one department a small saving while adding a larger cost to another department. A VE or VA programme seeks to assure that at every stage of design or manufacture there will be people from engineering, production, purchasing and marketing all thinking about cost versus function.

How it began—Value analysis began in the late 1940s at General Electric Co. The initial spark came, it is said, when a GEC design engineer asked plaintively: "Doesn't anybody around here CARE what things cost?"

The first users of value analysis were purchasing agents, and most companies that turned to VE and VA began their programme in the purchasing department to keep closer checks on the cost of parts. Thus the VE programme of General Motors Corp. was set up more than three years ago by procurement people, because "it was recognized that cost-saving techniques were not being applied as well as they should be."

The big spur to VE and VA in the US, however, came when the Defence Department offered to share savings with firms who used the system.

More recently, an increasing number of manufacturers of consumer goods and non-defence equipment have been adopting the cost-conscious twins VE and VA. In the opinion of Charles Warren, administrative engineer with the Towmotor Corp., "anyone who doesn't use the value analysis system is crazy".

Committee systems—Crazy or not, some companies still will have no part of VE and VA.

Walter Loeman at Parker-Hannifin lumps VE with quality control and reliability engineering as "catchwords" that grab ephemeral attention. "Companies have been doing these things for years," he says. "Dramatic cost savings and their association with value engineering are often coincidental. Value engineering came on the scene when companies were placing more and more emphasis on cost cutting. The savings would be just as dramatic if they were achieved by regular staff people."

Wholehearted formal VE programmes use various committee systems—frequently with full-time engineering people in charge.

Typical of one type is the programme at Westinghouse Electric.

Function versus cost—V. B. Baker, Westinghouse's director of product cost improvement in headquarters engineering, says that the first step is to set up a committee of "functional people"—from design, manufacturing, purchasing, industrial engineering and, often, marketing.

Management can perform another vital function in keeping VE within its proper and useful limits. In the view of Robert S. Codrington, who is manager of product engineering for the Analytical Instrument Div. of Varian Associates: "No design is ever completed that couldn't be improved in one way or another. But management at some point must say 'this design is good enough'."

Like other cost-efficiency techniques VE and VA are useful tools. But they need to be adequately managed. ∎

5.

New Techniques for Making Better Decisions

Improving your decisions

decision
decision
decision
decision

by A. R. Houseman
P.-E. Consulting Group Ltd.

LONG BEFORE THIS century bows itself out, we may see the general industrial worker with a 20-hour week. At the same time the executive will be on an 80-hour week unless he takes steps to organize himself and his work properly.

Our own experience of the past decade or two clearly points the way open before us. It is for management to keep abreast of new ideas and methods which will help it do its job more efficiently.

In a nutshell this means using scientific methods to make administrative problems more manageable.

The development and refinement of numerous such methods, perhaps symbolized best by the computer, have accelerated rapidly since the end of the fifties. They are giving us a whole series of new tools with which to work.

Barriers to progress—Firms that will need to use these new management techniques in the near future include some which even now have no proper understanding of their relevance.

Their misconceptions range from a belief that the new methods may replace managers with decision-making machines, to an acute scepticism that they are merely highly formalized, complex ways of doing what any experienced manager does naturally. These are misunderstandings based on ignorance and fear of change.

For management to ensure future administrative efficiency, its first step must be this:

Get to know the potential of these developments in scientific management and the many opportunities they bring with them.

The techniques now being brought into use by management fall into five main categories:

- Long-range planning and forecasting.
- Organization—cybernetics.
- Finance, value analysis, decision trees, integrated planning and control.
- Production—operational research, network analysis.
- Personnel—programmed learning, ergonomics.

All these techniques have been strongly influenced in their development by the systematic automation of management processes through the computer.

Computer limitations—Of course, the computer is far from being the answer to all management's problems, but its value is most noticeable when it is put to solving narrow and well-defined problems.

Computer programming, above all else, opens a way for the methodical setting out of a whole range of decision sequences which would otherwise be left largely to individual judgement and the lessons of experience.

This does not mean that the computer runs the company. The computer is programmed to incorporate certain assumptions; for instance, the price of raw material and the proportion of waste.

A key point for management here is, therefore, the attention it must pay to the examination of these various assumptions.

Let's now take a look at some of these techniques, both computer and non-computer based, and see where and how they fit in.

Forecasting

As a technique, this covers the analysis of statistical data and other economic, political and market information with an aim of reducing the risks involved in making decisions and long-range plans. It analyses what business conditions will be, whether the material requirements will be available, what manpower is needed and whether outside finance is required.

Business forecasting uses a number of different techniques because no single technique is perfect. And the cross-checking of different results is necessary to eliminate errors wherever possible and to arrive at conclusions that seem likely to be correct.

Cybernetics

This is an organizational science introduced about 20 years ago. It teaches management to treat a company as a complex, inter-reacting whole and not as a collection of unrelated units. Cybernetics shows that some aspects of this inter-reacting whole will never be understood clearly and that manipulation rather than dissection will be more successful.

The technique demonstrates that variety in the controlling machinery is the only way to deal with the variety existing in the system itself. It emphasizes that control, at any level, must be implicit and not explicit, with the feed-back of information being vital to the control system.

Value analysis

The object of value analysis is to eliminate all unnecessary costs in the design, manufacture and marketing of products or services.

The biggest savings are likely in four main areas. In purchases a ten per cent reduction in the cost of raw materials could have the same effect on profitability as if sales were doubled.

The second area is that of material stocks, where the levels are often far too high. This ties down capital which could more usefully be used elsewhere.

The third area of saving is in the basic product design and the possible use of alternative materials.

Lastly, quality and dimensional tolerances are often far in excess of those needed for the particular use to which the product will ultimately be put.

Some companies using value analysis have achieved a 30 to 60 per cent reduction in production costs.

The reason for this success is due to the deeply penetrating approach which a small team of specialists in different functions can bring to bear on the analysis of one product at the same time.

Decision trees

Problems of investment are of paramount importance today. The decision trees method helps to clarify the choice, risks, objective and financial gains of an investment scheme.

It represents, diagrammatically, the various decision points and the alternative courses of action. Each branch or line on the tree diagram represents an alternative course of action and each 'node' a decision point or an influencing factor.

The decision tree is built up by deciding what the alternatives are at each node, by estimating the probability of the results of the different alternatives and then by choosing which course to take.

The tree will show nothing not already known, but it presents a systematic analysis of the problem and therefore a better understanding of it.

Integrated planning and control

This method of management, commonly known as IPC, is a development of the existing conventional accounting system. Using this method, the individual manager sets his own targets and ensures that they are met. Instead of financial control being imposed upon him by the comptroller's office, he is told to produce a personal budget of what he can do to achieve improvements in his department and of the effect they will have on profits. He reviews his functions and selects those areas where improvements can be made.

The manager then details his aims, his proposed methods and their expected effects on profits.

This whole process brings an awareness of the individual manager's ability to contribute to the greater profitability of the company and forces him to take action.

Operational research

This method enables you to institute a routine way of handling many situations on a systematic basis. OR leaves a manager free to concentrate his time on those decisions which cannot be made on a systematic basis and on which he must use his personal judgement.

There are four steps in solving a problem by the use of OR: observation, hypothesis, experiment and deduction.

In general, the technique is to set up a model; usually a mathematical representation of what is likely to happen by means of a formula, or perhaps a computer programme. Several different ways are then tried to see which appears to be the best solution to the problem.

OR has been found to be of particular value in dealing with the increasing complexity of business operations, in dealing with conflicting interests of departments and in releasing managers from routine decision-making.

Network analysis

This is a technique for helping management in the planning and control of non-repetitive work. It incorporates the logical dependence of one operation on another and uses this information to define a period of time within which each operation must be carried out. It also shows levels of priority for management control purposes.

Network analysis is applicable to such projects as the introduction of new products, new plant, major repairs and maintenance work and limited production runs.

Network analysis enforces rigorous planning of the project and enables the forecasting of realistic completion dates. It allows the objective analysis of alternative plans in relation to the scheduled completion date and facilitates the consideration of any limitations in the availability of resources.

The system highlights those areas which are most likely to cause delay and indicates a sequence of priorities for management control purposes.

It also enables the programme to be updated quickly and cheaply and indicates where action is needed as a result of delays.

Programmed learning

In the personnel field, two important innovations have been developed to help solve the age-old problem of relating the employee to his working environment.

Programmed learning is a step-by-step system based on studies of how people learn. The subject to be learned is broken down into stages called frames. A programme is a complete series of frames, with each new frame building up on the last, so that the learner progresses at his own pace.

Both teaching machines and books are used, but there is a high initial cost and much work involved in preparing the course.

Ergonomics

This is the second personnel method. It essentially seeks the optimum conditions for man to carry out his work. As such, it is concerned with the practical application of energy and with the influences of working conditions.

The method depends on knowledge only recently acquired about human anatomy and physiological behaviour and is still in its infancy. But from results so far obtained there is an apparent need for companies to recognize the value of applied research into human performance.

These are the main tools being used. Applied correctly they can give far-reaching results. Both cybernetics and ergonomics, for instance, can help to get the maximum results from both manpower and machine operation. Programmed learning contributes to this by helping to improve operator and apprentice training.

Operational research can be used to estimate the cost of labour turnover and to calculate the possible savings of a reduction in the percentage of labour turnover. In this field it is possible to forecast the numbers likely to leave a company in the future and thus to plan the recruitment and training of replacements. This method leaves the executive free to concentrate on those decisions which require personal judgement. However, since some managers find it difficult to accept OR, the simpler the first project to which it is applied the better.

OR is also of particular use combined with a computer in scheduling production for a range of products, taking into account stock levels, manufacturing dates and expected product sales demands.

Stock control is among the most important applications of the computer. At the same time, it is able to compare gross requirements with free stocks, to calculate new balances, determine whether or not an order should be placed and if so for what quantity and for what delivery date.

In this respect, the computer is particularly valuable when frequent programme revisions are considered to be necessary. ■

Design trees aid decision

Alternative materials, finishes, components, processes, and many other factors combine to make the best choice difficult. Here's help.

DOUGLAS C. GREENWOOD

ARE you gambling with vital design decisions? If you're ignoring the interaction of design factors and still using intuitive decision procedures, as most design engineers are, you are indeed gambling—perhaps with your company's success, maybe with your country's safety.

Professor Martin Kenneth Starr in his latest book *Product Design and Decision Theory* makes this point and pleads for a more objective approach to design decision. As first aids to systematic judgment Starr has devised what he calls "design trees." These trees also show how complex modern design has become. Design engineers can clearly see just what a jungle they are actually trapped in—if they can bear the sudden light of revelation.

Aside from all the nonengineering aspects, such as sales, marketing, and even environmental operating conditions that influence the final design of a product, there are enough purely engineering problems to make it impossible to achieve significant optimization if ordinary methods are all an engineer has to work with. Most of Starr's work is devoted to showing how engineering "strategies," as derived from design trees, are applied to nonengineering factors in a "payoff" matrix—as in standard decision-theory mathematics. But a systematic way of finding the best combination of engineering alternatives is vital to good design.

So let us to our "trees." Example: If one part can be made in three different ways and in two different shapes but of only one material, then six variations are possible, see Fig 1. Add a second alternative material and you now have twelve variants, and so on.

So far, nothing worse than carrying a few chess moves in your head? All right. We'll now hit you with a slightly more complex design problem, represented by the tree in Fig 2. There are 5184 unique design configurations illustrated. Actual design problems generally involve even more parameters than the relative few in Fig 2 and would take many lifetimes to work through!

Can anything be done about this nightmare state of affairs? Well, if you treat the single components as though they were independent of each other, then there are only 24 alternatives for component 1, 24 for component 2, and nine for component 3, a mere 57 decisions.

But if you ignore component interaction in some products they'll fail completely. For example, you just can't pick the best rocket-engine design from a set of feasible rocket engines and then, ignoring the choice of engine, pick the best control system from a group of control systems. So if you can't ignore interaction of design factors, what's the answer? More systematic approach to design from now on, says Starr.

A system is a group of activities or components that can be bounded. The bounding rule is: all relevant interdependences and interactions must be enclosed.

Let's apply this rule to the example of Fig 2, where complete interaction gave us 5184 possible alternatives. We'll assume interaction now between only three interdependent factors, as shown in Fig 3, which is an extensive tree where the branches have been untwined. Now you have only 24 decisions to make. Evaluate each link, give it a number, multiply the number along each branch, and the values above some arbitrary cut-off point are the preferred combinations.

Evaluating design trees

Applying specific numbers is easy. In Fig 3 the numbers are merely expressions of preference for the particular material or material combinations with which the numbers are associated. You get the decimal numbers by

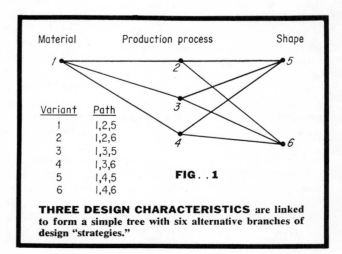

THREE DESIGN CHARACTERISTICS are linked to form a simple tree with six alternative branches of design "strategies."

assigning values for component 1 materials. In the example these were 3, 2, 4 and 1. Their sum is 10, and dividing each number by 10 gives the numbers shown. (If, however, the values were 1, 2, 3, and 2, the sum would be 8; dividing by 8 would give 0.125, 0.250, 0.375, and 0.250. These values would then replace those shown in the first row of Fig 3.) Now evaluate the combinations *ae, af,* and *ag,* which must also total one. Do the same for materials *b, c,* and *d.* Now, for link *ae,* decide what preference you have for finishes *j* and *k* of component 2. If it doesn't matter which finish will be used with the combination *ae,* give equal values to links *ej* and *ek.* If one of the links is totally preferred give it a value of 1. The other link would then receive a zero value, meaning that continuation of that line is pointless because the final result would be valueless, no matter how good the other combinations in the line were.

After assigning all link values, multiply the numbers successively along each branch, placing the results on the final row as in Fig 3. Thus the maximum value 0.108 for branch *a-g-k* was obtained by multiplying 0.3 x 0.4 x 0.9. Dots have been placed under all those evaluations that exceed 0.05. There are nine such branches. If our design decision problem consisted of just these three levels, we would begin our decision analysis with nine alternative strategies, which could be applied to a decision-theory matrix if further analysis were necessary.

This method of choosing alternative strategies is the first filter; it reduces the problem to a manageable size by filtering out the obviously unfit combinations. Analogous to the grade of a mechanical filter, the cut-off point of 0.05 can be varied, and in this case was chosen so that a sufficient number of contending designs would remain. Note, however, that as you move sequentially through a network, low-valued branches begin to appear. When they fall below a specified cut-off point, don't bother to proceed any further.

Here, then, is a systematic method for analyzing design problems even though, perhaps, the enormity of most design-decision problems now stands revealed in more detail than was realized. That we have managed so far to create good products by "green-thumb" engineering intuition is to our credit. But how much better, perhaps, could they have been with a more systematic approach to design decisions. It's certain that this approach, coupled with the rapid growth of technology, guarantees that the future belongs to the design engineers who recognize the problem and know how best to go about making the right decisions. ∎

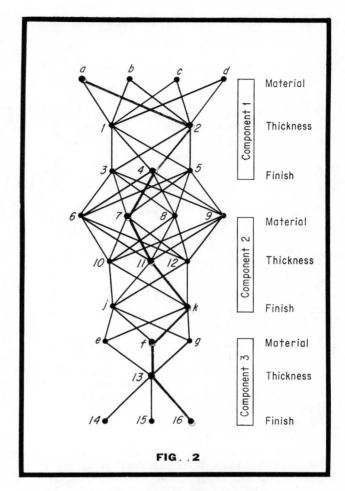

FIG..2

THREE-COMPONENT DESIGN TREE has 5184 unique design configurations.* One of these unique paths might be, for example, a-2-4-7-11-k-f-13-16. If your average decision time for each of the 5184 possibilities were only five minutes, you'd have eleven solid weeks of work ahead of you.
*1 X 4 X 2 X 3 X 1 X 4 X 3 X 2 X 1 X 3 X 1 X 3 = 5184

THREE INTERDEPENDENT DESIGN FACTORS in three components are evaluated to arrive at the best choice among many alternative combinations.

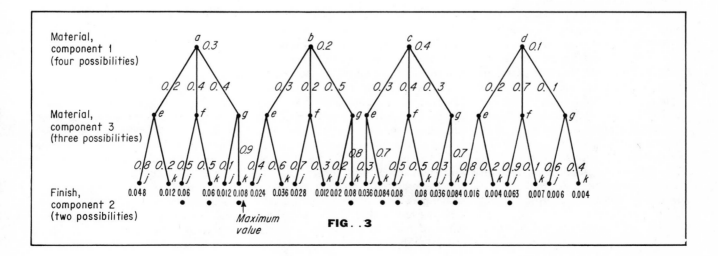

FIG..3

Several methods—both practical and theoretical—for solving industrial problems by operations research. A linear programming solution is applied to a quantity, storage, distribution problem.

Operations Research: For Industrial Use

LINEAR PROGRAMMING, Edward C. Varnum, Barber-Colman Co.

OPERATIONS RESEARCH is simply the application of scientific research techniques to management, engineering and manufacturing problems. For instance, an expenditure problem can be set up in mathematical form—a set of equations—that show how a change in any one of the variables will affect the overall results. Thus, a comprehensive algebraic formula could relate storage costs, shipping time, production time, cost of loss of business if shipment can not be made immediately, product costs, gross margin, selling costs, turnover rate, and others that would indicate the most profitable inventory policy for finished goods in a manufacturing plant.

Operations research is applied research in that it deals with measurable factors and produces specific answers to practical problems. Its purpose is to find a new way to clarify old problems that previously were not subject to quantitative analysis.

Mathematical approaches include tables of random numbers, Poisson distribution, normal distribution and others. The probability theory, optimization theory and variations of these are coming into use. These give the engineer additional methods of problem solution. The selected approach is related to the type of problem and the number of variables that need to be considered.

Practical Methods

In addition to the tables mentioned, other useful tables are the t, F, Chi-square and binomial probability. The numerical calculations may be performed on anything from a slide rule or nomogram, through a desk calculator to high speed digital computers.

Table of Random Numbers. Random numbers have been used extensively in setting up statistical theories and in quality control applications relating to inspection problems. Recently, they have been applied to a study of the efficiency of equipment subject to small probabilities of failure. Also: random numbers may be used to illustrate theories which can help in the production of components.

Table of Poisson Distribution. Again a method used for many years in sta-

tistical theory and quality control. Briefly, the distribution is concerned with the probabilities of occurrence of an exact number of events in a large population when the probability of this event happening to an individual is small. In industry such events occur, for example, in textile production. Many bobbins are involved on a single machine and the probability of yarn breakage for any particular bobbin is small.

Table of Areas and Ordinates for the Normal Distribution. In dealing with populations which can be assumed to be distributed normally, many numerical problems can be solved easily. An example is a merit rating control chart designed for use in determining unusual shifts in rating. This is an excellent example of where operations research leaves the bounds of production and inspection and enters the field of general management.

Theoretical Methods

Beside the theories mentioned here, the mathematical model technique is often used. This is a method by which a problem solution is modeled upon a similar set of circumstances. Additional variables may enter into the new problem but the basic method of solution can be followed. To some extent, the following theories all follow this mathematical technique.

Probability Theory. Little need be said about probability theory since its considerations are basic in the older techniques of statistical control, significance tests and acceptance sampling. Some of the newer developments are the search theory, Monte Carlo methods

and the theory of games. Specific examples of both the old and new techniques can be found in the literature; many of them mentioned at the end of this article.

Optimization Theory. The simplest examples arise when a cost function can be expressed as a simple relationship to a single variable. This cost function is then differentiated with respect to the single variable. By setting the derivative equal to zero and solving for the value of the variable, the cost becomes optimum (minimum).

The simpler aspects of optimization have been applied to the problem of economic lot sizes, machinery replacement, finding the optimum resistances in Wheatstone bridge circuits, minimizing moments of inertia of gear trains and deriving formulas for maximum slope angles for various radial cam motions. Other uses for the theory are in the field of sales forecasting in which trend lines are fitted to sales and production data so that the errors are minimized. The theory of least squares, an optimization technique, is also useful as a tool for sales and market analysts.

Linear Programming

This is a more complicated version of the optimization theory. However, its versatility and relative simplicity—compared to many of the other procedures—of application makes it applicable to a variety of problems and to companies of any size.

The method is used for solving problems involving many inter-dependent variables by maximizing or minimizing an outcome. The technique can be visualized in geometrical terms as follows:

The n variables define an n-dimensional space; a point of this space corresponds to a solution. Each limitation on the range of the variables corresponds to a hyperplane in this space, restricting the allowed solution points to one side of the hyperplane. By the time all restrictions are specified (negative production not allowed, maximum limits on storage capacity, limits of production, etc.), the entire region of possible solutions by hypersurfaces has been surrounded. There are two limiting hyperplanes: one corresponding to the largest value of the function and one corresponding to the smallest value. The outermost limit is the optimum solution if the function is to be maximized; the innermost point is optimum if the function is to be minimized.

For instance, the following example shows the basic steps in the solution of a simple transportation problem. Numbers are simplified and some of the more complicated details are omitted to emphasize the fundamental numerical processes.

Assume that three factories A, B and C produce 10 tons, 40 tons and 50 tons, respectively. This material is to be shipped to warehouses I, II, and III so that these warehouses receive 20 tons, 20 tons and 60 tons, respectively. The freight rate from A to I is $2.00 per ton, from A to II is $1.00 per ton and from A to III is $3.00 per ton. Factory B can ship to I, II, and III, for $4.00, $3.00, and $2.00 per ton, respectively, while $C's$ respective freight costs are $5.00, $2.00, and $4.00. The above information can be exhibited as shown in Table I:

TABLE I

Factories	Warehouses			Pro-duc-tion
	I	II	III	
A	2	1	3	10
B	4	3	2	40
C	5	2	4	50
Receipts	20	20	60	100

For a given matrix which shows freight costs along with tonnages for each factory and warehouse, the problem consists in scheduling the shipping so that the total freight bill will be the cheapest.

The first step is to make a schedule in an obvious way; that is, start with factory A and use up all its production starting with warehouse I; then use up $B's$ production, and then $C's$ by working to the right and downward in the Table. This easy schedule is shown in Table II.

TABLE II

	I	II	III	
A	10			10
B	10	20	10	40
C			50	50
	20	20	60	100

By comparison of Tables I and II freight charges will cost $340.00 as there are 10 tons at $2.00, 10 tons at $4.00, 20 tons at $3.00, 10 tons at $2.00 and 50 tons at $4.00. The problem consists of reducing this $340.00 freight bill.

Table III is made by first writing in the rates corresponding to the shipments in Table II. For clarity, these numbers are italicized to show that they are written in first. The notion of row numbers and column numbers are now introduced. Each italicized number in Table III shall be the sum of its respective row and column numbers. Assume that the upper row number is zero. Combine this 0 with the italicized 2 in square A I to find that the first column number is 2. Now, combine this 2 with the italicized 4 to find that the middle row number is 2. Combining this new 2 with the italicized 3, the middle column number is 1. The last column number is obtained from the italicized 2 and the middle row number which is also a 2; thus, the last column number is zero. The last row number is 4 because the last column number is 0 and C III is an italicized 4.

TABLE III

	I	II	III	Row Nos.
A	2			0
B	4	3	2	2
C			4	4
Column Nos.	2	1	0	

Having determined all the row and column numbers by means of assuming a zero and subtracting from the italicized numbers, Table III can be filled in as shown in Table IV, by adding respective row and column numbers. For example, A II is 0 plus 1, C I is 4 plus 2, etc.

TABLE IV

	I	II	III	Row
A	2	1	0	0
B	4	3	2	2
C	6	5	4	4
Column	2	1	0	

Now compare Table I with Table IV. Naturally, the italicized numbers in Table IV are the same as their mates in Table I. Thus, only the italicized numbers need be considered. Looking for the number in Table IV which exceeds its mate in Table I by the greatest amount, it is found in this problem that the 1 and 0 in Table IV do not exceed their mates, but that 6 is 1 more than 5, and 5 is 3 more than its corresponding 2. C II exceeds its mate by the greatest amount.

The next step in the solution is to place an x in the C II square of Table II as shown in Table V. To keep a balance of 20 tons in warehouse II, x tons must be taken away from the entry for B II. To maintain a balance of 50 tons from factory C, x tons must also be taken from C III. Finally, the totals can be balanced by adding x to the 10 tons in entry B III.

TABLE V

	I	II	III	
A	10			10
B	10	$20-x$	$10+x$	40
C		x	$50-x$	50
	20	20	60	

By examining Table V it is obvious that x cannot exceed 20 because otherwise B II would be negative. Thus, x is set equal to its largest possible value of 20 to obtain Table VI.

TABLE VI

	I	II	III	
A	10			10
B	10		30	40
C		20	30	50
	20	20	60	100

By comparing Tables I and VI the new freight bill may be calculated as follows:

$$10 \times 2.00 = 20.00$$
$$10 \times 4.00 = 40.00$$
$$30 \times 2.00 = 60.00$$
$$20 \times 2.00 = 40.00$$
$$30 \times 4.00 = 120.00$$

Total = $280.00

In this first refinement, the total freight bill has been reduced from $340.00 to $280.00.

To seek a further reduction, the process is repeated as follows. Table VII is obtained from Tables I and VI in the same manner that Table III was obtained.

TABLE VII

	I	II	III	Row Nos.
A	2			0
B	4		2	2
C		2	4	4
Column Nos.	2	−2	0	

Note in Table VII that the middle column number is −2 because the last row number is 4 and the C II is 2.

Now, fill in the blanks of Table VII to obtain Table VIII.

TABLE VIII

	I	II	III	Row
A	2	−2	0	0
B	4	0	2	2
C	6	2	4	4
Column	2	−2	0	

Comparing the numbers that are not italicized in Table VIII with their mates in Table I, 6 in C I exceeds its mate by 1 whereas no other number in Table VIII exceeds its mate. The next step, therefore, as shown in Table IX, is to put an x in C I and then adjust B I, B III, and C III accordingly.

TABLE IX

	I	II	III	
A	10			10
B	10−x	20	30+x	40
C	x	20	30−x	50
	20	20	60	100

By inspection of Table IX, 10 is the largest possible value of x, so in obtaining the revised schedule Table X, x is given this value.

TABLE X

	I	II	III	
A	10			10
B			40	40
C	10	20	20	50
	20	20	60	100

The revised freight bill then is:

$$10 \times 2.00 = 20.00$$
$$40 \times 2.00 = 80.00$$
$$10 \times 5.00 = 50.00$$
$$20 \times 2.00 = 40.00$$
$$20 \times 4.00 = 80.00$$

Total = $270.00

This bill is $10.00 less than before. To attempt a further improvement, calculate Tables XI and XII in the same way as before:

TABLE XI

	I	II	III	Row
A	2			0
B			2	1
C	5	2	4	3
Column	2	−1	1	

TABLE XII

	I	II	III	Row
A	2	−1	1	0
B	3	0	2	1
C	5	2	4	3
Column	2	−1	1	

By comparing, no number not italicized is as large as its mate in the original price Table I. This fact indicates that Table X gives the cheapest freight bill.

It is interesting to note that the best solution includes 10 tons at the $5.00 rate which is the maximum rate in the table and that the cheapest rate of $1.00 per ton is not used. The best schedule, as shown in Table X, is for factory A to send all its production to warehouse I, B should ship to III exclusively, and C should send 10 tons to I, 20 tons to II and 20 tons to III. The resulting freight bill of $270.00 cannot be further reduced.

The linear programming technique shown here can be readily extended to larger values and to more precise numerical values. Naturally, the arithmetic will increase in volume but the procedure is clear and there is no chance of becoming lost in a maze of equations. ■

How to conduct successful meetings

Don't—as many executives do—waste time in meetings. Here's some good advice on how to be more efficient

by John D. Foskett

GETTING WORK DONE through others is what most executives are doing all day, every day—through the process we now call "communicating". Most of us feel we're pretty good at this, but recent rather startling discoveries concerning this process raise some serious questions as to whether we're any good at all!

Most of us are too busy or too preoccupied with what we are saying to be sensitive to the reactions of the person we're addressing and to realize that all too often we are simply not "getting through". We never find out what this may be costing us in terms of misunderstandings, negative feelings, errors and inefficiencies, except when some extreme examples come to our attention.

If you don't believe this about "getting through", try this experiment: next time you find yourself in a simple argument with a friend, make an agreement that you must repeat each point in his argument back to him to his complete satisfaction before you can present *your* next point. Then he must be able to repeat that point *you* have made before he can continue, and so on.

Different ideas—You'll soon discover that what *you* think you say and what *he* thinks you say will be two vastly different things, and he'll say the same thing about what you say he has said. You will also begin to see the encouraging results you can get through getting this *feedback*, that is, from checking the two-way communication circuit. You will find the heat of the argument will start to fade.

In simple, everyday situations this problem between two people is irritating; but when it comes to complex matters or executive decisions, the barriers are formidable indeed and the results may be far-reaching.

The blocks are caused by such factors as plain physical distance, contrasting status and position, differences in how each sees the job, the amounts of information each has, differing scales of values, limits of intelligence and experience.

Many more subtle barriers also contribute to making accurate communication between two people a hazardous undertaking at best.

Group complexities — But if the situation is like this between two people, what about four, five or six? Is it any wonder that an executive meeting which doubles, triples or quadruples the communication complexities is a worrisome and frustrating affair for a president?

And yet, the meeting, as a communication tool, is potentially a most effective aid to real communication—perhaps the best a president has if he can understand its dynamics and exploit its possibilities for use.

Granted that you are looking for ways to improve your meetings, you probably won't read books on social psychology to find the answers.

You're not likely to settle for "The Ten Easy Steps to Better Meetings" either. There are no "ten easy steps" to *anything*, and you know it.

What you *may* find helpful are some focal points to help you concentrate your attention on the important aspects of meetings which you can do something about. Here are ten such focal points.

1. Plan to solve a problem, not to hold a meeting.
2. Use the meeting as your tool.
3. Pick each member as a resource.
4. See your meeting as others see it
5. Don't tolerate late attendance and interruptions.
6. Share the responsibility for starting out right.
7. Change your leader style to fit the type of meeting.
8. Harness a variety of skills to get sound decisions.
9. Diagnose and treat the "hidden agendas".
10. Build a bridge from the meeting to the goal.

Each of these particular points falls roughly within the framework of a conceptual model of the meeting, as shown in Figure 1. The meeting is viewed not as an activity or an event in itself but merely as a tool—a communication tool for getting action results, not at the meeting but somewhere else, later on. As you direct your attention to these ten focal points, try to relate them to this model of the meeting, as a tool for more effective communication.

Why is it that a top executive will carefully plan his own expenditure of time but will think nothing of calling in six very busy key executives, spending hardly a moment to plan how to use their valuable time?

In one company the top six managers, who said they spent one-half of their time in conferences, had average salaries of $15,000 (£5,300). They discovered their meeting time was costing them $45,000 (£16,000) per year in salaries alone!

A problem-solving approach which views planning as a mental process is what is needed. This is the way you plan financial moves or decide market strategy. Why not think this way when you consider calling a meeting?

What is the problem I'm trying to deal with?

What are the real facts of the case?

How could I go about solving it?

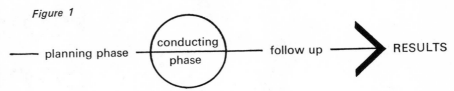

Figure 1

planning phase — conducting phase — follow up — RESULTS

Money savers—Too often we may *think* we're planning when we busy ourselves with finding a good meeting place, checking on time and availability of members and setting the date. This should come later. This is **scheduling**—the job of the secretary or the assistant. The important few minutes that you spend asking yourself hard questions, not about the **meeting** but about the **problem**, can be real money savers for you.

There are good reasons and bad reasons for calling a meeting, and a president needs to know the differences. Whether you are swamped with

John D. Foskett believes he is well qualified to write on the subject of corporate management meetings because he is a person who, as he puts it, "has attended too many meetings."

This tongue-in-cheek statement belies the true qualifications of this dynamic young executive who is president of American Screen Products Co.

Mr. Foskett gives more detailed coverage of the information contained in this article in "Conducting Management Meetings", his contribution to the "Top Management Handbook" published by the McGraw-Hill Book Co.

Readers may obtain additional information about this book from International Management Book Editor John Wasley.

meetings or hold very few of them, take another look at the pros and cons for calling them. The basis for either your use or your neglect of meetings may be worth questioning.

A meeting is only one of a number of communication tools. In many situations, other tools are often just as good or better. For instance:

1. **When you've got to act fast.** Obviously there are many occasions when phone calls are excellent substitutes for a meeting. Many executives find the investment in improved tele-

phone and interoffice communication facilities worthwhile for making the phone system more effective. (Conference phones are a useful combination of these two ways of communicating).

2. **When you've got a wide audience to reach.** Memos and letters will reach a wider audience. It often helps to supplement the communication by meeting with the crucial people who can also help to spread the word, again combining the methods.

3. **When reactions are needed, or wanted.** Sometimes you send out a directive which can hardly be misunderstood and which you don't care to have questioned. Why hold a meeting which would only raise questions that you don't intend to answer?

4. **When the problem is between an individual and yourself.** In the friendliest of staff meetings there are personal concerns with a subordinate which should not be shared with the others. Better to handle these with the individual alone. (Keep in mind that you, the superior, may not be as sensitive to this need for protecting the individual as your subordinate is.)

A meeting may also be used as an escape or excuse. Maybe all of us should ask ourselves these slightly self-searching questions from time to time.

Is a meeting really necessary to accomplish this task?

Could I get this job done at some other meeting, later on?

Am I calling this meeting to get some listeners and increase my own sense of importance?

Am I calling this meeting to get other people to do my homework?

Am I calling this meeting to get others to share responsibility for decisions which I should make?

A well organised meeting is, potentially, the best communication tool you have, and the proper use of this tool may be of great importance to your organization.

Here are some reasons which strongly favour calling a meeting.

1. When you must be sure your message will be understood.
2. When you want to get subordi-

Figure 2

If this is the type of meeting...		...this style is best suited
1. Information giving --	Such as: addressing a civic group, making year-end report to employees, explaining a directive to the staff.	Autocratic -- Because it's from you to them with little need for reactions from them or further explanation.
2. Information collecting --	Such as: interviewing new employees, hearing union committee opinions, getting staff member reports.	Shared (a better word for "democratic") -- Because lots of participation is important to get the facts out. Members stimulate each other.
3. Decision-making --	Such as: establishing new pricing policy, planning a cost reduction program, setting up the work schedule.	Shared -- Because almost every member can perform useful functions and members need to become committed to follow-up action.
4. Decision-selling --	Such as: getting staff members to accept new organization set-up passed down by the Board (not open to questions): getting subordinates to go along with your decision on capital equipment policy.	Autocratic -- As far as any questioning of the decision (which has already been made) but shared as far as carrying out the decision - because intelligent, individual commitments to action are needed.
5. Problem-solving --	Such as: figuring out how to handle a difficult customer, helping each other on best ways to hold talks with subordinates	Shared -- Because it calls for flexibility and the use of all resources available.

nates' reactions and stimulate two-way communication.

3. When you need more facts, expert opinions, and the like.
4. When you need creative new ideas, approaches and solutions.
5. When you must depend on others to carry out decisions.
6. When you want to build better teamwork.

Always try to see your meeting as others see it. When your members are with you and really going along with what you're trying to do in a meeting, the job is easy. But you can't assume this will happen automatically.

Too often the members have other purposes for attending your meeting and have other things in mind that they hope to get out of the meeting. These other goals may work at cross-purposes to yours unless you do something about them both before and at the meeting.

Plan ahead—You can take several actions beforehand which will help members to see the meeting better in terms of your planned agenda. Such actions will help them to have some of their needs met, too, so they will then be able to work for what you want.

1. Send them word of the problem to be discussed beforehand and tell them to do some thinking about it, even specify what kind of thinking you want. Here are some examples:

    What holes do you see in this plan?

    How can we put this plan into effect?

    What other approaches does this plan suggest?

    What difficulties can we expect to run into later on?

2. Distribute a tentative agenda and ask for comments or additions to it. Be sure you acknowledge their contributions at the meeting.

3. Brief them on the meeting's purpose and ask them to take some specific action beforehand, such as (for example):

    (a) Prepare statistics.

    (b) Interview several employees to get reactions to a proposal.

    (c) Prepare a plan, and the like.

You should *not* assume that announcing the agenda of the meeting beforehand will have eliminated conflicting interests at the meeting.

You must deal with them again at the start of the meeting, if you want to have the members with you. One way of handling this problem, especially in regular staff meetings, is through the use of "agenda budgeting" This method is simple enough, if you'll use it, and has the advantage of:

(1) getting people involved in the meeting right at the start, (2) getting their agenda items shared by the group. and (3) getting the members to share responsibility for the outcome of the meeting.

Here are the steps to take:

1. Use chart pad or blackboard to list agenda items you have selected for the meeting.

2. Ask members for additional items they would like to have covered.

3. Work with the group to give priorities to each item, labelling them as:

    Urgent.
    Important—today.
    Important—this week.
    Individual attention.

4. Work with group to budget time to be spent in each item.

5. From time to time during the meeting review and revise time budgets.

You may find that the joint agenda setting may take six or seven minutes. But this time spent in getting squared away, even for an hour meeting, is worthwhile expenditure in getting them with you.

Find a balance—Executives in many organizations view their president's behaviour in meetings as being either autocratic or democratic, usually the former. But if you are seen consistently as either one or the other, you are probably limiting your effectiveness. You should be both.

It all depends on the kind of meeting and its requirements. All meetings fall generally into five major categories, and for each category you'll find that one style of chairmanship is usually best. The five general categories of meetings are given in Figure 2, graphically as well as verbally, along

In Meetings, Watch Out for These Types

Tough guy — Likes to argue and make others angry. Don't lose your temper with him, ever.

Fuzzy thinker — He gets lost in irrelevant issues. Try to keep him on the right track to save time.

Antagonists — Clashing personalities can destroy a meeting. Your job is to keep them well apart.

Silent type—He's bored or indifferent. Ask him a question to get his interest. Careful if he's shy.

with the leadership style best suited for each category.

General guides to meeting chairmanship are given in the illustration, but let us take a closer look at things you can do, as chairman, during the meeting.

For most meetings where decisions must be made, it is recommended that you use the "shared" style. Why? Not just because this is the "good way", but because in the long run it's the most efficient. Let's look a little closer at the meeting to see why.

What makes a meeting tick? What are the things that must be done, the functions that must be performed if a meeting group is to reach its goal of making a decision or completing an agenda?

The meeting has got started.

Ideas must be proposed.

Facts must be presented and tested.

Solutions must be suggested.

These can be called getting-the-job-done action. Each of these is a function which must be performed if the job is to get done. But who performs them? Generally speaking, any member of the meeting, at times, may be able to perform one or two or maybe more of the functions.

Good teamwork—A meeting is a group of individuals interacting with each other in some pretty complex ways to try to get a job done. And so it is vital that they stick together as a group and develop teamwork en route to the goal.

What's more, most meetings don't reach the ultimate goal at the meeting. but through individual members' actions later on, back on the job. If a member is not really on the team during a meeting, he is less likely to do his share in carrying out the decision afterward. So another series of functions is required to hold the group together. Some of these may be less obvious:

Helping the quieter members to participate.

Complimenting the entire group on its progress.

Relieving tension with a joke or pleasant story.

Mediating in an argument.

These group-building functions, unfortunately, are less often performed than the getting-the-job-done type. They are usually performed by thoughtful members without sanction from others.

Often we feel a little bit irritated and frustrated that we have to spend time on people that is not related to the task. Yet these group-building functions are vital to the meeting in progress and to the results afterward and may be important with respect to future good relations between the members of the group.

Shared chairmanship — Shared chairmanship is when the chairman gets most of the job and group-building functions performed by members and takes the responsibility to guide the group. You can see the advantages of this style for most complex meetings; it gets more people working on the problem.

Under *autocratic* chairmanship, the chairman performs most of the functions. If the major function is simply information giving, there's no difficulty. But if this is a decision-making meeting, the autocratic chairman will have to be the starter, opinion-seeker, opinion giver, collaborator, co-ordinator, tester, summarizer, encourager, consensus taker, nose counter, standard setter, mediator, decision maker, evaluator and Lord High Everything!

Obviously a chairman such as this will have little time to think ahead and guide the group. The members, not being encouraged to help out, will look to him for the performance of all these functions and may sit on their hands.

In summary, don't assume you'll hold a meeting before first analysing the problem you face. Then you should consider the meeting as just one of several possible communication tools available to you. It is a useful tool for many purposes, especially as an organization builder. But be sure you are using it for the right purposes.

Under the *shared* style, the chairman delegates leadership to other members of the meeting, but he can never abdicate responsibility for seeing to it that the job is done. In that case he would be using laissez-faire chairmanship, a third style, but one not to be recommended for presidents!

Many kinds of people and resources should be considered in the planning of a meeting, for often we forget the resources our organization has to offer. But for members to be of maximum usefulness they need to feel involved.

Set standards—You should always plan in terms of their goals for the meeting; then they'll be able to accept your goals, too. The mechanics of planning (prior notice, prompt attendance, etc.) set standards for starting out right, but it's equally important to create a relaxed, informal atmosphere at the start.

The style of chairmanship should be used which best fits each type of meeting. Shared leadership which gets the functions spread about among all the members is generally most effective for important decision making meetings.

Executive groups can make better decisions by flexible use of the decision-making process, all the members performing functions as needed. But besides working on the surface agenda, the group must become more aware of and must deal with the hidden agendas, if there is to be good working communication among all the members of the group.

Assure follow-up—Finally, planning in terms of goals, selective recording and end-of-meeting rechecks can all help assure follow-up on the meeting.

While all these points can be helpful to you, they should not be expected to produce results in your meetings without a good deal of practice. They require, also, the development of skills—not only of your skills but of the skills of all the members of your meetings, encouraged by you. ■

Too Many Solutions

If a problem can be
solved more than
one way, how do you pick
the best alternative?
Linear programming may help.

G. F. HADLEY
School of Industrial Management
Massachusetts Institute of Technology

Most problems presented to engineering management ordinarily have too many—not too few—possible solutions, and making a single choice among the many alternatives may be even more ulcer-provoking than having no answers at all.

Mathematicians are developing a method that will help choose the most profitable or least costly alternative out of a large (perhaps infinitely large) group. The method is called linear programming.

The word *linear* places an important restriction on applicability of the method. All relationships between variables must be directly proportional. If the amount of a resource is doubled, so is its cost. Relationships cannot, for example, depend on the square of a variable. Some attempts have been made to study nonlinear programming, with little success.

To aid in visualization, here are three general areas into which many solvable problems fall.

Mixing problems involve a number of components, combined to form one or more products. The "mixing" may or may not involve a physical combination of components, but the final product will be a linear mixture of its component parts.

Gasoline blending is a good example. A number of raw stocks are to be blended to yield several grades of gasoline. The quantity of each raw stock available per day is known. In what quantities shall they be mixed (to meet the three or more gasoline specifications) to maximize profits? A further restriction might include the proportion of premium gasoline to regular.

Transportation problems call for the cheapest way to move a product from a number of origins to a number of destinations. Shipping cost between any two points is known. You also know the stock at each origin and the number desired at each destination.

Allocation problems attempt to determine optimum product mix and machine assignments for a given plant. How much of each product should be made and on what machines? Note that sequence or order of performed operations are not considered.

Blanket manufacture, for example, requires that each go through a number of machines, but several different machine combinations can be used. Each machine operates a limited time every day and sales restrictions determine maximum and minimum quantities of blanket types.

Personnel assignment is also a form of allocation problem. A number of men are available with given abilities (job categories). A number of jobs are available. Productivity of the men in each job is known. What assignment has best productivity.

GENERALIZATION AND GRAPHICAL INTERPRETATION

The general linear programming problem has n variables X_j which are non-negative

$$X_j \geqq 0$$

and m constraints ($m < n$, in general) of the form

$$a_{i1}X_1 + a_{i2}X_2 + \cdots + a_{in}X_n \geqq b_i$$

with any one of the relationships (equal to, greater than, or less than) possible.

It is desired to maximize or minimize a function of the form

$$\sum_i c_i X_i = c_1 X_1 + c_2 X_2 + \cdots + c_n X_n$$

These equations have a geometrical interpretation. A simple two-dimensional (two variables) problem might be defined by

$$X_1 \geqq 0, \qquad X_2 \geqq 0$$

with the constraints

$$3X_1 + 5X_2 \leqq 15 \tag{1}$$
$$5X_1 + 2X_2 \leqq 10 \tag{2}$$

Now maximize

$$b = 4X_1 + 3X_2 \tag{3}$$

Eq (1) and (2) are plotted in Fig. 1 and, because X_1 and X_2 must be positive, the inequalities limit the variables to areas between the straight line and axes. The combined area (in black) satisfies both inequalities and it therefore represents a feasible solution.

For any given value of b in Eq (3) a straight line can be constructed for values of X_1 and X_2. Two values of b will set up parallel straight lines, then b is varied with its line moving up and to the right until the largest value of b is obtained whose line still has at least one point in the shaded area (b_3 in Fig. 1). This point represents optimum values of X_1 and X_2.

Solutions to linear programming problems always occur at one corner of the area containing allowable solutions. The area in Fig. 1 has four extreme points. The simpler method for solving these problems is a procedure for moving from extreme point to extreme point until the optimum is reached.

Suppose Eq (3) were altered to read

$$b = 1.5X_1 + 2.5X_2$$

This equation has been plotted in Fig. 2 for some values of b. Note that here a group of values of X_1 and X_2 will all satisfy the requirements although there is a unique value for b.

A minization problem is shown in Fig. 3.

$$X_1 \geqq 0, \qquad X_2 \geqq 0$$
$$5X_1 + X_2 \geqq 5$$
$$X_1 + 6X_2 \geqq 6$$
$$X_1 + 1.2X_2 \leqq 6$$
$$2X_1 + 3X_2 = b$$

The three constraint inequalities limit the area to a triangular shape. The minimum b occurs at point 2.

AIDS TO SOLUTION

It should be evident without considering the mathematical methods in detail that a problem of any size (say, 20 equations and 50 variables) would require a tremendous amount of time to work out by hand. Simpler problems can, of course, be solved by any one of several methods, and there are many published papers describing such methods in detail (see references on the next page).

Codes for high-speed digital computers have been

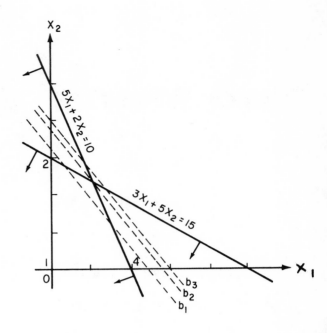

developed for the solution of linear programming problems. At least four programs are available for the IBM 650 and one of them will, in theory, handle up to 98 restrictions. It is possible to have up to 200 restrictions in the IBM 704.

Note that the decision to undertake a linear programming study usually entails fairly heavy expense. Potential savings must be reasonably large to justify such a study.

EXAMPLE I—GASOLINE BLENDING

To help establish the essential character of linear programming here is a symbolical presentation of some problems with an indication of how to solve them.

In gasoline blending, assume three raw stocks (A, B and C barrels available per day for blending into two grades of motor fuel. Let X_{ij} ($\geqq 0$) be the gallons of raw stock j blended to form fuel i.

Each fuel must meet three specifications. For these, let a_j be the lean octane number, b_j the rich octane number and c_j the Reid vapor pressure of raw stock j.

Let α_i be the lean octane number, β_i the rich octane number and γ_i the Reid vapor pressure of fuel i.

Availability restrictions set up three relationships.

$$\begin{aligned} A &\geqq X_{11} + X_{21} \\ B &\geqq X_{12} + X_{22} \\ C &\geqq X_{13} + X_{23} \end{aligned} \tag{4}$$

Equal-or-greater-than signs are introduced because it may not be desirable to blend all of any one raw stock.

Blending specifications for lean octane number establish

$$\alpha_1 \leqq \frac{a_1 X_{11} + a_2 X_{12} + a_3 X_{13}}{X_{11} + X_{12} + X_{13}} \tag{5}$$

Here each ratio $X_{11}/(X_{11} + X_{12} + X_{13})$ represents the ratio of raw stock No. 1 in fuel No. 1. Or rearranged

$$(a_1 - \alpha_1)X_{11} + (a_2 - \alpha_1)X_{12} + (a_3 - \alpha_1)X_{13} \geqq 0$$

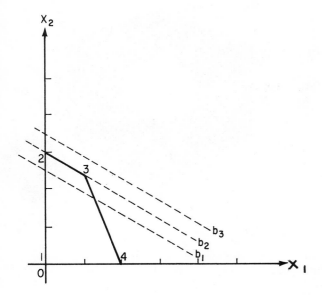

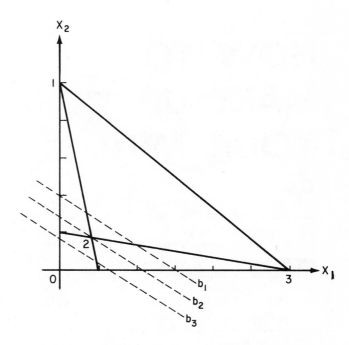

Similarly for rich octane number and Reid vapor pressure

$$(b_1 - \beta_1)X_{11} + (b_2 - \beta_1)X_{12} + (b_3 - \beta_1)X_{13} \geqq 0$$

$$(c_1 - \gamma_1)X_{11} + (c_2 - \gamma_1)X_{12} + (b_3 - \gamma_1)X_{13} \geqq 0$$

Equal-or-greater-than signs allow for going above the minimum specifications if it is profitable to do so.

A set of three inequalities may be based on the three specifications for the ith motor fuel in the general form

$$(a_1 - \alpha_i)X_{i1} + (a_2 - \alpha_i)X_{i2} + (a_3 - \alpha_i)X_{i3} \geqq 0$$

$$(b_1 - \beta_i)X_{i1} + (b_2 - \beta_i)X_{i2} + (b_3 - \beta_i)X_{i3} \geqq 0$$

$$(c_1 - \gamma_i)X_{i1} + (c_2 - \gamma_i)X_{i2} + (c_3 - \gamma_i)X_{i3} \geqq 0$$

Let λ_i be the revenue made on one gallon of motor fuel i and Ψ_j the cost of one gallon of raw stock j. Neglecting mixing costs, the profit to be maximized is

$$\sum_{j,i} (\lambda_i - \psi_j)X_{ij} \qquad (6)$$

to be summed over i and j. Eqs (4) and (5) set the restraints of the problem, and (6) the function to be maximized.

No sales restrictions were included. Suppose the quantity of fuel 1 cannot be greater than fraction f of all motor fuel made. Then

$$X_{11} + X_{12} + X_{13} - f(X_{21} + X_{22} + X_{23}) \leqq 0$$

EXAMPLE II—BLANKET MANUFACTURE

Suppose $X_1 \geqq 0$ is the quantity of blanket material produced on a given combination of machines. Several X_i may refer to the same type of blanket material because a given material may be made on several combinations of machines.

Let a_{ji} be hours required on machine j to process a unit length of material i. Let b_j be total machine hours available (say, per week) in machine j. Machine restrictions thus become

$$a_{11}X_1 + a_{12}X_2 + \cdots + a_{1n}X_n \leqq b_1$$

$$a_{m1}X_1 + a_{m2}X_2 + \cdots + a_{mn}X_n \leqq b_m$$

These equations state that for n variables (materials) and m machine types the sum of machine time spent on each material cannot exceed the hours available on that machine.

Sales restrictions may be included. Let d_k and e_k be maximum and minimum amounts of each blanket material to be produced

$$\Sigma X_i \leqq d_k$$

$$\Sigma X_i \geqq e_k$$

The summation is taken over all X_i referring to the same blanket.

If C_i is the profit per unit length of blanket X_i then it is desirable to maximize.

$$\sum_i C_i X_i = C_1 X_1 + C_2 X_2 + \cdots + C_n X_n$$

EXAMPLE III—TRANSPORT PROBLEM

Suppose there are a_i units of a product available at origin i and at least b_j units of the product are to be shipped to destination j. Let C_{ij} be the cost to ship one unit from origin i to destination j. Let X_{ij} be the number of units shipped from origin i to destination j. The restraints are

$$X_{ij} \geqq 0$$

The total amount shipped to all destinations from origin i cannot exceed a_i

$$\sum_j X_{ij} \leqq a_i$$

The total received from all origins at destination j must be at least b_j

$$\sum_i X_{ij} \geqq b_j$$

Now minimize the total cost

$$\sum_j C_{ij} X_{ij}$$

■

HOW TO MAKE UP YOUR MIND

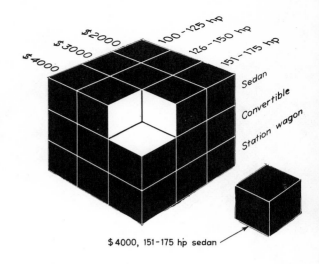

$4000, 151-175 hp sedan

"**T**otal think" is the name given by Dr. Fritz Zwicky, scientific advisor to Hycon Mfg. Co., to what he claims is a universal technique for solving problems. The system bears a strong resemblance to the theory of games of strategy, and is equally applicable to buying a new car (our example), choosing a direction for further research—or deciding on a dinner menu for the boss.

FIRST: Isolate the factors or areas of choice that influence the decision. Three factors might be all-important in buying a car: style, horsepower and price.

Note: In a simple game involving two persons, the factors would be limited to two: your strategy and your opponent's strategy. In a business decision the number of factors may seem endless: production cost, production quantity, selling price, product excellence, advertising influence, market attitude, political climate, etc. Simplification of these factors to a vital minimum is desirable if a definite decision must be made at once. But enumeration of all factors known to be influential may bring out relationships never before imagined.

SECOND: Isolate alternatives within each factor. Body style might be sedan, convertible, or station wagon. Market attitude might be favorable or unfavorable. Alternatives within a factor may be subdivided indefinitely (selling price: $4.50, $4.51, $4.52, etc.) but again it makes sense to reduce the number to a significant few to make the final solution a reasonable goal.

Now list the factors along the left edge of a page and the alternatives within each factor horizontally (See table below).

A table with three factors can also be conceived as a cube with each factor as one dimension and each choice a location along that dimension.

Any box in the cube represents a possible solution. (In illustration above, the removed box is a 151-175-hp sedan costing $4000; the 27 solutions represent all possible combinations of alternatives.)

Very often all combinations will not be possible—horsepower may be dependent on price and a $4000, 100-hp car not available. Elimination of some, or even most, of the combinations reduces total number of choices—but all that remain are practical solutions.

The arbitrary combination of all possible areas of choice may set up alternatives of decision never before considered practical.

THIRD: This step tells you which alternative is the optimum—if the problem is simple enough. If all factors are under your control, each combination of alternatives may be given an arbitrary value or estimate of desirability. The highest value combination is the logical choice if only one solution is permitted. But several interesting possibilities may be followed by different research staffs, for example, or you might simultaneously invest time or money in more than one business.

A variation on this method is based on game theory which, for all practical purposes, limits the number of factors (dimensions) to two and insists that while you have control of one, an opponent (Nature if need be) controls the second factor.

For Example: A research director must choose between two lines of work (see below). As far as he can tell they have equal chance of success. One is expensive but has great market potential, the second is cheap with poorer potential. The most conservative approach (always preferred by game theory) is to choose the solution that guarantees least loss—in this case the low research investment is called for.

These problems have been simplified so that solutions appear almost at a glance. Solutions are possible by rigorous mathematical analysis for far more complex situations though they may call for computer aid in the rather repetitious calculations required.

But whatever the problem, and independent of any optimum solutions that may exist, it will always be helped by enforced clarification of issues inherent in game theory and "Total Think." ■

Factors						Success	Failure
Body Style	Sedan	Convertible	Station Wagon				
Horsepower	100-125 hp	126-150 hp	151-175 hp				
Price	$2000	$3000	$4000	Research Budget — High		+$100,000	−$10,000
				Research Budget — Low		+$20,000	−$1,000

Each chain is a problem solution.

6.

How to Estimate Engineering and Product Costs

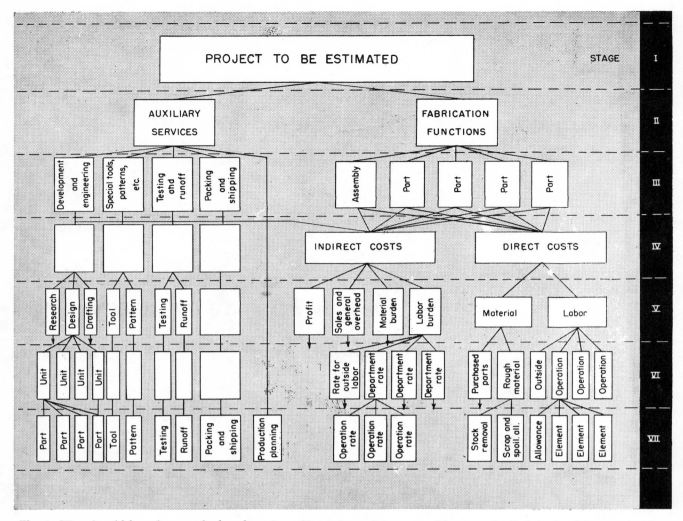

Fig. 1—Ways in which projects are broken down into elements to estimate costs. The more detailed the breakdown, generally, the more accurate is the estimate. Dotted horizontal lines indicate progressive stages th at usually are followed.

How to Estimate Costs

LAWRENCE E. DOYLE
Associate Professor of Mechanical Engineering
University of Illinois

A COST ESTIMATE IS AN ATTEMPT to forecast the expenses that must be incurred to make a product. It may be undertaken to:

1. Establish the selling price of a product for a quotation or contract.

2. Ascertain whether a proposed product can be manufactured and marketed profitably.

3. Find whether parts or assemblies can be more cheaply fabricated or purchased from a vendor.

4. Determine the most economical method, process or material for manufacturing a product.

5. Determine how much must be invested in tools and equipment to manufacture a product.

6. Study the economy of making revisions in existing production facilities and practices, and to initiate means of cost reduction.

7. Provide a standard of production performance and a control of actual operating costs at the start of a project.

The quickest way to estimate the cost of a project is to compare it as a whole with a similar project. An overall comparison is inaccurate in most cases for a number of reasons. The reference project may not be sufficiently identical to the one being estimated. It may have been made in larger or smaller quantities with different tools and methods from those justified at present, and overhead and material prices may change. However, estimating on an overall basis is satisfactory in some cases where the old and the new projects are practically identical. The estimate sheet shown in Fig. 2 has spaces in its lower left-hand corner for entering the identification and actual cost of a similar job for an overall estimate.

The accuracy of an estimate increases as a project is broken down into more and more elements. The amount of breakdown varies with different circumstances, Fig. 1. The fabrication cost of each part of a mechanical device is logically estimated by itself

TOOL NO. PX25691
PART NO. 7F6048

ESTIMATE SHEET

— DATE — 11/17

DET. NO.	NO. REQ'D	MACH. HRS.	MAT'L. & H.T. COST	DET. NO.	NO. REQ'D	MACH. HRS.	MAT'L. & H.T. COST	DET. NO.	NO. REQ'D	MACH. HRS.	MAT'L. & H.T. COST	DET. NO.	NO. REQ'D	MACH. HRS.	MAT'L. & H.T. COST
1	1	40	5.60	26				51				76			
2	2	15	3.10	27				52				77			
3	1	7	.95	28				53							
4	1	3	1.15	29				54							
5	3	6	.60	30				55							
6	5	11	2.30	31											
7	1	8	.75	32											
8	2	17	1.55	33											
9	1	4	.80	34											
10	1	9	2.70	35											
11	1	*	—	36											
12	6	*	—	37											
13	4	*	—	38											
14	7	*	—	39											
15				40											
16		120	19.50	41											
17				42											
18				43											
19				44				93							
20				45				94							
21				46				95							
22				47				96							
23				48			72	97							
24				49			73	98							
25				50			74	99							
							75	100							

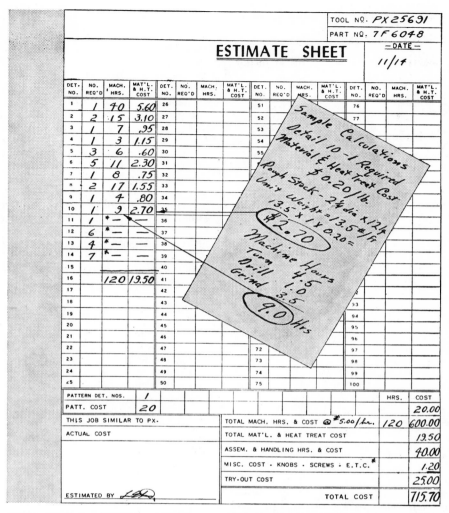

Handwritten sample calculation: Sample Calculations — Detail 10-1 Required — Material & Heat Treat Cost $0.20/lb. — Rough Stock - 2¾ dia x12¼ — Unit Weight = 13.5 x 12¼ — 13.5 x 1 x 0.20 = **$2.70** — Machine Hours: Turn, Drill 4.5, Grind 1.0, 3.5 — **9.0 Hrs**

		HRS.	COST
PATTERN DET. NOS.	1		
PATT. COST	20		20.00
THIS JOB SIMILAR TO PX-			
ACTUAL COST			
TOTAL MACH. HRS. & COST @ $5.00/hr.		120	600.00
TOTAL MAT'L. & HEAT TREAT COST			19.50
ASSEM. & HANDLING HRS. & COST			40.00
MISC. COST · KNOBS · SCREWS · E.T.C.*			1.20
TRY-OUT COST			25.00
ESTIMATED BY		TOTAL COST	715.70

Fig. 2—Typical cost estimate sheet for a tool, including charges for materials, labor, assembly, and tryout, but not for auxiliary services. Sample shows method for one item.

# of New Products

as indicated in Step III. Assembly of the parts is also a distinct fabrication function. At this or later stages, certain auxiliary services may be given individual attention.

The cost of a part is commonly based upon material, labor, and overhead as indicated in Step V. As the breakdown of direct costs becomes more detailed, indirect costs are correspondingly segregated. Where the labor for each part is found by estimating the time for each operation, as in Stage VI, or the elements of operations, as in Stage VII, overhead may also be allocated more precisely.

Each stage of Fig. 1 represents a general form of estimating procedure. However, many variations can be

found. For instance, direct labor and material may be estimated in accordance with Stage VI, indirect costs at Stage V, and auxiliary services at various stages as convenient. The procedure in almost every plant shows some difference. As a general rule, tool estimating is done at Stages I through VI, and product estimating at Stages V through VII.

Specific Cost Estimating Examples

The estimate form of Fig. 3 indicates the detail that may exist in estimating the costs of auxiliary services of a sizeable production project. Behind the figures that appear on the form is a still more detailed breakdown. For a preliminary estimate,

common practice is to analyze the part prints of the product to determine the quantities and kinds of patterns, tools, fixtures, jigs and dies needed. An overall estimate or a partial breakdown may be made of the cost of each tool. Various departments in the organization such as research, engineering and tool design, are required to submit estimates of the material, labor, and equipment each will have to furnish to complete the project.

A detailed cost estimate for a part of a large size production project is shown in Fig 4. The operations to make the part are itemized. Setup and cycle times for each operation entered in the first two columns on the left are obtained by adding standard elemental times. Setup and cycle times are multiplied by the labor and overhead rate for each operation, and the cost for each is entered just below the standard time. The unit setup and cycle costs are added to obtain the standard cost including labor and overhead. For operation 1, the standard setup time is 0.19 hr and the cycle time is 0.92 hr. The setup cost is $0.44 and the cycle cost is $2.11. The latter added to a unit setup cost of $0.04 gives a standard labor and overhead cost of $2.15. The product of the standard cost and a performance factor of 1.05 is the estimated labor and overhead cost of $2.26. Each type of operation in the process is assigned its own labor and overhead rate and performance ratio.

The weight, unit price, and a ratio enter into the calculation of material cost in each case.

A procedure for compiling the parts and assembly costs into a total figure for a major unit of a product, also for the headstock of a machine tool, is shown in Fig 5. The material, labor and overhead costs for parts and assembly operations are accumulated into sub-assembly groups in the manner illustrated in (B). The costs of the sub-assemblies are collected on the unit assembly sheet and added to the costs of the unit assembly operations as shown in (C). Figures for administration and selling costs and engineering and tool costs are added to the manufacturing costs to obtain the total cost for the major unit.

A cost estimate for a redesigned product that has been in existence requires a less complete treatment than for a new product. The parts of the redesigned product are compared with those of the old and classified as revised, added, and unchanged parts. The costs of the unchanged parts are found from production records. Detailed estimate sheets need to be prepared only for changed parts or added

Cost figures require multiplication by a correction factor for current use.

ESTIMATE OF DEVELOPMENT COST

				LABEL column			

PROJECT — Design and develop new high speed lathe to operate at range of 1,000 to 2,000 surface feet per minute to sell for $5,000..

NUMBER 207
DATE 11/15 — PREPARED S.A.R.
DATE 11/30 — APPROVED R.S.P.

DIVISION	SUB-NUMBER	DESCRIPTION	MATERIAL COST	LABOR AND OVERHEAD		OTHER COST	TOTAL COST
				Hours	Cost		
Research	100	High speed bearings at various loads	3,000	12,750	60,000	12,000	75,000
Design	200	Headstock	50	1,520	6,950	3,000	10,000
	210	Gearing	100	3,060	9,900	2,000	12,000
	220	Base	75	4,120	11,925	2,000	14,000
	230	Etc., etc.	250	15,075	55,750	8,000	64,000
Production	301	Headstock - Patterns	125	650	2,175	200	2,500
	302	- Tools, Jigs, Fixtures	750	1,945	6,250	500	7,500
	303	- Experimental Parts	1,250	500	1,550	200	3,000
	311	Gearing - Patterns	225	905	2,975	300	3,500
	312	- Tools, Jigs, Fixtures	1,245	1,420	4,855	400	6,500
	313	- Experimental Parts	975	520	1,925	100	3,000
	321	Etc., etc. - Patterns	4,575	24,200	84,825	3,000	92,400
	322	- Tools, Jigs, Fixtures	12,515	47,400	172,285	6,000	190,800
	323	- Experimental Parts	18,520	8,650	45,780	1,500	65,800
Testing	900		1,200	5,450	18,800	5,000	25,000

	MATERIAL	Hours	Cost	OTHER	TOTAL
Grand total estimated cost.............	44,855	134,165	485,945	44,200	575,000
Total quantity of machines.............	......	......	......	......	5,000
Estimated cost per machine.............	9	......	97	9	115

Fig. 3—Estimates of development, design, special tool, and tryout costs for a new product—in this case, a high speed lathe. This represents a summary of estimates.

assemblies. Costs for engineering, administration, selling, and new tools and the expected profit are added to the manufacturing cost to get the total selling price.

Estimating forms like those shown provide an excellent means of summarizing estimates, and are a necessary tool when an appreciable number of estimates are to be made. They provide a concise and uniform means for presenting the results of an estimate to others, for preserving information for future reference, and for systemizing the work of the estimator. In addition, the spaces for individual items provide a series of goals in compiling data for an estimate and a check list for completeness of results.

Estimating Direct Labor Costs

The total direct labor required for a job may be estimated by comparison with one or more similar jobs. For more detail, the work is divided into operations. That is the same as prescribing the method for the job, and must be done competently if the estim-

ate is to be verified by actual performance. If the estimator lists the operations, and many do, he must be well acquainted with the processes and methods involved.

Only a person with considerable background in the shop is competent to judge operations times with reasonable accuracy. Others need to refer to recorded experience. An estimator may go to the records in the cost accounting department to find the time for specific operations that have been performed. These are entries of time card readings that have been received from the shop.

To look for references for operations is arduous. Estimating can be made easier by compiling and using tables and charts that show at a glance the times required for common operations.

In many plants production procedures are standardized, and the estimator is in a position to divide operations into standard elements and ascertain their values from time study data. Operation time is commonly divided into setup time and cycle

time. The latter in turn may be divided into man or handling time and machine time. These divisions are estimated from their elements. Estimating can be systematized and simplified by means of tables, Fig. 6 of operation elements.

No overall or synthesized estimates of an operation can predict actual performance with certainty. Time may be lost from breakdowns, parts that do not fit as expected, tools that do not cut properly, defective material, and other faults. The best that can be done is to multiply all operation estimates by a performance factor to compensate for losses over a period of time. A performance factor may be derived by dividing the sum of actual times for a large number of jobs by the sum of the estimated times for the same jobs. This factor should be checked from time to time.

A performance factor often includes a correction factor for errors in estimation. An estimator may include a margin to allow for items he may have overlooked in doing rough estimating. One estimator found that when working from prints not to full scale, he had a tendency to underestimate the work required. He compensated for that by adding 25 percent to labor if prints were half-size, and 33 percent if prints were quarter-size.

Estimating Material Cost

The cost of material is based upon the size of the rough stock used per piece. If a piece is machined, the amount of stock removed is added to the finished dimensions. The volume is computed from the dimensions. If the piece is irregular, it is divided into components of simple geometric shapes. The volumes of the components are computed separately and added together. The volume is multiplied by the density of the material to obtain the weight, which is then easily converted into cost.

Materials in certain shops may be estimated in other ways. The length of bar stock, equal to the length of a piece plus facing and cutoff of stock, is multiplied by the weight of price per inch of the diameter of stock as given in tables. The dimensions of a blank may be developed from the dimensions of a formed piece. The area, including scrap per piece and gage size for a stamping is found from part dimensions, if the sheet steel used is purchased at a sheet price.

Some material normally lost in processing in scrapped pieces, butt ends, droppings, etc., must be accounted for in an estimate. Losses vary from 1 to 12 percent, depending upon the process, material and practice. An

PATTERN NUMBER	PART NAME			PART NUMBER	STANDARD COST				ESTIMATE		
P 19252	Headstock			19252	10, 1				11/1		
ORDER QUANTITY	MATERIAL SYMBOL	SIZE	LENGTH	TOTAL WEIGHT OR LENGTH	UNIT PRICE	MATERIAL	LABOR & OVERHEAD	ACCUMULATED COST	RATIO	MATERIAL TOTAL	LABOR & OVERHEAD
10	C.I.			278.	.085	23 63		23 63	110	25 99	
ROUTING 9/5 HM											
COST 9/20 DB											
ESTIMATE 9/											
					TOTAL	23 63				25 99	

SET-UP	CYCLE	DEPARTMENT WORK CENTER MACHINE TOOL	OPER. NO	DESCRIPTION OF OPERATION (Assembly Quantity and Part Number)	RATE	MATERIAL	LABOR & OVERHEAD	ACCUMULATED COST	RATIO	MATERIAL TOTAL	LABOR & OVERHEAD
19	92	183-01	1 05	Seal inside white, prime outside and bottom, putty, patch, fill outside two coats	30		2 15	25 78	105		2 26
44	2 11										
13	96	183-02	2 10	Sand fill surfaces, finish paint one seal coat outside bottom and top.	30		2 23	28 01	105		2 34
30	2 20										
43	45	111-04	3 15	Mill top	3 20		1 58	29 59	106		1 68
1 37	1 44										
78	48	111-04	4 20	Mill vee and flat	3 20		1 78	31 37	106		1 89
2 49	1 53	142	X								
26	28	140-05	5 25	Drill 7 holes and tap 5 holes S'Face 2 in bottom	3 00		92	32 29	101		93
78	84	207									
82	1 07	111-07	6 30	Mill 4 Sides	3 20		3 69	35 98	106		3 91
2 62	3 43	171	X								
06	40	180-01	7 35	Scrape	2 80		1 14	37 12	107		1 22
17	1 12										
19	1 27	141-03	8 40	Line bore pulley shaft, long and short int. shaft, rev. shaft and grind spindle holes.	4 00		5 15	42 27	101		5 20
76	5 08		X								
1 07	1 88	140-05	9 45	Drill 15, cham & tap 12, C'bore 7, ream 2 S'face 1 in top, front and back, drill, cham, tap 24 holes both sides.	3 00		5 96	48 23	101		6 02
3 21	5 64	210	X								
32	38	111-07	10 50	Mill pad	3 20		1 32	49 55	106		1 40
1 04	1 21		X								
29	14	111-09	11 55	Mill keyway	3 20		54	50 09	106		57
93	45		12 X								
			13								
14 11	25 05										

X See Tool Lists

	MATERIAL	LABOR & OVERHEAD			MATERIAL TOTAL	LABOR & OVERHEAD
TOTAL ABOVE	23 63	26 46			25 99	27 42
TOTAL MANUFACTURING						
ADMINISTRATION & SELLING						
ENGINEERING, TOOLS						
GRAND TOTAL						

COST AND ESTIMATE SHEET

(Cost figures require multiplication by a correction factor for current use.)

Fig. 4—Detailed breakdown of fabrication costs for the headstock of the lathe estimated in the previous summary. The required manufacturing operations are itemized.

average allowance of 5 percent is often added to material estimates to distribute the bulk losses over the pieces produced. Sometimes an amount to take care of bulk losses is included in unit cost or overhead rate factors.

The weight of a piece is multiplied by the unit cost of the material to find the cost of the piece. The unit cost may include a pro-rated amount for bulk losses, purchasing, and handling in addition to the market price of the material. In making estimates like those in Fig. 2, the estimator is guided by a list of unit costs that includes all relevant charges. The rates for materials that require heat treatment included a pro-rated charge per pound for heat treating. Another procedure is to multiply the weight of the material by its market price. That product is then multiplied by a factor to cover other costs.

A scale of unit costs decreasing with quantity is realistic for materials purchased as needed. In a typical case, the price of grey iron castings for tools is quoted at $0.25 per lb for pieces weighing from 1 to 25 lb, but is less for larger castings. For those weighing over 1,000 lb, the price is $0.16 per pound.

Unit costs need to be checked at intervals and changed if necessary. The intervals have been found to vary from 2 months to a year in various plants, with an average of about 6 months.

Estimating the Costs of Auxiliary Services

Just what auxiliary services are estimated individually for a specific job varies with circumstances. Engineering, testing, and run-off are commonly given individual attention. Production planning usually does not appear as a distinct item in an estimate except where a product is to be made in large quantities and not always then. Such services as are not estimated separately are included as overhead.

Services that involve creative work or the solution of unforeseeable problems are not amenable to standardization. Engineering design is one of

them. The amount of time required to design a mechanical device may be estimated on the basis of what has been found necessary for a similar job or on the basis of the judgment of the designer as to how much time he will need. Whenever a sizeable amount is at stake, it is always well for an estimator to seek an estimate of the time required from those who will have to meet the estimate in performance.

The time estimated for a service, such as engineering, is multiplied by an hourly rate to obtain the cost of the service. If several grades of designers, draftsmen, or other workers are employed on a job, the rate may be different for the time expended by each group. The hourly rate includes charges for supervision, housing, light, heat, and other expenses. Much design, research, development and experimental work is done that cannot be applied to specific salable jobs. Engineering may be done to develop proposals that do not materialize in orders. Such costs may be included in the engineering rate or charged to factory overhead. In some places general administration and selling costs and profits are included in the engineering rate. In other cases, these items are accounted for by an additional rate.

When packing and shipping are not included in general overhead, they may be accounted for in various ways. For estimates like Fig. 2, practice is to allow 10 percent of the material cost on the job with a minimum of $10. In other cases, shipping and packing costs may be pro-rated on the basis of total project cost.

Estimating Indirect Costs

Common practice in tool estimating is to apply a single rate to all time estimated for the tool room or job shop. Part of this rate is for direct labor. The remainder covers overhead. Periodically the cost department adds together all the charges against the tool room for supervision, light, heat, power, building, equipment, interest, taxes, insurance, maintenance, and many others. This sum is divided by the total hours of direct labor expended in the tool room during the same period. The quotient is the overhead rate. The direct labor and overhead rate together comprise the rate the estimator uses to estimate the costs of making tools.

Standard purchased parts and material are not generally required to carry factory and general overhead, although practice in this respect is not uniform. From a competitive

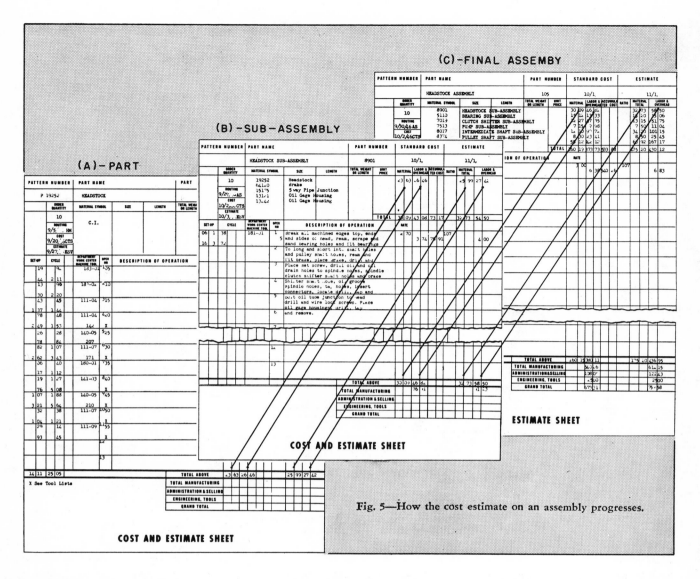

(C)—FINAL ASSEMBLY

(B)—SUB-ASSEMBLY

(A)—PART

COST AND ESTIMATE SHEET

COST AND ESTIMATE SHEET

ESTIMATE SHEET

Fig. 5—How the cost estimate on an assembly progresses.

standpoint, a manufacturer is not justified in adding a large markup to merchandise that can be purchased on about the same terms in the market by his customers. That the standard parts and material be charged with out-of-pocket expenses for shipping, purchasing, and handling is normally considered reasonable.

Overhead cannot be distributed equitably if one article is processed with little or no equipment but is burdened by the same labor overhead rate as another that requires expensive equipment. Different rates may be applied to work done in different departments or even on different kinds of machines to refine the distribution of overhead. That requires that the direct costs estimated for each department or for each operation be kept separated. Overhead is distributed mostly but not always on a labor cost or hour basis for estimating purposes.

The detailed form of product estimating depicted by Fig. 4 utilizes different rates for different kinds of operations. These rates are determined by the cost department which accumulates the cost of similar operations in work centers. Several work centers may be contained in one department under one supervisor. Benefits like space, power, and water are charged to each center in proportion to amounts consumed. The costs of services such as planning, methods, and inspection are divided among the work centers in proportion to the amount each center is judged to benefit. Depreciation, interest, insurance, and taxes are charged on the equipment in each center. Other expenses, such as for supervision, and personnel services, are charged in proportion to direct hours of labor. Direct labor is accumulated on the basis of wages paid plus fringe benefits. All the charges against a work center are added together for a period and divided by the number of direct hours worked in the center for the same period. The figure thus obtained is the rate charged against each productive hour estimated for work to be done in a given center.

For the product estimating procedure illustrated in Fig. 5, administration and selling costs are charged in proportion to the number of dollars of standard manufacturing cost of major assemblies of a product.

Estimating Costs for the Future

Present costs and quotations must serve as a start in preparing estimates for the future, but they may have to be modified by a forecast of conditions at the time of manufacture. An estimator must be in touch with economic trends, or seek advice from someone who is, to make a decision as to whether prices may rise or fall or whether the market will be more or less favorable.

Not only future prices, but anticipated volume and facilities must be studied. At a lower volume than expected, unit fixed and overhead costs tend to increase. A higher output may not only serve to alleviate fixed charges but also permit the utilization of more efficient work methods. Additional lines of products may absorb some of the overhead costs of a plant, or vice versa.

An estimator cannot hope to recognize the cost trends unless he understands the principles behind the cost accounting system that furnishes him with information. With such an understanding, he is in a position to appreciate why overhead rates are going up or down, the relation of overhead to shop activity, labor costs, and the general production picture.

The Chance Factors of Cost Estimating

Every estimator knows that almost all his estimated costs differ from eventual actual costs, Fig. 7. The percent error of each of 157 estimates of labor cost for making tools was calculated. Each bar of the chart represents the number of estimates within a certain range of 10 percentage points of error. The deviations range from 50 low to 450 percent high in this case. If an infinite number of estimates were plotted and the pattern remained about the same, the distribution of errors could be represented by a curve like the one super-imposed on the histogram.

When a project is broken down into elements, the errors of some elements may be large, but probably the errors of most elements are small. Some elements are above, others below actual cost. When the elements are added together, their individual deviations tend to offset each other. Consequently, the likelihood of large errors in the total estimate is small. Thus

projects are broken down into elements because it has been found that their totals generally deviate less from actual costs than do projects estimated on an overall basis.

A project must be divided into elements of approximately equal significance to benefit fully from the compensations of chance. If a large part of a job is estimated without being examined in detail and only minor details are estimated individually, the large part has a preponderant effect upon the accuracy of the whole estimate.

The spread of errors in estimating the costs of elements of a project is normally less than the spread when such projects are estimated on an overall basis. Likewise, the spread of errors in estimating small and simple elements should logically be less than the spread for large and complex elements if the same facilities are available for appraising both.

The breakdown of a project into smaller and smaller elements gives an approach to estimating with certainty, but never assures certainty. Consider a product that is not a commercial item itself but can be constructed from standard commercial details. The present costs of the individual details can be found from catalogs or quotations. Current plant costs can be studied to ascertain how much should be added for purchasing, handling and assembly. A series of such products could be estimated quite accurately in that way, but some of the estimated costs would naturally deviate from actual costs over a period of time. The estimator may make a mistake, market prices may

change, and some probability is always present that any estimate will show a certain amount of deviation from actual cost.

The Costs of Cost Estimating

With competent estimating, the average of the estimated costs of a large number of projects usually is about the same as the average of the true costs of the same projects. Even so, the estimate of each individual project creates some loss to the extent that it differs from actual cost. This is obvious if an estimate is low. High estimates may help to make up for low ones as far as immediate income is concerned, but each high estimate is a potential source of customer dissatisfaction, lost business, or misleading prices. Thus, the losses from excessively high estimates may very well be as costly as those from low estimates.

The greater the spread of deviations in estimated costs from true costs, the larger the real and potential losses from the estimates. The aim of good estimating practice is to make all estimates reflect actual costs as closely as possible.

Estimates can be made more accurate and reliable by breaking the individual projects into more and more elements. However, the larger the number of elements that must be considered, the greater the cost of making the estimates.

A Theory of Cost Estimating Procedure

A project can be estimated most efficiently when it is divided into a suitable number of elements. But what

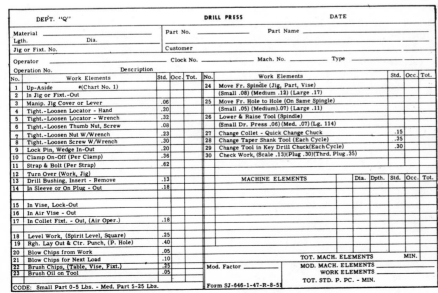

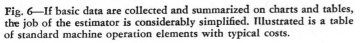

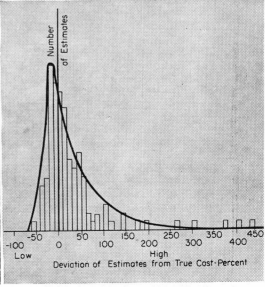

Fig. 6—If basic data are collected and summarized on charts and tables, the job of the estimator is considerably simplified. Illustrated is a table of standard machine operation elements with typical costs.

Fig. 7—Distribution of errors in 157 estimates for different projects. Theoretically, the errors should follow the statistical distribution curve.

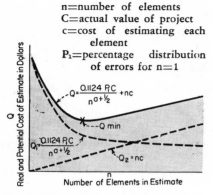

n=number of elements
C=actual value of project
c=cost of estimating each element
P_1=percentage distribution of errors for n=1

$Q = \dfrac{0.1124\ P_1 C}{n^{a+\frac{1}{2}}} + nc$

Q min

$Q_1 = \dfrac{0.1124\ P_1 C}{n^{a+\frac{1}{2}}}$

$Q_2 = nc$

Fig. 8 Effect of the number of elements on the real and potential cost of an estimate, including loss due to inaccuracies: Q_1 is the probable cost due to error; Q is the total cost, including the cost of the estimate; and Q_2 is the total cost of the estimate. Proper balance is essential.

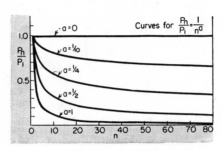

Fig. 9—Typical curves for the ratio $1/n^a$, where n is the number of elements in an estimate and a is an exponent indicating the accuracy of each individual estimate. The value of the exponent a normally falls between 0 and $\frac{1}{2}$. See text for discussion.

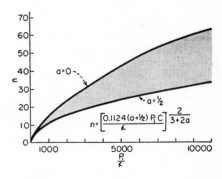

$$n = \left[\frac{0.1124(a+\frac{1}{2})\,P_1 C}{c}\right]^{\frac{2}{3+2a}}$$

Fig. 10—Theoretical numbers of elements desirable for estimating various projects. Number depends on exponent a and on a factor $P_1 C/c$ expressed in Eq. (7).

is the right number? General principles to guide the estimator may be deduced by making several simplifying assumptions.

A project is to be estimated by dividing it into n equal elements. When elements of this order are estimated, the distribution of their percentage deviations from actual cost is normal with a spread P_n corresponding to $\pm 3\sigma$ limits. This is an ideal situation that is only approximated even by the best estimating practices. Practically all the percentage deviations fall within the range P_n. If n equals a; then P_n has a value P_a; if n equals b, P_n has a different value, P_b. The errors in the estimates occur from chance causes and therefore at random.

The sum of the n elemental estimates is the estimate of the total cost of the project. Practically all the percentage deviations from actual costs of projects estimated in the way described fall within a range P_s. A fundamental theorem of statistics specifies that

$$P_s = P_n \sqrt{n} \qquad (1)$$

Thus, the spread of the percentage errors of projects of the kind under consideration is less than the spread of percentage errors of the elements. If P_n remains the same or decreases, P_s decreases as n increases.

As a project is divided into more and more elements, its elements become smaller and simpler. With the same effort, small elements can be estimated more accurately than large ones. That means that P_n decreases as n increases. Let P_1 be the spread of the distribution of percentage errors when projects of this type are estimated on an overall basis; that is when n equals 1. At that point the ratio P_n/P_1 has a value of 1, but it decreases as n increases. However, the ratio P_n/P_1 can never reach zero, no matter how large

n becomes, because that would mean certainty in estimating, which can never be. A relationship that expresses these conditions is

$$\frac{P_n}{P_1} = \frac{1}{n^a} \qquad (2)$$

The rate at which the ratio P_n/P_1 decreases as n increases depends upon circumstances controlling the estimating procedure. A value for the exponent a can be selected to make the expression approximate any rate of decline over a reasonable range of value of n. A series of curves for several values of a is depicted in Fig. 9. Thus, if the estimating situation in a plant is such that little or no elemental data are available, and small elements can scarcely be estimated more accurately than large ones, the ratio P_n/P_1 decreases very little, if any, as n increases. That situation is reflected by Eq (2) with the exponent a equal to or very close to zero.

On the other hand, adequate records in another plant may make it possible to estimate the elements of a project much more accurately than the project as a whole. That is expressed by a rapid decline in the ratio P_n/P_1, which can be reflected by Equation (2) with a value for the exponent a of $\frac{1}{2}$ or larger. Experience indicates that in most cases, small elements can be estimated more accurately than large elements in a proportion expressed by Equation (2) with a value for the exponent a somewhere between 0 and $\frac{1}{2}$.

From Eqs. (1) and (2)

$$P_s = P_1/n^{a+1/2} \qquad (3)$$

The term P_s is equal to six times the standard deviation of the normal distribution of errors in estimates of the total cost. The probable percentage error, high or low, in total cost of the project is 0.6745σ. This is the

percentage error that is as likely to be exceeded as not on either the high or low side, and is designated by

$$P' = 0.1124\ P_s = 0.1124\ P_1/n^{a+1/2} \qquad (4)$$

The real and potential loss suffered from an error in estimating a project of this type is assumed the same as the difference between the estimated and actual cost. If C is the actual value of the project, the probable real and potential loss is

$$Q_1 = C P' = 0.1124\ P_1\ C/n^{a+1/2} \qquad (5)$$

A straight line function expressing a proportional rise of the cost of making the estimate as n increases is nc; where c is the average cost of estimating any element. This is the straight line Q_2 of Fig. 8. The total real and potential cost of the estimate is then

$$Q = 0.1124\ P_1\ C/n^{a+1/2} + nc \qquad (6)$$

The value of n for $Q_{\min}$ is found by setting the derivative of Eq. (6) equal to zero and solving for n. Thus

$$\frac{dQ}{dn} = -(a+1/2)\frac{0.1124\ P_1\ C}{n^{a+3/2}} + c = 0$$

and $n_{\min} = \left[\dfrac{0.1124\ (a+1/2)\ P_1\ C}{c}\right]^{\frac{2}{3+2a}}$ (7)

For $a = 0$

$$n_{mo} = 0.147\left(\frac{P_1 C}{c}\right)^{1/3} \qquad (8)$$

and $\quad Q_{mo} = 0.44\ (P_1 C)^{2/3} \times c^{1/3} \qquad (9)$

For $a = 1/2$

$$n_{m\ 1/2} = 0.336\left(\frac{P_1 C}{c}\right)^{1/2} \qquad (10)$$

and $Q_{m\ 1/2} = 0.67\left(\dfrac{P_1 C}{c}\right)^{1/2} \qquad (11)$

Fig. 10 shows curves of the variable $P_1 C/c$ plotted against n for a equal to 0 and a equal to 1/2.

Uniform Estimating Practice

A curve like that typified in Fig. 8 for Eq. (6) is fairly flat for a wide range of values of n on both sides of the minimum. As an example, when a equals $\frac{1}{2}$ the total real and potential cost of estimating is not more than 10 percent above the minimum over a range equal to about 90 percent of the number of elements that gives the minimum cost. If in a particular situation, the theoretical minimum cost of estimating is obtained when a job is divided into 20 elements, the cost should be no more than 10 percent above the minimum if the job is divided into any number from 13 to 31 elements. If the optimum number of elements is 2,000 for another job, any number of elements from about 1,300 to 3,100 will not increase the estimating cost more than 10 percent. Furthermore, the smaller that the value a is, the larger the choice of the number of elements becomes. When a equals 0, the range for n over which the cost of estimating does not increase more than 10 percent is about $1\frac{1}{2}$ times the range when a equals $\frac{1}{2}$.

Departures in practice from the simplifying assumptions of the theory have an effect similar to decreasing the value of the exponent a in Eq. (6). That effect is favorable because the selection of number of elements is thereby increased.

The theory indicates that a project may be divided as convenient, into any number of elements within a wide range. That supports conventional estimating practice where a certain procedure is established for estimating all jobs of a particular class. Each job is broken down into elements at a particular stage. The number of parts and the number of elements vary from one job to another. Even so, a variety of jobs in one class are served quite well by the uniform procedure. The theoretical lowest estimating cost is likely to be realized in only a few cases, but otherwise the results are economical for all practical purposes.

The Economical Number of Elements for an Estimate

The number of elements into which a project or class of projects should be divided depends theoretically upon an exponent a and a factor P_1C/c as expressed in Eq. (7). That relationship may be visualized as a surface that cuts two plane normal to an a axis perpendicular to the surface presented in Fig. 10. The planes a equals 0 and a equals $\frac{1}{2}$, and the intersections are indicated by the curves. The shaded area between the curves is a projection of the surface between the two planes.

The path of a curve on the surface representing Eq. (7) is determined by the estimating procedure. Such a curve has a projection on the plane of Fig. 10 within the shaded area and a trend between the curves for a equals 0 and a equals $\frac{1}{2}$. For an established procedure, the optimum number of elements, n, in any applicable case depends upon the factor P_1C/c.

The factor P_1 designates the difference between the highest and lowest percentage error that may occur if a project is estimated on an overall basis. If a project can be compared with a recent identical job, P_1 may be small, and a value of n equals 1 justified. If doubts exist about an overall comparison, the indication is that P_1 is large and the project should be divided into a number of elements. In general, a probability of large errors at any stage of estimating calls for a more detailed breakdown.

The term C stands for the total cost of a project. A production job with a risk of many thousands of dollars warrants a more detailed breakdown than one worth a few hundred dollars if other considerations are approximately the same. However, the difference in the number of elements for two such jobs is numerically only a fraction of the difference in values. For example, a device made as a special item might cost $300. If 100 are to be produced, the unit cost is $100 and the total cost is $10,000. The amount of money risked in producing the lot is 33-$\frac{1}{3}$ times that involved for the special item, but the production estimate may require no more than about 10 times as many elements as the estimate for the single device for comparable efficiency.

A pertinent observation at this time is that each successive stage in estimating, as suggested in Fig. 1, is associated with a multiple increase in elements. This can be seen in a simple case of the labor to make a device consisting of five parts. Assume that an average of 6 operations are needed to make each part. If the cost of each operation is estimated, 30 elements constitute the total labor cost. If each operation is divided into 5 elements at the next stage, the total number of elements becomes 150. An estimate for a project may consist of 25 elements at stage V, 100 elements at stage VI, and 500 elements at stage VII. Modifications may be made in an estimating procedure to meet specific situations, but in general each typical stage is best suited to projects in certain cost ranges. In other words, if a job is efficiently estimated at stage VI, it is not likely to be estimated economically at either stages V or VII.

Projects of the same class may differ considerably in cost but will be efficiently estimated at the same stage because the more costly has many parts and the less expensive has few parts. For example, a complex machine tool costing around $20,000 may have several hundred parts. In contrast, a simple machine worth $1000 may have 10 or 20 parts. The $20,000 machine tool should be estimated on the basis of 10 or more times as many elements as the $1000 machine. That is possible with a uniform estimating procedure because the larger number of parts in the larger machine provides the needed greater number of elements.

The Unit Cost of Estimating Elements

The term c stands for the average direct cost of estimating each element. If the cost of estimating each element is large, the number of elements should be small to keep down direct estimating expense. Such a situation may exist where estimates of a certain kind are made infrequently and the collection of data for extensive estimates would be uneconomical. On the other hand, where a sufficient volume of estimating exists, the standardization and tabulation of basic data makes it possible to decrease the cost of estimating each element, to resort to larger numbers of elements, and in the long run to minimize the total real and potential costs of estimating.

Tables of basic data for estimating purposes are costly to compile but do help to reduce the time needed to make each estimate, are conducive to accurate results, and make it possible to use a lower order of skill on some of the estimating work. Such tables can never replace competent and skilled estimators entirely, but they do fit into routines where much of the work can be assigned to clerks under the supervision of the estimator. If the cost of assembling and recording data can be spread over a large enough number of elements, the expense per element can be low. ∎

Estimating the Profit Potential of a New Product

SIDNEY SOBELMAN

chief, Special Analysis Branch, Picatinny Arsenal

**Product planning chooses those products
that will make the most money. But don't just subtract estimated
development costs from estimated profits, warns the author.
Here is a strategy that will always give better results.**

What is the awesome challenge facing new-product managers today? Simply this: How to choose a money-maker from a pile of potential new products, when development costs are several times greater than they were 20 years ago . . . and product life is several times shorter.

This predicament can be traced to two recent trends. First is the sophisticated level of our technology. It makes significant scientific developments increasingly hard to come by and pushes development cost up. Second is the pace of technical progress. It can make products obsolete before they have completed their anticipated market life.

Unfortunately, there is no magic answer. A thorough job of market research can weed out those products for which there is no real need and those which, for one reason or another, have small chance of commercial success. Evaluation by a competent engineering staff can eliminate those in which the technical objectives have a small chance of being realized. There are formulas which include these two factors (see "The Economics of Research and New Product Planning," (starting on p. 156) but in the final analysis, both factors are really matters of economics: Chance of commercial success is only a measure of how much money is invested in market analysis; chance of technical success is, except for those products which will be rejected by the engineering staff as too far beyond the present state of the art, simply a matter of how much the development effort will cost.

Therefore, after the rough screening, there are really only four components to be evaluated in considering any new product to be added to the present product line:
1. Average development cost/year, c

2. Years of development time, t
3. Average profit/year of product life, p
4. Years of market life, T

Each factor involves a guess, but some of them can be estimated more closely than others. Assume for the moment that such estimates can be made. (We will have more to say about *how* in the last part of this article.) What is the best way to put these factors into an equation to determine the payoff for the product under consideration?

Strategy comes first

Obviously, the aim of a company is to get as many products with as much payoff as possible on the market as quickly as possible. Each product, then, should be assessed in terms of its own return and investment. This gives maximum payoff at minimum cost for that product, even though total cost for the group may not be minimized. A replacement strategy is applicable only when two products (the old one and its newer counterpart) compete for scarce dollars, skilled personnel, floor space or transportation facilities.

With this strategy, clearly the simplest and most direct relationship between the factors is to subtract total development costs (cost per year, c, times number of years t) from total net profit (profit per year, p, times years of product life, T). The value of any one product, z, can then be expressed,

$$z = pT - ct$$

Every product characteristic and its magnitude affect one

110

HERE'S HOW IT WORKS

The tables at the bottom of the page compare two different methods for choosing new products—Profit and Cost chooses those projects which give largest z; Dynamic Payoff chooses those projects which give largest z'. In both cases the projects are chosen from those available for that year (shown in the big table) or from projects started the previous year. Company strategy requires that only three projects can be developed in any one year but any number can be in production. Also that projects not started in the year available become useless in future years. Old projects are reevaluated each year (computing a new value for t) and compete with the five new projects available for that next year.

Hypothetical projects were generated using Monte Carlo methods. Average times, T' and t', (for computing z') are 3 years. Totals show that projects chosen using Dynamic Payoff formula were more profitable for the company by $2,630.

Hypothetical Projects / Computations

Year	No.	P	T	c	t	pT	ct	z	T_1	t_1	pT_1	ct_1	z'
1	1	450	4	120	4	1,800	480	1,320	3	3	1,350	360	990
	2	350	3	210	2	1,050	420	630	4	2	1,440	420	1,020
	3	500	3	90	3	1,500	270	1,230	3	3	1,500	270	1,230
	4	350	3	120	3	1,050	360	690	3	3	1,050	360	690
	5	550	3	90	4	1,650	360	1,290	2	4	1,100	360	740
2	6	450	4	180	5	1,800	900	900	2	4	900	720	180
	7	550	4	120	2	2,200	240	1,960	5	1	2,750	120	2,630
	8	500	3	90	2	1,500	180	1,320	4	2	2,000	180	1,820
	9	450	2	210	3	900	630	270	2	4	900	840	60
	10	400	3	120	1	1,200	120	1,080	5	1	2,000	120	1,880
3	11	500	4	120	4	2,000	480	1,520	3	3	1,500	360	1,140
	12	350	5	90	1	1,750	90	1,660	7	-1	2,450	-90	2,540
	13	350	5	120	4	1,750	480	1,270	4	2	1,400	240	1,160
	14	400	3	90	3	1,200	270	930	3	3	1,200	270	930
	15	400	3	90	2	1,200	180	1,020	4	2	1,600	180	1,420
4	16	550	3	120	4	1,650	480	1,170	2	4	1,100	480	620
	17	400	4	120	1	1,600	120	1,480	6	0	2,400	0	2,400
	18	450	2	210	2	900	420	480	3	3	1,350	630	720
	19	450	4	150	3	1,800	450	1,350	4	2	1,800	300	1,500
	20	550	5	150	3	2,750	450	2,300	5	1	2,750	150	2,600

Profit and Cost Method

Year	Project	z	Cost per year	Profit per year	Comments
1	1	1,320	120	....	....
	5	1,290	90	....	....
	3	1,230	90	....	....
2	1	1,440	120	....	....
	5	1,380	90	....	....
	3	1,320	...	....	Cancelled
	7	1,960	120	....	....
3	1	1,560	120	....	....
	5	1,470	...	....	Cancelled
	7	2,080	120	....	Development complete
	12	1,660	90	....	Development complete
4	1	1,680	120	....	Development complete
	20	2,300	150	....	....
	17	1,480	120	....	Development complete
	7	.....	...	500	....
	12	.....	...	350	....
5–10	1	.....	...	1,800	....
	20	.....	300	2,200	Complete 6th year
	17	.....	...	1,600	....
	7	.....	...	1,650	....
	12	.....	...	1,400	....
Totals			$1,650	$9,200	
				−1,650	
			Net	Profit = $7,550	

Dynamic Payoff Method

Year	Project	z'	Cost per year	Profit per year	Comments
1	1	990	120	....	....
	2	1,020	210	....	....
	3	1,230	90	....	....
2	1	1,560	......	....	Cancelled
	2	1,540	......	....	Cancelled
	3	1,820	90	....	....
	7	2,630	120	....	....
	10	1,880	120	....	Development complete
3	3	2,410	90	....	Development complete
	7	3,300	120	....	Development complete
	12	2,540	90	....	Development complete
	10	.....	......	400	....
4	17	2,400	120	....	Development complete
	19	1,500	150	....	....
	20	2,600	150	....	....
	3	.....	......	500	....
	7	.....	......	550	....
	10	.....	......	400	....
	12	.....	......	350	....
5–10	3	.....	......	1,000	....
	7	.....	......	1,650	....
	10	.....	......	400	....
	12	.....	......	1,400	....
	17	.....	......	1,600	....
	19	.....	300	1,800	Development complete, 6th yr
	20	.....	300	2,200	Development complete, 6th yr
Totals			$2,070	$12,250	
				−2,070	
			Net Profit	$10,180	

of the four parameters on the basic equation on page 110.

While this equation is a basic and complete expression of payoff for one product, it has one very serious shortcoming. It does not include a provision for the economic value of time. That is, two projects which have equal payoff z will be considered equally desirable even though the development time, t, or product life, T, may not be the same for both. This is not realistic. Near money is more valuable than distant money or, stating it another way, the dollar that is earned today is worth more than the dollar that is earned tomorrow because today's dollar will increase in value by the interest it will return as an investment.

The long and short of it

So the basic equation must be modified to maximize both long-range and short-range profits. Getting both is not necessarily incompatible. From the short-range viewpoint, the equation must be adjusted to penalize those projects which have a longer than average development item. And from the long-range point of view, the equation must be modified to reward those projects with a longer than average life because a project with a long life will spread profit-taking out over several years, saving the cost and necessity of developing a new project to cover those years.

Thus, a new equation can be derived which includes correction factors based on average development time, t', and average market life, T'.

$$z' = p\,[T + T'\,(1 - t/t')] - c\,[t + t'\,(1 - T/T')]$$

Notice that when both times are average (that is, when $t = t'$ and $T = T'$) the equation reduces to the original basic relationship.

Defining two new variables,

$$T_1 = T + T'\,(1 - t/t')$$
$$\text{and } t_1 = t + t'\,(1 - T/T')$$

the equation reduces to

$$z' = p\,T_1 - c\,t_1$$

This modified equation reflects the exact relationship between the parameters for the best selection strategy of future projects. The average times, t' and T', depend upon the class or type of project. But the existence of such figures is generally recognized in each industry. (For example, recent figures indicate 10 years' development time for a guided missile, 5 years for a new electrical appliance, 3 years for a major modification of an automobile).

Estimating the parameters

Development time is estimated primarily on the basis of how long it will take to lick the technical problems and produce a set of working drawings. But the estimator must also take into account possible delays: backlogs of uncompleted work, insufficient funds or delays in making funds available, demands on time and money arriving at random from outside agencies or internal organizations, necessity for rejustification through formal or informal reports . . . and many others. Market "ripeness" can also have an effect on development time. Knowledge of customer needs and the probability of competitive developments are the most important factors to be considered here.

The formula should be used to reevaluate programs periodically. Therefore, t must always be defined as the remaining years required for completion. Thus, a product is always evaluated on the basis of its future worth to the company, regardless of how much money has been spent on it in the past. In some cases, it may be to the company's advantage to scrap a project on which development money has already been spent in favor of a product that has a higher payoff.

Development costs will depend to a certain extent on development time. The remarks concerning time apply equally to cost. But within limits it is possible to play one off against the other—a decrease in time will require an increase in manpower or facilities and an increase in cost. However, there appears to be an optimum size for the project group, beyond which additional manpower has little effect in decreasing development time.

Manufacturing cost or market price of the completed product have very little to do with development cost. It depends, instead, on the newness of the proposed product and the experience of the design and development team in whatever field is involved. Best estimates can be made when there is a history of costs for similar projects to draw from. Companies commonly make such estimates in terms of man-years and then convert these figures to dollars. Costs of a man-year can usually be predicted with considerable accuracy for a given type of industry and so such conversions can be made quite easily.

Product life, T (also called market life), is the useful life of the product—"useful" in that the product is still desired by the customer and still profitable for the manufacturer. The typical curve for net profit vs years shows a rapid buildup in the first few years followed by a slow decline because of technological and competitive obsolescence. What point on this curve should be chosen as the virtual end of product life? There are a number of criteria; some companies use the 80 per effectiveness cutoff—a measure of technological decay. Others consider that product life has ended when return on investment has dropped to 10%. Whichever point is chosen, the criteria should be consistent for all products under consideration so that z's can be compared directly.

Net profit per year is, of course, simply gross profit less total cost. Total cost includes all costs except those incurred during development: cost of production (including packaging), of marketing, maintenance, replacement, and malfunctions. Gross profit includes number sold multiplied by the selling price plus the scrap value of unsold items and capital equipment.

Selling price depends upon market strategy. At one extreme, there is the policy of skimming the cream off the market—at first the product is priced extremely high and when demand drops at that price, it is lowered to skim the cream off the next market layer. At the other extreme, is the policy of blitzkrieg penetration. Here, the objective is to establish a solid long-term competitive position by pricing low to capture a large share of the market in the shortest possible time. ∎

How to Use Price-Weight Curves for Preliminary Estimates

Competitive cost analysis, using weight-price correlation, may be a better barometer during initial design stages than a detailed cost estimate. Breakeven charts and progress curves also are valuable pre- and post-design tools.

GEORGE H. KENDALL
Consulting Engineer

ASSURANCE of an essential margin of profit on new or redesigned machinery or equipment is contingent not only on final selling price but also on the relationship of the price and performance with competitive lines of machines. During initial design and development stages, these comparative costs are often more important than a detailed cost estimate—and of more help in making design decisions.

Such comparisons may provide the answers to many of the policy questions that invariably arise in discussions among engineering, sales, and management departments, and be an excellent guidepost for the project engineer who is responsible for a given line of machines. One method of obtaining such information is to correlate weight with price for machines already on the market.

These weight-price relationships represent basic information regardless of whether the manufacturer is large or small or whether his production equipment is obsolescent or of the latest design. Taxes, selling and merchandizing costs, shop bonuses and incentives, and all overhead costs are represented in his price. Mark-ups differ, so that they become an individual problem, but even so are included in price-weight ratios.

In the past, many views were held as to whether weight and price could be correlated. Some engineers maintained that no such correlation could exist, particularly in view of changing labor and materials prices, fluctuating taxes, and other variable conditions existing between different plants. Others claimed that it was impossible to obtain satisfactory results on machinery built on special order. Still others were sure that the effects of special attach-

ments or services would upset any possibility of correlation.

However, research has demonstrated that, once a line of machines is designed and placed on the market as a "type," the shape of an average price weight curve changes very little over a period of years. While specific cost values will vary, these can be taken care of by correction factors computed from the difference between a current base and the base that was originally used to obtain the curve.

Curves must be based on the price

and weight of similar combinations of mechanisms. A lathe, for example, consists essentially of a base, headstock, tailstock, ways, cross slide, chuck, gearing, and associated drives and controls. If all types of lathes were placed on one graph, however, the figures would be meaningless. It is necessary to plot data only for machines designed for similar functions, so that tool room lathes would be represented by one graph, veneer lathes by another, and automatic chucking machines by still another. In Tables I and II are lists

Table I—Range of Weight and Price for Various Types of Products*

Equipment Similar to	Range of Weight, lb.		Range of Price per lb.	
	Min.	Max.	Min.	Max.
Floor scrubbers and polishers	10	150	$1.160	$3.210
Veneer lathes	7,500	45,000	0.230	0.520
Wire and ribbon stock reels	75	600	0.180	0.350
Marking machines	400	8,000	0.580	3.050
Vending machines, automatic coin	75	250	3.580	7.350
Shredder machines, waste-paper	1,000	5,000	0.940	1.220
Automatic gas water heaters (galv. outside flue)	100	700	0.300	0.410
Garden tractor, disk-harrow (hand directed)	150	600	0.720	1.560
Milk-can coolers	500	1,100	0.400	0.530
Food freezers	200	750	0.690	1.180
Motion-picture projector	6	18	4.550	18.50
Farm field mowers, horse- or tractor-drawn	500	800	0.290	0.525
Harvesters, cornhusker	1,500	3,500	0.300	0.350
Harvesters, corn-sheller	1,000	3,500	0.310	0.390
Grain blowers	300	450	0.300	0.320
Magnets, rail-lifting	2,000	7,000	0.670	0.780
Dollies, low truck	20	100	0.190	0.610
Unloading chutes	25	150	0.230	0.440
Wheelbarrows, steel	60	150	0.145	0.230
Dump carts, two-wheel (chassis only)	300	650	0.300	0.500
Coal stokers	300	2,500	0.190	0.590
Food deep-pan fryers	25	700	0.760	1.710
Overhead traveling crane	15,000	105,000	0.280	0.820
Hammers, single-frame forging	5,000	110,000	0.070	0.330
Hammers, double-frame forging	30,000	400,000	0.070	0.190
Chain hoists	20	1,500	0.510	1.490
Air compressors, single-stage	1,500	9,000	0.390	0.610
Air compressors, two-stage	5,000	130,000	0.290	0.640

* Figures require multiplication by a correction factor for current use.

Table II—Effect of Production Quantity on Equipment Cost*

Type of Machine	Design Cost per lb.	Total Cost for Various Productions Quantities, per lb.												
		1	2	3	5	10	15	20	25	30	40	50	100	200
1. Fertilizer spreader	4.22	11.0	10.8	10.7	10.5	10.0	9.30	8.95	8.20	7.70	6.58	5.70	1.00	
2. Plows	5.50	16.1	16.0	15.8	15.5	14.6	13.8	13.0	12.1	11.3	10.1	8.30	1.00	
3. Harrows	2.07	12.2	12.1	12.1	12.0	11.7	11.4	11.1	10.8	10.5	10.0	9.50	6.60	1.00
4. Road bulldozer, power grader	0.43	4.35	4.12	3.95	3.65	3.00	2.35	1.68	1.00					
5. Metal chamfering machines	0.80	8.00	7.62	7.27	6.63	5.20	3.80	2.44	1.00					
6. Diesel road rollers	0.51	4.25	4.09	3.95	3.62	2.95	2.30	1.66	1.00					
7. Trailor wagon, chassis and rubber wheels	0.67	2.39	2.31	2.24	2.11	1.84	1.57	1.28	1.00					
8. Diesel tractor	0.74	6.25	5.97	5.71	5.23	4.13	3.10	2.04	1.00					
9. Gasoline tractor	0.90	8.55	8.15	7.80	7.15	5.56	4.02	2.52	1.00					
10. Gasoline tractor, rubber wheel	2.19	19.3	18.1	17.2	15.6	12.0	8.27	4.63	1.00					
11. Low bed trailer	0.67	6.58	6.25	5.95	5.46	4.34	3.22	2.12	1.00					
12. Road graders	0.16	1.61	1.58	1.55	1.51	1.37	1.24	1.11	1.00					
13. Grader—snow plow	0.47	4.68	4.43	4.23	3.90	3.18	2.48	1.73	1.00					
14. Dump wagon trailer	0.40	4.20	4.02	3.86	3.57	2.94	2.27	1.62	1.00					

* Figures require multiplication by correction factor for current use.

of similar combinations of mechanisms, along with minimum and maximum prices and weights.

As can be seen from Fig. 1, price-weight relationships will scatter over a band throughout the entire range of weights, rather than fall on a line. This band will indicate the highest and lowest cost per pound at which the given type of machinery has been successfully produced. A smooth, faired curve can be drawn through this band to indicate the average price variation that might be expected, based on past American practice. To assure strictly impartial information with the ultimate aim of the largest scope of general use, the greatest width of the band can be indicated on the curve by plus and minus values in cents per pound.

The weight and price of each machine of a given type should be thoroughly checked and plotted into the material for just one graph. Data for many machines, representing the entire cross section of the industry, must be plotted. While the curve that is drawn through this plot will represent a compromise among all machines in a particular classification, it will be indicative of the best modern practice. In general, any long range program of development should be aimed at producing equipment that will cost less than the average to assure a proper margin of profit.

While this is not the entire story, it is the hard, cold, basic fact on which analysis should be based. It is entirely possible that creative design may produce a machine with greater capacity than its competitors and so command a higher price for a given weight. It is also possible that certain patented features will permit marketing of a machine at a higher price per pound than competition. It is also possible that certain low cost constructions, plus large volume of manufacture without any patentable features whatever, may result in a price lower than the average. This in turn might result in a greater margin of profit.

In some of the machine classifications the range from the smallest size to the largest size is so great as to warrant establishing light, medium, and heavy zones purely for analysis of local size studies. The cross-section lines clearly show the trend characteristics of the particular type of machine. As the weight of machines increase and, particularly in the heavy classes of equipment, the width of this "band of machines" decreases.

A wide band width may indicate several other things. Generally it exemplifies a new machine classification with many patentable features, or a class of lightweight equipment, such as instruments or appliances, that are costly. Data for older lines of machinery or equipment for which most basic patents have expired will fall within a much narrower price band.

The more sensitive zones of any particular graph are indicated by the max-

Fig 1—Typical price-weight chart. This indicates the definite correlation between price and weight of similar classes of equipment, and can be used to establish specifications during initial stages of design. Note effect of light weight.

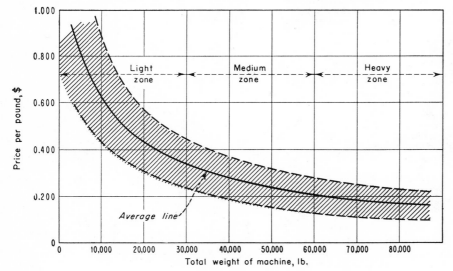

Table III—How Price Weight Curves Differ for Various Equipments

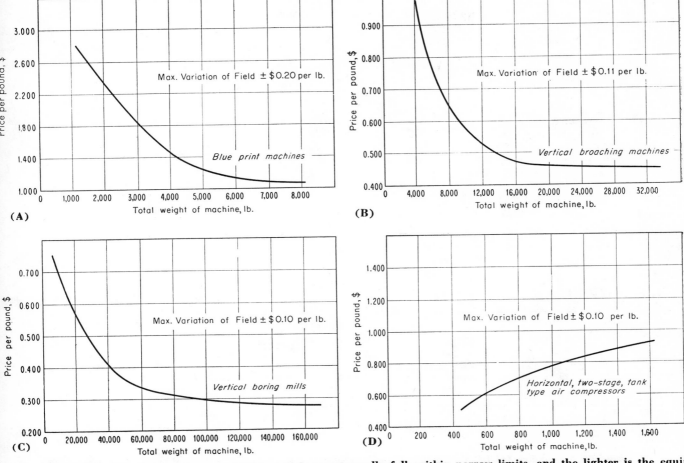

(A)—Price of equipment in an established industry generally falls within narrow limits, and the lighter is the equipment, the more sensitive is the price-weight relationship. All data are from Kendall Harris Reference Guide.

(B)—This curve indicates an extreme sensitivity of cost to weight in smaller machines—probably a result of heavy overhead costs. Engineering costs alone are high on this type of equipment, which is large even in small sizes.

(C)—Price line for well established equipment in an older industry. Maximum price variation is extremely small, even though curve covers a wide range of equipment sizes. This is normal for industries that have been long established.

(D)—Unusual weight-price graph results when increasing the limits of operating conditions—temperature or pressure, for example—requires "beefing up" of the equipment. The curve would be similar for some hydraulic devices.

imum degree of change of the average curve. In these zones, slight changes in weight or price will have a considerable effect on the competitive position of the machine, and may greatly influence the overall margin of profit. Conversely, in the least sensitive zones, the curve is relatively flat and a considerable weight change is possible with but little effect on unit price. In other words, overall price varies almost directly with weight in the latter instance, while in the more sensitive zones, a decrease in weight may cause an increase in price.

Once experience has been obtained with the curves—and these may take several forms, as illustrated in Table III—several other features may be added based on personal experience and company records on former products. The curves might be broken down

to show the proportion of design and tooling cost to total cost, or to other costs making up the total. And, as previously mentioned, factor can be developed to correct for changes in economic conditions.

Once charts have been developed for a given type of machine, answers to questions such as the following can be easily obtained:

1. What is the cost range of competitive lines of a proposed machine?
2. What is the range of weight of this type of machine?
3. What are the extremes of weight and price for this type of machine?
4. How does price vary with weight? How fast?
5. To sell at a certain cost, how much can the proposed machine weigh?
6. Can more weight be added and

still leave the machine within the general price range?

7. Does the indicated cost show that further design revision is advisable?
8. Would the use of other mechanisms reduce cost?
9. What is the range of cost of other constructions?
10. Would a combination of other mechanisms result in lower cost?

The importance of knowing weight-price relative and comparative values cannot be overlooked for those who desire facts and an assured margin of profit. When it is realized that the shape of all of these curves are different, and that each one represents the successful performance of manufacturers with the recognized best skills in the world, then basic value for the design and development program are understood and practiced.

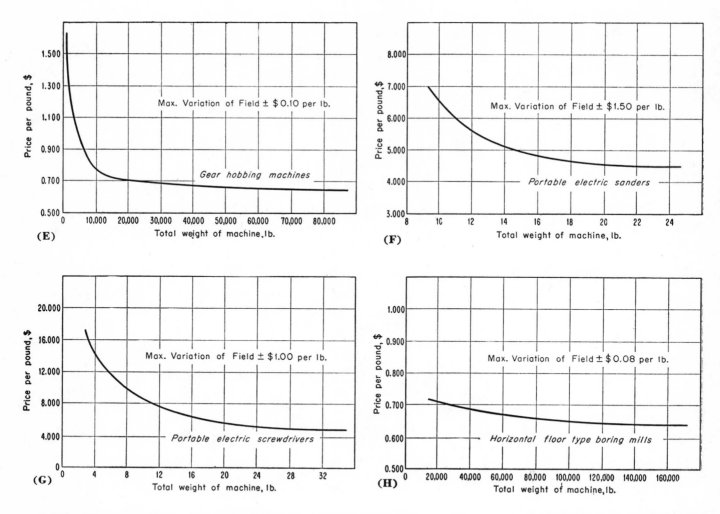

(E)—When capacity or size are far below normal, the weight-price curve has almost a vertical slope. However, distinctive patentable features may support a higher price level. Competitive features are always a factor in design.

(F)—Lightweight equipment. The relatively large variation in price per pound indicates a line of products not yet established as an industry. Good engineering can make a product an industry standard on some equipment lines.

(G)—This equipment is costly but designed to close limits. A new company entering this field should definitely investigate weight-price relationships before establishing design specifications, else the product be sold at a loss.

(H)—The average line of this curve is indicative of constructions made of all basic structural shapes or all castings. Material costs per pound remain essentially the same regardless of product size, so the curve has very little slope.

Break Even Charts

Another type of cost curve that can be put to excellent use in the engineering department is the so-called break even chart. This chart contains two curves: One shows accumulative anticipated income; the other, accumulative anticipated cost. The point at which the curve of income crosses the curve of costs is the break even point in terms of units that have to be produced before the company recovers all direct and indirect expenses and starts making a profit.

For example, assume that a new product is under consideration by the engineering and sales departments. From preliminary designs, the engineering department can estimate the development and tooling costs, as well as determine the unit cost of the product. In Fig. 2, $100,000 is taken as total

development and tooling costs. Assuming that direct and indirect costs equal $325.00 per unit, the curve of costs can be plotted. If, based on market analysis, the sales department estimates that the product can sell for $475, 670 units must be produced before profit. This gives the sales department a preliminary figure that can be checked against sales estimates, and indicates to the engineering department the necessity for design modifications or reductions in tooling and development.

An additional expenditure for jigs and semi-automatic tooling ($50,000 on curves) might reduce unit costs by reducing the slope of the cost line, and lower the break even point (dotted line). So the curve can be used to compare production methods as well as to determine feasibility of development, economics of different designs, or

worked backwards, the efficiency of the engineering program.

There are several factors to keep in mind, however, if break even down charts are to be used:

(1) They are based on preliminary estimates, and so if the error is to be on the safe side, the estimates should be conservative, yet as accurate as possible.

(2) The selling price may effect unit sales, and so should be based on actual market conditions. It is frequently better to establish limits, both minimum and maximum, for market price as well as limits on sales potential.

(3) Development costs should include engineering, drafting, models, testing, allowance design changes, and other preproduction costs, including tools, jigs, fixtures, material, and labor cost and also the cost of such new

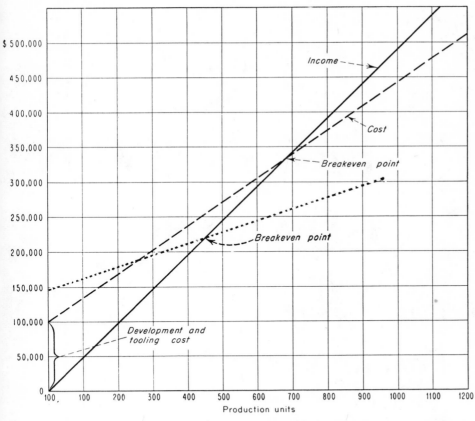

Fig 2—Break even chart. Point at which income crosses the cost line indicates the number of units that must be produced before profit.

equipment and expanded facilities as are necessary.

Like price per weight curves, break even charts are easily prepared once preliminary calculations have been made and should be more widely used than they now are in engineering department planning. They also are an effective tool for management.

Progress Curves

The greatest inaccuracy in break even charts is that they are based on uniform product cost regardless of quantity produced. Actually, unit costs decrease with increasing production quantities since indirect and overhead costs are spread over a greater number of units and the efficiency of labor,

tooling, and machine use becomes greater as production runs become longer. When cumulative costs are plotted vs. the cumulative number of units produced, a hyperbolic curve similar to that shown in Fig 3 results.

Since the rate of decrease of cost with quantity for one product often can be predicted from curves for another, progress curves can be used by both the engineering and production department for cost estimating purposes. They can also be used to ascertain how several production costs making up the whole vary with production or to show the effect of quantity on material, tooling, engineering and overhead costs.

Three types of progress curves can be plotted: One of cumulative average costs vs units produced; one showing cumulative costs at any given unit; and another showing unit cost vs production quantity. The first can be used to estimate break even points and to check total anticipated production costs vs actual costs.

These can be plotted from historical data on the following basis:

Cumulative Average Cost Curves

$y = bx^m$, where y is product cost, x is the number of products produced, b is the cost of the first product, and m is the slope of the progress curve on logarithmic paper.

Unit Cost Curves

$y^1 = b(x - \frac{1}{2})^m (m + 1)$, where y^1 is the unit product cost at x and x is the unit number.

Cumulative Cost Curves

$y = b x^{m+1}$ ∎

Material for this article based on Kendall-Harris Reference Guide (unpublished).

Fig 3—Progress curves indicating the effect of quantity on decreasing unit cost. Improved methods and machines plus labor improvement are primary causes. Both plots are so-called 80 percent progress curves common to the aircraft industry.

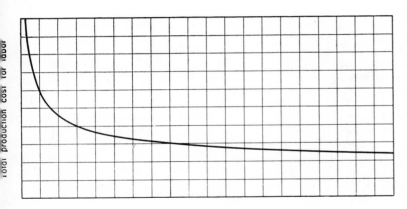

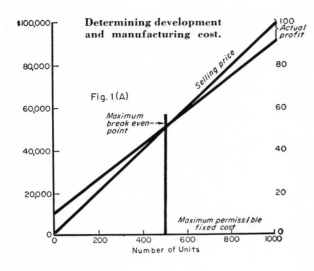

Determining development and manufacturing cost.

Fig. 1(A)

Maximum break even point

Selling price

Actual profit

Maximum permissible fixed cost

Number of Units

BREAK-EVEN CHARTS:

They'll Tell You If A Product Should Be Made

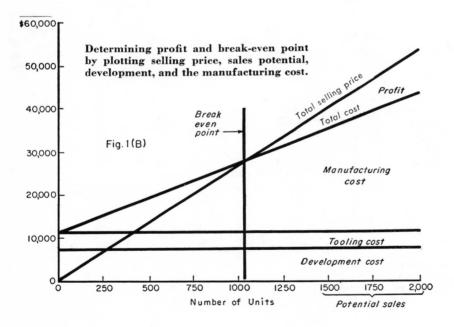

Determining profit and break-even point by plotting selling price, sales potential, development, and the manufacturing cost.

Fig. 1(B)

Break even point

Total selling price

Total cost

Profit

Manufacturing cost

Tooling cost

Development cost

Number of Units

Potential sales

W. A. SCHUETTE
Office & Contract Supervisor
Allis-Chalmers Manufacturing Co.

USE OF A BREAK-EVEN CHART to predict the volume in which a product must be made before the company starts making a profit is often the simplest method of answering one of the most difficult questions faced by the engineering department: "Should we recommend development?"

In basic form, such a chart is a plot of anticipated income from sale of a product versus the cost of developing and manufacturing it. Readily determined is the unknown factor—the volume necessary before all indirect charges are paid for, direct costs are covered, and a profit is made.

Break-even charts can be used also in other ways: To compare virtues of one design with those of another; to determine whether unit costs will be too high to insure sales; or even to aid in the selection of production equipment, determine whether plant mechanization is practical, or decide whether manufacturing shifts should be expanded.

In new product development, the break-even chart can reflect the economic survival of a project, whether the factor to be determined is the point of *profit and break-even,* or the cost of *development and production.*

Where profit is unknown, Fig. 1(B), estimates calculated for plotting should be as accurate as possible. If these estimates are also conservative a clearer picture for decision will be obtained.

Factors from which these estimates are derived should include:

1. Projected Selling Price based on market potential and the competitive situation. It might also prove advantageous to establish minimum and maximum limits. *On the chart:* $26.50 per unit

2. Sales Potential based on competitive considerations such as market conditions, quality of product, and selling points. Range between minimum and maximum expectations should be included. *On the chart:* 1,500 units minimum; 2,000 units maximum

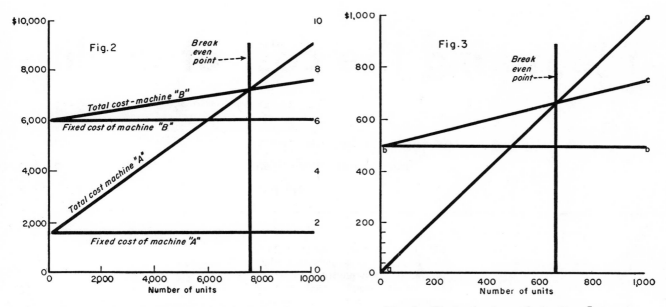

Fig. 2—Selecting Equipment. Fixed cost of equipment is plotted with unit production cost. Choice is determined by production.

Fig. 3—Mechanization substitution. Intersection of device's labor cost and previous hand labor cost represents break-even point.

3. Development Cost
   a. Development engineering
   b. Development drafting
   c. Pilot model or models
   d. Preliminary testing
   e. Allowances for modifications of drawings and models
   f. Other pre-production costs exclusive of tools
On the chart: $7,500.00

4. Cost of New Tools and Expansion of Facilities. *On the chart:* $3,400.00

5. Manufacturing Cost *On the chart*: $15.85 per unit.

When this factor is plotted on the chart, the economic survival of the product is more evident. If the position of the break-even point permits an acceptable profit despite the conservative estimates—and adverse price and market conditions based on lowest selling price and minimum sales potential—the product can be considered worth investment and further development can be justified.

If the break-even point indicates a marginal return or a loss, the project may warrant modification, but in all likelihood, it should be dropped. As actual development progresses or important modifications are made, the new data obtained can also be charted so that if the break-even point does fall beyond safe economic limits, that fact will be brought out. In Fig. 1(B) the location of the break-even point indicates that profit will begin at less than the minimum sales potential.

Where development and production costs are being determined, Fig. 1 (A), the chart can show whether economic restrictions imposed by a required profit and break-even point are prohibitive. Assume that the sales force advises the engineering department of a customer's request for the production of a new device with a total sales potential of 1,000 units and a total price of $100,000.00. Management has giv-en a conditional approval based on the assurance of a ten percent minimum profit and a break-even point at 500 units. Plotting the limitations shows the engineer that approximately $9,000.00 must cover costs of development, tooling and facilities, and manufacturing. These data combined with experience will then enable him to advise Management as to the practicality of the project.

OTHER USES FOR CHART

The flexibility afforded by the break-even chart can be applied to a variety of other engineering problems in addition to new product analysis.

Equipment Selection: The break-even chart is a practical means of comparing two or more sets of data. In determining which of two machines is more economical, Fig. 2, the fixed cost of the equipment is plotted with the unit production cost achieved with each:

	Machine A	Machine B
Initial Cost	$1,500.00	$6,000.00
Unit Production Cost	.75	.15

The chart shows that it is more economical to purchase Machine A if production will not exceed 7,500 units. For higher quantity production the economy lies with Machine B. The selection of equipment will, therefore, depend upon the sales forecast, production schedule, obsolescence of product, or depreciation and maintenance factors.

Mechanization Substitution: Break-even charts offer a particularly convincing argument of their effectiveness when employed to show the advantages of mechanized production over those of hand labor. Assume that a new wrapping device, costing $500, is being considered for a job where 1,000 units are handled yearly. Complete manual labor costs per unit total about one dollar, but the use of the wrapping device is expected to reduce the labor cost to 25 cents. The "break-even" chart, Fig. 3, is constructed quickly from this data. Line *b-b* represents the fixed cost of the device, line *b-c* its labor cost, and *a-a* the hand labor costs. The intersection of *a-a* and *b-c* is the break-even point—at approximately 670 units the wrapping device is paid for and mechanization is indicated. ∎

Measuring the cost of quality

LAD J. BAYER chief industrial engineer, Warner & Swasey Co.

A method to provide tangible information that will permit manufacturing cost control during early stages of design reducing cost and time between development and production

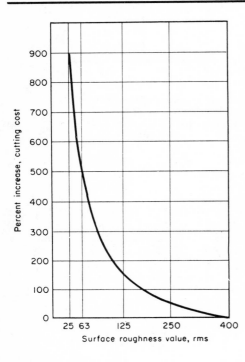

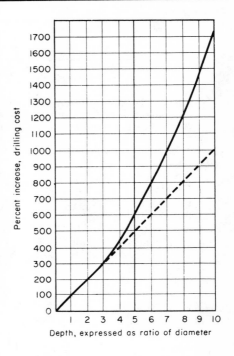

Fig. 1 Left—SURFACE QUALITY: Representative cost-comparison chart in which cost is plotted with respect to surface quality standards, and limited to the turning process as done on turret lathes. Using ths chart the choice of functional surface quality for any application can be made, with full knowledge of comparative cost.

Fig. 2 Right—DRILLED HOLES: From the chart it is readily apparent that deep holes are expensive. Beyond the depth of three times the diameter, the cost rises more rapidly than equal increments of depth. The dotted line is shown to highlight the accelerated cost. Only standard drilling facilities were covered by the data, special oil-hole drills or trepanning tools would reflect cost patterns at extremely wide variance with this chart.

Fig. 3—PLANNING AND FACE-MILLING: The cost-behavoir chart on planning, (A), demonstrates the effect of two quality variables; surface quality and dimensional tolerance. The variables can be judged separately or in combination. Surface quality being defined by coded numbers supported with visual samples, since RMS values do not express the desired control.

The cost behavoir chart on face milling, (B), combines two variables, surface roughness and tolerance. Extremely wide cost differentials exist throughout the range of defined quality.

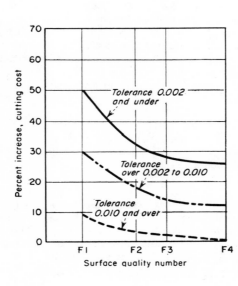

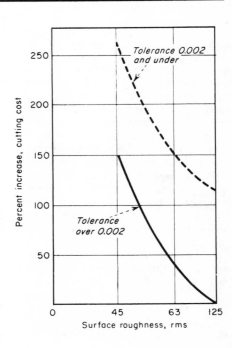

MANUFACTURING costs are largely decided by the quality desired in the product produced. Unfortunately, very little information is available on the relationship of cost to acceptable quality standards. Quality, however, may be defined as the function, durability and appearance of a product. Therefore quality can be related to definable and measurable increments. Standards of dimensional tolerance and surface roughness are a few of the indicators of quality that may be well defined and easily measured.

Time being a measure of cost it is possible to tabulate a time or cost relationship for quality standards. Fig. 1 to 6 are plots of variables of cost against variables of quality. These charts were plotted to test the practicability of using industrial engineering data to establish tangible information about the cost-quality relationship desired.

Variation in facilities, processing methods and differences in quality range will affect the character of the cost behavior pattern. The idea or principle, however, is applicable to any manufacturing operation and charts can be compiled for any requirement. The ease with which these charts can be drawn up depends on the degree of standardization and availability of industrial engineering data. ■

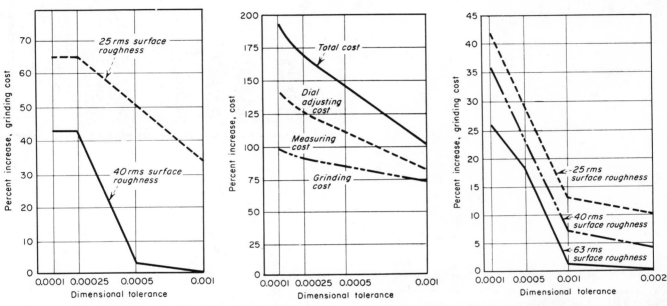

Fig. 4 — CYLINDRICAL, INTERNAL AND SURFACE GRINDING: Cylindrical grinding cost, (A) show a nonuniform cost-behavior pattern. The 40 rms surface quality line shows a minor cost rise between the 0.001 and 0.0005 in. tolerances followed by an abrupt rise between the 0.0005 and 0.00025 in. tolerances. The 25 rms surface quality line reflects the usual cost behavior relative to tolerance reduction.

Internal grinding cost, (B), as related to dimensional tolerance, plus some of the elements that make up total cost are shown. As reduced tolerance increases the cost of grinding, additional costs occur in the form of increased gaging and adjustment time.

In reciprocating or surface grinding, (C), the dimensional tolerance range has greater cost effect than the surface-quality range. Cost rises sharply with tolerances less than 0.001 in.

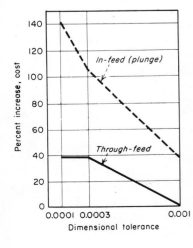

Fig. 5 Left—CENTERLESS GRINDING: The possibilities of incorporating quality features other than surface roughness or tolerance is illustrated by comparing two grinding methods. In order to gain the benefit of the low cost "through-feed" method on the centerless grinder, the ground diameter must be the largest dimension on the part. If this is impractical, a generous tolerance will minimize cost when using "in-feed".

Fig. 6 Right—ROTARY SURFACE GRINDING: Rotary surface grinding figures are presented primarily to demonstrate that cost is not always severely effected by quality variation. Here the cost increase over the given tolerance range is only 15 per cent and more than half the cost increase occurs between the 0.001 and 0.0005 tolerances.

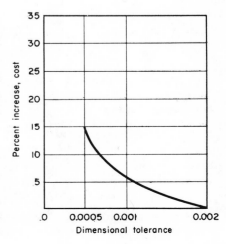

How to Get Realistic Drafting-Time Estimates

GEORGE R. BECK

A UNIQUE APPROACH to design and drafting work measurement, combining the work measurement techniques of industrial engineers with employee participation, and the motivational techniques of behavioral scientists is now being used at TRW to develop time standards for drafting work and the equally important factors of time spent on related and non-related activity. The operational process is a powerful management tool for improving drafting department performance and morale. The resulting standards are accurate enough to be useful to management in setting budgets and schedules, and at the same time are acceptable to the employees because they participated in all phases of establishing them.

A work measurement program can provide widely useful drawing time standards. These standards can be the basis for:

Cost estimates or proposals
Manpower forecasting
Scheduling drawings
Manpower assignment and loading
Budgeting labor
Budgeting cost
A basis for cost control and reduction
Methods and procedures improvement
Measurement performance

Work measurement can provide the details needed for Value Engineering analysis of documentation function and cost, with the objective of providing required documentation at reduced cost. This effort has high potential for realizing good performance improvement and cost reduction.

Generally accepted methods for establishing factors useful in determining work, schedules, and budgets include: estimates by an experienced drafting supervisor; time study—use of stop watches and other timing devices; time and motion analysis of movies taken of drafting; analysis of historical records of actual times of drafting; motion analysis using a predetermined time data system; and work sampling observations taken at random times. Work sampling is well established by industrial engineering. This method can give the greatest variety of detail for how time is spent but does not necessarily measure efficiency. Too often the work sampling is conducted by outsiders so both they and their results are resented by the draftsman.

In the record analysis approach, the total hours divided by the number of drawings produced becomes an index useful for estimating and manpower forecasting. In some cases, these cost factors are weighted for drawing complexity. This method can relate efficiency to a norm but cannot identify details useful for analyzing work performance.

Using industrial engineering with behavioral science techniques retains the advantages of detailed analysis for how time is spent and adds the advantage of employee motivation. The employee helps determine what work is to be sampled, helps gather the time data, helps evaluate the meaningfulness of the data and adds his judgment in setting the final work standard. During this process, he is also able to provide suggestions for improving work situations. This system works well with supervisors and employees who are objective about their jobs. It is not as well accepted or implemented by supervisors of the "irreplaceable" type who keep performance knowledge "in their heads" and are not willing to have factual data brought out.

System description

In applying the industrial engineer/behaviorial science approach, TRW management makes certain assumptions about how people relate to their job, and their commitment toward achievement of organizational objectives. Individuals are seen as wanting to take initiative and to seek out and accept responsibility. They are seen also as being concerned about their work and as having the ability to participate in decisions regarding their work. A comparison of the traditional industrial engineering approach with the TRW approach is shown in Table I.

Consistent with this the industrial engineering role is one which recognizes that line management is responsible for use of the program, and the controls developed are meaningful only if they are meaningful to him. In this role the industrial engineer is a technical resource to the supervisor. The supervisor identifies his problem, determines solutions and plans the program, calling on the industrial engineer as an advisor.

The TRW approach to time measurement is unique. *First,* our assumptions about the objectives of time measurement are different: we believe that time measurement is an aid to the line supervisor—not a club in the hands of his manager.

We believe that time measurement is an aid to improved productivity—not a cleaver for cost reduction.

We believe that time measurement is a means to an end—not an end in itself.

Second, our approach to accomplish time measurement is different.

We will help the line supervisor decide what to measure and how to measure it—but we will not make these decisions.

We will help the line supervisor gather the data necessary for time measurement, but we will not do it for him.

We will help the line supervisor to analyze the data and develop meaningful standards, but we will not do it without his participation.

Finally, our recommendations regarding the use of standards for performance reporting is different.

We recommend that performance reports be issued by the line supervisor, not by an outside staff.

We recommend that performance reports function as a method of "self measurement", not as a measure of someone else.

We recommend that performance data assist the decision-making process, not become the sole criteria for it.

To accumulate the work-time data, an activity log is maintained by each person while the supervisor conducts a work sample study. Figure 1 shows an example of an individual activity log. Every 15 minutes the person marks his activity according to a code. At the end of the day, the

data from these activity logs is accumulated on a daily input form (Figure 2) when computerized compilation techniques are used. This may also be done by hand. The supervisor's work sampling consists of a brief periodic review of activity throughout his area, indicating activity at that moment. The results are summarized and compared weekly to the results of the activity log data. Some typical comparisons of these two data sources are given later in this paper.

When the work sampling is analyzed and is discussed with those who took the data, it is possible to establish work standards for those tasks which show reasonable correlation of data. Some of this data points out problem areas. This is good source data for creative group discussions which result in performance improvement.

WORK MEASUREMENT - METHODS COMPARISON

Traditional Approach	TRW Experimental Approach
I	**I**
Cost Reduction is the main objective.	The objective is to find better tools (for the line supervisor) to apply in the performance of his required responsibilities, especially cost and manpower control.
II	**II**
The program is imposed from above.	The program belongs to line management. (The industrial engineer is a professional consultant to each level of line management, particularly to first line supervision.)
III	**III**
Industrial Engineering decides the technique of measurement, what will be counted, etc. The line supervisor contributes only his knowledge of operations.	The line supervisor is involved in day-to-day decisions on what to measure, how to count it, what measurement technique to use, and the reporting system.
IV	**IV**
Performance reports are issued by the Industrial Engineering Department concurrently to all levels of management. Industrial Engineering often explains the variance in levels of performance.	The performance report is forwarded by the line supervisor to his superior. The supervisor is responsible for any explanation with assistance from the industrial engineer when desired.
V	**V**
Standards (and the resulting performance reports) motivate increased productivity. (Carrot and Stick approach).	High levels of productivity and effectiveness cannot be achieved only by standards. Standards by themselves can be negative motivators.

Name: John Smith				Date: 2/11			
Dwg Group No. Code: 130*				Dwg Type Code: 37**			
Dwg No. Prefix: T Body: 220081				MJO: 2430 SO: 02 UI: 01			
Dwg or EO Rev Letter: A							

Period Ending	*** Activity Code			
	06/01	12	15	17
8:45	X			
9:00	X			
9:15	X			
9:30		X		
9:45			X	
10:00			X	
10:15				X
10:30				X
10:45				
11:00				
11:15				
11:30				
11:45				
12:00				
1:15				
1:30				
1:45				
2:00				
2:15				
2:30				
2:45				
3:00				
3:15				
3:30				
3:45				
4:00				
4:15				
4:30				
4:45				
5:00				
5:15				
5:30				
Totals	4	1	2	2

*Drawing Group Number Codes are three digits to record the following:

First Digit	Function
0	Administration
1	Checking
2	Designing
3	Drafting

Second Digit	Group
0	Administration
1	Power Equipment
2	Ground Equipment
3	Communications Equipment
4	Guidance Equipment
5	Product Integration and Test
6	Special Projects
7	Runner
8	Clerical

Third Digit	Drawing Level
0	Formal, released drawing
1	Pre-released or preliminary drawing ("X")
2	Upgrading drawing (removing the "X" prefix)

**Drawing Type Codes are listed in Table II.

***Activity Codes are listed in Table I. To indicate rework, a Rework Code shall follow the Activity Code. 01 indicates the first rework, 02 the second, etc. For example, 01/01 = the first recheck of a drawing or EO.

FIGURE 1—*Daily activity log.*

The Work Unit Measurement Program provides an efficient, flexible method for collecting accurate work time data from the various design and drafting groups and for reducing this data into computer tab runs. When a complete range of data is available, it provides management with three extremely valuable tools.

(1) It gives a detailed breakdown of all design and drafting activity during the working day, showing how personnel actually spend their time, in terms of total manhours per activity. This visibility highlights particularly time-consuming activities, and actual and potential problem areas. The breakdown is useful as the basis for improving standard practices, streamlining operations, and increasing effective cost control.

(2) It gives a comprehensive list of standard times required for the preparation and checking of each type of drawing. Based on actual past performance data, and constantly checked against current performance, standard times can enable more accurate manpower forecasts, and more efficient work assignments. In addition, they can help to provide better criteria for personnel evaluations.

(3) It gives a weekly performance rating for each individual design and drafting group. This rating is derived by applying standard drawing times to the number of drawings completed during the week to compute the total earned hours. The actual hours charged by the group for the week, excluding supervisior and clerical support, are then measured against the total earned hours to obtain the performance rating by the formula:

$$\frac{\text{Total Earned Hours}}{\text{Total Actual Hours}} \times 100\% = \text{Percent Performance}$$

For example:

$$\frac{1325 \text{ Earned Hours}}{1540 \text{ Actual Hours}} \times 100\% = 86\% \text{ Performance}$$

This rating can be used to monitor the validity of standard times by comparing them with actual performance, develop specialized time data for follow-on or minor redesign programs (versus new projects), and provide early warning of potential problems.

By varying the data collected (that is, changing the activities reported) the Work Measurement Program can be adapted to changing situations or tailored to different organizations. Currently, computer programs have been developed which have a built-in updating capability; that

124

WORK UNIT MEASUREMENT PROGRAM DAILY INPUT FORM

Emp No.	Drawing No. Prefix	Body	Dash	EO	Date Mo	Da	Yr	Active ted type	Over Ct iom e	Hours	Re w o r k	Cost Cntr Code	Group No.	W Lo ars ks	MJO	SO	Card ode	UI	T Dy W pg e	B L ld g	Si ze	For Completed Drawings N So,h	EC lo em cp	D Pe kn ngi s	N t No.s	I t Ne o.s	L Na y e Nm o.s	Co mp	Ch ks Code	Ch ks Code	C C C C
2 4 6 8 0	T	2 2 0 8 1 5			2	1 2	6 6 0 6			4 0 0		7 4 1 3	1 3 0	K	2 4 3 0	0 2	1 0 1 3 7 6 0													2
						1 2	1 2 5																							2
						1 5	1 7 5																							2
	G	2 3 7 4 9 6			0 1	X	1 0 0 0 2					1 2 0		2 4 3 3	1 1	1 0 3 6 2														2

This portion of form for keypunch use only; not to be completed by Design and Drafting personnel.

NOTES:
1. Activity Codes are listed in Table I.
2. Rework and Drawing Group Number Codes are explained in Figure 1.
3. Work Classifications are:

Classification	Code	Classification	Code
Design Engineer	5	Sr Clerk	F
Sr Designer	K	Intermed Clerk	D
Designer	J	Clerk	C
Sr Checker	4	Clerk Typist	B
Checker	K	Jr Clerk	A
Sr Draftsman	I	Sr Secretary	E
Draftsman	F	Secretary	C
Jr Draftsman	D		

To indicate contract personnel, place an "X" in front of the code letter.

FIGURE 2—Daily input form.

is, the programs provide for the automatic comparison of the latest data with that previously collected to continually verify the standard time figures used. This flexibility assures greater confidence in the results achieved, better analysis of the data compiled, and generally more effective use of the data.

Implementing the program

Implementing the program requires careful orientation of all personnel. This is to make certain that *all* management understands its "hands-off" role, that supervision understands its initiating responsibility, and that all employees fully understand the purpose of the program and how they will participate in all phases of the effort. To help gain employee confidence that management is interested in improving work situations, management must follow up the suggestions brought out by individual interviews. This feedback is used only with the permission of the employee. Also data collected during the time-data collection phase is acted upon by management only after employees have first evaluated and commented upon the data. Throughout the time-standards development phase, this identification of the program as the "employees' own" is maintained. As a result, the employees help develop correction and improvement of work situations. Also they willingly accept the final standards as well as time allocation of non-productive work.

To illustrate the difference between the traditional approach to implementing a work measurement program and the approach used by TRW, the chronological steps of each system are listed below.

Chronology of traditional approach.
(1) Basic Fact Gathering.
(2) Work Distribution Analysis.
(3) Selection of Key Jobs.
(4) Job Analysis.
(5) Time Data Collection.
(6) Developing Standard Time.
(7) Installation of Reporting and Control Procedures.

Chronology of TRW approach. Numbers shown in parenthesis refer back to steps in the traditional approach.
(A) A Management/Industrial Engineering (IE) discussion of approach and objectives.
(B) Input to IE—basic facts of organization, procedures, operational interfaces, demotivating problems. (1).
(C) Presentation of Program approach and objectives to Design and Drafting (D/D) supervisors.
(D) IE interviews with individual D/D supervisors—basic fact gathering. (1).
(E) IE/Management discussion results to date, selection of key (pilot) area and key jobs. (3).
(F) Presentation to key area personnel—program approach and objectives.
(G) IE interviews with key area individuals. (1).
(H) General/Orientation of all interested management supervisors, and employees on Work Measurement techniques.
(I) IE discussion with key area supervision regarding work distribution and job analysis. (2, 4).
(J) Feedback from D/D to IE data for I above.
(K) IE develop (D/D approve) work measurement system including work breakdown, activity coding, data collection and reporting. (4, 5).
(L) Collect data—all performed by D/D personnel, IE as advisor to supervision. (5).
(M) Data evaluation—supervision and employees using IE as advisor.
(N) Set initial time standards. (6).

(O) Adapt and apply system wherever appropriate. (7).

In each of the steps, the Industrial Engineer participates in presenting the program or advising those involved in performing the work. He keeps constantly aware of the level of understanding and acceptance. Personally involved, he maintains continuity of the program, makes sure that the desired approach is held to, and guides the work to the objectives established.

Typical results

Interview Comments. When supervisors were asked how they viewed their work situations they made such comments as:

"There is difficulty defining responsibility between engineering D/D supervision."

"Much time is lost in preparation of engineering changes due to incomplete engineering information."

"Drawing approval requirements cause long delays."

"Piece-meal budgeting makes manpower forecasting and work scheduling inaccurate and uncontrollable."

"Cost analysis data for different types of drawings would help in estimating and budgeting."

"A formal supervisor training course is desired."

Each of these comments was acted upon by management and D/D supervision. Engineering communication improved and D/D morale soared.

Work Sampling/Activity Log Correlation. Work sampling (WS) performed by supervisors or observers had reasonably good correlation with activity log (AL) data recorded by each employee. Only the following five activities were observed by supervision and only for correlating purposes.

Work Sampling (WS) Activity Log (AL) Correlation: Typical activity, observed by different methods, is expressed as per cent of total time.

Activity	Area A		Area B		Area C	
Observation Method						
	WS	AL	WS	AL	WS	AL
Checking	53	66	70	70	50	60
Talking	23	23	16	20	24	29
Out of Area	8	5	8	6	16	6
Walking	6	–	3	–	4	5
Personal	10	6	3	4	6	5
	100%	100%	100%	100%	100%	100%

Activity Distribution. Typical activity distribution expressed as per cent of total time is given below. Not all activity is shown.

Activity	Area D	Area E	Area F
Checking	56.0	56.5	61.0
Obtain Reference	2.3	7.7	1.1
Use Reference	3.3	2.6	1.8
Talk with Designers, etc.	6.7	7.9	4.7
Talk with Checkers	8.7	6.6	3.7
Talk with Shop	2.4	1.5	1.8
Personal	5.8	4.7	3.1

The activities to be monitored can be set up to cover any special needs and the data obtained can be used to help evaluate the effect of changes on performance.

Time Standards. After the activity log data is evaluated, it is possible to establish the standard times required for different types of drawings. These types can have "level of complexity" weighting and can also be factored according to drawing size. The actual value of the standard is very dependent upon the activity needed to complete the particular drawing. Consequently the standards developed for TRW electronics drawings would have little meaning for any other company. They even require modification for use on different products within TRW electronics. However, some typical results are given below showing time for checking an E size drawing of moderate complexity.

Drawing	Checking Standard Time
Schematic	9.80
Wiring Diagram	7.70
Multi-layer artwork layout	41.00
Mechanical layout	9.10
Top assembly	13.90
Optics assembly	13.00
Welded Circuit Module	10.50

Program Material. Before active work measurement begins in a new area, a program plan is prepared describing how activity log and work sampling data collection will be performed, what reports will be prepared, and what information coding systems are to be established. The coding eliminates written description for an activity and permits using numbers useable in manual or computerized data compilation. These codes and activities are best worked out generally for the overall areas and then detail codes added for special applications.

Remarks

The program described above has provided several positive advantages and has been able to win over some supervisors whose reaction could be phrased "I have always done it another way that has always worked for me." Advantages realized from this system include:

(1) Performance problems are highlighted with enough data to help solve the problems.

(2) Knowledge of how time is spent provides background for working out methods for improving time effectiveness.

Factual time data has gained the expected usefulness described at the beginning of this paper. ■

The Author

GEORGE R. BECK is Manager, Cost Reduction and The Right Way Program, Value Assurance Staff, TRW Systems, One Space Park, Redondo Beach, Calif. 90278.

7.

How to Schedule and Control Engineering Projects

Plan projects scientifically with
Critical-path scheduling

To hit your target date without paying crash-program prices, focus first on the important jobs.

CHARLES J LYNCH

Diagram your project this way to discover four benefits

First, the relationship between jobs is clearly evident. Each arrow represents a job; each circled number a completion point. All jobs preceeding a circled number must be finished before following jobs can be started. Dashed arrows (dummy jobs) show that job at the tail of the arrow must be completed before starting job at the head of the arrow.

Second, you can quickly estimate how long the project will take. Working with a table of normal time estimates for each job, find the path through the diagram (see the gray line) that represents the greatest total time. This is the critical path.

Third, trimming time from the project is simply a matter of trimming time from jobs on the critical path. Of course, if you shorten a critical job too much its time may be less than a parallel noncritical job. Now you've got a new critical job. Although it gets a trifle complicated (and here's where computers come in), you can continue to shorten critical jobs—and noncritical jobs as they become critical—until the project is reduced to minimum time.

Fourth, you save money because, even with this "shortest possible" schedule, many jobs proceed at a normal pace and at normal cost.

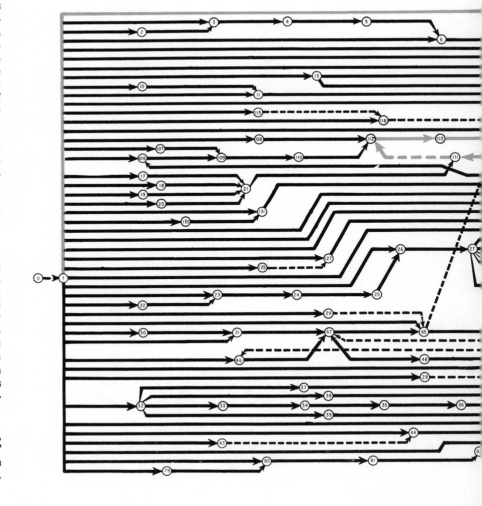

A "CRASH" program is traditionally just what its name implies— a dizzying plunge through the stratosphere of cost-plus contracts, doubled manpower requirements and overtime schedules, all of which comes to an abrupt and noisy conclusion against the unyielding commitment of a firm deadline date.

A better solution is provided by a new tool called Critical-path Scheduling (also known as the Critical-path Method or CPM). It is based on the seemingly obvious idea that the time needed for the whole project depends on the sum of times needed for only a small number of essential jobs (usually less than 20% of the total); speeding up the other jobs does nothing to hasten the completion date. By concentrating on these critical phases of a project, the reasoning continues, you will get the same result as an across-the-board crash program without paying an across-the-board cost penalty.

The scheduling procedure that evolved from this kind of reasoning is, today, more than an idea. Beginning with a trial run at DuPont's Louisville plant in 1957 (where it saved an estimated $1 million a year) it has since proven its usefulness in construction work, maintenance and plant improvement. A somewhat simplified scheme called PERT (for Program Evaluation and Review Technique) helped to expedite the Polaris program. And the Air Force uses a similar project-monitoring method called PEP (Program Evaluation Procedure).

The key to the critical-path method is a graphical plot, called an arrow diagram, which shows each phase of the project and its relationship to other phases. Like a Gantt chart (see *PE—Nov* 4 '57, *p* 34), the arrow diagram allows you to arrange the individual jobs and, based on the time required for each, you can estimate how long the project will take. But the arrow diagram goes further than this. With this new method of plotting, you can easily spot the critical jobs—those that will delay the whole project if they are delayed—and concentrating on these, you can decide where to speed it up and what it will cost.

The first step in the critical-path method is to list all the jobs that have to be done to complete a project. These will probably be listed roughly in sequence, but the order isn't important at this stage. Include only

of the critical-path method

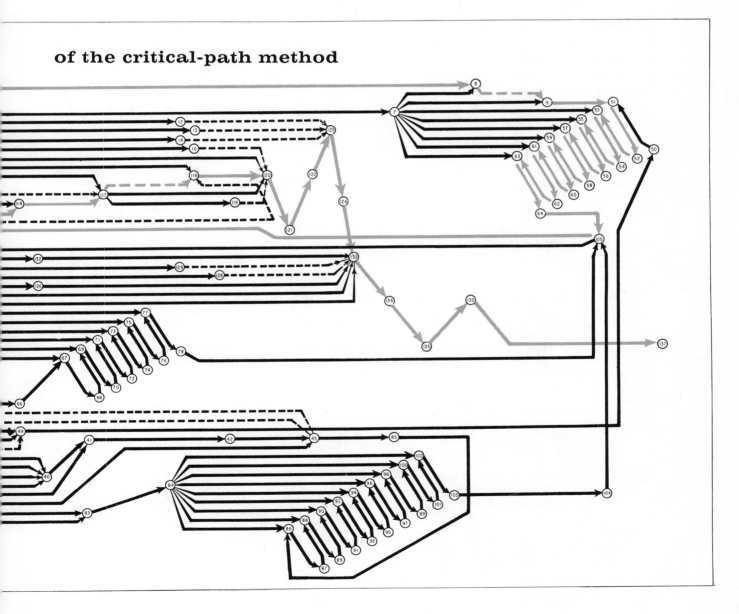

How to schedule a small design

FOR this example, we've chosen a gearbox—actually, the scheduling of a prototype gearbox for a new machine tool. The diagram is simple, there is no need for a computer, but the steps in the critical path method are the same no matter how large or small the project.

drawn to represent this. This is followed by three jobs, all of which can be started as soon as the design is complete: (B) drafting, (D) ordering special materials, (E) ordering bearings, oil seals and other purchased parts. Three arrows sprouting from the head of the first show

Shafts, housing and gears can all be made during the same time interval so these are shown as parallel arrow paths. All arrows terminate at the beginning of the assembly phase where they meet the arrow representing delivered and inspected purchased parts.

Now, referring to the normal job times previously agreed upon, it is easy to establish the critical path— the one requiring greatest total time. And these critical times tell how much float is available in parallel paths.

The project engineer is now ready to estimate how much time he can squeeze out of the project and what it will cost. Subtracting crash time from normal time and normal cost from crash cost and dividing the two gives him the cost slope which he enters as another column of the table. This is a measure of how costly it will be to speed up each job. Looking first at the job with zero float and lowest cost slope, and then moving on to more expensive critical jobs, he finds his expediting steps break down like this. (For purposes of computation —though this may not be true in practice—he assumes that it is possible to expedite a job to any desired point between the normal and crash times at a pro rata portion of the cost for an all-out crash program on that job.)

● The least expensive critical job is D. Because of the allowable float in parallel jobs B and C, he can cut **one week** at a cost of $20. Now B, C and D are all critical. But no more time can be pared from these

		Normal			Crash		
		Time, Weeks	Total Float, Weeks	Cost, $	Time, Weeks	Cost, $	Cost Slope, $/week
A	Design	2.5	0	450	1.5	700	250
B	Drafting	0.8	1.0	140	0.5	200	200
C	Check drawing	0.2	1.0	35	0.1	45	100
D	Deliver special materials	2.0	0	10	1.0	30	20
E	Deliver bearings, oil seals	1.5	3.3	10	0.5	20	10
F	Inspect purchased parts	0.1	3.3	20	0.05	25	100
G	Pattern for housing	2.3	0	350	1.3	550	200
H	Cast housing	0.2	0	50	0.1	75	250
I	Machine housing	0.4	0	100	0.3	150	500
J	Turn shafts	0.8	1.8	175	0.3	375	400
K	Heat treat shafts	0.3	1.8	75	0.3	75	. . .
L	Machine gear blanks	0.8	0.6	175	0.4	325	375
M	Cut gears	1.0	0.6	250	0.5	450	400
N	Heat treat gears	0.5	0.6	125	0.5	125	. . .
P	Assemble	2.0	0	300	1.0	600	300
				2265		3745	

Here's how it's done:

The project engineer starts with the gearbox specification prepared by the machine design group. Drawing on his experience with similar projects, he lists all the jobs that need to be done to deliver an assembled unit meeting these specifications. The list contains 15 jobs. He then calls in his chief designer, drafting-room supervisor and shop foreman, and they estimate time and cost of each job on both a normal and "crash" basis. In making the estimates for crash time and cost, they consider such expediting measures as overtime work, hiring additional manpower, and subcontracting special jobs.

The next step is to prepare the arrow diagram. The first job is obviously "design," so an arrow is

this relationship. Shop work can't begin until the drawing is checked and special materials arrive, so both these arrows terminate at the beginning of the shop work (4).

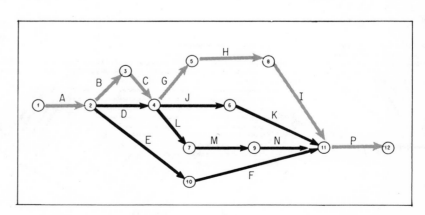

project

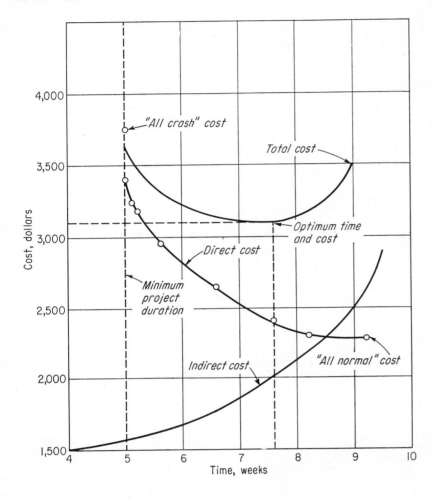

because D has already been reduced to the allowable minimum.

- He can save **0.6 weeks** by speeding up G. This costs him (0.6) (200) or $120. He could have saved a full week but there is only 0.6-week float in jobs L, M and N. With this compression, G is still the least expensive critical job. But to cut any more from G, he would have to cut an equal amount from L (the least expensive job in the parallel critical path) at a cost of $200 + $275 = $575 per week.

Continue to shave time from critical jobs and re-examining non-critical jobs as they become critical, he finds he can save

- **1 week** in A at a cost of $250
- **1 week** in P at a cost of $300
- **0.4 weeks** by trimming G and L at a cost of 0.4 (575) = $230
- **0.1 weeks** by compressing H

and M at a cost of 0.1 (650) = $65
- **0.1 weeks** by expediting I and M at a cost of 0.1 (900) = $90

At this point the project has been reduced to the minimum. Total time is 5 weeks, which is equal to the time of an "all-crash" project. But total cost is $3340 compared with $3745 for the "all-crash" project.

The curve above shows the relationship between project cost and time. This is combined with the curve for indirect project costs, using the established overhead figures for the departments involved. The total cost curve has a minimum point at 7.6 weeks, meaning he can produce the gearbox at minimum cost by expediting jobs D and G while allowing the other jobs to proceed on a normal schedule. This adds only $120 to the direct cost.

those jobs that are directly related to the project but don't be disturbed if the list gets long and cumbersome; the diagramming will straighten out the mess (it can handle as many as 1000 jobs if necessary).

To make the diagram, begin with the job that must be done first and draw an arrow to represent it. The length and direction of the arrow aren't important, although this first arrow will probably be a horizontal one pointing to the right. Now ask yourself which job follows the first job and whether there are other jobs that can be done at the same time. Draw an arrow (or arrows) to indicate this second job starting from the head of the previous arrow and pointing in whatever direction is convenient to provide space for other arrows. Jobs that can be done at the same time are drawn in parallel, like an electrical circuit, while jobs that must follow one another are drawn in series. If a job on one parallel path must be done before another job on another parallel path, show this relationship with a dotted arrow from the head of the first job to the tail of the second. Continue drawing arrows, working from left to right, until all jobs are represented.

What you have constructed is a progress chart—what must precede each job, what must follow it, and what can be done at the same time. Though its real usefulness is not yet evident, it has already yielded one important benefit: Because you were forced to think in terms of what must be done at what time, you have had to include every phase of the project.

Now go back to the list of jobs and add the time required to complete each. These time estimates are usually based on previous experience with similar jobs. If there is difficulty getting a reliable time estimate, try dividing the job into several smaller tasks for which more accurate estimates are available. Or, for research and development work, you might make three estimates—an optimistic one, a pessimistic one and a "most likely" one—combining them statistically to give an estimate which reflects a 50% probability that the job will be completed within the estimated time. Make all estimates, including the combined, three-level estimates, on the basis of normal working effort. Ignore speedup measures such as overtime or additional facilities and personnel for the moment.

With these time estimates in one hand and the arrow diagram in the other, you can quickly find the critical jobs. Trace a path through the diagram from left to right and add the time for each job on the path. Repeat this for all possible paths; the one with the longest time is the critical path and the jobs on it are the critical jobs. Tracing all possible paths through the diagram may sound like tedious work but it's actually much simpler than it looks. Even a complicated diagram can usually be divided into several smaller diagrams which are then attacked individually.

Notice that by defining the critical path you have eliminated from consideration a large number of noncritical jobs. Rushing these jobs can have no effect on the completion date for the project. Even a delay, providing it does not exceed that of the parallel critical jobs, will have no effect. The leeway between the time required for the critical jobs and the time required for noncritical jobs is called "float." If several series-connected, noncritical jobs are in parallel with the critical path, the amount of float assignable to any particular job will depend on when the preceding and following noncritical jobs are scheduled. For purposes of tabulation, the usual practice is to make all the float available to each series-connected job and decide how it will be divided later.

It is clear that to speed up a project, the critical jobs—those that have zero float—will have to be expedited. And the least expensive way to do this is to start with the jobs that cost least to expedite per unit time. From the table of time estimates, make an estimate of the total direct cost of each job assuming normal work effort. Then add another column to show the cost and time required if the job is done on a crash basis. Combining these four columns gives the cost slope—the cost increment divided by the time increment.

The table is your guide to compressing the project's schedule. Find the job that has zero float and the lowest cost slope. If this job is done on a crash basis, the length of the project will be reduced accordingly and its cost will go up by an amount equal to whatever it costs to "crash" this one job. Remember, however, that compressing one job may cause parallel jobs to go critical. Also notice that the over-all time saved by crashing a particular job can be no more than the available float.

For a project of practical size (say 100 jobs or more) you will need to draw up a new table for each reduction in project length. Otherwise, after one or two compressions, it will be difficult to tell which jobs are critical, which jobs have been compressed to the minimum, and how much float is available. By continuing to shave

time from the critical jobs, starting with the least expensive and working up, you can eventually pare the project to minimum length (equal to the "all crash" project length).

The sum of job costs—whether crash or normal—for the minimum length project is the most that needs to be spent. Notice that it is (probably) less than the cost of the "all-crash" program.

Direct project costs are not the whole story, however. There are also indirect costs or overhead (the cost of staying in business) and these must be added to the project cost. Generally, overhead increases directly with time, in contrast to direct costs, which decrease with time. These relationships emphasize the importance of preparing a complete direct project cost curve, from maximum time, minimum cost to minimum time, maximum cost. Adding the direct cost curve to the indirect cost curve gives a total cost curve that usually has a minimum point. This represents the least expensive schedule for the project.

Though the critical-path method will handle projects of almost any size, the tedious hand work required for a large project is more than most scheduling staffs would be willing to bear. This is particularly true for schedules that need continual revision (and even the best schedules do) to meet changes in cost and time as work

Rear Adm. William F Raborn, head of Special Projects Officer of the Navy, was chief promoter for PERT (the Navy's version of the critical path method). His insistence on using this method for scheduling the fantastically complex Polaris missile and submarine program was responsible for this weapons project being completed two years ahead of schedule.

proceeds. For these detailed calculations and recalculations, a computer is the only answer.

Several computer programs are presently available for the purpose. IBM has a program called LESS (Least cost EStimating and Scheduling). Sperry-Rand has a critical-path scheduling program for their Univac computer in addition to PERT and PEP programs, and Burroughs is working on a PERT program for their new B-5000 system. RCA recently announced a PERT program which they have used on their own scheduling problems and are now prepared to offer for general use. One of the most recent additions to the group is GE's CPM program for use on their 225 general-purpose computer.

Besides eliminating paperwork, computers offer other advantages. Time saving is, of course, one of them. With a computer spewing out new and revised schedules, management can stay on top of the project and head off potential problems before they get costly. Moreover, a computer can digest more information than its human counterpart and give answers in more detail. The GE program, for example, has provision for a priority weighting function that can be applied to each job. With this feature, noncritical jobs can be scheduled at a time that best suits the available resources and facilities by appropriate asignment of float.

Even more sophisticated developments are on the way. It is expected that there will soon be a method for scheduling several projects at once, interlacing them to make best use of the available equipment and personnel. Also, work is being done to combine the critical-path method with other modern management tools. Mathematical simulation, for example, could be used to examine particular parts of the critical path in detail. ∎

Brief course in PERT

M. Silverman

Whereas line of balance, Gantt charts and similar systems of management control are best applied to routine repetitive tasks, PERT (Program Evaluation Review Technique) really shows its power on research, development, and design projects. This is because PERT is designed to handle uncertainties in producing a single item or design—and it does so exceedingly well.

You start a PERT analysis by making an arrow diagram of events (circled numbers) joined by activities (arrows). Arrow length is not significant, but the sequence and interconnection must give a true picture of the activities which must be completed before the next activity becomes possible.

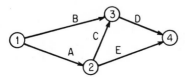

Here we have four numbered events joined by five lettered arrows. Assume that at event 1 engineering has released to drafting a design layout of a simple device plus a packet of sketches of the component parts. In PERT you list the events and the three estimates each manager makes for the length of time an activity will take. The optimistic estimate assumes everything will go better than expected. The most likely estimate indicates the time the job is expected to take. The pessimistic estimate assumes everything will go wrong.

Activity	Optimistic	Most likely	Pessimistic
A — detail drafting...........	2	3	5
B — list hardware required....	½	1	2
C — add critical tolerances....	½	1	4
D — draw master assembly...	2	3	6
E — make list of materials....	1	2	3

Two calculations are based on these figures. The first establishes the earliest expected time to accomplish each activity, t_e.

$$t_e = \frac{\text{(optimistic)} + 4\,\text{(most likely)} + \text{(pessimistic)}}{6}$$

The second calculation is of the variance (σ^2) for each activity.

$$\sigma^2 = \left[\frac{\text{(pessimistic)} - \text{(optimistic)}}{6}\right]^2$$

Activity	Optimistic	Most likely	Pessimistic	t_e	σ^2
A	2	3	5	3.2	0.250
B	½	1	2	1.1	0.063
C	½	1	4	1.4	0.341
D	2	3	6	3.3	0.445
E	1	2	3	2.0	0.111

Now, on the basis of expected times, t_e, trace through the diagram from left to right and find the earliest expected time at which each activity can be completed. Note that all activities leading to a given event must have been completed before the next event can start. List the time (T_E) in the table.

Tracing backwards with event 4 at 7.9 (the longest T_E, 1—2—3—4) you can find the latest expected time that each activity can be completed, T_L.

Slack is the difference ($T_L - T_E$). It tells you when the activity is on the critical path (slack = 0) and which activities have extra resources which may be used to expedite the more critical activities.

Activity	T_E	T_L	Slack
A	3.2	3.2	0
B	[(B) 1.1]	[(A-C) 4.6]	3.5
C	4.6	[(A-C) 4.6]	0
D	[(A-C-D) 7.9]	[(A-C-D) 7.9]	0
E	[(A-E) 5.2]	[(A-C-D) 7.9]	2.7

Now sum the variances for the critical path (A—C—D) and take the square root to find the standard deviation of the critical path.

Activity	Slack	σ^2
A	0	0.250
C	0	0.341
D	0	0.445

$$\Sigma\sigma^2 = 1.036$$
$$\sigma = 1.017$$

Now if the scheduled date is T_S (say 10 days in this example) the probability of meeting the schedule, P, can be estimated from $(T_S - T_E)/\sigma$ in the chart, which is a type of cumulative normal distribution.

$$\frac{T_S - T_E}{\sigma} = \frac{10 - 7.9}{1.017} = 2.065$$
$$P = 97$$

In this case there is roughly a 97% probability of meeting the schedule. If the scheduled completion date were 8 days there would be only 55% likelihood of meeting the schedule.

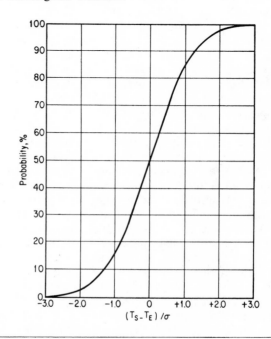

When PERT's too much, manage with MOST

Here's a procedure that helps you keep the smaller projects on schedule. Unlike PERT, it needs no computer

PERT has revolutionized the management of research and development. By breaking down every project into fine detail and identifying potential trouble spots, PERT networks have enabled managers to get submarines, missile systems, and other projects finished on schedule.

But what if a project is only a $50,000 contract to improve, say, a gas turbine? The customer wants it by a definite date, and the project manager had better meet the date if he wishes to keep the customer. For a small, relatively simple design job such as this, and even on some large jobs, PERT, though usable, is often inappropriate. It requires a computer, and the project may not warrant this expense.

Today the manager has a practical alternative in MOST (an acronym for Management Operation System Technique). MOST borrows ideas from PERT but displays project evolution on charts that are easy to read instead of in a computer tabulation. The technique was developed by Anthony Iannone, management planning specialist for Lycoming Div of Avco Corp in Stratford, Conn, who dubs his creation "poor man's PERT."

At a glance. In place of a computer, MOST relies on bar charts that show every step in a project, the latest possible date for starting each of these jobs to meet the deadline, and the progress made on each job. At a glance these charts show project managers where they stand. If work is falling behind, the manager knows in time that he must authorize overtime, hire more men, shift men from a job that's ahead of schedule to the one behind, or take other action.

A MOST chart does not give as much mathematical information as a PERT computer analysis, Talbert warns. But project planners at Lycoming have found that it gives enough information to make sound decisions. "MOST raises red flags

early enough that we can get back on schedule," says Talbert.

How it's done. The first step to a MOST chart is to draw a PERT-like network that breaks a project down into all its steps and indicates which steps can be accomplished simultaneously, which depend on prior solution of another, and how long each step should take. A critical path is established, showing the sequence of steps that will depend on one another and take the longest to accomplish. Delays on the critical path are special menaces to meeting a deadline, experience shows.

The PERT-like network is drawn after consultation with everybody responsible for a portion of the project. These people may include design engineers, test engineers, draftsmen, purchasing agents, and manufacturing engineers. Once they establish the PERT tracery, Iannone's group rearranges the data in bar chart form, working backward from the date the project must be finished.

Step by step. Take a simple case illustrated in the chart (right), which plots the design history of, say, a prototype actuator. It must be designed, tested, and assembled no later than the end of September. At that time, all the work on the critical path — represented by the long bar in the middle — and all five parallel paths must be complete.

The project engineer, getting this master plan from Iannone, knows he must begin inspection of in-plant designed parts no later than the first week in September. To meet this date, he must begin fabrication of these parts no later than the third week in August.

As the job goes along, Iannone and the project engineers meet periodically to discuss progress. If they conclude that the actuator is on schedule, Iannone blackens the bar. If it's behind, he leaves it white to show this.

Thus, the chart here shows that it

is the end of June — the vertical black line indicates the last progress meeting. (The line, incidentally, is a strip of tape that can be lifted up and laid down again after each meeting.) The chart also shows that the project manager is having trouble procuring forgings for special parts of the actuator and in procuring the tooling for these parts. But the chart tells him he is on schedule or ahead of schedule elsewhere.

Varied uses. The MOST charts also show other management control data, including cost and manpower loading. The number 3.0 (arrow) indicates that the job should take the equivalent of three men working three weeks to complete. The entry 2400 (arrow) represents anticipated cost of completing the design analysis and layout, including labor and overhead. A running total of actual manpower loading and costs at the bottom of the chart keeps management aware of whether the project is staying within budget or not.

This relatively simple MOST chart can be adapted to many other management control applications. It can do things PERT can't. The most important variation, says Iannone, is Multi-Project Planning (MPP). In many cases a member of the engineering staff will have three unrelated jobs to manage simultaneously. In addition to the actuator, he may be responsible for developing a valve system for corrosive fluids and completing a prototype of a new engine shroud.

The MOST planners graph these three projects as shown in the chart. Again they work back from the date each phase must be completed, to determine the very latest date when each phase of the three projects must be started. The charts show the manager at a glance how much manpower will be needed for each project, and they spotlight possible conflicts that may develop. The chart may show, for example, that test facilities will be overloaded in August. The project manager knows this early enough to start one of the projects earlier or to shift engineers over to the test department for the heavy period that is foreseen. ■

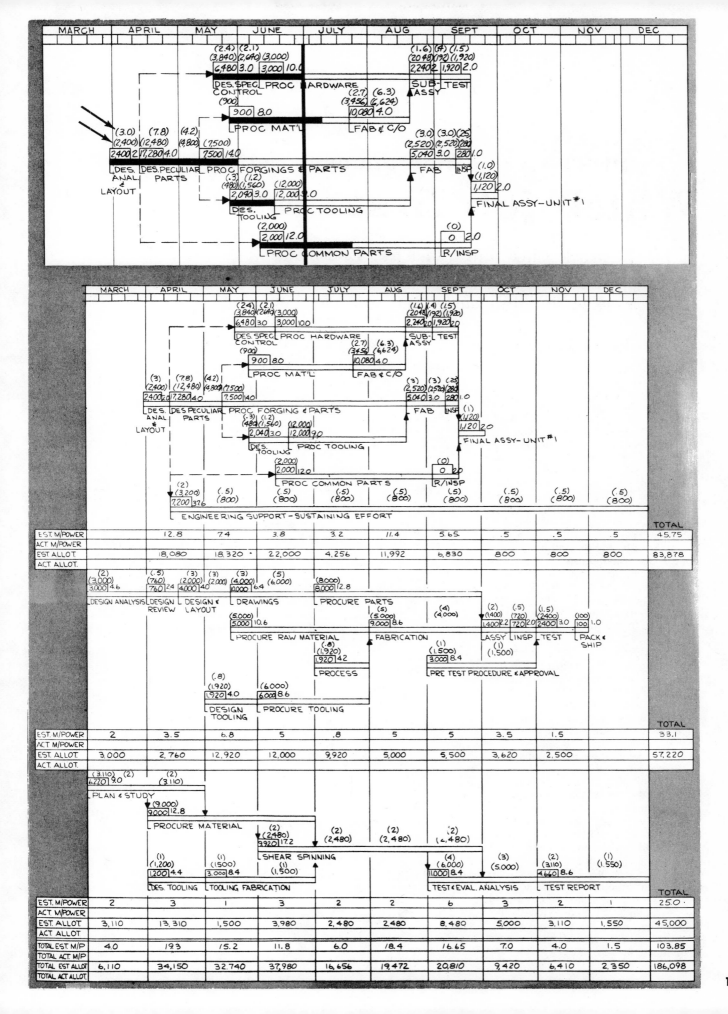

Which job first?

Network scheduling (such as PERT) assumes all parallel branches can be worked simultaneously. But suppose they can't?

DON R. TAYLOR, Utica, Mich

YOU have decided to use **PERT** (program evaluation and review technique, see the article on p. 128) on a small project. Carefully you list all the job activities and then draw up the network (Fig 1) and add estimated times. You are about to check for the critical path when suddenly you realize that as it stands the network is impossible. Activities 2-3 (prepare letter), 2-5 (prepare questionnaire), and 2-9 (visit designer) are assumed to run simultaneously, but they all have to be done by one man—you.

Of course, after 2-3, 2-5, and 2-9 are completed the other activities (to event 10) *can* run simultaneously because they are accomplished by others. But which of the three should you do first?

Every day we face the problem of sequencing jobs we have to do ourselves yet are prerequisites for action by others. If we sequence correctly the time required for project completion is at a minimum. If we sequence incorrectly the time required is sure to be longer.

Let us define the activities involved as composed of two sets: the activities which must be accomplished in series by the "individual", and the activities which can be accomplished in parallel by "others". Thus activity 2-3 (preparation of a letter) must be done by the individual, and activities from 3 to 10 (typing and sending of the letter, and receipt of an answer) although not accomplished by the same person are accomplished by others and will be thought of as one activity for sequencing purposes (Fig 2).

In what order should we sequence activities 2-3, 2-5, and 2-9 so that the

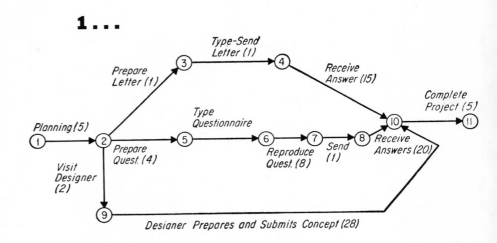

1...

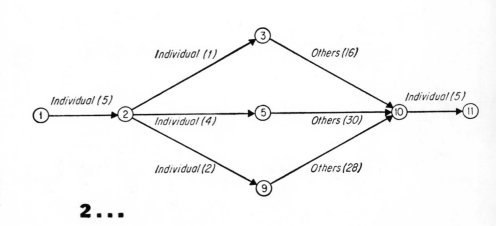

2...

calendar time required to move from event 2 to event 10 is a minimum? You might say, "I'll perform activities which require the least amount of time first." If this rule were applied the sequenced activities would appear as in Fig 3. The critical path from 2 to 10 (represented by the dotted line) requires 37 units of time for completion. But this does not give us the shortest critical path.

Derivation of a rule to aid us in optimum sequencing is deceptively short. Take two individual tasks A and B, followed by tasks C and D respectively which must be performed by others. Only two sequences are possible (Fig 4). What formula would always give sequence 1 a shorter criti-

cal path than sequence 2 regardless of the relative lengths of tasks A, B, C and D? The answer is:

$$(A + C) < (B + A + C) \ (1)$$

$$(A + B + D) < (B + A + C) \ (2)$$

Equation 1 reduces to $O < B$, which is self evident as long as B exists. Equation 2 reduces to $D < C$ or, in words:

Place first those activities performed by others which require the longest time for completion.

Application of this rule to the activities shown in Fig 3 will result in the arrangement shown in Fig 5.

The critical path is now 34 units of time in length. In this example

we saved 3 units of time through application of the rule. We have now provided optimum sequencing with respect to time and can now proceed with network development as desired (Fig 6).

After the rule is committed to memory it becomes a way of life and you will sequence your activities in an optimum manner automatically.

An interesting sidelight to the rule is that optimum project planning is dictated not by your work but by the work of others. Therefore the ability to work with people and the ability to predict and control their efforts as well as your own is once again shown to be the most important part of project management. ∎

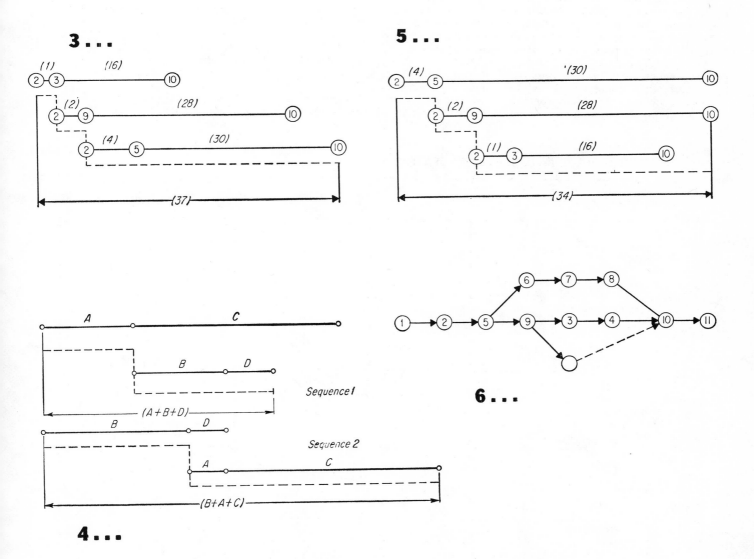

3...

5...

4...

6...

To smooth and speed development, assign

Design responsibility

The path of a new product is beset with
delays and "gray areas" of authority.
Here is a way to clear out the briers.

ADOLPH NEADERLAND, Engineering Manager, Utility-Industrial Div, Burndy Corporation

PROVIDING for the continuity of flow from product concept to consumer often means the difference between success and failure in penetrating a market with a new product. With so many producers searching for new-product areas, it is essential to minimize the developmental and **initial** production time. Many companies are trying to streamline their prod-

uct-development sections to cope with this increased pace of activity, remain flexible enough to handle a variety of assignments and reduce interdepartmental friction.

New products generally follow a typical cycle (chart), and many opportunities for queueing delays prevail. It can also be assumed that excess capacity in these departments is not such

that work could start immediately. Conversely, it can be assumed that the output of the engineering department is a continuum, and all service sections are loaded relative to capacity; hence each new service requirement arrival will face some delay.

The developmental nature of the first stage (design) precludes accurate scheduling, the deviation possibly ex-

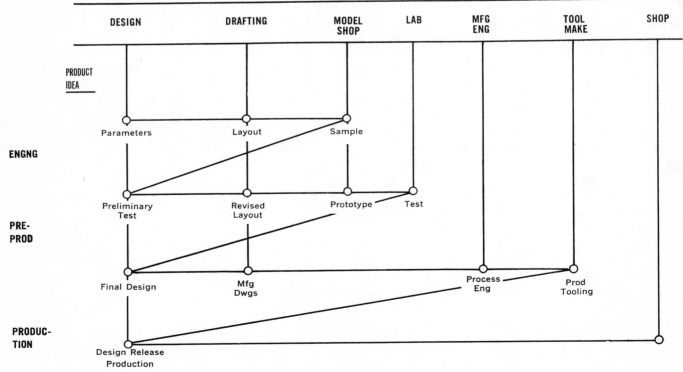

SIMPLIFIED LIFE CYCLE OF PRODUCT DEVELOPMENT

(Many important sub-sequences, such as purchasing, value analysis, reliability and quality-control activities, are left out for simplicity in charting.)

ceeding the total scheduled time. This is certainly true where some "state of the art" is being pressed, perhaps in new-material applications or delicate fabrication requirements. The first developmental cycle is often repeated in the process of narrowing the design parameters to commercial acceptability. These secondary cycles again increase scheduling difficulties, adding waiting time to the calendar life of a product development. Incremental waiting times may exceed the actual working time by a factor of two.

Historically, however, the major point of delay has been the transition from design engineering to production. In most manufacturing organizations, the engineering and manufacturing departments report, in classical fashion, to independent top-level executives. Because the line organization is faced with daily maintenance problems, new-product co-ordination takes on the onus of interruption and is attended to grudgingly. Thus up through the late 1940s, products were essentially completely designed in Engineering, largely without manufacturing guidance (or knowledge) and literally dumped on the manufacturing organization for production. Repercussions were many and serious:

a) Delays from redesign for production.

b) Delays from personality clashes between the two groups, as a result of (a).

c) Production costs excessive for proper profit levels.

d) Disruption of production schedules by the introduction of the new item(s).

All the above are interrelated and reflect subjective feelings of limited responsibility. Engineering feels responsible only for design; someone else will make it. Production feels responsible for making "something" but, not having had a hand in design, assumes incomplete responsibility for cost (and sometimes function) or schedule.

In the late Forties, a trend developed to strengthen the liaison with Manufacturing at an early stage, providing the definitive responsibility transfer at the time production drawings were officially turned over to the line manufacturing organization. Interviews with many such groups indicated that the "responsibility" problem was not resolved by this action, although considerable redesign delay was eliminated.

Many engineering groups suggested that the Production "veto" (ie non-approval of the production drawing) limited the scope of design to conventional manufacturing processes. The traditional search for broader tolerances to ease manufacturing operations could stratify design effort.

The problem of responsibility and its relation to job satisfaction by the participants is the key to this dilemma. An organization based on the approach of "unity of responsibility" is proposed. To evolve such an organization, it is first necessary to examine the responsibilities of the various groups involved, and their inter-relationships.

Three primary factors are involved in design of a new product:

1) Function (technical requirements)

2) Cost (economic requirements)

3) Schedule (marketing requirements)

Product design in its totality requires a functional product, produced at a cost to return a predetermined profit, to be marketable at a predetermined date. If each factor were considered a vector, there would appear to be a "maximin" criterion needed to satisfy all conditions. Attempts to maximize profit, minimize schedule or optimize function independently clearly will not optimize the total situation. To optimize function, vector components are created that tend to drive costs up and to lengthen schedule. Minimizing cost would form vector components tending to lengthen the schedule and make the function marginal. Similarly, attempting to minimize the schedule would also force a marginal design with excessive costs.

It is clear, therefore, that for each product problem condition a unique solution exists of manpower and internal schedule to satisfy the parameters of Cost-Function-Schedule. Unfortunately, most such conditions are difficult, if not impossible, to quantify, making it necessary to seek other logic. Systems engineering, or a major project effort, would warrant the attention of a staff group to oversee the coordination of the many technical and administrative disciplines that become necessary. Much has been published on this subject; it is not the purpose here to expand in this area.

It is the smaller project, representing the bulk of the industrial technical effort of our economy, that faces the basic problem of coordination. It would seem reasonable, and consistent with the earlier argument of responsibility and job satisfaction, that primary responsibility for the over-all project should rest with the group whose function represents the most critical (sensitive) components. The assignments of such responsibility are shown in the table below.

The difficulties encountered by many organizations result from non-recognition that emphasis varies from project to project, requiring flexibility to shift primary responsibility as is required. Each group's participation should be weighed carefully at the outset. Organizational responsibilities for implementation should then be specified.

Responsibility for the "producibility" function will vary with the emphasis on the factors noted previously. The various transitions from phase to phase are diagrammed on the next page. *A* illustrates the situation in which the manufacturing group assumes primary responsibility as soon as the basic design concepts have been solidified. *B* illustrates that situation which requires the engineering groups to maintain primary responsibility until initial production is verified and the project stabilized.

Many engineering departments will find themselves unprepared for the responsibility which will be properly assigned, as a result of the specific project under consideration. In fact, many organizations will find that the nature of their general effort would place basic coordination responsibility (ie, design through initial production) for a large percentage of their new products in Engineering. To support the design engineers in this new

WHICH GROUP KEEPS THE MAJOR RESPONSIBILITY?

RATIO	MAJOR RESPONSIBILITY	
	Manufacturing	Engineering
High labor/material cost High material/labor cost Long development/mfg toolup time Long mfg toolup time/development time	Cost Schedule	 Cost Schedule

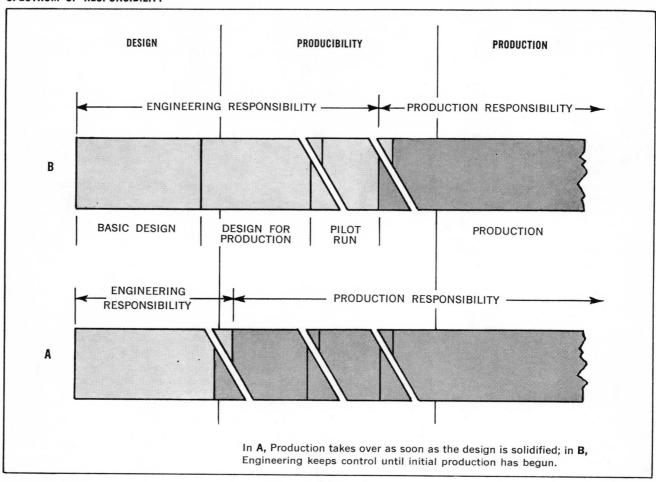

DESIGN　　　　PRODUCIBILITY　　　　PRODUCTION

←——— ENGINEERING RESPONSIBILITY ———→ ←— PRODUCTION RESPONSIBILITY —→

B

BASIC DESIGN　　DESIGN FOR PRODUCTION　PILOT RUN　　PRODUCTION

←— ENGINEERING RESPONSIBILITY —→ ←——— PRODUCTION RESPONSIBILITY ———→

A

In **A,** Production takes over as soon as the design is solidified; in **B,** Engineering keeps control until initial production has begun.

role, it is necessary to provide the "producibility" information required for proper design (ie, fulfilling the restraints of cost, in addition to function).

If design engineers can be adequately trained (and kept current) in modern production practices, the ideal solution has been found. Generally, however, this is not the case. As a substitute, it is desirable to form the nucleus of a production engineering group in the engineering department. These qualified manufacturing engineers would be assigned to work with the design engineer and guide the design in manufacturing practice. It would also be their responsibility to communicate and coordinate the progress of the project with all of the live organizations—Manufacturing, Production Control, Accounting, Purchasing, Quality Control, etc. Because this group would report to the senior engineering executive, it could be held accountable for the performance on the project by the chief executive officer.

Where the organization has a high proportion of engineering "projects," this producibility group would be large. On the other hand, where the number of engineering projects varies, the group could fluctuate with personnel on temporary assignment from Production. Keeping such personnel current with shop practice is most important. A cross-training program with production personnel should be instituted, rotating personnel on a regular basis.

All these factors, properly coordinated, will reduce friction within the organization by placing responsibility where it belongs, thus reduce delays. ∎

To preserve ideas, reduce duplication

Keep a project docket

Here is a systematic way to record the history of a project—and all that was learned on the way.

STEPHEN E. LEHMANN, Project Engineer, Surface Armament Div, Sperry Gyroscope Co, Div Sperry Rand

MOST complex equipment takes years to develop and produce. Thousands of manhours are spent, hundreds of ideas conceived and then incorporated into the final drawings. But drawings and specifications do not record experience, define purpose, or evaluate equipment. So we set up a special file.

We call it a docket, because it will contain a lot more than drawings and specifications. It records the purpose, characteristics and history of the project, the reasons for the design, its accomplishments and shortcomings, improvements made, future considerations. It is the only way a company can hope to learn from experience.

The project docket contains 12 sections, each with an outline of the material to be included or a questionnaire requiring specific answers. A milestone chart is added to guide the engineer as to the time particular entries should be made. The docket is periodically reviewed by the project engineer's supervisor to check its completeness. A summary sheet records responsible participants, a list of project reviews, and a distribution list.

1

FUNCTION

This is the engineer's assignment to provide a design for a particular purpose. The section will be referred to by designers, publication writers, sales, field and manufacturing engineers, so that the project engineer need not repeatedly explain the purpose of the device.

The section should include:

1) Function of the device in the over-all system — its reason for existence.
2) How the device is expected to perform.
3) How the device accomplishes its function or purpose.
4) Physical description, including size, weight, material, etc.

PROJECT DOCKET

TITLE: ___TRACKER___   P/N ___1040931___

DESCRIPTION:

 Function in overall system
 Performance characteristics
 Functional description
 Physical description (size, weight, material, special components).

Function in System

 The function of the Tracker is to align the L/X band video with the C band video by automatically correcting for any delays due to relative Doppler shifts between the two videos.

Performance Characteristics

 The Tracker will align the C'l gate (which is centered with the C band video) with the L/X band video (which is delayed before being supplied to the Tracker for reasons described later). This is accomplished by measuring any misalignment and supplying a correction voltage to the Integrator, UD115410 (see description), causing a shift of the video to its correct position. The unit is capable of tracking two [...]

DESIGN CONSIDERATIONS

2 Here the engineer describes all the alternative designs considered, giving advantages and disadvantages of each and reasons for the final selection. This section may be a duplicate of the engineer's note book and his progress reports but in the project docket the ideas are preserved for others. This section is reviewed when problems arise. It should prevent pseudo solutions and duplication of past experiences and should foster new approaches. It is a defense of the present design.

PROJECT DOCKET

TITLE: TRACKER   P/N   1040931

DESIGN CONSIDERATIONS:

List all designs considered with advantages and disadvantages of each including analytical considerations and reason for the selection of this design.

DESIGN CONSIDERATIONS

The major consideration in the design of the Tracker was the shape of the video. The shape of the main lobe is parabolic

INFORMATION TO DESIGN

3 This includes reference to specifications, manuals, parts, etc., required by company practice, product requirements, or the contract. This section will vary in accordance with company operating procedures. A check list is a worth-while approach for forwarding information in an organized manner.

PROJECT DOCKET

TITLE _TRACKER_   P/N _1040931_
                U.D. _115425_

E. I. CHECK LIST

    SUAD
    Design Manual
    Reference

         1. Electrical Review
            A. Consistent with System Functional
               Requirements   Yes ✓ No ___
            B. Conformance with Operating
               Conditions
               1. Variations in line voltage and
                   frequency (including transients)   Yes ✓ No ___
               2. Temperature and humidity   Yes ✓ No

RELIABILITY

4 This section should be formulated in accordance with reliability requirements, company policy, product requirements, specifications, or the contract. It may vary from brief statements of policy to an elaborate check list. Here you can compare tested reliability of a device with intended or calculated reliability.

PROJECT DOCKET

TITLE: _TRACKER_   P/N _1040931_

RELIABILITY-MAINTAINABILITY DESIGN REVIEW CHECK LIST

Product No. _936_   Schematic No. _2389138_   Unit Engineer _W. GRUENEBAUM_

Unit Desig. No. _115425_   Designer _R. GIRGENTI_

Unit Name _TRACKER_   Reliability Engineer _A. KALINOUSKY_

Design Review Date _11/6/61_   (Date all entries made after Design Review)

DESIGN CONSIDERATIONS	YES	NO	REMARKS

TEST REQUIREMENTS

5 This includes the purpose of the test, its procedure, and the amount of engineering participation required. This section will guide the test department in planning and performing the tests. Field engineers will also refer to this section to fulfill field test requirements.

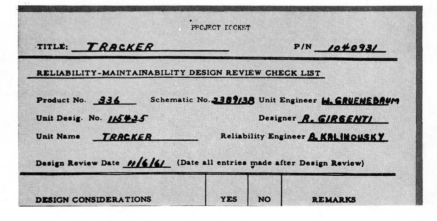

PROJECT DOCKET

TITLE: _____ TRACKER

TEST REQUIREMENTS: (Include tolerances and accuracies involved):   P/N ___ 1040931

    Special areas or test fixtures
    Standard Test equipment
    Product equipment
    Power supplies

PROJECT DOCKET

TITLE: TRACKER   P/N 1040931

DESIGN PARTICULARS:

Limitations of present design
Future design considerations

Limitations of Present Design

The present desi...

DESIGN PARTICULARS

This section covers two areas: 1) limitations of present design because of space, weight, environmental requirements, invoked specifications, etc. and 2) design improvements and value engineering recommendations that cannot be included in a present order but should be considered on new orders or any contemplated redesign.

6

PROJECT DOCKET

TITLE: TRACKER   P/N 1040931

MAJOR PROBLEMS:

(significant problems encountered in development, mfg. test and in the field)

Date	Outline Each Major Problem & Corrective Action Taken
10/9/62	Gain stability of coincidence amplifiers did not suffice

MAJOR PROBLEMS

Here are listed the problems encountered in development, manufacturing, testing, and field performance as well as the corrective action taken. A major problem can be defined as one that should be recorded for future reference or one that requires changing previous entries in the docket. The main purpose here is to provide a means of evaluation and avoid repeating past errors.

7

PROJECT DOCKET

TITLE: TRACKER   P/N 1040931

RECOMMENDED SPARE PARTS

P/N	Description	P/N	Description
2392251	Transistor		
1507016	Diode		
2392261	Diode		
1632374-1	Electronic Tube		

RECOMMENDED SPARE PARTS

If the device or a component cannot be replaced in the field without elaborate test or assembly techniques the engineer will recommend replacing the entire unit. Also listed here are replacement parts that should be kept on hand. This section is to be used by purchasing and spare parts provisioning groups.

8

PROJECT DOCKET

TITLE: TRACKER   P/N 1040931

MAJOR NUMBERS OF THIS ASS'Y

Number	Title	Qty
2389138	K/A Schematic (electrical)	
4073268	K/A Wiring Diagram	
T1177505	K/A Test Spec.	
EB629572	K/A Engineering Bulletin	
2006543	K/A Signal Flow Diagram	

DRAWING AND SPEC NUMBERS

This is simply an index of pertinent numbers: drawing numbers, wiring diagrams, test specifications, etc.

10

GENERAL INFORMATION

This section records such items as contract numbers, quantities ordered, serial numbers assigned, similarity to other units, special processes and tools required, names of vendors or subcontractors, and cost information. This section is to be used as a reference for future quotations and orders.

PROJECT DOCKET

Title: TRACKER   P/N 1040931

General Information:

1. List special or unusual processes, vendors, tools, and their costs.

2. Other pertinent data. (Including similarity with other units)

A.O.	Qty	Serial Number used

11

DOCKET TRANSFER QUESTIONNAIRE

This section is used when a project engineer is transferring his responsibility to another. It is a statement of engineering status. The responsible engineer fills out this section in the presence of his replacement. The supervisor approved the answers. This questionnaire should enable the new project engineer to assume his responsibility with minimum effort.

PROJECT DOCKET

TITLE: TRACKER   P/N 1040931

DOCKET TRANSFER QUESTIONNAIRE

DATE AUGUST 8, 1961

FROM E. FULLER   TO H. GRUENEBAUM

SECTION HEAD R. KNECHT   SECTION HEAD R. KNECHT

A. This questionnaire should be answered at the time of the transfer of responsibility of a unit. It should supply the recipient of the responsibility with sufficient information to assure a smooth transfer.

B. The following questions should be answered by the present responsible

12

SUMMARY SHEET

The first portion, "Responsible Participants," records the names of individuals concerned in the development, design, and manufacturing phases. This portion is used to trace people who may contribute or advise currently responsible engineers and others when questions or problems arise.

The second portion, "Docket Distribution," records location of particular sections to enable the engineer to inform those relying on the docket for information about changes.

The third portion, "Docket Review," records changes and reviews. Docket reviews should be conducted periodically by the engineer's supervisor.

DOCKET SUMMARY SHEET

Title TRACKER   SFN 1040931

RESPONSIBLE PARTICIPANTS

ENGINEERING			PRODUCT METHODS			QUALITY CONTROL		
From	To	Name	From	To	Name	From	To	Name
JUN/61	AUG/61	E. FULLER	AUG. 61	–	P. GAETA	AUG. 61	–	B. KALINOWSKY
AUG/61	–	H. GRUENEBAUM						

Design Layout by W. MARX   Checked by: P. AIELLO

Date Layout Completed 12/8/61   Date Dwgs. Released 12/14/61

DOCKET DISTRIBUTION

Date	Name	Dept.	Dept. No.	Sections	Remarks
11/22/61		QC/PUBS.			
12/11/61		PUBS/F.S.		1	
12/18/61		PUBS/F.S.		1	

DOCKET REVIEW

Date	Eng.	Appvl. Sys. Eng. or E.S.H.	Sections Revised	Date	Eng.	Appvl. Sys. Eng. or E.S.H.	Sections Revised
8/61	E. FULLER	R. KNECHT	NONE				

13

MILESTONE CHART		
MILESTONE	SECTION	DOCKET ENTRIES
1. . Assignment of responsibility	1	Purpose of unit Function in overall system
2. . Release of engineering information to design	2 3 4 5 7	List of design considerations Engineering Information check list Reliability check list and work sheet Preliminary test requirements Major problems during development
3. . Signing of design layout	1 2 3 5 6 Summary sheet	Physical description of unit Additional design considerations during layout Reliability Review and revise test requirements Design limitations Add names of responsible participants in the design
4. . Release of drawings for manufacturing	All 8 9 All Summary sheet All	Assign identification or part numbers Recommend parts to be spared List major drawing and specification numbers Review entire docket Obtain required approvals record docket distributions File docket in department file
5. . Production and use	7 8 6 11 Summary sheet	List major problems and corrective action taken Monitor spare recommendations List future design considerations Transfer of responsibility questionnaire Keep up to date
6. . Completion of production or company responsibility	11 All	Transfer of responsibility questionnaire Review and file in archives

MILESTONE CHART

This sheet tells the project engineer when entries are to be made in the docket. It puts entries and additions in logical sequence and prevents neglect of a particular section.

14

FILING

The sections of the docket can be clipped to the right-hand side of a filing folder, the summary sheet and milestone chart to the left-hand side. The sections should be readily removable for duplication and the contents legibly recorded for future reference. The folders should be placed in a departmental file in accordance with a company's identification procedure. ∎

Special Visual-Control Board

GRAYSON D. KIRTLAND
Wassell Organization, Inc.

MOST CHIEF ENGINEERS or administrative engineers will agree that all engineering projects must be scheduled and controlled. But the big questions are how much scheduling and control, and what kind.

The chief engineer of a small group usually keeps his schedules and control procedure in his head, while the chief engineer of a large engineering staff may need an elaborate system of paperwork and several administrative assistants to help him. In between, some responsible engineers work from their heads when they should be using a formal control system, and others who go too far in the other direction.

Just enough scheduling and control serves two purposes: (1) It improves engineering department operations and, (2) it enables top management, sales, advertising and production to keep tabs on engineering, whom they are frequently inclined to regard as the bad boys of the organization.

Just what is enough control? Defined loosely it is control to a degree which enables the chief engineer or

Fig. 1—Typical visual control board showing horizontal and vertical tape pegs. Job order cards at left serve as reference.

Job Number	↓	Proposal Prep 1	Prelim Layouts 2	Prelim Design 3	Prelim Aero, Stress, Weights 4	Design Layout 5	Detail Design 6	Assembles 7	Aero, Stress, Weights 8	Tests 9	Final Check 10		AUGUST 2 4 6 8 10 12 14 1 3 5 7 9 11 13 15
Peg hole - - - -		- - - - 10	20	30	40	50	60	70	80	90	100		10
67x-D-a	1											1	
67x-D-b	2					▨						2	◯
67x-D-c	3				▨							3	◯
67x-D-d	4					▨						4	
67x-D-e	5					▨						5	
67x-D-f	6			▨								6	
67x-D-g	7			▨								7	
67x-D-h	8			▨								8	◯
67x-D-i	9				▨							9	
67x-D-j	10				▨							10	

Peg hole number is for convenience in counting off spaces

Current status of job

Date current operation started

Fig. 2—Section of visual control board showing scheduling and control

other responsible head to have, at his finger tips, the whole story about every significant phase of the engineering operations.

A visual control board can be used to good advantage if there are many points to check in the process of maintaining control. This board is the apex of a paperwork production control system and sums up all production data. The department head has, in the board, a visual record of the progress on all projects, what ones are off schedule and whether anything is being done to get them back on schedule.

A picture of one such control board is shown in Fig. 1. Physically the board is a grid of punched holes into which small pegs can be inserted. Some of the pegs are attached to elastic tapes that run under the left hand panel covering this portion of the board. The pegs and tapes can be used to set up horizontal lines on the board. Other pegs connected to tapes can be inserted in the board to make vertical lines. In addition, individual pegs can be inserted any place on the board to record specific information.

For discussion purposes, we can assume a hypothetical aircraft development design project. The engineering groups working on the project and some of their jobs follow. The number of the project is 67X.

From previous designs, we can assume also that sufficient performance data is available to schedule each group. This includes specifying the number of men working on the project, the time allowed for each operation, and the starting and finishing dates. This is a big job, but not particularly difficult provided the scheduling group uses the performance data available and avoids wild guesses. Performance data may be based on pounds of structure per engineering man-hour, square feet of drawing per man-hour, number of parts per man-hour, or any other reliable index that has been found to work. Each company develops its own units of performance to measure man-hour output. It is sufficient to say that there are few companies who cannot work up some reliable performance data.

Returning to the aircraft project, the next step is to post the schedule on the control board. In Fig. 2 is shown the control board setup for one group only, the design group. The rest of the board setup for other groups is the same except that the vertical column headings, which break the jobs down to successive operations, will be different. On the sample board shown all jobs have started before August 1, hence no starting peg locations are shown. The scheduled finish dates, however, for each job (such as 67X-D-d) are posted using pegs shaped as horizontal arrows. In posting the overall schedule for each job on the board, detailed information relating to that job is entered on a job card.

This card is put in the cardex on the left side of the board and identifies each horizontal line on the board. The cards overlap so that the last line only is seen. Listed on the card is the job, the operations involved, the scheduled starting and finish dates, and other information needed for job analysis and future projects.

Next, the schedules for the current operations (for example, Design Layout on job 67X-D-d) for each job are posted. As shown, round pegs are used to show the starting and finishing dates. Note that the operation schedule dates shown at any one time apply only to the operation indicated by the rectangular peg in the current status section of the board.

The next feature is the "today's date" line, which is advanced day by day. If, on any one day, the "today's date" line passes the round peg indicating when the current operation of a job is scheduled to be finished, the indication is that the operation is lagging behind schedule. If this happens, a follow-up peg can be posted to indicate that action must be taken on the operation that has fallen behind. One color follow-up peg can be used to call for follow-up action and another color follow-up peg to show that action has been taken.

If, on the other hand, an operation is finished before the scheduled date, the schedule clerk removes the scheduled dates for that operation and posts the scheduled dates for the next successive operation, thus keeping the board up to date. ∎

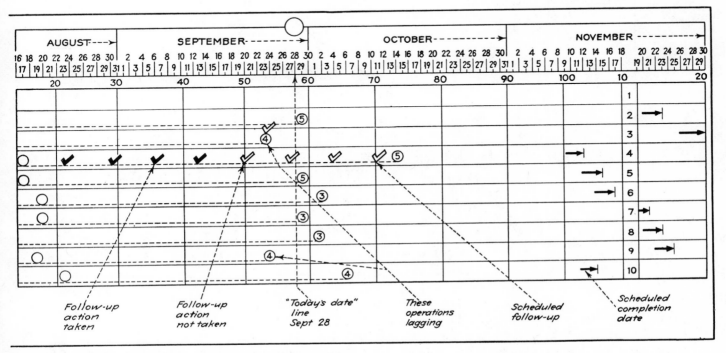

information for a design group working on an aircraft project.

How to keep score on an engineering project

J. G. ADILETTA

*American Machine & Foundry Co.
General Engineering Laboratories,
Greenwich, Conn.*

Are your projects late? Do 90% of the costs suddenly accumulate in the final 10% of the time? Do delays catch you unprepared?

If the answer to any of these questions is "Yes", you need a control system—some way of recording and transmitting information. Written reports, tabulations, and charts or graphs are the three common methods; each has advantages in particular applications.

A written report will record a simple fact or two about the progress of a project, or an item within it. A tabulation or graph wastes time and effort in this case; the graph may even cause inaccuracy if specific figures must be found by interpolation.

Information for a number of projects of items is usually best presented in tabular form. Associated elements can be grouped; exact figures are in systematic arrangement. Time and effort are saved for both recorder and reader as long as the number of categories or items is not unwieldy.

Both written and tabular methods, however, offer complications if direct comparisons (of schedule and performance, for example) are desirable. Too many words, or too many column headings, are required, so the data become confusing.

Charts and graphs, however, show clearly a comparison between performance and planned activity for a number of items or projects at regular intervals. They easily relate progress to manpower, schedule dates, and over-all project costs. Two of the most common graph types and their applications are shown here. Both are simple to produce and to read; they will show you the score without delay or waste of time. ∎

How to present manpower data

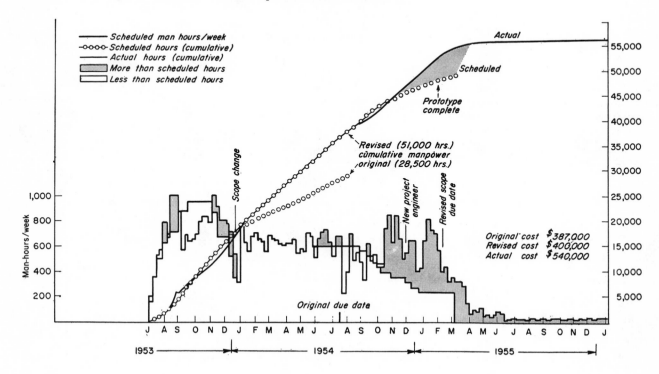

Scheduled man-hours per week, actual and scheduled man-hours cumulative, more-than-scheduled and less-than-scheduled hours—all these are shown on one chart with calendar dates as the abscissa. Notations at certain dates record program changes. Useful in planning and estimating, this chart is too all-encompassing to provide day-to-day control.

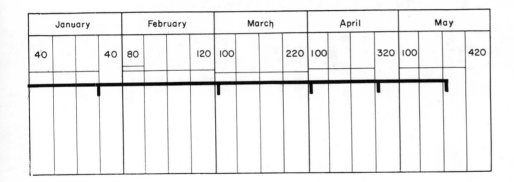

January		February		March		April		May	
40	40	80	120	100	220	100	320	100	420

A project can be monitored with a Gantt chart

Horizontal bars or lines compare schedule and actual work done. In the 5-month example shown, for a typical manufacturing operation, each month is divided into quarters. These do not represent time, but units produced, and the value changes with the monthly budget. As charted, the Jan. budget is 40 units (figure at upper left); Feb. 80; and the remaining three months, 100 each. This makes the value of each division in Jan., 10 units; in Feb., 20; in the other months, 25.

Units actually produced are: Jan., 30; Feb., 100; Mar., 100; Apr., 75; May, 75. These totals are shown as light black lines. The Jan. line covers 30/40 of the width (showing 75% of budget completed), Feb. line covers 100/80 (showing 125% completed), etc. Lines for adjacent months are stepped up or down slightly so there is no appearance of continuity, and any overproduction (i. e., Feb.) appears as a second line above. Thus, month-by-month comparison of scheduled and actual work is charted in an easily interpreted form.

Total accomplishment for the period can also be charted against that scheduled—in this case by the cumulative line (shown in color). In Jan., lines are the same length. In Feb., however, 10 units must be applied to complete the Jan. schedule (last division), so 90 are left. This carries the cumulative line through Feb. (80 units) and 10 units into Mar. (where each division is 25 units). In Mar., the full schedule is completed, so the cumulative line projects 10 units into Apr. But in Apr. and May (25-unit divisions), only 75% of the budget is completed, so one full division is lost in each month. Thus, at end of May, the job is 1.6 divisions (or 40 units) behind schedule. This can be read at a glance.

Is is customary also to show cumulative scheduled output as a number in upper right-hand corner of each monthly division. This type of chart is named after Gantt, its inventor, has been used for decades in production control, and is still one of the most effective and graphic methods.

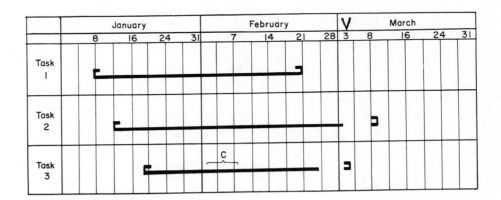

		January				February				March			
		8	16	24	31	7	14	21	28	3	8	16	24	31
Task 1														
Task 2														
Task 3					C									

Engineering progress can be Gantt-charted too

Any human activity can be shown on a Gantt chart, because it relates actual progress of each task to scheduled progress relative to a time scale, and spots problem areas. Here is an adaptation charting engineering progress. Note that each month is divided arbitrarily into eight sections by dates, so the value of each division in Jan. and Mar. is 31/8 days, while in Feb. it is 28/8 (or 3.5 days). A 3-sided box (colored) shows initiation and scheduled-termination dates for each task. The V in color (at Mar. 3) signifies chart-drafting date.

It is immediately apparent that Task 1 was completed on schedule, Task 2 is one day behind schedule, Task 3 is seven days off.

Additional information can be shown on this chart by suitable notations. For example, a short vertical line with an identifying letter over it can indicate a delay and its cause, or two bracketed lines can show the duration of a delay. On Task 3, a time loss of seven days is thus shown, with an explanatory "C" for engineering changes.

149

A New Scheduling Technique...
The "Production-Line-of-Balance"

M. SILVERMAN

A relatively new technique, line of balance (LOB), is actually a monitoring tool to be used in a control system. Its purpose is to give the manager a measure of where his project is with respect to where it ought to be according to the original plan. Line of balance was first applied to the production line and here its greatest advantages still remain. It assumes that you have a number of parts which must be purchased, manufactured, or processed. The parts will make subassemblies and then be combined to make completed products which can be shipped to the customer.

The monitoring is usually not a continuous process—it is done at monthly or weekly intervals—but the analysis will show clearly where the delays are, if any, and where certain processes are moving faster than expected.

To set up an LOB for a project you start with a forecast of deliveries. This production schedule will also carry the cumulative plot of assemblies actually shipped, so horizontal differences between the two lines are a measure of time delay or advance. Vertical differences indicate quantity delay or advance. Slope differences indicate variations in production rate.

Next draw up a flow chart showing when the parts are to be made or bought and how they flow together to make subassemblies and assemblies. Work backwards from the finished product (0 time) to the major and then the minor parts. Measure line lengths horizontally according to a scale of working days. This entire chart might be based on a PERT diagram, but note that here the line length *is* important and the individual branches may start at widely varying points along the time scale. (In the sample above the sleeve actuator need not be started until some 15 days after the rod-end extension has started in production—74 days minus 59 days.)

Now number the important milestone or benchmark points which you will be monitoring. The various supervisors will report progress at all of these points to you at the monitoring intervals. Number from left to right in time sequence so that a lower number is always to the left of the next higher number. The shipping date has the highest number. Keep the number of benchmark points to the minimum needed to give you a clear idea of what is going on—the more benchmark points, the more laborious the monitoring job.

The last chart is simply a bar chart plotting the number of parts or subassemblies that have passed each benchmark to date. On this chart you will actually draw the line of balance. Suppose today is March 23. Benchmark number 12 must be passed 36 days before final delivery according to our flow chart, and on the delivery schedule

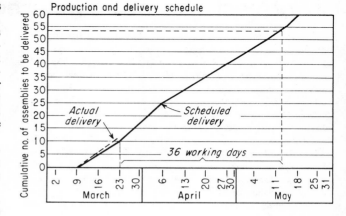

Production and delivery schedule

PRODUCTION REPORT — 23 March

CHECK POINT	DESCRIPTION	LOB REQ'D	LOB ACTUAL	CORRECTIVE ACTION
2	Procure Rod End Ext.	60	58	2 pieces due in tomorrow
4	Insp. Rod End Int.	60	55	5 pieces in process
9	Insp. Mach. Sleeve Act.	60	53	7 pieces in process
10	Insp. H.T. Rod End	60	50	Vendor delay — 15 pieces tomorrow
12	Insp. H.T. Cyl. Res.	53	23	Vendor delay — 40 pieces tomorrow
15	Insp. Mach. Cyl. Res.	40	20	Holdup — checkpoint 12
21	Cyl. Res. Into Stock	28	17	Holdup — checkpoint 12

36 days forward from March 23 brings us to May 13, when we see that 53 assemblies are to be delivered.

On the bar chart we draw (in gray) the March 23 LOB crossing benchmark 12 at 53. It crosses benchmark 15 at 40, benchmarks 13 through 24 at 28. This line of balance tells us exactly how many parts and assemblies should have passed each benchmark by the date under consideration if the scheduled delivery is to be met.

Finally, a periodic production report lists each benchmark that lags behind schedule and notes the corrective action that has been or will be taken.

A production line-of-balance (LOB) chart shows the minimum requirement of each component that goes into an assembly or the maximum number of dollars that should have been spent to meet some distant delivery requirement. It enables each supervisor to see how much of his task must be completed at that time to satisfy the over-all project demands. It also enables the manager to evaluate the performance of the supervisor in satisfying the demands. It is one of the most useful and easily applied tools available to the manager. Even without other data, he can predict posible trouble areas and eliminate them before they become major ones. For example, examination of the LOB shows that even though there are enough cylinder reservoirs (check point 21) to satisfy present deliveries, there are not enough in stock for the future. ■

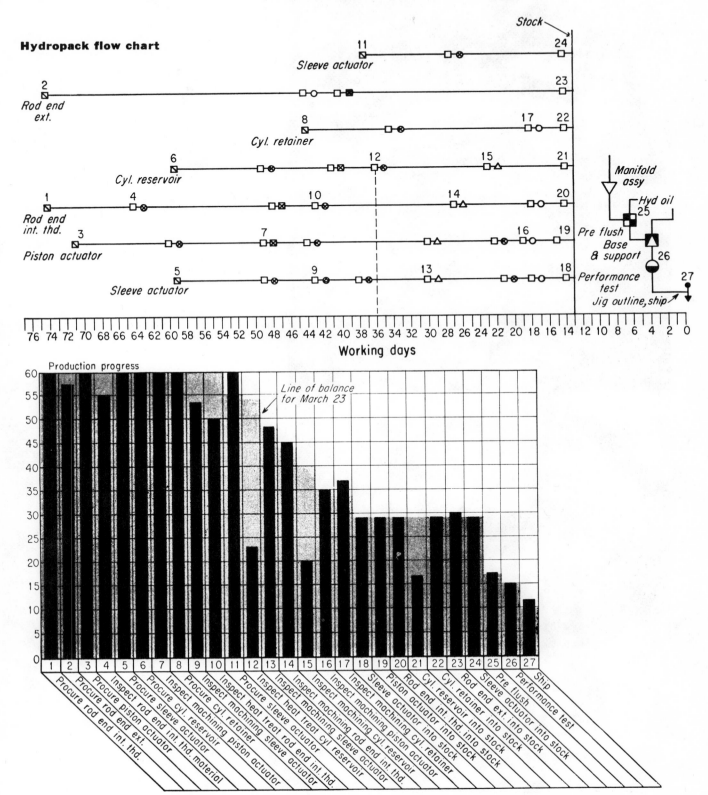

Hydropack flow chart

A

A . . TAPE NEEDS NO DRYING: as soon as it is in place, work can be continued without danger of ink smudges.

B . . TAPE-PEN feeds a 1/64 to 1/16-in.-wide tape that can be guided round french curves.

C . . BEAM COMPASS holds Tape-pen that applies tape. Circles from 2 to 18 in. diameter can be drawn with tape in this manner.

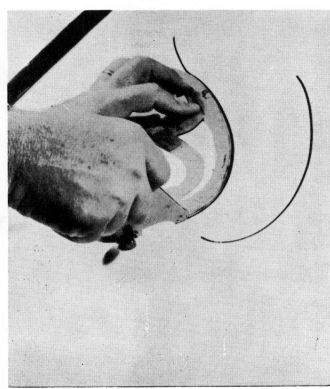

B

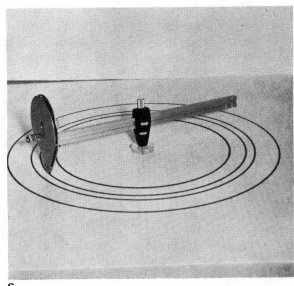

C

"Don't draw it, tape it," is a new slogan for engineers who . . .

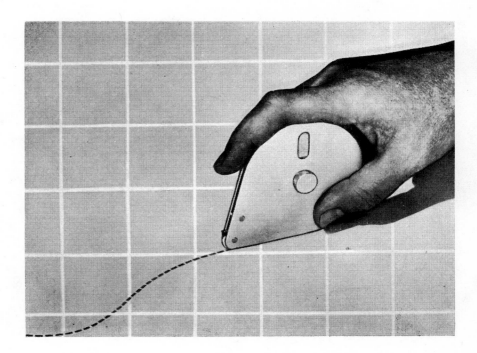

. . . CUT CHARTMAKING TIME WITH TAPE

Engineering chart-work becomes quick and easy with preprinted, pressure-sensitive tapes and papers that eliminate tedious pen-and-pencil drawing. Preprinted with symbols and designs in black or colors, these tapes and sheets, slit to a variety of precise widths, are fast becoming a favorite aid in engineering offices. Here's what they can do—

Office layouts: Symbols for all office equipment and scaled templets, for use on a grid, permit arrangements for interiors to be moved around until final layout is settled on. Walls, partitions, and other structural components can be indicated with patterned tapes.

Plant layout: Patterned tapes indicating power lines, material conveyors, and piping allow scaled representations for guides in material flow plans. Templets representing machinery can be made from templet sheets.

Maps: Patterned tapes representing railroad tracks, telephone lines, streets and other important routings can be quickly laid down on map surfaces.

Statistical visuals: Pictorial symbols representing numbers of persons, foodstuffs, money, automobiles, ships and the like permit rapid construction of easily appreciated graphs.

Organization charts: Rectangles, circles, and triangles, and tapes for connective lines make possible quick assembly of these much-used charts.

Advertising and art: A complete selection of tapes imprinted with border patterns for use in newspaper advertising and other art is aiding in new reproduction processes available; for example, photo composition techniques.

Special tools available—

Tape-pen—an ingenious tape holder that permits the user to roll on a line of tape, freehand or following a straightedge or french curve.

Multiple Tape-pen—this lets several parallel lines of varying patterns be laid down simultaneously.

Beam compass holder for Tape-pens —with this, engineers can make accurate circles or arcs with narrow tape.

Sheets, grids, planning boards, knives, and other tools are all planned to let the user work to precise tolerances and scales.

Electronic Symbols

Available are hundreds of symbols used in electronics design and printed circuitry, produced to engineering and government specifications. Draftsmen need not waste time drawing each symbol—a supply, razor-cut from a backing sheet, speeds the work.

Other special symbols, eg, often-used fasteners, can be custom-made.■

8.

How to Improve Research and Material-Specification Operations

the ECONOMICS
of RESEACH and
NEW PRODUCT PLANNING

You can take some of the gamble out of R & D bets with a bit of realistic market analysis and a careful budget estimate.

RUSS EGGERS

The American Alcolac Company of Baltimore has a simple, but effective, formula for rating the profitability of an R & D project:

Chance of technical success
× Chance of commercial success
× Annual volume × (Price−Cost)
× Product life ÷ Total costs = Project number

This is a ratio of the *total expected profit over the life of a product* to its *total development cost*. The formula provides no radically new information, but it forces you to take an objective look at the project.

Suppose the chances of coming up with a better mousetrap are estimated at 80%. The sales manager guesses a 60% chance of commercial success. If you can make it for 13 cents he says he can sell 500,000 traps per year at 18 cents each to the retailers over an 8-year period; then something new will come along. Estimated research costs are $20,000; market development, $40,000; engineering and production design $40,000—total costs: $100,000.

$$\frac{0.8 \times 0.6 \times 500,000 \times (\$0.18 - \$0.13) \times 8}{100,000} = \frac{96,000}{100,000} = 0.96$$

This project is a honey. They'll lose $4000 for their trouble! But if they could cut the research cost to $10,000, market development to $20,000, engineering and production design to $20,000; the total cost becomes $50,000 and the ratio 96,000/50,000 = 1.92 is a very different story.

A similar method is used at Armour Research where a paying research program must be established for their cus-

tomer-companies. The Engineering Economics Research Dept uses a three-step process: designating the alternative courses of action; estimating the outcome from each alternative course; estimating the probability of success.

They evaluate each alternative in terms of: cost of research; time of research; probability of technical success; effect of volume; probability of commercial success; exploitation investment; time span of profitability; profitability; rate of return on investment. With these estimates the company executive committee can evaluate various programs on a comparable basis and one, or more than one, program may be actively pursued. Note that re-evaluation at semiannual or annual intervals is also possible and desirable.

Evaluating a project and plugging numbers into a formula looks easy, but the estimates, if they're to be worth using, will take some careful thinking and inspired guesswork. According to one survey, even the more successful of the research-minded companies find that fewer than 50% of their carefully thought-out new products show a profit. And the failures aren't owing to a lack of good ideas or technical success.

Despite these risks, research for new products is still very profitable. But the profit curve on a new product—unlike that of conventional products—is often reversed. Instead of building up your market over a long period, getting costs down, knocking out your competitors—you take a quick profit on the new product and then start worrying (see chart). This short-lived but lucrative monopoly that

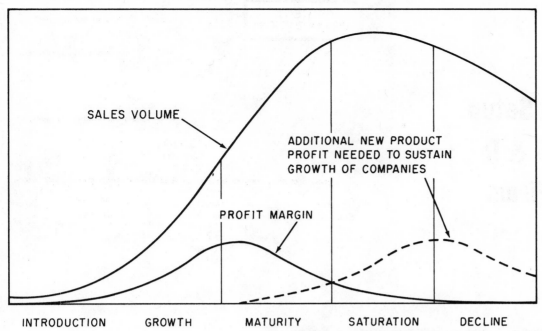

SALES VOLUME

ADDITIONAL NEW PRODUCT
PROFIT NEEDED TO SUSTAIN
GROWTH OF COMPANIES

PROFIT MARGIN

INTRODUCTION   GROWTH   MATURITY   SATURATION   DECLINE

In this age of innovation a company needs a continuing flow of new products to sustain profit margins. The early monopoly pays off handsomely. Late arrivals are just in time to be caught in the profit decline. Sources: Booz, Allen & Hamilton

goes with a successful new product is important—for it often gives the small adventurous company a chance to beat the big boys. Large corporations tend to move slowly, testing the market, probing—before making any large scale commitments of capital.

So, new products are risky, profitable and anybody can play at the game. How does a company judge the profitability of a new product in advance? Two rule-of-thumb methods were given above; now let's take a look at W R Grace & Co.'s Polymer Chemicals Division to see a check list in depth.

Grace puts a big emphasis on the early screening of new product ideas, since this is the source of a company's most expensive mistakes. In order to get a profile on each new product up for consideration, Grace takes a close look—and classifies simply as VERY GOOD, GOOD, AVERAGE, POOR or VERY POOR—for the following:

The stability factors: How durable is the market for the new product? Is it steady, like the market for sulphuric acid; a slowly declining one such as textiles; a Hula-hoop market? Is the product one which can be used nationwide and abroad? Is it easy for other manufacturers to copy? Have you a captive market for the product within the company? How would its market hold up in a depression? Would wartime shortages of critical materials give you trouble?

The growth factors: Is the product (or process) really a unique one? Will demand for the product grow? Can the product ride a big new technological change that is coming up, or will new technology probably make it obsolete? Do export possibilities add to its growth prospects?

Marketability: Can you sell the product through your present sales setup? If it's in a new field, will your present reputation help any? How well has competition been handling this market? Will you sell the product in large

volumes to a few customers? How many variations or styles in the product will be required? Is it free from seasonal fluctuations or can you sell it all year round?

About your company's position: Are you well established in the field so that you can commercialize the new product quickly? Do you have any special advantages in purchasing materials? Do you supply your own raw materials? If not, will the new product put your purchase of raw materials into the carload or tank car class, so you get a break on costs?

The research and development factors: Can you develop the new product idea with your current knowledge? If not, will the product give you information you can use or take you down a side street? Would it utilize existing laboratory or pilot plant equipment? Can you get enough R & D personnel to handle the additional work?

The engineering factors: Do you have all the process know-how or are there unknowns which may add to the costs? Will you use a high proportion of standardized equipment to produce the product? Will it overload your engineering staff?

The production factors: Will the new product put idle capacity to work? Does it use familiar production techniques? Will it require substantial investment for new utilities—power, water, gas? Is it free from hazards, difficult maintenance problems, waste disposal headaches?

These are among the 39 specific questions which Grace uses in its economic thinking about a new product. Viewed in so comprehensive a way, you find out quickly whether the product is at all promising for your company. Profiles of different suggestions can be evaluated, compared and screened.

Nobody, of course, has been able to come up with *the* magic formula for predicting the profitability of a new product, but one thing is certain: the more objective the analysis, the more likely the profit. ■

Combined Setup Best for R & D of Small Firms

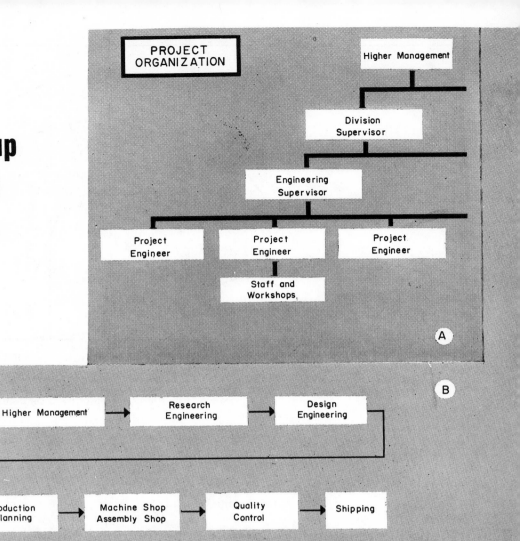

PROJECT ORGANIZATION

Higher Management → Division Supervisor → Engineering Supervisor → Project Engineer / Project Engineer / Project Engineer → Staff and Workshops

Ⓐ

Ⓑ

DEPARTMENTAL ORGANIZATION

Higher Management → Research Engineering → Design Engineering → Drafting Laboratory Technical Editing → Production Planning → Machine Shop Assembly Shop → Quality Control → Shipping

T. W. JARMIE
President, Engineered Electronics Company

Most research and development companies do not mass-produce their products. Usually their customers require just a few custom-designed products—or maybe only one. Engineering time, therefore, accounts for much of the final cost. Anything done to use engineers more efficiently will thus affect final costs far more than for a mass-produced article.

A major source of inefficiency can be the way operations in the company are organized. The Service Organization described here should not be regarded as just another operations chart. A genuine change of mental attitude is required. It assumes that the real "boss" is the customer, who rules through the contract or purchase order. The project engineer, once he is chosen to work with and for the customer, must be given the utmost freedom to get the project completed. All other departments should be regarded as services upon which the project engineer can call for assistance. For example, his supervisor controls central pools of test equipment, space and other facilities that can be directed as necessary within the company to the main end of getting the project completed efficiently. The division supervisor can supply more project support, where necessary, such as production planning, over-all material control

and accounting functions. Priority questions can be referred by the project engineer to his own supervisor. If project operations can be rescheduled the problem goes no further. If not, the division supervisor may be able to reschedule operations of other departments.

The operating departments must also look upon themselves as service functions. Their work is not an end in itself; its purpose is to produce a good product. ∎

Project Organization	
Faults	**Advantages**
1. Develops "Jacks of all trades."	1. Consistent supervision.
2. Excessive load on project engineer.	2. One learning period.
3. Nonstandard product.	3. No loss of data (one information source).
4. Inconsistent operating policies	4. Minimum Writing of instructions
5. Multiple outside representation.	
6. Duplication of facilities	
7. Inefficient use of personnel	

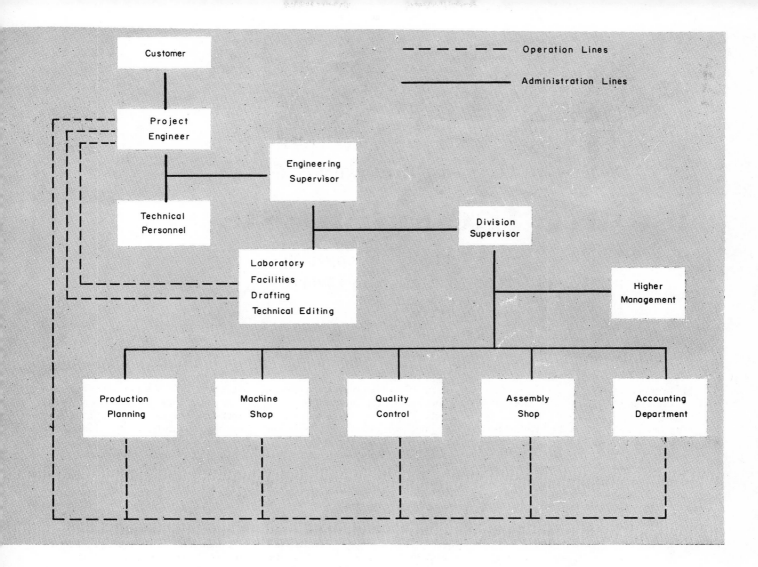

- - - - - - - Operation Lines

——————— Administration Lines

Both basic types . . . (opposite page)

(A) Project organization and (B) Departmental organization tend to be inflexible. They are bound more by "policy" than the idea of getting a job done efficiently and satisfying the customer. Justification for an action is often of more concern than whether the action furthers the end. Often, when he is promoted, an engineer is required to do less actual engineering and more administration. Engineering skill can, thus, even become a barrier to promotion—a good engineer is difficult to replace.

Departmental Organization	
Advantages	**Faults**
1. Permits specialization.	1. Multiple supervision.
2. Distributes workload.	2. Increased writing of instructions.
3. Produces standard product.	3. Multiple learning.
4. Consistent outside representation.	4. Loss of data.
5. Consistent outside representation.	
6. No duplication of facilities.	
7. More efficient use of people (because of specialization)	

Service Organization . . . ▲

joins together the good points of other types of organization, and has added advantages as well. To the engineer it gives; opportunity to advance with a minimum administrative burden and dilution of effort, opportunity in his junior days to learn by handling small projects or portions of large projects, opportunity to become acquainted with and be an important part of the over-all company picture—as a project engineer he is, and must be regarded as, an important member of the management team. It gives the customer ease of contact, ability to obtain decisions and information quickly and reliably, excellent relations, lower cost resulting from a higher efficiency. It gives vendors easy access to technical information without losing the security of a central purchasing decision. It gives the company flexibility, speed of action, ability to establish a standard of quality, appearance, and design philosophy, a cost situation which is more than competitive, ability to utilize the technical ability it possesses, ability to provide incentive and opportunity for individual progress and growth, ability to diversify its effort readily.

◀ Advantages are combined . . .

when two basic types become a service organization. Faults of the two do not occur in the third, which is based on the fact that the customer is "boss." Lip service is frequently paid to this dictum but, in practice, no real effort is made to re-arrange company structure so that the customer is boss. Switching to the service type not only combines existing advantages but gains extra ones.

Want better engineering?

Isolate the scientists

Lockheed finds scientists and engineers
are two different "breeds." They work
best when they work separately.

MARGARET RALSTON

The management of Lockheed Aircraft and Missiles took stock of the company's technical activities a few years ago and found room for improvement. The problem, they concluded, was that the organizational structure made no distinction between research and engineering, even though the two are very different functions. Since then the technical division has undergone a gradual metamorphosis that ended this spring in complete separation of the two activities.

"Before reorganization," says Dr John P. Nash, director of research and engineering under the new organization, "engineering wasn't controlled enough and research too much."

In engineering, he and his associates have found, time is very important. The staff is responsible for designing a system or complex apparatus for a customer, who is usually impatient, or for the open market where a small time lead may give a company a strong competitive advantage. Because of ever-looming deadlines, it is essential for the managers of a project to keep close tabs on its progress, particularly when several groups contribute to the final design. They must know where trouble is developing before it becomes a serious time delay, and to do this they need weekly and even daily engineering reports.

In research, on the other hand, time is not important. The skill of the scientist depends upon identifying and solving long-range problems. Scientists operate best with a great deal of freedom and without time limits, reporting their progress only quarterly.

Lockheed management also found considerable waste of technical help in management jobs. "There has been

a lot of phony emphasis on getting into management in this country," says Kenneth T. Larkin, associate director of engineering for electronics. This took a particularly severe toll of scientists under the old organization. When scientists and engineers were intermixed in research groups, the scientist who got a promotion into management spent most of his time scheduling, budgeting, and generally setting up the controls necessary for a project. This use of scientists was wasteful and unnecessary, Larkin adds. Under reorganization, Lockheed hopes to reclaim some of its lost talent.

A glance at the old and new organization charts reveals Lockheed's thinking. The old chart lists some 30 research project groups, all of them with individual managers and most of them oriented towards a product. In the new chart, engineering is completely divorced from research. And the research division is very informally organized. On the chart it shows simply as four long boxes, one for each of the company's four labs—physical sciences, mechanical and mathematical sciences, materials sciences, and electronic sciences. Each box lists a director, assistant director, and the senior scientists.

Engineering, by contrast, is more formally organized. There are five major divisions—spacecraft and missiles, advanced system, dynamics and navigation, electronics, and information processing. Each of these is subdivided into specialized departments—electronics, for example, has 17, including such product areas as ground digital equipment, vehicle digital equipment, microwave applications, electromagnets, instruments and me-

chanisms, infrared and optical devices.

At first the reorganization caused considerable apprehension, particularly among scientists, even though the changes were instituted gradually. Larkin explained it this way:

"A man can take considerable comfort in an organization chart, since it shows him where he is in comparison with others in the group and shows his progress. He can count the number of blocks between him and the president. But we feel that a rigid organization chart is an artificial way to motivate and meaningless on the research side. We think it is better to remove the rigid structure—take away that ladder. People can tear themselves apart worrying about the boxes in an organization chart."

Larkin, who formerly headed a group combining electronics research and engineering, lists several advantages for separation.

"Under the new system," he says, "we can promise scientists long-term support." In essence, the company says to them: we think highly of you and you have our confidence. You're better able than we to determine what needs to be done in your field, so you choose your project and we'll back you in it as long as necessary.

Administratively, he adds, it is now simpler to classify programs. If someone wants a set of engineering drawings, it's an engineering project; if he wants a report on what's new in solid state physics, it's a research project. Before, engineers and scientists were all mixed in together, making it difficult for management to figure out which man might be best at a job.

"And," Larkin continues, "in a joint research and engineering group, sci-

BEFORE—Scientists and engineers work together

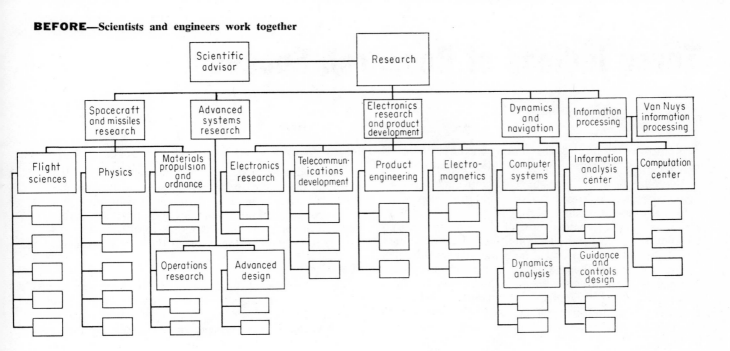

entists frequently got sidetracked into strictly engineering projects instead of turning them over to the engineering people, who should properly handle them. Materials people, interested in checking the properties of materials, got involved in building machinery to test the projects. Separation of scientists and engineers makes it easier to pull this sort of project out and turn it over to the engineering department where it can be run under engineering discipline."

"Previously," he adds, "we filled out weekly pink sheets indicating problem areas in various projects. These were essential for engineers, but not appropriate for scientists. Now they are made out for engineers only, and have become a hardboiled scheduling tool."

There are advantages on the re-search side as well. William F. Main, director of the electronics sciences lab, notes that under the old system a scientist who wanted to bring together a group of people from several disciplines—solid-state physics, computer electronics, and digital techniques, for example, became involved in a complicated bookkeeping routine to get people out of one group and into another. Sometimes projects died aborning strangled in red tape. Now, new groups can be put together with little or no administrative interference. Communications have been vastly improved by breaking down artificial departmental barriers and interdisciplinary reviews can be conducted simply and at greater depth.

Despite separation of research and engineering, communications between the two are kept open. Frequent meetings cross-linking the groups are held. Dr Wayland C. Griffith, director of the research half, meets weekly with his laboratory directors. Frank J. Bednarez, director of engineering, meets weekly with associate directors of the engineering sections. The two directors meet to exchange information.

Lockheed management feels the importance of good research cannot be overemphasized. It is encouraging scientists to stay in the lab by setting up parallel routes of progression and parallel salary structures, with men advancing as managers or scientists. Some ten levels from scientist or research assistant to senior member of the lab have been established on the technical side, with broad and overlapping salary brackets. ∎

AFTER—Scientists work in loosely organized labs

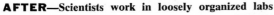
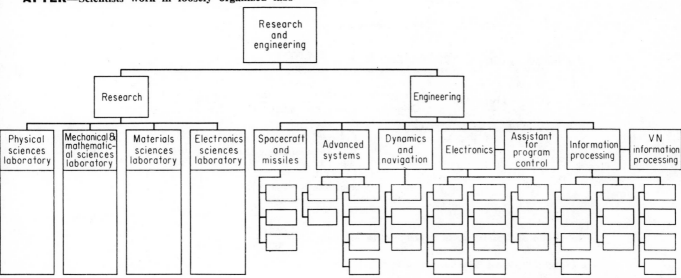

Three Indices of Research Success

ARTHUR A. LYTLE

Industry carries on R & D programs for the sole purpose of improving its position—whether this represents profits, prestige, size, or what have you. This motivation rules out support for industrial research that would be "nice to do." It further rules out products already invented but which do not promise an adequate return for the company. Given a demonstrable economic, or other, incentive rest assured the products will be invented and produced by someone.

The key words here are "demonstrable incentive." Normally a company appraises new products or processes in the same way it appraises its mature, standardized products. There are three common methods. The man to convince in your corporation will be using one or more of them.

Return on total sales

This method measures the ratio of average yearly profit to average yearly sales. This ratio gives direct information on the effectiveness of the sales and production efforts. However, from the standpoint of business management, it has the very serious fault of ignoring the factor of original investment in sales and production.

Return on investment

Two products which offer the same potential total sales and profit may differ appreciably in equipment-to-produce, buildings, cash, or inventory required. A company would, of course, greatly prefer the lower-capital-cost product. The return on investment criterion is, therefore, widely used to relate profit before taxes to the total investment.

Cash Flow

But accounting, like all other activities of modern business, has become progressively more sophisticated. Newer concepts attempt to introduce the rate of flow of money in and through the company and the time value of money.

These methods integrate the complete picture of all costs including R & D; inventory, operations, sales costs, sales income, return on investment, and the value of dollars spent in the future in terms of their value at the start of a project.

The cash-flow method requires a running record of income and outgo on a project as far into the future as possible and so, once accepted, it becomes a guide for the execution of the project as well as a means of evaluation at the start. ■

A PRODUCT'S FUTURE

ORIGINAL INVESTMENT: $1,000,000

		Sales	Cost	Profit
	1	0	$90,000	−$90,000
End	2	$500,000	300,000	200,000
of	3	1,000,000	600,000	400,000
Year	4	1,100,000	650,000	450,000
	5	400,000	200,000	200,000
Totals		$3,000,000		$1,160,000
Average		$600,000		$232,000

SALVAGE OF ORIGINAL INVESTMENT: $400,000 after 5 years

A — Return on sales $= \dfrac{\text{Average Yearly Profit}}{\text{Average Yearly Sales}} = \dfrac{232,000}{600,000} = 38.7\%$

B — Return on Investment $= \dfrac{\text{Average Yearly Profit}}{\text{Original Investment}} = \dfrac{232,000}{1,000,000} = 23.2\%$

C — Present Worth of Cash Flow @ 10% Interest:

$$\left. \begin{array}{r} \$-81,700 \\ 165,000 \\ 300,000 \\ 308,000 \\ 124,000 \end{array} \right\} \text{Profits and losses}$$

$248,000$ Salvage value

$$\$1,063,300$$

D — Ratio of Present Worth to Original Investment $= \dfrac{1,063,000}{1,000,000} = 1.063$

E — Actual Interest Rate Earned = 11.8%

How to Control Cost of Research and Development Projects

H. J. FINISON

RESEARCH ENGINEERS often think that the work of control of cost of the research project is valuable time lost from the more creative technical tasks. Yet experience indicates that adequate systems of cost control, applied with an understanding of their true functions and philosophies, can aid research teams to a better understanding of the technical problems and better plans for attacking those problems. Cost control systems closely integrated with the technical problems of the research program often stimulate applied research teams to higher levels of creativity.

The nature of the activities, the character of the research organization and its organizational position all influence the type of cost control systems that is most effective. It would be unwise to suggest that the methods to be dis-

cussed are directly applicable to most research laboratories. Rather, the nature of the research operation for which the controls have been devised, the nature of the controls, and the reasons for which the particular controls have been established will be described. Thus each research administrator can select those principles and practices that may be helpful for his own activities.

One classification of the various areas of scientific and engineering work is: 1. Fundamental research; 2. Applied research; 3. Development; 4. Design; and 5. Application.

This classification is particularly applicable to work leading toward products, although similar ones might be used for work pertaining to processes. The cost controls to be described are intended to be applicable to programs

dealing with applied research and development. Some of the methods may be applied to design but it is doubtful if they would be suitable for fundamental research or application.

Among the laboratories available for work in the scientific and engineering fields are: 1. University; 2. Company; 3. Association; 4. Institute; and 5. Government.

Research institutes carry out research and development programs under sponsorship of industrial companies, associations or government. They have tended to become somewhat regional in character since many of their programs are carried out for industry in their immediate area. In general, the work is carried out for the sponsor at cost since most of the organizations are on a not-for-profit basis. Usually pat-

CONTROL PROCESS		
PRODUCT QUALITY	MANAGEMENT PROBLEMS	PROJECT COST
Standard	Budget	Plan
Tests	Statement and Analysis	Review

Fig. 1—Similarity between control of product quality, management problems, and costs of a research project.

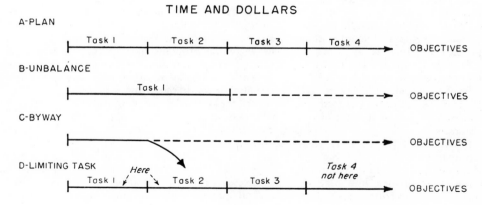

Fig. 2—Pattern for planning approaches to the various tasks required to complete a project.

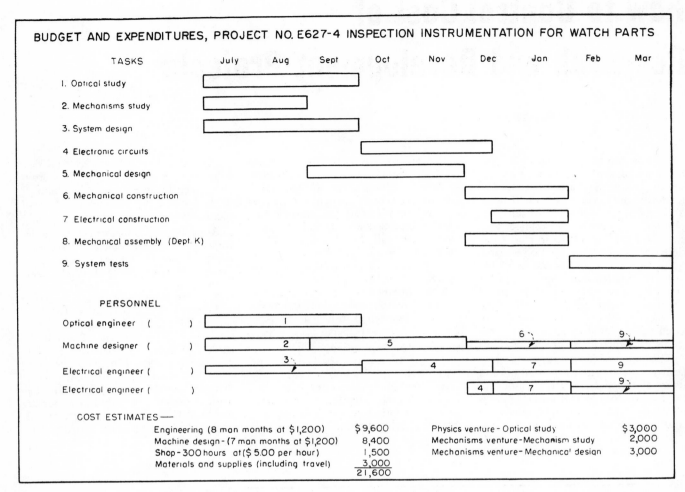

Fig. 3—Project plan for the development of an inspection instrument with specific desired operating characteristics.

(Cost figures require multiplication by a correction factor for current use.)

ent rights are assigned to the sponsor.

The research staff usually covers many different fields of science and engineering. The larger research institutes may range in staff size from a few hundred to more than two thousand.

Research institutes have grown to positions of prominence in the industrial research field because they:

1. Offer a large and diversified staff. Few companies can afford as varied a technical staff.

2. Provide ability to handle peak research and development loads without long-term commitments.

3. Provide specialized laboratory facilities not available otherwise.

4. Provide stimulation for the research and development staff of the sponsoring company as a result of outside contacts.

5. Provide new viewpoints, ideas, and approaches.

At Armour Research Foundation* the organization is divided into nine departments, each covering a specialized

field of science or engineering. In general, the departments range in size from 50 to 150 people. The ratio of professional to supporting personnel is usually higher than is typical of industrial laboratories.

Each department is divided into four to ten sections by specialized fields. A section is headed by a supervisor and may include two to eight senior level engineers and scientists capable of serving as project leaders or specialists.

Projects are assigned to a particular section, a project engineer is placed in charge of the program, and appropriate supporting personnel is provided for work within the scope of his own section. For work requiring engineers and scientists in other sections and departments, phases of the program are "farmed out" by "ventures" or subcontracts as needed. The project engineer assumes technical charge as well as financial control of his project.

Successful execution of an industrial research and development program re-

quires both superior technical performance and close financial control. The wide variety of research programs makes a high order of specialization undesirable. Yet the research engineer or scientist must rapidly gain a knowledge of the particular specialized field and produce effectively in that field.

A project leader must make good cost estimates prior to the initiation of the program, then follow through on problems of project organization and execution, including cost control. While the controls described here are not unique, their form of organization may offer possibilities for application in other laboratories.

The Control Process

The chart in Fig. 1 shows the similarity between the problems of product quality control, a management or business problem, and the control of costs of a research project.

For control of quality of a product

Now the ITT Research Institute

in production, one must first establish the characteristics of the product that are significant to the quality or acceptance of that product. The quantitative values to be used as a determinant of acceptability must also be defined. These establish the standards or specifications for the product and their establishment is a vital first phase of the quality control process. Quantitative standards or specifications must define the limits of acceptability.

The second step in quality control is establishing adequate tests to determine whether the product conforms to the established standards. In modern technology these tests may be on a sampling basis. Tests or measurements should be more refined than the values specified in the standards. A continuing control chart will show trends in measureable values so that detection and correction of production difficulties may be made prior to the production of units that fall outside of the limiting acceptable values.

In management problems, the standard set is usually in terms of a budget. The budget is an operating plan expressed in dollar terms. The purposes underlying budgeting and management control have been summarized in Ref. 1. Mr. Anderson indicates that the budget is "a summary in financial terms of the standards of performance established for all departments of the business;" or, it is "a coordinated plan for the operation of the business expressed in financial terms."

In business, management control is exercised by setting standards in the form of a budget and by establishing measuring techniques in the form of accounting statements to indicate conformance, deviation from the budget, and need for corrective action. As with quality control, forms of measurement that are sufficiently sensitive to detect the trend away from conformance to the budget are desirable. Hence, frequent accounting periods are usually necessary for adequate control of the business.

Research project control is a management problem with the research engineer or scientist acting in the management capacity. Many of the factors that must be considered for control, however, are not readily expressed in financial terms. The highly technical character of the research problems requires extensive scientific or engineering training, often to the exclusion of training in fields that would be helpful in the management phases of project leadership. Yet the project leader must gain an understanding of the meaning of budgets and accounting statements.

The standard or budget for the re-

Table I — General Requirements of the Project Plan

1. Planned by persons responsible for the project.

    A plan is a process as well as a product.

2. Formal yet flexible:
    (a) Change plans where needed but change consciously
    (b) Written:
        A tool not a ritual
        Avoid the "paper" work problem.

3. Plan before authorization of funds and initiation of the work.

4. Use exploratory project for projects that cannot be planned immediately.

5. Plan in terms of specific individuals for the research team.

6. Time spent in planning is well invested and should be adequate for the particular project.

search project is here called the Project Plan. This title implies that much more is involved in the plan than financial terms. The tests or statements to determine conformance with the plan as the work progresses are designated the Project Review. Again, the review must be in more than financial terms.

Approach to Project Planning

A summary of the general principles of project planning is given in Table I. Some questions that one might ask when setting out to plan a project are:
1. For what purpose?
2. Who should plan?
3. How formal?
4. When should the plan be made?
5. How long should it take?
6. How can unknowns be planned?

The answers to these questions are somewhat interrelated.

Many of the advantages to be gained from the preparation of the project plan stem from the process of making the plan. Project planning is a process of living through the carrying out of the program in the imagination of the research team doing the planning. Hence, the development of a research plan serves not only to establish budgets of time and money, but it serves to orient the research staff in the nature of the technical problem and the interrelationships of the parts of the entire plan.

The process of planning helps in assuring that the various tasks required for completion will be carried out in an orderly fashion with appropriate emphasis. A desirable approach is indicated in Fig. 2 (A). If a pre-established plan is not available, dangers such as excessive emphasis on early tasks with little time left for later tasks, or the pursuit of interesting byways are more likely to occur.

The tasks that appear to be most doubtful of achieving success should be carried out as early in the research program as possible; Fig. 2 (D). Often such tasks may mean delay of other tasks where economy is more important than time in completion. If the tasks that are limiting success prove unsuccessful, wasted efforts on other tasks will have been avoided.

It should be emphasized that few projects should progress as directly from beginning to achievement of objectives as indicated in Fig. 2 (A). Unless some effort is allowed on the interesting byway, there is danger that a sufficiently imaginative approach will not be taken on the project.

Similarly, unless some unbalance is permitted in the face of a promising possibility, there is danger that the program will be terminated just short of success. Yet it is essential that these deviations from plan be kept under control and carried out with complete realization of their implications to achievement of the final objectives.

It is desirable that the research team that will carry out the project do the planning. Supervisory and management personnel may participate in the planning but should carefully avoid directing the planning or inhibiting the planning discussions. Various specialists from the same or other departments may also participate, depending on the nature of the project. It is desirable for the planning of a project to be carried out in a small conference with the supervisor or project leader acting as the conference leader.

Unfortunately, in the work at Armour there is a lag between planning of a project during preparation of a proposal and the initiation of a research project. Hence, the particular people who planned the project may be assigned on other programs when the new project is initiated. The knowledge that this situation may occur makes it difficult to plan projects since it is important to know the characteristics of the people who will carry out the work. It has been found helpful to assign specific individuals for each task, even though their work schedule may make it unlikely that they will be assigned to the project.

Careful selection of the personnel finally assigned is essential for the plan to be valid. Replanning of the project in terms of personnel actually assigned at the time of initiation of the work is sometimes necessary. Fortunately, these revisions seldom affect over-all cost and time estimates.

The question of formality is one requiring good judgment and some compromise. There must be a formal requirement that a project plan be made prior to the authorization and initiation of a project. An adequate formality means that the plan should be in written form. A verbal plan, even though understood by several people, will inevitably be constantly revised to fit the exigencies of the moment. Project plans should often be changed as the project progresses. But the plans should be consciously changed with full realization of the effects of the changes on all phases of the project.

Yet with the requirement for a formal written plan, there are real dangers in the planning programs. The temptation is for the research administrator to require plans that are ends in themselves—plans that are physically beautiful. Then the research team may prepare the plan with the end product as a goal of the planning rather than a thorough understanding of the research problems. They become slaves to a system and the planning becomes a ritual to be performed rather than a tool to achieve higher effectiveness.

Similarly, excessive formality may result in failure to change the plan when necessary. A "paper plan" in the administrator's office and the real plan in the minds of the research team will be the likely result.

There will always be projects that

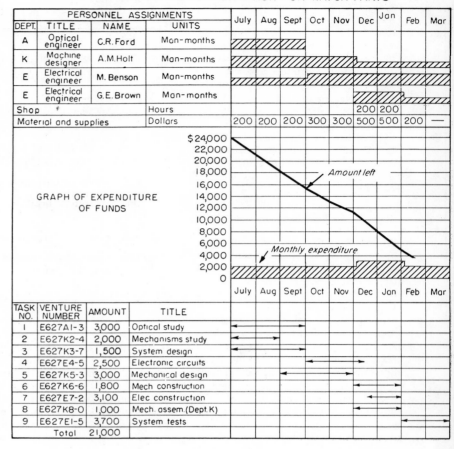

BUDGET AND EXPENDITURES, PROJECT NO. E627-4
INSPECTION INSTRUMENTATION FOR WATCH PARTS

DEPT.	TITLE	NAME	UNITS	July	Aug	Sept	Oct	Nov	Dec	Jan	Feb	Mar
	PERSONNEL ASSIGNMENTS											
A	Optical engineer	C.R.Ford	Man-months	/////	/////	/////						
K	Machine designer	A.M.Holt	Man-months	/////	/////	/////	/////	/////	—	/////	/////	/////
E	Electrical engineer	M. Benson	Man-months	/////	/////		/////	/////	/////	/////	/////	/////
E	Electrical engineer	G.E.Brown	Man-months							/////	/////	/////
Shop			Hours						200	200		
Material and supplies			Dollars	200	200	200	300	300	500	500	200	—

GRAPH OF EXPENDITURE OF FUNDS

$24,000 — 22,000 — 20,000 — 18,000 — 16,000 — 14,000 — 12,000 — 10,000 — 8,000 — 6,000 — 4,000 — 2,000 — 0

Amount left
Monthly expenditure

July | Aug | Sept | Oct | Nov | Dec | Jan | Feb | Mar

TASK NO.	VENTURE NUMBER	AMOUNT	TITLE
1	E627A1-3	3,000	Optical study
2	E627K2-4	2,000	Mechanisms study
3	E627K3-7	1,500	System design
4	E627E4-5	2,500	Electronic circuits
5	E627K5-3	3,000	Mechanical design
6	E627K6-6	1,800	Mech construction
7	E627E7-2	3,100	Elec construction
8	E627K8-0	1,000	Mech. assem.(Dept.K)
9	E627E1-5	3,700	System tests
Total		21,000	

cannot be planned, since by their very nature the programs deal with unknowns. When a project cannot be planned based on present knowledge, it is well to carry out an initial exploratory program. The definition of some of the unknown factors would be the objective of the exploratory program for use in planning the full scale research or development project.

Finally, how long should be spent in planning the research project? The only answer can be: as long as necessary. Many small projects can be planned initially in a few hours; others take a full day. Some large projects may require a week or more during which the project is subdivided into smaller projects, each with its own detailed research plan.

The Project Plan

The elements of a project plan are: Objectives, tasks, task schedule, manpower estimate, personnel schedule, cost estimate, project organization, and provision for review.

Clear statements of the objectives toward which the research program is directed are essential to successful applied research work. Often an appreciable portion of the time spent in planning a project will be involved in determining such statements of objectives. Once they are clearly stated, the remainder of the planning process proceeds easily. The objectives sometimes cannot be finally stated until some of the project is planned. And often as the planning progresses, the statements of objectives may be repeatedly modified as better understanding of the problem develops.

In work at Armour, the statements of objectives of the research program are included in the proposal, which if accepted becomes a part of the research contract. Where supplementary or revised objectives are developed as the project progresses, these are made part of a report or letter so that all people associated with the project will be clearly familiar with them and will be oriented toward their accomplishment.

There are two levels of objectives; first, the sponsor's reasons for carrying

ARMOUR RESEARCH FOUNDATION

OF ILLINOIS INSTITUTE OF TECHNOLOGY

AUDITED AND APPROVED FOR $_____

DATE _____ RESIDENT AUDITOR _____

SHEET NO._____ OF BUREAU VO. NO. _____

PROJECT, TEST OR VENTURE NUMBER	SPONSOR	MONTH OF	CONTRACT DATES FROM	TO	AUTHORIZED APPROPRIATION	FIXED FEE	NET APPROPRIATION	PAGE NO.
E 598	2 XYZ CORP	3 54	10 31	12 31 3			28000 00	

PROJECT, TEST OR VENTURE NUMBER	TYPE CHARGE	PREVIOUSLY EXPENDED	CURRENT MONTH	TO DATE	TOTAL EXPENDITURES
E 598	2 PRCH MAT SERV	490 62	58 21	548 83	
E 598	2 TEL & TEL	15 95	3 38	19 33	
E 598	2 TRAVEL	124 90	7 00	131 90	
E 598	2 STORES & AUX SV	325 48	73 01	398 49	
E 598	2 SERVICE LABOR	7 80	22 65	30 45	
E 598	2 SERVICE OVERHD 120 %	9 36	27 18	36 54	
E 598	2 STAFF SALARIES	5425 18	1341 97	6767 15	
E 598	2 STAFF VAC PROV 8 %	434 01	107 36	541 37	
E 598	2 STAFF OVERHEAD 100 %	5425 18	1341 97	6767 15	
E 598	2 STAFF VAC INC 8 %	434 01	107 36	541 37	
E 598	2 TOTAL EXPEND	12692 49	3090 09	15782 58	15782 58
E 598	2 FIXED FEE				
E 598	2 TOTAL VOLUME	12692 49	3090 09	15782 58	
E 598 A01-9	TOTAL EXPEND	4222 40	422 00	4644 40	4644 40
		16914 89	3512 09		20426 98 *

2140 0
TOTAL COMMITMENTS

BILLING INSTRUCTIONS
☐ BILL PER COST SHEET TOTAL
☐ OTHER INSTRUCTIONS _____

COST SHEET APPROVED:

DEPARTMENT FORECAST:
ESTIMATED EXPENDITURE FOR MONTH OF _____ APPROX. $ _____
ESTIMATED EXPENDITURE FOR MONTH OF _____ APPROX. $ _____

IS NEED FOR A TIME EXT. ANTICIPATED?
☐ NO ☐ YES _____ MOS.
IS NEED FOR ADDITIONAL APPROPRIATION ANTICIPATED?
☐ NO ☐ YES $ _____

757302 *
BALANCE OVER (CR) OR UNDER EXPENDED

IF ADDITIONAL CONTRACT FUNDS AND/OR TIME IS ANTICIPATED TO COMPLETE PRESENT PROJECT REQUIREMENTS (OR TO EXTEND SCOPE OF PROGRAM), INDICATE THE ACTION TAKEN OR PLANNED, (NORMALLY ACTION SHOULD BE INITIATED AT LEAST 4 MONTHS IN ADVANCE ON GOVERNMENT CONTRACTS AND 2 MONTHS IN ADVANCE ON INDUSTRIAL CONTRACTS):

BILLING SUMMARY
BILLED PREVIOUSLY_____
BILLED_____EXPENDITURES: $
INVOICE NO._____DATED_____
BILLED TO DATE_____

DEPARTMENT CHAIRMAN

Fig. 4 (Left)—Project plan in which graphs of expenditures and amount of authorized funds remaining are shown and plotted by months.

Fig. 5 (Above)—Monthly cost sheet prepared by accountants and supplied to project leaders. A sheet for each project task is often prepared.

out a particular project. These are usually of an economic character, although they may have social implications. For example: it may be desirable to devise an instrument to carry out a particular inspection function, even though there are no cost savings over manual methods of inspection. The gain may be in the elimination of an extremely fatiguing operation that is difficult to man.

Knowledge of the sponsor's broader objectives may lead the research team to a broader outlook and permit bringing of approaches or ideas to the attention of the sponsor, even though they do not pertain to the specific objectives of the project.

The second level of objectives is a clear definition of the technical results desired. For example: The development of an inspection instrument with specific desired operating characteristics such as speeds, sensitivity, selectivity; sufficiently simple for production line use; and with a final manufacturing cost not to exceed a specified amount.

The next four elements of a project

plan are so closely related that they cannot be discussed separately. These are tasks, task schedules, manpower estimates and personnel schedule. These can be discussed best by considering a typical plan like that shown in Fig. 3. Such a plan can be prepared on 11 by 17 in. section paper, 4 by 4 squares to the inch.

Presumedly an appropriate printed form could be developed that would be suitable for many project plans. But when projects are extremely varied in size, duration, and complexity, there is danger in a fixed form with appropriate blanks to be filled in by the planners. First, there is danger that too little thought will go into the planning and, second, there is danger in bounding the thinking of the research team in the planning stage. There is usually negligible time saving in the printed form and it may be a serious obstacle to successful planning.

A project plan need not follow any prescribed arrangement. In planning the project, the research team first lists the appropriate tasks that must be carried out for the completion of the

project. A considerable portion of the total effort in planning is the naming, discussing, definition, and grouping of these tasks. In the process, the research team tries to get as exact an understanding of the problems as possible and finally achieves a list of meaningful tasks appropriately interrelated. On the left side of Fig. 3 such a list is presented.

As soon as the framework of the project begins to be formulated by definition of the tasks, the task schedule can also be started. In Fig. 3 the task schedule is shown by months at the right of the tasks; the bars show only the relationships of elapsed time. No attempt is made in the task schedules to show the magnitude of the effort involved. In some projects, the task schedule is laid out without previous consideration of the completion date. In others, rather clear ideas of desired completion time may place restriction on the possible task schedules.

Concurrently with the schedule, appropriate manpower is listed and a manpower schedule made below the task schedule. These bars may be to scale and symbols used to designate the corresponding task.

As with most design problems, the first attempt at the project plan may not be completely successful. Usually the plan may be reworked several times during the planning session as more concrete understandings of the problem evolve. Revision to meet sound personnel practices are also required. For example, continuity of personnel or limited appropriate personnel may be important factors in the layout of task and personnel schedules.

It may be helpful for the research team to write additional information about each task; this information may be included in the proposal submitted to the prospective sponsor. Thoroughness of understanding, however, is the important criterion in adequately planned projects.

From the manpower schedule together with a summary of other costs such as materials, travel, and shop costs the cost estimate may be prepared. Either salary rates for the particular personnel or appropriate standardized rates may be used. The latter are almost a necessity where the estimates are prepared by the research team.

Project organization may be a problem to be considered, depending on the nature of the research laboratory. In work at Armour, the project is usually assigned to one section and a project leader selected. Services of specialists in other sections and departments are obtained by "farming out" with "ventures" or subcontracts appropriate phases of the work. Other than selection of appropriate personnel, there is usually little more to the problem of project organization.

In some laboratories, particularly where very large long term projects are carried out, a new group may be created to work on the project. This group will generally include specialists in several fields. In this form of operation, problems of organization must be more extensively considered in planning the project.

Project plans for large projects may be much more complex than that shown in Fig. 3. An example of a larger project is shown by Fig. 4. In this plan only the tasks and task schedules are shown. A project plan was also prepared for each of the tasks with the additional detail on objectives, subtasks, manpower estimates and schedules shown for each.

The project plans are complete at the stage shown by Fig. 3 with the additional information such as objectives included in the proposal. When a project is initiated, the supervisor or

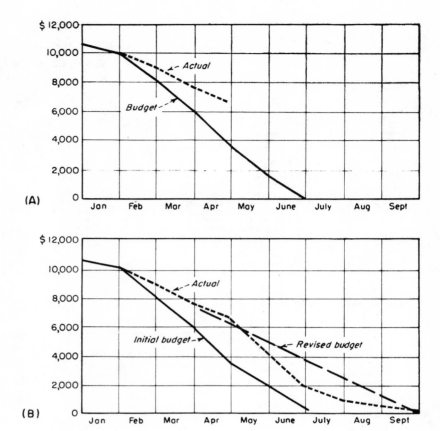

Fig. 6—Review expenditure graphs. (A)—Actual expenditures are considerably less than estimated; investigation revealed that the project was in difficulty. (B) —Extended time and revised budget needed to overcome difficulty in project.

project leader may elect to place the plan in some different form for ease in control of the project. One method is that shown by Fig. 4, where graphs of expenditures and amount of authorized funds remaining are shown by months. In some instances, additional graphs may be used for each task. In this approach, expenditures may be graphed as the project progresses and serve as a part of the project review.

Finally, the plan should make provisions for adequate review of the project.

Project Review

The review of a research or development project involves two phases: (1) Financial review; and (2) technical review. These two cannot be separated; they must be carried out at the same time and by the same people.

Complete information in suitable form covering actual expenditures on projects must be supplied to the project leader promptly to allow him to appraise the financial status of the project at frequent intervals.

In establishing a project accounting

system, it is well to remember that its prime purpose is to aid the project leader in making appropriate decisions for the future conduct of his project. Timeliness and completeness of the cost information are important. If these conditions are not well met by the accounting organization, there is danger that the research team will waste time in keeping a separate accounting of cost information or in failing to achieve adequate control.

The IBM Card Programmed Calculator is used in the Computer Center at Armour to provide the cost information on each project. It is used the first three working days of the month for accounting activities and the remaining time for scientific and engineering calculatons. On the sixth working day of the month, cost data are supplied to the project leader in the form shown in Fig. 5. A monthly cost sheet of this type is prepared for each project and for each task of a project if the project leader desires.

Note that the cost sheet provides the following information:

1. Authorized time and funds

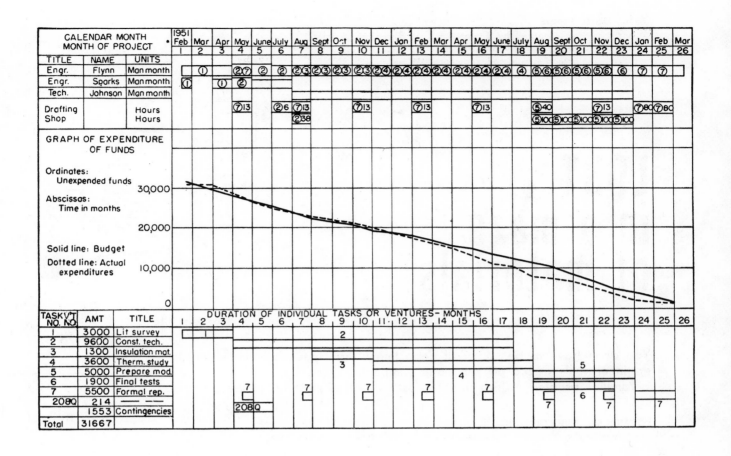

Fig. 7—Review graph in which expenditures closely follow amount budgeted. To achieve this result, changes in staff were required as project progressed.

2. Totals of expenditures by classes
   (a) Previously expended
   (b) Expended in current month
   (c) Total expenditures to date
3. Remaining authorized funds
4. Total commitments (purchase orders outstanding)

Additional detail is supplied with supplementary sheets of which Fig. 7 is a simplified example.

Research and development projects change rapdly. It is difficult for a project leader to accurately appraise a project with cost information that is a month old.

The project leader must review the entire project at monthly intervals with the new cost information at hand. In some laboratories, an attempt is made to have the technical personnel place an evaluation on the percent completion of a project so that others may compare the work completed with the cost information. The comparison is rarely worthwhile. It is better to place the emphasis on remaining funds and remaining work; whether they are properly matched requires very careful evaluation of the technical problems.

Additional forms of review may be classified as technical review, although at all times financial factors may also be involved. These forms of review include: Direct contact; Reports; and Meetings.

The direct contact of supervisory and management personnel with the work as it progresses is essential for an appraisal of the progress of the work; also, whether appropriate facilities and personnel are being applied to the project. Even though the supervisory and management personnel are not specialists in the particular field, it is possible to gain a fairly good appraisal of the problems if a cooperative atmosphere exists.

Reports also serve as more than a medium of review of the project. Often much of the most exact and complete analysis of problems and formulation of conclusions is actually carried out in preparation of reports. Technical reports covering the technical work in considerable detail should be prepared at reasonably scheduled intervals.

Meetings of the entire research team and supervisory personnel are important to the successful execution of a project where a number of people are working on the same program. These meetings afford opportunity for the staff to visualize ideas and approaches and are a helpful supplement to report writing. They also assure coordinated efforts on the program where several phases are carried out simultaneously.

Perhaps it is equally important that the research staff learn from each other and stimulate each other to do more effective work.

Control of research and development projects deals with supervisory and management problems. In addition to some of the factors that have been discussed, the process involves important personnel relationships (Ref 2). The establishment of specific goals and budgets for projects inevitably creates some pressures on research personnel. The human problems must be carefully considered to avoid destroying initiative and creativity of the staff. ■

Data sheets . . .
prepared by a Materials
Engineering Department, can
help lead bewildered engineers
out of the maze.

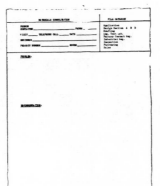

LOST
in a maze
of materials?

You don't have to be. A small department that specializes in materials
engineering has paid off for many companies faced by
a familiar problem—which metal, plastic or other material to use.

NICHOLAS J. PETRELLA
Chief Material Engineer, Brown Instruments Div., Minneapolis-Honeywell Regulator Co.

Want to relieve a growing burden that eats into
engineering time? A good answer is setting up a section
devoted to materials engineering: it not only relieves
the burden—it may mean the difference between success or failure of a new product.

It isn't lack of materials that is the problem; it's the
complexity of choice. For example, there are almost
two dozen basic plastics . . . 40 varieties of stainless
steel . . . 35 different aluminum alloys. And as the list
keeps growing, keeping pace becomes a full-time job.

Here is where materials engineering enters as a service department. It does more than keep the designer
posted on new developments. It helps him select the
right material for new products. Or it may suggest redesign with a material that does the same job at less
cost. The production, purchasing and inspection departments receive valuable help too—as part of its
duties, materials engineering tests new materials, gets
reactions from vendors, prepares materials specifications.

SETTING IT UP

Where to put the new department on the organization chart depends on a company's complexity and raw
materials requirements—on what departments are to be
served and the kind of service required. Some companies
call it a part of the engineering department. Others
make it a staff function that reports to top management. Still others include it in quality control.

Organizing the unit may take considerable time—
often a full year before it operates smoothly. Responsibility for its success lies largely with the man chosen as
chief materials engineer. There is always some criticism and resistance to change, so he must be forceful
and able to "sell" his group to others.

Size of his staff will vary. Typically, it will include
about three or four engineers with differing backgrounds,
assigned to handle specific problems in such fields as
metals, nonmetals, raw materials. These men should
be good salesmen, too, and the best sales qualities are
a knowledge of the field, a pleasing personality, and an
ability to give quick answers to difficult or poorly defined problems.

How will operation of this service group be financed?
Two popular methods are: charge costs to company
overhead; or tax each department using the service.
Either way requires keeping track of time spent with
each department. A convenient method is to assign a
charge number to each department and charge time to
this number whenever the service is used. Records then
give a quick annual review of who has used the service
and how often.

The company must also provide a place to file data
and a working space where experiments can be performed. Working space can sometimes be found in
the testing lab which is already doing some materials
engineering. Or possibly a small, vacant area can be
found in the plant.

10 THINGS MATERIALS ENGINEERING DOES

— Advises engineers on selecting proper materials

— Suggests substitution of materials

— Prepares materials specifications

— Tests samples and makes trial applications

— Maintains file of manufacturers' literature; samples of materials

— Interviews salesmen

— Reviews drawings for adequacy of materials specifications

— Helps develop specialized materials to meet company needs

— Passes materials information along to design and engineering departments

— Arranges for periodic educational programs on materials

THE TOOLS

A filing system is the group's key to efficient operation—quick access to vital information expedites solution of complex problems. Several systems are possible but one with two breakdowns—one for manufacturers' literature and one for specifications—is very often valuable. Further division can be into two groups—metallic and nonmetallic—with coded subdivisions. If each materials engineer has a copy of the code, it will be easy to find information and file new data properly.

A small reference library should back up the files with quickly available textbooks on materials and engineering. Handbooks and manufacturers' data books should also be included.

A consultation sheet will simplify keeping score on requests for assistance. It should be used for any project requiring more than one hour's consulting time; should include such information as person contacted, date, project number, hours spent, description of problem, and recommendation made. Reviewing these forms from time to time will indicate trends in materials problems and show where materials emphasis is needed.

Raw materials specifications are often the basis for decisions made by the materials engineer. These specifications may come from military or ASTM standards, or from other companies and suppliers. They make it possible for company buyers to purchase the best materials at lowest cost. Without such specifica-

tions, the inspection department could not determine if submitted materials meet established quality levels.

A list of qualified suppliers is a logical companion to materials specifications. It names manufacturers who have met company requirements. The purchasing department may have primary responsibility for furnishing such names and contacts new vendors only when a new source of supply is needed. This prevents vendors from taking advantage of the company's testing facilities. One way is to have vendors send data first. If data is acceptable, samples are tested and the vendor informed of qualification—or disqualification—and why.

THE CHALLENGE

In its early months, the materials engineering section can expect some resistance. Here are a few familiar roadblocks.

● Acceptance of new materials standards. It is one of the toughest problems that will be met, and there are no easy solutions. The old standards always seem good enough—and it takes forceful selling to overcome this built-in inertia.

● Friction between purchasing departments and materials engineering. This arises because of overlapping activities. Purchasing people usually feel they have exclusive prerogative to deal with vendors. It will be necessary to develop a working relationship by showing them how the materials section can free them from spending time with vendors on matters purchasing is not equipped to handle.

● Delay in getting to the problem. Often the materials engineer is not called in early enough; instead of solving the problem properly, he performs a post-mortem. If the departments being serviced are shown the advantages of consultation early in the problem, they will learn to respond more quickly.

● The key to gaining group acceptance is confidence; best way to establish it is by quick, accurate solutions to problems. Some people may never learn to use the service because of their unwillingness to accept help from others. But acceptance will be hastened by: providing good service; setting a deadline on each problem and sticking to it; finding out what the person presenting the problem really needs and trying to satisfy him; and avoiding a blatant show of your knowledge. Simply ask questions and make suggestions—don't argue.

● A descriptive booklet will help define functions of the group and explain how it works. Some departments will be unfamiliar with the purpose of a materials engineering section. The booklet should tell what the group does and sell its importance.

● A monthly materials bulletin is a useful sales tool too. It can run from two to four pages. In short, easily read paragraphs it should describe new materials, give news of projects under development, and list materials specifications issued during the month. Besides finding the summaries valuable, engineers will be reminded that the materials engineering department is alert—and ready to help. ■

How to Set Up a Material Specification System

Basic content of a company specification.
Use of National standards and recommended practices.
Suggestions for a numbering system and index, format and distribution.
A check list and method of periodic review.

PLANNING A SPECIFICATION

In preparing specifications, planning is a necessity. Details not handled properly ultimately become major problems. Here is the order in which such details should be considered:
1. Numbering system.
2. Specification format and method of duplication.
3. Index and method of preparation.
4. Method for distribution of information.
5. Check sheet.
6. Adequate record file.
7. Trade name file.
8. System of periodic review.

JOSEPH GURSKI

Manufacturing Research Department, Ford Motor Company

THE CONTENT OF A SPECIFICATION is the most important single thing about any system of company specifications. Other factors are of importance in that they influence the physical work of a specification activity, and minimize much confusion. However, the requirements of the specification itself are vital, since they determine the cost of the material being purchased, its suitability for processing, and finally its serviceability.

The basic thinking in the choice of materials for a product should be to select the least expensive material that will do the intended job. Anything else is economically wasteful of both money and material. Obviously, the inclusion in a specification of requirements which serve no useful purpose should be discouraged. Similarly, to restrict the range of requirements is also wasteful. For one thing it will increase the cost of acceptance inspection. More important, it may restrict the number of suppliers, thereby lessening competition and certainly adding to the cost of the material, because the supplier must exercise greater care or be subject to rejections.

In setting up a system, the following five main headings may be used: 1. Scope; 2. Application; 3. Requirements; 4. Approval of Suppliers; 5. General Information.

The "Scope" contains a complete, but preferably, non technical description of the desired material.

The "Application" describes where the material is generally used, or under what conditions it is to be used. This is not a basic requirement of a specification, but is a concession to expediency. This section may not stay correct as new uses may be found; however it does give an indication of application.

The "Requirements" list the mandatory attributes needed to control the quality of the material. They contain realistic limits consistent with typical manufacturing tolerances.

"Approval" describes the conditions under which new suppliers receive certification. This paragraph indicates whether a simple laboratory test is adequate, or whether shop trials are needed.

"General Information" headings are used to list such things as typical analyses, annealing procedures, or method of specifying on part prints.

Fig. 1 shows a typical specification with the above headings mentioned.

NATIONAL STANDARDS

The use of national standards is always desirable. Specifying bodies such as the Society of Automotive Engineers, American Society for Testing Materials, American Standards Association and others develop specifications which are recognized throughout industry, and through wide usage make the purchasing of materials relatively easy.

At the author's company such specifications are used when possible—particularly SAE specifications, because some of the company personnel were on the committees which developed them.

In some cases specifications as developed by other specifying bodies do not adequately describe the materials that a company will use. In such cases it is possible for a company to supplement the information issued by these national bodies, and build its specifications with their

MATERIAL SPECIFICATION

FORD MOTOR COMPANY

MFG ENGR **2015**

M 4B1

NITRATE HEAT TREAT SALT

1. SCOPE: The material desired under this specification is a heat treat salt consisting of a mixture of potassium nitrate (KNO_3) and sodium nitrate ($NaNO_3$) salts.

2. APPLICATION: The material shall be suitable for use for low temperature heat treating baths generally used in martempering, tempering, or austempering operations.

3. REQUIREMENTS:

3.1 Composition:

Potassium Nitrate (KNO_3)	50-60%
Sodium Nitrate ($NaNO_3$)	40-50%

3.2 Melting Point: 450 F maximum

3.3 Operating Range: 500 - 1000 F

3.4 Color: Salts shall be tinted red in a manner which will not harm the performance of the material.

3.5 Packaging: Material must be packaged in weather resistant and moisture proof containers.

3.6 Supplier's Responsibility: All material supplied to this specification must be equivalent in all characteristics to the material upon which approval was originally granted and shall be suitable for the intended application.

4. APPROVAL OF NEW SUPPLIERS: All new suppliers to this specification must be laboratory approved by the Divisional Quality Control Laboratory or Chemical Engineering Department for Divisional application or by the Quality Laboratory, Manufacturing Staff, for Company wide application. Recommendations for addition of suppliers to the approved list must be made in writing to the Manufacturing Research Department. Test data upon which the recommendations are based must be attached. This material must be given a Divisional shop trial. The shop trial and laboratory report must be approved by Manufacturing Research Department.

5. GENERAL INFORMATION:

5.1 Safety: Safety precautions must be followed as outlined in Process Specification MS 8-1.

5.1.1 Under no circumstances are CYANIDES to be allowed to come in contact with these highly oxidizing low temperature baths either as carry over from other heat treating operations or by direct addition.

Fig. 1—A Specification Sheet used at the author's company, listing the five main headings that are employed to completely define the part or material.

information as a nucleus. In addition, there are many materials for which specifications are not written, and probably never will be written by national bodies. In such cases, a company can develop its own information.

RECOMMENDED PRACTICES

While Recommended Practices do not strictly qualify as company specifications, nevertheless they have extremely important functions. Through the medium of recommended practices one can achieve standardization and simplification of materials. The SAE defines Recommended Practices as, "Recommendations based on sound engineering principles intended as guides for standard engineering practices." These recommended practices take a variety of shapes. However, they have one thing in common in that they establish some requirements of materials as a basis for their selection for various applications. These requirements may be dimensional, chemical, metallurgical, or any other which affect their suitability.

Recommended practices highlight the pertinent factors that should be considered in the selection of materials, and point out the need for an evaluation of new materials. These practices are difficult to develop in that it is desirable to develop simple Recommended Practices which can be understood by everyone. Fig. 2 shows a Recommended Practice developed for the Selection of Cutting Fluids.

NUMBERING SYSTEM AND INDEX

Numbering systems specifications can be compared with filing systems. If it is anticipated that a file will not grow beyond the stage of one cabinet, then no particular system is necessary. One could look at every piece of paper in

The following charts list recommended coolants and cutting oils for various machining operations and materials when using high speed tool steels. Approved equivalent coolants may be substituted although the listed ones are preferred. For carbide tools, M-589-B Standard Soluble Oil, Petroleum Base is recommended in those instances where a coolant is desired. Use in a concentration that will keep corrosion at a minimum. Recommended dilutions are between 24:1 and 60:1.

The chart is to be read as follows: M-589-B, 24:1 means that M-589-B is mixed with water in the ratio of 24 parts of water to 1 part of oil; M-501 and M-4635-A, 5:1 means that 5 parts of M-501 are mixed with 1 part of M-4635-A. In those instances where two different fluids are given for the same operation on the same material, the top fluid is recommended and the second or bottom fluid is optional.

FERROUS METALS

Type Of Material	Automatic Screw Machines	Boring, Milling, Profiling, Chucking	Broaching	Drilling	Gear Cutting	Gear Shaving	Hand Screw Machines & Lathes	Threading and Tapping	Honing	Grinding	Thread Grinding
Carbon Steels	M-3C5	M-589-B 24:1	M-501 and M-4635-A 5:1 ---or---- Sol. Oil*	M-589-B 24:1	M-3C5 ---or--- M-589-B** 24:1	M-3C3	M-589-B 24:1	M-3C5	M-4640-B	M-589-B 60:1 ---or--- M-3C6	M-4635-H
Alloy Steels	M-3C5	M-589-B 24:1	M-501 and M-4635-A 5:1 ---or---- Sol. Oil*	M-589-B 24:1	M-3C5 ---or---- M-589-B** 24:1	M-3C3	M-589-B 24:1	M-3C5	M-4640-B	M-589-B 60:1	M-4635-H
Stainless Steels	M-501 and M-4635-A 5:1	M-501 and M-4635-A 5:1 ---or---- Sol. Oil*	M-501 and M-4635-A 5:1	M-501 and M-4635-A 5:1 ---or---- Sol. Oil*	M-4635-H	M-3C3	M-3C5 ---or--- Sol. Oil*	M-3C3 ---or--- M-4635-H	M-4640-B	M-3C2 60:1	M-4635-H
Steel Castings		M-589-B 24:1	M-501 and M-4635-A 5:1 ---or---- Sol. Oil*	M-589-B 24:1	M-3C5 ---or---- M-589-B** 24:1	M-3C3	M-589-B 24:1	M-501 and M-4635-A 5:1	M-4640-B	M-589-B 60:1	M-4635-H
Cast Or Malleable Iron		M-589-B 24:1	M-589-B 24:1	M-589-B 24:1	M-3C4 40:1	M-4635-H	M-3C4 40:1	M-3C4 40:1	M-532-A-B ---or---- M-4640-B	M-3C4 40:1	M-4635-H

NON-FERROUS METALS

Aluminum	M-501 and M-4647-B 19:1	M-3C2 40:1	M-3C2 40:1	M-3C2 40:1	M-3C2 40:1	M-3C2 40:1	M-3C2 40:1	M-3C2 40:1	M-4640-B	M-3C2 40:1	M-3C2 40:1
Copper and Copper Alloys	M-501	M-589-B 40:1	M-589-B 24:1	M-589-B 40:1	M-501 ---or--- M-589-B** 24:1	M-589-B 24:1	M-589-B 40:1	M-501	M-532-A-B	M-589-B 60:1	M-501 and M-532
Magnesium	M-501	M-501 or Dry	M-3C5	M-501 or Dry	M-501	M-501 or CO₂	M-501	M-501	M-4640-B	M-501	M-501
Zinc		M-589-B 40:1	M-589-B 24:1	M-589-B 40:1	M-589-B 40:1	M-589-B 40:1	M-589-B 40:1	M-589-B 40:1	M-4640-B	M-589-B 60:1	M-589-B 60:1

* Consult divisional metallurgist.
** Only where construction of machine permits its use.

Fig. 2—Recommended practices do not exactly come under the heading of company specifications; however, they do serve as a guide to unify thinking on a particular subject and promote the use of standards.

order to find a particular item. When a file grows too large, this hit and miss method is no longer applicable, and some sort of system must be developed. So it is with a numbering system for specifications. As long as there is only a handful of specifications, any system such as 1, 2, 3, 4, etc., will do. When one can in time visualize hundreds or thousands of numbers, then some sort of system must be developed.

It is necessary to have some idea of the volume of specifications that will be involved before grouping related materials into some system. Obviously, groups with only a few specifications are no more desirable than file folders with only several sheets of paper. A system which carries a breakdown too far is almost as bad as no system at all.

An example of a coding system is shown in Fig. 3.

In the author's company the prefix letter "M" has had a long history as identification for a Material Specification.

In order to continue with the prefix letter "M" and still use another letter to identify groups, numbers such as M-5B1 are used. In all cases "M" establishes the fact that a Material Specification is being discussed; the second letter, "B", denotes that the material is a chemical; the first digit, "5", denotes that the chemical is a washer and cleaner compound; and the second digit, "1", indicates the first of a series.

The use of a system such as illustrated in Fig. 3 does have a number of advantages. It tells anyone familiar with the system: the type of material involved; minimizes the chance of issuing numbers for very similar materials; groups like materials and aids in selection; and provides identification for an infinite number of specifications within the initially selected groups. Incidentally, once a specification has been obsoleted for some reason, the number should not be re-used even at some later date. References

MA—METALS
1. Ferrous, Misc.
2. Non-Ferrous, Misc.
3. Tool, Die & Equipment
4. Welding & Brazing Filler Metal
5. Spring Steel Wire
6. Electrical (Contact Points, Resistors, Bi-Metals)
7. Anodes
8. Bearing Metals
9. Shot-Grit
10. Powder

MB—CHEMICALS
1. Soaps
2. Plating Compounds
3. Conversion Coating Compounds
4. Heat Treating Compounds
5. Washer & Cleaner Compounds
8. Alcohol & Antifreeze
10. Metal Polishing Compounds
11. Organic Finish Polishing Compounds
12. Solid Fuels
13. Flux
14. Draw Compounds & Hot Die Lubricants
16. Acids
17. Gases
97. Organic, Other
98. Inorganic, Other
99. Miscellaneous

MC—PETROLEUM PRODUCTS
1. Lubricating Grease
2. Lubricating Oil
3. Machining Coolants
4. Liquid Fuels
6. Hydraulic Oils and Fluids
7. Rust Preventives
8. Multiple Purpose Oils
99. Miscellaneous

MD—RUBBER & PLASTICS
1. Friction Materials
2. Rubber
3. Thermo-Setting Plastics
4. Thermo-Plastic Plastics
97. Rubber Mfg. Materials
98. Plastics Mfg. Materials
99. Rubber & Plastics, Misc. (Excluding Gaskets)

ME—PAPER
1. Paper
2. Paper Boards
3. Pyroxylin or Vinyl Coated Boards
98. Paper Mfg. Materials

MF—LEATHER
1. Genuine Leather
2. Artificial Leather
3. Quilted Artificial Leather
98. Artificial Leather Mfg. Materials

MG—NON-METALLICS (Not Otherwise Listed)
1. Trim Bindings
2. Adhesives
3. Tapes, Adhesive
4. Sealers, Fillers
5. Mastic Sound Deadeners
6. Anti-Squeak
7. Refractories
8. Gaskets
9. Waxes
10. Asphalt, Tar, Pitch
11. Wood
12. Glass

MH—TEXTILES
1. Body
2. Sidewall Cloth
3. Carpet
4. Curtain & Top Cloth
5. Headlining
6. Seat Cover Material
7. Webbing
15. Threads
16. Felts
17. Padding

MJ—PAINTS
1. Air Dry Paint
2. Baking Enamel
25. Dual Purpose Baking Enamel
3. Polishing Enamel
31. Satin Polishing Enamel
4. Lacquer
41. Satin Polishing Lacquer
5. Maintenance Paint
6. Primers
7. Shellac, Varnish, Stains
10. Pigments
11. Resins
12. Enamel Mill Bases
13. Lacquer Mill Bases
14. Solvents and Thinners
98. Paint Mfg. Materials

ML—ELECTRICAL
1. Multiple Wire Assemblies
2. Single Wire
3. Insulating Material

MR—CASTING & STEEL MANUFACTURE PROCESSING MATERIALS (Other than fuels)
1. Ferrous Melting Metals
2. Non-Ferrous Melting Metals
3. Fluxes
4. Core & Mold Materials

Fig. 3—In an index such as this, the method by which it is made up is important, since frequent revisions will be necessary. Any method which requires only the retyping of those lines that need changing is desirable.

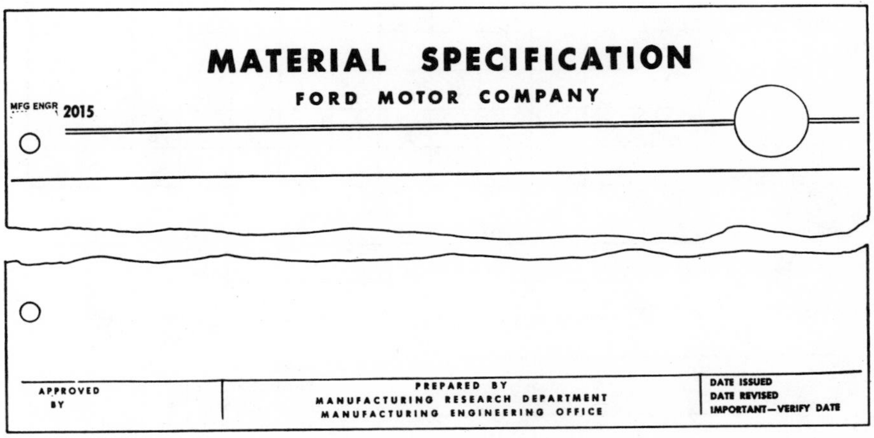

MATERIAL SPECIFICATION
FORD MOTOR COMPANY

MFG ENGR 2015

APPROVED BY | PREPARED BY MANUFACTURING RESEARCH DEPARTMENT MANUFACTURING ENGINEERING OFFICE | DATE ISSUED DATE REVISED IMPORTANT—VERIFY DATE

Fig. 4—Format of a specification shows company's name, and in this case that a material specification is contained. At bottom is the issuing department, and a space for approval. The ideal format uses a minimum of space, and leaves most of the room for information.

to specifications persist for remarkably long periods of time, particularly on product drawings. The use of a number of an obsoleted material as a designation for an entirely different material could result in complications. Also, care should be exercised in the initial selection of a numbering system, because changing a system once established could be very confusing, and result in costly engineering errors. The best indexing method, of course, is that which requires only the retyping of those lines that need changing.

FORMAT OF A SPECIFICATION

A format should be developed which will suit the purpose for which the specifications will be used. Fig. 4 shows an example of a format that has been found to be satisfactory.

The format clearly indicates the company's name, and that a Material Specification is the content. It has a prominent place for the title and identifying number. The bottom indicates the issuing department, and provides space for specific approval. The space for issue and revisions is important, since dates are a prerequisite of any discussion to insure latest available information.

There are many things about the actual specification sheet that should be considered. Final decisions can be made only after all factors are weighed. Generally speaking, the least expensive method of accurate preparation and reproduction, consistent with desired speed and available manpower, is what all companies strive for. The appearance of the finished specification and the number of copies required influence the selector of typewriter and reproducing method. One thing that is not generally considered is the time consumed in retyping a specification to make a slight revision in one or two paragraphs. A photographic method of reproduction, changing only the affected paragraphs should be considered to reduce the work and produce a more accurate copy.

A format should be designed which uses a minimum of space and leaves most of the room for information. Printing should be done on both sides of the sheet to minimize the number of sheets to reduce collating costs.

DISTRIBUTION OF SPECIFICATION INFORMATION AND SPECIFICATIONS

To acquaint various departments in the company with the latest information on specifications, an Information Letter is usually circulated. This letter is sent out at approximately monthly intervals and lists the numbers assigned to new materials, indicates that certain specifications have been written or revised, and states that other specifications have been obsoleted. Such a Letter in effect, becomes a supplement to an Index.

New or revised specifications are not sent out with an Information Letter, because all areas of the company are not interested in every specification that is written. While this procedure results in some delay in getting information, it also eliminates the necessity of numerous receiving locations handling a tremendous volume of paper for which they have no use. Specifications are sent out immediately on request to speed up service as much as possible.

The Engineering Department's Materials Engineer must have available information on specifications in order to have an adequate selection of materials for particular applications. The Manufacturing Engineer and Chemical Engineer are interested in materials used for "non-production" applications, and must know what materials are available. Purchasing agents must have specifications available to them in order to buy materials properly. Also, they must have a supply of specifications on hand for vendors who are bidding. Quality Control Laboratories must have specifications available to them in order to test materials adequately, and to determine whether they meet all requirements.

SPECIFICATION CHECK SHEET

There are many facets to the problem of writing, issuing, and keeping specifications and specification references accurate. Without a formal check sheet, many details are overlooked, and before long it becomes a matter of continually correcting mistakes that are found, instead of a positive approach to prevent their occurrence.

Fig. 5 indicates the type of check sheet that has been found to be satisfactory. Basically, it indicates the items that are initiated by a specification activity and shows

SPECIFICATION CHECK SHEET

Name: _____ No.: _____

_____ Date: _____

Specified For: _____ Written By: _____

_____ Date Typed: _____

	1	2	3	4	5	6	7	8	9	10
"M" No Assigned	A	B	B	B	A	A	B			A
Revised "M" No.	A	B	B	B	A	A	B			A
Obsoleted "M" No.	A	B	B	B		A		B	B	A
New Specification	A	B		B	A	A	B	B		A
Revised Specification		B		B	A	A	B	B		A
Obsoleted Specification	A		B	B		A	B	B	B	A
RP Specification	A				A	A	A	A		A

Requested By: _____ Dept. _____ Engg Request No. _____

Request Filed With: _____ Flash Point: _____ Class: _____

Other Numbers Affected: _____

_____

Copies To: _____

_____

_____

_____

_____

CODE
1. Index
2. Trade Name File
3. Flash Point
4. Approved Suppliers' List
5. Periodic Review
6. Information Letter
7. Other Numbers Affected
8. Material & Process Handbook
9. Recommended Practice
10. File

Supplier: _____

Supplier's Designation: _____

Fig. 5—A formal check sheet like this keeps many of the details connected with specification writing from being overlooked. Primarily, it lists items of a particular specification group, and shows how each item affects other lists and records.

how each item affects other lists and records for which the specification group is responsible. For example, when a specification number is assigned, this action affects the index, a periodic review list, an information letter, and the file. It may or may not affect a trade name file, a listing of material flash points, an approved suppliers list, or other specifications. As the various items are done, the individual who does the job initials the appropriate box.

Similarly, revisions, obsoletions, and other items all have definite effects on the various records. By taking care of the details as soon as they occur, the possibilities of errors creeping into a system are minimized and information is kept current.

RECORDS

Adequate records play an important part of any specification function. At the time a number is assigned, detail records may seem like a nuisance because the information is fresh. However, if a specification exists for any length of time, the records will be referred to many times, and often three, four, and five years later. Such information as: who requested the material, where it is used, its chemical analysis, any physical tests that were run, any shop trials that were run, all becomes important. This is particularly true when comparisons have to be made to approve a second source. Consequently, the greater the number of specifications that are handled by a specification activity, the more complete such records must be.

TRADE NAME FILE

The consideration of a Trade Name File and a system of company specifications perhaps does not seem compatible. However, through the aggressive sales techniques of suppliers, brand names of various materials are constantly brought to the attention of users. The circulation of technical magazines with their materials advertising is constantly increasing; memberships in technical societies offer opportunities for personal contact to extoll virtues of materials; and active selling on the job all contribute to make the user aware of materials which could help him do a better job.

Consequently, since many of the materials referred for approval are generally described by a trade name or a supplier's code, it has been found necessary to keep such a file. With it, one can determine the kind of material it is, whether it has been investigated, and the purpose for which the material is intended. Also, it will tell whether or not the material has been approved for one of the specifications.

Many of the advertised materials are good, but they are similar and will do similar jobs. Consequently, when similar materials are approved to a specification the company gets the benefit of a certain amount of competition. Permitting the use of brand names would make it difficult to take advantage of either lower prices or new products.

PERIODIC REVIEW

One of the problems which arises in a specification activity is that of keeping up to date. Conditions change constantly, new materials are brought forth, errors were introduced into the original writing of the specification, and limits were too broad on certain requirements. These reasons and many others make it necessary to institute some method by which materials can be reviewed without creating a crisis that must be handled as an emergency.

As a specification number is assigned, it should be automatically listed for review at an appropriate interval. The interval may be six months, a year, or possibly two years, depending on the type of material and other circumstances. After it is reviewed, it should be relisted for another review at some later date.

APPROVAL OF SUPPLIERS

A specification's purpose has been defined as being "to insure a flow of uniform material." Accomplishing this purpose is relatively simple for many materials that are used in a company's operations. Those materials which can be readily described, and for which adequate inspection procedures can be employed, present no problem. Steels, non-ferrous metals, ferro-alloys, pig iron, lubricating oils and similar materials are in such a class. However, it is also true that many materials which are purchased to specification are difficult to describe exactly. Analyses are difficult to make, or if made, the results of the analyses are difficult to correlate with actual job performance.

In those cases, it is best to have suppliers who are familiar with the materials that one requires. A supplier who has furnished the material previously, generally has records which indicate to him that what he furnished was satisfactory for the intended application. Once it has been established that a specific supplier's material conforms to the specification, he is entered as an approved source.

The amount of work required to approve a supplier depends to a large extent on the detail requirements of the specification. If laboratory determinations are all that are required, the job is easy. When the specification requires that in addition a shop trial must be run, the situation is complicated.

PROCESS SPECIFICATIONS

So far, only Material Specifications have been discussed. Process specifications are a necessary adjunct to "company specifications." They can assume two forms.

One type describes what is desired in an end product without indicating exactly how that requirement is to be accomplished. This type of specification usually belongs on a part drawing. The reasoning behind this type of specification is that one does not tell a supplier what he wants and how to do it too. Either one or the other has to be specified. An example of this is a plating specification in which is indicated a thickness of coating and other requirements such as salt spray resistance, color, resistance to peeling, etc. A supplier is not told how to apply the plating, and such a responsibility is left to him.

Another type of Process Specification describes how chemical or metallurgical processes are carried out. It establishes sequence of operations, times, and temperatures. Materials required in the processing are indicated, since it is obvious that even acceptable materials can be improperly used with results that leave much to be desired.

This type of specification is used to insure uniformity of operations from day to day, and as a check point to indicate any deviations from operations which have proven satisfactory in the past. ■

MODEL SHOP SAVES DEVELOPMENT TIME

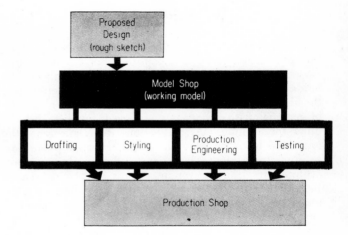

Let's call it the ABC company. A typical manufacturing organization, it isn't very large: 900 employes, 75 of them engineers; and about 200,000 sq ft of plant area. ABC makes small pumps and has just recently branched out into a line of specialized compressors. But what interests us is the company's model shop.

Here we find four drill presses, three lathes, two milling machines and a variety of other typical metal-working tools. Full-time staff consists of two trained modelmakers and a young machinist. They do most of their work on developmental models—new types of pumps or standard pump designs modified with new materials to fit some special application.

Why the model shop? "Three years ago," says the engineer in charge, "before we bought these machines and set aside an area exclusively for model building, we farmed out most such projects. Or if the job was small, we would sometimes steal half a day on one of the production machines. This interfered with production schedules and the production people were always in our hair or on our backs. Subcontractors weren't a good answer as too much time was lost between their shop and ours.

"It's different now," he said. "Engineers supervise modelbuilding right at the elbow of the model maker."

Expensive—but cheap

But isn't this costly? If an expensive machine sits idle half the week it isn't very economical, is it?

"No," said the engineer, "it certainly isn't. But balance that loss against the time saved—or the money saved when impractical ideas or design errors are stopped before they reach the really costly stage. Time savings alone will balance the loss. Our philosophy is this: When the design group comes up with the rough design for a new product, every day that product is not on the market the company is losing money. And if too much time is spent in development, it may never make money at all."

Many companies, large and small, have also found that a model shop, far from being a luxury, is a necessity. Some feel this shop has almost as important a place in product design as the engineering staff. One medium-size industrial design outfit allots half its floor space and capital investment to model-shop activities and half to engineering. It has found that engineers learn more from models than from drawings—are able to see flaws, improvements, or can suggest changes for ease in manufacture. Completion of the first model often marks only the half way point in the design process.

Model shops can tackle a variety of jobs. Developmental models are the most common. These test a principle of operation or a new material. Another place where the model shop helps out is for building unusual test equipment and one-of-a-kind experimental apparatus. At some companies, full-scale, wood-and-clay appearance models are major output of the model shop. In addition, these shops usually take on working models, which mimic the action of a proposed machine, and reduced-scale models for display or promotion.

But the model shop must not be turned into a catch-all for small machining jobs or a shop for equipment repair. Skilled modelmakers are expensive and hard to find. It is wasteful and an insult to a craftsman to give him a job that does not utilize his ability or tax his skill. Repairs and routine machine work should be done in a machine shop set up for that purpose and staffed with machinists —or it should be farmed out.

Do it yourself

Why not farm out all modelmaking work? There are several reasons. First, drawings at this stage of the game are very likely to be incomplete: dimensions missing, standard parts not shown in detail—perhaps they're only a rough sketch on a piece of squared paper. If the job is done outside, the vendor will want the drawings in detail and that means additional time. Even then, errors will show up and time is spent in communication between company engineers and vendor's machinists before getting difficulties ironed out.

In addition, your own shop will take a personal interest in the product that an outsider wouldn't have. Modelmakers get to know the engineers they work with and can make constructive contributions. They often give suggestions that make the product more manufacturable.

Security is another reason. In government work the vendor has to be cleared—this eats up time. And for reasons of company security, unpatented prototypes and experimental models should be circulated as little as possible.

Although it saves money in the long run, a model shop is not an inexpensive venture. Top-grade toolroom machinery and skilled craftsmen cost money. One model-shop manager puts it this way. "For real economy you want the best equipment and personnel the company can buy. This is not the area to save money. Back of each model is a staff of people—engineers, draftsmen, technicians. Any delay delivering the model means holding up these people. Saving time is much more important than saving model-shop costs." ∎

9.

How to Speed up Drafting and Reproducing Operations

How to organize your
Design drafting function

Here's a graphical breakdown of the function of the drafting department—the objectives and purposes of each drafting category

DELMAR W. KARGER, Dean, School of Management, Rensselaer Polytechnic Institute
and ROBERT G. MURDICK, Professor, State University of New York

PRESSURE to reduce drafting costs continues to mount, despite the publicity given to various plans for improving efficiency of the drafting operation. For any plan to succeed, good organization is basic. How does yours measure up?

The charts provide a yardstick with which to compare your organization. Chart 1 breaks down the classes of drafting into types of design and their objectives, plus the why, how, when, and background required. Chart 2 examines the design-draftsman function similarly.

Since the organization of the drafting operation is directly related to, and inevitably influenced by the total engineering and research function, you cannot deal with drafting as a separate entity. And, what fits one company will not exactly fit another. If, after checking the charts, you find a need for improvement, take these key steps:

1. Establish the objectives of the drafting organization and reduce them to writing.

2. Determine the total work necessary to meet these objectives and break down the work into broad classes of actions to be taken.

3. Divide these classes of actions into work elements.

4. Divide the work elements into positions and the positions into manageable groups. Document these by means of position guides, function charts, and suchlike.

Much can be done to abbreviate position guides or descriptions by omitting repetitive detail and by listing separately the definitions of terms and general responsibilities common to the various positions in the drafting organization. The following are basic terms in job descriptions concerned with drafting:

• **Quality design layouts** define the original concept of the design and establish the basis for the preparation of detail and/or assembly drawings. They must be extremely accurate. A complete layout drawing will show the basic design configuration plus other essential engineering information such as critical dimensions and tolerances, finishes, and strength and hardness requirements. Preparation of these layouts must include a thorough consideration of operation, reliability, field adjustment, safety appearance, ease of manufacture, clearances, tolerances, maintenance, and cost.

• **Geometric layouts** show paths of motions; they are therefore a motion analysis of moving parts.

Class of Drafting	Objectives	When
PRODUCT DRAFTING A	Preparation of graphical or written instructions for manufacturing, assembling, erecting, installing, or servicing products, systems, or any component thereof.	After design layouts and other data needed for preparing specific instructions are available.
PRODUCT DRAFTING B	Preparation of graphical or written instructions for manufacturing and assembling products or product components. Revising existing graphical or written instructions for manufacturing, assembling, erecting, installing, or servicing products, systems, or any component thereof.	After design layouts and other data needed for preparing specific instructions are available.
PATENT DRAFTING	Preparation of the drawings necessary to properly describe inventions, for which patent applications will be processed.	After it has been determined advisable to apply for patent protection and after patent attorney has established requirements for drawings.
TOOL DRAFTING	Preparation of graphical instructions for manufacturing new tools. Revision of graphical instructions for modifying existing tools.	After tool designs have been established and data for preparing specific instructions are available.
TECHNICAL ILLUSTRATING A	Preparation of necessary finished technical illustrations in color or black and white.	
TECHNICAL ILLUSTRATING B	Preparation of necessary copies and revisions of graphical and written engineering documents and the recording of engineering instructions and data.	After planning, layout and composition have been determined.
COPYING	Preparation of necessary copying and revisions of graphical and written engineering documents and the recording of engineering instructions and data.	

- **Clearance layouts** show possible interferences, the amount of clearance, and tolerances allowable under operating and production conditions.
- **Sketches** are free-hand drawings. Such sketches are often used in advance of layouts in order to help organize thought, record known factors, and retain design concepts. Sketches are also prepared for use in detailing, and free-hand sketching will often be used in the actual drafting operation to reduce the cost of producing a drawing.
- **Checking layouts** are prepared to check the accuracy of design, the relationship of mating parts, sizes, clearances, develop links, etc, as dimensioned on detail and assembly drawings.
- **Tolerance accumulation layouts** show the results of accumulated tolerances and should indicate where tolerances may be changed to better meet production requirements.
- **Quality drawings** are detail and assembly drawings that meet such requirements as conformance with design layouts, functional fitness, clarity of presentation, conformance with standards, accuracy, ease of manufacture and assembly, adequate clearances, sufficient wall thicknesses, proper part names and numbers, realistic tolerances, reproduction legibility, correctness of materials, finishes, heat treatment, gear data. There are many kinds of such drawings. Typical examples are wiring diagrams, development of cams, depiction of sheet-metal parts, springs, castings, and forgings.
- **Quality checking** is used to assure quality drawings.
- **Drawing schedule** must show estimated time to completion, the drawing involved with a particular component or task, drawing numbers (where applicable), completion dates, and other information needed by engineering.

Common sense in simplified drafting

In spite of tremendous technological progress and scientific advancements, it seems paradoxical that drafting, a tool that has been used in bringing about such progress, has itself remained almost unchanged and today is done with nearly the same amount of elaboration of detail as it was in the early 1900s. Many drafting organizations have been so engrossed with product design and development that they have not realized their practices were lagging behind the general trend of industrial progress.

Today, more than ever before, the challenge of modern industry is to produce more and better goods with less

DRAFTING WORK

How	Why	Knowledge Of –
By organizing available information and by preparing finished drawings, parts lists, diagrams and related documents.	To provide specific and precise instructions to any function of the Company, or customers and vendors, amplifying upon the work of the design draftsmen -- for ordering material, and for producing, shipping, erecting, installing and servicing products and systems or any component thereof.	Company and departmental drafting practices, and understanding pre-established material uses. Manufacturing, erection or installation practices. Shop or field standards. Arithmetic, algebra, geometry and trigonometry, including skill in solving problems, skill in graphical presentation – mechanical or freehand, and skill in interpreting instructions given on layouts, sketches, notes, etc.
By organizing available information and by preparing finished drawings, parts lists, diagrams and related documents.	To provide specific and precise instructions to Manufacturing or vendors for producing products or product components, amplifying upon the work of design draftsmen.	Company and departmental drafting practices, and understanding of pre-established material uses. Manufacturing practices and shop standards, skill in solving arithmetical problems, skill in graphical presentation – mechanical or freehand, and skill in interpreting instructions given on layouts, sketches, notes, etc.
By first analyzing drawings, layouts sketches, photographs, samples, written instructions and/or other pertinent information. Secondly, by recognizing patent drawing requirements. Third, by preparing drawings on government authorized or approved forms.	To help describe inventions and to meet the drawing requirements of the U.S. and foreign patent granting agencies.	"Rules of Practice" of the U.S. Patent Office. Drafting fundamentals and ink rendering, and skill in preparing 3 – dimensional pictorial illustrations. Nomenclature of mechanical, electrical, chemical and other required terms.
By organizing available information and by preparing finished tool drawings.	To provide specific and precise instructions to the tool room or tool vendors when the tool designer has not produced finished drawings.	Fundamentals of tool drafting. Company and departmental drafting practices, skill in solving arithmetical problems, skill in graphical presentation – mechanical or freehand, and skill in interpreting instructions given on layouts, sketches, notes, etc. Application of standard tool components.
By analysis of drawings, layouts, sketches, photographs, model samples, written instructions or other source materials. By planning layout and composition of cutaway, exploded, phantom, sectional, interior, exterior or other views needed to communicate necessary information. By preparing finished illustrations.	To help communicate data and information to the features and functions of products and systems for manuals, cooperating, service, erection, etc., or for marketing publicity or any other necessary company communication purposes.	Artistic layout and composition. Drafting fundamentals. Projection illustrating methods; oblique, isometric, trimetric, and perspective; and freehand artistic sketching. Color applications, dry brush, air brush, water color wash, and skill in artistic presentation.
By a study of drawings, photographs, sketches, objects, similar illustrations, or other similar source materials. By preparing finished illustrations, charts, graphs. By revising existing illustrations.	To help communicate data and information on parts and assemblies or other similar product features for instruction books, renewal parts bulletins, manuals, and similar publications.	Drafting fundamentals. Projection illustrating methods oblique, isometric, trimetric, and perspective. Ink rendering, and skill in graphical presentation.
By applying drawing preparation fundamentals.	To provide documents which can be satisfactorily used as reproduction masters.	Drawing preparation fundamentals and skill in graphic presentation and lettering.

effort and expense. As a key function, therefore, drafting must help meet the challenge. The old concept of drafting which permitted and often demanded that professional pride find expression in beautiful and artistically executed mechanical drawings with numerous accurately projected views and sections, is today as outmoded as the horse and buggy. A new concept of drafting values is needed. Drafting must be stripped of its frills without losing either clarity of presentation or accuracy of dimension.

Three of the easiest and most effective ways to reduce drafting costs are: 1) simplification of delineation, 2) elimination of non-essentials, and 3) extensive use of free-hand drawing. All of these practices have been followed to some degree, but not nearly to the extent they should.

Hard and fast rules of procedure are not to be recommended; however, here is a summary of common-sense, time saving practices used successfully in industry today:

• Where practical, use description to eliminate delineation and projected views.

• Eliminate views where shape can be described.

• Show only partial views of symmetrical objects.

• Avoid elaborate and repetitive detail.

• Omit, or cut down on thread detail.

• Omit details of nuts, bolts, etc when they can be described. Use plain outlines to indicate position.

• On assembly drawings, omit the detail of any parts which are included merely to show the part location.

• Do not make use of unnecessary dotted lines.

• Use partial cross-sectioning for clarity.

• Use symbols to delineate holes and their interiors.

• Make the drawing as small as practicable: A small drawing is usually made more easily and quickly.

• Use the smallest standard sized tracing that will accommodate the drawing.

• If two parts are similar and only differ to a small degree, complete delineation of both parts is not ordinarily required. Use description "same as except......"

• Drawings made for the purpose of modifying stock or commercial parts should be as plain as possible.

• Reduce cost by drawing objects out of scale but proportional as to size.

• Omit circles around reference numbers and the arrows on leader lines where it will not cause confusion.

• Do not duplicate dimensions.

• Substitute descriptions or recognized symbols for washers, studs, nuts, etc.

• Omit inch or foot marks when dimensions cannot be confused with other data.

• Use notes to eliminate repetitive data.

• Omit center lines except when absolutely necessary.

• Use free-hand drawing wherever possible. It is 20 to 30% faster than conventional drawing with instruments. Neither clarity nor completeness need be sacrificed.

• Do not use hand or machine lettering when typing will save time.

• Use tabulated arrangements in place of unnecessary repetitive views.

• Use datum lines to simplify dimensioning. The following rules will aid in utilization of this technique:

1. A datum line may be established in any plane: Indicate by a prominent "O" or other symbol.

2. Establish only one datum line per plane. The preferred locations for datum lines are on an edge, center line, or coinciding with datum of mating parts.

3. Indicate distances from the datum line to a point by line extensions parallel to datum line. Place the numeral representing distance at end of extension line.

4. Dimension only one side of symmetrical parts.

5. Both simplified and conventional dimensioning may be used on the same drawing, if necessary. ■

Type of Designing	Objective	Why	
ADVANCE PRODUCT *	Conceive ideas for new product designs and for improvement of existing products. Develop advanced engineering design concepts. Conceive principles and establish basic design configurations.	To satisfy a recognized or defined engineering requirement. Give graphical expression to ideas or concepts in such form as will facilitate analysis, consultation, and communication.	
PRODUCT	Design new products. Redesign existing products by conceiving functional and design improvements.	To determine whether functional design requirements are satisfied by graphical means. To establish spatial relationships, electrical and mechanical clearances, configurations, and dimensional limitations.	
PRODUCTION	Revise existing designs to reduce cost (at equal or better quality) by facilitating manufacture and assembly. Eliminate product weakness. Eliminate "bugs" discovered in the production phases.	To determine design revisions which will reduce cost, eliminate production difficulties and increase the value of parts components and products — maintaining equal or better quality.	
SYSTEMS	Arrange products or components into equipments, systems, or other combinations to satisfy established requirements.	To determine clearances, spatial relations and other dimensional features of the products, components and other elements used in the system in order to facilitate installation and servicing.	
PRODUCT ADAPTATION	Modify established designs to satisfy special requirements for manufacturing, erection, installation, servicing, match and line-up or other requirements, or to standardize a line.	To establish new dimensions, configurations, clearances and spatial relations without changing functional design.	
APPEARANCE	Make new or existing products more efficient, useable and/or saleable by design of exterior (may affect arrangement of component parts or even basic design).	To fully consider human, utility, functional, manufacturing and marketing requirements in the design of the product's exterior.	
TOOL DESIGNING A	Design new tool for parts having new configurations fo: Hold or guide work during processing Guide cutting tools Form parts Perform assembly operations Inspect work.	To aid and make possible the manufacture of the concerned products at minimum cost.	
TOOL DESIGNING B	Design new tools for parts having "Similar to" existing configurations; revise existing tool designs. To accomplish same purpose as listed for Tool Design A.	Same as above but mostly involving simpler problems or tools for parts similar to those for which tools already exist.	

*Enlarge by adding required specific skills or understanding, such as: knowledge
**May be further subdivided into product components, ratings, electrical or

How	When		*Knowledge Required Of —	**Typical Work
	After	Before		
By an analysis of engineering requirements; recognition of design problems; relating problems to engineering data; conception of practical solutions. By preparing basic design layouts, sketches, diagrams and graphical analyses and studies in order to test solutions. Written report sometimes required.	Management (Engineering, Marketing or others) has recognized a need and defined a requirement for a new design.	Functional details have been worked out or design problems have been solved.	Assigned engineering field and understanding of the industrial arts. Properties and application of materials. Proper application of proven manufacturing methods and processes. Availability and sources of pertinent engineering data. Basic steps required to develop a product. Historical knowledge of product or product line, both that of the company and of competitors. Functional principles embodied in the product. Specialized technical knowledge peculiar to the given product's requirements. All influences which will affect the product design or operation. All drafting fundamentals and principles.	Advance Designing of products or equipment such as missiles, engines, turbines, etc.
By analyzing design requirements, relating requirements to design data and solving design problems. By preparing functional design layouts, sketches, diagrams, graphical analyses and studies. Written report sometimes required.	Engineering problems have been solved and design specifications have been established.	Design for function has been completely worked out.	A specialized area of an assigned engineering field and an understanding of the industrial arts. The utility and limitations of materials. Proper application of proven manufacturing methods and processes. The availability and sources of design data. Basic design procedures. Historical knowledge of similar company products. The required function of the product. Specialized technical knowledge peculiar to a given product's requirements. The influences which will affect the product's design or operation. The requirements for information expected of drafting. All drafting fundamentals and principles.	Designing of products such as washers, dryers, lamp ballasts, rectifiers, etc.
By obtaining costs of existing parts, components, and products. By analyzing tolerances, fits, manufacturing and assembling operations and raw materials requirements. By evaluating materials and processes employed and investigating, recognizing and defining production difficulties. By preparing sketches, layouts, and/or written instructions for design changes.	Prototype has been built, or after first run of parts or products.	Should be done before high production tools are made.	Value analyses techniques. Properties, workability, and application of materials. Manufacturing processes and methods. Shop practices and manufacturing standards (fits, tolerances). Production tools and machines. Basic mechanical design principles. Comparative costs of materials and processes. Technical features of concerned products. All drafting fundamentals and principles.	Production Designing of any and all products designed and/or manufactured by the company.
By first graphically arranging the parts of the system and then analyzing arrangement requirements. By preparing layouts, sketches, finished drawings, and diagrams to graphically describe relationships of products, devices, and connections.	General design parameters have been established.		Function of two or more products (The Company's or others). The utility of materials. The application of related products. Availability and sources of design data. All drafting fundamentals and principles. Specialized technical knowledge peculiar to a particular system.	Designing systems of the type manufactured by the company or division of the company.
By graphically determining and expressing modifications to existing designing. By analyzing design modification requirements and relating requirements to available design data. By preparing layouts, sketches, diagrams and graphical representations of required modifications of established designs.	Functional design has been established.		A specialized area of an assigned engineering field and an understanding of the industrial arts. The utility and limitations of materials. The proper application of proven manufacturing methods and processes. The availability and sources of design data. Basic design procedures. Specialized technical knowledge peculiar to a given product's requirements. The product function. Drafting fundamentals and principles.	Adaptation Designing of company products.
By graphically expressing the integration of function, materials, appearance, color and distinction, which involves analyzing functional design, recognition of utility, materials, and human requirements. By preparing sketches and constructing models. By preparing finished drawings, sketches, and/or layouts.	When expedient but preferably before product design		Appearance and industrial design principles. Company principles of product distinction. Technical knowledge in the field of industrial arts. The application and finished appearance of materials. External influences on the product (weather, acids, etc.) Human requirements and preferences. Graphic arts; sketching, color applications; perspective.	Appearance, Designing of any of the company's products.
By recognizing, defining and analyzing tool design problems. By conceiving tool designs. By preparing layouts, sketches, of finished drawings of tools, dies, molds, jigs, fixtures, etc.	Product part configurations and dimensions have been established. Subassemblies and other components have been established.		Properties, workability and application of materials. Machine tools and their utility and versatility. Production processes and methods. Principles of tool design. Shop practices. Manufacturing standards. Tool drafting fundamentals as well as drafting fundamentals and principles. Availability and source of supply of standard tool components.	Typical tool designing work will be determined by the tool requirements of each department.
By understanding and recognizing tool requirements. By preparing layouts, sketches or finished drawings of tools, dies, jigs, and fixtures. By revising existing tool drawings.	Basic tool designs have been established.		Workability and application of materials. Machine tools and their utility and versatility. Production processes and methods. Fundamentals of tool design. Shop practices. Manufacturing standards. Tool drafting fundamentals. Availability and sources of supply of standard tool components.	

of thermodynamics, pneumatics, fluid flow, high voltage insulation, electric arc phenomena, circuit relaying, mechanical features, or other distinguishable product or systems features.

THERE ARE TIMES when it is mandatory to measure the performance of the design and drafting department and the individuals in it. The need for evaluation may arise when the department head is faced with a mass layoff due to contract termination and wishes to keep the best people as a nucleus on which to rebuild the department, or when he wants an equitable basis on which to give merit increases, or an aid in the preparation of periodic ratings. Having met all three of these situations a number of times, I have arrived, with the assistance of my chief draftsmen, at a system which, while far from perfect, is better than no system at all.

Reflection on the problems of supervising a design and drafting department brings to light one significant fact: the people in the department are creative and, like all creative people, are subject to fits of temperament. During the course of an engineering career which spans thirty years, I have seen design and drafting departments of all kinds and sizes. My association with these departments has ranged from casual contact to Chief Engineer of Design and Drafting. Repeatedly, I have heard the same departmental complaints: bad lighting and drafts.

Two years ago, a major corporation

EVALUATING WORK EFFECTIVENESS

IN THE DRAFTING

FIGURE 1

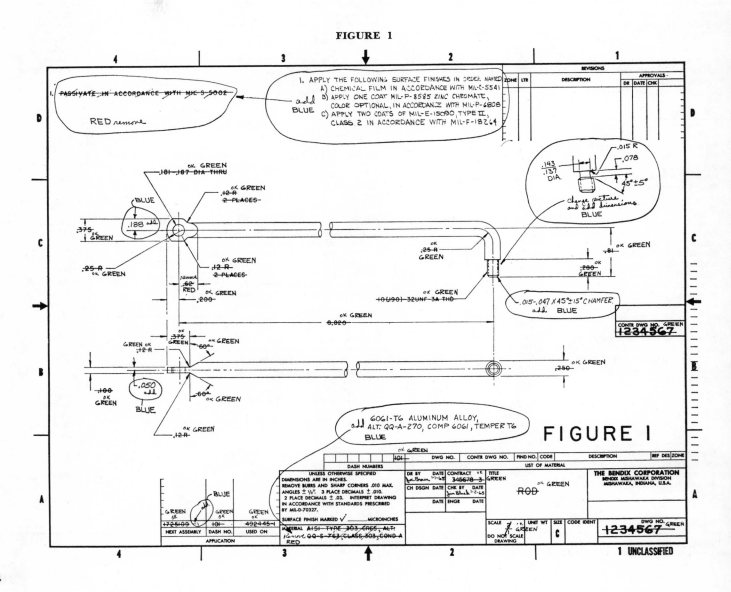

FIGURE I

built a new drafting room with a high level of diffused lighting and in which drafts were reduced to a minimum. Deprived of these two common causes for complaint, the people found other things to complain about, such as the body of a dead pigeon on an adjoining roof and small errors in the standards manuals. The supervisor's first reaction is, "let's get rid of these chronic complainers." This is sometimes justified, but just as often the chronic

by Parker G. Cox

DEPARTMENT

complainer is your best man—hence the need for a system which eliminates emotion in the evaluation of performance. The system outlined here is a step in this direction.

To measure the performance of a design and drafting department and its individual members requires the measurement of accuracy and rate. Accuracy is measured as a percent of correctness of drawings before checking. Rate is measured as hours per square foot required to prepare and check drawings.

Accuracy is measured by counting the marks which the checker places on the drawing. Three colored pencils are used by the checkers at the Bendix Mishawaka Division: items lined out in red are to be removed, items marked in blue are to be added or corrected, and items lined out in green are correct. Accuracy equals the number of green items divided by the sum of the red, blue, and green items expressed as a percentage. Note that this is accuracy before checking. An example of a check print marked as above is shown in Figure 1. A curve showing the drafting accuracy of the entire department by months for the years 1962 and 1963 is given in Figure 2. The accuracies of some individual draftsmen and individual drawings are given in Table 1.

In using the accuracy figures arrived at in the above manner, prob-

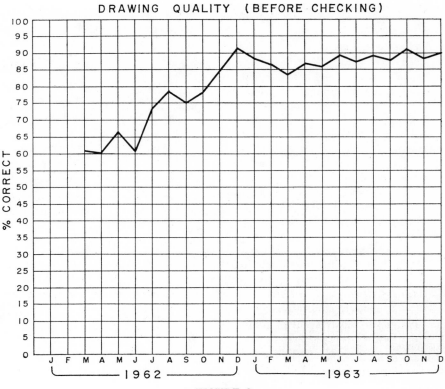

FIGURE 2

DRAWING NO.	SIZE	SQ FT	HRS	HRS/SQ FT	BLUE CHECKS	RED CHECKS	GREEN CHECKS	% ACCURACY	PERFORMANCE
DRAFTSMAN A									
JX190−361	D	5.2	16	3.08	7	1	20	71	.768
JX190−360	C	2.6	10	3.84	6	0	20	76	.650
JX190−368	C	2.6	8	3.07	7	0	14	67	.730
JX190−359	C	2.6	8	3.07	8	1	23	71	.770
JX190−369	C	2.6	10	3.84	15	0	50	76	.664
JX190−367	C	2.6	6	2.30	4	2	15	71	1.028
JX190−366	B	1.3	2	1.53	1	0	12	92	2.005
JX190−363	B	1.3	4	3.07	1	0	17	94	1.022
JX190−365	B	1.3	2	1.53	1	0	6	85	1.848
JX190−364	E	10.4	36	3.36	72	25	72	42	.417
TOTALS		32.5	102	3.1	122	29	249	62	.666
DRAFTSMAN B									
1562770	C	2.6	3	1.15	9	0	10	53	1.548
1562771	C	2.6	3	1.15	5	0	11	68	1.970
1562680	C	2.6	4	1.54	6	0	23	79	1.712
JX182−2565	E	10.4	10	1.00	4	3	60	89	2.975
1563307	D	5.2	5	.96	8	0	72	90	3.120
JX187−493	C	2.6	2	.76	3	0	77	96	4.200
JX182−2562	D	5.2	8	1.54	6	1	33	82	1.778
JX182−2563	D	5.2	10	1.92	2	6	30	78	1.352
JX182−2566	J	17.5	30	1.71	25	10	200	85	1.660
TOTALS		53.5	75	1.40	68	20	516	85	2.025

TABLE I

TABLE II

SIZE	SQUARE FEET
A	0.65
B	1.3
C	2.6
D	5.2
E	10.4

The Author

PARKER G. Cox is Chief Engineer, Design and Drafting for the Bendix Mishawaka Division of Bendix Corporation, Mishawaka, Indiana.

lems appear. Some of them are:

(1) How to evaluate the errors committed in the light of the complexity of the drawing.

(2) Weighing of errors. (A misspelled word should not count as heavily as an incorrect dimension.)

(3) Personal equation. The opinions of checkers versus draftsmen; both may be correct. The variation among checkers.

(4) Comparison of junior and senior people.

(5) The evaluation of special skills—for example, the design of a casting in comparison with the creation of an electrical schematic.

Rate is measured by keeping track of the hours spent in preparing each drawing and the hours spent checking each drawing. A work sheet used in accumulating this data is shown in Figure 3. The hours spent preparing the drawing divided by the number of square feet in the drawing gives the rate in hours per square foot. The same method applies to the checking rate. A curve showing the drafting plus checking rates of the entire department by months is given in Figure 4. The drafting rate for some individual draftsmen and individual drawings is given in Table 1. The number of square feet used for the various drawing sizes is given in Table II. The data used in plotting Figure 4 is given in Table III.

One final step in this system is a method to evaluate the percent correctness against the rate in hours per

FIGURE 3

WORK SHEET FOR DESIGN & DRAFTING USE ONLY

PRIME WORK REQUEST NO. 8122   PROJ. NO. IOSNOOO   CONTRACT NO. ROw69-01 COG. GR. LEADER MAXWELL

LAYOUT OR TOP ASSY. NO.   TEST FIXTURE   LD NO.   MODEL

DIGITAL SUBMODULE T.S.

ITEM	BXM NO.	SIZE	REQD	TITLE	DR BY	DATE	CKD BY	DATE	KIND REL	TIME HRS DFTS SUP	CKR	OTHER GRS GR LEADER	GRS WR
	1416146	E		TEST FIXTURE, ANALOG	DY S2	8/6	Coop	8/24	TE	5.0 1.0	2.0		
	1416147	E		CHASSIS MODIFIED	DY S2	8/5	Coop	8/24	TE	5.0 1.0	2.5		
	1416148	D		SCHEMATIC	DY S2	8/9	D.G.	8/26	TE	2.0 .5	1.0		
	1416149	C		TERMINAL BOARD ASS'Y	DY S2	8/22	D.G.	8/23	TE	2.0 .5	1.0		
	1416159	E		TEST FIXTURE, READ	DY S2	8/7	D.M.	8/31	TE	5.0 1.0	1.5		
	1416160	E		CHASSIS MODIFIED	DY S2	8/8	D.M.	8/31	TE	4.0 1.0	1.5		
	1416161	D		SCHEMATIC	DY S2	8/9	D.G.	9/1	TE	2.0 .5	.8		
	1416162	D		TERMINAL BOARD ASS'Y	HART	8/30	MAX	9/11	TE	7.2 1.0	1.0		
	1416163	D		TERMINAL BOARD ASS'Y	HART	9/3	MAX	9/11	TE	6.8 1.0	1.0		

FIGURE 4

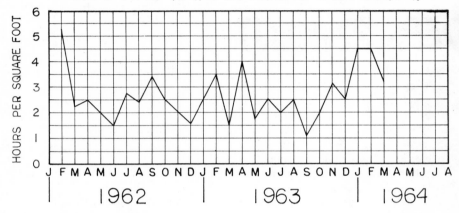

DRAFTING RATE IN HOURS PER SQ. FT.

TABLE III

1962	DRAFTING	CHECKING	TOTAL	PERCENT
FEBRUARY	3.46	1.26	5.26	36.3
MARCH	1.45	.79	2.24	54.4
APRIL	1.579	.847	2.42	53.6
MAY	1.161	.748	1.91	64.4
JUNE	.91	.59	1.50	65.3
JULY	1.625	1.095	2.72	67.0
AUGUST	1.753	.617	2.37	35.0
SEPTEMBER	2.017	1.361	3.38	67.0
OCTOBER	1.732	.758	2.49	43.7
NOVEMBER	1.436	.663	2.10	46.2
DECEMBER	1.050	.569	1.62	54.0

1963				
JANUARY	1.727	.685	2.412	40.0
FEBRUARY	2.463	1.051	3.514	43.0
MARCH	1.003	.559	1.562	55.0
APRIL	2.992	1.021	4.013	34.0
MAY	1.224	.524	1.748	43.0
JUNE	1.660	.960	2.620	57.8
JULY	1.231	.724	1.96	59.0
AUGUST	1.990	.579	2.57	29.0
SEPTEMBER	.77	.34	1.11	49.0
OCTOBER	1.461	.514	1.98	35.0
NOVEMBER	2.558	.570	3.13	22.0
DECEMBER	1.824	.764	2.59	42.0

1964				
JANUARY	3.33	1.26	4.59	38.0
FEBRUARY	3.30	1.27	4.57	38.0

CORRELATION CHART

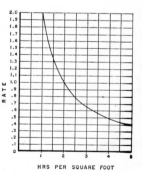

ACCURACY = % CORRECT / 60		RATE = 2 / HRS/SQ FT	
% CORRECT	ACCURACY	HRS/SQ FT	RATE
30	0.500	1.0	2.000
35	0.584	1.2	1.665
40	0.666	1.4	1.430
45	0.750	1.6	1.250
50	0.834	1.8	1.110
55	0.917	2.0	1.000
60	1.000	2.2	0.910
65	1.082	2.4	0.833
70	1.167	2.6	0.769
75	1.250	2.8	0.714
80	1.332	3.0	0.666
85	1.418		
90	1.500		
95	1.583		
100	1.666		

TABLE IV

square foot. This tells us whether or not some individuals are producing rapidly at the expense of accuracy. Stated mathematically: average accuracy times average rate equals average performance, or individual accuracy times individual rate equals in-

dividual performance. If we establish norms of 60 percent accuracy equal to one, and two hours per square foot rate equal to one, we have a performance norm of one for a draftsman who produces a 60 percent accurate drawing at the rate of two hours per square foot. A correlation chart for

accuracy and rate is given in Table IV.

As stated previously, the system is far from perfect and should be used judiciously. It cannot give an absolute rating of a draftsman. It can be used, however, to compare an individual with his group. ∎

How to Make Best Use of Available Drafting Space

Allotment of drafting room space is often a serious problem . . . here's how to use yours to the best advantage

A. D. Kaill
Editor

Is space at a premium in your drafting office? Have your rental rates been increased lately, forcing you into retrenchment? Are you faced with the problem of accommodating more men in the engineering office without any increase in your allotment of floor space?

These are serious problems in many engineering and drafting sections. It seems that wherever we travel we find supervision are trying to squeeze more people into an already overcrowded working area.

There are solutions, of course, but like all worthwhile projects, they require considerable research and development. And this is the one thing that is usually not available.

How many times, for instance, have you seen the location of the drawing office equipment left to the discretion of the janitoring or bull squad? Have you ever arrived for work one morning to find that an additional drafting board had been brought into the office overnight — with space being made for it by closing up the clearances between the established equipment? Maybe this has never happened in **your** office — but from our observations it does happen in far too many.

Comfort is important

It is indeed surprising that while many companies insist upon continual study of their production opera-tions to ensure minimum costs and maximum profits, they fail to make even cursory examination of their drafting and engineering departments. When something goes wrong, or a design or development project gets behind schedule, management will often jump in with both feet in the expectation of unearthing another case of maladministration by those directly involved with the drafting operation. Otherwise they usually leave well enough alone. But this is not enough. The drafting office is the one area where it is important that the employees work in comfort all the time, to obtain maximum productivity.

Yet we are all familiar with the drafting office where, with expanding work load, more tables are crammed into spaces already inadequate, and where makeshifts must be used because of management's unwillingness to provide proper facilities. Crowded conditions should never be tolerated in the normal routine of a drawing office. It is true that such conditions can be put up with for very short periods, but it is just as true that eventually they will have a noxious effect upon the quality and quantity of the work.

How serious is the problem?

Management should never look upon this problem lightly. It is one of the malignant diseases penetrating the very inner workings of our Canadian industry, hence our national economy.

Most drafting offices that we have observed are laid out very poorly. Often, like Topsy . . . they appear to have "just growed".

Cabinets of reference material, drawing storage files, catalogue cupboards, print-making equipment and the general supplies cupboard are usually placed in one of two spots:
● In the most inaccessible corner, where everyone has to take many steps to reach them, or
● Right in the geographical centre of the office, effectively cutting off all light and communication.

There is no one best location for all this equipment; in fact, we hesitate to even make a suggestion. The best location for each individual piece can only be determined when you have full knowledge of all the other factors involved in the layout of your particular office. The best location in most cases, must be a compromise between the need for accessibility and for minimum interference with other office functions.

Adequate space is a must

But the decision where to locate these extras is only incidental to the one big decision. The chief problem to be resolved in the layout of a drafting office, quite logically, is where to locate the draftsmen. And the major factor influencing this decision is the space required per man. Here is where you must bow to the limits put upon you by the type of equipment you have to work with.

Modern drafting machines and adjustable boards provide for optimum utilization of available floor space.

If your office is the old-fashioned type, with flat horizontal boards, of necessity you are forced to make the most uneconomical use of floor space. And remember that space costs money. If your office further cuts down on your efficiency and working comfort by failing to provide individual reference tables, we suggest it's time you began looking for another job. Unless you are a government employee (and for some reason government drafting offices are generally the poorest equipped in the country) it's a fairly safe bet that your employers will be forced out of business within the next few years by their more progressive competitors.

But what can be done about it? How can output be increased without increasing drafting office space or upping operating costs?

Two step solution

There's a simple two-step solution available to all. It will entail some capital outlay, but this will be compensated for by lowered operating costs per drawing produced. This solution requires that:
● Your office be equipped with modern drafting facilities — drawing machines, adjustable boards, and matching reference tables.
● The office layout be made a matter of engineering methods study, so that optimum use of space will result. That's all there is to it. No hokus-pokus . . . no mumbo-jumbo . . . just plain ordinary sound engineering methods.

The accompanying diagrams give some idea of what can be accomplished. It has been our practice to use a rule of thumb, the figures of 400 to 500 square feet for each group of ten draftsmen under normal operating conditions and using modern equipment. Where it is absolutely necessary to expand facilities temporarily, we agree that up to 20 draftsmen can be accommodated in about the same space — but we emphasize, this must be for a short time only.

The space figures given in the diagrams make the savings self-evident. These can be used as a sound basis upon which appropriations for actual installation can be made.

We have used Kuhlman products for the standard dimensions quoted in these examples because they are typical of the modern equipment available for drafting rooms. Other manufacturers have similar equipment which also can save space and cost.

We usually make it our business to look in on the drafting office when we are privileged to visit a plant —we find that the conditions there are an excellent indicator of the state of the company's management. Make certain that those who visit your engineering and drafting offices are impressed with the same forward thinking that you put into your other facilities. ■

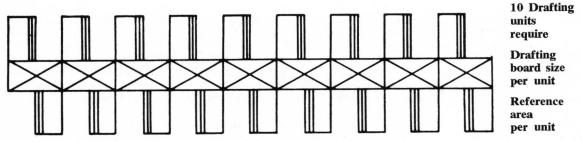

10 Drafting units require	386
Drafting board size per unit	12.5
Reference area per unit	7.6

Another excellent layout with 36 x 50 boards and 30 x 60 reference tables.

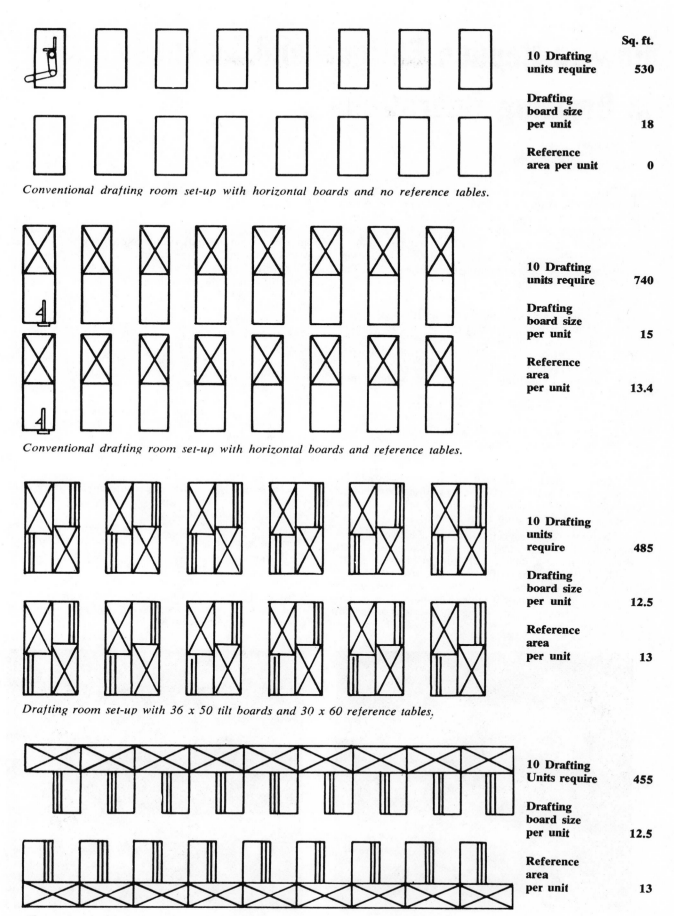

	Sq. ft.
10 Drafting units require	530
Drafting board size per unit	18
Reference area per unit	0

Conventional drafting room set-up with horizontal boards and no reference tables.

10 Drafting units require	740
Drafting board size per unit	15
Reference area per unit	13.4

Conventional drafting room set-up with horizontal boards and reference tables.

10 Drafting units require	485
Drafting board size per unit	12.5
Reference area per unit	13

Drafting room set-up with 36 x 50 tilt boards and 30 x 60 reference tables.

10 Drafting Units require	455
Drafting board size per unit	12.5
Reference area per unit	13

Alternative drafting room set-up with same size equipment as immediately above.

How to Reduce Fatigue and Sickness in Drafting Operations

W. STRAUBE

Kuhlmann Straube Co., Ltd.

This article is based on a report of tests carried out by the Battelle Institute of Columbus, Ohio, and points to the need for thought on the subject of production in the drawing office where all production begins.

Just how big a part does the draftsman's equipment play in his efficiency? For the purpose of tabulating results, each type of test equipment is indicated by the initial letter shown.

TH. T-square and set squares on a horizontal board.

PH. Counterbalanced parallel motion and set squares on a horizontal board.

PU. Counterbalanced parallel motion and set squares on an upright adjustable board.

DH. Standard drafting machine on a horizontal board.

DU. Standard drafting machine on an upright adjustable board.

DZU. Drafting machine with an adjustable zero head on an upright adjustable board.

Test drawings made included an uncomplicated engine part, an architectural drawing and a fairly difficult assembly drawing with main group arranged about centre lines inclined at different angles.

To create a measuring standard, the average time taken to produce the first drawing was estimated, each draftsman using a standard drafting machine at an upright adjustable board. This average time of 55 minutes is expressed as 100% in the tables below and is compared proportionately with the times taken to produce the same drawing using the various other test equipment.

Drawing equipment	DU	PU	DH	PH	TH
% Working time	100	117	123	128	139

This test clearly shows the advantage of the drafting machines at an upright adjustable board. It is interesting to note that the test was completed in faster time with the parallel motion unit and an upright board than with a drafting machine at a horizontal board, indicating that for this test, board position was more important than the drafting machine.

The second test was designed to produce conditions said to favor the use of T-squares and parallel motion units.

It has long been held that the drafting machine cannot compete with this equipment where the design demands the drawing of long horizontal lines. But the test drawing disproved this theory. In fact, test drawings produced with a parallel motion unit at an upright board required 25% more time, and with a T-square 31% more time, than with the drafting machine. The final test drawing was of a four stroke internal combustion engine. The results show great advantages in the use of drafting heads with adjustable zero for this type of work. These heads permit the necessary contant change of drawing base angles without calculation. Actual times were as follows:

Drawing equipment	DU	DZU	PU	PH
% Working time	100	84	120	141

The above individual tests and the following figures prove conclusively that the drafting machine on an upright adjustable board is the most suitable equipment from the aspect of speedy working.

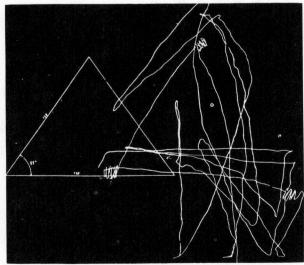
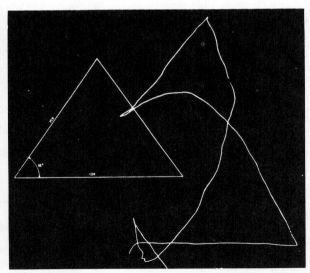

Fig 2. Before and after studies. At left is seen the work of draftsman's hand when drawing a triangle using an ordinary T-square. Same task when performed on modern drafting machine at right. Notice how work is reduced.

Drawing equipment	% Working time simple drawing	% Working time difficult drawing	Mean % work time
DU	100	100	100
DZU	100	84	92
PU	115	125	120
DH	120	130	125
PH	130	140	135
TH	130	150	140

To eleminate the fatigue factor, short tests of one minute were carried out and in order that only the purely mechanical work of drawing was involved, each draftsman was allowed practice time on each piece of equipment making drawings of the simple figures chosen for the test.

As in previous tests, the time taken when using a standard drafting machine and an upright adjustable board, were taken as the measuring standard and are again expressed as 100% to the following tables.

Examining these figures it will be seen from DU, DH and PU, PH that board position has made little difference to the working times with similar equipment. The mean times for PH, TH, PU are similar but they are more than 100% longer than those for DU and DH, thus proving absolutely the simplification of work made possible by the drafting machine.

Drawing equipment	Triangle	Rectangle	Mean % working time
DU	100	100	100
DH	98	99	99
PH	210	200	205
TH	225	194	210
PU	247	189	218

The movement diagrams in figure 2 illustrate that even on the most simple drawings, the drafting machines can save a great deal of movement and so reduce fatigue. Results from 10,000 tests made on horizontal boards, show that between 50 and 75% of drafting errors and inaccuracies occur when working at the top of the board where maintenance of a convenient working position is most fatiguing.

The draftsman's working position and the equipment he uses have an effect on his health also, quite apart from its influence on his efficiency.

The tests carried out by Battelle were not of long enough duration to reach definite conclusions but the following observations are nevertheless of interest.

Four working positions were involved in these tests —sitting or standing at a horizontal board and sitting or standing at an upright adjustable board.

When working at a horizontal board the draftsman perspired more freely and both pulse and respiratory rates increased.

This rate increase lasted for an average of four to six minutes before being returned to normal by the body's regulating function.

Interviews with 300 draftsmen produced information on the incidence of common complaints and are shown as percentages in the presentation

It was found that the energy consumed by the person who maintains a stooping position is 40% to 50% greater than that consumed in a normal standing position. The increased use of back muscles to maintain a convenient working position accounted for much of this increase and is undoubtedly responsible for the much higher incidence of backaches. Foot complaints must be expected from draftsmen who stand to do their work. ∎

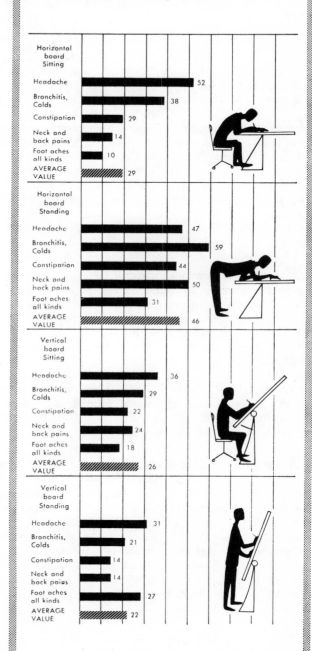

Fatigue vs. sickness rate in the drafting office in %

The main physical strain put on an engineer or draftsman working at the drawing board, such as regular fatigue, and many symptoms caused by working on a horizontal or slightly inclined board, can be greatly reduced, if not eliminated, by the use of modern drafting equipment.

Statistics shown are excerpts from the Battelle Report on drafting fatigue and efficiency.

13 ways to cut DRAFTING COSTS

**Check this list of modern methods and materials
compiled by an expert in drafting-room procedures.**

A F GAGNE, *Consultant*
Binghamton, NY.

To reduce drafting time: **Don't draw unnecessary lines.** One approach, the "Simplified Drafting method, omits all lines that have no importance to shop personnel. But if carried too far, the time saved in drafting may be swallowed up in production. A better method is to avoid drawing lines when they can be printed, traced, stamped, constructed with a machine, or otherwise mechanically applied. Here are the tools available today. Are you using them?

1 **Preprint all repetitive material.** Provide cut-to-size, pre-printed forms in all common sizes. They save lettering title blocks and drawing borders, and get rid of odd-size tracings. Stock forms can be purchased for not much more than cost of paper in rolls.

Parts of the drawing itself can even be preprinted. Optional material can be printed in non-reproducing blue lines, and traced as needed. Wiring and pneumatic diagrams, chassis with different hole layouts, studs, spacers, cams and springs can be printed in black for the draftsman to complete by filling in. This saves time in checking as well as in drafting.

2 **Prepare tracing templets for common components.** A file of standard component drawings or assemblies, suitable for tracing, are cheap to prepare. An increasing number of component suppliers offer tracing templets of their products to customers. But you can make your own. A file of full, half and quarter-scale drawings of proprietary parts and components will save drafting time when the assembled product has many standard parts. Ingersoll-Rand Co, for example, estimates that the templet file in their Machine Assembly Section saves 30 percent in drafting time.

3 **Supply rubber stamps and self-adhesive appliques for frequently drawn symbols and diagrams.** Rubber stamps are popular for applying title blocks and standard notes but have four limitations: drying time, uncertain quality, gray lines and uncertain positioning. New inks and pads help solve the first two problems, while the recently introduced stamps made of transparent rubber and plastic have overcome the positioning difficulty.

Appliques, those transparent, pressure-sensitive drawing aids, are also useful. Standard symbolic components and custom forms (hole or drilling patterns, mechanical components, special notes or warnings, title blocks) can be purchased in strips or rolls at nominal cost compared to equivalent drafting time. Some firms are completely sold on them; others find that adhesives sometimes bleed, picking up dirt, or that they separate, wrinkle, or leave heavy "ghost" backgrounds when several generations of intermediates are made. This will not be a problem when tracings are microfilmed or otherwise reproduced in a manner that does not depend on light passing through the paper.

4 **Templets do a uniform job.** When a symbol consists of but a few simple lines, the cutout or stencil templet is faster than the appliques or any of the tracing methods. They are inexpensive and make short work of squares, circles, ellipses and such specialties as fluid fittings drawn to precise scale. It may seem that such painstaking delineation is a waste of time, no matter how speeded up. But careful component layouts provide visual guarantees against interference—important as equipment becomes more complex, more compact.

Leroy, Variograph or Wrico scriber templets are inherently faster than cut-out templets because no shifting is required to create a complex symbol. But, they are limited in the size of character that can be made.

5 **New pens and pencils solve some long-standing problems for the draftsman.** Pencils sharpened with pen knife and file (or sandpaper block) can cost as much as $75 per man-year according to a time check made by the author. Instead, provide manual and electric rotary sharpening devices, vibrating sandpaper blocks (good for compasses as well as pencils) or mechanical pencils with thin leads that need no sharpening (recommended for a series of long lines, rather than for detail work). Also, an electric eraser can easily save fifteen minutes per day, returning purchase cost (around $22) in one month.

Push-button ruling pens refilled from a cartridge in the handle, and wide-blade pens hold more ink and are less apt to run dry at the wrong time. There are also special fountain pens and spring-leaf brushes that provide constant-width lines for hand lettering.

6 **Take advantage of recent developments in drafting paper.** The cost of drafting paper is negligible when compared to the value of the drawing after it has been prepared. Therefore, don't buy inexpensive paper; instead look for those qualities that reduce drafting effort.

If, for example, a harder pencil can be used without gouging, embossing, or reducing contrast between line and background, there will be fewer stops for pencil sharpening and tracings will be cleaner, sharper, and probably more accurate. Other points: does the material take pencil or ink well after erasing; does it pucker after erasure or when humidity changes; is it sufficiently transparent for good prints; will it resist tears and wrinkles.

Some of the new polyester films such as DuPont's "Cronaflex" score outstandingly on all counts. They are unusually transparent; a 6H pencil produces an intense line that can be speedily erased; they are virtually indestructible, with none of the tears, rips and dog-earing so often experienced with vellum. A film thickness of four mils is suggested to prevent embossing by hard pencils. Cost is around 21¢/sq ft in quantity.

7 Use intermediates to save tracing time. These "reproducible reproductions" will restore worn-out tracings, generate duplicate "originals" for more economical printing, and facilitate engineering change and redesign. This last application is one of the most valuable and perhaps the least common. With intermediates, drawings are edited, not redrawn or traced. Unwanted areas are masked out when the intermediate is printed. Lines are erased by chemical or mechanical means (or, if a negative intermediate, by rapidly brushing a special opaque paint over undesired portions). New drawings are composed from scissored pieces of old drawings.

8 Specify photographs in place of drawings. This is especially useful for showing changes in existing equipment; these are marked over a photoprint. Other applications: assembly drawings, diagrams for instruction manuals, exploded views of complex mechanisms. Because the camera does not have a discriminating eye, distracting backgrounds must be minimized.

9 Tell draftsman how accurate the drawing needs to be. There are a number of occasions when an accurate, mechanical drawing is unnecessary and a freehand sketch will be quite adequate. On the other hand, special parts can sometimes be prepared by making very precise, full-scale drawings and printing directly on the surface of the metal. Thus, one precise layout in drafting saves many layouts in the shop.

10 Provide a comfortable, efficient environment. If you can afford posture chairs for the secretaries and the factory girls, get good chairs for the much better-paid draftsmen. The board is also important. With the new, fast-adjusting board, the work is always at the right angle and the right height. Easy-shift boards not only make substantial contribution to output, drawing quality, appearance of drafting room and morale, but can save up to 40% in floorspace.

11 Typewriters are faster, cleaner than lettering pens. Special purpose typewriters or conventional typewriters with long carriages are faster and neater than other methods for those long lists of materials, specifications, notes and instructions. But all too often, these parts of the drawings are hand-lettered because the firm doesn't think it can afford a special machine. This is not good reasoning: the cost of the machine is small compared to the cost of equivalent drafting time.

Another easy job often done the hard way is drawing guide lines for lettering. This can be accomplished with a cross-section backing sheet under the drawing, such as K & E's Laminene board covering, or by providing drawing paper that has non-reproducing cross-hatch lines.

12 Drafting machine does the job of straightedge, scale, protractor, triangles. Combining these tools, comfortably in the left hand can save 10 to 50% in drafting time. The new X-Y track-type machines overcome many of the objections to the steel band or linkage-controlled machines. First-cost, habit, and training time are other problems each firm must evaluate for itself. For those who prefer to stick with the string-type parallel rule (recently improved with ball bearings) a triangle is recommended that has a knob for lifting and stencil cut-outs for symbols and machine elements.

13 Special tools make short work of special jobs. Ellipsographs, "circular drawing machines" and templets do away with classical methods of constructing ellipses. Other 3-D devices include semi-automatic machines for perspective rendering and specially ruled paper.

Art projectors are, unfortunately, little known outside the art department. But they have many applications in the drafting room. Photographs, small drawings or parts can be traced on the spot, without distortion or lost time. Price is around $430.

Light boxes are a time saver when tracing poor prints, comparing details with assemblies, or checking interferences through several layers of tracing paper. Other uses include inspection of transparencies and X-rays, and stripping-in and opaquing of negatives. Compared to tracing tables, portable light boxes will not occupy space in the drafting room, can be stored like a book and conveniently brought to the user's board when needed. Prices start at about $32.50.

Another gadget is the cross-hatcher. It permits faster and better-appearing work than cross-hatching positioned by eye. Some are built into the drafting machine (Nestler); others are a separate piece of equipment to be used with parallel rule or drafting machine. Also consider having such time-and-work savers as adjustable curves, proportional dividers, dotting pens, double-line pens, quick adjusting compasses. ■

New Methods Speed Making and Handling of Drawings

Norbert Stahl

THE ivory tower of engineering has produced a paper empire all its own which is about to crumble. Not only has this paper stuffing process, called "documentation," become increasingly costly (results of questionnaires indicate that up to 90% of the engineering dollar is being used for documentation), it is also the cause of endless duplication in other branches of the company.

It is not enough to point to the problems. How do you correct them? Change is never popular; however, it seems inevitable that top management will sooner or later attempt to do something about the waste. The best plan would be an integrated documentation system based on "action papers." With the end-use in mind, only those papers which can actually be used by Manufacturing, Sales, Service, etc., would be created. The end-user and not the engineer would determine the content. Reproduction facilities would be centralized, and the amount of paper work strictly monitored by this integrated line function. Objective measuring tools, such as the ratios given at the end of this article, would permit company officials to determine proper use of manpower, facilities, and money and enable the documentation group to do its job effectively. Here are some specific suggestions collected in the course of this survey:

1) Take greater advantage of electronic data-processing.

2) Produce drawings from computer-stored information.

3) Reduce the size of drawings in general—to facilitate microfilming and to reduce printing, handling, and mailing costs.

4) Resort to greater use of aperture cards and other microfilm techniques for storage, reproduction, and direct use at point of requirement.

5) Simplify procedure for making engineering changes.

6) Adopt complete decimal system of dimensioning to facilitate arithmetical calculations and to present information in linear form compatible with electronic data-processing equipment.

7) Promote greater integration between national standards (ASA) and military specifications for engineering documents.

8) Extend the use of simplified drafting practices.

9) Employ symbols for commonly used components, particularly for piping, structural work and electrical diagrams.

10) Extend use of geometric tolerance symbols in lieu of long descriptive notes for expressing geometrical relationships.

11) Extend the use of work abbreviations for parts lists, bills of material, and the like.

12) Do more documentation by photographic means when there are samples, models, or products which must be modified.

13) Use more adhesive appliqués for repetitive configurations, notes, legends, tables, etc.

14) Provide punched tapes for numerically controlled machining in lieu of drawings.

Trends in machines and methods

"The manufacturing plant of the future will be a grand and glorious thing. Machines and processes will be automatically controlled, yet will permit a surprising variety of output. Product designers will feed instructions to the plant and anticipate production reaction immediately and product shipment within days, if not hours. . . ." (from *Design Automation: System Approach to Engineering Data Processing*—an IBM press release).

Simplified drafting: Proponents claim that freehand tracing cuts drafting work in half. Normally the original concept is first sketched by an engineer, then redrawn by a draftsman. For simplified drafting, the detailer places a transparent drawing form over the portion of the layout and traces freehand the outline of the part, omitting all but the essential details. All "unnecessary work," "work-that-should-never-have-been-done," is eliminated. For instance, if it is possible to convey information by word description alone, no supporting delineation whatsoever is needed. The slogan at General Electric, where this method is practiced extensively, is "A superfluous line is a waste of time."

Panoramic design: This system takes simplified drafting one step further. Engineers put their ideas directly on wall-size blackboards. For permanent records, the blackboard sketches are photographed. TAB Engineering Inc, developer of the method, says it has cut drafting, design, and engineering costs 33 to 55%.

Originally blueprint-size photographs were made of all detail and assembly drawings. However, it was found that the people in the shop could read the dimensions right off the pocket-size print and that they actually preferred the small photographs. Bulky rolls of drawings were eliminated, and so was the practice of running back and forth between the shop and the office where the prints were laid out. This process now makes use of Polaroid cameras for instant prints and 35-mm cameras for permanent recording of engineering data.

The most important skill required in this changed procedure, according to TAB, is to persuade the engineers to accept this new method and acquire the proper new habits.

Photographically produced drawings: Torrington Mfg Co says that it can save $300 on a relatively simple assembly drawing by putting a camera instead of a draftsman to work. Log Etronics Inc offers equipment it claims will save from 50%, for a relatively simple drawing, to 95% for drawings with many parts and complex spatial relationships.

Photodrawings do not eliminate the draftsman completely. He must still add dimensions, parts callouts, labels, and hidden lines, but accuracy is assured and the work is greatly simplified. The process takes four steps:

1) Using a conventional camera, a photographer makes one negative for each view required on the assembly drawing.

2) A positive transparency is made from the negative, and adjustments by *dodging* the exposure produce a uniform density.

3) Linework is added to the posi-

tive by a draftsman.

4) Prints are made either by diazo or by any other standard reproduction process.

Rehabilitation of drawings: This method facilitates quick drawing changes by creating a second original from a soiled or torn original drawing or by creating new sections of a drawing, without the need to copy the entire drawing.

Rehabilitation can be done photographically, as with a 40 x 40-in. copy camera and a 10 ft x 40-in. contact printer, or on diazo "intermediates." After smudges, rips, or imperfections in the original have been removed from the intermediate and new data have been added, the intermediate becomes a new original from which prints may be made.

Modernized print systems: It is still staggering to executives to learn how much paper their company uses. The Boeing Co estimated for its officials that the engineering blueprints needed to produce the average 707 jet weighed more than 50,000 lb. The payload of the plane itself is 57,000 lb. This company requires 40 copies of each print, and there are 22,000 original drawings. So 880,000 sheets of paper are printed.

Boeing's reproduction program, with the aid of specialists from the Paragon-Revolute Division of Charles Bruning Co Inc, now produces half-sized white prints to save between $11,500 and $25,800 per month. No dollar value can be placed on the ease of handling the tremendous number of drawings as they go through the various departments, but this considerably influenced introduction of the change.

Microfilm: This method provides an "inviolate reservoir" of drawing information which can be used quickly without depleting the original source. As in the past, an engineer requests the file for a drawing. The clerk takes the microfilm from the file and, with a card-to-card printer, makes an exact duplicate on diazo film, which is mounted in a similar aperture card. The duplicate is given to the engineer, and the master card is returned to its file. The engineer now has a microfilm drawing, which he takes to a reader. There he can view the microfilm as an enlarged image to obtain the information he desires. If he now wants a print of this drawing for marking or any other purpose, he inserts his microfilm card into an enlarger-printer near by—and in seconds he has his print.

Many who have modernized their printing system have resorted to xerography, or its equivalent, in conjunction with microfilming and offset units. The diagrams on page 86 show typical microfilm workflow. In addition to the standard aperture card a variety of jackets and readers is available for other than 35-mm film. Many of the spokesmen interviewed have expressed a preference for 16-mm film for descriptive material.

Aperture cards require about 5% of the space taken by the original drawings and can be mailed for a fraction of the cost. They can be taken from files to make prints or study details in half the time needed to pull an original. Prints are 50% smaller—a 75% reduction in square footage of paper. And the cards are permanent records that can be stored in fireproof files.

Micro-image technology: National Cash Register Co has developed a new method for storage and dissemination of micro documents. This new technique, called Photochromic Micro-Images, has made very high-density document storage feasible at linear reduction of 200:1, representing an area reduction of 40,000:1. This means that 400 3x5 index cards can contain 1 million document pages. With this system it would not be necessary to have automatic-retrieval equipment, only a desk-top semi-automatic viewing console. These advantages are claimed:

1) Photochromatic films provide very high resolution with no grain.

2) They require no development and are sensitive to a range of grays.

3) They permit both erasing and

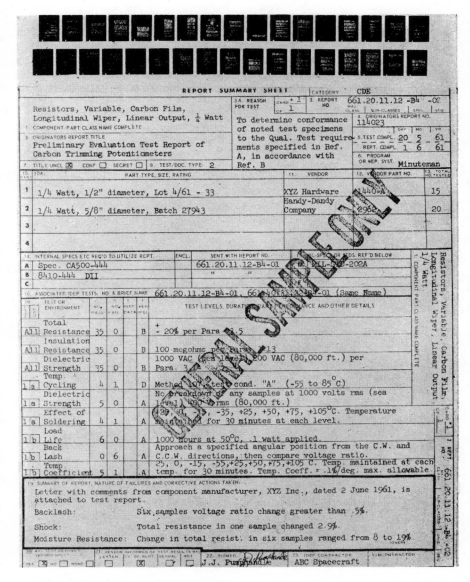

COMPLETE MICROFILMED REPORT (small squares) is attached to a summary sheet giving test results on Government "shelf items."

rewriting, allowing for editing, updating, and error correction.

4) Duplicates or hard copies can be made.

Electronically produced drawings: Using information in mathematical-code form supplied by a computer, a new microfilm recorder pencils in (with a beam of electrons) lines, curves, symbols, and dimensions. The recorder, developed by General Dynamics/Electronics, will turn out finished drawings in less than half a second. The images are displayed on the face of a Charato Shaped-Beam tube and photographed on 35-mm film. Drawings are made in the same computer code that produces tapes, which operate automatic production equipment so that the engineer can check the tape output before it is used in actual production.

Computer output can also be used to transmit the design to other locations either in the form of tape code or pictorially on television cameras. Prints can be made from the 35-mm negatives by standard microfilm processes.

An "action document": General Electric Co at Johnson City, NY, has developed a new technique for electrical and electronic modules. Circuit design and layout are presented on a single drawing. The innovation in this system consists of positioning all components on a standard 0.1-in. grid, which is defined by numbers and letters in the vertical and horizontal margins. This method eliminates dimensions from the drawing and is aimed to serve the assembler and inspector, while it also simplifies design and drafting of the module.

Here again, the one major obstacle to be overcome was the engineer's reluctance to accept the method. Careful human-relations program had to be used before this rather minor change became acceptable to engineering.

Design automation

The use of computers to help in layout of piping, valves, meters, heat exchangers, and pressure vessels is common among engineering firms. But some companies (IBM, Burroughs, Remington) have started to use design automation concepts for highly repetitive tasks that are difficult to do manually and are subject to human error.

The concept is less than five years old. It was started to speed both engineering and production on solid-state circuitry, to obtain detailed and optimum engineering configurations, analytical or diagnostic data about the design, numerical instructions for automatic tools, and manufacturing control data.

It is anticipated that, in the future, the system engineer will simply write out his requirements symbolically and present them directly to the computer, eliminating the need for preliminary

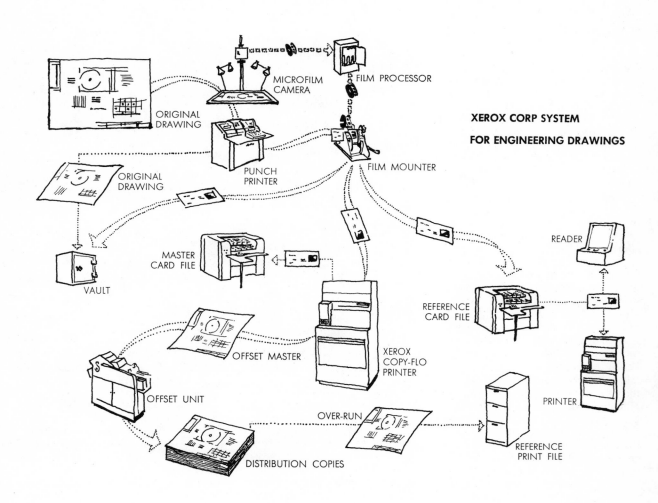

XEROX CORP SYSTEM

FOR ENGINEERING DRAWINGS

drawings. This may mean stating the desired logic in Boolean symbols. From this basic information, the computer will then produce the necessary drawings, corrections, and listings, as well as maintain a complete design record. The value of this tool does not stop here. The computer also provides the tape for automatic wiring to the factory and the necessary records for production planning and controls inventory and purchasing schedules.

DOCUMENTATION TODAY

Many who responded to this survey spoke of evolution, not revolution; of steady rather than radical change; of allowing the new things to become accepted before they would adopt them. But does our highly competitive economy permit slow evolution? Aren't whole industries being wiped out because they could not, or would not, undergo radical change? Or for

that matter, aren't segments of labor being made obsolete because they were not prepared for automation?

It is doubtful that much radical change will take place if engineering departments are left to their own devices. Certainly very little integration of engineering into the total production capacity of a company will take place unless top management first takes an active part in learning what isolation really exists and then participates in planning the long-overdue changes.

This study has shown that a surprising number of companies have arrived at a level of streamlining far above that anticipated. These are the leaders in the field, and they provide an excellent standard against which the other companies may be measured. Here are some of the current practices and cost ratios:

Only 3% of the companies are now using freehand sketches in all of their

work. No company is using blackboard drawings in all its work. About 5% of the companies use photos of models with dimensions added in some of their work. The change will come, of course, eventually, but as the companies that are now using simplified drafting have shown, this need not be a lucky shot in the dark. With top management as a catalyst, crystallization can occur much sooner.

It is startling to note that 15% of the companies are now using computers in design. Further, 56% of the companies say they use data processing in their engineering system activity. All the companies in aircraft and rocketry, aerospace accessories, and communication do so. Of the eight companies that reported they had been able to decrease documentation costs, seven stated they make use of this method. Looking further into the type of data-processing system in use, we can see that not all the companies

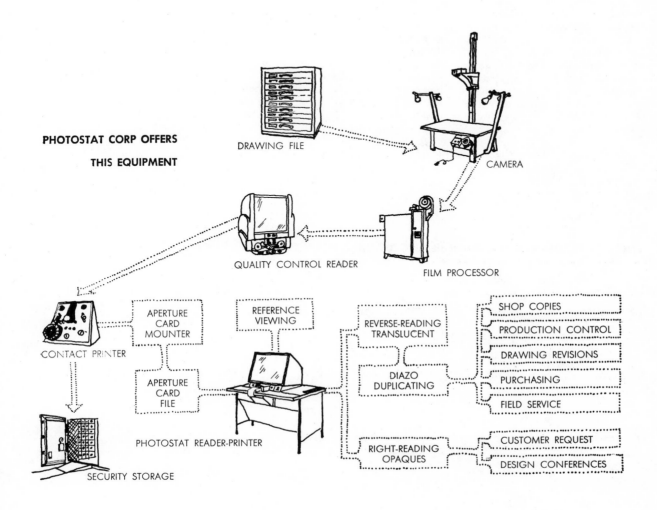

PHOTOSTAT CORP OFFERS

THIS EQUIPMENT

DRAWING FILE

CAMERA

QUALITY CONTROL READER

FILM PROCESSOR

CONTACT PRINTER

APERTURE CARD MOUNTER

REFERENCE VIEWING

REVERSE-READING TRANSLUCENT

SHOP COPIES

PRODUCTION CONTROL

DRAWING REVISIONS

APERTURE CARD FILE

DIAZO DUPLICATING

PURCHASING

FIELD SERVICE

PHOTOSTAT READER-PRINTER

SECURITY STORAGE

RIGHT-READING OPAQUES

CUSTOMER REQUEST

DESIGN CONFERENCES

engaged in defense work have as yet installed aperture-card systems, although MIL 70327 is a **DOD** requirement.

Electronically produced drawings and the use of coordinates for tape-controlled machines will find more and more use in industry, although they are only in embryonic stages today. Note, however, that many companies now using tape-controlled machines still depend on manufacturing engineers to convert the conventional drawings into coordinates. The trend seems to be to eliminate the conventional drawing and supply Manufacturing with just the coordinates and a written description of the part. Those companies which now produce drawings by computers are doing just that.

We asked several questions about anticipated changes: Will your drafting procedures change radically in the future? Is there a plan that will bring about these changes in an orderly fashion? Has your drafting process undergone radical change in the last 20 years?

Only 12% answered all of these questions in the affirmative. More than 45% of these answers were made by the companies which stated they had already been able to reduce their engineering documentation system costs. It is also noteworthy that 40% of the respondents who believed the company would make radical changes did not think there was any plan for making these changes in an orderly fashion. Some commented that change was constant and occurring in evolutionary rather than revolutionary steps.

The questionnaire asked, "Do you use ink?" This apparently shamed many respondents. Almost none of the companies engaged in defense work answered this question; the few that did answer said that they were required to do so by contractual agreements or that aperture cards make ink necessary in order to achieve sharper lines. This was, I am sure, not the intention of DOD. Other companies that resort to ink do so for their art work and not for the generation of engineering drawings.

The question, "How does your company produce parts lists, bills of material, genealogy charts, status of completion lists?" evoked a considerable number of comments. Most of these lists are handwritten, many on separate sheets. Many defense activities now require either a print-out or a set of punch cards with each set of documents and this may have encouraged some companies to use this method in their commercial work. Others use both methods simultaneously. Some have been using tabulating equipment for many years.

Another trend seems to be for engineering departments to go into the printing business in reproducing these lists; 11% report using offset equipment.

Efficiency ratios

The tables on these pages are based on figures from more than 70 major engineering organizations. The columns in Table II have been arranged so that the lower the figure, the more efficient the operation. In the case of the percentage of people employed in Engineering, as given in Table I, the most efficient proportions will vary considerably and must be established for each organization.

Each boldface figure in Table II is the average of the companies. This average is by no means an optimum but probably constitutes the lowest acceptable limit of efficiency. Thus approximately half the companies operate less efficiently than they might. The small figures above and below show how great the spread is above and below the average.

Table I gives various types of personnel serving in the drafting and engineering of new products and changes.

(Note: The term *drafting,* for the purpose of this study, includes originating, reproducing, storing, distributing, and organizing engineering drawings.)

Table II lists the following ratios:

Column 1) Percentage of the total engineering budget consumed by changes.

Column 2) Ratio of space devoted to drafting to the total investment in drafting equipment ($ft^2/\$$).

Column 3) Ratio between the total investment in drafting equipment and the total number of prints made per year ($\$/print$).

Column 4) Ratio between the space devoted to drafting and the total number of employes in Engineering and Drafting (ft^2/man).

Column 5) Ratio between the total investment in drafting equipment and the total number of employes in Engineering and Drafting ($\$/man$).

Column 6) Ratio between the total number of employes in Engineering and Drafting and the total number of drawings handled per year.

Column 7 to 11) Percentage of prints made per year of: detail parts (7), assemblies (8), schematics (9), parts lists (10), and bills of material (11).

Column 12) Number of times an original drawing is handled in one year.

Column 13) Percentage of cost of the total engineering budget devoted to drafting.

One is first struck by the great

TABLE II. SOME OTHER ENGINEERING DOCUMENTATION RATIOS DISCOVERED IN THIS SURVEY

	1	2	3	4	5	6	7	8	9	10	11	12	13
Maximum	58.0	707	19	5730	3950	0.143	98	88	30	38	36	100	90
Average	22.5	18	0.6	101	460	0.014	55	16	7	9	12	29	47
Minimum	2	1	0.1	15.5	88	0.0004	18	0	1	0	1	2	15

TABLE I. PERCENTAGES OF PERSONNEL IN THE ENGINEERING DEPARTMENT

	Drafting Engineering Changes		
	New Products		
Clerical	33.0	22.5	48.0
	7.1%	**9.5%**	**14.0%**
	0	0	0
Draftsmen	100.0	80.0	82.5
	62.5%	**37.0%**	**45.0%**
	14.0	9.9	0
Engineers	78.5	91.0	93.0
	30.5%	**53.5%**	**41.0%**
	0	10.0	11.0

scatter of responses. However, there seem to be definite clusters and definite trends. In a number of questions most companies seem to follow a certain flow from one question to another, while others make a very different response. But certain trends are clear.

It was anticipated that companies would employ less clerical help in engineering new work, and progressively more in drafting new products and making changes. It was also anticipated that most engineering personnel would be used in engineering new work and that fewer would be required in drafting and an even smaller number in changing existing designs.

Here are the underlying reasons. It was believed that clerks become increasingly important as documents near their release date and would remain active for a considerable time after the initial release had been made. Drafting personnel would be most active in the initial design and in the final drafting, less so in the period devoted to changes. Engineers would spend most of their time on the new product, then progressively less as the project neared completion.

A small number of companies (about 35%) do follow approximately the anticipated responses. Companies using a smaller percentage of either clerical or drafting help use a noticeably larger percentage of engineers. Companies with more drafting help seem to get along with less clerical help and fewer engineers. One is tempted to say that both drafting and engineering personnel seem to fulfill some of the functions of the clerical help.

This is further brought home by answers to the question on the total engineering budget consumed by changes (column 1). Companies with fewer engineers assigned to the change work spend less.

Most companies seem to be careful about the amount of space devoted to drafting in relation to the total drafting investment (column 2), but close to 20% of the companies use a ratio far above the anticipated maximum of 15. One company has a ratio of 706.7/1!

There is a fairly good agreement in the ratio of total investment in drafting equipment to the number of prints made (column 3). But there appears to be no correlation between the space allotted to drafting personnel and the number of people employed (column 4), between the amount of investment in drafting equipment and to the number of people employed (column 5), or between the number employed and the total drawings made (column 6). There is, however, a close relationship between the amount of money spent on the engineering documentation system activity and the aforementioned three ratios.

Finally, there seems to be a startlingly clear correlation between the amount of defense work done by a company and the cost of documentation. Companies with less than 15% defense work as a rule spend more on their documentation than companies with more. At both ends of the defense work scale, those that have the most, or the least, spend less on documentation. In other words, indications are that companies set up to do only commercial work or only defense work spend less than companies that try to do both under one roof. ■

Make More Use of Camera-Made Drawings

Take a photo of the model or prototype, let the draftsman sketch in the details, and you've got an assembly drawing that's faster and cheaper to produce, easier to read.

Suppose we have to reverse the usual procedure. What method—in assembly drawings, for example—will transform the 3-dimensional prototype back into a 2-dimensional drawing? Traditionally, this has meant another full-dress drafting job. But why not exploit the advantages of a very common instrument—a device that turns three dimensions into two at the click of a shutter?

Putting a camera to work this way is not a new idea. But until recently most results with photodrawings have been disappointing because of technical limitations.

It's difficult to get ideal lighting for an entire piece of hardware, so some parts of the negative are bound to be overexposed, others underexposed. The result in either case is loss of detail. And to produce the abundance of prints necessary, it is preferable to use the same diazo reproducing machine that's used for line drawings; but with ordinary techniques diazo prints are too contrasty to be acceptable, particularly when a second generation of prints is made from diazo intermediates.

Two improvements in the photodrawing method have changed all that. An electronic enlarger has been developed that automatically compensates for poorly exposed negatives; and use of a halftone screen ensures detailed, magazine-quality diazo prints for copies beyond the first generation. These two methods are primarily responsible for the renewed interest in photodrawings.

Photodrawings don't eliminate the draftsman. He is still needed to make drawings of individual parts of the assembly—and any other drawings where there is no physical part to photograph. Even the photodrawings require some drafting work—dimensions, part callouts, labels, hidden lines.

Why make an assembly drawing if the machine has already been assembled? Usually, of course, this first machine is only a prototype, put together from sketches and notes; and undoubtedly with the project engineer breathing down the machinist's neck. The photodrawing tells production personnel how to repeat this process. It's not necessary to have a complete, working prototype; full-scale appearance models, mockups, even small-scale models can serve the same purpose. Photodrawings are also convenient when engineers want to make changes or custom modifications of a machine that is already in production. Their advantages over line drawings are:

Low Cost. Except for simple shapes, photodrawings are considerably cheaper than comparable line drawings. Because cost of materials is about equal, the major difference is cost of drafting effort. Savings range from 50% for a relatively simple drawing to as much as 95% for drawings with many parts.

Speed. Only a small amount of time is required to take the photo and process it to the point where the

From 3-D to 2-D prints—four simple steps

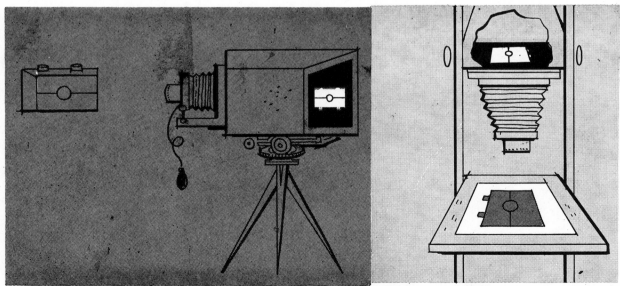

1 CONVENTIONAL CAMERA gives negative image; photographer makes one negative for each view required on the assembly drawing

2 POSITIVE TRANSPARENCY is made from negative and "dodged" to adjust for variations in exposure. Halftone positive is made when requirements are critical.

GORDON O F JOHNSON,

LogEtronics Inc, Alexandria, Va

ELECTRONIC ENLARGER made by LogEtronics Inc automatically eliminates unwanted variations in contrast on the negative. The schematic shows how it works. The light source, a cathode ray tube, scans negative and exposes the print, one spot at a time. Intensity of spot is monitored and controlled by the feedback photomultipler between negative and lens. Two light-sensitive probes permit photographer to adjust image brightness-range and contrast to match emulsion on print.

draftsman can add the necessary lines. The major portion of the time required to produce a photodrawing is still the drafting time. Hence, as with cost, time savings are roughly in proportion to saving in drafting effort.

Accuracy. Cameras don't make mistakes, so the drawing checker only has to look at the lines added by the draftsman. Further, the photo shows shading, texture and depth, making the assembly easier to visualize and reducing error at the production level. The symbols, sections and special pictorial representations of line drawings can easily confuse personnel unfamiliar with standard drafting notation.

THE FOUR STEPS

Start With a Good Photo

The sketches above show the four steps in making a photodrawing. First requirement is a good photo of the prototype, model or mockup. Usually it is taken by the firm's own photography department. The small company that does not have its own cameraman can call in a commercial photographer without adding much to the cost of the process.

The photographer should be cautioned to avoid shadows or highlights that obscure needed detail. He should also choose a camera angle that minimizes perspective as much as possible. He should not try to include too

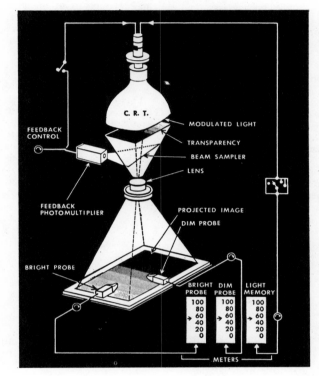

3 LINEWORK IS ADDED to the positive by a draftsman. It's done directly on matte-surface positive or on a drawing film taped over it.

4 PRINTS ARE MADE in the conventional diazo machine with the same sensitized paper used for line drawings—no special skill or materials needed.

PHOTODRAWINGS IN A LARGE COMPANY

General Electric's Large Jet Engine Department in Evendale, Ohio has its own photography department, with a staff of 12 photographers and lab technicians. Since 1951, GE has been using photodrawings to replace some of its line drawings; today, virtually all engine-assembly drawings are made this way.

A typical jet-engine assembly drawing is shown in the photo at right. The sheet of screened, positive transparencies (master photodrawing) is being microfilmed as required for military records.

The drafting-group supervisor estimates that this drawing, if conventionally prepared, would require at least 600 hours of drafting time, over a period of probably six to eight weeks. The photodrawing was produced in 30 hours—10 in the photography lab and 20 in the drafting room. Thomas E. Ware, supervisor of photography, points out that the 20-to-1 cost and time reduction is not the only benefit: there is more information in the photo and chance of error is reduced.

The Large Jet Engine Department has a LogEtronic contact printer (a simpler device operating on the same principle as the enlarger) in its photo lab and it is used to make all positive transparencies for photodrawings. These are printed on Eastman Kodak Autoscreen film. The special printer is a later acquisition—the first jet-engine assembly drawings were made without automatic contrast control. These had several drawbacks. First, the master photodrawings did not give clear prints and many detailed parts of the assembly were obscured. This made it necessary to add supplementary close-ups to the medium-distance photos in the drawing. An average of 30 photos was needed to show the assembly in all its detail. With the electronic printer this number has been reduced to 10.

Moreover, because there was a wide variation in contrast among photos, each of 30 views was previously put on its own 11 x 17-in. sheet, and the diazo machine frequently had to be reset when a new view was printed. With the LogEtronic printer, contrast is consistent and detail is increased. Thus, the same size views can be put on one size E (34 x 44 in.) sheet and processed together. The single sheets are more convenient, require less storage space. When changes are necessary, the master drawing can be modified by stripping in a new view.

much information in one view by taking photos from oblique angles—one picture for each of the views, as they would appear on a line drawing, is the best practice. Whenever convenient, the assembly should be photographed in a studio where there is better control of lighting and camera angle.

Make a Controlled-contrast Positive

Loss of detail because of lighting variations in the negative can be overcome by careful preparations of the positive transparency. One way is by skillful "dodging"— a good photographic technician can use a conventional enlarger to compensate for uneven exposure by blocking off light from the lighter parts of the negative while allowing darker parts to receive more exposure.

A more precise solution is with the special enlarger that automatically makes properly exposed prints from poorly exposed negatives. Such an electronic enlarger is made by LogEtronics Inc.

Add Linework

When the positive transparencies have been prepared, next step is to add the necessary linework. There are two common methods.

Suppose the desired photodrawing is to include three views of the assembly—top, side and elevation. The three positive transparencies can simply be taped in their proper position on the back of a piece of drawing film or vellum and the lines drawn on the top.

The other way is to make a contact print on an intermediate film. Here the problem is to make a composite positive intermediate from the individual positive transparencies. The individual transparencies can either be arranged in their proper positions on a single sheet of matte-surface, direct-positive, sensitized film and a contact print made; or the transparencies can be placed on a sheet of diazo-sensitized, matte-surface film-intermediate and exposed in the diazo reproducing machine. In either case, the additional lines, dimensions and labels are added directly on the matte surface of the film. This then becomes the master photodrawing.

Make Prints on Standard Machine

Master photodrawings prepared this way can be handled the same as conventional line drawings. They are stored and revised in exactly the same manner and prints are made in the diazo machine as before. Reproduction is the final step. No special skill is required and, with equal-density masters, the same machine setting gives perfect prints for every photodrawing.

The quality of prints is very good indeed. The screened positives ensure good definition, and a tonal quality equal to the best magazine photographs. Many companies have been so pleased with the quality of photographs made on their diazo machines that they regularly use the process to make copies of photographs. Numerous copies of photos for booklets, reports, sales brochures and many other individual uses can be made quickly and inexpensively by this process. ■

More Hints for the Drafting Manager

WILLIAM J. IRWIN

(1) *Try to salvage as much of the old drawing as possible.* This can be done by cutting out the worthwhile sections of old drawings and inserting them into a new printed sheet. Transparent mending tape can be used to hold these sections in place and, at the same time, produce a good diazo print.

(2) *Trace as much of the old drawing as possible.* This is usually done better if a print of the original is run off and slipped under the drawing being prepared. Use of a light board will increase the degree of transparency considerably. See Figure 1.

Figure 1—Draftsman is shown using light board to trace an extremely opaque print.

(3) *Use underlays to draw repetitive details.* Never redraw repetitive details. Trace them whenever possible. Here, again, a light board proves helpful.

(4) *Reproduction methods.* Thoroughly familiarize yourself with the latest reproduction materials and the flexibility of your whiteprinter.

Consider the possibility of making a free-hand sketch rather than a lined drawing. Our drawing files contain more sketches than any other type of drawing. For the most part, these sketches cover jobs that are never again duplicated. Consequently, the file drawers are gone through once a year and the worthless sketches are discarded.

One original drawing can be superimposed on another original drawing so that a composite print or intermediate can be obtained from a Whiteprinter.

Cardboard templates can sometimes serve as original drawings. When run through a whiteprinter they come out a deep shade of blue.

Certain sections can be cut out of originals so that they are not reproduced and replaced on a sepia with the appropriate information.

Sensitized Mylar is being widely used to produce copies better than the original in most cases. This material offers a degree of durability which cannot be matched. Mylar is easily corrected by removing the emulsion with a sharp blade, such as an "Exacto" knife.

Water-soluble sepia and mylar is also available which eliminates the need for any kind of correction fluid.

Make maximum use of layouts and preliminary designs. By inserting them into a standard size sheet, they can very often serve as an assembly drawing.

A Xerox 914 Printer can reproduce any 8-½ x 11" print on any kind of paper, including vellum. A Xerox camera can enlarge or reduce the size of drawings or sections of drawings, depending on what the requirements might be.

Use photo drawings whenever possible. Photo drawings can be reproduced on any type of paper that will serve very nicely as original drawings. This reproduction method is extremely useful in the preparation of assembly drawings.

The Polaroid camera quite frequently gives us the quickest and best method of obtaining engineering information. The pictures are stapled to a stiff drawing mat and are filed the same as any other drawing. Additional copies can be obtained through photography.

Very often, additional copies are required of blueline prints. These cannot be used as originals with any degree of success because they are too opaque. If the print is a good one it might be possible to make an auto-positive of it which, in turn, could be used as an original. Auto-positives are made through a photographic process, which is considerably cheaper and faster than tracing a print.

THE SIMPLE RULES

Remember these simple rules in producing original drawings:

(1) Always apply functional drafting techniques.

(2) Never be over-functional so that the drawing will be confusing to the person who must interpret it.

(3) Before making a drawing conventionally, try to apply any time-saving reproduction method possible.

(4) With any original drawing, determine the quickest method of preparing it in the beginning.

(5) Acquaint yourself with your company's reproduction equipment and the methods of reproducing original drawings available to you.

(6) Above all, if you can trace it, don't draw it. If you can photograph it, don't trace it. Always keep in mind the best reproduction method.

My company has a small drafting section. It is unlikely that it will ever be much larger. Therefore, every draftsman must do his share of the work and be on the constant lookout for new, functional drafting techniques and improvements to old ones.

Our draftsmen are certainly not regarded as Michaelangelos for the drawings they turn out, but they are held in esteem by top management for doing the job that is expected of them. This adds real security to each man's job and fosters a deep feeling that each individual is a vital member on the drafting team. ■

The Author

WILLIAM J. IRWIN is Chief Draftsman for the Consumer Products Division of the International Latex Corporation, Dover, Delaware.

How computers are becoming draftsmen

By J. A. Weller, *Editor*

SO FAR, THE use of computers in industry has been chiefly concerned with an output in various numerical and word forms, or 'alphanumeric' forms as they are called in the computer business.

But we are on the threshold of major developments in the use of computers for the presentation of information in graphical forms. In fact, some computer technologists believe that, ten years from now, graphic data processing will be as extensive as alphanumeric data processing is today.

If this is so, it is easy to see that the next decade will herald profound procedural, educational, and social changes for design and drawing office personnel. It is therefore appropriate to draw attention to some of the current trends in computer controlled drafting. This article is based largely on information provided by IBM Canada Ltd., and is intended to indicate areas of application and development for the benefit of the uninitiated.

Definition

Graphic data processing supplements a computer's ability to handle large amounts of information at high speed with an ability to display this information, as required, in the form of sketches, drawings, diagrams, bar-charts and graphs.

Since computers vary widely in power and capability, the graphic uses to which they can be applied vary widely in sophistication. However, here are some of the basic ways in which a computer can be used to supply graphical through the use of various types of output:

Printer output methods

The printers of computers have been used for several years as graphic output devices using standard numerical and alphabetical characters. By substituting special characters such as corners, arrow-heads, etc., in place of standard characters additional 'drafting' capability is available.

XY plotting heads

These consist of a pen mechanism moved over a sheet of paper by pulses from a control unit. When operated 'on line,' these pulses come directly from the computer. When operated 'off-line' the computer prepares instructions for putting on paper tape, cards, or magnetic tape.

The accuracy of an XY plotter is low, usually less than 0.01 inch. Speeds range from 80 in./min up to 600 in./min.

Table sizes range from 10 x 15 in. to 42 x 58 in. although one uses continuous roll paper which allows the preparation of drawings up to 29 x 120 in.

Automatic drafting machines

These represent the current ultimate in drawing preparation. Some machines have pens giving different

Printer

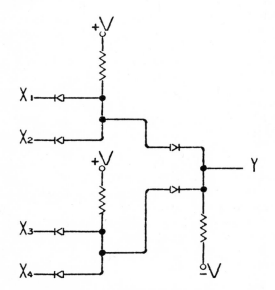

TWO-LEVEL AND/OR GATING CIRCUIT

Electrical schematic produced on printer output in 15 seconds.

XY plotter

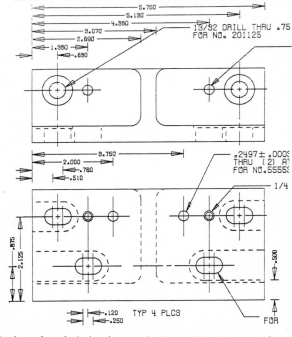

Portion of typical drawing produced on XY plotter attachment.

line widths and colors. Complex curves can be programmed to considerable accuracy. Some drafting machines also have print heads for use on drawings which include large amounts of written notations. Automatic drafting machines are usually run off-line from a computer and can be driven by paper tape, magnetic tape or punched cards prepared by the computer. Some automatic drafting machines are fitted with tables for the preparation of drawings up to 6 ft wide and 20 ft long.

In terms of speed, drafting machines currently draw at 200 to 300 in./min and can print characters with the print head from 100 to 400 characters/min. Some automatic drafting machines give a line accuracy to within plus or minus 0.001 in.

An important characteristic of automatic drafting machines is their ability to be used as graphic input devices. Thus, a finished drawing can be placed on the table and the drawing head unhooked from the drive so that it can be operated manually. In this way a drawing can be traced and the coordinate positions automatically punched on paper or magnetic tape or cards, then entered into the computer for processing or storage. In this way files of old, but active, drawings can be easily converted to computer language in preparation for a comprehensive graphic data processing system.

Some automatic drafting machines generate sufficiently high torque to carry scribers and cutting blades.

Cathode ray tubes

In systems employing tubes as the output device, information is displayed on the 'television' screen in the form of lines, points and other types of graphic symbols. This display can then be recorded on film. Alternatively, micro-film images can be 'read' for conversion into digital form for storage. With a special display unit the user can modify 'images' stored in the computer and can also create original drawings for

Look for these applications

Schematic, dimensional and scale drawings

Isometric, axonometric and perspective drawings

Verification drawings for numerical control machining tapes

Layouts for printed circuit boards

Process layout and unit operation drawings for petro-chemical industries

Display of engineering and management information

Template preparation on sensitized sheet metal or Mylar for full-size lofting

Graphic checks on moments of inertia of rotating members

Engine performance charts

Stress analysis drawings

Temperature and pressure distribution drawings

Mathematical analysis

Pattern recognition studies

Quality control displays

Wave research drawings

direct entry into the computer for storage.

In this system a 'light pen' is moved over the image displayed on the screen by the operator. This instantaneously detects light emanating from points on the screen under the pen. These responses are transmitted to the computer which can alter its digital representation of the image being displayed, under program control. After the image has been modified, under control of a user's program, it can be recorded on 35 mm film developed and viewed on the film recorder's rear projection screen within seconds. ∎

Automatic drafting machine

Cathode ray tube

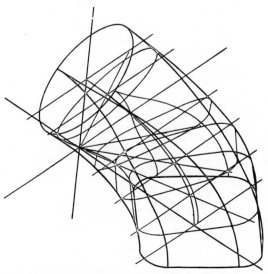

Twin-hull drawing by Boeing made on automatic drafting machine.

In under 4 seconds this perspective view of a duct was produced by North American Aviation engineers on a cathode ray tube.

Simplified Drafting Reduces Costs

From (1) General Electric Company Manual "Simplified Drafting"; (2) "Simplified Drafting Practices" Rau & Healy, John Wiley & Sons

THE TIME ELEMENT has compelled the adoption of a new yardstick for the measurement of drafting values. This yardstick is drafting stripped of its frills, yet surrendering nothing in either clarity of presentation or accuracy of dimension. This results in workable drawings, but with a low time and money investment.

The new standard or concept embraces many modern economical drafting practices, recognized by many as a method of increasing overall productivity by improving individual performance. Three of the easiest and yet most effective practices which can be applied immediately to reduce the effort and time required to make drawings are:

- Simplification of delineation.
- Elimination of non-essentials.
- Extensive use of free-hand drawings and free-hand sketches.

In the most simple terms simplification of delineation and elimination of non-essentials means merely leaving off drawings and layouts those things which add nothing to their accuracy, completeness or clarity.

Complex parts can obviously be described more economically with illustrations than with words. For such parts a drawing is made that serves as a framework to support dimensions and other necessary information. Explanations can, however, complement the illustrations and make it unnecessary to draw extra views. Use no more delineation than is necessary to present the story with clarity and completeness (see below).

Tests have proved that free-hand drawing, when used judiciously, is both practical and economical. All factors being equal, actual drawing time for the average draftsman is reduced between 20 and 30 percent.

It is generally conceded, however, that to effect the maximum economy it should be confined to the presentation of detailed parts of simple contour. But even large and complex drawings lend themselves readily to a combination of free-hand and instrument use. On assembly drawings, for example, small radii, holes, hardware and other parts can be effectively drawn free-hand with no sacrifice in clarity or accuracy.

Standard drawing forms are available imprinted with non-actinic blue cross-section lines over the drawing area. This facilitates and makes it

SIMPLIFIED

Stud 1-¼-7 NC2A x 9" long

Thd. ends 2" long

125/ both ends

ELABORATE

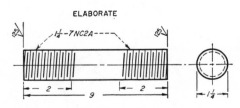

Use description to completely eliminate delineation. Do not hand letter where typing or a Varitype machine can save time.

Avoid the use of elaborate, pictorial or repetitive details.

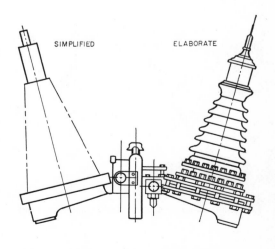

quite easy to make a good, neat free-hand sketch.

Progressive dimensioning is being used extensively in the industry. This method requires less space on the drawing for dimensions and the drawing is clarified and time is saved.

Progressive dimensioning resembles the well-known method of dimensioning a chart or graph, in that a datum line is selected and all dimensions originate from this line. Some of the points to remember when using this method are:

- Only one datum line may be established in any one plane.
- Preferred locations are on an edge, centerline or point which coincides with the datum line of mating parts.
- A figure at the end of an extension line represents the total distance of that line from the datum line to which it is parallel.
- when dimensions are symmetrical about a datum line, they may be given on only one side.
- Simplified and conventional dimensioning may be combined on the same delineation.
- When a dimension is not taken from a datum line, the conventional dimension line should be used.

Simplified dimensioning allows a large portion of the measurements to be made from a given datum line by one setting of the measuring device. This is especially useful and time saving when machines equipped with built-in measuring or gaging devices are used such as jig-borers.

Drawings need not be drawn to scale. A small drawing can be made more easily and faster than a large one. This is especially true for installation drawings where the drawing indicates only relative position or mounting arrangement. Here, the small drawing, with unnecessary detail deleted, can be rapidly depicted without any loss of delineation or accuracy.

The following illustrations offer some practical suggestions in the application of these principles. They are intentionally elementary and some are not to be considered complete. They have been selected merely to illustrate various points of simplifications. Although the drawings are of small and simple parts, the same principles can be applied to more complex drawings with even better results. ■

Eliminate views where the shape can be given by description: for example, hexagon or channel.

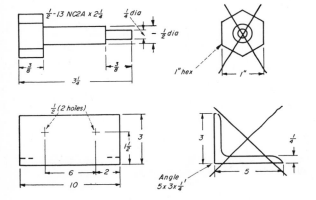

Use tabulated arrangement instead of unnecessary repetitive views especially when shape of part or location of holes is the same.

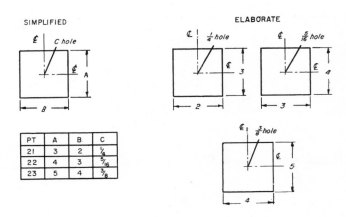

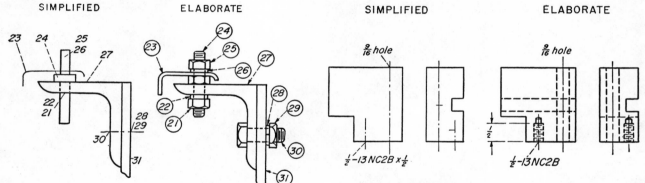

SIMPLIFIED   ELABORATE

SIMPLIFIED   ELABORATE

Omit reference part circles and arrow heads on leader lines when it will not cause confusion with other data.

Avoid dotted lines that do not add clarification. The purpose of the drawing is to help, not confuse.

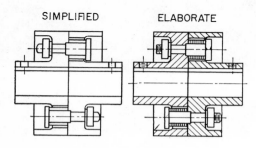

SIMPLIFIED   ELABORATE

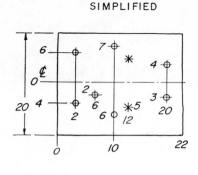

SIMPLIFIED   ELABORATE

Cross sectioning should be used only when the clarity of the drawing depends upon it. Partial cross hatching saves time.

Use progressive dimensioning to reduce the number of dimension lines. Use free-hand sketches wherever possible.

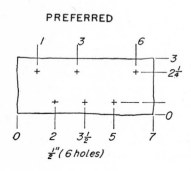

PREFERRED   UNDESIRABLE

Draw objects to scale only when absolutely necessary. Otherwise, draw out of scale but proportionately to size. Note progressive dimensioning.

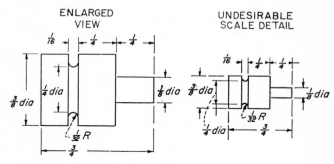

ENLARGED VIEW   UNDESIRABLE SCALE DETAIL

Draw small parts large enough to avoid crowding so that they can be read. Make lettering larger.

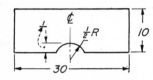

ENLARGED DETAIL

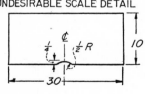

UNDESIRABLE SCALE DETAIL

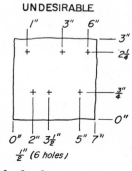

Enlarge small details on larger parts for clarity when necessary.

ELABORATE

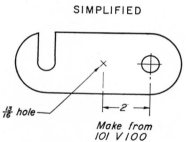

SIMPLIFIED

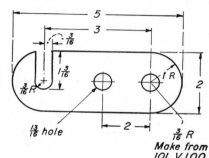

Drawings made to modify stock or commercial parts should be as plain as possible, with no unnecessary detail or dimensions.

208

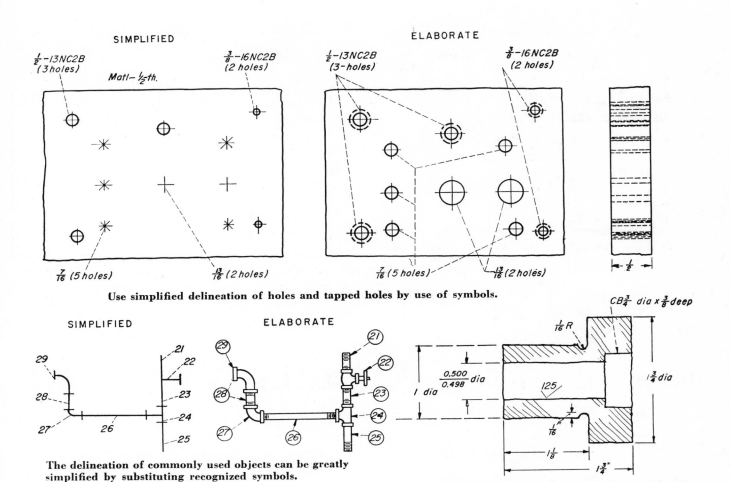

Use simplified delineation of holes and tapped holes by use of symbols.

The delineation of commonly used objects can be greatly simplified by substituting recognized symbols.

When delineating, use as much free-hand drawing as the nature of the work will permit.

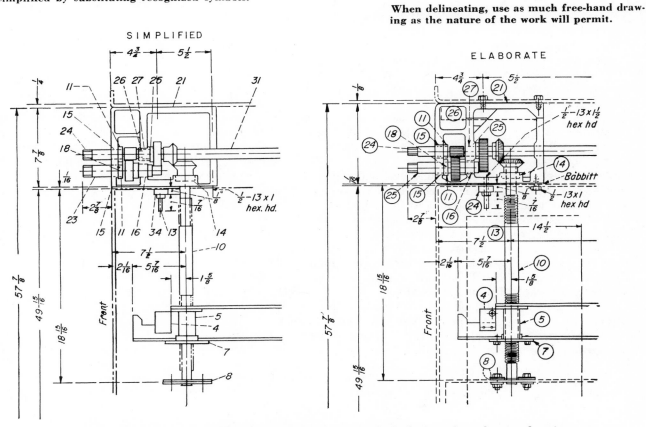

Omit detail of parts on assembly drawings the function of which is to show the part location.

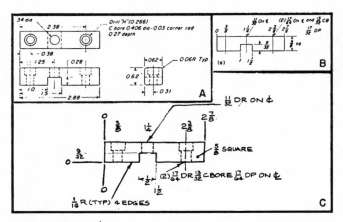

Fig. 1—Three drafting conventions are compared for ease of interpretation and drawing speed. (A) Conventional practice uses three views standard dimensioning and notation. (B) Views reduced to one, dimension lines and arrows omitted, centerline notations and abbreviations used. (C) Freehand sketch includes hidden lines, ordinate dimensioning.

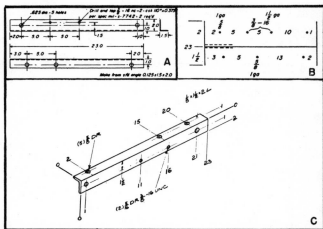

Fig. 2—Similar conventions on L-shaped section in (A) conventional practice, (B) extreme simplification and (C) freehand sketch plus ordinate dimensioning.

Functional Drafting... Another Viewpoint

Similar objectives but with a different approach characterize these suggestions. Hidden lines are included but freehand drawing and ordinate dimensioning are emphasized.

R. E. MEYERS Head, Value Engineering Branch San Francisco Naval Shipyard

THE VALUE ENGINEERING GROUP, U. S. Navy, Bureau of Ships, has assigned a group at the San Francisco Naval Shipyard the task of investigating the simplification of engineering practices. This paper is an outline of the drafting phase of this program.

In the development of a common sense drafting room system the cooperation and advise of the shop is mandatory. As the largest user of drawings the shop deserves first consideration in all simplification methods. The dimensioning system should be functional and suit shop methods of measuring and manufacture. No pencil work should be required in the shop in order to use the drawing. The drawing should be devoid of superfluous frills or views that add nothing to clarity or completeness.

Some of these comments may infer adding to the drawing and not simplifying. Actually, by adding clarifying information, employing functional standards and conventions to the fullest extent and using minimum views required for complete clarity, two purposes are accomplished; that of furnishing more necessary information and taking less time and space to accomplish this end. With this basic philosophy in mind a sensible drafting room system may be formulated.

In setting up a functional drafting system it has been found that, in general, the shops are very co-operative, and when trial drawings have been evaluated little trouble is

encountered in understanding. Most shops care little if the drawing is freehand, if only one view is shown, or if the drawing is to scale (as long as proportion is about right). They are interested in having all the necessary information for manufacture or assembly shown in clearly understandable fashion. In the drafting room however, adoption of new methods often becomes an emotional human problem.

The cardinal points of functional drafting can be summed up as freehand drawing, simplified delineation, and functional dimensioning.

Freehand Drawing

The tools of drafting do not constitute the subject of drafting, and may often be dispensed with to great advantage. (This is not to advocate their elimination for the design layout, of course.) Freehand drawing is applicable to all phases of engineering drawing in various degrees. In mechanical detailing it can be employed almost exclusively with probably lesser application in other fields. Complexity of detail need be no problem and most competent draftsmen can learn to do neat and readable freehand work.

Freehand drafting can be divided into the following types: freehand tracing from assemblies; scaled freehand using grid underlays or printed grid paper with nonactinic lines; freehand using no scale or guide. Freehand drafting does not compromise clarity and, of course, is not license for sub-standard or sloppy work. It does, however, provide a time saving factor of 20 to 50 per cent.

Opinions expressed herein are those of the author and not necessarily those of the Navy Department.

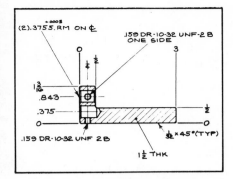

Fig. 3—More complex part showing use of crosshatch, conventional holes and ordinate dimensions. (From actual production drawing.)

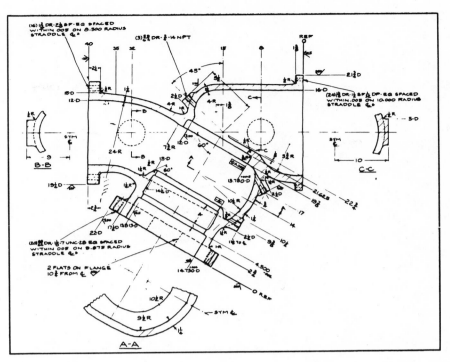

Fig. 4—Freehand traced valve casting with supplementary views as required for clarity. Ordinates start from bottom and right hand flanges.

Simplified Delineation

Reduction of a drawing to only essential views makes good sense. At the shop interpretation level it is generally agreed that the briefer the physical rendering of the picture, if all required information is indicated clearly, the better the drawing. Most important are the dimensions and how they are shown. Of the errors that do occasionally occur in manufacturing parts, the greatest majority are errors in size, not in shape.

In contrast to some opinions, however, it is felt that whatever views are shown should be complete, with all necessary holes and lines giving an undistorted picture of the part. The danger of over-simplification and consequent misunderstanding cannot be overemphasized.

Functional Dimensioning

No other single factor has more influence on the use of drawings than the dimensioning practice. It is not sufficient to have dimensions numerically correct. It is of equal importance to have dimensions placed so as to be of direct use without rearrangement or computation at the shop level. Included in the scope of this concept is ordinate dimensioning. Ordinate dimensioning is functional and logical for practical shop and drafting room use on many intricate parts, castings, and turned work, but it must be imployed correctly. Ordinate dimensioning, as shown in the illustrations, eliminates actual dimension lines and arrowheads. This is incidental to its use and does not sacrifice clarity.

Advantages of simplified delineation and ordinate dimentioning are:

1. Large scales without increase in format size.
2. Dimensions large and clear. Little or no crossing of dimension or leader lines.
3. Eliminates unnecessary views and lines.
4. Not limited to ordinate dimensioning.

5. Consistent with photo reduction methods without sacrificing readability.
6. Functional for shop measuring methods.

On the negative side, it has been found that probably better judgment must be exercised when using functional techniques and ordinate dimensioning since fewer rules and generalizations apply. Also, it has been found that thorough training in classical methods is an aid to functional drafting.

Sample Applications

Fig. 3 shows detail using the minimum views and ordinate dimensioning. This type of drawing is acceptable and readable to the shop and is taken without change from an actual production drawing used at San Francisco Naval Shipyard.

Fig. 4 is a detail of a valve casting shown in simplified form and using ordinate dimensioning. Note the clear delineation and absence of frills. The original drawing of this part had three more views, a larger drawing format, and offered no greater clarity.

The soundness and practicability of functional drafting is being proven. Shop acceptance and response has been enthusiastic. Engineering Department adoption is only a matter of time and is urged on by the policy of shop trial and evaluation.

The ultimate aim of the Navy Group is to have drafting practices, and the use of standards and conventions consistent throughout all Naval activities. Actually, consistency depends on supervision and enforcement rather than the existence of a uniform drafting room manual. The rate of progress to date indicates that adoption of functional methods is a matter of a few years. ∎

10.

How to Release and Control Engineering Drawings

Release and Control Procedures for Engineering Drawings

JAMES E. THOMPSON

These drawing-release procedures are applicable to a wide variety of companies and manufacturing plants. Included are typical forms for assignment records, release requests, job tickets and drawing control.

THE function of the release group within the engineering department is to obtain required authorization, checking, corrections and approval of all drawings before prints are released to the factory. After the drawing is processed, prints are obtained and forwarded to the correct destinations. Records maintained by the release group show the status of each drawing, and the location of each print.

The basic step-by-step operation of the drawing release procedure is shown in Fig. 1. Each completed drawing is given by the draftsman to his group supervisor, who checks new drawings for functional designs, and changed drawings for correct execution of the change. Drawings meeting with the supervisor's satisfaction are then forwarded to the release group for processing through the checking and approval system. Each drawing is recorded and forwarded to the engineering checking group who check for production design, accuracy of change incorporation, dimensional exactness, correctness of material and proess data, and conformance to drafting standards. Incorrect drawings are returned to the draftsman. When all errors are corrected each drawing is signed by the checker, and returned to Release for forwarding to the special checkers.

These special checkers include stress analysts who examine each drawing to insure that all parts have necessary strength; weight engineers who ascertain the weight of each part and make certain that no part is heavier than necessary for the required strength and rigidity. A production engineer may check each drawing to determine the practicability of manufacturing the parts. A tool engineer may examine the drawings to make certain that the design does not require unnecessarily complicated tooling.

The number of special checkers is governed by the nature of the product to meet the needs of the engineering de-

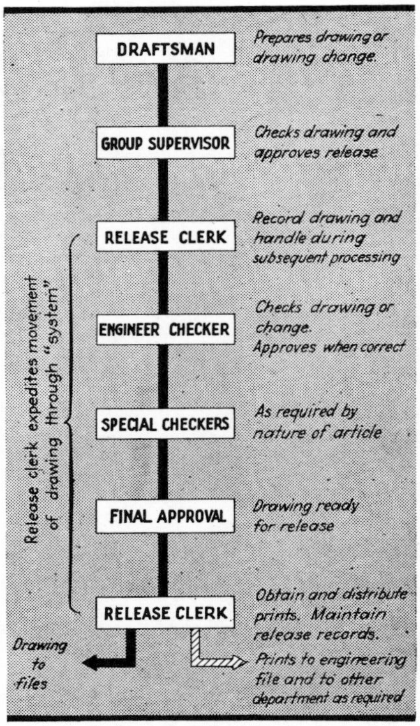

Fig. 1—Flow chart showing basic procedure for releasing engineering drawings.

partment. Drawings are returned to the release group by each special checker after the required corrections have been made. Release forwards each to the next special checker, and records the location of the drawings in the system.

After final check, drawings are forwarded for final engineering approval. This is usually a function of the chief project engineer or chief engineer with new drawings, and of the chief draftsman or project engineer with changed drawings. The release group obtains the necessary quantities and kinds of prints from each approved drawing, forwards these prints to their destinations, and sends the drawing to engineering files. Records maintained by Release show the destination of each print.

The release procedure will vary somewhat according to the nature of the drawing. There are three basic functional types of drawings prepared in the engineering department: layout drawings; test drawings; and manufacturing drawings. Layout drawings define basic structural or mechanical designs, and serve as the basis of subsequent manufacturing drawings. Only in rare cases are other than engineering reference prints made from layout drawings. Because these serve as the basis for future manufacturing drawings, positive control must be maintained to insure that all layout drawings are properly checked, approved and recorded.

Test drawings are prepared when it is desired to make a mechanism or structure for functional test, structural test or mock-up purposes. The release of these drawings varies only in that the required prints are few in number, and bear special identification to preclude the possibility of use for manufacture.

Manufacturing drawings form the large majority of the drawings released by an engineering department. They are prepared to provide manufacturing instructions for parts to be assembled to form complete articles; including production, experimental, spare and service units—but excluding test and mock-up parts. The detail release procedure is practically the same, whether the drawing is for experimental or production articles. It is equally important to check and approve both experimental and production drawings. The release of manufacturing drawings will be considered first, as the procedures for releasing layout and test drawings are modifications of the basic procedure.

Releasing Manufacturing Drawings

Detail procedure for the release of manufacturing drawings is shown at Fig. 2. The method is used by a large

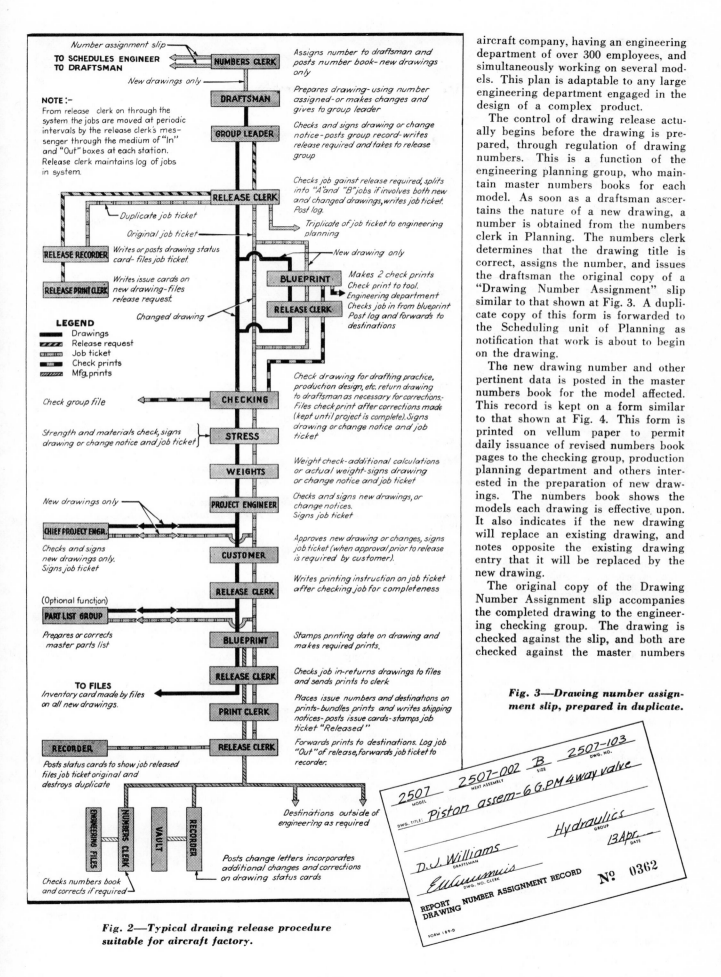

aircraft company, having an engineering department of over 300 employees, and simultaneously working on several models. This plan is adaptable to any large engineering department engaged in the design of a complex product.

The control of drawing release actually begins before the drawing is prepared, through regulation of drawing numbers. This is a function of the engineering planning group, who maintain master numbers books for each model. As soon as a draftsman ascertains the nature of a new drawing, a number is obtained from the numbers clerk in Planning. The numbers clerk determines that the drawing title is correct, assigns the number, and issues the draftsman the original copy of a "Drawing Number Assignment" slip similar to that shown at Fig. 3. A duplicate copy of this form is forwarded to the Scheduling unit of Planning as notification that work is about to begin on the drawing.

The new drawing number and other pertinent data is posted in the master numbers book for the model affected. This record is kept on a form similar to that shown at Fig. 4. This form is printed on vellum paper to permit daily issuance of revised numbers book pages to the checking group, production planning department and others interested in the preparation of new drawings. The numbers book shows the models each drawing is effective upon. It also indicates if the new drawing will replace an existing drawing, and notes opposite the existing drawing entry that it will be replaced by the new drawing.

The original copy of the Drawing Number Assignment slip accompanies the completed drawing to the engineering checking group. The drawing is checked against the slip, and both are checked against the master numbers

Fig. 3—Drawing number assignment slip, prepared in duplicate.

Fig. 2—Typical drawing release procedure suitable for aircraft factory.

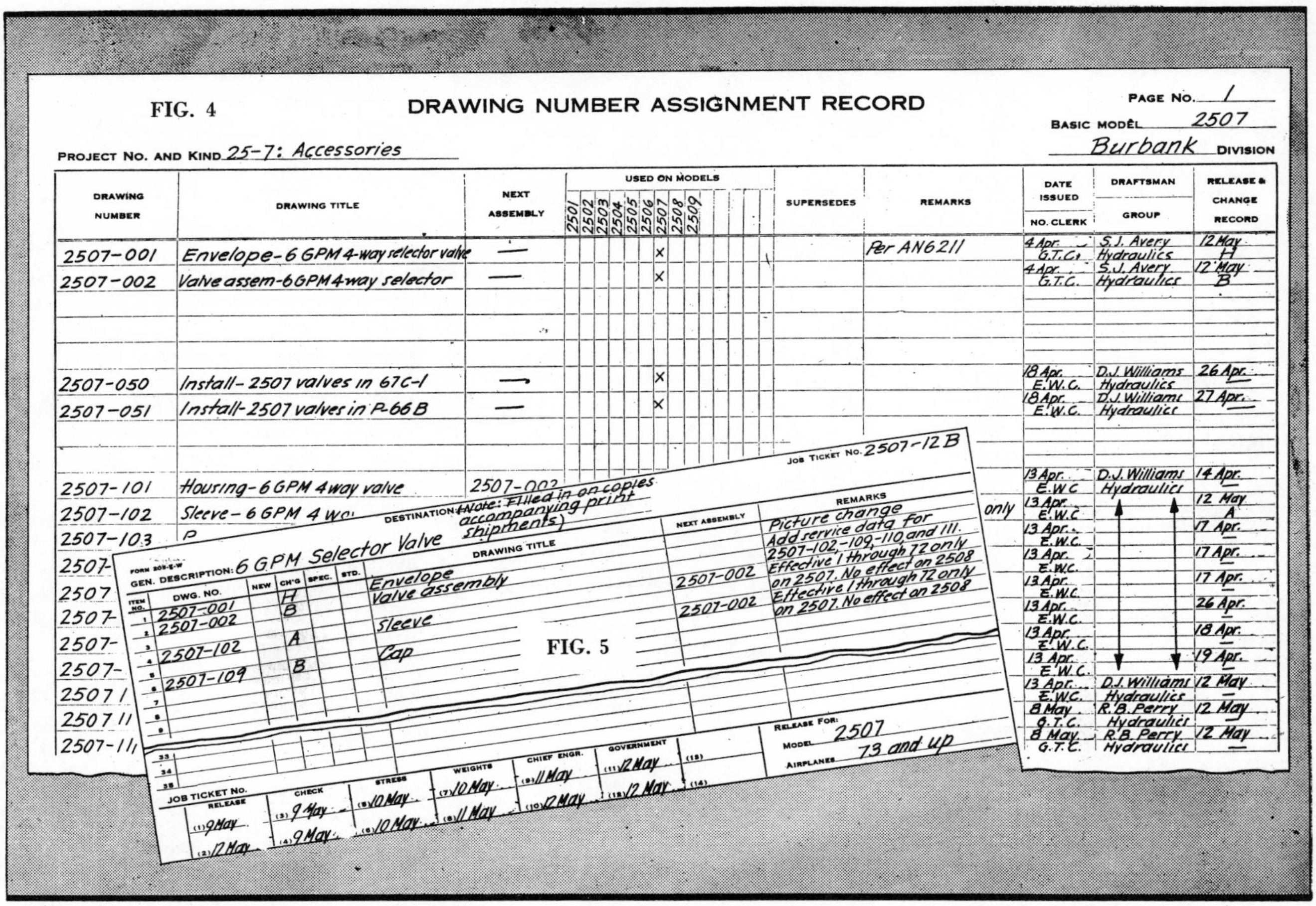

FIG. 4

DRAWING NUMBER ASSIGNMENT RECORD

PAGE NO. 1
BASIC MODEL 2507
Burbank DIVISION

PROJECT NO. AND KIND 25-7: Accessories

DRAWING NUMBER	DRAWING TITLE	NEXT ASSEMBLY	USED ON MODELS (2502 2503 2504 2505 2506 2507 2508 2509)	SUPERSEDES	REMARKS	DATE ISSUED / NO. CLERK	DRAFTSMAN GROUP	RELEASE & CHANGE RECORD
2507-001	Envelope- 6 GPM 4-way selector valve	—	X		Per AN6211	4 Apr. G.T.C.	S.J. Avery Hydraulics	12 May H
2507-002	Valve assem- 6 GPM 4 way selector	—	X			4 Apr. G.T.C.	S.J. Avery Hydraulics	12 May B
2507-050	Install- 2507 valves in 67C-1	→	X			18 Apr. E.W.C.	D.J. Williams Hydraulics	26 Apr.
2507-051	Install- 2507 valves in P-66 B	→	X			18 Apr. E.W.C.	D.J. Williams Hydraulics	27 Apr.
2507-101	Housing- 6 GPM 4 way valve	2507-002				13 Apr. E.W.C	D.J. Williams Hydraulics	14 Apr.
2507-102	Sleeve - 6 GPM 4 wa...					13 Apr. E.W.C.		12 May A
2507-103	...					13 Apr. E.W.C.		17 Apr.
2507-...						13 Apr. E.W.C.		17 Apr.
2507-...						13 Apr. E.W.C.		26 Apr.
2507-...						13 Apr. E.W.C.		18 Apr.
2507-...						13 Apr. E.W.C.		19 Apr.
2507-1						13 Apr. E.W.C.	D.J. Williams Hydraulics	12 May
2507 11						8 May G.T.C.	R.B. Perry Hydraulics	12 May
2507 11						8 May G.T.C.	R.B. Perry Hydraulics	12 May

JOB TICKET No. 2507-12 B

DESTINATION (Note: Filled in on copies accompanying print shipments)

FORM 805-E-W   GEN. DESCRIPTION: 6 GPM Selector Valve   DRAWING TITLE   NEXT ASSEMBLY   REMARKS

ITEM NO.	DWG. NO.	NEW	CH'G	SPEC.	STD.	DRAWING TITLE	NEXT ASSEMBLY	REMARKS
1	2507-001	H	B			Envelope	2507-002	Picture change Add service data for 2507-102,-109,-110, and 111.
2	2507-002	B				Valve assembly	2507-002	Effective 1 through 72 only on 2507. No effect on 2508
3	2507-102	A				Sleeve		Effective 1 through 72 only on 2507. No effect on 2508
4	2507-109	B				Cap		

FIG. 5

RELEASE FOR: MODEL 2507   AIRPLANES 73 and up

JOB TICKET NO. RELEASE (3) 9 May (4) 12 May   CHECK (5) 9 May   STRESS (6) 10 May (7) 10 May   WEIGHTS (8) 11 May   CHIEF ENGR. (9) 11 May   GOVERNMENT (12) 12 May (13) 12 May   (18)   RELEASE FOR MODEL 2507

Fig. 4—Drawing numbers are posted in the master numbers book on the form shown.
Fig. 5—Drawing release request, used when a job is ready for release to manufacturing.

book, so that drawing number, title, next assembly and other data are the same as originally authorized by the numbers clerk. Discrepancies are investigated, and suitable corrections made in the record.

After the new drawing is completed, or the required changes have been made to an existing drawing, it is given by the draftsman to his group supervisor for checking and approval before it is placed on the release system. The group supervisor is responsible for the functional correctness of the design shown on a new drawing, and for the correct incorporation of all change data on a changed drawing.

Job Release Procedure

Individual drawings are rarely sent through the release system. Instead, groups of related drawings, known as "jobs," are processed and released as units. It is rare that an individual drawing is changed without affecting other drawings. The one changed drawing is of little value to the factory departments unless prints of other affected drawings are received simultaneously.

A single new drawing is of little value to the manufacturing department. An assembly without its details cannot be properly planned, nor can materials be ordered. On the other hand, a detail without its next assembly is of little value. The material can be ordered, but assembly planning and tooling cannot be established, and the manufacturing planning must remain partially completed until the assembly print is received.

New drawings are ordinarily released in jobs comprising an assembly and its details. Changed drawings are released in jobs comprising all drawings affected by the change, together with any new drawings involved. If the change is of considerable magnitude, it is likely to be released as several jobs, each comprising a complete group of related drawings. In general it is good practice to maintain jobs at a maximum of 25 drawings.

When a job is ready for release the group supervisor prepares a Drawing Release Request, similar to that shown at Fig. 5, listing the drawings involved. Suitable explanatory remarks and a schedule of reference data forwarded with the job are also shown. This reference data usually comprises layout

drawings and copies of all Engineering Orders, Advance Drawing Changes and Change Requests noted in the drawings.

Separate Release Requests are made for the new and changed drawings forming the job, but both requests and all drawings involved are forwarded to the Release group as a unit. This is particularly necessary when the routing of new and changed drawings is different, as shown at Fig. 2. Segregating the drawings at the source greatly simplifies the Release group's work. Engineering departments wherein the system routing is the same for all drawings will find it advantageous to list the entire job on one Release Request.

The Release Request provides the Release group with definite authorization to begin processing the job, and also provides a means of approving "rush" jobs. There will be occasions when it is important that one drawing or group of drawings be processed and prints released to the factory as soon as possible. These are handled as "rush" jobs, and given preference over all other jobs in the system. The approval of the chief draftsmen must appear on the request authorizing a rush job.

When the Release Request with re-

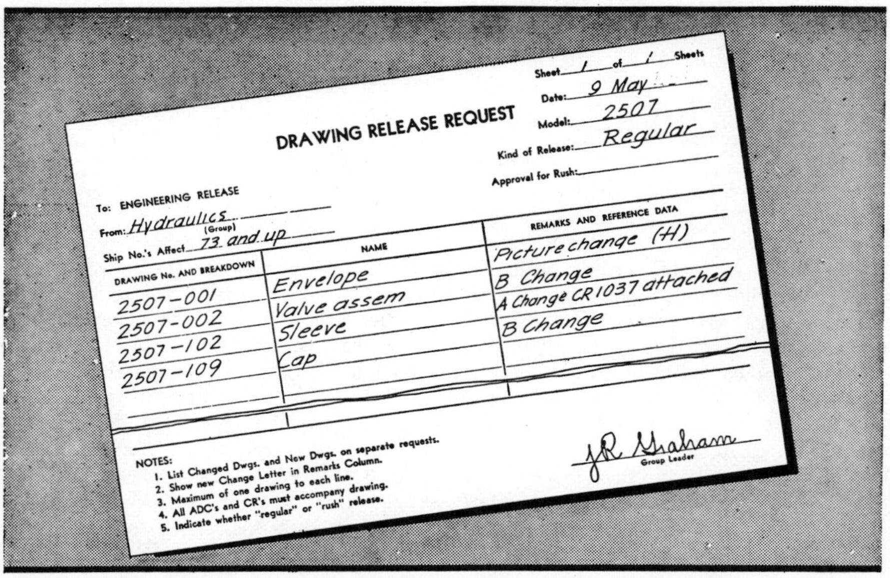

Fig. 6—Job ticket prepared in triplicate after job is received by Release group.

lated drawings and data is delivered to the Release Group, the actual processing of the job by the release "system" begins. The work of the Release group in handling jobs is divided into three prime functions of recording, dispatching, and print distribution. All three functions can be done by one person in a small engineering department, whereas a large department requires a chief release clerk with lead personnel in charge of each function.

Each new job delivered to Release is assigned a job number and checked against the Release Request or requests to ascertain that all listed drawings and reference data are attached.

When the system routing is different for new and changed drawings it is necessary to split jobs comprising both new and changed drawings into two parts. These are identified by "A" and "B" suffixes to the job number. The job number consists of the model designation for the article covered by the drawings, followed by a serial number. For instance, the specimen Job Ticket shown at Fig. 6 covers job 2507-12B. This indicates that it comprises the changed drawings forming a part of the twelfth job relating to model 2507.

After the job is checked a Job Ticket is prepared in triplicate, using a form shown at Fig. 6. The Job Ticket is an invoice of the drawings forming the job, a traveler to accompany the job through the system, a log of the location of the job in the system, a record of the job's checking and approval, and finally a notice to those receiving prints when the job is released.

The original of the Job Ticket accompanies the job through the system, and is signed by each person checking or approving the job. The duplicate copy is sent to the release recorder for use in posting the Drawing Status Cards, see Fig 7, and remains in the Release active-job file while the job is in the system. It is posted to show the dates the job is delivered to and received from each station in the system. The traveler strip at the lower margin of the Job Ticket is used for this purpose. The triplicate copy is forwarded to the engineering Planning group, as notification of the drawings entering the release system.

Drawing Status Record

Prior to actually placing the job in the system, the Drawing Status Record card for each drawing is posted. A specimen status record card, intended for use with a visible filing system, is shown in Fig. 7. This card is the master release record for each drawing, showing each release, together with all Advance Drawing Changes and Change Requests issued against the drawing. The drawing change incorporating each of these are included, together with a record of all Engineering Orders issued against the drawing. Stop Orders issued to halt manufacturing are also listed, together with a record of their release.

Advance Drawing Changes are documents issued to authorize drawing changes in advance of actual change. Their use expedites issuance of change information to the factory. Engineering Orders are similar documents which provide engineering authorization for items not requiring a drawing change. For instance, an *EO* should be used to issue special rework instructions for salvaging incorrectly manufactured parts.

Each Drawing Status Record card provides the following up-to-the-minute information, available to all interested parties, for one drawing: drawing number; drawing title; model that card relates to; other models used on; date of original release; date of all changes released; time in system on each release; job number of each release; *ADC*'s outstanding and incorporated; *EO*'s relating to the drawing; Change Requests outstanding and incorporated; and Stop Orders active and released.

It is the responsibility of each draftsman assigned drawing change work to contact Release and obtain the current status of the drawing before proceeding to work. The checking group contacts Release when the drawing is received for checking—to make certain that all outstanding *ADC*'s and change Requests have been incorporated. If an active Stop Order exists against the drawing, this must be released simultaneously with the drawing change—for a stopped drawing cannot be re-released.

Colored signal flags, affixed to the lower margin of each card, give visual indication of the drawing's status. These cards are placed on visible filing boards supported by stands. Thus, all concerned with each model may immediately obtain a "mass impression" of its progress from the colors displayed on the cards. In some cases it may be found advantageous to use alphabetical signals on the cards to show the latest change letter. The card shown at fig. 7 provides this feature.

The following signals are used on the Drawing Status Card visible files:

LETTER—Indicates latest change letter.
ORANGE—Indicates drawing number issued.
PINK—New drawing in system (orange signal removed).
GREEN—Drawing released. Remains until drawing cancelled. (pink signal removed).
YELLOW—Drawing in system on change. (removed when change released).
RED—Active Stop Order (removed when Stop is released).
BLUE—Unincorporated Advance Drawing Change or Change Request. (removed when all incorporated)
BROWN—Drawing void or cancelled.

A complete set of Drawing Status Record cards is maintained for each model. When a drawing is used on more than one model there is a Status card for the drawing in each model file. The space on the card marked "Basic Model" and "Other Models Released For" records the cards existing for each drawing. The "Basic Model" space always shows the model that the file relates to, while the "Other Models Released For" shows the other model files in which cards for the same drawing will be found. When a drawing change is released it is necessary to post appropriate information on all Status cards existing for the drawing. The same action is taken when an Advance Drawing Change, Engineering Order or Change Request is issued. The issuance and release of a Stop Order is shown only on the card for the model affected.

This duplication of Status cards may seem unnecessary at first glance, but investigation will reveal that it is necessary to have a complete release record for each model—for the release procedure is for the purpose of controlling the release of data required by the factory to construct a certain model. It will also become apparent that certain drawing changes, Advance Drawing Changes, Stop Orders, and the like, may have different effects upon the various models covered by the drawing—so again a complete Status file for each model is imperative. For instance, a Stop Order may be issued to halt manufacture of a part for one model only, without affecting its use on several other models.

Should it be found undesirable to use a visible file for the Drawing Status Record cards it is possible to rearrange the identical card for use in a box file. It is only necessary to move the record strip from the bottom of the card to the upper margin, and place the signals along the top of each card.

Handling of Jobs

Jobs placed in the system cannot be expected to carry on under their own momentum. Instead, the Release dispatcher has the responsibility of delivering each job to the next station in the System, picking up all completed and approved jobs and personally forwarding these to the next station. Boxes at each station for incoming and outgoing jobs provide specific places for the dispatcher's deliveries and pickups. The dispatcher also has the responsibility of expediting jobs which appear to lag, through urging speedier action by the station at fault.

The dispatcher records the location of each job, using the traveler strip along the lower margin of the duplicate Job Ticket in the active-job file. The original copy of the Job Ticket is signed and dated in the same spaces by the person in charge of each station, upon the job being completed and ready for the dispatcher.

Release prepares a daily report showing the location of each job in the system, together with notation of jobs which appear unduly delayed. Copies are forwarded to Engineering Planning, the Chief Clerk and the Chief Draftsman. The necessary corrective action is taken by the Chief Draftsman or Chief Clerk, depending upon the station at fault. Planning is thus constantly advised of each drawing's progress, and assists in cases where delay is caused by lack of personnel at a particular station.

Releasing the Job

Upon receiving the customer's approval a job has completed the system and is ready for release. At this time the *A* and *B* portions of a job split because of containing both new and changed drawings are collected to form one job. Occasionally the complete, approved job must be routed to the Parts List Group prior to actual release. This is desirable when a Master Parts List is maintained for each model or article, and copies are distributed throughout the factory. In such cases the Master Parts List is the only authentic record of active drawings, and should be revised and reissued concurrently with the daily release of jobs.

Every station added to the release system increases the time required to process a job, and it may be advantageous to eliminate the Parts List Group from the system. If so, prints of each job can be forwarded directly to the Parts List Group by Release, as authority to make appropriate corrections to the Master Parts List.

When the completed job is received the release clerk checks to ascertain that it contains all drawings shown on the Job Ticket, and then prepares instructions regarding the quantity and kind of prints required. The information is entered in the space provided at the upper margin of the Job Ticket. The job is then forwarded to the Blue-

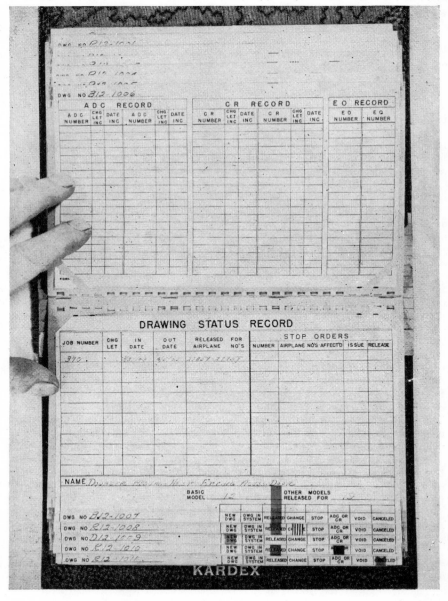

Fig. 7—Drawing status is recorded on a visible indexing card. Colored signals placed over appropriate squares indicate drawing status.

print Group for preparation of the necessary prints. Prior to sending the job to Blueprint, the release clerk removes all reference data and returns these to the proper files.

The Blueprint group stamps the printing date on each tracing, opposite the appropriate change letter in the alteration-block, and makes the required prints. Placing the printing date on the tracing eliminates entering the date on each print. The drawings, Job Ticket and prints are then returned to Release.

The release clerk checks the job in, returns drawings to the engineering file, and forwards prints to the print-clerk. Each print is marked with issue-number and destination to provide positive individual identity, and the print issue-record cards are posted. The prints are then gathered in bundles for each destination. A shipping notice is prepared in duplicate for each bundle, and the original copy of the shipping notice is delivered with the prints. The duplicate is signed by the recipient and retained by Release as proof of delivery.

Completion of Job

When prints are delivered, the Job Ticket is stamped "Released" and forwarded to the release recorder. The recorder posts the affected Drawing Status Cards to show that the job is released. The duplicate Job Ticket is removed from the active-job file and destroyed, and the original Job Ticket placed in the closed-job file.

In some cases a copy of the Job Ticket is forwarded to each destination with the prints forming the job. This is good practice and provides information on the general nature of the job and its relationship to the model or article affected. Choice of this method is governed by comparing the value of this information with the cost of preparing additional copies of the Job Ticket. These additional copies are prepared just prior to release of the job, to avoid errors caused by possible changes in the nature of the job which might have occurred during its course through the system.

The prints intended for the engineering files are routed to the numbers-clerk prior to delivery to the files. This permits the numbers-clerk to check the prints against the numbers books, and makes appropriate corrections or entries in the books.

One print of each drawing release is designated as a "vault copy," and is intended for a master file, in which is maintained one print of every change on each drawing. This vault-copy print

Table I—Print Distribution for Model 10

Destination	Quantity	Issue Numbers
Production Planning	6	00, 10, 20, 30, 40 and 50
Engineering File	3	01, 11 and 21
Inspection	3	02, 12 and 22
Parts List Group	1	03
Vault	1	04

is first routed to the release-recorder for posting the incorporated Advance Drawing Changes and Change Requests on the Drawing Status Cards. This information appears on the Notice of Change attached to each changed drawing.

Print Distribution System

Prints are furnished the purchasing, manufacturing, quality control and shipping departments as authority for procurement of material, fabrication, assembly, inspection and packing of the parts described thereon. A definite effort is made to maintain print delivery points at the minimum. Each delivery point gets one print of all the drawings pertaining to a given model or article. Whenever a delivery point requires more than one print, the same number of additional prints of all the drawings for the model is furnished. The only exception to this rule applies to sub-contracted parts where the print quantities are sometimes greater than for parts made within the factory. The drawings of these parts are identified by a large asterisk immediately following the drawing number. The regular-release print quantity is shown within a space provided in the drawing title-block. The release group can then order the prints required on each drawing release.

When print delivery points and basic quantities are determined for each new model, these data are issued in the form of a bulletin to the release group, blueprint unit, and all print delivery points. This bulletin serves as authority to prepare and deliver the specified prints to each delivery point. When a change becomes necessary, the bulletin is replaced with a corrected issue.

To maintain accurate record of print distribution and loans, each print must have individual identity. This is achieved by assigning an "issue number" to each print, marked in the title block area with red crayon prior to delivery of the print. A two-digit issue number provides: (1) A serial number for the print; and (2) identification of the delivery point. The first numeral indicates the serial number of the print. The second numeral indicates the delivery point. Thus, should the engineering files receive three prints of each draw-

ing, the prints are identified as issues 01, 11 and 21, where "1" indicates the engineering files, and "0", "1" and "2" indicate the first, second and third prints. Should engineering-files release be increased to four, the fourth print would bear issue number 31. Table I gives a typical distribution list for a given model.

This print issue-number system provides for ten destinations and a maximum of ten prints to each destination. When more than ten destinations are required, a four-digit issue number can be used, with the first two numbers indicating the print serial number, and the second pair designating the delivery point. For example, "0000" indicates the first print supplied the first designation. Likewise "0306" indicates the fourth print furnished the seventh delivery point, while "1411" identifies the fifteenth print supplied the twelfth delivery point. A four-digit issue number provides identification for a hundred prints to each of a hundred delivery points.

Once a basic issue number is assigned to a specific destination, it is never used to identify another destination. If a delivery point requires prints of one model, and not of another model, then the basic issue number for that delivery point is not used in the release of prints relating to the second model. The only conditions under which an issue number can be reassigned is the complete elimination of a particular delivery point, and the recall of all prints furnished that point.

Special-issue prints are assigned issue numbers beginning with one for each drawing number, and a prefixed "S". Thus, the first special-issue print of a given drawing is issue number "S1", the second "S2", and so on.

Prints reissued on a drawing change bear the original issue number suffixed with the change letter, and are forwarded to the same destinations as the original issue. Thus, "02A", "15C", "28E", and the like are issue numbers for regular release prints. Special issue prints are suffixed with the change letter appearing on the drawing at the time the print is made, and no attempt ordinarily is made to keep these up to date by forwarding prints of succeeding drawing changes. ∎

Release and Control of Advance Engineering Information

JAMES E. THOMPSON

Essential to efficient engineering management are these systems for issuing advance information and temporary engineering orders so that manufacture can continue while drawings are being made or revised.

EVERY engineering department requires simple, practical means for rapidly issuing instructions to the manufacturing departments. To issue a new drawing or a drawing change usually consumes too much time when manufacture of a part must be stopped, information in advance of a drawing change is needed, and special engineering authorization for tests, drawing deviations and parts salvage are required.

A small engineering department will have less need for a system of advance drawing changes than a large department, wherein a week or more may be required to process the drawing through the release system. In all sizes of departments there is a genuine need for stop orders and engineering orders. A positive method of halting manufacture is necessary; a record of drawing deviations and salvaged parts must be kept.

Three forms are used to convey advance engineering information; namely, a Stop Order, Advance Drawing Change, and Engineering Order, as shown in Figs. 3, 4 and 5. Separate, distinctly different, forms are used for each. Possibility of confusion is thereby eliminated, and maintaining records of them is simplified. Each form is 8½ x 11 in. preferably a hectograph master to permit rapid duplication of copies. The same form upon tracing paper for blueprint duplication serves almost as well.

Stop Orders

A Stop Order is issued when manufacturing operations on a part must be halted immediately and when impending changes will require the reworking or scrapping of parts or the disassembly of units. Judgment must be used in the issuance of Stop Orders, for sometimes halting work on a large assembly is more expensive than the completion of some parts, even though the parts may be scrapped later.

Stop Orders originate in the engineering department initially as proposed Stop Orders, which serve as requests for parts-status surveys, and later as orders that actually stop work. Parts-status reports are obtained from the manufacturing planning department.

A typical Stop Order is shown in Fig. 3. In the proposal stage the following data are entered on the form: the production serial number of the unit upon which the stop will be effective; the model; part name; part number; dash-number parts affected (only those listed are stopped); and the reason for the stop. The effect of the stop upon the raw materials required for manufacturing the part is also shown.

The proposed Stop Order is delivered to the engineering Release group for forwarding to the manufacturing planning department. This does not constitute release of the stop, but is simply an official request to manufacturing planning to furnish a work-status report on the part.

Upon receipt of the proposed Stop Order manufacturing planning makes an investigation to obtain information on materials, tooling and parts affected by the proposed stop. These data are entered in the spaces on the stop order marked "raw stock," "tooling" and "parts status." The Stop Order is then returned to its originator in the engineering department.

After receiving the work-status report, the engineering supervisor who initiated the proposed stop decides upon the advisability of its issuance. It may be found that while a change is desirable, the quantity of completed parts makes the change not feasible. On the other hand large quantities of raw-stock materials may have been received, and the delay required to obtain new materials would be prohibitive. A considerable quantity of expensive tooling may have been completed, and the change would necessitate either scrapping or reworking of them.

In each case it is necessary to weigh the cost of the change against the improvement gained by the change. This assumes that the proposed change may be classified as desirable, rather than mandatory as the consequence of design deficiencies or changes in customer requirements. In the latter case there is no question about issuing the Stop Order as soon as possible. The work-status report is then useful only in determining the best methods of salvaging as much as possible of the completed tools and parts.

If the final decision is to issue the Stop Order, the approval of the project engineer is obtained, and the Stop Order is forwarded to engineering Release for duplication and distribution of the required copies. The original Stop Order is filed after duplication; copies are attached to each print.

Should the decision be against issue, the Stop Order is marked "void" and forwarded to Release. Copies are distributed only to the engineering department and to the manufacturing planning files; none is attached to prints. This procedure informs the manufacturing planning department of the disposition of every Stop Order that served as a request for a work-status report, and avoids uncertainty regarding pending stops. This is necessary in fairness to manufacturing planning, for each stop disrupts their schedule of production, and even the suggestion of a stop is cause for concern.

There may arise circumstances that make mandatory the issuance of an immediate stop on a certain part. This can be done without securing a work-status report from manufacturing planning, upon authorization by the chief engineer.

Stop Orders on parts for experimental models are not sent to manufacturing planning for a work-status report, as shown by the routing in Fig. 1. The quantity of parts and materials for an experimental model is small, and speed in issuing the stop is the paramount issue.

The issuance of a Stop Order not only halts all work in the factory on the part affected, but also prevents further release of its drawing. In other words, the stop must be released before the drawing can be released again under the next drawing change letter or revision.

Release of Stop Order

After the necessary drawing changes have been made, the Stop Order is released by entering the appropriate information at the

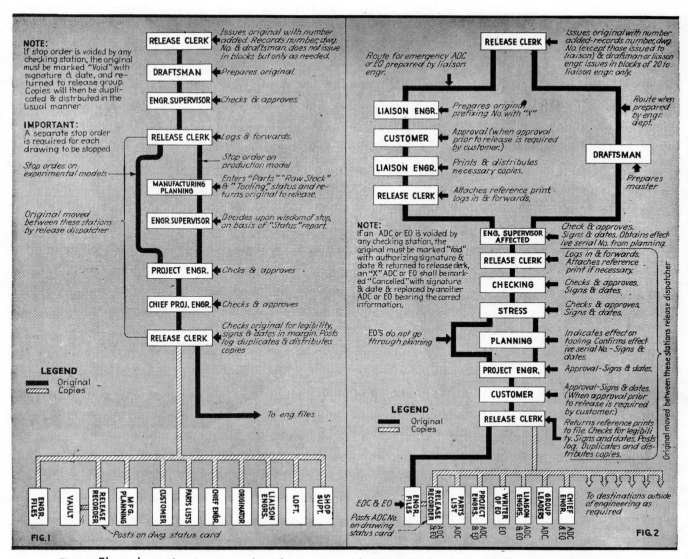

NOTE:
If stop order is voided by any checking station, the original must be marked "Void" with signature & date, and returned to release group. Copies will then be duplicated & distributed in the usual manner.

IMPORTANT:
A separate stop order is required for each drawing to be stopped

Stop orders on experimental models

Original moved between these stations by release dispatcher

RELEASE CLERK — Issues original with number added. Records number, dwg. No. & draftsman, does not issue in blocks but only as needed.

DRAFTSMAN — Prepares original.

ENGR. SUPERVISOR — Checks & approves.

RELEASE CLERK — Logs & forwards.

Stop order on production model

MANUFACTURING PLANNING — Enters "Parts" "Raw Stock" & "Tooling", status and returns original to release.

ENGR. SUPERVISOR — Decides upon wisdom of stop, on basis of "Status" report.

PROJECT ENGR. — Checks & approves

CHIEF PROJ. ENGR. — Checks & approves

RELEASE CLERK — Checks original for legibility, signs & dates in margin. Posts log duplicates & distributes copies

LEGEND
Original
Copies

To eng. files

ENGR. FILES · VAULT · RELEASE RECORDER · MFG. PLANNING · CUSTOMER · PARTS LISTS · CHIEF ENGR. · ORIGINATOR · LIAISON ENGRS. · LOFT. · SHOP SUPT.

Posts on dwg. status card

FIG. 1

Route for emergency ADC or EO prepared by liaison engr.

RELEASE CLERK — Issues original with number added-records number, dwg. No. (except those issued to liaison) & draftsman or liaison engr. issues in blocks of 20 to liaison engr. only.

Route when prepared by engr. dept.

LIAISON ENGR. — Prepares original prefixing No. with "X"

CUSTOMER — Approval (when approval prior to release is required by customer.)

LIAISON ENGR. — Prints & distributes necessary copies.

DRAFTSMAN — Prepares master

RELEASE CLERK — Attaches reference print logs in & forwards.

NOTE:
If an ADC or EO is voided by any checking station, the original must be marked "Void" with authorizing signature & date & returned to release clerk, an "X" ADC or EO shall be marked "Cancelled" with signature & date & replaced by another ADC or EO bearing the correct information.

EO'S do not go through planning

ENG. SUPERVISOR AFFECTED — Check & approves. Signs & dates. Obtains effective serial No. from planning.

RELEASE CLERK — Logs in & forwards. Attaches reference print if necessary.

CHECKING — Checks & approves. Signs & dates.

STRESS — Checks & approves. Signs & dates.

PLANNING — Indicates effect on tooling. Confirms effective serial No. - Signs & dates.

PROJECT ENGR. — Approval - Signs & dates.

CUSTOMER — Approval - Signs & dates. (When approval prior to release is required by customer.)

RELEASE CLERK — Returns reference prints to file. Checks for legibility. Signs and dates. Posts log. Duplicates and distributes copies.

Original moved between these stations release dispatcher

LEGEND
Original
Copies

EDC & EO
Posts ADC No. on drawing status card

ENGR. FILES ADC & EO · RELEASE RECORDER ADC & EO · PARTS LIST ADC · PROJECT ENGRS. ADC & EO · WRITER OF EO EO · LIAISON ENGRS. ADC & EO · GROUP LEADERS ADC · CHIEF ENGR. ADC & EO

To destinations outside of engineering as required

FIG. 2

Fig. 1—Flow chart showing procedure for issuance of a Stop Order. Fig. 2—Flow chart showing the procedure in approving, checking and releasing Advance Drawing Changes and Engineering Orders.

---

bottom of the stop original, and substituting the word "RELEASE" for the word "ORDER" at the top of the form, Fig. 3. The original used to issue the stop is employed to effect its release. Thus both the stop and its release bear the same serial number to insure immediate coordination. The Stop Release accompanies the new or changed drawing through the engineering checking and approval system. In no case is the Stop Release forwarded separately.

The Stop Release always indicates the disposition of finished parts in stores. All drawing change notices associated with the stop must show identical stock disposition instructions, and bear the notation, "This releases Stop Order (number)."

Sometimes it will be found that a stop has been issued in error, or subsequent investigation may reveal facts which make the stop unnecessary. In such cases the Stop Order is cancelled. This is accomplished by placing the notation "use without change" in the stop release block entitled "special," and forwarding the stop original to the

Release group for distribution of the copies.

A record of each Stop Order and Stop Release is maintained by engineering Release, using the drawing status record cards for that purpose (see the article on release and control of drawings, p. 214). The Stop Order number, date and effective production serial number are recorded at the time copies of the stop are distributed. Upon release of the stop, the date of its distribution is posted on the record. A red signal is placed upon the status card for the stopped drawing when the stop is distributed. It remains there until the stop is released.

Stop Orders should be released as soon as possible, as each causes a production delay. The stopping of one part usually results in hindering the completion of others. A part upon which work has been stopped prevents completion of its subassembly, and lack of that subassembly may prevent completion of the final product. A weekly summary of Stop Orders and Stop Releases is prepared and distributed to all engineering

supervisors and executives by engineering Release. The report lists all active stops, and those released during the preceding week; and serves as a reminder to take action on unreleased stops.

Advance Drawing Changes

The form shown in Fig. 4, Advance Drawing Change or ADC, is used by the engineering department when the need to authorize a drawing change is so urgent that it cannot be handled with sufficient rapidity through the regular release procedure. The issuance of an ADC is a guarantee that the drawing will be changed accordingly and released again as soon as practicable. An ADC may be issued in lieu of a drawing when time does not permit preparing and releasing a new drawing in the usual manner. In such cases a new drawing number is assigned for the new part described.

The ADC is used only for information to be incorporated in a drawing. The issuance of special information not relating to draw-

STOP ORDER NO. 73

THIS STOP AFFECTS ONLY THOSE DASH NUMBERS NOTED HEREON. STOPS ON ASSEMBLIES DO NOT STOP DETAILED PARTS

EFFECTIVE ON AIRPLANE NO. *34-375*

MODEL	PART NAME
34	*CLEVIS ASSEM-ARRESTING GEAR CYL PISTON ROD*

PART NO. *10122*
SERIAL NO. *402*
DASH NOS. *-4 8 -6*

TO BE FILLED IN BY PLANNING

PART NO.	SHOP ORDER	PROJ. NO.	DEPT.
(for entry of data on copies supplied manufacturing planning dept.)			

REASON FOR STOP

ARRESTING HOOK MUST BE PROVIDED WITH POSITIVE STOPS TO LIMIT MOVEMENT

STOP MATERIAL: YES ☐ NO ☒

ENG. APPROVAL
DRAFTSMAN *E.J. Klein*
GROUP LDR. *Burrows*
PROJECT ENGR.
CHIEF ENGR. *R.W. Hart*
BY *issued 9/7 B.E.B.*

(TO BE FILLED IN BY PLANNING) **PARTS STATUS** DATE *9/6*

ASSEMBLED IN PLANES *169*	ASSEMBLED IN SUBS. *0*	COMPLETELY FABRICATED *131*	IN WORK *100*

(TO BE FILLED IN BY MATERIAL CONTROL) **RAW STOCK STATUS** DATE *9/6*

MAT'L ORDERED *for 600 pieces* DUE DATE *11/15*
MAT'L IN STOCK *for 321 pieces*

(TO BE FILLED IN BY TOOLING) **TOOLING STATUS** DATE *9/6*

LIST TOOLS COMPLETED *All machine shop fixtures & assembly jig*
INCOMPLETED

PLANNING
PROJ. SUP. *R.M. Masters 9/6*
DATE STOPPED *9/7*
SIGNATURE *W.D. Spies*

STOP ORDER IS RELEASED AS FOLLOWS

BY NEW DRAWING	COMMENTS	BY DWG. CHANGE	BY A.D.C.	SPECIAL	DISPOSITION OF STOCK *Scrap all -4. Use -6*
DWG. NO *10283*		CHG. LET.	P.S. NO.		
DATE *9/15*		DATE	DATE		
Burrows		SIG.	SIG.	DATE	
R.W. Hart				SIG.	TO BE FILLED IN AT TIME OF RELEASE

Fig. 3—A typical stop order. An 8½x11 in. hectograph form permits rapid duplication. When the Stop Order is released the spaces at the bottom of the form are filled in and the word "Release" is substituted for "Order".

ing changes is accomplished by the Engineering Order shown at Fig. 5. The two forms keep information relating only to drawing changes segregated from that which is not shown on drawings.

A copy of each ADC is attached to every print of the drawing affected. Their use permits immediate issuance of change information without the necessity of reprinting the drawing and of issuing revised prints to all departments.

Each ADC is prepared by, or under the direction of, an engineering supervisor. It lists the reason for the change, the drawing number, the part name, and other information. See Fig. 4. Sketches and explanations clearly indicate the action to be taken by the manufacturing departments.

After an ADC is prepared it is forwarded to the Release section for routing through the system. The ADC is routed in a manner shown at Fig. 2 for a large aircraft company. The release system includes checking and approval by the checking group, stress group, manufacturing planning department, project office and customer's representative. A small engineering department, or one engaged in the design of comparatively simple products, will not usually require the complete system shown in Fig. 2. In such cases the system can usually be confined to checking, followed by the chief engineer's approval. Accuracy of the change information given on the ADC is the liability of the engineering supervisor responsible for its issuance.

Since the only justification for the usage of an ADC is to decrease the time required to issue information to the manufacturing departments, the routing of ADCs through the checking and approval system cannot be left to chance. It is made the prime duty of an alert, aggressive member of the Release group. This employee personally forwards ADCs between release system stations and maintains a record of the time at each station in the system. A total time within the system of four hours is the maximum that can be allowed for an ADC, and it is the duty of the ADC expediter to prevent their release from being delayed beyond this period. When an ADC is delayed by circumstances beyond the authority of the expediter, he immediately refers the case to the chief draftsman or chief clerk, depending upon who is at fault.

Copies of the ADC are duplicated and distributed by the Release group. In addition to copies for various files throughout the company, one copy is attached to each regular-issue print of the drawing. A small hole is punched in the margin of the print, directly below the title block, each time an ADC is attached. This provides a ready check upon the completeness of the ADCs attached to the print. There should be the same number of ADCs attached as there are holes punched in the print margin. If not, the user of the print should obtain from Release the serial numbers of all active ADCs issued against that drawing. The missing attachments can then be identified, and copies obtained from Release.

When the ADC form does not provide sufficient space adequately to describe the change, it is necessary to make a supplementary sketch on tracing paper to accompany the ADC. In such cases the ADC is prepared in the usual manner, except that it is plainly marked "Sheet 1 of 2 sheets." The supplementary sketch is not assigned a drawing number, but instead is identified in the lower right-hand corner with the corresponding ADC serial number. It is marked "Sheet 2 of 2 sheets." All signatures appearing on the ADC also appear on the sketch. The ADC title block is placed on the sketch by the use of a rubber stamp.

The ADC and sketch are routed together. After the blueprint unit has prepared the

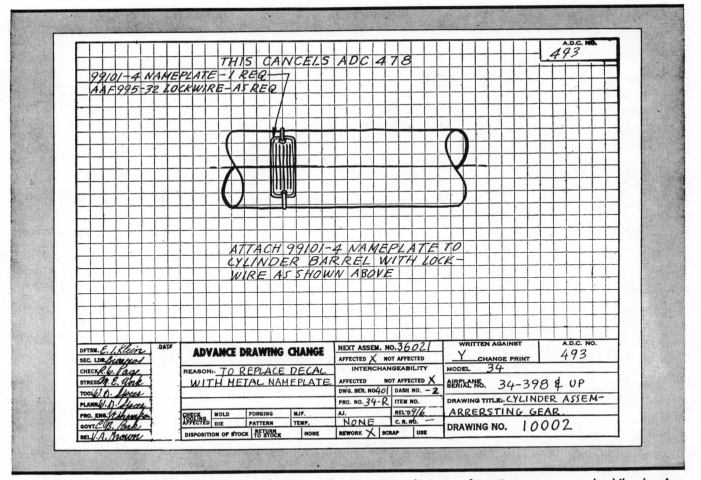

THIS CANCELS ADC 478

99101-4 NAMEPLATE - 1 REQ
AAF995-32 LOCKWIRE - AS REQ

A.D.C. NO.
493

ATTACH 99101-4 NAMEPLATE TO
CYLINDER BARREL WITH LOCK-
WIRE AS SHOWN ABOVE

DFTSM. E. I. Klein	DATE	**ADVANCE DRAWING CHANGE**	NEXT ASSEM. NO. 36021		WRITTEN AGAINST		A.D.C. NO.
SEC. LDR.			AFFECTED X NOT AFFECTED		Y __CHANGE PRINT		493
CHECK R. G. Page		REASON: TO REPLACE DECAL	INTERCHANGEABILITY		MODEL 34		
STRESS M. E. York		WITH METAL NAMEPLATE	AFFECTED NOT AFFECTED X		AIRPLANE SERIAL NO. 34-398 & UP		
TOOL			DWG. SER. NO. 401 DASH NO. -2				
PLANN.			PRO. NO. 34-R ITEM NO.		DRAWING TITLE: CYLINDER ASSEM-		
PRO. ENG.		CHECK TOOLING AFFECTED MOLD FORGING MJF.	AJ. REL'D 9/6		ARRERSTING GEAR.		
GOVT.		DIE PATTERN TEMP.	NONE C. R. NO. —		DRAWING NO. 10002		
REL. V. A. Brown		DISPOSITION OF STOCK RETURN TO STOCK NONE	REWORK X SCRAP USE				

Fig. 4—An Advance Drawing change provides urgent information so that manufacturing can proceed while drawings are being revised. The issuance of an ADC is a guarantee that the drawing will be changed to correspond.

required prints, the supplementary sketch is forwarded to engineering files for filing with the ADC original.

In every manufacturing enterprise of any size there is usually an engineering liaison function. The person or persons assigned to this duty serve as direct contact between the engineering and the manufacturing departments, receiving and answering all requests for engineering information and assistance. This insures that all requests from the manufacturing departments will be quickly and accurately answered, as well as provides complete coordination between the engineering and the other departments. In the absence of an engineering liaison function an unreasonable portion of an engineering supervisor's time is spent handling requests from the factory. Even worse, misinformation may be supplied the manufacturing departments—as the inevitable result of decentralized responsibility.

The liaison engineers are experienced, competent engineering personnel. They are authorized to issue emergency ADCs, without the necessity of formal checking and approval after normal working hours of the engineering department, or when the need for engineering authorization is so urgent that it cannot be handled through the regu-

lar release procedure.

Each emergency ADC has its serial number prefixed by "X" for identification. In some cases it may be necessary for the liaison engineer to obtain approval of the customer's representative prior to releasing the ADC. Only sufficient copies are distributed to take care of the immediate need. The ADC original is forwarded to the Release Section for processing and checking in the regular manner. After an emergency ADC has been approved in the regular manner, the "X" is removed from its serial number and copies are distributed in the usual manner.

If the emergency ADC is found undesirable, or in error when checked, it is plainly marked "cancelled." Another ADC, cross-referenced to the cancelled emergency ADC, is issued to provide the correct information. When competent personnel are assigned to liaison engineering, the quantity of incorrect emergency ADCs will be small.

All ADCs show, in the space marked "written against—change print," Fig. 4, the change letter appearing on the drawing at the time the ADC is written. Thus, the letter "D" appearing in the change-letter space indicates that the ADC affects the "D" revision of the drawing, and should be incorporated in the "E" drawing change. A

copy of the ADC should be attached to each regular-issue "D" revision print. ADCs written against drawings that do not bear a change letter show a dash in the change-letter space.

Changes cannot be made on an ADC after its release. Should it be found incorrect, another ADC is issued with the note: "This cancels ADC (number)." Should it be necessary to provide additional information, another ADC is issued, bearing the note "This supplements ADC (number)."

A change affecting several drawings requires a separate ADC for each drawing. In no case does one ADC relate to more than a single drawing. Several dash numbers on one drawing, however, can be covered by a single ADC. This procedure insures an orderly release of ADCs and a record of the distribution of them.

The production serial number upon which an ADC takes effect is obtained from the manufacturing planning department, except in the case of mandatory changes which must take effect upon a certain unit regardless of the disruption of production schedules. The desired effective serial number is shown on the ADC when it is forwarded to manufacturing planning for confirmation. If the requested serial number cannot be

ENG'R ORDER NO. *132*

PROJECT NO. *X-293*   MODEL *202 & 204*   DWG NO. *20109*
DWG SERIAL NO. *6309*   AIRPLANE NO. —   DWG TITLE *Valve Arm-Sequence*
DASH NO. —   REQUESTED BY *R.E. Brison*   SALVAGE TICKET NO. —
DEPT. NO. *73*

TEST ☒   LOFT ☐   MOCK-UP ☐   NEW ST'D ☐   DEVIATION ☐

REWORK 6 ONLY 20109-4 AS FOLLOWS:—

NOTE:— 0.0005 MAX ALLOWABLE TAPER ON I.D.

.6300 +.0005 / -.0000 I.D.

REWORK 6 ONLY 20109-5 AS FOLLOWS:—

HARD CHROME PLATE O.D. OF FLANGES ONLY TO .631 +.001 / -.000 THEN GRIND TO .629 +.000 / -.001

GRIND GROOVE TO .424 ± .001 DIA.

DELIVER COMPLETED PARTS TO R.E. BRISON, ENGR. DEPT.

WRITTEN AGAINST A CHANGE PRINT

REASON FOR E.O. *TO AUTHORIZE MANUFACTURE OF TEST PARTS FOR LEAKAGE CORRECTION INVESTIGATION*

				DISPOSITION OF STOCK	
DFTSMAN. *R.E. Brison* DATE *9/2*	CHECK *D. M. Hart* DATE *9/3*			RETURN TO OVERSTOCK	☐
SEC. LDR. *R.E. Brison* *9/2*	GEN. REL. *B.E. Brown* *9/6*			NONE ☒ SCRAP	☐
PRO. ENG. *R.S. Brown* *9/2*	GOV'T *G.C. Nyggo* *9/2*			REWORK ☐ USE	☐
STRESS *H.L. Watro* *9/2*	RELEASED *9/3*				

Fig. 5—An Engineering Order is used, as an aid in manufacturing and assembly, to supply special information that does not appear on drawings.

met without disrupting production schedules, it will be changed by manufacturing planning to one that can. Selection by the engineering department of a reasonable effective serial number is simplified when manufacturing planning uses a block-release system for issuance of shop orders. Thus, all changes within a given calendar period accumulate against the starting serial number of the next production release.

In general it is not economical to issue ADCs against small drawings, such as the "A" and "B" sizes, i.e. 8½x11 and 11x17 in., respectively. Instead, the change should be made directly upon the drawing affected. Exceptions to this rule are emergency ADCs listed by liaison engineers.

Whenever an ADC is incorporated in its drawing, the ADC original is marked "Incorporated," with date, change letter and the signature of the person obsoleting the ADC. The obsolete original is then returned to engineering files.

The drawing change notice accompanying a changed drawing lists the serial numbers of all ADCs incorporated by the change in the "authority for change" column. This authorizes Release to list the ADCs as incorporated on the status-record cards for the drawing affected. The drawing-status record cards provide for listing all ADCs issued against each drawing, as well as a column for indicating the change letter. This information is entered by engineering Release; first, when the ADC original passes through Release, and later when the changed prints incorporating the ADC are released.

The prime reason for an ADC is speed in conveying information to the manufacturing departments, and in most cases freehand sketching is entirely adequate. Accurate information is the important consideration, which can be conveyed quickly and conveniently by well-drawn sketches.

It may be found desirable to route all ADCs affecting production models to the tool design department, prior to release. This will prevent release of ADCs that ad-versely affect tooling, and avail the engineering department of information on alternate methods of accomplishing the change at less expense. When this practice is followed, the tool-design department checks all production ADCs for effect upon tooling and approves those found satisfactory. Objectionable ADCs are referred to the project engineer, who arranges a compromise satisfactory to both engineering and the tool design department.

Engineering Orders

The Engineering Order, EO form, Fig. 5, is used by the engineering department to effect the rapid release of information not incorporated on a drawing, such as drawing deviations, parts salvage, test instructions and authorization for the manufacture of mock-up parts. Engineering orders are not issued to cover design material or dimensional changes. An EO should affect as few units as possible, and never be issued to cover large portions of a contract. An ADC should be issued when a quantity of units are involved.

A deviation EO is frequently issued to authorize the re-work of parts in cases where the actual drawing change will show a different alteration of the parts. Parts that deviate from their drawing in a manner that cannot be re-worked to the drawing dimensions are often usable. In such cases the parts are not scrapped, and an EO deviation authorizes their acceptance by the inspection department as salvage.

The basic procedure for releasing EOs is similar to that used for ADCs, as shown in Fig. 2. The only variation is elimination of manufacturing planning as a station in the release system. Engineering Orders do not affect tooling. The effective serial number is usually based upon actual need for a drawing deviation.

When an EO is issued to authorize fabrication of a new test part or to aid an installation, a drawing number is assigned to identify the part or installation. The serial number of the EO is shown in the drawing number assignment record. If the test part is found to be satisfactory for production, a drawing or an ADC is issued to release the part for manufacture. If unsatisfactory, the drawing number is cancelled. When the EO describes an assembly, dash numbers are used to identify the detail parts thereof, unless they are already described by detail drawings. Dash numbers used for EO part identification are not dash-numbers of a drawing.

The general rules governing use of advance drawing-changes also apply to EOs. The principal difference in procedure for the two forms is the fact that EOs are never incorated in the drawing. They are listed on the drawing status record cards for reference purposes only. One copy of the EO is attached to each regular-issue print bearing the same change letter. ∎

Handling Drawing Changes in Small Companies

JAMES E. THOMPSON

Drawing changes are costly, yet unavoidable. Regardless of the reason for making the change, its request and execution must be put through in an orderly manner. Here are flow charts, drawing-change forms and procedures for handling eight classes of drawing changes.

DRAWING CHANGES are undesirable, but unavoidable. It is impossible to foresee all the conditions that will be encountered during the manufacture of a product and therefore changes may be necessary during fabrication and assembly to reduce cost, facilitate production or simply manufacture. Also, changes may be required to correct engineering errors, or rectify unsatisfactory operating conditions experienced by customers. Articles manufactured on contract may require drawing revisions to meet changes in the customer's requirements.

In planning the operation of an engineering department it must be considered that simple designs may require relatively few engineers assigned to drawing changes but complex equipment will require a larger percent of the engineering personnel assigned to making drawing revisions. One leading manufacture of four-engine bomber aircraft, with an engineering department of approximately 1,800 employees, found that 136 persons were required to handle the average of 350 drawing changes that were necessary during each week of the model's production.

Another prominent aircraft manufacturer estimates that the time expended upon drawing changes, after production begins, will approximately equal the engineering time required to complete the original design. A surprising number of changes are also necessary during the transition from an experimental prototype into a production design. A twin-engine night-fighter airplane produced by a western manufacturer had a total of 4,857 drawings, in which 4,727 drawing changes and 3,787 advance drawing changes were made during its production engineering phase. (The purpose and use of advance drawing changes is explained in an article.

Because drawing changes are a normal engineering department operation, it is necessary to establish an orderly method of making and recording revisions. Drawing revision methods are primarily concerned with: (1) drawing change request procedure; and (2) drawing change system. The first includes establishing a method that insures prompt action on all changes requested by other departments. The second requires a logical, efficient method of preparing and identifying drawing revisions.

Drawing Change Requests

Drawing change requests may originate with the customer, sub-contractors or other departments of the company. Revisions desired by the customer are usually requested through the sales or contract departments, either by correspondence or by special procedure established by the customer.

The originator of a drawing change request prepares either 4 or 5 copies as indicated on the flow chart, Fig. 1. All drawing change requests no matter whether they originate within the engineering department, other departments of the company or from sub-contractors are made on the same Drawing Change Request form, Fig. 2, which is referred to as a Change Request or CR form.

A Change Request may originate in any department, but it does not have official recognition until delivered to the engineering release-group for recording and engineering investigation. The CR form is prepared as an original and three carbon copies, except that CRs to be forwarded to another division are prepared as an original and four copies. The original and all copies except the last are routed as shown in Fig. 1. The last copy is retained by the person originating the request.

A CR originating in a manufacturing department is signed by the person requesting the change, endorsed by the originator's immediate superior, and then routed to the inspection department for approval. If approved by the inspection department, all forwarding copies of the CR are routed to manufacturing planning. If rejected, a statement of the reason for the rejection is placed on the back of all copies, followed by routing to manufacturing planning. Planning will either approve and forward to engineering release, or reject and forward with a statement of the reason for rejection. This procedure provides engineering with the viewpoints of inspection and manufacturing planning, and makes sure that all requests originating in the manufacturing departments reach the engineering department.

Change Requests are used within the engineering department when one design group desires changes upon a drawing within the control of another design group. Liaison engineers use this form to request changes to facilitate production, investigate engineering errors, and the like. The request is prepared by the person desiring the change, endorsed by the originator's immediate supervisor, and then forwarded to engineering release-group for routing. Some engineering departments, route all change requests through engineering planning, to assist that activity in maintaining control over work assignments. Engineering release-group upon receipt of a CR, detaches the third copy, and files this in an "incomplete CR file" as a record of its receipt and subsequent routing. The remaining copies are routed to the proper group leaders after suitable notations of date and names have been entered on the release file-copy. The remaining copies, one and two, are returned to release-group for distribution after an investigation by the engineering department is completed. The original copy is returned to the originator of the CR, and the second copy is sent to the group leader. Suitable entries on the Release file-copy indicate the date of this distribution. All approved change requests are posted on the Drawing Status Record (see p. 218) card or cards affected, and the Release file-copy is placed in an "approved CR file." Disapproved CRs are filed in an "obsolete CR file."

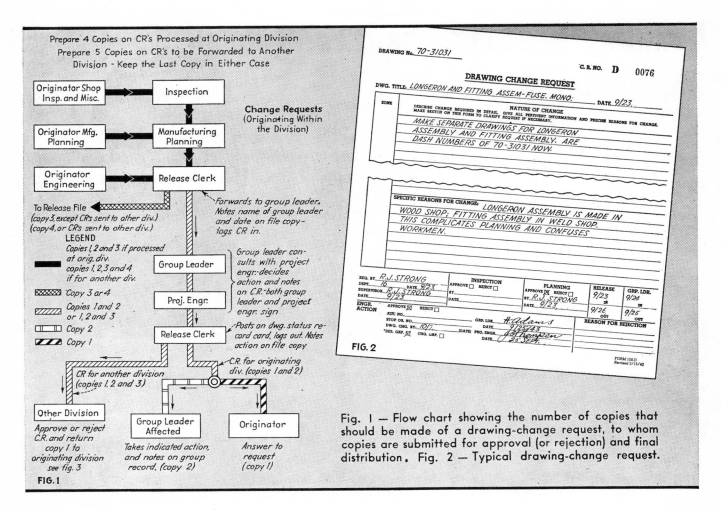

Fig. 1 — Flow chart showing the number of copies that should be made of a drawing-change request, to whom copies are submitted for approval (or rejection) and final distribution. Fig. 2 — Typical drawing-change request.

The group leader determines the action to be taken upon the CR through consultation with the project engineer who will be affected by the change request. Final engineering approval or rejection is entered in the "Engr. Action" block, Fig. 2, which bears the signatures of both the group leader and the project engineer.

If the Change Request is rejected, it is only necessary to check the "Reject" square, Fig. 2, and note the reason for the rejection in the space provided. If approved, the square marked "Approve" is checked, and the action to be taken is indicated on one of the three lines below it. If an Advance Drawing Change, ADC, is being issued, its number is listed. When a Stop Order is issued, its number is listed. If neither an ADC or Stop Order is being issued and the request will be handled by a drawing change, then the estimated date of the change is noted on the line provided. When a change-group exists, it is necessary to indicate whether the change will be made by that group or by the design-group affected. Only one of the three lines on the CR form for the action on approved change requests is used.

Regardless of the final action, the CR must bear the signature of both the project engineer and the group leader affected, before final distribution. An approved Change Request covered either by an ADC or by a Stop Order should not be distributed until the latter document is actually released. The coordination required to effect simultaneous release of an approved CR and the relevant advance engineering information is a responsibility of the release-group.

Records of the issuance, approval or rejection, and incorporation of Change Requests are maintained by the engineering release-group. An "incomplete" file contains all requests upon which action is pending, and an "approved" file contains a copy of each authorized request. A copy of each rejected change request is placed in an "obsolete" file.

Drawing Changes

A clearly defined procedure for handling drawing changes is necessary to insure efficient, accurate revisions. The method to be described for processing drawing changes is used by many engineering departments. Briefly the method comprises the following tasks:

1. Group leader assigns job to draftsman.
2. Draftsman obtains affected drawing from engineering files, and checks with release-group to obtain a list of all unincorporated ADCs and Change Requests.
3. Draftsman ascertains if change will affect interchangeability. Changes that affect interchangeability require special handling.

4. Required revisions are made, including incorporation of all outstanding ADCs and CRs, in addition to changes requested by the group leader and approved by the project engineer. A change letter is assigned to identify the revision.
5. Change is recorded in the drawing title block.
6. A "Notice of Change" is prepared, describing the change.
7. The drawing, Notice-of-Change, copies of all ADCs and CRs incorporated, and other reference data are returned to the group leader.
8. The group leader inspects the change, and signs the Notice-of-Change if the work is approved. Group leader then writes a "Release Request" covering the drawing affected, and forwards request and drawing with all reference data to release-group.
9. Release places drawing in release system for checking and approval.
10. Draftsman makes required checker's corrections.
11. Corrected and approved drawing is released, and prints distributed.

When a change is made that affects interchangeability, two drawings of the part are required—one of the part in its initial form, and one of the re-designed part. Both drawings must remain active to permit ordering and manufacture of spare parts. Service data notes are placed on each drawing to indicate the serial numbers and models to which it applies and to give a cross-reference to the other drawing number. These notes are placed to the left of the drawing title-block, except that "A" size (8½ x 11 in.) drawings carry the note above the title.

Each successive drawing change is identified by a letter, beginning with A for the first change and continuing in alphabetical order, except that the letters I, O, Q, R and X, are not used. Each change on the drawing is identified by a symbol comprising the change letter circumscribed by a 5/16 in. diameter circle, placed adjacent to the affected portion of the drawing. When more than one item is changed, sub-numerals, for example, A_1, A_2, A_3, are added to the change letter to identify each item. Some engineering departments identify drawing changes by numerals, rather than letters although the majority prefer the letter system.

The change letter, with the highest sub-numeral of the change, is entered in the drawing title-block revision record. The date of the change and the name of the draftsman are entered in columns provided for these data. The government representative usually signs in the "approval" column when the drawing relates to government contracts.

The use of a Notice-of-Change, Fig. 3, eliminates the need for describing the change in the title block revision space which ordinarily does not provide sufficient area to describe the revision adequately. The same deficiency is usually present even in cases where the drawing revision space is separate from the title block. Some companies use a drawing title-block that provides only for listing the change letter, date and signature.

The Notice-of-Change accompanying a changed drawing must be carefully prepared. Its purpose is to indicate what change has been made, which ADCs and CRs are incorporated in the change, what is to be done with the stock (in work or stores) of existing parts, and when the change becomes effective. It also provides a clear record of how drawing appeared prior to change.

Many changes become effective during a project with the result that some parts must be fabricated according to the drawing prior to the change, and others according to the drawing as changed. Thus the drawing and the attached Notice-of-Change should clearly set forth complete information for both old and new parts. The complexities of mass production require that the Notice-of-Change accompanying a revised drawing provides a variety of information to guide the manufacturing planning department in applying the change. The information required makes impractical the use of the revision space in the title-block. Use of a separate Notice-of-Change is advisable for all production drawings. The Notice-of-Change Fig. 3 is an 8½ x 11 in. form printed on tracing paper.

When extensive revisions are made to a large drawing it may be found that several pages are required for an adequate Notice-of-Change. Changes of this nature become so complicated that manufacturing planning usually prefers to process the change as though it were a new drawing, rather than attempting to correct the records for each changed item individually. Further, the printing and distribution of long Notice-of-Change is costly, and serves little useful purpose. It is wise to limit Notices-of-Change to six pages.

When more than six pages will be required for the complete Notice-of-Change, two separate notices can be prepared, each bearing the same change letter. One is complete, listing every changed item, and is prepared only for record purposes. The second notice is distributed with copies of the changed drawing. It does not list the changed items, but simply bears the statement "Drawing Completely Revised." Both notices accompany the drawing through the release system, but the complete notice is detached by release-group after the drawing completes the system. It is forwarded to engineering files. The single-page notice accompanies the drawing to the blueprint unit for preparation of copies for distribution with the drawing prints. The complete notice is always available for reference, and the wasteful distribution of an extensive Notice-of-Change is avoided.

The current Notice-of-Change is blueprinted adjacent to the right-side edge of the

Dwg. No. 70-31031	NOTICE OF CHANGE	Contract No. NXs 1053
Chg. Letter C		Project No. 70
Model X4-R		Job No. 70-1231
Date 9/7		Sheet No. 1 of 1

Title LONGERON & FITTING ASSEM & -FUSELAGE MONOCOQUE

Letter No.	Zone	Kind of Change	Detail Description of Change	Effective on	Authority for Change	Disposition of Parts in Stock
1		REVISE AND REDRAWN - SAME NO.	SEPARATE DETAILS MADE FOR LONGERON ASSEM & FITTING ASSEM.	707 & SUB	CR-76	USE
						USE
2		CHG PART NO.	70-31017 WAS -2	707 & SUB	ENGR	USE
			70-31017-1 WAS -3	707 & SUB	ENGR	USE
3		CHG PART NO.	70-31016 WAS -4 & -5	707 & SUB	ADC-2731	USE
4		REMOVE PART NO.	1S270P36-0128 REMOVED & CALLED OUT ON 70-31016	707 & SUB	ADC-2731	USE
5		REMOVED DIM	MFG DIMENSIONS REMOVED & SHOWN ON 70-31017 & 70-31016	707 & SUB	ENGR	USE
6		REMOVED NOTE	NOTES REMOVED & SHOWN ON 70-31017 & 70-31016	707 & SUB	ENGR	USE

| REASON FOR CHANGE: 1 THRU 6-TO FACILITATE PRODUCTION BY SEPARATE DWGS FOR WOOD & METAL PARTS | Affects Dash Numbers -2, -3, -4 & -5. |

SHOP		H. ADAMS 10/1	W. JONES 10/5	J.E. THOMPSON 10/5	W. HALE 10/6	M. ROBERTS
Requested By	Date	Group Leader	Date	Stress	Date	Project Eng.	Date	Gov't Approval	Date	Blueprint	Date
E.C. WISEMAN	9/30	BRAVERMAN 10/4	R. HARVEY 10/5	--	R.D. RAY 10/7	--
Changed By	Date	Checked By	Date	Weights	Date	Parts List	Date	Release	Date	Form 242-E

Fig. 3—A Notice-of-Change furnishes complete information about drawing changes and revisions to keep not only the users of the drawing up-to-date but also to provide adequate records of the changes.

Table I—Guide for Classifying and Making Drawing Changes

Class	Title of Change	Instructions	Remarks
1	ADVANCE DRAWING CHANGE	....	Changes requiring immediate action can be economically and rapidly made by use of an ADC.
2	DETAIL CHANGE All changes involving revisions and additions without re-drawing.	Place date, name and change letter in the title-block space.	Write Notice-of-Change, assign change letter and list changes.
3	VOID Drawings that have not been released.	No Notice-of-Change required. Group supervisor writes "VOID" on margin of drawing below title block, with date and signature — draws two red lines through number, and forwards to files for storing with obsolete tracings.	Check next assembly and remove requirements for part. Notify numbers clerk.
4	CANCELLED — NO LONGER USED Drawings which have been released and which are no longer required.	Write Notice-of-Change giving reason for discontinuing part, and listing as cancelled all ADCs and CRs against the drawing. Place change letter in title and cross out with a neat "X", that leaves the letter legible. Draw two red lines through dwg. no. in title block and write "CANCELLED" below number, with date and signature.	Must not affect interchangeability. Give detailed explanation. Remove part from next assembly with change or ADC. Notify numbers clerk.
5	SUPERSEDED Drawings which have been released and later replaced by a non-interchangeable part.	Old drawing remains active with service data note added to dwg. Notice-of-Change required. New drawing service-data note is also required.	Applies to changes involving interchangeability. Notify numbers clerk.
6	*REDRAWN — SAME NO. NO CHANGE	Old drawing requires no Notice-of-Change, but change letter in block, and notation in "Change" space. Cross out change letter and dwg. no. as with Class 4 change. Write "REDRAWN — SAME NO. — NO CHANGE" below number, with date and signature. For new drawing write Notice-of-Change, and note change in size, if any. Same change letter is used on both old and new drawings.	Does not affect interchangeability.
7	*REDRAWN — SAME NO. WITH CHANGES	No Notice-of-Change required on old drawings. Cross out change letter and dwg. no. as in Class 4 change. Write "REDRAWN — SAME NO. — WITH CHANGES" below number, with date and signature. Same procedure for new drawings as outlined in Class 6.	If next assembly is affected, correct by drawing change or ADC.
8	TO REINSTATE A VOIDED OR CANCELLED DRAWING	Assign next change letter. Write Notice-of-Change, stating "REINSTATED" and explain reason. Remove red lines from dwg. no., and cancellation note below number.	Same as Class 7. Notify numbers clerk. Additional change items may be listed on the "reinstating" Notice-of-Change.

* Notes on Redrawing.
(a) Copy (do not imitate) all signatures, lettering them exactly as they appear on the old drawing.
(b) Do not copy previous change letters either on the face of the drawing or in the change block.
(c) Indicate the new changes, forming the revision being made, in the conventional manner, and list them in the Notice-of-Change.
(d) Always note full name for signature (not initials).

drawing so that a copy thereof accompanies each print. This method eliminates all possibility of the notice becoming detached from the print. Use of staples, or other mechanical means, of attaching the notice to prints should be discouraged.

The current Notice-of-Change should be filed with the drawing at all times. Obsolete notices are stored by drawing number in the engineering files. A Notice-of-Change written to cancel a drawing should always state whether or not the cancelled drawing is replaced by another. One of the following notes should appear on it:

"CANCELLED—REPLACED BY (XXXXX)"
or "CANCELLED—NOT REPLACED"

New drawings that replace existing drawings should carry the note "REPLACES (old dwg no.)." A space is provided usually in the title block for this purpose. Otherwise,

the drawing can carry the information as a general note, adjacent to the title-block.

All drawing changes can be grouped into eight classes, and simple rules can be stated to guide the making of the changes in each class. The classes and instructions on making the changes are given in Table I. The statements appearing in capital letters should be used verbatim on drawings and on Notices-of-Change as they provide simple, positive identification about the change.

Some engineering departments have established change groups for the purpose of relieving design groups of the burden of routine changes. This arrangement has not been altogether satisfactory. The resultant decentralization of drawing control often introduces drawing errors that will not occur when the design group-leader retains complete control over all drawings relating to

his work. The condition is aggravated by the tendency to consider the change group as a training center, and staff it with inexperienced draftsmen.

Duplication of effort is frequently experienced when a separate change group exists; resulting from the design group-leader making design changes just before or immediately after a routine incorporation of ADCs and CRs by the change groups. Both could have been achieved by a single change.

The logical conclusion drawn from experience with many change groups is that more efficient utilization of personnel can be had from placing junior draftsmen in each design group for the express purpose of making routine changes. They can be placed under the direct supervision of a senior draftsman, who then acts in the capacity of the responsible assistant group leader. ∎

How to Reduce Confusion Caused by Design Changes

- Pointers on getting a new product into production.
- Suggestions for reducing confusion in the factory due to design changes.
- Methods of handling part interchangeability when engineering change notices are issued.

Assembly of television station equipment. Engineering change notices on a component for a product such as this should specify cut-in point of change and disposition of obsoleted parts in inventory.

ALLEN T. WILSON
Communications and Sound Sections,
R C A Victor Division
Radio Corporation of America

THE NUISANCE OF ENGINEERING CHANGES can be greatly reduced if: (1) engineers become more familiar with factory operation; (2) a system is set up that is realistic toward changes, and all personnel involved admit that changes are normal; (3) the first new piece on every shop order is submitted to the engineering department for approval—and this can easily be done since a sample can be made during the tool trial before the tool is forwarded to production; (4) pre-production runs are made whenever possible; (5) a method is established that will allow the systematic assimilation of changes into a production order; and (6) detailed disposition of obsolete parts and assemblies as well as cut-in points are indicated to all department that will be affected.

Following are recommendations that may help the engineering department in setting up a workable design change system, particularly with respect to relations with the factory.

ESTABLISH A CLOSE ENGINEERING-FACTORY CONTACT. It is absolutely necessary that the design engineer be acquainted with production facilities and problems, or at least that he check basic considerations with production personnel. Review of engineering drawings by factory people prior to sign off is of little value in reducing the number of design changes required. Checking of black line prints usually is sketchy, time consuming, and uncoordinated, and is helpful only when limited to a few prints and when personally followed up by an engineer.

Many times gross or obvious errors that are apparent to the design engineer occur in the initial production run of a product. There are several ways to correct this situation: The engineer can circulate within the factory during the initial production phase; the first inspection piece can be forwarded to the engineering department for comment; or a pre-production run of a number of pieces can be made to check the design and prevent errors.

GIVE CHANGES PRIORITY. Changes during a shop order follow a fairly uniform pattern. After release when parts are being procured and made, purchasing and parts fabrication want alternates or derivations from drawings which must be confirmed by drawing changes; these ·changes generally involve no cost as they take place prior to parts being made. Starting prior to assembly and during the initial assembly phase of the shop order, the engineering department will need changes to correct errors; these changes are the costly ones requiring scrap, reworking, or new parts. Then as the assembly plant becomes more familiar with the design during the same phase, the assembly process department and the assembly line will want changes; these changes will generally be to facilitate manufacture, assembly, processing, and stocking of parts which are required to build the product in conformance with the most economical methods.

As the sales department gets some of the first units and starts to get customer reaction, other changes are required. Here again these changes are costly. A problem results from the fact that the people who see and have to account for the costs of changes do not also see how the product benefits from those costs. Establishing a priority system for such changes will substantially reduce costs.

USE FORMS FOR TEMPORARY CHANGES. An engineering change notice Fig. 2 is (1) an authorization to change a drawing as specified; (2) instructions to the factory as to disposition or action on the part or assemblies changed; (3) instructions to replacement parts as to disposition or action on the part changed. Other activities may also be affected such as writing of instruction books but the above three are the main ones. Of course on changes affecting the saleability or performance of the product, sales and product administration are also intimately concerned.

Engineering change notices should not be issued to cover all deviations from drawings. Such deviations arise from several conditions. They may result from engineering errors in the drawing, intentional deviations which are required to produce parts and which will be reflected in every part made, factory errors or unintentional deviations which are correctable, and substitutions. Engineering change notices should be written to correct all errors in the drawing, all intentional (approved) deviations from the drawing, and substitutions which are permanent or are approved alternates. Other deviations from drawings can be covered by the use of forms that

1. Approve use of parts from an alternate supplier.

2. Approve deviations in the first sample parts submitted by a supplier.

3. Approve temporary substitutions in materials for parts supplied by the factory.

4. Transmit engineering information to the shop.

5. Approve or reject deviations from drawings for production parts.

Whenever a temporary change is affected, either a form should be used or the change should be confirmed in writing. Verbal agreements are subject to misinterpretation and often lead to subsequent controversy.

However, other factors are present. Many people will contact the engineer to cover relatively minor items or interpretations of notes and dimensions. Many of these relate to standards which will supersede the drawing. (Standards must be intimately known.) Unless such items affect costs or methods of manufacture normally no drawing changes need be made.

CONSIDER PART INTERCHANGEABILITY. The biggest problem introduced by changes, except for cost and sched-ule, is the problem of interchangeability of parts. Interchangeability is a very nebulous item. First of all interchangeability must operate in both directions; that is, the old part must be interchangeable with the new and vice versa. Or it may be necessary that one part must be interchangeable with two or more parts. There should be no preference between the interchangeable parts. There should be consideration given to costs because if the difference in costs between two interchangeable parts is great, the cheaper part is preferred. Finally consideration needs to be given process interchangeability in the fabrication plant. Two functionally interchangeable parts may require entirely different processes, and may barely resemble one another in appearance. Special attention needs to be given replacement parts, and whenever possible, the stock problem simplified. Many times it is possible to stock the new part or several parts which will be an interchangeable unit in all products built. Notes may be used on the engineering change notice to help clarify this interchangeability problem. Because the engineering department is apt to change drawing numbers and interchangeable parts may not have the same drawing number, replacement parts may assign its own stock number to the part which is different than the drawing number. Then several different parts can be stocked under the same number.

AVOID MARKED PRINTS. Reworking of parts made always requires some consideration of interchangeability because there is a preference between parts made to the latest drawing and parts made to a previous drawing.

However, since the factory usually does not maintain its stock by change number, a change involving rework may be a difficult thing to handle. The assumption can be made that all parts to the same drawing number are interchangeable. When two or more parts must be correlated on a rework, it is generally easier to change part numbers just to accommodate the factory. At all times, the engineer must base his disposition instructions on the assumption that all parts are made.

The change column for a drawing Fig. 3 should completely describe the drawing change as the factory follows those instruction to rework. If reworking parts is not to be done in accordance with the desired drawing change, the rework must be specified on the engineering change notice. This should be done by means of a note or a sketch. The engineer must particularly mastermind any rework instructions. Costs and schedule are the two considerations. In some cases it is cheaper to scrap parts already made and make new parts. If this is so, such action must be specified.

Reworking parts usually involves moving in on the change fast and supplying the factory with new prints immediately. Marked prints are to be avoided for several reasons. (1) They are hard to "kill" Instances have been known where marked prints were in use for several years. (2) They are not applicable to extensive changes correlating several parts. (3) They are only applicable to small changes in a part. A large number of changes requires a new print as duplicating several marked prints involves too many opportunities for error and requires more time than changing the print. (4) Marked prints cannot be recorded; thus, they may be duplicated by unauthorized individuals.

SPECIFY CUT-IN POINTS AND PART DISPOSITION. The changing of assembly drawings is far more complex than changing detailed part drawings. One particular problem results from the fact that many normal changes on an assembly drawing actually are "future" changes. For instance, if a detailed part on an assembly drawing is changed and the parts made are usable, then the assembly drawing does not reflect the product as it is being currently produced. This same situation occurs when parts are changed and the new parts are not immediately available. Or this same situation can occur when the change requires the reworking or salvaging of parts and the resulting part or parts are not like they would be if made from raw material. Therefore, the engineering change

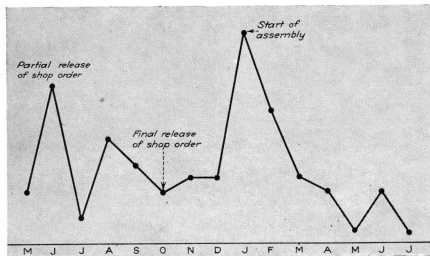

Fig. 1—Activity on engineering change notices. The number of changes on a new product usually reaches a peak at start of assembly.

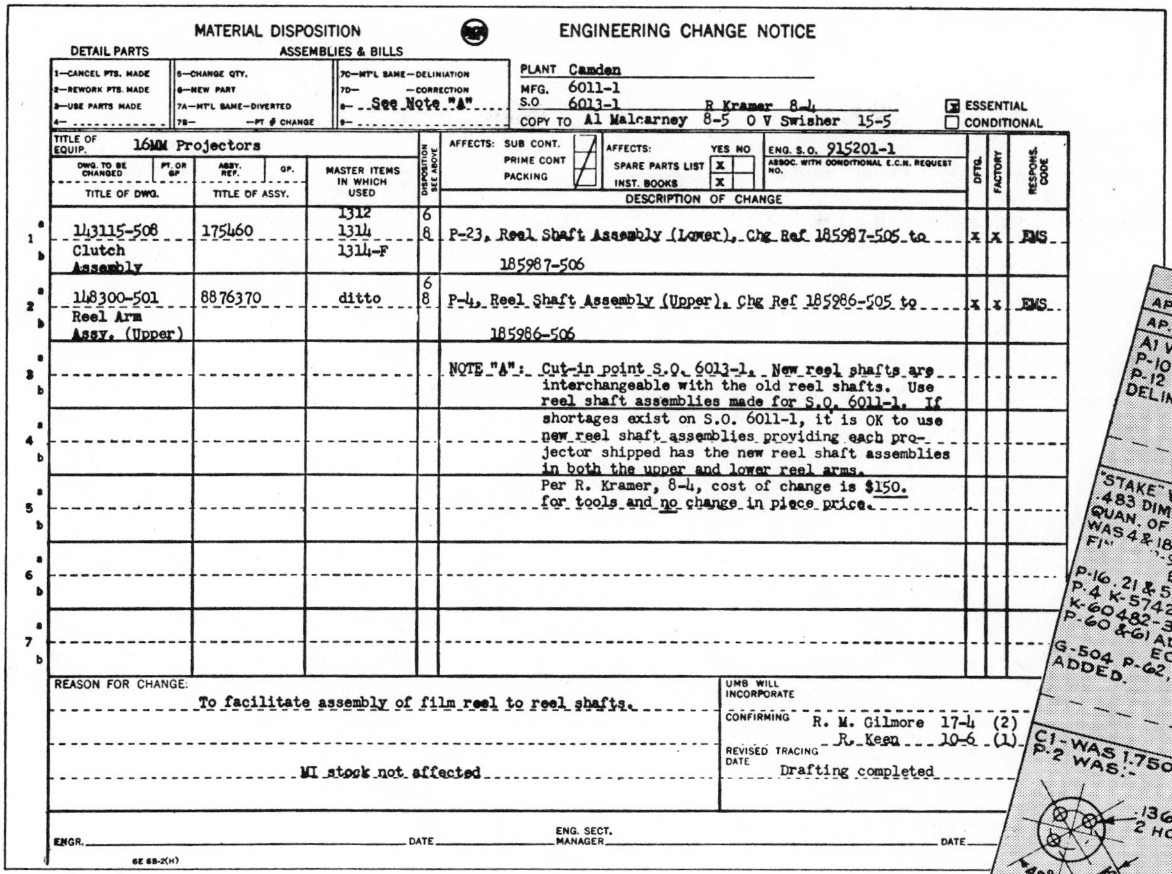

MATERIAL DISPOSITION   ENGINEERING CHANGE NOTICE

DETAIL PARTS		ASSEMBLIES & BILLS	
1—CANCEL PTS. MADE	5—CHANGE QTY.	7C—MT'L SAME—DELINIATION	
2—REWORK PTS. MADE	6—NEW PART	7D— — CORRECTION	
3—USE PARTS MADE	7A—MT'L SAME—DIVERTED	8—_See Note "A"_	
4—	7B— —PT # CHANGE	9—	

PLANT Camden
MFG. 6011-1
S.O 6013-1   R Kramer 8-4
COPY TO Al Malcarney 8-5 O V Swisher 15-5

☑ ESSENTIAL
☐ CONDITIONAL

TITLE OF EQUIP. 16MM Projectors

AFFECTS: SUB CONT. / PRIME CONT / PACKING
AFFECTS: SPARE PARTS LIST X / INST. BOOKS X   YES NO
ENG. S.O. 915201-1
ASSOC. WITH CONDITIONAL E.C.N. REQUEST NO.

	DWG. TO BE CHANGED / TITLE OF DWG.	PT OR GP	ASSY. REF. / TITLE OF ASSY.	GP.	MASTER ITEMS IN WHICH USED	DISPOSITION SEE ABOVE	DESCRIPTION OF CHANGE	DFTG.	FACTORY	RESPONS. CODE
1	143115-508 Clutch Assembly		175460		1312 1314 1314-F	6 8	P-23, Reel Shaft Assembly (Lower), Chg Ref 185987-505 to 185987-506	X	X	RMS
2	148300-501 Reel Arm Assy. (Upper)		8876370		ditto	6 8	P-4, Reel Shaft Assembly (Upper), Chg Ref 185986-505 to 185986-506	X	X	RMS
3							NOTE "A": Cut-in point S.O. 6013-1. New reel shafts are interchangeable with the old reel shafts. Use reel shaft assemblies made for S.O. 6011-1. If shortages exist on S.O. 6011-1, it is OK to use new reel shaft assemblies providing each projector shipped has the new reel shaft assemblies in both the upper and lower reel arms.			
4							Per R. Kramer, 8-4, cost of change is $150. for tools and no change in piece price.			
5										
6										
7										

REASON FOR CHANGE:
To facilitate assembly of film reel to reel shafts.

MI stock not affected

UMB WILL INCORPORATE

CONFIRMING R. M. Gilmore 17-4 (2)
    R. Keen 10-6 (1)
REVISED TRACING DATE Drafting completed

ENGR. _____ DATE ____
ENG. SECT. MANAGER _____ DATE ____
6E 6B-2(H)

Fig. 2—Engineering change notices being used by one manufacturer. Note that a point is made of giving all information considered pertinent.

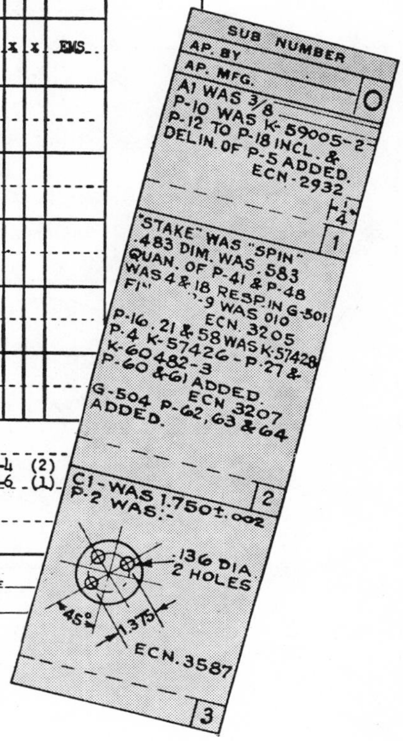

Fig. 3—Typical drawing change column. This should describe changes made since the factory follows these notes when reworking parts.

notice on an assembly should specify not only the cancelling of a shop order on parts, reducing the quantity of parts, or adding new parts, but also the disposition of parts that have been obsoleted and the point at which the factory is to cut-in with the change. Sales needs it to know when important changes are cut-in. Manufacturing needs it to maintain a semblance of continuity of scheduling and control of costs. Replacement parts may need to know 10 years from now what part to supply a customer, and Engineering needs it so that they can coordinate the change.

Generally these cut-in points should be based upon economical production quantities, and should consider the assembly rate. Only "stop" production changes should be allowed at other times, and such changes should require approval by the top level of sales, product manufacturing and engineering.

Such a procedure reduces costs of changes and solves the interchangeability problem as units within any cut-in point can be assigned different factory numbers. Thus upon release

the model number MI-1300-1 might apply to the first two thousand units; MI-1300-2 might apply to the second two thousand units, etc. By pre-assigning these numbers and by accumulating the engineering change notices for cut-in at these points, much confusion can be resolved.

Changes involving vendor's requests, factory's requests, or engineering errors can be cut-in at any time, providing (1) no increase in cost is incurred (2) no change in parts involved and (3) no change in the assembly line is involved.

One of the difficult problems occurs when the factory is building one shop order and engineering is working on an evolutionary design based on the same product drawings. Changes may be desired in a part currently in production. If the part is changed for the new shop order, but not the old, then the factory may be in the position of trying to build a part different from the delineation. This is a "future" engineering change notice and should not be used. However, whenever a change is made and the engineer specifies the disposition "Use Parts

Made", the engineering change notice is essentially a future engineering change notice. In these cases there is generally no preference between parts made to either sub on the drawing. To avoid future engineering change notices, it may be advisable to add new parts to the drawing or to make a new drawing. Thus it can be seen that in some respects, drawings apply to one shop order only.

All of this points out that the manufacture of a product within a factory is a great cooperative effort. In some respects the engineer is the unifying force between the individuals within the factory. Many times he becomes the arbitrator when differences arise— and the cohesive force to tie the loose ends together. He can build a product consciousness in the minds of everyone which will overcome the departmentalism inherent within the factory. Or he can destroy the cooperative viewpoint by his failure to work with or cooperate with various individuals on their requests to ease their jobs. The adoption of suggestions and changes from factory personnel will help sell the product to the organization. ∎

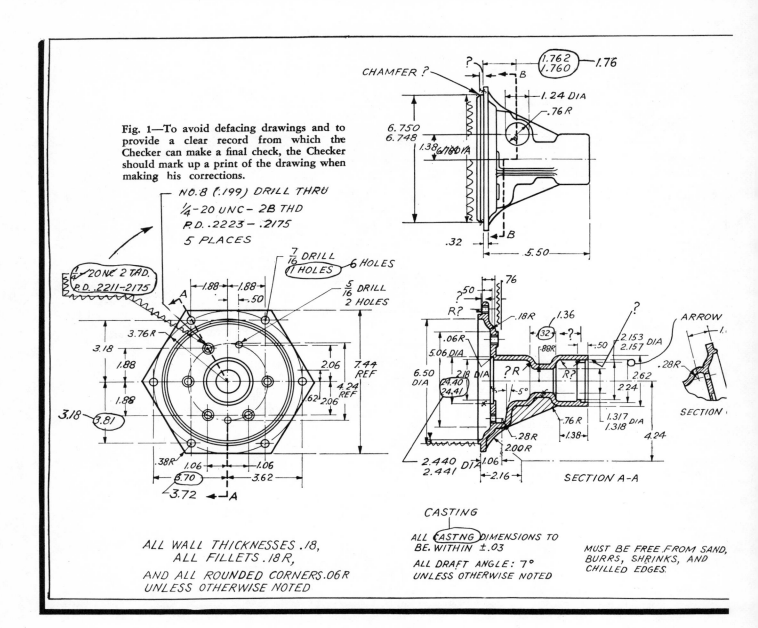

Fig. 1—To avoid defacing drawings and to provide a clear record from which the Checker can make a final check, the Checker should mark up a print of the drawing when making his corrections.

ALL WALL THICKNESSES .18,
ALL FILLETS .18R,
AND ALL ROUNDED CORNERS .06R
UNLESS OTHERWISE NOTED

CASTING
ALL CASTING DIMENSIONS TO BE WITHIN ±.03

ALL DRAFT ANGLE: 7°
UNLESS OTHERWISE NOTED

MUST BE FREE FROM SAND, BURRS, SHRINKS, AND CHILLED EDGES.

Competent Engineering Checkers Promote
Economical Production

GEORGE E. ROWBOTHAM

IN ANY ENGINEERING DEPARTMENT, the main functions of a Checker are to see that costly errors are not made, to insure uniformly correct interpretation of drawings, and to avoid confusion in engineering instructions, specifications and requisitions issued to the purchasing and manufacturing divisions of his company or organization.

The competent Checker has a sound engineering background and a thorough knowledge of manufacturing. His experience usually consists of a minimum of ten years in drafting and shop work. He probably started as a tracer, became a detailer, then a layout draftsman, and so on up the rungs of the ladder.

Not every ambitious draftsman, un-fortunately, has the proper adaptiveness to be a Checker. The outstanding characteristic needed is a facility and feeling for detail and precision. Because of this trait draftsmen like to refer to Checkers as "cranks" and "old fuss-pots". The nature of the Checker's work makes him a critic. Since it is his job to catch the draftsman's errors, he is often an unpopular man around a drafting room. The draftsman's

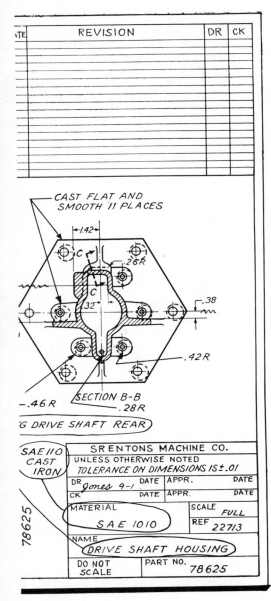

Table 1—Drawing Details and Notations

That Must Be Checked

1. Is general appearance of the drawing satisfactory?

2. Is tracing free from dirt and tears? Is back of tracing clean?

3. Are figures, letters and lines correctly formed, clean and dense enough to assure good reproduction and legibility?

4. Does the drawing conform with Company Engineering Drafting Standards?

5. Are necessary views and sections shown, and are they in proper relation to each other?

6. Is drawing to scale?

7. Are all necessary dimensions shown?

8. Do witness lines extend to the correct surface?

9. Do arrowheads extend to the correct witness lines?

10. Do the dimensions agree with the layout and related parts?

11. Has consideration been given to dimensioning to avoid unnecessary calculations in the shop?

12. Are necessary notes, data and charts provided?

13. Does any duplication of information exist? For instance, are dimensions duplicated or does the same information exist on both the detail and assembly drawings?

14. Is there a duplication of parts?

15. Are all necessary symbols for finishing, grinding, welding, and other operations shown?

16. Are sufficient notes, including concentricity. parallelism, squareness, and flatness shown?

17. Has the title block been filled in completely, and is information correct? Is the title correct?

18. Are all required approval signatures recorded? For instance, has the drawing been signed by authorized laboratory personnel for material, heat-treatment and finished specifications given?

19. Are material and heat-treatment specifications given?

20. Are plating and painting specifications, either for protection or decorative purposes, given?

21. Are the correct drawing, die, casting, pattern and forging numbers given?

22. Is the stock size specified?

23. Is the hand of left and right-hand parts correctly designated, and is the part drawn in its correct position?

24. Are Standard Parts used wherever possible, and are they properly specified?

25. Are proper finish allowances provided?

26. Will the part interfere with other parts in assembly and operation?

27. Are proper limits or tolerances for desired fits given?

28. Are undesirable limit accumulations present?

29. Are stationary and moveable clearances sufficient?

30. Are proper draft angles, fillets and corner radii given?

31. Is the approximate developed length of finished part shown?

32. Are required trade mark, and manufacturer's identification instructions given?

33. Is the part designed to facilitate production?

34. Is the part sufficiently strong and suitable for the work it has to do?

35. Is there proper alignment of oil holes, drilled holes, and studs with mating parts?

36. Has accessibility been provided for welding and riveting tools?

37. Can the part or parts be assembled and disassembled with the necessary tools? For instance, is there provision for adequate wrench clearance for all nuts and bolt heads?

38. How does the drawing compare with previously released drawings of similar parts?

39. Has the assembly drawing been changed to agree with the revised detail drawing?

40. Have installation drawings been revised to agree with latest production drawings?

41. Has the original drawing, when redrawn, been properly marked?

42. If consideration should be given to the prevention of dirt, grit accumulation and other foreign matter on oiled or greased working parts have provisions been made so they can be easily cleaned and inspected?

feelings are easily understood—most of us, being human like him, dislike being shown our errors.

Checkers are often accused of everything from changing drawings because of a personal grudge to the desire to impress the Chief Draftsman. Nothing could be further from the truth. Contrary to such false accusations, many draftsmen owe their continued employment to the skill and ability of a Checker.

In any disagreement between a Checker and draftsman, the Checker should take the initiative to bring out a workable understanding. He should understand and appreciate the draftsman's feeling and work attitude based upon his own experience as a draftsman. He should exercise extreme patience with the draftsman and be willing to explain the reason for each change. The Checker's experience, if properly applied, will become part of the draftsman's "know-how" through constant association and application.

The success of drafting standards depends largely upon the Checker. These important critics of drawings can do much toward directing the draftsman in the application of standards until familiarity has been thoroughly established. Checkers are definite safeguards against laxity in the application of standards.

When questions arise concerning practices not covered by accepted standard practice, the Checker is often confronted with the fact that the draftsman has employed practices contrary to the Checker's personal preference. In all such events, if it is apparent that the drawing in question will be clear to the user the Checker disregards personal preference and approves the drawing. If any shade of doubt exists regarding the intent of the drawing, however, or if it is definitely incorrect, the Checker recommends that the draftsman change the drawing.

If a general inspection of the drawing reveals that it contains errors as a result of outright negligence on the part of the draftsman, the Checker returns the drawing for a complete review by the draftsman without further check.

In performing the duties called for in Table I, it is within the Checker's province to suggest design changes when he sees fit to do so. When his suggestion would make a change in design necessary, the change may be made only upon the approval of the engineer responsible for the design.

In addition to checking the dimensions and views shown on a drawing, the Checker constantly checks for information that is lacking because either of carelessness or lack of knowledge on the part of the detailer.

The checker uses a print, Fig. 1, for the corrections to avoid defacing the drawing and to provide a clear record from which he can make the final check.

The Checker's signature on a drawing carries definite responsibility. The accuracy and legibilty of the information on the drawing, conformance with accepted standard practices, the application of the part, both in relation to itself and to associated parts, as well as the completeness of the drawing, are all the responsibility of the Checker.

After a draftsman has "gone through the mill" and has proven to be good material and is at last ready to be elevated to the post of Checker, he is frequently extremely reluctant to accept the job. This reluctance is not surprising because, unfortunately, the Checker does not enjoy the high rank in the engineering department to which his services should entitle him. However, there is one definite advantage to a Checker's job. It is a stepping stone to the positions of Assistant Chief Draftsman, Chief Draftsman, Project Engineer, Standard Engineer, and other positions on a staff level. There are many Chief Engineers who were once Checkers. The wise draftsman will accept a Checker's job any time the opportunity is offered. ∎

Why a Design-Review Committee Pays off Dividends

D P SIMONTON
RCA Missile & Surface Radar Dept

The designer thinks he is doing fine as he plans new equipment. What he doesn't realize is that he is calling for specially machined gears where standard off-the-shelf items would do just as well . . . or that he is specifying indicator lamps that can't be replaced without taking off the front panel. Such boners aren't anything new. But they can be caught in time if designs are checked at certain stages along the way by a Design Review Panel.

The entire engineering staff will profit from these get-togethers—the old-timer and the newcomer; the inexperienced, and the seasoned veteran. Such reviews are based on a pair of pretty safe assumptions; anybody can "goof" in design; several heads are better than one.

So at certain stages, the design undergoes the critical scrutiny of a committee of senior engineers. The makeup of the committee recognizes another principle—older heads know things that younger ones don't. This is particularly important nowadays. Systems are more complex and experienced engineers are in short supply. This pushes the seniors up into coordination and management groups and places more and more responsibility on younger, less-experienced shoulders.

It's Good Training

Training of these younger men is a major byproduct of the reviews. In the press of an urgent project, it is often impossible to seek out senior men who have had previous experience with a particular design problem. Design reviews bring such individuals together as a matter of course—not only to solve known problems but to unearth others. Newly hired engineers get acquainted with "the oracle" in each specialized field and when new problems arise, they can go straight to him. This kind

10 Areas Where Review Pays Off

Here are the kinds of challenges and questions that a review committee may throw at the design engineer.

● **Reliability.** Have environmental tests been conducted to prove reliable operation in shock, vibration, humidity, salt spray? Has the selection of parts included only those whose lives have been proven (or are being proven) through adequate testing?

● **Maintainability.** The customer spends about 10 times as much money to maintain electronic equipment as he does on the initial purchase price—let's not make it any worse. Can burned-out indicator lamps be replaced readily from the front, or must the whole panel be removed? Can a man get his fingers around each tube shield or will he need a special tool? . . . will he burn his fingers? More basic, just what is the maintenance philosophy of the equipment? Will maintenance be by unit replacement, or trouble-shooting? Will chassis be in the cabinet or on the bench? In a shop or in the field? It makes a difference. Does the assembly under review meet requirements for minimum downtime?

● **Adherence to specifications.** Are insulating materials fungus-proof? Does the equipment have to operate in an explosive environment? If so, get rid of open relays or other arc-producing parts. Is the finish the right color?

● **Value Engineering.** When specs don't make sense, they should be questioned. Does indoor equipment really have to operate at −65 C? Does stationary gear really have to withstand 50-g shock? Should you pay $20 apiece for stainless-steel jigs that straighten tube pins, when you can buy diecastings off the shelf for $1.25?

● **Standardization.** Don't do unnecessary design work. Use beefed-up sections when weight is not a major consideration, and forget about special high-strength alloys. Why machine special cluster gears when standard ones are available off the shelf? Is the grounding problem really critical enough to require a silver-plated chassis? Why use a special blower? The same one throughout may mean throwing away a few cfm, but this will be a lot cheaper than preparing an extra drawing, finding a new vendor and testing, stocking, processing an extra part. There may be several "right" ways to accomplish a design goal, but there is only one standard way—use it.

● **Reproducibility.** Possibly the modelmaker was able to trick an assembly together and make it work, but can the man in the production shop do it economically or at all? Does the design depend on a part made by a single-source vendor? If an undimensioned radius is changed by the vendor, will parts still fit together?

● **Safety.** Are areas surrounding knobs and access doors free of "knuckle nibblers"? Are test points well removed from dangerous voltages and hot spots? Are high-voltage controls well insulated from their shafts? Does the operator risk getting his fingers into a power gear mesh or a fan blade?

● **Finishing.** Does the paint finish include an adequate primer? Will electrolysis result from intimate contact of dissimilar metals? Will weldlaps permit ready draining of finishing reagents, or will there be entrapment and corrosion?

● **Human Engineering.** To work really well, machines have to fit people. Are controls logically arranged and labeled? Does the operator have to lie on his belly to read a meter? Will room lights glare into his eyes when he's seated at the console? Will he bark his shins on a brace across the back of the knee hole in a console? Can he reach controls without stretching, or removing his attention from indicators?

● **Drafting.** Are notes complete and comprehendible? Is proper part-marking called for? Do dimension groupings and datum lines make sense? Are tolerances reasonable? Do backlash limits on gear trains specify which shaft is locked and which is deflected.

---

of horizontal communication is very effective in reducing delay. It also avoids the destructive ill feeling that results from "going over the head" of responsible designers.

The very existence of the program makes itself felt in everyday decisions of the young designer. When pressed for delivery it is all too easy to say, "I'll push it through half-designed . . . and fix it up later." Those who have been through a job or two realize that "later" never comes; the first guess actually goes into the field —if it can be made to work at all. Knowing the design will have to run a ganlet provides a sort of subconscious design-quality control.

The designer may go into his first review so nervous he can barely hold a pencil, but after a few sessions his composure and self-assurance return. He develops "stage presence," a quality traditionally lacking among technical people.

The engineer whose design is being reviewed must be prepared to answer questions and justify design decisions. There is no better way to analyze a design than trying to explain it to somebody else. Even the preparation for the review often uncovers mistakes. It also develops thoroughness—a must for all engineers, but particularly important for good product designers.

Who Participates

A mechanical-design-review committee should consist of the following people:

Chairman who coordinates the meeting and writes the report. He is usually not a member of management —if so, he is certainly not in the higher echelons.

Mechanical-design engineer whose design is being reviewed. He comes equipped with calculations, sketches, layouts, drawings and (if possible) a laboratory model. Unless design is straightforward, sketches or drawings should be distributed to each member of the committee before the meeting.

Lead mechanical engineer who is responsible for the subsystem or major unit of which the particular design is a part.

Mechanical engineering supervisor.

Senior mechanical engineer who has experience in the type of design under review. He acts as a consultant, preferably with no direct responsibility for the design. He usually has a reputation for a "gimlet eye and a long nose" and may well be the most important member of the committee.

Project engineer who answers specialized questions

A DESIGN REVIEW (cont.)

Scheduling the Design Reviews

At RCA, design reviews are specified for both the electrical and the mechanical aspects of a newly designed equipment. Electrical design reviews come first. Here such things as circuitry, electrical part selection, reliability and critical circuit configurations are established.

When these specifications are set, detail mechanical design begins. The schedule calls for regular mechanical design reviews. However, if work is incomplete, reviews can be postponed until they can become meaningful. Or if a number of similar assemblies are used in the system, a complete program of reviews is probably not necessary; details can be thrashed out on a "guinea pig" while all similar mechanisms get only a routine pre-release review.

Type of review depends upon design status. In general, reviews are of four different types:

- Concept review, as soon as mechanical layout is sufficiently complete to indicate adequacy of general design features. It determines whether or not the designer is headed in the right direction before committing too much in the way of time and material.
- Pre-release review after drawings are complete enough to make a detailed check on the design, but before drawings for developmental model are released to the model shop. This review knocks out excess cost by taking a fresh look at the application of parts, materials, finishes and processes.
- Large-quantity release review (if such quantities are indicated) considers reproducibility of that particular quantity (weldments vs sand castings vs forgings). Purchased parts also get a careful screening for standards, procurability and status of reliability testing.
- Miscellaneous or electromechanical review may be held during any phase of the project. Combined electrical-mechanical reviews might cover such areas as high voltage circuits, timing mechanisms, servo systems, and assemblies presenting special heat, shielding or environmental problems.

on other phases of the system and keeps himself abreast of design progress.

Drafting supervisor who assures good drafting practice is followed. He may not be present if finalized drawings are not a part of material being reviewed.

Additional consultants who are invited from Methods Engineering, Human Engineering, Reliability, Field Service, when their particular interests are at stake.

But there are problems

By nature a design engineer is an individualist who likes to inject his own personality into his work—the things he designs. This is particularly true of the younger men, some of whom still display traces of the independence and secretiveness required of them in school—but a hindrance to a good design team. Setting these beginners straight is not a matter of, "OK, junior, bring in your little treasure so your elders and betters can tear it apart." No one would think of conducting a design review on that basis. The diplomatic approach is better. Here the senior man says candidly, "I tried that once, and here's what happened. . . ."

Creativity could be stifled if raw authority were used

to push design changes through—or to veto what the reviewer happens merely to be prejudiced against. The equipment would suffer because the state of the art would stagnate. And a damper would be put on the designer's creative imagination. But when suggestions for improvements are made with tact and supported by logical reasoning, such reviews can catalyze better design. And the designer is reassured that changes are reasonable, not just a whim, pressured through by a senior engineer.

Gloves or Fist?

Recriminations are not allowed at the review table. As soon as participants start playing the old game of "Who struck John?" the program has lost its usefulness. The theme is, "Is this a good design?" and if not, "What should be done to fix it? Who should do it?" Never mind who made the error. The thing under review is the design, not the designer.

Teeth are nevertheless required. Without strong, decisive leadership, engineers may let their duties slide and, as a result, the whole program will suffer. If a committee chairman writes a report containing the most masterful recommendations for saving a bad design from almost certain failure—and then allows that report to get lost in the file—he has wasted his own time and the time of the committee. Management must stand squarely behind the program and see that action results from the review—not necessarily 100% incorporation of the committee's recommendations, but at least some effective correction of recognized faults or justification for leaving the design alone. Faults that are discovered are usually not just mere peccadillos—some have been so knotty that outside consultants had to be hired just to solve them.

Concentrated effort is necessary to get the review program off the ground. Behind a successful program are one or two missionaries who keep pushing and advertising. Once established, however, it tends to be self-sustaining. It fits comfortably into the scheme of things—so much so that designers want reviews. But they must be scheduled early enough in a project so recommended changes are incorporated without upsetting drafting schedules, and certainly without having to rework jigs, tools or, in the extreme case, completed hardware.

Sales Psychology

Selling the program is probably not so much a matter of organization as it is personality. A good salesman, almost anywhere in the engineering organization, could be responsible for pushing the thing through. But it is probably easier if the design review chairman is given responsibility, deriving his authority directly from management. This way, management acts mostly as an advisor to the local chairman, who deals directly with his everyday associates. It seems less like outside interference—at least initially.

Final payoff of a successful review program is improved equipment and a more experienced engineering team. The equipment requires a minimum of debugging, rework and engineering changes; it is compatible and easily maintained. The design team learns and matures through the shared experience of each man, and is better able to benefit as a team from the particular specialties found in its members. ■

11.

How to File, Number and Retrieve Drawings and Technical Data

a system for . . .
your
Personal File

A place for everything and everything in its place is fine — if you can remember the place. This system helps you keep tabs on any kind of subject matter — even if you've forgotten author and title.

RAY A KELSEY *professional engineer, Texas*

Can you find the information you're after in that collection of catalogs stashed away in the bookshelf and the scramble of spec sheets filed higgledy-piggledy in your bottom drawer? Probably not. Most engineers can't be bothered with the mechanics of a methodical filing system. So they develop an adequate, but not very flexible system to meet present needs. The trouble here is that as new material arrives and new interests are cultivated there is simply no place for them—and the thing gets quickly out of hand.

Here is a system, adapted from the "Uniterm" system originally developed for the Armed Services Technical Information Agency, that organizes any kind of subject matter and expands to meet increasing needs. It requires only a filing cabinet and a 3 x 5 card file. There are only two steps, shown in photos at right. The Uniterm system has these advantages:

- Any kind of material can be filed—even catalogs with vastly different products.
- It's easy to arrange and keep up to date.
- Needed material can be found on any subject without knowledge of author or title.
- All material on one subject is listed on one card. ∎

A—Storing the Data

Start your filing with the number 1. As each new catalog, tearsheet, data sheet is filed, assign it the next number—regardless of subject matter, size or source. Place number so it shows in upper right corner when in the file drawer. For example, PRODUCT ENGINEERING reprint of article about microfilming (above) is number 136 because it was the 136th item filed.

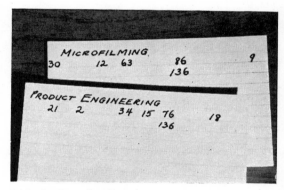

B—Indexing the Data

The 3 x 5 file cards are index to all material in the big file. When numbering a document also enter that number on all reference cards that may be helpful later. Each card covers a certain topic, and is filed alphabetically in the 3 x 5 file drawer. For example, the number on the microfilming article (136) has been entered on two cards: "Microfilming" and "PRODUCT ENGINEERING." Note that numbers appear in columns on the card. The column chosen depends on the last digit—a number ending in 0 appears in the first column; ending in 1, it goes in the second column, etc. This makes it easier to find same number on several cards—which is useful when hunting a specific topic that may have been filed under several headings.

Tips and Shortcuts

1. Place loose sheets and small pamphlets in numbered file folders. Same number should appear on documents (or document) so they can be returned to the correct folder and won't get lost.

2. When entering numbers on file card, use a guide templet to aid getting numbers in proper column. This can be simply a 3 x 5 card with numbers 0 to 9 along the bottom.

3. When old material is weeded out of the file, replace each document with a sheet titled "Material Outdated and Destroyed." This way, there is no need to correct cross-reference cards.

It takes only moments

To retrieve a design

Woodward Governor has over 60,000 drawings, part and product specs, assembly lists, and engineering documents in a parts analog system

E. J. TANGERMAN

"DESCRIBE a desired part and in moments you can have drawings of all the parts Woodward has designed like it. You can avoid duplication, encourage standardization and simplification in design, and identify everything Woodward buys or makes by a 7-digit retrieval number."

Thus, Giles Lovelace of Lovelace, Lawrence & Co, Toledo, describes the system developed for Woodward Governor Company, Rockford, Ill, and

installed recently. Woodward makes governors and control systems for hydro and diesel installations, propellers, and fuel-supply setups, many of which are special designs for the job. Thus duplication of design and consequent increased cost is inherent and was growing more prevalent as products proliferated.

There *was* a coding system, similar to that of most companies—a 6-digit code in which blocks of numbers were

reserved for "common parts" and others allocated to parts "peculiar" to given end products. As parts and products grew, blocks were filled and new blocks were assigned. A given part might be in any of three different number ranges, so any significance the system once had was gone. There were 2000 pages of tabulations to cross-reference parts, and they only covered about a third of the parts for retrieval. A study of the problem

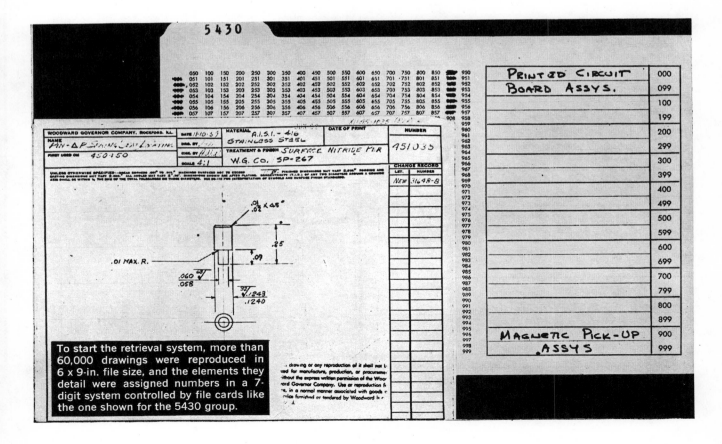

To start the retrieval system, more than 60,000 drawings were reproduced in 6 x 9-in. file size, and the elements they detail were assigned numbers in a 7-digit system controlled by file cards like the one shown for the 5430 group.

showed that a change was desirable because designs of new parts were rapidly increasing. With each new design problem it was becoming increasingly difficult to determine whether satisfactory items already existed or new parts would have to be designed. The company concluded that a more effective system of design retrieval was required.

After preliminary study of the work involved, it was decided to seek outside assistance. Lovelace, Lawrence & Co, a consulting company specializing in the design of information storage and retrieval systems, was hired to analyze and to detail the complete system.

The consultants recommended a conceptual approach, to be based on a comprehensive system of classification and coding that includes all engineering and manufacturing documents.

The new system classifies all proprietary items into six mutually exclusive categories in which 1 identifies commercial parts, 2 is primary materials including castings and forgings,

3 & 4 proprietary single-piece parts, 5 & 6 assemblies, 8 end products, and 9 manufacturing information, plant, equipment, and tools.

Within this general class structure, similar items are grouped together regardless of where they are ultimately used—in categories of 10 to 20 parts. Each such category has 1000 numbers assigned to it, so the 7-digit system provides for at least 50 times expansion without jumping the number bracket. All Woodward part drawings were copied on 35-mm film, then reproduced in 6 x 9-in. Xerox copies.

All commercial parts, fully identified and classified by function, were tabulated showing commercial availability, conformance to industry and government standards, and pertinent design features, to allow direct specification in design. Tabulations are entered on a standard loose-leaf code-sheet form. This permits updating with a minimum of codebook reprinting.

Castings and forgings were first grouped into five size categories, each group being further classified by shape descriptions. Single-piece

parts were classified into two main groups according to their general configurations. Parts machined from bar, sheet, or plate—"Regular Form"—were separated from those which are preferably cast or forged—"Irregular Form."

Within each category, items were designated as either "Specific Purpose" or "General Purpose" and are described differently for effective retrieval. The specific-purpose group includes such items as springs, gears, and cast product-enclosures that are all classified according to their functional characteristics.

General-purpose parts, comprising over 90%, are classified by pure shape classification, bringing all similar parts together regardless of function or end use. Parts made from sheet or plate are separated from those turned from bar. Flat, uniform-thickness parts are similarly separated from those of bent steel or plate. Thus similar parts can be easily batched for production.

Assemblies were broken into the same two groups. "Specific Purpose" assemblies are those that are ma-

| Woodward Governor Company Rockford, Illinois | | | SUMMARY OF CLASSES | |
Fort Collins, Colorado Schiphol, Netherlands	Slough, England Tokyo, Japan			
				0
COMMERCIAL PARTS		- STANDARD		1
		- SPECIAL		
MATERIALS CASTINGS, FORGINGS, BLANKS, SINTERED FORMS INCL. UNFINISHED FABRICATIONS,				2
COMPONENT PARTS	METALLIC	REGULAR FORM		3
		IRREGULAR FORM		4
	NON-METALLIC			
ASSEMBLIES	GENERAL PURPOSE ASSEMBLIES			5
	AUXILIARY-DEVICE ASSEMBLIES			
	PRODUCT MODULES	BASIC-PRODUCT ASSEMBLIES		6
		AUXILIARY-PRODUCT ASSEMBLIES		
				7
PRODUCTS	FLOW CONTROLS GOVERNORS, ACTUATORS AUXILIARY PRODUCTS SPAREPARTS KITS, CONVERSION KITS TEST STANDS & ACCESSORIES, AUXILIARY INSTRUMENTS			8
INFORMATION, SPECIFICATIONS, SYSTEM LAYOUTS PRODUCTION TOOLS & EQUIPMENT PROCESS & ASSEMBLY DATA, STANDARD CONSTRUCTION DATA				9

WOODWARD

| Woodward Governor Company Rockford, Illinois | | | COMPONENT PARTS METALLIC - IRREGULAR FORM NON-METALLIC | 4 |
Fort Collins, Colorado Schiphol, Netherlands	Slough, England Tokyo, Japan			
METALLIC-IRREGULAR FORM	SPECIFIC PURPOSE	PRODUCT ENCLOSURES	BASES, ADAPTERS. FRAMES, HOUSINGS, SUBCAPS, BODIES, CASES, COLUMNS. COVERS, CAPS. INCL. w/w SERVO CYLS. & COVERS.	40
			POWER CYLINDERS, CASES, COVERS & ADAPTERS. VALVE BODIES, CASES, COVERS. FLUID MOVEMENT ELEMENTS, COMPONENTS	41
			HOUSINGS & ENCLOSURES o/t ABOVE INCL. FLUID CONTAINERS, FLOATS	42
			BEARINGS, MOUNTINGS, BRACKETS	43
			CRANKSHAFTS, LEVERAGES, LINKAGES INCL. SHEAVE & PULLEY SEGMENTS.	44
			BALLHEADS, BALLARMS, FLYWEIGHTS, CROSSHEADS BRAKE BANDS. WEIGHTS o/t FLYWEIGHTS.	45
	GENERAL PURPOSE		w/ CYLINDRICAL PORTIONS	46
			w/o CYLINDRICAL PORTIONS	47
				48
NON-METALLIC				49

WOODWARD

Basis of the system is eight classes. In searching for a component such as a specific lever, for example, the engineer would first enter a book page to find class 4, then go to

a page subdividing components (group 4). Say it was a metal link or lever with an angle less than 90 deg, and for a specific form. On the second sheet, he moves rap-

jor functional elements of the product —"Product Modules"—and as such are peculiar to one product family. These are classified by specific functions and arranged in product groups. "General Purpose" assemblies are classified by general engineering function regardless of where used. This group includes 75% of the assemblies.

Finished products are grouped on the basis of similar operating characteristics and coded for separate identity of each model within its product family.

All miniature drawings and specs are numbered and filed in cabinets with twin 6 x 9-in. sections. Only commercial parts are tabulated; others are itemized in a codebook which has item-families coded with 4-digit numbers that lead to the corresponding group of drawings in the file.

With this setup, any engineer can follow a six-step procedure:

1. Retrieve all existing designs suitable for a new part.

2. Choose part appropriate for new design.

3. Review existing similar parts for combination and elimination of items.

4. If a new design is required, attempt to eliminate one or more existing designs through interchangeability with the new part.

5. If new production methods are desirable for future production, extend the new-methods study to all closely similar parts where practical.

6. Assign new part numbers only after searching the system to avoid duplication.

Given the shape or design features of *any* component part, an engineer using the system can determine conclusively whether there is a duplicate in his files, identify those parts from which it might be made, whose tools might be used, or which should possibly be made interchangeable with it. He can also identify the castings or forgings which could be used, as well as synthesize accurate cost estimates from *actual cost experience* on similar parts. Given very old, out-of-date, service-part requirements, he can quickly determine whether a current production item, if modified, would suffice.

In application, the system becomes the principal reference medium for most activities of the company concerned with design and specification, and proves equally useful in planning and control. The main body of the system, including the classified microfilm prints, is in the Engineering Department where designers have direct access to the drawings. Reference to originals is seldom necessary, reducing wear and tear on tracings. All prior design effort is instantly available for reference on easily handled 6 x 9-in. drawings. Each new drawing will be filmed when finished and a photocopy will be added to the file.

The designer specifies parts and materials, utilizing the system as a form of Engineering Standards, which clearly indicates the most economic choices of items. All current items are indicated and part numbers for desired new items that have to be added, particularly commercial parts, are self-assigning. Simplified ranges of "Preferred" and "Non-Preferred" items are set out for many item categories to limit unnecessary variety further by

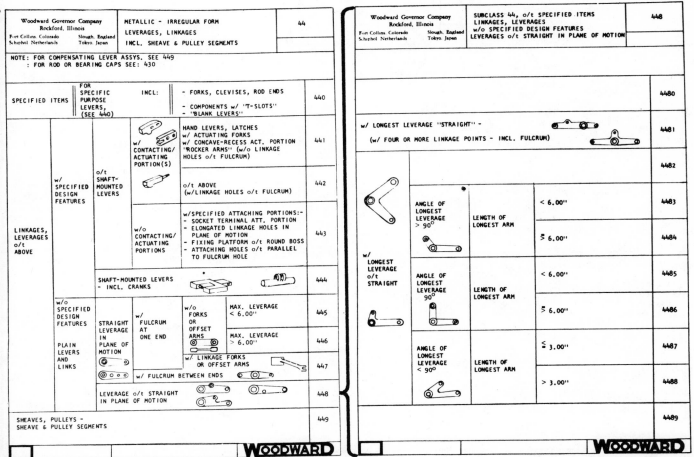

idly through "metallic-irregular form" and "specific purpose" and finds "leverages" as 44. He then goes through "linkage, leverages" and "without specified design features" to "leverage o/t straight in plane of motion," and comes up with 448. Then on the sheet headed 448 he finds his lever as 4487 or 4488, depending on length.

concentrating usage on common varieties where possible.

The system is available to personnel in various activities. The microprint file is made available to all operating departments. The functions of each of these activities may benefit from reference to past experience with similar parts. Similar parts have similar production characteristics, materials requirements, cost of manufacture, operation sequence, handling characteristics, time requirements, tool requirements, and can often be made from the same casting or forgings. The primary materials and purchased commodities sections of the system also find use in Inventory Control, Purchasing, Receiving and Stores.

During the design of the system, all duplicate parts were revealed and drawings were marked accordingly. All duplicates of the same item received the same code number. In the commercial-parts category, the final accounting showed 216 duplications (4.2%) in 5147 items active at the start of the project, and 294 duplications (2.3%) in a 12,628 total. In 1240 new items added in the following two years, 91 (7.3%) were duplications, and of 247 electrical items, 48 (or a walloping 19.5%) were duplications. Further, there were 108 clevis pins, of which 30 were ultimately designated as "preferred"; 244 headless set-screws, of which 150 were preferred. With specials designated as "non-preferred," future reuse is discouraged, and large reductions can be made in number of types and sizes used.

While a great deal of work remains to be done to achieve a minimum necessary variety of "Woodward designed" parts, a means is now available to avoid any further proliferation of unnecessary designs. With an easily used retrieval system forming the basis for assignment of all new part numbers, virtually all existing parts suitable for any new design requirement will be found, eliminating unnecessary design activity at its source. The result is a capability to implement a corporate standardization policy while gaining added flexibility in design—two objectives which are not often found hand-in-hand.

Because duplication of the existing part numbers was avoided in the design of the new system, it was not necessary to change all old part numbers. Instead, they were retained for the time being and the two systems are operated in parallel. New codes are assigned to all new designs, and old part numbers are changed only when required by design revisions.

By way of history

A type of parts analog system originated in Soviet Russia over a decade ago in S. P. Mitrofanow's concept of "group technology," wherein apparently dissimilar parts were grouped in families built around similarities of form rather than function or end use. West Germany, with the help of Prof H. Opitz of Aachen Technical University, expanded the concept to include machine and product design, even plant layout. Edward G. Brisch, an expatriate Polish engineer, developed the idea in England after World War II, designing systems for a number of clients there as well as in this country.

Early American users of the Brisch system were DeVilbiss, Underwood, Clark Equipment. Allis-Chalmers Industrial Group has a quarter of a million drawings classified in this way.

Others follow specially designed systems developed by Remington-Rand. Meantime, there are a number of coding and classification systems in use, but most differ from department to department within a company or permit undesirable duplication in greater or lesser degree. Proliferation of plant locations is also causing considerable confusion.

The Woodward setup described here, while not as large as some of the others, is however probably the widest based. ∎

Woodward Governor Company Rockford, Illinois — Fort Collins, Colorado; Slough, England; Schiphol, Netherlands; Tokyo, Japan	COMMERCIAL PARTS STANDARD & SPECIAL — Summary of Sub-Classes			1XXX
NON-ELECTRICAL	STRUCTURAL HARDWARE	FIXINGS & FASTENINGS GENERAL PURPOSE	THREADLESS	10XX
			THREADED	SCREWS: WOOD, TAPPING, SET, SOCKET HEAD CAP, MACHINE, HEXAGON HEAD incl. HEXAGON HEAD BOLTS	
				o/t ABOVE	
		FINISHING HARDWARE incl. LOCKS, HANDLES, KNOBS		11XX
	MARKERS, WIRE ROPE, CONTROL CABLE, FITTINGS & ACCESSORIES			
	PACKING, SHIPPING MATERIALS & ELEMENTS			
	FLUID MOVEMENT ELEMENTS & DEVICES	PIPE, TUBE FITTINGS incl. PIPE FLANGES, FLANGED PIPE FITTINGS HOSE FITTINGS, HOSE ASSEMBLIES LUBRICATION, AIR LINE FITTINGS PIPE, TUBE, CONDUIT, HOSE FIXING DEVICES		12XX
		COCKS, VALVES STRAINERS, FILTERS, TRAPS, BELLOWS PUMPS, COMPRESSORS, FLUID/AIR MOTORS, SEALING, JOINTING, PACKING ELEMENTS incl. 'O' RINGS, OIL SEALS		13XX
	POWER TRANS-MISSION ELEMENTS & DEVICES	BEARINGS: PLAIN, BALL, ROLLER, SPHERICAL ROD ENDS, CAM FOLLOWERS, SHAFT SUPPORTING UNITS COUPLINGS, JOINTS CLUTCHES, BRAKES GEARS, GEAR UNITS, SPEED REDUCTION UNITS		14XX
		COLLARS, KEYS, BELTS, BELTING, PULLEYS, SHEAVES CHAIN, CHAINWHEELS, SPROCKETS, SPRINGS ELEMENTS & DEVICES o/t ABOVE		15XX
ELECTRICAL ELECTRONIC SUPPLIES & ACCESSORIES	WIRING DEVICES, incl. FITTINGS BOXES, ENCLOSURES, PLUGS & RECEPTACLES			16XX
	CIRCUIT ELEMENTS	FUSES, FUSELINKS, RESISTORS, CAPACITORS VACUUM TUBES, CELLS, CRYSTALS, PIEZOELECTRIC DEVICES PICK-UPS, SEMI-CONDUCTORS, RECTIFIERS, TRANSFORMERS		
		SWITCHES, RELAYS, CIRCUIT BREAKERS, SOLENOIDS LAMPS, ELEMENTS o/t ABOVE		
	DEVICES, incl. MOTORS, POWER SUPPLIES, MOTOR CONTROL GEAR			17XX
	COMMUNICATION SUPPLIES			
	INSTRUMENTS: INDICATING, RECORDING their ACCESSORIES AND SPARES			18XX
	TEST EQUIPMENT and ACCESSORIES TOOLS			19XX
	PARTS o/t ABOVE			

WOODWARD

The knotty problem of commercial (purchased) parts is broken down this way.

An Easy Filing System for Catalogs and Data Sheets

L. GALOCKIN

The time and effort saved by grouping can be considerable. New companies and new products are constantly being introduced, flooding the engineering library with catalogs and design data. This is a welcome flood to the engineer—when it is channeled efficiently.

The grouped system classifies catalogs and other publications under nine main headings: a general division and eight numbered divisions. Each main division, in turn, is subdivided into lettered groups that list specific items. For example, catalogs and other material on Belts and Pulleys will be found in group 2B under Division 2—Mechanical Machine Parts. Any specific area of interest thus becomes a number and a letter found by consulting simple index sheets. Additional index sheets, arranged alphabetically by company or product, will provide a convenient and useful cross-reference if desired.

The most efficient procedure for arranging the filing system is:

1. Sort catalogs into eight main divisions and one general division.

2. Divide main divisions into related subdivisions containing not more than 15 to 20 catalogs each.

3. Label each catalog with the main division and group to which it belongs. Pressure-sensitive labels can be used conveniently.

The sample headings and groupings presented here are applicable to a machine tool manufacturing company and are necessarily slanted to meet its specific needs. This list, however, may serve as a guide for other engineering libraries—just expand or shorten groups to satisfy individual requirements. ∎

GENERAL

Catalogs from large supply houses, because they include parts and supplies under several main headings. Also product directories.

DIVISION 1 . . . MATERIALS

1 gen—Catalogs covering several subdivisions of Division 1. Also material charts.
1 A—Ferrous Metals: steels, cast iron, etc.
1 B—Nonferrous Metals: aluminum, bronze, bearing metals, etc.
1 C—Rubber, Rubber Products, & Adhesives
1 D—Plastics
1 E—Nonmetallic Materials: glass, ceramic, cork, etc.

DIVISION 2 . . . MECHANICAL MACHINE PARTS

2 gen—Catalogs covering several subdivisions of Division 2
2 A—Gears, Transmissions & Gear Reducers
2 B—Belts & Pulleys
2 C—Chains & Sprockets
2 D—Mechanical Clutches & Brakes
2 E—Couplings & Flexible Shafts
2 F—Ball, Roller & Needle Bearings
2 G—Bushings & Sleeve Bearings
2 H—Fasteners
2 J—Machine Hardware: springs, vibration isolators, knobs, etc.

DIVISION 3 . . . HYDRAULIC & PNEUMATIC EQUIPMENT

3 gen—Catalogs covering several subdivisions of Division 3
3 A—Valves
3 B—Hydraulic and Pneumatic Motors, Pumps & Accumulators
3 C—Hoses, Tubing & Fittings
3 D—Filters & Strainers
3 E—Lubricating Systems & Parts
3 F—Seals, Packings & Gaskets
3 G—Grease, Oil & Hydraulic Fluid

DIVISION 4 . . . ELECTRICAL EQUIPMENT

4 gen—Catalogs covering several subdivisions of Division 4
4 A—Motors & Generators
4 B—Motor Controls
4 C—Switches, Fuses, Relays & Resistors
4 D—Electrical Instruments
4 E—Transformers and Rectifiers
4 F—Parts for Electrical Installation: conduit boxes, panels, etc.

DIVISION 5 . . . MACHINE TOOLS & FACTORY EQUIPMENT

5 gen—Catalogs covering several subdivisions of Division 5
5 A—Lathes
5 B—Milling Machines
5 C—Drilling Machines
5 D—Grinding & Polishing Machines
5 E—Planers, Shapers & Broaching Machines
5 F—Pipe Bending & Threading Machines
5 G—Sawing Machines
5 H—Sheet Metal Working Machines
5 J—Machine-Tool Attachments
5 K—Small Hand Tools, Portable Electric Tools
5 L—Gages, Recorders & Regulators
5 M—Molding & Casting Equipment
5 N—Furnaces & Heat Exchangers
5 P—Forging Equipment
5 Q—Welding Equipment
5 R—Painting & Finishing Equipment
5 S—Material Handling & Storage Equipment
5 T—Engraving & Marking Machines
5 U—Heat-treating Equipment
5 V—Special Machines

DIVISION 6 . . . TOOLING

6 gen—Catalogs covering several subdivisions of Division 6
6 A—Cutting Tools: drills, milling cutters, etc.
6 B—Jigs & Fixtures
6 C—Tool Holders: chucks, arbors, mandrels, etc.
6 D—Punches & Dies
6 E—Measuring Instruments for Tooling
6 F—Setup Equipment

DIVISION 7 . . . MISCELLANEOUS MACHINERY

7 gen—Catalogs covering several subdivisions of Division 7
7 A—Packaging Materials & Machines
7 B—Screens, Sifters & Separators
7 C—Food & Dairy Processing Equipment
7 D—Processing Equipment for Rubber, Plastic & Textiles
7 E—Earthmoving & Farming Equipment
7 F—Refrigeration & Air-conditioning Equipment
7 G—Laboratory & Test Equipment
7 H—Woodworking Machines
7 J—Engines & Turbines
7 K—Heating, Plumbing & Building Equipment
7 L—Office & Drafting-room Equipment

DIVISION 8 . . . SERVICES

8 gen—Engineering, grinding, metal finishing, stamping, spinning, advertising, photography, etc.

FIRST, pull out of the file box all cards with headings that pertain to subject matter you want. Example: for documents dealing with analog computer networks, you might select the punched cards shown here.

NOVEL INDEXING DEVICE
solves technical filing problems

Sight through holes in home-made punched cards—then go directly to all pertinent information in your file drawer. It's a desktop version of the **Peek**-a-Boo information-retrieval system developed for libraries containing up to 40,000 documents.

R E WENDT JR, *manager*
Advanced Manufacturing Techniques
Westinghouse Electric Corp

If your file drawer is like most technical files, you're in trouble. You know what you have but don't know where to find it. Or even worse—you've forgotten what you have. This indexing device will make you master of the situation. You can build it yourself, or have the shop make one. And with it on your desk, you can keep track of up to 1000 documents. Here's how it works.

For filing, each technical paper, catalog, tearsheet, reprint, is marked with a number and filed in numerical order. Don't worry about arranging this file by subject, source, type, size, author or any other order—only the sequence of numbers is important. For the index you have special file cards. There are as many file cards as there are categories; and categories can be anything from color of the document to the author's company affiliation. Each card has space for 1000 numbered holes. Each hole you punch represents a different document number.

Now suppose you want to find a certain technical paper.

SECOND, put the selected cards in the viewer on the front of the file box and note the numbers for the holes that line up. Such viewing is done by placing the cards on a transparent plastic window and covering them with a card-size, plastic plate that has been ruled to speed identification of the current number. When not in use, the ruled plate is stored in the box.

TO FILE A DOCUMENT

CARD PUNCH is built into the back of the file box. When a new document is filed, it is given the next consecutive number in the file and the cards for each subject heading pertaining to that document are punched with a hole corresponding to the document number. Holes in this 25 x 40 matrix are numbered left to right, top to bottom. The card is being punched to show that document number 666 contains some material about standards. Punch is made of hardened-steel rod; die plates are steel, separated by 0.025-in. spacer and aligned with dowel pins before assembly.

You remember it had a blue cover and dealt with use of analog computers in automotive design. Remove the file cards for "blue cover," "analog," "computers" and automobiles." Next, stack them together and hold the stack to the light. The number corresponding to the hole where you can see daylight is the needed document.

The device shown in the pictures above is a file box combined with viewer and card punch. In the box you store a separate 3 x 5 card for each category you select as being the most significant and memorable. Choose broad topic headings, ones that will include a large number of documents in the file drawer. (If headings are too specialized, you'll be hunting through too many cards—destroying the efficiency of the system.) One of the system's advantages is that headings don't need to be specialized—combining cards with broad headings gives a combined narrow heading. Naturally, the more cards in a combination, the narrower the span.

Cards are punched in the jig provided on the back of the file box. The jig has 1000 holes in its 25 x 40 matrix. This capacity is adequate for most filing purposes; with more holes in a 3 x 5 card, tolerances become critical, cards become mechanically weak and the system is generally more difficult to use. If you want to expand, it is better to divide the card file into two or more groups and provide a different color card for each category.

Read the number of any open hole by placing the stack of cards against the transparent plate on the opposite side of the file box. The overlaying transparent plate is ruled to allow you to read the number that corresponds with any hole. Finding all the documents that pertain to any combined group of subjects is quick and easy: simply read the numbers of the holes in the cards and pull the material corresponding to that number. If an item is misfiled or if you miss an applicable heading when punching the cards, the needed information can probably still be found by pulling those documents indicated by faint holes (holes in which light is blocked by only one thickness of card). ∎

How to Set up a Numbering System for the Engineering Department

S. ULRICH
Industrial Controller Division
Square D Company

THERE ARE TWO MAJOR SCHOOLS of thought concerning numbering systems, the basic difference between them being whether the numbers should or should not impart information in themselves. Serial systems consist only of numbers assigned consecutively as required—there is no relationship between a number and what it identifies. Mnemonic (memory-aiding) systems are, by definition, based on specific relationships that increase the efficiency of their use. In actual practice, there are innumerable combinations embodying features of both systems; the make-up of each depends upon the application.

Serial System

Completely meaningless numbering systems are purely numerical systems in which the numbers or their sequence are purposely kept from betraying any information about the document or item in question. This is justified as avoiding the tendency to make up non-existent numbers based on existing numbers. It is further claimed that it promotes accuracy, since the user cannot possibly become familiar with thousands of six- or seven-digit numbers and must rely on an actual check rather than on his memory. Systems of this type are used by many large concerns.

One of the primary advantages of the serial system is the ease with which numbers can be assigned. The log of number assignments grows only from one end and filing within the system is restricted to revisions. The fact that the drawing file expands from only one end is a great advantage when compared to the logical system which literally grows in all directions. This feature of the mnemonic system results in extensive interfiling and occasional refiling of much information as the file expands in the middle.

The experience of large firms with serial systems indicates flexibility is needed when a system must be used by geographically or functionally separate units. It is a simple matter to assign blocks of numbers to the various divisions and achieve a standard operation. The logical system, being more susceptible to interpretation and variations in actual practice, cannot so easily be standardized throughout a widespread organization. If the company products fall into a relatively small number of categories, the serial system can be modified by the assignment of blocks of numbers to specific categories. As this procedure is continued and expanded, the system becomes mnemonic and begins to involve filing and interpretation difficulties inherent to the logical system.

In serial systems, it is generally difficult to distinguish between the kinds of items to which the numbers pertain. A distinction can be made between drawing numbers, part numbers and specification numbers, for example, by allotting blocks of numbers to the various classes. This involves the adoption of a classifying system and at least partial use of a mnemonic device. If such distinctions are not made,

Useful Tips for Setting Up a Numbering System

In any system of documentation, there are many factors to be considered. Not all of them directly affect the numbering system to be adopted, but all should be kept in mind while the system is being devised and during the early stages of use.

1. How many different kinds of documents must the system be able to assimilate?

2. Can system apply easily to both part and drawing numbers without making it necessary to use extensive cross-referencing?

3. Can system be expanded when new kinds of documents must be incorporated?

4. Is system restricted as to kind of equipment to which it can pertain?

5. Can extent of coverage expand indefinitely as volume of business grows?

6. Should numbers be usable for purposes not connected with documentation?

7. What sizes of documents will be numbered and should size be identified?

8. In the case of engineering drawings, should the material on which drawing is made be identified by number?

9. Should provisions be made to indicate class or kind of equipment in certain cases?

10. Does number distinguish simply and quickly between individual parts and assemblies?

11. Can parts that appear only on assembly drawings be easily identified as individual parts?

12. Can abstract or general data be numbered according to a logical pattern?

13. Does method of designating revisions fit logically into the numbering system?

14. Can numbers be easily remembered or are they long meaningless series of digits?

---

it is usually necessary to maintain an extensive cross-reference of part numbers to drawing numbers, thereby introducing errors into the system.

There are other advantages in a serial system, such as facility of use with automatic tabulating equipment. But to sum up the case for serial numbering systems: They are most advantageously used when filing ease is of major importance and when several more or less autonomous units must be covered by the same system. If a firm produces products that, by their nature, are active for only a few years, the advantages are even more apparent.

The Logical Approach

Another, and entirely different, group believes that the utmost advantage should be taken of features that permit the user to learn as much as possible from the number alone. This group contends that the logical system can be made to apply to all engineering documents, and points out that in many cases, where a meaningless system is used in part, it has been abandoned in favor of a mnemonic system for common items such as hardware, tools, pipe fittings, and raw materials.

The main argument for logical systems is simply that it is desirable to be able to look at a number and immediately identify it as pertaining to a drawing, part, raw material, manufacturing specification or other type of engineering document. Such aids to the memory that can be built into the system return large dividends in facility of use and effectiveness of effort.

A logical numbering system of this type has been in use by the Industrial Controller Division of the Square D Company for some thirty-five years. A few minor changes were necessary in the very early years, but no major revision has been necessary during the past quarter century.

Drawings, specifications, and part numbers are the ingredients of this system, which correlates all three categories accurately. There is no need for auxiliary cross-references because items are easily distinguishable. Another feature is the ease with which the system has been expanded over the years to incorporate additional kinds of information. It has also lent itself readily to the development of different systems (for raw materials, etc.) in similar form.

Typical Mnemonic System

The Industrial Controller Division's numbering system consists essentially of a three- or four-digit prime number identifying the type of product or item. This is followed by a letter indicating the form or size of the document, and then one, two, or three digits that identify the specific drawing or subject involved. Individual parts on assembly drawings or lists are identified by an additonal letter and one to three digits as described in following paragraphs.

Engineering Drawings. When used for engineering drawings, the first digits (prime number) denote a particular major item or class of common part, Fig. 1. The first letter designates both the sheet size of the drawing and whether the original drawing was made on tracing cloth or paper. The last set of digits is assigned serially as the drawings are made. Code letters are given in Table I for size designations.

It has not been necessary to distinguish between cloth and paper in the larger sizes and thus *AA* and *A* are used for either. The distinction is required for smaller sizes to

Table I—Drawing Sizes and Corresponding Letter Symbols

Document	Symbol	Size, in.	Material
Tracing (Part)	X	5 x 8	Paper
Tracing (Assembly)	G	5 x 8	Paper
Tracing	D	8½ x 11	Cloth
Tracing	L	8½ x 11	Paper
Tracing	C	11 x 17	Cloth
Tracing	F	11 x 17	Paper
Tracing	B	17 x 22	Cloth
Tracing	E	17 x 22	Paper
Tracing	A	22 x 34	Cloth or paper
Tracing	AA	Larger	Cloth or paper
Curves, Data	J	8½ x 11	Graph paper
Material List	M	8½ x 11	Paper Form
Manufacturing Spec	S	8½ x 11	Paper Form

avoid the difficulties encountered when interfiling cloth and paper, i.e., *B* and *E, C* and *F, D* and *L* for cloth and paper, respectively.

Both *G* and *X* drawings are the same size (5 x 8 in.) and are prepared only on paper. The *X* number is used for drawings that show only a single part, while *G* numbers are for drawings of simple assemblies. This notation is also used in the adaptation of drawing numbers to part numbers and is considered a most useful feature of the system.

Part Numbers. A part number is derived from a drawing number by adding *G* or *X* to the drawing number and then the required serial digits. As in the 5 x 8 in. drawings, *G* applies to assemblies and *X* to individual parts. The *X* and *G* drawings show only a single part or simple assembly and carry the drawing number as the part number. On all larger drawings, it is important that parts and assemblies, as well as drawings and parts, be distinguishable from each other.

As an example of how the numbering system functions, assume that development work on a new product, Model Z, has been completed and production drawings are required. Prime number 4444 was taken out to cover this new product when it went into development. This number was recorded in a card file because new numbers are constantly being assigned within the system rather than serially, as in a purely numerical system.

The 17 x 22 in. cloth tracings will be numbered 4444-*B*1, 4444-*B*2, etc; the 8½ x 11 in. cloth tracings will be listed 4444-*D*1 and so on. Individual parts detailed on 5 x 8 in. drawings will be numbered 4444-*X*1 and up, and small assembly drawings will be numbered 4444-*G*1 and up. For individual parts or assemblies appearing on the larger drawings, a part number is formed by adding appropriately an *X* or *G* and the next unused serial number. Thus, individual parts not detailed on individual drawings that appear on 4444-*D*1 will bear part numbers 4444-*D*1-*X*1, 4444-*D*1-*X*2 and so on. If a sub-assembly on 4444-*C*2 requires a part number, the sub-assembly will be listed as 4444-*C*2-*G*1 in the record.

This example illustrates how the system completely avoids the need for a cross reference of part numbers to drawing numbers. It also reduces detailing and results in greatly

simplified maintenance, because only the prime numbers must be indexed and the majority of allied information is associated under a given number.

There are a few other features of the system worthy of mention. All finished drawing sizes are multiples of 8½ x 11 in. letter size sheets and thus will fold for vertical filing of office and shop prints. While very common today, this practice was somewhat of an innovation when first adopted some thirty-five years ago. The separate designation of cloth and paper tracings is also of value since it is impractical to file both kinds of tracings intermixed in the same drawer. And last, the useful life of tracings can be extended by cutting them somewhat oversize and using trim lines to show the actual print size. Tracing sheets usually measure from one to two inches larger on each dimension than the drawing sizes shown in Table I.

Manufacturing Specifications. The system extends to other forms of engineering documents and permits a closer correlation of all engineering information. One of the most desirable extensions arises from the fact that industrial electrical control equipment is sold in an infinite variety of arrangements of standard devices and components. There is a continuing problem of setting up new devices that differ only in arrangement from other devices, yet must be positively identified. This problem is overcome through the use of manufacturing specifications that detail—without drawings—the makeup of specific arrangements. The prime number is the same as that assigned to the major item concerned and the letter *S* is used to designate the specification. To return to the example above, Model Z can be supplied in a variety of enclosures to meet varying conditions of use and with a multitude of accessory arrangements to meet specialized requirements. These variations will be listed as manufacturing specifications 4444-*S*1, 4444-*S*2, etc.

Material Lists. Certain specialized devices manufactured from common parts would have an assembly drawing that merely lists the components. For devices of this type, which do not require instructions as to sequence or method of assembly, *M* lists, keyed to the appropriate prime number, are used. Thus, if a major assembly in Model Z is identified by part number 4444-*B*2-*G*12, and if a part of this assembly is modified slightly for a specialized purpose, the parts showing the change are listed on Material List 4444-*M*1, and a notation is made to the effect that no drawing is involved.

Performance Data. In some cases, it is necessary to associate data on performance with the devices concerned. This is accomplished by use of *J* drawings normally made on 8½ x 11 in. graph paper. The first performance curve prepared on Model Z would be drawing number 4444-*J*1. Here, too, cross-referencing is avoided.

Preliminary Sketches. During the development of Model Z, many drawings and sketches were made. Though they were preliminary in nature and merely indicative of design trends, some of them are used for quotation and other purposes, and therefore require a number. To keep their identity separate from other drawings, they are assigned numbers in the *K* series. Thus, Original Idea No. 1 on Model Z is preserved under the 4444-*K*1 designation.

Special Part Numbers. In connection with the use of part number suffixes *X* and *G* (added to drawing numbers to form part numbers), there are other classes of information that require special part number treatment. There may arise a class of product (such as magnet coils) where many basically similar, yet distinct, items are manufactured. Although it is desirable to distinguish among them, it is equally important to identify all according to their common characteristics. This problem has been solved by writing an *S* specification on the class and then assigning individual part-number suffixes, using letters other than X or *G*, i.e., all magnet coils of a given size and shape are covered by a single specification; variations in wire size and number of turns are indicated by special part-number suffixes.

Returning to Model Z, there may be a series of components designed for use with this product and manufactured in multiples of two-inch lengths. A specification 4444-*S4* is written on the general construction of these components and the individual lengths identified as 4444-*S4-L2*, 4444-*S4-L4* and so on.

Revisions. The final feature of the regular part numbering system is the method of designating revisions to all the above types of numbered documents. To afford maximum flexibility, straight alphabetical suffixes were adopted.

When more than twenty-six revisions are made, a double letter system is used starting *AA, AB, AC,* and so on through revision 52; then *BA, BB, BC,* etc. More than 700 revisions can be used before a new drawing or specification number is required.

It should be noted that only drawing and specification numbers are revised. The problem of using letters in three positions is thus avoided, i.e., there may be a part number 4444-*B2-G12*, but revisions are made to the drawing as 4444-*B2-A* or 4444-*B2-B* and not to the part number. The case involving the small X and *G* drawings for which part and drawing numbers coincide is a special one. In a sense, revision of these drawings constitutes a revision to the part number. But since the drawing or part number initially contains a letter in only one position, there is no added complication of the tabulating operation.

General Information. One aspect of engineering data not adequately covered by this or any other drawing number system is general engineering information that exists in one form or another. Classification of this information is handled by the Universal Decimal Classification, a version of the Dewey Decimal Classification modified for use by commercial firms as well as libraries.

Auxiliary Systems in Similar Form

Along with the drawing and part numbering system just described, there is also the need for identifying raw materials and purchased common parts not covered by local drawing or part numbers.

Raw Materials. Designations for raw materials are basically specifications, yet they cannot be assigned prime numbers from the drawing number series because the prime drawing numbers pertain primarily to devices. A system similar in form to the drawing number system was devised. This consists of a three-digit prime number followed by the letter *R*, and a number identifying specific characteristics, grades or dimensions. The prime numbers identify the basic material by the first two digits, and a particular class or type of that material by the last digit.

Purchased Common Parts. The system established for common parts purchased from outside sources is basically a part number system. It was devised to resemble the drawing number system and consists of a four-digit prime number followed by the letter *W* and a number for a particular part. The first two digits of the prime number identify a class of part, such as round head screws, hex nuts, lock washers, solid rivets or electrical components; the last two digits refer to a particular type of that part such as round-

head iron machine screw or round-Phillipshead iron machine screw. These are in turn broken down by suffix digits according to specific characteristics.

Universal Decimal Classification

The general engineering information not identified by specific document numbers presents a serious problem of classification. For many years, modifications of the Dewey Decimal Classification have been used to classify information of this type. The Dewey system suffers the disadvantage of having been designed especially for library use, therefore, efforts to improvise a system for business use have been underway for many years by the International Federation of Documentation. Information on the Universal Decimal Classification, Fig. 2, is available through the American Standards Association.

The use of U.D.C. appears to be fully justified. First, some such system must be devised or the mass of abstract information collected over the years is unusable. Secondly, the system is already "engineered," has been published, and requires only familiarization by the personnel. Lastly, its international and universal nature is assurance that, once in effect, it may be extended but not altered.

For drawing and parts numbers, the U.D.C. offers an opportunity to provide readily available engineering information. As each prime number in the drawing number series is assigned, the proper location for the subject of the number in the U.D.C. is determined. A cross-reference card file shows exactly which drawing number series has been assigned to any given subject.

To locate pertinent drawing number series easily, it is sometimes necessary to cross reference a prime number to two or more subjects and then make multiple entries in the file. It is then possible to locate rapidly all the drawing number series pertaining to a subject regardless of the viewpoint from which it is approached. ∎

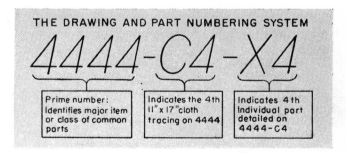

Fig. 1—Example to show how a drawing number can be amended to form part number by adding X-number suffix.

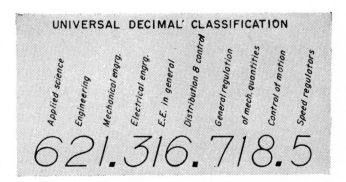

Fig. 2—First three or more digits are frequently replaced by abbreviations in order that references will be more concise.

In this system, many parts need no drawings at all

The key is a numbering system that classifies parts
and identifies them with relatively few master drawings
that serve as a basis for the distinguishing details

A new system for classifying and numbering parts used in manufacture reduces a mountain of engineering drawings to a manageable and hard-working minimum. Besides relieving the load on the drafting room, the new system cuts other paperwork and eases production control.

H. F. Gatzow, standards engineer, and F. M. Eiche, supervisor of drafting practices, devised the system for Allis-Chalmers Mfg Co, after a study of the 200,000 engineering drawings in the company's active file. Their study revealed that 10% to 15% of these drawings were duplicates.

This was not so surprising as another discovery they made: More than 100,000 drawings were so simple that they could have been grouped and tabulated according to size, shape, and material, with only one key drawing at the head of numerical data columns for identification purposes. From this finding, Gatzow and Eiche worked out their new index of standard parts.

Cut to the bone. The Gatzow-Eiche system has eliminated drawings for whole categories of parts, such as those consisting solely of cutoff or cutout pieces of standard raw materials. It has reduced drafting time in many more instances to the mere adding of details to master drawings.

An added dividend is that the entire system has proved "open-ended." Allis-Chalmers can now extend the system to include more complicated, but still multiple-purpose, parts.

The basic system got its start by providing a means of pre-assigning part numbers to types of parts that require no detailed drawings. These are parts obtained by cutting off required lengths from bar stock, tubing, angles, and other structural forms or by cutting out square, rectangular, circular, or triangular parts from plate, sheet, or strip.

Initially conceived as a semi-automatic arrangement requiring contact between engineering and Eiche's Operations Standards Service Dept, the system has evolved into a do-it-yourself operation. This evolution makes it even easier to work with than anticipated—hence more enthusiastically received.

Pick a number. The new system is based on 11-digit numbers, the same for a part and its drawing, if any. Such numbers are used in bills of material, automated or manual manufacturing process sheets, stock records, computer data storage. They remain part of any number assigned to a component that is made by subjecting a standard part to further machining or processing required to adapt it to specific designs.

To generate a new number for a cutoff part, a number in a two-digit series is assigned to indicate first whether a metallic or a nonmetallic material is to be used. A digit is then added to represent the shape (rectangular bar, tube, angle) that is being specified. The next two digits show the specific material to be used (steel, brass, polyester). Two more digits indicate the size of the raw material being used, and the final three digits give the desired length of the cutoff part, to one decimal place.

For cutout parts, the numbering formula also calls for 11 digits, but it is more complex since it must convey more information.

Anyone who wants to know if a part of a particular combination of shape, size, and material exists in the new Allis-Chalmers index of standard parts looks it up in a periodically revised publication

Allis-Chalmers — Parts selector chart (left)

ISSUED NOV. 15, 1965
REISSUED JAN. 29, 1966

FROM STOCK PLATE OR SHEET MATERIAL

EXAMPLE: RECTANGLE, CARBON STEEL PLATE, CP NO. 00-573-251-011, 10" W. x 20" LG. = 68-281-039-258
EXAMPLE: DISK, FLAT, CARBON STEEL, CP NO. 00-575-251-011, 10.5" DIA. = 68-281-900-105

SHAPE AND SIZE GROUP SELECTOR

		RECTANGLE No. 22	TRIANGLE No. 51	FLAT RING No. 63	DISK No. 61
MATERIAL NO. PLATE	MATERIAL NO. SHEET OR STRIP	BASIC DRAWING NO. 68-999-999-401	BASIC DRAWING NO. 68-999-999-402	BASIC DRAWING NO. 68-999-999-403	BASIC DRAWING NO. 68-999-999-404

ELEVEN DIGIT PART NO. GROUPS

MATERIAL	FIRST FIVE DIGITS		6TH	7TH THRU 11TH	6TH	7TH THRU 11TH	6TH	7TH THRU 11TH	6TH	7TH THRU 11TH
ALUMINUM	68-000 THRU 68-040	68-041 THRU 68-090	**0** IF WIDTH IS ≤ 12.6		**3** IF WIDTH IS ≤ 12.6		**6** IF WIDTH IS ≤ 12.6			
BRASS	68-091 THRU 68-100	68-101 THRU 68-120								
BRONZE	68-121 THRU 68-140	68-141 THRU 68-160								
COPPER	68-161 THRU 68-180	68-181 THRU 68-200								
COPPER-ALLOYS INCLUDING NICKEL COPPER	68-201 THRU 68-220	68-221 THRU 68-240	**1** IF WIDTH IS > 12.6 BUT ≤ 43.2	FOR CUTOUT SIZE DESIGNATION NUMBER, SEE INDEX PAGES	**4** IF WIDTH IS > 12.6 BUT ≤ 43.2	FOR CUTOUT SIZE DESIGNATION NUMBER, SEE INDEX PAGES	**7** IF WIDTH IS > 12.6 BUT ≤ 43.2	FOR CUTOUT SIZE DESIGNATION NUMBER, SEE INDEX PAGES	**9** FOR ALL SIZES	SPECIFY DIA. TO TENTH INCH EXAMPLE: 10.5 DIA = 00-105
IRON	68-241 THRU 68-265	68-266 THRU 68-280								
STEEL CARBON	68-281 THRU 68-500	68-501 THRU 68-720								
STEEL STAINLESS	68-721 THRU 68-770	68-771 THRU 68-810								
STEEL ALLOY	68-811 THRU 68-840	68-841 THRU 68-880	**2** IF WIDTH IS > 43.2		**5** IF WIDTH IS > 43.2		**8** IF WIDTH IS > 43.2			
RESERVED	68-881 THRU 68-940	68-941 THRU 68-998								

Parts selector pictures cutout parts and tabulates numbers for combinations of material, shape, size.

Allis-Chalmers — 50-Series Part Numbers for Centrifugal Castings (right)

SHAPE & MATERIAL

ISSUED NOV. 3, 1965
REISSUED

50-SERIES PART NUMBERS FOR CENTRIFUGAL CASTINGS

CASTING SHAPE	MATERIAL & SIZE GROUP					
FIRST FIVE DIGITS	BRONZE 6 Thru 8	BRONZE ALLOY 6 Thru 8	STAINLESS STEEL 6 Thru 8	ALLOY STEEL 6 Thru 8	6 Thru 8	6 Thru 8
50-455	000 THRU 398	399 THRU 598	599 THRU 698	699 THRU 798	799 THRU 898	899 THRU 999
50-456	000 THRU 398	399 THRU 598	599 THRU 698	699 THRU 798	799 THRU 898	899 THRU 999
50-457	000 THRU 398	399 THRU 598	599 THRU 698	699 THRU 798	799 THRU 898	899 THRU 999
50-458	000 THRU 398	399 THRU 598	599 THRU 698	699 THRU 798	799 THRU 898	899 THRU 999

PAGE - 1.02

Centrifugal castings from material and shape selector show how system works for more complex parts.

---

called a "Materials-Shape Group Selector." This pictorial tabulation guides the reader to pages where the desired part is listed, if it exists.

Master drawings. Backing up this no-drafting numbering system is a set of 160 master engineering drawings. These are used for parts that are fairly simple but are still more complex than those that consist solely of cutoff or cutout sections of raw materials. Each master drawing pictures a shape and combination of details common to a group of parts.

To use the drawing to depict a given part, the engineering designer or draftsman simply adds distinguishing details: exact dimensions, tolerances, material specifications, processing instructions. These master drawings, already delineate a variety of finishing operations such as bends, cutoff and notched corners, bolt circles, threads, chamfers, hole and slot patterns, irregular cutout patterns. Specifications for such parts as bolts, connectors, nuts, O-rings, pins and shims, screws, springs, spur gears, studs, and washers are also provided.

Just requisition them. These semi-completed, standard drawing forms are available to all Allis-Chalmers engineering and manufacturing operations from central stores.

With a master drawing in front of him, the engineer or draftsman only has to number the part in accordance with the department's assigned series.

A print of each such completed drawing must then be submitted to the Operations Standards Service Dept. Drawings selected for listing in the index are stamped "standard part," signaling that interchangeability and conformity to listing must be controlled. The regularly revised index shows delineating details of each part and abstracts the variables. Looseleaf copies of the index are available to all engineering and manufacturing units concerned.

Besides reducing drafting time and providing a simplified, more informative parts numbering system, Allis-Chalmers has also eliminated substantial amounts of paperwork, reducing space requirements for filing and microfilming. Parts duplication has also been eliminated, simplifying production planning. ∎

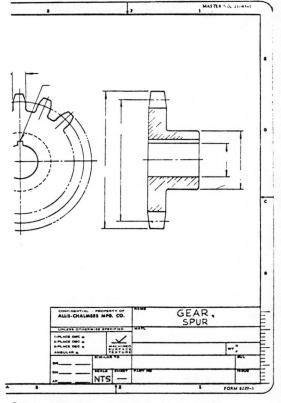

Spur gear master drawing of type used in various sizes and materials is ready for delineation of details, making it a finished drawing for a part that will be incorporated in a final design.

Instructions for Folding Prints of Drawings

Dimensioned fold lines for protective folding are shown in Fig. 1; for exposed folding in Fig. 2; and for book filing in Fig 3.

Size	Dimensions, in.	Comments
A	8½ x 11	No fold required.
B	11 x 17	Fold into halves. Cannot fold to bring title-block into correct location. Auxiliary number block required as shown in Fig. 2. For book filing, fold back to expose title-block.
C	17 x 22	Fold into halves and quarters. For book filing of size C and larger, fold into narrow horizontal concertina parallel to top edge, then into vertical concertina.
D	22 x 34	To locate title-block to best advantage, ignore that this size is 2 x 11 in. by 4 x 8½ in. and instead treat it as approximately 3 x 8½ in. or 25½ in. by 3 x 11 in. or 33 in. Fold into thirds both ways.
E	25 x 40	Or approximately this size. Fold short side into thirds, the long side into multiples of 11 in. as shown.
	Up to 28 x 44	Treat same as size E. Folded print will be 9⅓ x 11 in. If 9⅓ in. is too wide, must fold same as size F.
F	34 x 44	Fold top three-quarters into a triple concertina on horizontal lines. Then fold into quadruple concertina on vertical lines. Finally fold into two halves along horizontal line. Alternatively, for protective folding, fold into halves and quarters on vertical lines instead of concertina fashion; this method gives a dog ear over the title of a single thickness instead of triple thickness.

How to Fold Prints

Instructions for folding standard sizes of engineering drawing prints to letter size. Fold lines are given for protecting the viewing side of prints, for exposing the viewing side of prints, and for prints that are filed in book binders.

W. L. GOVAN

ONE IMPORTANT, though often neglected, engineering department operation is that of folding prints. Usually, in the performance of this operation, little thought is given as to how the original folds affect convenience in future handling, use, and filing of the prints.

A print refolded along new fold lines still retains the creases of the original folds and is awkward to handle in a flat unfolded state. For this reason, few prints are ever refolded to a new overall size.

Unless prints are originally folded to a uniform overall size, many inconveniences ensue in handling, mailing, loose filing in letter-size drawer type cabinets, binding in loose leaf books, or binding with sales proposals, contracts, and instructions.

Prints received through external or

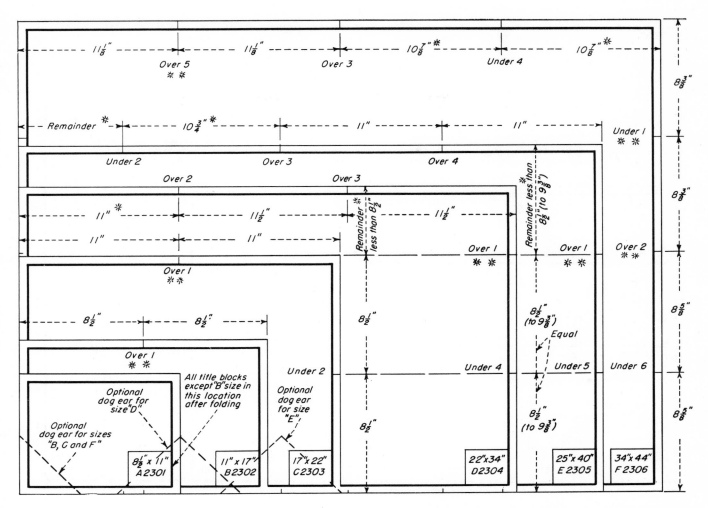

Fig. 1—Fold lines for protective folding that exposes only the blank reverse side. For protective folding only, folds marked with a single asterisk must be shorter than adjacent folds. For exposed folding, folds marked with double asterisk are reversed.

to Standard Letter Size

internal company mail are usually filed still folded in miscellaneous sizes as received. The results are bad housekeeping and an inefficient use of filing space. This undesirable situation could be avoided if both company prints and those received from outside sources were all folded to a uniform size.

Presumably to facilitate folding to a uniform filing size, most standards call for drawing sizes to be multiples of $8\frac{1}{2}$ x 11 in. letter-size paper. Few engineering departments, however, spe-

cify how folding is to be done. To be folded down to the letter size, drawings do not need to be a multiple of $8\frac{1}{2}$ x 11 in. as long as fold lines are selected accordingly.

Many good reasons may be given for completely ignoring the relationship of the standard letter size to the overall dimensions when folding prints. Some of these reasons are: It is easier to fold a print when all the folds are not exactly the same size; standard mailing envelopes will take larger than letter size; the title-block should be in its

normal lower right-hand position after folding; and because a binding edge is often required beyond the folds.

The preferred method of folding prints, indicated in Figs. 1 to 3, and the accompanying instructions, are based on the following considerations:

The final folded size should approximate letter size, $8\frac{1}{2}$ by 11 inches.

The thickest fold should be made in as few thicknesses of paper as possible, say a maximum of four to six. Somewhat in contradiction to this objective, a minimum of fold lines is

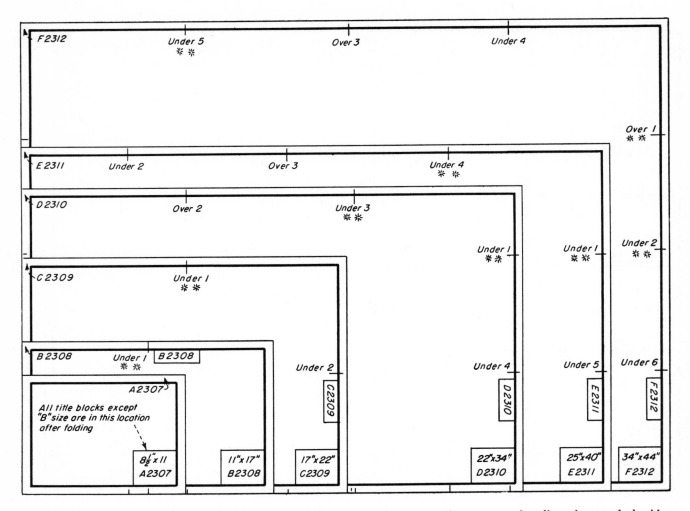

Fig. 2—Fold lines for exposed folding. For dimensioned location of fold lines see Fig. 1, except that dimensions marked with a single asterisk may be equalized for exposed folding. For protective folding, folds marked with a double asterisk are reversed.

desirable. Folding by halving, then quartering, and so on, requires a minimum number of folding operations, but the folds are bulkier than when the print is folded concertina fashion.

For filing in a letter-size cabinet, the top edge of the print should be a single fold line. This type of fold helps to avoid any possibility of filing a later print inside the folds of a former one.

Title-blocks should appear, if possible, in the lower right-hand corner of folded prints. This requirement can be readily fulfilled with every usual standard size except 11 x 17 in., commonly called "B" size.

The fold lines for protective folding shown in Fig. 1 satisfy the needs of engineers who prefer that prints be folded so as to protect their viewing side. This method is especially good when the folded print receives rough handling either in or out of the files.

In Figs. 1, 2, and 3, the word "under" means that the portion of the print above the horizontal fold line, or to the left of the vertical fold line, is to be folded underneath, away from the observer. The word "over" means that the fold is upward, toward the observer.

Only the blank reverse side of a print is exposed when the preferred fold lines shown in Fig. 1 are followed. The title-block is obscured. It can be made visible, however, by folding back one corner of the print in a triangle or dog ear.

Alternatively, another title-block can be stamped on the reverse or white side of the print in the most suitable corner. The laborious task of copying the title and drawing number into the new title block obviously makes this method impractical if there are many prints to be filed.

A title-block in a corner of the re-

verse side of prints received from outside may be stamped on when a local filing number and additional information are to be added.

The fold lines for exposed folding shown in Fig. 2 meet the requirements of engineers who prefer that prints be folded to expose the viewing side and title-block. If the print is to be studied a section at a time, this method is probably the most convenient.

Note that the same fold lines and the same sequence of folding can be used both for protective folding, Fig. 1, and for exposed folding, Fig. 2. The only difference is that some of the folds are reversed.

With the exposed type of folding, Fig. 2, the title-block is clearly visible. Offices that produce prints destined to end up in some other company's files can cater to the requirements of the ultimate user by:

1. Providing additional blanked-out

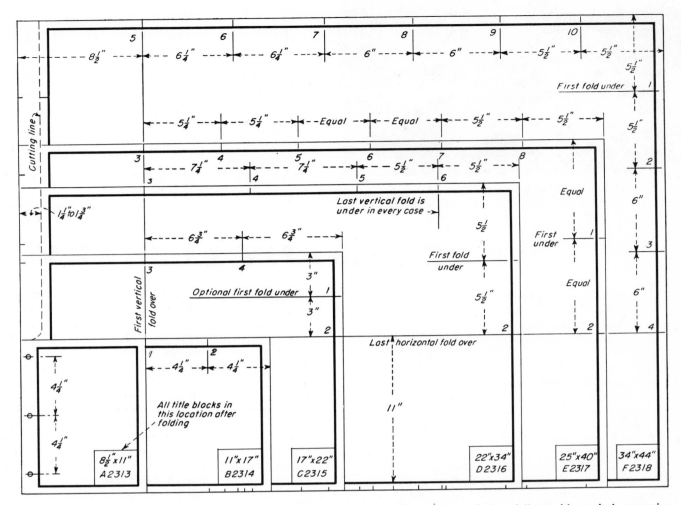

Fig. 3—Fold lines for book filing. First make all horizontal folds in concertina fashion and then follow with vertical concertina folds. For prints enclosed with text matter, this method provides a binding edge, exposes the tile block, and makes a neat package.

spaces in the title-block for local filing numbers and additions to be the title, such as location of the equipment.

2. Repeat the drawing number in an auxiliary box so that it appears on the top right-hand corner of the folded print when placed in the file.

3. Repeat the number a third time in inverted form in the top left-hand corner of each drawing, so that unfolded prints and drawings can be identified from either top or bottom.

Preferred fold lines for prints that are filed in book form binders are shown in Fig. 3. The horizontal folds are made first in concertina fashion and are then followed by vertical concertina folds, thus the total thickness of any one fold is reduced. This method provides a binding edge and exposes the title-block. For prints enclosed with text matter, this method makes a neat self-contained package, but is very awkward with large prints;

that is, if anybody takes the trouble of studying them in connection with the text.

When folded as indicated in Fig. 3 and bound in a book, only the viewing side of the print is visible from the front. No section of blank paper, especially the white side of the blue prints, mars the appearance of an open book. The title-block is exposed in the customary lower right-hand corner. Depending on the format of the drawing, the exposed upper right-hand corner of the print may be an advantage since the bill of material or other data usually placed there would be visible.

For book filing of any print wider than 11 in. it is, of course, necessary that a binding tab projects out about $1\frac{1}{2}$ in. wide by 11 in. high along the lower portion of the left hand edge of the unfolded print. A special off-set cutting line and border for this

tab may be printed on the drawing form. For any type of binding, draftsmen should keep clear a binding margin about $1\frac{1}{2}$ in. wide along the left side of all drawings.

Fold lines should be indicated on the printed drawing forms in the margins. Such indications are not only a help to the staff who do the folding, but enable draftsmen to avoid putting figures on or near a fold line. In many instances, zoning lines can be made to coincide with fold lines if zones are used. It is not necessary to identify the fold lines by abbreviations or numbers to indicate the sequence of folding, or whether the lines are for book or loose filing. The personnel concerned with the routine operations of folding prints can be readily instructed with regard to sequence. They will probably mark off or arrange their working table to facilitate folding to standard sizes. ■

Eyecatching displays . . .
alert the engineering staff-member to newly published
material and draw him into the library.

*Even if it concentrates on one subject,
your company library can't hope to compete with the Library of Congress. Being
relatively small, it must get the most
out of the facilities it can afford. Here's
a guide to . . .*

MORE SERVICE
FROM YOUR
COMPANY LIBRARY

You walk into your company library. You are looking
for only one thing—information. Today you want a
phase diagram for gold-aluminum alloy—or a magazine
article you remember reading several months ago. What
you need tomorrow may be the latest information on a
lubricant for nylon bearings, or the name of a manufacturer of Teflon O-rings. And the library that provides
the precise information in the shortest possible time . . .
that's the best library.

To give such service a library can get by with modest
physical assets; very few can afford to stock all the books
covering even a very narrow field. But although a small
library is limited in capital equipment it can supply the
engineer with all the information he needs—if the
librarian energetically exploits and develops all resources
at her command.

But simply getting the facts, quickly and accurately,
is only part of the well-run library's job—the passive part.
It will also actively reach out to the engineer, without
being asked. It will pass on information he may need,
encourage him to bring in his problems, stimulate his
thinking with information he might otherwise miss. Performing this two-part service adds up to a big job.

When Information Is in the Library . . .

As in all other types of libraries, the card catalog is key
to needed information. But a small company library
must go beyond the usual cataloging of books and pamphlets by subject, title and author cross-references. Literature must be scanned with company projects in mind, and
pertinent facts either cataloged or abstracted on file cards.
Ideally, every fact worth storing on library shelves should
be instantly available—that ideal is difficult if not impossible to attain. But an efficient, comprehensive catalog
system should be the goal of every company librarian.

Periodicals for the current year should be stacked on
easily accessible open shelves. Abstracts of selected articles should be printed on catalog cards, then filed by
subject and author. This file helps locate articles you
"remember reading" but aren't sure when or where; more
important, it will quickly find all available articles on a
given subject.

Books and pamphlets will be filed, of course, according
to accepted library techniques—Dewey Decimal System,

Library of Congress System, or whatever. In addition,
subject cards must be handled in detail with emphasis on
the subject content of each book. One book may spawn
many subject cards with page numbers noting where the
specific information can be found.

Commercial literature, such as catalogs, bulletins, data
sheets, is arranged alphabetically in some libraries, by
product in others. Another convenient way is to assign
each manufacturer an arbitrary file number, and to place
all company literature under this number. Two file cards
are made. One lists file number, name and address, and
local company representative; and on the reverse side,
products under which the company is listed. This card
is filed alphabetically with other company cards. The
other card is a cross-index, filed alphabetically by product,
listing companies and their corresponding file number.
Filing by number allows adding a new catalog without
rearranging the file.

In a small library the three sets of cards—one for
periodicals, one for books and pamphlets, and one for
company catalogs—can all be placed in the same cabinet.
Its separate sections permit two or more persons to search
simultaneously for information. The system is so simple
that do-it-yourselfers can help themselves to a magazine
or book in the librarian's absence, recording title and
number on conveniently placed or easily accessible check-
out cards.

Other Services

To give full service, small company libraries must
expand other typical services too. Some things to do are:

• Prepare bibliographies on any subject requested by
an engineer. Also collect any listed reference material.

• Scan magazines for new products in the company's
field and for literature offered by competitors or companies in related fields.

• Check catalogs and company data-handbooks periodically to be sure the latest are on file.

• Offer to order books and magazines through the
library. This is not only a convenience for employees,
but avoids duplication and allows the company to benefit
from the economy of central purchasing.

• Keep a "list of interest" file for all staff engineers.
If the librarian knows what topics interest each staff

No Library?—Some Tips on How to Begin

Perhaps the first step for the newcomer is to contact the Special Libraries Association. This organization, with 31 chapters in the US and Canada, is a group of libraries owned by manufacturing concerns, banks, law firms, insurance agencies. A letter addressed to the main office at 235 Park Ave. S., N. Y., N. Y., will put you in contact with the chapter in your area. Each chapter maintains a staff consultant who, for a fee, gives advice on how to set up your library. Consultants have had much experience helping small technical libraries get started and will answer: How many books are needed? How much space? How large a staff? What will it cost?

Next step is to find a librarian. Even a small library should be run by a trained librarian who will organize literature so that it is readily accessible, and do the most with available resources. Special Libraries Association can help here too—with its placement service for personnel trained in Library Science. But be patient. It may be several weeks before you can find the librarian with training and background you require.

Until the Doctor Comes

Here are some quick answers a trained librarian or special consultant can be expected to develop in detail:

Location

The new library, preferably in a room by itself, should be within easy reach of research and development personnel and away from noisy areas. Books are heavy—about 140 lb per sq ft for a bookshelf seven shelves high—so take this into account when planning floor space. Allow room for expansion too. It's estimated that the library with 1000 books today will contain over twice that many eight years from now. Stacks of periodicals alone grow at the rate of about 7 in. per year. The room should be air conditioned and all reading surfaces illuminated with 40 to 60 ft-candles of shadowless light.

Cost

This depends, of course, on size of the library, which depends in turn on size of your organization and breadth of the technical field involved. As a starter, 1000 books is average. This means a floor area of between 600 and 1000 sq ft—including space for desks, filing cabinets, reading tables. Such a setup would probably require one full-time librarian and an assistant. Initial outlay for books and office equipment would be about $10,000, of which perhaps half would go for equipment, one-third for books, the remainder for subscriptions and miscellaneous supplies. You can save money by rounding up company-owned books, presently scattered around the building in the private libraries of your engineers.

Yearly budget would be about $20,000–24,000 (not including heat, light and rent and other overhead items). The bulk of this will pay salaries of librarian and assistant. Out of the total, also figure on spending about $3,000 for new books and $300–400 for subscriptions.

member, publications can be screened and items of particular interest sent immediately without waiting for a request. This list should be revised every six months to keep it up to date.

• File engineering notebooks and research reports. One central file permits quick checking, especially where several staffs and laboratories are involved.

• Make patent searches and collect patent information when the company has no patent department to do this job. Patent searching is specialized work, but many company libraries have become proficient at it. Thousands of dollars can be saved if a search is made before filing a patent claim or starting a new project.

When the Library Needs Help...

There are a number of external sources for books and periodicals which, in effect, expand the fund of information upon which a small library can draw.

Commercial abstracting and indexing services provide quick reference to many more publications than most libraries can have on their shelves.

Technical societies usually maintain some kind of technical library. Perhaps the most extensive of these, as well as one of the most complete technical libraries in the country, is the one in the Engineering Building in New York City. Here are the collected libraries of many engineering societies. Branch offices of technical societies in cities all over the country also maintain their own libraries.

Nearby company libraries are another source. Two neighboring libraries often agree to concentrate on fields of peculiar interest to their engineers and reduce or eliminate overlapping holdings. This way, one library may stress electrical engineering, the other the physical sciences, with an arrangement to borrow freely when necessary. Together, they can answer many more requests and stretch book budgets farther.

Reaching Out—the Active Library

Besides expanding the services normally provided by any library, a company library must extend activities to meet the engineer more than halfway, providing him with technical information and making him aware of available facilities.

Library displays, exhibiting recent acquisitions or showing sample material keyed to some area of current interest, will often help draw the engineer into the library. These should be placed prominently in the main stream of traffic where technical personnel are certain to see them. A number of books and pamphlets on plastics, for example, could be displayed to show increasing impact of this material on a company making pipe fittings. Sometimes needed data is found right on the display table.

Library publications keep technical personnel aware that the library is standing by, ready to help. Library notes, circulated to all engineers describe new books and pamphlets available on loan. Other memos should be sent out periodically: some to announce new library facilities, services or procedures; others to suggest new uses for existing facilities . ■

RUTH R BOYLE and ROBERT C MAY
Automatic Switch Co

The How and Why of Microfilming

In itself, microfilm is not new as a security and space-saving trick. During World War II, thousands of rolls of microfilmed papers were cached away in vaults, and this form of insurance has since grown into a big business. What is new and becoming popular among large manufacturers is the active-storage method for filing their engineering drawings.

Here, instead of storing the film and keeping the original handy for reference, it's the other way around. The original is stored. Microfilm becomes the reference copy.

This method also means the film copies are no longer stored on rolls. Instead, individual frames are cut from the roll and put directly into envelopes, or mounted in cards provided with an insertion hole. Such cards can be either the conventional 3 x 5 file type or EAM (Electronic Accounting Machine) cards. The EAM cards are most popular because they can be punch-coded and processed on standard accounting machinery to provide fast access and convenient storage.

What's to be gained

An active microfilm file in a completely mechanized system has all the advantages of roll microfilm plus a few more:
- Security—valuable drawings, representing many thousand dollars of drafting and engineering time, can be stored in compact film form in a disaster-proof area.
- Space-saving—depending on size of the originals and the reduction ratio used, microfilms can often be stored in less than 1% of the space needed for full-size tracings and prints.
- Labor-saving—if automatic sorting machines are used, desired drawings can be selected automatically. Drawings stored in a film file are small; easier to work with than the original tracing. Also, all drawings are filed sequentially, regardless of size of the original.
- Time-saving—engineers can get prints of microfilmed drawings in about a minute, and in even less time with automatic-feed, high-volume printers.
- Better reproduction—microfilm copies are often superior to contact copies: smudges and stains that show up when light is passed through the tracing will be hardly noticeable on microfilm—it photographs only the surface.

For engineering drawings, most common microfilm sizes are 35mm, 70mm, and 105mm. The 35mm frames are usually mounted in cards; 70mm and 105mm are stored in envelopes. Companies having many large drawings (aircraft and ship-building, for example) or companies whose drawings show much busy detail, may choose the larger film sizes to get good working prints. Proponents of 35mm, on the other hand, claim large drawings can be reduced to 35 mm and still give prints as good as the original.

Who is using it

The advantages of microfilm vary, depending on size of the company. Very large corporations and government organizations have files active enough to allow them all the advantages of a completely mechanized system. The full battery of equipment is expensive but will save a large corporation enough money to more than offset the capital investment.

At other end of the scale, smaller manufacturers choose microfilm for only one reason—security. Microfilm, in this case, doesn't save money; it's an expense. But it's the only kind of insurance that will replace valuable drawings when they are lost, stolen or destroyed.

What about the "man in the middle"—the large-to-medium manufacturer? How big does the reproduction operation have to be to make a microfilm system more economical than standard diazo reproducing processes? Suppliers of microfilm and equipment are reluctant to quote a figure.

"It depends," they say, "on the number of drawings presently in the file, floor space occupied, labor involved, activity of the file, what the drawings are needed for, and—not to be underestimated—the ingenuity and experience of the engineer who sets up the system."

One thing is clear: It's not necessary to have several million drawings and a costly array of equipment to get—in a modest way—the cost-saving advantages of microfilm. For example, a company need not own a camera; microfilm service centers are spotted all over the country and will microfilm drawings—often on a same-day basis. Cost here depends on film size, quantity ordered, and intended use.

The system

Once the user has microfilms in his file, he has two ways to put them to work: He can turn them into enlarged copies (called "blow-backs"), or he can make duplicate film copies. The film copies can be made somewhat faster than the enlargements. They are small; the engineer can put many in his desk drawer; they can be easily mailed or carried around. Blow-backs, on the other hand, are often preferred because they don't require a viewer—can be used in the same way that contact copies of the tracing have served in the past.

Both types of copies can be made on a customer-service basis, but to take full advantage of an active microfilm file, most plants will prefer to have their own reproducing equipment. Blow-backs can be made on photographic paper, with standard photographic darkroom techniques, but this is expensive. There are a number of enlarging machines, however, that expose and develop the blow-back within the machine, without need for a darkroom. The principle is similar to that of photographic processing but is much quicker and less expensive—to the point of being almost competitive with diazo contact prints from the original drawing.

In addition, there are other enlarging machines—some only recently on the market—that operate on electrostatic or diazo principles and promise further savings in operating cost. One cost-saving feature when printing from microfilm: Satisfactory working prints needn't be full size, saving considerably on paper costs.

Duplicate film copies printed from 35mm microfilm require a reader for convenient inspection; 70mm and 105mm films can sometimes be scanned simply by holding them to the light. Readers, in many styles, are available for all sizes. Some, of the projection type, give an enlarged image on a translucent screen, others are simply handheld magnifiers and the image is viewed with room light.

Convenience at the drawing board

Draftsmen find microfilm convenient, and time-saving too. No longer is it necessary to roll and unroll bulky tracings on a reference table. A projection viewer at the desk side gives an easily viewed image to work from. And tracings of microfilmed drawings can be made quickly on a special ,translucent-topped drafting table which shows a full-size image, projected from underneath, on the working surface.

Microfilm is growing fast. New equipment is announced almost every month and operating costs decline steadily. This means microfilm and its inherent advantages are coming within reach of the pocketbook of many companies. ∎

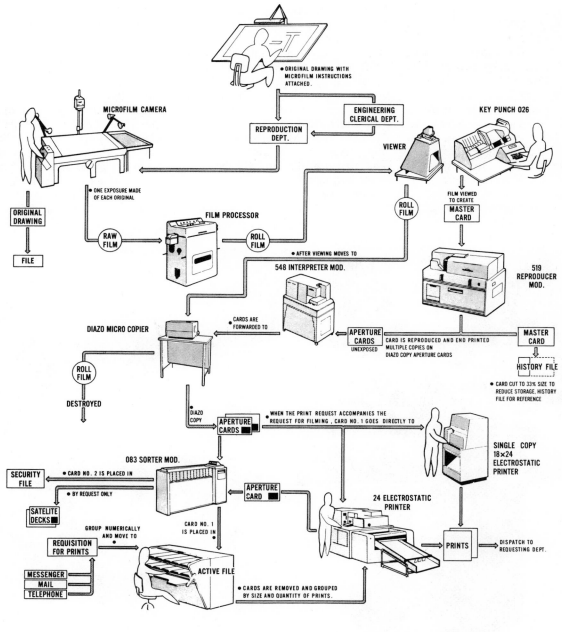

THE CINCINNATI MILLING MACHINE COMPANY
ENGINEERING REPRODUCTION DEPARTMENT
UNITIZED MICROFILM SYSTEM

• ORIGINAL DRAWING WITH MICROFILM INSTRUCTIONS ATTACHED.

ENGINEERING CLERICAL DEPT.

KEY PUNCH 026

MICROFILM CAMERA

REPRODUCTION DEPT.

VIEWER

ORIGINAL DRAWING

• ONE EXPOSURE MADE OF EACH ORIGINAL

FILM PROCESSOR

FILM VIEWED TO CREATE

ROLL FILM

MASTER CARD

FILE

RAW FILM

ROLL FILM

• AFTER VIEWING MOVES TO

548 INTERPRETER MOD.

519 REPRODUCER MOD.

DIAZO MICRO COPIER

• CARDS ARE FORWARDED TO

APERTURE CARDS
UNEXPOSED

CARD IS REPRODUCED AND END PRINTED MULTIPLE COPIES ON DIAZO COPY APERTURE CARDS

MASTER CARD

HISTORY FILE

ROLL FILM

DESTROYED

• CARD CUT TO 33% SIZE TO REDUCE STORAGE, HISTORY FILE FOR REFERENCE

• DIAZO COPY

APERTURE CARDS

WHEN THE PRINT REQUEST ACCOMPANIES THE REQUEST FOR FILMING , CARD NO. 1 GOES DIRECTLY TO

SINGLE COPY 18×24 ELECTROSTATIC PRINTER

083 SORTER MOD.

SECURITY FILE

• CARD NO. 2 IS PLACED IN

APERTURE CARD

24 ELECTROSTATIC PRINTER

• BY REQUEST ONLY

SATELITE DECKS

GROUP NUMERICALLY AND MOVE TO

CARD NO. 1 IS PLACED IN

REQUISITION FOR PRINTS

PRINTS

DISPATCH TO REQUESTING DEPT.

MESSENGER
MAIL
TELEPHONE

ACTIVE FILE

• CARDS ARE REMOVED AND GROUPED BY SIZE AND QUANTITY OF PRINTS.

Chart from *Design Engineering*

259

Microfilm drawings retrieved automatically in seconds

The design engineer is beginning to bring the paper blizzard under control. Two equipment manufacturers that have independently attacked the problem announce almost parallel solutions—random access systems for storing microfilm drawings and other documents, with retrieval units that deliver in a few seconds.

Up to 200,000 tabulating or microfilm aperture cards can be stored, retrieved, copied, and refiled in a unit designed by Mosler Safe Co, Hamilton, Ohio. A system worked out by IBM can handle 504,000 microfilm images of documents. Both systems offer fast retrieval and automatic refiling, but they work on different principles.

Hole-and-notch. In Mosler's setup, 3¼ x 7⅜ in. aperture cards containing microfilms are filed at random in cartridges of 100 cards. Along the lower edge of each cartridge are 35 holes for access to holes and notches that identify each microfilm card so it can be retrieved instantly on demand.

Requests for delivery of a document—an engineering drawing, specification sheet, photograph, or whatever—are entered through a keyboard, punched paper tape, or computer program. The desired card is either presented to the operator or is set aside for viewing, automatic transmission, or copying. With the necessary keyboard and closed-circuit television for viewing, the system can be used from as many as 48 remote locations.

Prices for Mosler's automated filing system start at under $30,000. The first installation will be in a bank late next year.

Film chips. IBM's filing system is based on 70 x 35 mm rectangles called "chips," coated on one side with a diazo emulsion. A magnetic oxide stripe on each chip can accommodate 100 eight-bit coding characters. An image is created on the chip by contact with the microfilm in an aperture card; to copy this image, the area of one or more images is contact-printed on a blank aperture card. The aperture card is the input-output medium.

Chips are stored, 32 at a time, in a plastic cell in which they are also transported through the system in movable trays. Cells are manipulated pneumatically in the trays.

To retrieve any cell in the file, the appropriate tray is moved automatically to one of five positions until the row of cells is aligned so the desired cell is opposite a tube-like transport channel. Switching devices above the trays link any transport channel with a pneumatic tube that serves the entire file. The system is said to be able to handle 1000 requests an hour. ■

From command to readout, entire Mosler retrieval averages 6½ sec, with a maximum of 10 sec. Refiling takes only about 3 sec. Card stays in the system all through operation.

Copying process takes less than 2 sec with IBM system, and entire operation from request to completed copy needs 3 to 6 sec. System can handle 1000 requests per hour.

12.

Creativity, Inventiveness and Patent Law

CREATIVITY ...

Mark Twain's familiar remark about the weather might also apply to creativity—but out of all the talk some facts begin to emerge. Here are summarized those brought to light at a 3-day Harvard Conference.

E J TANGERMAN

Fundamental discoveries are usually *not* accidents, much as they may appear to be. They result from attention to troublesome detail that the ordinary mind discards. The innovator does not throw away "spoiled" photo plates or bacterial cultures; he digs back to find out *why* they were spoiled. Many plates showed atomic action, many cultures showed penicillin, but for years researchers discarded them as faulty because they did not fit the pattern of what was already known. The researchers who stopped to find out *why* they were faulty made the discoveries. The basic characteristic is *driving curiosity,* something all children have, but adults grow out of. To increase creativity, we must start by preventing this growing up.

Creativity is a function of *people,* not of organization, or luck, or conditions, or desire, so any study of the subject must begin with some definition of the creative person and how to recognize him. This is not easy; there is good evidence that most of our colleges, as well as our industries, have rather carefully weeded such people out. One study by a college showed that the aptitude scores of those students who failed for academic reasons were higher than those of students who were graduated!

The Creative Man

Real creativity apparently occurs most often in the unconventional—even eccentric—individual. He has intense faith in himself and a willingness, or desire, to work alone. He is impatient with conventionality, whether it be rules and regulations, working conditions, or mentalities. Creation is a highly personal thing—whether it be artistic, scientific or emotional.

Says Dr H. B. G. Casimir, director of the Philips Research Laboratories in The Netherlands, "Most creative scientists have a number of idiosyncrasies—or perhaps even slightly neurotic tendencies—and they will feel happiest in surroundings where these are least evident. This is one of the advantages of a university as compared with an industrial organization."

Another point of importance: the creative person is usually young. Experts say the top age for basic innovations among theoretical physicists and mathematicians is 30 to 35, for experimental physicists 35 to 40, for biological and medical scientists 40 to 45. Thus the man with greatest potential usually is without reputation or experience, and the man with both reputation and experience is unlikely to produce anything basic. Creative scientists have much more in common with athletes than with artists and writers, whose creativity covers a much wider time span.

Tests during the past six years by UC-Berkeley's Institute of Personality Assessment and Research indicate that intelligence is much more important in creativity than education level. Tests covered creative people selected by their professional colleagues. Among those chosen, only the women mathematicians averaged high educational levels; the architects, writers and painters were most commonly without degrees—they'd left or been invited to leave college—yet their IQ's were all in the 150 to 160 range.

But not all intelligent people are creative—most lack the will or desire. And many lack the independent judgment. (This characteristic was tested in an interesting way. The subject was set for the test in a group of nine other people, presumably also testees but actually stooges. They were primed to give false answers to certain questions, so the testee had to pit his own judgment publicly against theirs!

Other fairly uniform characteristics are: an openness to experience (almost naïveté) even if the experience involves disorder and irrationality; esthetic sensitivity to beauty, particularly in form and dynamic balance, very deep concern with the philosophical issues and with the freedom and lawfulness in nature (a strong need for order, but *not* for conformity unless he's sure it meets nature's laws); and a willingness to stake his future on the meaning of his work. He has, as one expert put it, "good taste in selecting a project."

He is likely to be strongly anti-social, anti-authoritarian, may find refuge in excess in his personal habits. He regards his work as an expression of his own personality; it expresses and fulfils his personality and he assumes it shows his humanity. Thus he appreciates the opportunity to talk his problems over with qualified people to attain cross-fertilization of ideas, but he is likely to insist upon working alone. No organization can really deter him, and he is likely to feel that he can do everything on the job better than

the facts behind the fad

anyone else—even the shopwork, the ordering and the expediting. He is an inveterate gambler with his time and effort and the organization's money and facilities.

What is Creativity?

Creativity is basically the ability to produce new and interesting results from nature. But the word has been applied so broadly in recent years that it can represent any of four steps in science and engineering:

1. *Pure, basic research of the Nobel-prize level*—which perhaps 100 Americans are capable of doing. (After all, there have been only 60 basic papers presented on physics since Newton formulated his laws in 1687 up through 1933. With these 60, you could write any physics text.)

2. *Innovation and discovery*—say 1000 people.

3. *Invention*—say 10,000 can do.

4. *Problem solving*—say 100,000 people do this.

Actually, the common concept today is more likely to embrace Classes 2 and 3, with Class 1 hoped for and Class 4 questionable for inclusion at all.

You need not blush—nor will I—at our inability to define the word more exactly. Everybody has been trying to arrive at an acceptable definition, and none is known. But hundreds of experts are discussing it. This summer, for example, Prof John Arnold conducted his two-week seminar at Stanford, basically like his controversial seminars given at M.I.T., with industrial supervisors and teachers. Dr Alex Osborn and his Creative Education Foundation and the University of Buffalo co-sponsored a 3-day "creative problem-solving institute." And Harvard University invited 70 of the world's best-known creative minds from education, industry and government to a 3-day conference on "creativity in an organization setting." I audited the latter; it was stimulating, interesting and valuable, but it didn't catch the will-o'-the-wisp either—and it had the best chance. It did, however, picture the creative man, suggest how he can be selected and handled, and suggest as well how to use him effectively in an organization.

How to Find the Creative Man

There are as yet no effective tests for creativity—no way to guarantee you've found the man, nor any way to evaluate his work. Finding him after he's proved himself may be too late—unless you're seeking a manager or reputation. However, creative people seem to be able to spot creative ability, so a successful technique is the personal interview by—of all things—a committee of four or five people: the director of the lab, the candidate's potential superior, and a couple of creative people. Previous experience, degrees, and other usual criteria are of little help—you judge on faith, knowing the characteristics as described earlier.

The Setting

Authorities agree that the physical setting for creativity is less important than the mental or psychological one. Equipment should be adequate, but need not be elaborate; too much has historically been worse than too little. There should be few distractions; as Yeats replied once when asked if he had no telephone because he didn't like them: "No! I like them too well!" And there apparently should be some resistance; Dr Hatch of 3M said after retirement that the successful research project was invariably opposed by the management, and was carried out by a man who was willing to lay his job on the line in the face of this opposition.

There is evidence, also, that the creative person shouldn't have too much familiarity with the field, nor should people with whom he associates. Experts know all the reasons why the idea won't work, know all the rules—one or more of which must be disproved if any advance is made. Wisdom and experience, in the vicinity of creativity, turn out to be merely entrenched opinion and prejudice. Put these into a control or advisory committee and you have introduced rigor—the first word of *rigor mortis*.

Creativity doesn't countenance regulation either, so the really creative person won't observe usual employe rules or office hours. (Remember Steinmetz' ultimatum his first day at GE: "No smoking—no Steinmetz!") Nor will he countenance a static situation; if the organization is content with things as they are, the creative man goes out—or his creativity does. This is the problem of universities; the academic atmosphere dear to the creative mind is becoming obscured by poor management. Most universities manage research just as they always did—despite a 10-fold increase in funds. The creative person on the faculty has teaching, committees, fund-raising, and endless other interferences with his work. Also, he suffers from rigidity of equipment because many universities have invested in now-obsolete assisting units like computers and X-rays that they cannot or will not discard. Committees there are also on the increase, while in industry there is some evidence of decline. (The new president of one of America's largest corporations eliminated all committees—and nobody has missed them.)

How to Evaluate Creativity

Most measures of creativity thus far offered seem rather to be measures of productivity; they are largely quantitative. Technical papers (either in research-society journals or in all technical magazines) and patents are the criteria. One pair of researchers have even equated five papers as equal to one patent, simply because there are that many more papers than patents. The purist, however, argues that, regardless of jury, reviewer and editor standards, there are good papers and bad ones, significant and insignificant ones, basic and trivial patents. One study, for example, shows that in the tree-shaped development of one basic idea, there were six additional Nobel-prize winners—so even a Nobel prize is no guarantee of a basic contribution.

One company shows productivity of 0.28 papers and patents per professional in a 500- to 600-man lab, a gradual rise from 0.20 to 0.27 in another as the staff increased from 40 to 150. (This company discovered, incidentally, that up to 30 or 40 men in a lab require almost no management, between 40 and 100 a loose departmentalized structure is necessary, and above 100 a formal organization with definite channels of communication and an increase in management levels is required. Morale problems are bad during changeover.)

An extensive study of productivity, made by Arthur D. Little, Inc., is about to be published by the Office of Naval Research. This includes some rather surprising results, among them the indication that publication rate among physical scientists is high until the man receives his doctorate, then drops off rapidly to about 20% of the earlier value. Fellows of the physical society publish ten times as much as non-fellows; the ratio of academician publications to those of non-academicians is astronomically high. Also, only 20 to 30% of the doctors in physics and chemistry stay in research, but half of these write 70 to 80% of the papers. At right is a table from the same study, showing some relationships in money, men and papers.

Costs and Their Control

My own survey of R&D indicated that companies are trying to divorce this budget from operating budgets—to make it a capital investment just like plant, independent of sales. Actually, two factors work together to establish budget anyway: (1) number of professional people, (2) capital equipment. For each professional worker, the annual budget will be something between $20,000 and $25,000 (or more, see Oct 6, '58, p 23). Thus, costs can be controlled by controlling number of professional people. Capital equipment (without buildings) will be 10-12% of the cost per year of the staff. This figure, incidentally, shows why it is advisable to discard slow or obsolete research equipment promptly—the potential loss in working time is far greater than the investment represented by the equipment. In one case, a British lab completed a $500,000 mechanical computer, just as a far-cheaper and far-faster electronic one was announced. The discreet move was to discard the new unit after it had handled only a few problems.

The creative man wants freedom of choice in projects; the laboratory must show results in certain directions. How can these two be reconciled? If the sponsor is smart and sensible, he can control results in two ways: (1) by initial selection of his men, so their interests and his coincide at least roughly; (2) by explaining what his objectives and interests are in clear terms. If he can outline his general area of interest, the researcher then has full freedom of decision within the area as to problem, method and development. His close association with the field

RATIOS OF MONEY, MEN AND PAPERS IN RESEARCH

Type of Organization	Basic-research Expenditures, %	Publication Rate, % of Total	No. of Researchers % of Total
Government	11	9	7
Industry	39	19	27
Education & non-profit	50	72	66

Note: No correlation was found with patents, probably because of the vagaries of patent law. George Washington University has just reported that 55 to 65% of patents granted are, or have been, commercially used, as against the usually quoted figure of 5%.

Not all societies are interested in creativity. Insects, for example, stopped evolving a long time ago (ants nearly five million years ago). They are satisfied with what they are, see no reason for change. They discourage originality or creativity by eliminating innovators . . . Among men, only two societies have been truly creative, Athens from the sixth to fourth century BC, and after the Renaissance in Europe. Sparta was too moral, Egypt too religious, China too contemplative . . . The society must be stable, but interested in change (hence not static), must be more concerned with what you produce than the way you live, must be impressed by action and future, not contemplation and life after death.—Dr J Bronowski, England

---

will suggest which doors are open, which ajar, which closed, and he can best choose between them. He must be reassured, however, of the sponsor's understanding that blind alleys will occur, that time-tables are for routine workers, that a given project may pall.

Yet the time advantage in innovation is vital; a year or two years of time advantage is all a present-day sponsor can expect out of his investment. This means that development phases must be rapid once an idea is discovered—it was the concensus at Harvard that a major present Soviet advantage is the ability to capitalize faster on new science. Our scientific knowledge is as good as theirs, but they make hardware while we fight encumbrances such as company and governmental secrecy.

The need for speed in developing ideas is in direct conflict with the creative mind's desire to present its findings to its peers in a technical-society paper. This may delay disclosure for a year or more, may jeopardize or lose the sponsor's time advantage. Usual procedure now is to patent only products; processes are kept secret; this gives no competitor a blueprint of procedure. Thus GE announced artificial

diamonds but did not divulge the catalyst in the process.

Basic research always appears to be thoroughly disorganized; but there is plenty of evidence that good organization results in trifling research. The slipshod university atmosphere has up to now resulted in far more basic discoveries than has the more shipshape company atmosphere. This should be a warning that the lay idea that all research should be centrally planned and organized for efficiency will result in chaos—lots of projects but no results.

Dr. W. D. Lewis, director of systems research at Bell Telephone Labs, gives these rules for directing group research:

1. "Direct" means "guide," not "specify"—The important output of research is new information, new understanding, and new techniques. Because the commodity to be produced is not known in advance, it is inherently impossible for a research director to specify close deadlines and narrowly defined goals. It could be said that goals and time limits are for research what adrenalin is for the heart. The right amount can stimulate, but too much can cause failure. Goals should be presented as opportunities or

---

Growth (in science and technology) has been so rapid that 90% of all of the scientists who ever lived must be alive today. Science and technological change had almost no impact on the outcome of World War I, while it was a major factor in War II. The great economist Lord Keynes didn't recognize technological innovation as a factor in the economy twenty years ago, yet today it assumes major proportions.—Dr Guy Suits, GE Research

challenges, but only rarely as obligations.

2. Researchers are human too—They need to be appreciated, encouraged, and fairly rewarded just like anyone else. The rewarding must be done with particular care in group research where there is some danger that individual credits will be submerged.

3. Provide help—This means physical help, laboratory apparatus, and adequate technical assistance. Genius may be 1% inspiration and 99% perspiration, but these need not be provided homogeneously by all people in a research organization. Those who are more capable of inspiration should be able to delegate a judicious share of the perspiration. Furthermore, they should be made as free as possible from the ever-encroaching tangles of red tape and onslaughts of Parkinson's Law.

4. Stimulating atmosphere—A more crucial kind of help is that provided by an atmosphere loaded with ideas. Ideas come from people, so this means bringing clever people with different backgrounds into contact with the group and encouraging the interchange of ideas. Shockly has conjectured that inventive creativity is strongly enhanced by the ability of the brain to be aware of more than an average number of ideas simultaneously. The arrangement of these ideas in a new combination must occur first in the mind of a single individual, but the availability of these ideas around him greatly increases the likelihood that this will occur.

The number of simultaneous but independent great inventions and discoveries force us to believe that the climate of ideas may be as essential to technical creativity as the presence of minds capable of combining them. No savage, however brilliant, could have invented radio.

5. The creative group must not demand conformity—A characteristic of most human groups—military, religious, industrial, and social—is that they impose conformity in one way or another on their members. This can be dangerous in a creative group. Creativeness is not just the ability to lay bricks. The component ideas and lines of thought which go into a discovery or invention must be different from each other, and the result must be different from anything that existed before. Crossing of strains is known to be as fertile in science and technology as in botany. A well-known example is the impact of physics on electronics, especially on radar in World War II and in the creation of the transistor. It took mathematical logic as well as engineering to bring forth the electronic computer.

When put in terms of people, this means that the most creative group is likely to be the one which least demands conformity, except possibly to one thing—belief in the importance of creativity. Different members of the group must have different

characteristics, different skills, and make different contributions. Some will be highly creative, others skilled technicians, still others project engineers. These different sorts of people will probably have different work habits, and these differences should be understand and approved by all members of the group.

Individual vs Team

Evidence and opinion point to solo operation by researchers—most patents are granted to individuals and most papers have one principal author. Basic research flourishes in solitude. But there is so much work to be done, and the need for speed is so obvious, that multiple work should in theory speed up the process.

A study by GE of 239 articles in the *Physical Review*, Vol 113, Nos 1-5, showed 89 papers with one author, 99 with two, 35 with three, 13 with four, two with five, and one with six. Average is two authors per paper, or 4¼ if collaborators are counted.

At Bell Labs, there are 280 professional people in Research Division A, 80% of whom work as individuals, and 170 in Div B, 80% of whom work as groups. Based on discoveries and technical papers, Div A is more creative; Div B when measured by inventions and patents. On one accepted equating basis (5 papers per patent), Div B is 50% ahead of A; on another (2 papers per patent), they are equal. If patents and papers are added, the groups are equally creative on a contribution-per-man basis.

Tests by psychologists show that groups get better solutions to problems than individuals, but not more *per member*, and dividing the problem among individuals and adding all the answers gives an even-higher total. Groups tend to correct each other's mistakes, so the group *judgment* reduces quantity and improves quality—the individual produces more good designs, also more bad designs. The rule:

The individual is better at action, the group at judgment.

Yet the new PhD needs guidance—usually welcomes assignment of a problem. Later he develops individuality, but it often is not there initially. He is too diffident, too herd-bound, too inexperienced to want to strike out on his own at first. Later on, when he does, any effort to stop him will only make trouble.

What to Do with the Older Man

Assuming the evidence on youth of creative people is correct, and your goal is creativity of the basic type, the older man will be non-productive. But he certainly should be neither discarded nor misused. He should not become a paper pusher nor janitor at high salary—he'll only become dissatisfied and jealous. The latent desire for decision-making is there, stimulated by both social and technical pressures. He can appreciate and understand the creative work of younger men, can advise and help. And running the lab itself is a truly creative job. He can see that jobs are rotated so boredom doesn't kill initiative, he can teach, write papers and books, spark creativity types 2, 3 and 4. He can do the committee jobs, supervise the collecting of information, can make administrative decisions that will be acceptable to younger creative men. From the company standpoint, here is a man with proved creative ability plus experience which should not be wasted. The alternative is to use the younger man, still in his creative phase, for less-creative work—a procedure which may bring us to scientific bankruptcy in ten years.

Incidentally, R & D lab heads should be changed in six to ten years. Otherwise, the creativity and results both drop off. ∎

A solo chess player can always beat a committee, because the committee inevitably agrees upon the best next move, while the individual plays to a long-term, over-all strategy. So it is with creativity. One man makes no compromises, deals in fundamentals . . . Man is the only social animal who works alone.—Dr J Bronowski

---

Creativity jeers at time clocks, and this complicates administration. Said the former head of the Philips Research Labs (Holland): "I don't resent a man who is two hours late (his technicians assume he was at the patent office, head office or elsewhere on business), but I do resent a man who is always just ten minutes late."

Can Self-Hypnosis Boost your Creative Thinking?

The technique, called FMC, is the outgrowth of self-hypnosis under medical supervision. It directs the brain into creative channels.

ROBERT W. BRADLEY, Senior Staff Engineer, United Shoe Machinery Corp

THIS disclosure of an advanced system of mental control for creativity results from 25 years of study of what makes us "tick" mentally. We all know how hypnosis can be used to accomplish the unusual. So it is with controlled self-hypnosis (under a doctor's initial advice); for almost everyone using this system can increase his particular level of creative-problem solution by ten times, both in quality and quantity.

From scientific studies and experiments, it has become apparent that if you can put your mind into a primitive, uninhibited state, deeply centered with respect to the solution of a problem, it is possible to attain a free-running, non-conscious, computing mind. This mind is capable of producing new ideas, which are expanded into more ideas until a wholly unexpected innovation is produced. You will be conscious only of knowing the final answer as an obvious solution to your problem. These are controversial findings, but are my conclusions resulting from many years of introspective analysis, group seminars, study and evaluation. Persons of stature in the pertinent fields of science, business, education, medicine and industry have been involved.

How many times have you had a radiant idea while shaving? Is the idea a revolutionary way to dry the family laundry or an improved way to roller-paint the outside of the house? Usually you are quite happy about the whole affair, for the idea is apparently produced effortlessly, although you may have previously deferred action on a specific problem. The mental concept and associated operations happen in a flash. Interestingly, the solution is so complete in detail that there is a feeling that the new idea is basically correct. At no time is there a stop in the thinking to evaluate the mental steps with logic and reserve.

Most individuals can solve a problem by taking a step at a time. They gather facts, take a step and evaluate that step with caution. This is our basic school system of teaching. The world has moved along slowly by this "logic-thinking" method. But the really important advances result from what we have called the "breakthrough"—or even from serendipity. In our rapidly expanding competitive world, the logic approach is simply not fast enough, nor does it give us unique answers.

The creative person usually has an average IQ (as measured by traditional achievement aptitude tests), plus a tremendous personal drive to succeed. To compete with high-IQ logical individuals he develops a mental control to allow a free-running mind. In the beginning this free-running mind is shaky. The person is not sure of his mental results, but he has a feeling he knows what the answer is. Over a period of time, after gaining more background information and thinking about his answers, he gains confidence. The creative answers given by this non-logical, non-conscious, self-calculating, free-running mind are as reliable as the logical step-at-a-time approach.

Superb new scientific control conditioning and complete functional direction of the mind, at any desired time, under any environmental conditions, to allow the mind to run freely for both logical and creative individuals, is the target of this system.

How does F M C work?

The power of F M C (*F*ree-running mind, with *M*edical relaxation and *C*ontrol) can be best understood by examining experimental test results.

The F M C system has been screened by approximately 70 people, including doctors, a college president, teachers, engineers, directors of research, housewives and students. During the final two years of pre-system work, two Salem Hospital staff doctors and a surgeon-hypnotist were consulted specifically with reference to bio-chemistry of the brain and practical self-hypnosis. Some consider F M C to have advanced the understanding of the mechanics of the mind by a decade. Others feel sure that it is a breakthrough in creative mental computation.

Medical men explain that brain cells must have fuel to operate, for they are accomplishing work. The sugar and oxygen of the blood, pumped by the heart to the brain, is this fuel. If a cell is excited but cannot get enough fuel to satisfy its demands, then it cannot create, amplify or modify computation chains of command at top-level performance. It is the same as when an automobile carburetor is plugged; the fuel is limited, resulting in poor engine performance.

When we are asleep, blood flow to the brain is at a minimum. Many references support the idea that blood is furnished to cells calling for the fuel as long as there is enough fuel to satisfy all cells in operation. When we are in hypnosis, on the other hand, there is a high level of brain-cell activity in the brain cells being operated, demanding large quantities of fuel.

A blood-flow regulator in the brain attempts to keep the amount of blood flow to the brain constant regardless of the blood-flow requirements to the rest of the body.

In F M C, the brain blood-flow regulation system is temporarily tricked into increased flow. Physical exertion can be used to make the heart pump faster, increasing the blood pressure (for example deep breathing a few times). This is followed by restricted breathing which increases the CO_2 level of the brain. CO_2 is a profound vascular dilator, increasing the cerebral flow as much as 40% (*Physiological Basis of Medical Practice*—Taylor & Best).

What are we trying to accomplish?

Mentally we are trying to provide peak controlled conditions for a high-speed, effortless, self-calculating, non-conscious mind.

Practically we can expect to produce a mind with total recall of bit information, freedom from mental bias or pre-conceived ideas, prevention of side shift of interest from a disturbance, elimination of "jell" or problem thinking time, fineness of detail of the finished product, and answers which are new concepts.

How to solve a problem with F M C

1) Mentally set a time for the start to finish of the brain computation time —say two minutes. Then add a thought that you will awake and feel fine when the two minutes are up.

2) In thoughts (not words) talk to yourself to the effect that you are going to solve the given problem. You know what goes on in the brain and you want peak brain operation specifically for this problem solution only. You state the problem to yourself forcibly in thoughts, purposely with no preconceived idea of the answer and no idea of how to solve the problem.

3) With thoughts you drop the blood out of the unwanted brain sections.

4) Mentally you perceive that the brain arteries are enlarged to allow a greater blood-flow to the desired brain areas.

5) You momentarily tie your mind up with something silly like "a green feather" that requires only low-level brain activity.

6) You let yourself go into deep medical relaxation.

7) At the end of the two minutes time, you will "awake" and feel fine.

8) Answers to your problems will come immediately or within an hour as an obvious solution.

Recommendations and cautions concerning the use of deep medical relaxation are:

1) Check out physically with a competent doctor. Have him teach you deep medical self-relaxation control. Doctors vary the method of going into an uninhibited state somewhat according to the individual's personal mental approach.

2) The seemingly unlimited power requires serious caution and restraint in demands on the human mental and physical system. A slow building of use is a requisite.

3) You may have a habit which it is desirable to eliminate. This habit may result from an entirely different serious previous event in your life which has long been forgotten and is not consciously recallable even with hypnosis. In this case, removal of the habit may be replaced with a more unpleasant condition. Professional pre-mental analysis in some cases may be desirable.

Possibly you are wondering what it is like to be in self-hypnosis with F M C. This is simply a precise scientific method of complete release of brain-cell tension and commanded operation for brain-cell computation. Generally you have a feeling of falling or regression yet safely suspended in space.

ABOUT THE AUTHOR

Robert W. Bradley was born in Lynn, Mass. After graduation from high school he requested an extra year of work in the classics, later was graduated *magna cum laude* in engineering from Tufts. While an engineering student, he served as instructor in physics in the school of liberal arts. Upon graduation during the Depression, he took a job as fire-insurance inspector to get into industry, then went with Sylvania designing electron tubes. After designing for two other radio-tube companies, he returned to Sylvania, where he was in charge of gas-filled regulator tubes, tube ruggedizing, and high-speed assembly of tubes in turn. When Sylvania moved its tube plant to Pennsylvania, Mr Bradley moved to United Shoe Machinery, where he has been for 16 years. He has also conducted creativity experiments at the West Shore Laboratories, which is a small medical electronics company, and at the Digit Company in Marblehead, where he is a director. He has developed about 15 new products, among them the electronic sensor marketed by United Shoe to locate unwanted projecting metal inside finished shoes. His medical work has been in human-body electrical characteristics, muscle shock stimulation, electric-shock therapy and dust precipitation. He is a resident of Marblehead, an ardent sailor, radio amateur, and active in social and civic organizations.

Sounds from far away sound the same as those from nearby sources. You can hear everything going on but you now have a feeling that these sounds mean nothing to you. You are deeply relaxed, so why care?

The feeling is difficult to describe because each person feels a little differently. It is a feeling of complete release for seemingly eternity. A feeling of nothingness, of no pain.

A quiet positive mental approach is important to progress in deep medical relaxation. As assistance, these books are recommended:

1 *The Power of Positive Thinking* —Dr Norman Vincent Peale

2) *How to Live 365 Days a Year*— Dr John Schindler

F M C findings and control of the mind are practically and directly applicable to the broad expanse of everyday living. It is useful from the simplest to the most difficult of problems in all categories ranging from mechanics, business and money to the depths of life, fear, faith and prayer.

As one scientist puts it, "An approach which can be useful in all walks of life—and put to use in the world today."

While specific pre-background information concerning a problem is important, F M C is not limited to brilliant individuals. In fact, when used by average intelligent people with a minimum of background information, more unique and often further advanced answers are produced.

The stages of progress that most students go through are interesting. First the student wants to believe but is skeptical. This is followed by a false belief that he is accomplishing true deep medical relaxation. In his false trials, no results are accomplished. Next comes a stage of belligerency toward himself and his doctor. Finally after he works quietly at the system, there is a feeling of continued buoyancy, of success.

Some accomplish F M C control in thirty minutes. From one to six months of work is the more usual case. At this level the student can go into deep medical relaxation in thirty seconds.

People who have achieved successful deep medical relaxation state that they can accomplish one or more of following acts, which may indicate individual progress toward F M C:

1) Immediately relieve a headache.

2) Immediately relieve muscular pain.

3) Quickly control blood flow from a cut.

4) Reduce effects of eye strain.

Some of the usual comments concerning F M C are, "But isn't this like old-fashioned logic concentration," or "Isn't this just relaxed thinking?" My answer would have to be, "Have you ever been in hypnosis? How can you evaluate what you don't know until you have tried it? It is like trying to perceive what it is like to be in outer space without being there."

Proof of F M C effectiveness on a problem is nearly impossible. One must use it to jump creatively ahead from known bits of information and by experimental evaluation conclude on its validity. The concept of a Supreme Being is the same thing: You can't prove it but you accept it. ∎

How to Support and Encourage Creativity

Four basic principles are outlined
and the problems exemplified
by four "boss types"

ALVIN L. SIMBERG, General Supervisor, Salaried Personnel, AC Spark Plug Division, GMC

In developing tests and a management training program for creativity over ten years ago, I learned that the ideas were there—**everyone had ideas and, under the right circumstances, could express them and make contributions which had never before been made.** One annoying thought, however, was: Although an individual could be given the tools and taught to use them, how could we see that he had the opportunity? What could we learn about the supervisor's part? How could he help, and what might he be doing, without intent or awareness, to stifle ideas?

Answers to these questions have resulted in principles which have been tested and found valid. However, the department head or supervisor must **want** a true understanding of his employes. **No principle works without someone wanting it to, and no employe becomes motivated until and unless there is something or someone to motivate him.**

Four basic principles deal with the supervisor-employe relationship. These are detailed and explained overleaf, with examples of how managers go wrong.

Motivations

What are some of the motivations that people have on the job? In other words, other than having to earn a living, what brings them to work every day? The literature of psychology lists many acquired drives and needs which people possess, which affect them as strongly as the more basic, inborn drives of hunger, thirst, sex, survival, and so on. Some of these are: recognition, accomplishment, security, friendship, prestige, understanding, possession. Each of these drives or needs is usually demonstrated by definite signs which an alert supervisor can detect. This is not the place to go into detail on this subject. There are many books on human relations and courses available for this purpose.

In addition to the drives listed, the recent flourishing literature seems to point out these other kinds of needs that creative people apparently have:

Love of inventing. Although this is more often attributed to the independent inventor, it can be an equally important force in the departmental team member. This drive would be much more meaningful to a creative person than would decision-making or getting things of a more routine nature completed. Such a drive would be likely to affect the individual's work in several ways. He shows a preference for developmental work, is the type who will "outproduce" others at the start of a project, while it is new.

Work freedom. The idea man prefers more of a voice in deciding where he can make the greatest contribution. He has a need to work on projects that inspire him, that have, in themselves, many creative possibilities. Insofar as practical, he seems to desire the responsibility to do his own planning. This drive would be likely to affect his work effort in other recognizable ways: He might dislike conforming to standards and specifications set by someone else; working for a supervisor who exercises close control of his employes, telling them exactly what to do and not to do.

Constructive discontent. This need is one which we attempt to measure by determining an individual's "problem-sensitivity." It explains the person who appears to be somewhat disturbed by unsolved problems, inefficient operations. Characteristically, he might feel that all things can be improved. Having this need, an individual is likely to show a great amount of frustration on his job. Because he recognizes problems, he quite often feels that it is his duty to tell someone about them or do something about them himself. Ordinarily, this does not endear him either to his coworkers or his supervisor. Their usual reluctance to agree with him heightens his frustration. Thus the vicious cycle gains in momentum. The word "constructive" is used in terming this drive, to differentiate it from the chronic complainer, who only has discontent, but does not really do anything or even care to do anything about the problems

268

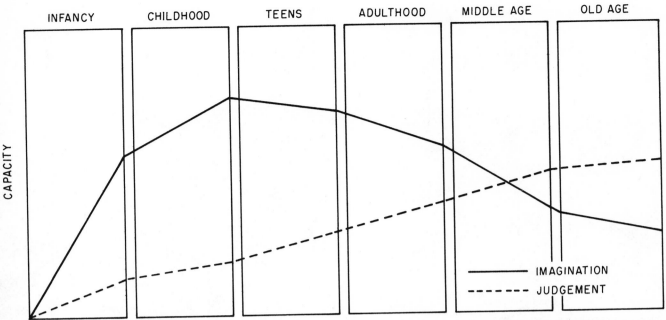

INFANCY CHILDHOOD TEENS ADULTHOOD MIDDLE AGE OLD AGE

CAPACITY

——————— IMAGINATION

– – – – – JUDGEMENT

As judgment develops, imagination declines. Why? Imagination could conceivably parallel judgment — but doesn't. Or are they incompatible? Creative Education Foundation Inc

which arise.

Curiosity. This is a need which many people have that causes them to inquire, investigate, analyze. They seem to want to find out how everything works. They will spend time thinking things out, puttering in the laboratory. They seem to be always asking questions, may have their desks piled high with odd pieces of equipment.

The background of these drives should put the second principle (next page) in better perspective, for the supervisor can now implement it. He can take the time to learn about which specific drives or needs his employes display. This can be accomplished by observation, talking to the employe, but above all listening to what the employe says and looking for what he means.

Furthermore, stimulating an individual means providing him with the opportunity to solve his own problems first—not stepping in until needed. This appears to be a great source of concern for many supervisors. By worrying about an employe's chances of failure, they may take away the project too soon or turn it over to someone else prematurely. This situation is analogous to the over-protective mother shielding her children from all possible dangers, so that the child grows up not knowing what problems

are nor how to cope with them. "Failure" is not necessarily bad; it may even be turned to advantage—if it results in learning on the part of the individual, if he can profit from his mistakes. Therefore the good supervisor, especially with a young, new member of the organization, should allow "freedom to fail." This last statement is made on the assumption that failure, in this case, will not materially damage the individual or his opportunities in the organization in the future.

Support creative effort

1. The supervisor should actively support the creative activities of his employes. He should assist his people in getting the help or information they need from other departments or individuals. He can use his authority as supervisor to support the ideas he feels have merit, even when things are not going well. Sometimes it is only his active support and encouragement which will keep alive something which everyone else would prefer to bury.

2. The supervisor should maintain effective communications within his own and with other departments. One of the major goals of the supervisor is to have everyone thoroughly familiar with departmental activities and objectives so that all have full opportunity to see possibilities for improve-

ment. Over and above this, however, another way of supporting creativity actively is by job rotation. This can quite often help to insure that fresh viewpoints are continually brought to bear on departmental activities. Many supervisors like to trade people with other departments where the experience will be mutually satisfactory and beneficial to employes.

3. A definite and formal system should be established for the fair and consistent consideration of all ideas. Once a formalized suggestion system is seen as necessary or desirable, everyone involved in its participation should be made thoroughly familiar with it. This would include the purpose, the procedure, and especially the basis upon which awards or merit of ideas are judged. There must be confidence in the system by those expected to use it, and here it would be incumbent on the supervisor to insure that objectivity and fairness are always present. Another integral aspect of a good idea system is that it must operate promptly, notifying suggesters immediately upon the receipt of ideas and processing them as quickly as possible. When investigations occasionally require longer periods of time, contacts should be made in a systematic fashion with the suggester to keep him informed of progress.

text continues, next page

Four bosses, and how they react

Sammy Surefoot is a supervisor of long standing with lots of reliable experience. He is highly practical, very cautious and conservative. He lacks confidence in his people because they haven't been on the job as long as he has and aren't as cost-conscious. He will tolerate very little experimenting; his conservatism and emphasis on practicality will resist any employe's love of invention. His caution and lack of confidence in his people will cause him to set up limitations and incline him to tell them how to do their work—there is no work freedom.

Bizzi Busbee is very conscientious and a steady worker. He keeps close control of the time people spend on their particular assignments and expects them to keep their noses to the grindstone. He follows a close work schedule, allows no intellectual curiosity; there's no time for anything but the specific work of the department. If an investigation does not contribute to the immediate job, it should be postponed; there is no time for individual interests. He emphasizes doing first things first, so the person who is constructively discontented is stymied.

Four principles should guide the supervisor of creative people. They minimize the resistance to ideas and changes which are often an integral part of normal supervisory practices. To dramatize how some supervisory practices frustrate the creative person, we show four supervisor types above and give their reactions to each principle.

Principle No. 1: Strive to build an atmosphere which encourages ideas and changes.

1. Openly urge your people to be alert constantly for improvement possibilities in their own and others' jobs.
2. Personally be alert for improvements and put them into effect whenever possible.
3. Urge your people to cooperate with each other in developing and trying out new ideas.
4. Carefully explain changes and new ideas to all those affected by them and sell the benefits of these changes.
5. Present department problems to the members of your group, as opportunities for creative action.

Sammy Surefoot: *There's no point in changing something unless we're sure it's going to save us money.*
Bizzi Busbee: *We don't have time to sit around dreaming up ideas.*
Ronnie Recluse: *I can't possibly keep my people informed of everything that crosses my desk.*
Oaf MaGoof: *I've got a working atmosphere in my department. Is that any different from a creative atmosphere?*

Principle No. II: Design a positive approach to stimulate and encourage creativity in each individual.

1. Study the drives that stimulate creative activities. Put this knowledge to use in dealing with the employe, particularly the creative one.
2. Attempt to maintain interest in worthwhile ideas, should such interest begin to lag.
3. Provide all of your people with the opportunity to solve their own problems before you, or others, step in to "help out."
4. Provide as much opportunity as possible for an individual actually to try out his idea.
5. Contribute to an idea from your own knowledge and experience where it will help.

Sammy Surefoot: *If I let a man work on something I'm not sure of, I'm sticking my neck out.*
Bizzi Busbee: *The regular work is what we're here for. That's more important and should come first.*
Ronnie Recluse: *If a man stops trying to push his idea through, it's a sign to me that he thought it over again and decided it wasn't any good.*
Oaf MaGoof: *I've got to treat everyone alike. I can't show favoritism just because a guy is supposed to be creative.*

to four creative principles

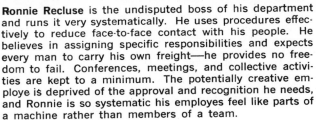

Ronnie Recluse is the undisputed boss of his department and runs it very systematically. He uses procedures effectively to reduce face-to-face contact with his people. He believes in assigning specific responsibilities and expects every man to carry his own freight—he provides no freedom to fail. Conferences, meetings, and collective activities are kept to a minimum. The potentially creative employe is deprived of the approval and recognition he needs, and Ronnie is so systematic his employes feel like parts of a machine rather than members of a team.

Oaf MaGoof is very outspoken, says exactly what he thinks. He is considered to be fair in all his dealings, judges people strictly on the basis of their ability to get things done. He considers creative people a problem, but doesn't believe they should be treated differently from anyone else. Actually, he doesn't understand creative people, will strongly disapprove of their eccentricities, considers them problem employes. He will favor the more practical, down-to-earth people whom he understands, will assign them the responsibilities because "they are more dependable."

Principle No. III: Be a good listener.

1. Be sympathetic and have a sincere interest in understanding a person's ideas.

2. Be open-minded on ideas and avoid biases or prejudices, either related to the individual or the idea.

a. Always keep in mind that conditions change; yesterday's impractical idea may be practical today.

b. Avoid personal antagonism or preference.

c. Don't allow a person's performance in other areas or his level of responsibility to influence your reception.

d. Don't judge a given idea by the quality (or lack thereof) of previous ideas a person may have submitted.

3. Give each person with an idea as much personal time and attention as possible (and as is practical).

4. Learn to treat complaints as suggestions and show appreciation for them.

5. Indicate by your mood and manner that you are genuinely interested in the person's idea.

Sammy Surefoot: *I'll listen to any reasonable idea. I judge an idea partly on what I know about the originator.*
Bizzi Busbee: *If a man is wasting my time, I can't resist letting him know about it.*
Ronnie Recluse: *If people would only follow procedures, all these lengthy discussions could be eliminated.*
Oaf MaGoof: *Some people are always bringing in hare-brained ideas.*

Principle No. IV: Give recognition for all new ideas and further commendations when deserved.

1. Recognize and commend the person privately by:
   a. A special conference, meeting, or conversation
   b. Appropriate memo, certificate, note, etc
   c. Entries on permanent records (employment, suggestion, etc)
2. Commend the individual publicly by:
   a. Announcing or presenting the idea before groups
   b. Appropriate articles in papers, journals, or periodicals
3. Recognize and commend the group or department as a whole when deserved.
   a. By publicity in various media
   b. By the supervisor in group meetings
   c. By banners, posters, signs, in the department

Sammy Surefoot: *A lot of things that my men are coming up with these days are things we worked on a long time ago. We paved the way.*
Bizzi Busbee: *If you make too much fuss about people's ideas, eventually they'll neglect their regular work in favor of idea work.*
Ronnie Recluse: *If a man doesn't hear from me, he's doing all right.*
Oaf MaGoof: *If you encourage a person too much, he'll make a pest of himself* ■

Simple Creativity Tests Can Be Helpful

ALVIN L SIMBERG
Supervisor of personnel research & development, A C Spark Plug Div
Dr RICHARD H HARRIS
Director of employe research, General Motors Corp

No one pretends that psychological testing is the complete answer to personnel selection; and few responsible companies makes selections solely on the basis of psychological tests. Actually the more responsible the company the fuller use it will make of *all* the measures of a man's suitability for a particular position.

But certainly every responsible company will attempt to improve its selection procedures, and carefully controlled studies suggest that some of the newest psychological and technological concepts show considerable promise.

What we are after is an instrument or tool that will give a supervisor some estimate of the creative ability of his staff—an estimate that can be used independently of job performance as a check and as a predictor of performance.

The *AC Test of Creative Ability* was an original work by the authors. It was based in part on earlier research by Prof J. P. Guilford of the University of Southern California. He had investigated the different factors involved in creativity and tried to measure them. The factors he isolated were: fluency, flexibility, ability to change set, ability to visualize new uses for common objects and, finally, a certain discontent with things as they are. Later studies have proved that the AC test can reliably differentiate individuals considered creative by their supervisors from those who are not.

Definitions Are No Problem

The most frequent objections to tests of creativity are that creativity has not been adequately defined, that the characteristics of creative men are unknown or unknowable, and that there are "different types" of creativity. All these are, in fact, quite academic and of little practical significance. Whenever we have set up an experiment and asked supervisors about creativity they were in substantial agreement on which men are or are not creative. As with intelligence, or the force of gravity, we all *know* what the characteristics are, even if we don't know precisely what causes them.

Our test was designed as an indicator of a person's ability to produce a number of unique ideas for a given situation in a given amount of time. The result is not an absolute measure of creativity but a relative ranking of the individual in his own company group.

In our company, we have established separate norms for engineers, supervisory personnel, and hourly rated personnel. We have found statistically valid differences in range and test scores for these groups.

The Test Itself

The test is in five parts. Each part is separately timed and the total working time is 80 minutes. There are no multiple-choice or true-false questions. Each answer must be created in the imagination of the person taking the test. Here is an example of each type:

1—In a thick fog in a major American harbor, a passenger liner moves cautiously toward its berth. The liner has the latest radar equipment, but the equipment is inoperative and the radar operator is unaware of this fact. Another boat approaches the liner amidships, and it is obvious that neither ship is aware of the other's presence. List all the things you think might happen as a consequence.

This test contains five such situations. You list as many possible consequences of each situation as you can. Scores are a function of quantity and a uniqueness of the imagined consequences. (20 min.)

2—List as many reasons as possible to explain the truth of this statement: Residents of Chicago consume, on the average, more Brazil nuts than residents of Omaha.

This is a test of general reasoning. Five unusual and not necessarily true statements are presented. You must marshal your arguments to make them seem reasonable. This part also yields a quantity and a uniqueness score. (10 min.)

3—List all the things you think are wrong with, or could be improved upon, in a wrist watch.

A test of awareness of the problems in five common appliances. This part yields a uniqueness score. (15 min.)

4—An Air Force pilot is told to take samples of air at five different altitudes up to 10,000 feet. For this purpose he is given a small plane with a nonpressurized cabin and five bottles with small openings that can be sealed with a cork. When he is ready to take off, it occurs to him that the bottles already contain ground-level air. This air has to be removed so that air at the varying altitudes can be collected. Rather than go to the trouble of locating a pump or other special device to create a vacuum in each bottle, how can he accomplish the assigned task?

This is a test of practical judgment. The five problem situations call for solutions that are least expensive and least time-consuming. This part yields a quality score. (20 min.)

5—How many uses can you think of for a common paper clip?

This is a test of originality. The five common objects yield both a quantity and a uniqueness score. (15 min.)

Scoring

The test produces three types of scores: Quantity (in Parts 1, 2, 5), Uniqueness (1, 2, 3, 5) and Quality (4). The measure of uniqueness is derived from a statistical tabulation—answers given infrequently get more points than the more common answers. Quality of a solution (in Part 4) is measured against a scale set by a panel of judges. The judges award highest scores to the least expensive and least time-consuming solution.

As you can see, though the test measures flexibility, fluency, problem sensitivity, and so on, imagination is still the prime requisite for a high score.

The Results

We insisted on two requirements for anyone wishing to use this test. The user first had to send someone to our offices to learn all aspects of administration, scoring and interpretation. Then a validation study had to be made, consisting of testing carefully selected groups within the user's company. These restrictions were not for our own benefit but rather to help the organization wishing to use the test—one might almost say for its protection. In this way we have a growing mass of data on the performance of the test itself plus a set of representative norms against which individual scores may be measured.

The original validation study was conducted on 36 engineers from two divisions of our company. Half of the 36 engineers had been rated by their supervisors as consistently producing many unique ideas; the others had rarely produced ideas of any kind. We found that the test differentiated between the two groups at the 1% level of statistical significance.

A second group of 35 engineers was selected, consisting of an entire design and development department. Superintendent and assistant superintendent had independently judged the individual's performance on creative tasks. Of the group, 22 were reported as consistently satisfactory, while the performance of the remaining 13 in this respect had, at one time or another, been unsatisfactory.

The difference in scores was remarkable. Individual scores varied from under 1000 to over 6000 but the mean of the low group was about 2200 while the mean of the high group was over 3500. So large a difference in means, combined with the relatively close clustering of the scores in each group around its mean, could not have been obtained by chance in more than one case out of one hundred. Thus the test again differentiated between two groups at the 1% significance level.

Thus far, we had been correlating the tests with ratings or opinions of superiors. A third study was then conducted, using the number of suggestions turned in by hourly rated employes as an objective measure of creativity. The study involved 28 pairs of individuals. Each pair had one man with an outstanding suggestion record and one with a poor suggestion record. Each pair was matched as nearly as possible—both men in the pair were from the same department, with the same supervisor, the same job classification and equivalent seniority. It was found that the quantity scores on the test were again related at the 1% level to the number of suggestions turned in by these people.

Still other types of criteria were sought. At MIT, 45 senior engineering students enrolled in a product design course were given the test. This course strongly emphasized imagination because of the nature of the material covered and the projects assigned. The instructor, Prof John Arnold, did not see the test results until after final grades had been assigned. The differences on test scores between students earning grades of A and students earning grades of B were again significant beyond the 1% level. In addition, the instructor had made subjective comments about the observed creative ability of each student. These were based upon his observation of their methods, questions and performance during the semester. Again, the test found differences closely associated with his comments.

The *AC Test of Creative Ability* has been tried in many divisions of General Motors Corporation as well as in many companies outside of General Motors. Complete validation studies have been undertaken at Underwood Corp, Dow Chemical, Smith-Kline-French, etc. All results were positive and significant. In other words, the test successfully differentiated between groups of people considered creative and not creative.

Everyone is looking for the man with ideas. It really does not matter so much whether he searches his own experience for ideas or whether he solves his problems piecemeal or whether he uses analogies. What is important, and most often overlooked, is that in all of these approaches he is using his imagination and developing ideas. If you can find a person who has ideas, and who is not reluctant to give them, you can infer that he would be a better risk than someone who does not demonstrate this ability. The *AC Test of Creative Ability* purports to measure the number of unique ideas which an individual can develop for a given situation.

Try It Yourself

We have no intention of making a profit out of this test and so it was offered to the Industrial Relations Center, University of Chicago, which is now making it available to interested users. This nonprofit organization is observing the cautions stated above and requests careful consideration before the test is used. The charges only cover printing costs.

Let us repeat, tests should never be used as the sole determinant in making personnel decisions. The employment interview can yield excellent indicators of interest, personality, maturity and appearance. A thorough interviewer will pay careful attention to references—the types of people listed and what they say. Former employers can help corroborate what the references say about honesty, stability, dependability and other character traits. Resumes of education and experience are also useful in assessing an individual. ■

are you CREATIVE?

ask your wife

Dr. J. H. McPherson, staff psychologist of the Dow Chemical Co., put together these statements about the nature of creative man. Alongside each statement, Mrs. McPherson (who also has her doctorate in psychology) has added the reaction of a wife who must live with such a man. In tests of engineer and scientist groups, it has clearly separated creative and non-creative men.

Do not attempt to measure your own creativity with the reaction list—give it to your wife and judge yourself by her reaction.

THE PSYCHOLOGIST SPEAKS

The original man seems to prefer the complex asymmetrical, unbalanced, vital, dynamic designs to the orderly symmetrical balanced designs.

A WIFE REACTS . . .

I like the living room to look "balanced", but no — he has to put it all off center.

He feels that a person should have the courage to probe deeply into his feelings, he shouldn't just take things as they are.

He has to understand everything. He talks about his feelings, his thoughts, asks me questions I can't answer. Why won't he let well enough alone?

When caught up in the process of putting ideas together he is apt to be so deeply engrossed that he appears out-of-contact and insensitive to human problems.

When he is in one of his deep periods he'll promise anything and promptly forget about it. Someday I'll fix him.

There is little doubt that most people dislike being confronted with disorder. In individuals who turn out original work in science or in art, however, a reversal of the usual attitude may be observed.

He seems to like a mess. I can't touch a thing.

His universe is more complex and in addition he usually lead's more complex life, seeking tension for the pleasure he obtains upon its discharge.

He seems to like having a problem to solve. Can't he just rest a little bit?

He likes to fool around with new ideas even if they turn out later to be a total waste of time.

Always ideas, some don't work at all. Costs money, too.

He can accept people whose manners and appearance are repulsive to others.

And the people he collects, ugh!

He often seems very gullible because he tends to be open to experience.

A crack-pot will corner him somewhere, he'll bring him home to dinner and you'd think we were entertaining Einstein.

The gullibility that contributes to his creativity may also make him a sucker for unscrupulous people.

He got so excited about a new potato peeler that he bought six. He was going to rig up a device where you pour a peck of potatoes in one end, turn a crank, and get peeled potatoes out at the other.

He seems to be haunted by problems and may feel that he deserves no credit for working on them.

I try to tell him how everybody appreciates his work but he acts like he shouldn't get any credit.. as if it were something he _had_ to do.

He may also tend to talk over his feelings with good friends and really let his hair down recognizing that by doing so he will be able to expend more of his energies toward his creative tasks.

I'd think he could keep a ~~few~~ things to himself.

He is frequently unimpressed by titles and other symbols of status success.

We could afford a Cadillac but he's got to keep that old Chevrolet.

He may, in the process of analyzing the kind of work environment that benefits him, devise strange habits that others don't readily understand.

Can you imagine, he says he thinks better out on a hill on the farm. He built a shelter so he can go there in the rain.

He can be a relentless worker when he starts on a project and tends to forget usual social commitments.

We'll plan to go somewhere, have the tickets and everything, the party all arranged, and he'll forget to come home.

Because the solution has not been verbalized, it is difficult for him to discuss it.

Sometimes I'll make the mistake of asking him about his work when he seems depressed. He'll glower and saw the air with his hands and say nothing. Wish I hadn't asked.

He has trouble accepting the usual theological arguments.

Our minister doesn't come to call anymore. Always arguments and the children don't know what to believe.

He seems possessed of a constant constructive discontent, an almost chronic dissatisfaction with things as they are.

It doesn't matter how well somebody's house is built, he can always think of a better way to do it. It's embarrassing at times. ■

How to Set up Brainstorming Sessions

Brainstorming is the name Alex Osborn (author of the much-quoted book, *Applied Imagination*) gives the uninhibited group approach to idea-getting. It requires green-light thinking, makes maximum use of free association as ideas ricochet from one person to another. Sessions are always less than an hour, often as short as 15 minutes. But concentration is intense. Best results seem to come when 8 to 12 people sit in—people with similar interests but with varied backgrounds.

Goal of the brainstorm is to get at least 50 ideas per session. Willard Pleuthner, vice president of Batton, Barton, Durstine & Osborn, the advertising firm that has wrung the most spectacular successes from this method, says 6% to 10% of the ideas generated in these "mental hitchhiking" sessions are worth following up.

BBD&O's four rules for brainstorming emphasize an unfettered atmosphere as participants "go to play" on a problem unhampered by judicial reasoning, "must's," "do's," "don't's," and "can't's."

Rule 1. Don't criticize ideas. There's time later for judicial thinking. Anybody who snipes or pooh-poohs is penalized—pays for a round of coffee or puts a dollar in the kitty.

Rule 2. Welcome free wheeling. The wilder the idea, the better. It's easier to tame down ideas than to think them up. A "can-you-top-this?" attitude is encouraged. Participants use others' ideas as jumping-off places for their own.

Rule 3. Strive for quantity. Even remote connections and screwy suggestions sow the seed for fruitful thoughts. Top-of-the-head pacesetters break the ice for reflective contributors.

Rule 4. Combine and improve. Since ideas are like building blocks, panel members are encouraged to suggest how others' ideas can be made better—or how two or more can be turned into one idea that's still better than either one alone. Pleuthner also advises this procedure for fruitful brainstorming:

...*Brief panelists a couple of days ahead* of time with a one-page memo. Give two examples of the type of methods or solutions needed to fit the limitations of procedures now in use. For example, suppose you want to find a new method for improving communications. Your memo might sum up the problem, present pertinent information, then state that lots of plans are already under way to improve *written* methods. But you want ways to improve *face-to-face* communications—such as 5-min. Monday morning quarterback talks by the plant superintendent to insure at least one weekly conversation with every worker.

...*Allow the man who poses the problem* to answer questions for the first 5 minutes of the session. After that, the wraps are off.

Other pointers—Charles S. Whiting offers some advice on group idea-getting. He was a member of a group in Professor George F. Doriot's Harvard Business School class on manufacturing that wrote "Imagination—Undeveloped Resource," an evaluation of programs and techniques for stimulating creative thinking in business. Here's what he suggests:

...*Be sure ideas are recorded*—On a blackboard, or by tape or secretary. Good ideas may be forgotten or lost in the shuffle.

...*Hold sessions in the morning*—If people are to continue work on the same problem in the afternoon. Otherwise, hold sessions late in the day. The excitement of a brainstorming session continues for several hours, may interfere with an employee's routine task.

...*Keep rank of participants fairly equal.* It takes a lot of warming up for a foreman to mix his ideas freely with those of the plant manager.

IS BRAINSTORMING NEW?

Maybe you've been noting something familiar about brainstorming and creative thinking. Because in the main we are rediscovering ideas that are centuries old. But we're bringing together in one package some of the methods that have been systematized and popularized only within the last 25 years. Here are a few of them:

...*Work Simplification.* A. H. Mogensen, high priest of Work Simplification, was probably the first industrial engineer to realize that almost anybody in industry—if properly taught—can apply the principles of motion-and-time study.

...*Job Methods Training.* Good old JMT from World War II days was the next try to formalize and direct workers' and foremen's thinking toward improving methods in the plant. Remember the formula for developing new methods? *Eliminate, combine, rearrange, simplify.* Alex Osborn enlarged upon these four steps in his "idea needlers."

...*Suggestion systems.* Cash awards and prestige help provide the incentive that makes people *want* to create. This stimulus is essential to anybody's creativity—yours or your employees'.

...*Buzz sessions*—As Phillips Petroleum does in its well-known "66" method, split big groups into real small ones, to attack a problem quickly, to kick ideas around freely to find better ones.

...*Problem-solving conferences*—especially those employing the "laundry list" technique. In this method the leader takes any suggestion whatever from the floor and writes it on the blackboard. He doesn't permit any challenge or evaluation at this stage. The technique differs from buzz sessions in that there is a formal approach to getting the ideas for solving the problem.

Teamwork gets you more ideas than lone-wolfing

How A. C. Studt of Hotpoint initiates ideas:

As an imagination ice-breaker at each session, Studt narrates an involved and harrowing tale. Just when his listeners are gripping the edge of their chairs, Studt breaks off, says, "Now you finish the story." Supervisors must do this in writing. He reads several completions before the class, notes their uniqueness and the variety of turns the story takes in the minds of different people.

Three new attacks—Group brainstorming is the central theme of the course, but Studt recognizes it won't handle every problem that comes up. Instead he suggests management people try the following entirely new approaches. Two can be used by two men working together; the third, by a man working alone.

. . . *Tear-down method.* Two men pick an operating practice to brainstorm. Man No. 1 takes the attitude that everything about the present way is wrong, then suggests another way (not necessarily better, just different). Man No. 2 is forbidden to agree with him. He must, in turn, suggest another way. Man No. 1 disagrees, suggests still a third way. This continues. Eventually one suggestion clicks. The two men get together, engineer their idea down to earth.

. . . *And-also method.* Same problem as above, but this time each must agree with the other's suggestion, then add to it. For example, Man No. 1 suggests a way to improve scheduling. Man No. 2 says, "Good idea. *And also* we could improve upon it by . . . ," and he adds to the idea. This goes on until they reach a sound solution.

. . . *17-solutions method*—to be used by one man working alone. Before a conference, the problem under study is written out and sent to each departmental supervisor concerned. Ticket of admission to the meeting is a list of 17 solutions. By the time duplications and impossible solutions are struck out of 100 or more answers, there may be only five or six good ones left. But this is an encouraging start. How did Studt pick 17 as the magic number? He says, "The number of solutions you request is up to you; 17 just happened to sound good to me." ∎

HOW TO KILL IDEAS

These comments sound familiar? Look out then. They're 24 idea chillers selected from a list of 56 put together by the New York Chapter of the American Society of Training Directors at a Brainstorming Workshop last year.

- Don't be ridiculous.
- We tried that before.
- It cost too much.
- That's beyond our responsibility.
- It's too radical a change.
- We don't have the time.
- That will make other equipment obsolete.
- We're too small for it.
- Not practical for operating people.
- The union will scream.
- We've never done it before.
- Let's get back to reality.
- That's not our problem.
- Why change it, it's still working o.k.
- You're two years ahead of your time.
- We're not ready for that.
- It isn't in the budget.
- Can't teach an old dog new tricks.
- Top management would never go for it.
- We'll be the laughing stock.
- We did all right without it.
- Let's shelve it for the time being.
- Let's form a committee.
- Has anyone else ever tried it?
- Too hard to sell.
- It won't work in our industry.

Have trouble coming up with new ideas?

Program your inventions

Try this step-by-step approach.
It won't make an Edison of you, but it's
guaranteed to improve your idea output

JOHN H. BICKFORD, Senior Development Engineer, Veeder-Root Inc, Hartford, Conn

A great deal has been written about creativity in the last few years, but most of the articles have concentrated so heavily on the management or psychological aspects that they have been of little practical help to the man on the board. It is possible, however, with our present understanding of creativity, to define a concrete procedure for the man who wants to multiply his ideas. The procedure is similar to a computer program; it consists of a series of questions that lead a designer in a logical progression from a problem to a solution. The most sophisticated computer in the world is helpless unless the questions it is asked are reduced to its level of intelligence. Man's brain is far superior to the best computers, yet even the brain can be aided by formal procedures or programs that reduce a complicated task to a series of easier steps.

The program given here won't convert you to a Master Inventor, however. True invention requires such things as intuition, inspiration, and imagination—creative mental processes we really can't define or control. Maybe some got it and some ain't! Past experience plays a large part, too, and this the program cannot supply. But the program is still useful. Most employers neither expect nor want real invention from their designers. They can't afford it, at least not as a steady diet. They want ingenuity; practical, patentable designs. This program should help you produce ideas of that sort.

A few general comments are in order before we push the START button. **As you go through the program, write down your ideas.** No computer could operate without a memory of some sort, and you will need one too. Don't depend on the one you were born with; it's too unreliable when you're dealing with complex problems. It's likely to forget things it doesn't think are important, yet an unimportant idea, combined with another idea later on, may lead to the solution you are looking for. Putting your ideas down in black and white also helps you clarify and refine them; so record your thoughts with words and sketches.

Another rule of equal importance: **Work hard! You may not look like you're working when you're trying to come up with a new idea; but in fact you are working as hard as you ever have before if you are doing it right.** It's downright exhausting; maybe that's why so few people ever really do it. But if you are a designer, it is part of your job, and after awhile your boss will realize that the results justify the time you spend staring at the wall. He must do the same thing at times.

Another rule: **Don't skip any of the steps or questions in the program because you don't think they apply to your particular problem.** The program is specifically intended to lead you in directions you would not normally go. The best ideas are often found in the least likely places. Make a conscious effort to answer each question, then make a second effort to relate that answer to your actual problem.

One final rule: **Don't be too critical of your ideas at first.** Record and study even the ones that seem pretty far out. Combined with another idea later, or modified in some as-yet-unseen way, they may be just what you are looking for. Better still, a wild idea may

Don't forget! Record all your ideas!

Table I . . . Possible Specifications for New Products

Functional life (consistent with price)	Strength	Other costs
	Stiffness	Resistance to:
Stability vs time or environment	Fits available space	Wear
Accuracy	Dynamic balance	Vibration
Safety	Stress levels	Corrosion
Ease of operation	Strength-weight ratio	Dirt
Noise	Overload capacity	Vacuum
Ease of maintenance	Speed capability	Heat
Appearance	Operating costs	Cold
Ease of installation	Operating time	Humidity
Flexibility, versatility in use	Meets legal requirements	Fatigue
Efficiency	Size	Shock
Compatible with associated equipment	Weight	Other performance requirements
	Configuration	Other functional requirements
Sales features not otherwise covered	Manufacturing cost	Human-engineering requirements
	Assembly cost	

lead you into a whole new area where you will find practical solutions as well as impractical ones. Try to avoid talking to the boss or to fellow workers when you're chasing the wild ones. They'll shame you out of this approach and get you "back to work." But you've got to be different to be novel, and it really helps to overdo the novelty for a while to force your mind off the beaten track.

Well, let's try it! The general procedure is simple: Start at the beginning and answer every question as thoroughly and as thoughtfully as you can. Work! Try to think of other questions that will help you, and answer them too. Then go on to "Add-Combine" and subsequent steps and do the same. Ready? Good luck!

Start—define

What?—What have I been asked to do? What specifications apply? (Everything you can think of: See Table I for some possibilities.)

Are all these requirements really necessary?

What is the problem *behind* the stated problem? (Eg, we want a better hammer in order to drive nails. The problem behind the problem is "to drive nails.")

Would we be willing to solve the problem behind the problem instead of the stated problem? (Eg, instead of designing a new hammer, we find a new way of driving nails.)

Is there a problem behind the problem behind the problem? (Eg, we want to drive nails in order to fasten wood together.)

Do we want to solve *this* problem instead? (Keep digging deeper until you reach a point beyond which you don't care to go. Your boss may or may not be interested in having you suggest new ways of joining wood when he asks for a better hammer!)

Why?—Why is *this* a problem? (Can't drive nails with our bare hands because they go in too hard. Can't use other tools because they haven't been designed to drive nails. Again, probe the "whys" until you've gone beyond a practical limit.)

Subdivide—Can I break the problem down into smaller parts that I can understand more clearly? (For example,

a machine problem might be broken down into a clutch problem plus a drive problem plus a frame problem, etc. Block diagrams are often helpful in this step.)

Re-define—Do the definitions of the problems suggest specific solutions?

If so, can I redefine the problems to avoid these suggestions?

How many ways can I restate the problems I have defined? (Use a dictionary or a thesaurus to find new words that are equivalent to key words in your original definitions. New words often suggest radically different solutions.)

Now that I have probed the problem and the prob-

Instead of designing a new hammer, perhaps we should find a new way to drive nails.

lems behind it, can I think of new specifications? New sub-problems? New sub-parts?

Program—Can I think of any other questions which will help me define and understand the problem? (This program won't be ideal for every designer on every problem. Try to modify and extend it as you work.)

Think big

Use the list below to locate all of the general areas where a solution to all or part of your problem might be found. Don't overlook combinations of two or more areas, even though combinations don't appear on this list.

General Areas

Mechanical	Optical	Acoustical
Electrical	Hydraulic	Thermal
Electronic	Pneumatic	Nuclear
Chemical		
	Other?	

Explore—Have I really marked all possible areas of solution, or did I only mark those where I have a tentative solution in the back of my mind?

If cost were no object, would I mark others?

If I adopt one of my other definitions of the problem, would I mark others?

Have I avoided areas where my own experience is limited? (If you admit there may be solutions here in spite of your own inexperience, try to talk to someone who is familiar with the area in question.)

Think small (but hard!)

Select—Now select one of the general areas you have marked on the list and use the questions below to find as many specific solutions to your total problem as you can. If your total problem is very complex, start by finding programmed solutions to sub-problems. Then use the program again to combine these to solve the whole problem.

Remember, don't be too critical of your ideas at this stage; you'll get to that later. Besides, many of the answers to the questions below won't really be solutions to your problem. It is hoped that the answers will suggest solutions, but they can do that only if you temporarily accept even the wild ones.

When you have run dry on one category or one sub-problem, try another. Sometimes it helps to keep a separate piece of paper going on each, doing all categories simultaneously; an idea in one classification often suggests similar ideas in the others.

Work hard! This step is the toughest, and, in the final analysis, is the one that counts the most. There is no particular order to most of the questions in this group, so you may skip around if you wish; but answer them all.

How—How has this been done in the past?

Why?—Why was it done this way? (Tradition? Patent reasons? Limit of skill or of technology? Cost? No known reason?)

Are the original reasons still valid?

How would I do this if I were the original designer?

Way out—How would I have done it if I were designing it in 1000 BC?

How would I design it if it were to be used as a prop in a science fiction movie?

Back—Is there anything in Nature that suggests a parallel? (Consider animals, insects, plant life, natural structures and systems.)

Consider insects.

Is there an "unnatural" way to do this?

Have we ever done anything like this before on any project?

Beauty—If appearance were the most important requirement, how would I do it? (Don't laugh at this one! Superb design is always beautiful.)

Invert—How is this done in other products?

How is this done in other civilizations?

Can I reverse the parts of this thing? (Eg, hold the shaft and let the frame rotate?)

Can I turn it inside out? Upside down? Mirror image? Backwards?

Imagine you are part of the machine.

Table II

Mechanical	Electrical	Acoustical, Hydraulic, Pneumatic
Force	Voltage	Pressure
Displacement	Charge	Volume
Velocity	Current	Volume Flow
Mass	Inductance	Mass Flow
Spring Compliance (1/K)	Capacitance	Capacitance (cavity)
Friction (viscous)	Resistance	Resistance (restriction)

Inside—How would I do this if I were part of the machine? (Most machines are extensions of man.)

Convert—Is there an electrical analog for the mechanical method of doing this? Or vice versa? Table II is a brief list of analogs to help you.

Cycle—Can I improve the analog? Simplify it? Find alternates? Now reconvert to original area (from electrical back to mechanical).

Refine—Do any of the following words or phrases suggest solutions? (Take them slowly, one at a time.)

    Combine features or parts

    Expand function

    Reduce function

    Eliminate parts or features

    Share function (one part do several jobs)

    Scatter (part here, part there)

    Change location of major parts

    Change sequence of operation

Jog—Does a specific solution or type of solution keep forcing itself on my mind? If so, why? Afraid I can't find others? Custom? Habit? Some special feature that looks good? (Watch out for this too. It's easy to fall in love with a novel idea if it's yours. Don't stop at one; go back and try again.)

How—How would I do this if my life depended on it?
How would I do this if cost were no object?
How would I do this underwater?
How would I do this in space?

Play—How would I do this if it were to be used as a toy? (Want maximum play value.)

Clarify—How would I do this if it were to be used to teach others how to do it? (Most easily understood way.)

Program—Any other questions that will help suggest solutions? (Extend and improve your program.)

Add—combine

Now use a matrix to find combinations of the ideas you have produced so far. List five or so of your better ideas across the top and list the same five down the side (see example, next page). Don't hesitate to include a few "impractical" ideas. This is your best chance to combine them with others to produce something both practical *and* novel. Think carefully about each combination suggested by the matrix. The key to most invention is "a new combination of old ideas," so study your list for every valid association of ideas it reveals.

Now build a second matrix with some of your other ideas. Add a few of the better ideas produced by your first matrix. Keep combining until you run dry.

Select

By now you should have a pretty good list of possible solutions. Some will sound good because they are so familiar you know they will work. Others will sound good because they are really different and they're yours!! Now is the time to show you're a man, not a boy. You've got to pick the one idea that is most likely to meet the required specifications; not the idea most likely to satisfy your ego. You've shown you could be an inventor, and hopefully one or more of your inventions will satisfy the requirements established and like those listed at the beginning of this article. But have the strength of character to pick "the old way" if that is still the best. Whichever way you do it, stick with it; don't be deflected easily by outside "advice" and suggestions. Sometimes a man with ideas needs more protection from his friends than from his enemies—friends can help and protect you into mediocrity.

Pick a solution by intuition if you wish, mentally comparing the most promising ideas to your list of specifications. If you prefer instead to continue a step-by-step approach for this part of the job, read "Forced Decision for Value," by John Fasal in the April 12, 1965, PRODUCT ENGINEERING. Mr Fasal uses probability techniques to identify the most likely solution from a long list of suggestions. His procedure takes a lot of the guess-

Maximum play value.

	1.	2.	3.	4.	5.
1. Ratchet, slip clutch, transparent plastic housing	▨				
2. Step motor, movable base, pneumatic indicator		▨			
3. Solenoid and pawl, cycloidal gearing, mechanical indicator			▨		★
4. Geneva, torque motor, row of colored disks				▨	
5. Audible "indicator", pneumatic motor, bellows and pawl					▨

Column headers: 1. Ratchet, slip clutch, transparent plastic housing; 2. Step motor, movable base, pneumatic indicator; 3. Solenoid and pawl, cycloidal gearing, mechanical indicator; 4. Geneva, torque motor, row of colored disks; 5. Audible "indicator", pneumatic motor, bellows and pawl

Matrix for combining tentative solutions—The square marked with a star suggests combinations of solutions 3 and 5. One possibility: pneumatic motor, pawl, mechanical indicator with audible overload signal.

work out of complicated design decisions by reducing them to a programmed series of simplified questions and calculations.

Develop

In spite of all the work you have done so far, the chances are excellent that you still don't *really* understand the problem. You made headway in Part I, and your attempt to find solutions probably brought you farther; but you're not there yet. This step should do it, however.

Take the solution you have just selected and develop it. Work out the details. How would you make it? Size, shape, materials, everything. Keep working until you see all the ramifications of this approach. Don't stop when you hit the first unexpected problem (there will be many!) but keep working on this "solution" until you have a design of sorts. Your understanding of the problem, and of the sub-problems, is now really deep. And yet, if you have followed the program faithfully, you can *still* be objective and imaginative in your final design; you will understand that the idea you have just developed isn't the only way, or you will be able to combine this idea with others to solve the problems you have uncovered.

Recycle

If you have picked your "most promising" solution carefully, and the design development revealed no overwhelming new problems, you can now fold your pencil and silently (and proudly) steal away. If you have doubts about your design, however, or think you see other solutions that should be carried at least this far, then you should re-cycle (like a computer) to an earlier part of the program and repeat some or all of the steps you have taken. It's often helpful, after working out the first design, to repeat the *whole* program; your understanding of the problem is so much better you can often re-define it and find many new solutions.

It's also helpful at this point to work on another problem for a while. Let your mind rest on this one, if your schedule permits it. Your "computer" will continue working on the problem even though you aren't conscious of this effort and your second trip through the program will be improved as a result.

Stop

Well, that's it! Write it down; work hard; and don't skip any steps. See you in the *Patent Gazette*. ∎

Pick a solution by intuition, if you wish.

SHOULD YOU USE OUTSIDE INVENTORS?

GEORGE S. HASTINGS
Vice-president in Charge of Patents
American Machine & Foundry Co.

Should a company solicit ideas from outside inventors? Corporate consensus on this question is emphatically no! First of all, any sort of solicitation greatly increases the number of ideas to be screened without a corresponding increase in the number of useful ideas received.

Secondly, solicitation increases the legal risk. There is an implied obligation to pay for ideas used and it might not be at all easy to prove that you had the idea long before it was submitted.

And suppose a number of different people submit the same idea? If it is a good one it would be almost impossible to use it with fair credit (and remuneration) to everyone concerned.

1 Initial screening

2 Secure an option on the new product

3 Determine technical feasibility

4 Determine patent feasibility

5 Determine marketing feasibility

6 Study the relationship of the submitted idea to the company's business. A good way of doing this is to compare a list of the company's manufacturing and other facilities, skills, selling ability, research and engineering background, and so on against the requirements of the submitted product.

7 Test for degree of completion (see chart.

There are several steps common to good evaluation procedure. The procedure first applies those tests which are inexpensive and most likely to determine the unsuitability of the particular product.

A number of companies have considered this problem and have decided that it is still worth the risk. They have set up procedures somewhat as follows:

1 Personnel likely to receive such disclosures are instructed to send them immediately to a single, responsible, administrative person. Such disclosures are not seen by technical or engineering personnel until ground rules have been established with the outside submitter.

2 Ground rules are established by sending the submitter an agreement form which he is asked to sign and return. This form sets forth the basis on which the company will receive the disclosure. It has a number of conditions: no confidential relation; no commitment is made to compensate; the company does not agree to do more than state whether it is interested; it is suggested that the submitter's sole remedy is to enforce his rights under the patent laws.

Inventors tend to be somewhat suspicious of corporations. Anything which relieves suspicion helps negotiations.

Inventors tend to put too high a value on their inventions. The remedy is a sense of values on the part of the corporate negotiator. Where significant facts are missing, allowance must be made for the possibility that the missing facts are adverse.

Do not narrow the company's future. Be stiff about agreements to keep the invention confidential, about grant-back clauses (particularly exclusive ones) and about agreements not to use or not to enter the same field for a period of time.

How is a fair royalty determined? The inventor must be paid out of the profits. He will be getting about one-third of the pre-tax income if the figure is 5%. This is probably about the top royalty for a profitable invention developed to a point just short of the going-business stage. ■

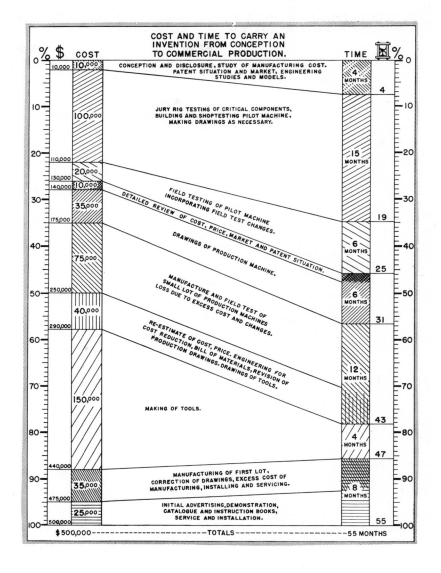

COST AND TIME TO CARRY AN INVENTION FROM CONCEPTION TO COMMERCIAL PRODUCTION

Patent Law—and the Characteristics

A patentable invention is a concrete, workable expression of an idea that is new and useful. It can be a new and useful proposal derived from an old combination of parts or steps in a process; or from a new combination; or from partly old and partly new elements or steps. It can be a new article of manufacture, a process, a machine, a composition of matter, a plant, or a design. It must not be merely a thing that is more convenient, easier to operate, cheaper, lighter, adjustable, simpler, or any one of the ordinary comparative advances in an industry resulting from the application of ordinary mechanical skill, standard electrical technique, or engineering or scientific knowledge.

Art or Process

A manufacturing process is clearly an "art", within the meaning of the law. Goodyear's patent was for a process—vulcanizing india-rubber by subjecting it to a high temperature when mixed with sulfur and a mineral salt. The apparatus for performing the process was not patented, and was not relevant to the patent. In Nielson's patent for applying a hot-blast to furnaces by forcing the blast through a vessel situated between the blowing apparatus and furnace, the form of the heated vessel was stated by the patent to be immaterial.

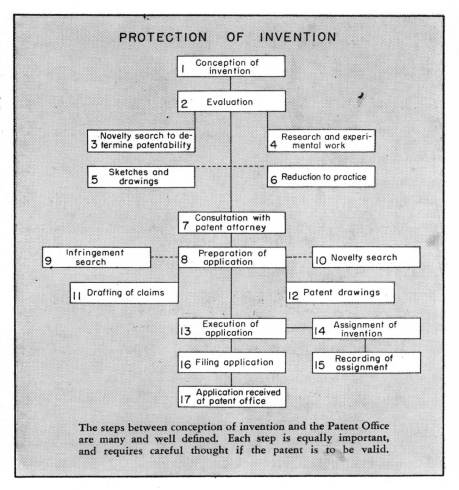

PROTECTION OF INVENTION

1 Conception of invention

2 Evaluation

3 Novelty search to determine patentability

4 Research and experimental work

5 Sketches and drawings

6 Reduction to practice

7 Consultation with patent attorney

9 Infringement search

8 Preparation of application

10 Novelty search

11 Drafting of claims

12 Patent drawings

13 Execution of application

14 Assignment of invention

16 Filing application

15 Recording of assignment

17 Application received at patent office

The steps between conception of invention and the Patent Office are many and well defined. Each step is equally important, and requires careful thought if the patent is to be valid.

Machines

The term "machine" as used in the patent statute includes every mechanical device or combination of power units and devices to perform a function and produce an effect. However, a person cannot describe a machine that will perform a specified function, and then claim he has patented the function itself and all other machines that might be invented to perform such a function. Function is not patentable as defined in the statute.

Manufactures

The term "manufacture" as used in the patent law, has a comprehensive sense, embracing whatever is made by man, not including a machine, a composition of matter, or a design. Articles of manufacture can be new in the commercial sense, and not new in the sense of the patent law. New articles of commerce are not patentable as new manufactures, unless it is proven that the production of the new article involved the exercise of invention or discovery beyond what was necessary to construct the apparatus for its manufacture or production.

Improvements

Mere improvement without invention is not patentable, and the fact that a substituted device is greatly superior to the one it replaces is not of itself proof of invention. To be patentable, improvement must be a product of original conception—the more extended application of an original idea is not invention.

The law regards a change as evidence of novelty. It also recognizes degree of change, dividing inventions into primary and secondary, and giving proportionate dominion to the claims granted. Thus, an invention can be broadly new, subjecting all that comes after it to tribute; or, it can be only a step in a series of developments, and limited, therefore, to its precise form and elements. The latter type has as firm a right to protection as the former.

A patent for an improvement will be granted if invention is proved, even though the patentee of neither the original device nor the improvement can use his invention alone. This may lead to a deadlock. The only way out of such a situation is by common ownership or cross licensing.

# of Invention

H. A. TOULMIN, JR.
Toulmin & Toulmin, Dayton, Ohio

Some Highlights of Patent Law

- A person other than the inventor can file a patent application if the real inventor has sold the invention to another and then refuses to sign the application. Likewise, when there are two or more joint inventors if one or more of them refuses to sign, his co-inventor can sign for him.
- If an innocent mistake is made as to who are joint inventors, either before or after the patent issues, the mistake can be corrected when it is proven to be an honest one and the facts show it is a mistake.
- New uses for old processes, articles of manufacture and products can be patented.
- If an idea is new, useful and inventive, it can be protected. It makes no difference whether an idea is born of continuing research or came suddenly; whether it is the work of a genius or a moron; it is still patentable.
- A person can infringe a patent not only by taking all of it, but also by taking a part of it or even inducing another to do so. This is "contributory infringement." Likewise, anyone selling a component of a claim on a patented machine, combination, composition, material or apparatus for use in practicing a patented process, which is an especially adapted part of the patented combination, is an infringer of the patent. This infringement takes place even though only one element of the patented claims especially adapted to the claim is sold or furnished to complete the invention covered by the patent.
- If the Government decides an idea is too "hot" to be made public, it can be held in the Patent Office under orders of secrecy. During this time, the inventor or his company will be compensated by the Government for this action in keeping the invention under wraps. The penalty for disclosure of such ideas is very severe.
- Taxpayers who conduct research and experimental work are given the right to deduct these experimental expenditures as an expense of doing business. No longer must one capitalize such expenditures and write off the capitalization in small increments over a number of years. Now they can be wiped off in the year they occur.

Note: Proposed changes in patent law are outlined on pages 292 to 294.

Composition of Matter

According to a court decision: "A patentable composition of matter may well result or be formed by the intermixture of two or more ingredients, which develop a different or additional property or properties which the several ingredients individually do not possess in common."

The discovery, that acetone used as a solvent for acetylene gas made a solution having none of the explosive properties of either substance singly and therefore could be safely handled, was held patentable.

Designs

The Act of Congress which authorized the grant of patents for designs contemplated appearance more than utility. It is not the manner in which the appearance is produced but the appearance itself, that is the patentable element.

Some designs can be protected under the design patent law, the copyright law, or the new trademark law, and the owner of the design can choose the law under which he will seek protection.

Scientific Principles

Scientific principles and laws of nature belong to the common storehouse of public knowledge. Therefore, discoveries that reveal new fundamental scientific principles are not patentable. However, as soon as such a discovery is given a concrete application for the creation of a new art, or the advancement of a known art, it becomes invention.

Personal Factors

Legally, an inventor can only be a natural person, not a corporation. When two inventors work together for a common end, finally accomplished by the contributions and united efforts of both, the invention is joint. Neither can secure a valid patent as the sole inventor.

Even when one person conceives the entire invention, and another makes a suggestion needed to make the conception a success, it makes them joint inventors.

A person directing others to carry out his general ideas can be an inventor, even though he is not the actual discoverer of the particular thing that constitutes the final invention. The accomplishment of the associate is considered an expression of the intellectual activity of the principal.

Because the law protecting invention is based on the idea of promoting public welfare, it requires that the patent be sufficiently explicit to enable others to benefit from the ideas. The proposer must have something more than a general idea; he must show in what manner it can be done.

The law encourages sufficient delay on the part of the inventor, before he makes his disclosure, for him to determine that his invention is workable. However, an inventor must not abandon his idea, but must complete it and disclose it promptly. If he drops it and another person completes it and makes it known to the public, then the second person is the inventor. Invention is based on successful accomplishment. Mere experimental work is not recognized as invention.

The standard of success can be low; the invention need not have achieved complete commercial form. It need not be in such shape that it can be sold to the public. The invention must merely be sufficiently operable so that any one skilled in the art, by applying knowledge and engineering talent in that art to the proposal of the inventor, could make it practicable.

The latter step is not necessary on the part of the inventor. Most important inventions have been crude in their initial stages, but their disclosures have been sufficient to teach

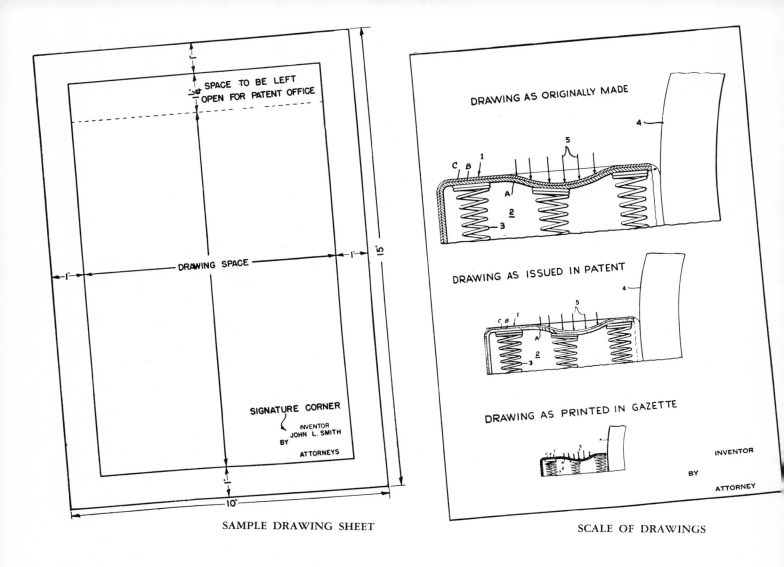

SAMPLE DRAWING SHEET

SCALE OF DRAWINGS

Drawings that accompany a patent application should be made in a definite size and style. A better drawing does not guarantee a valid patent; however, anything that can be done to point out salient features of the invention to the examiner will save time, and avoid possible litigation later. Drawings also help determine intended coverage. Information as to size, lettering, shading, dimensions, standard symbols and other patent drawing practice can be obtained from the U. S. Patent Office.

the principles involved and to show the way to full utilization of the invention. That is all the law requires.

It is not important that the inventor specify all the uses to which his invention can be put. To mention one legitimate use is sufficient. It would be impossible for the inventor to predict the wide range of uses to which his invention might be applied over a period of seventeen years.

Patent Procedure

THE INVENTOR usually passes through the first stage of speculation, investigation and finally conception. This takes place first in his mind and then in drawings and sketches. Then follows reduction of the development to a working model, to enable tests of the workability of the idea to be made.

As far as the patent law is concerned, an inventive idea can be merely on paper; if it is clear, workable, and new, a valid patent can be obtained. For commercial reasons, however, it is desirable that some development work be done. It is usually safer for the average inventor to do this work before securing a patent rather than do it later in haste.

The patent application consists of a petition; specification; oath; a drawing if necessary; claims; filing fee; and usually a power of attorney to the lawyer, which authorizes him to act before the Patent Office on behalf of the inventor.

The first step in obtaining a patent is to furnish a patent lawyer with a description of the invention, together with drawings, photographs or a model. An inventor can file and prosecute his own application, but he will not find it easy to do this in view of complex Patent Office practice.

The attorney should be qualified to practice before the United States Patent Office, and must be on the roster of such attorneys, in good standing. A patent attorney should be skilled not only in law, but also in the arts and sciences, preferably in engineering. He should have had practical experience in patent litigation in the United States courts.

The attorney will search the Patent Office records in Washington and the literature of the particular art, to see whether the idea is new. If he finds it new, he prepares a description of the invention stating its objectives, its accomplishments and how it works.

Specification

The scope of every patent is limited to the invention described in the claims, and in accordance with the specification. According to the courts: "The specification and claims of a patent constitute a contract between the United States and the patentee and they should be read and construed together, not for the purpose of limiting, contracting, or expanding the claims, but for the purpose of ascertaining from the entire agreement the actual intent of the parties." However, the claims, not the specifications afford "the measure of the grant to the patentee."

The specification concludes with a series of numbered paragraphs, called "claims". Each of these claims covers the particular property of the invention which the inventor hopes to monopolize. Some of the claims are broad and are usually brief. Others are somewhat narrower and more detailed, and some include practically all of the separate elements.

In making up his claims, the inventor should keep in mind that there are several classes of patents: Mechanical patents for manufactured products and machines—these include electrical, aerodynamic, and hydraulic constructions; chemical patents for materials and chemical processes; and design patents, which cover form and appearance, usually emphasizing artistic features not essential to mechanical operation of the device.

Patents can be classified in another way: Some deal with the apparatus itself, and others cover the method of operation of the apparatus. An apparatus patent, for example, can have claims that call for the combination of a wheel, an axle, a body, and a steering gear. In a method patent claims must not be tied down to any particular mechanism. The number of necessary claims is not limited.

Drawings

The drawings accompanying a patent and its claims are illuminating when the question of prior art and intended coverage is at issue. Drawings can be referred to for illustration and can be used to interpret the specification or claim. Drawings cannot fill the absence of a written description; however, they serve to add clearness and certainty to what is actually described.

The description of an invention as contained in the claims; interpreted in the light of the specifications, is neither restricted nor extended by the drawings. An evident mistake in a figure in the drawings will not render a patent invalid.

When the application is filed in the Patent Office it is accompanied by a government fee of thirty dollars, with an additional fee of one dollar for each additional claim over twenty. The application is then assigned to the particular part of the Patent Office which examines that class of inventions.

After the application is filed and examined by the examining division, the Patent Office replies to the attorney, allowing or rejecting the claims and indicating any objections to the drawings, or the subject matter of the specification and its wording. Usually the Patent Office refers to anticipating patents and publications, which must be ordered, studied, and discussed in detail when replying to the Patent Office. The inventor or his attorney has six months to reply to this action. Failure to reply to the Patent Office, or an incomplete response within six months after the Patent Office replies to the inventor or his attorney, causes abandonment of the patent. Under certain conditions, it can be restored.

At this stage the applicant, or his attorney can amend the claims, so they will not conflict with the prior art; or he can cancel them; or his answer can be a combination of claim cancellation, amendment and argument. This correspondence terminates in a final allowance or final rejection of the application.

Upon final allowance, the final fee of 30 dollars is paid and the patent is made ready for issuance. When it is issued, a summary of it is published in the Official Gazette of the Patent Office.

The File Wrapper

THE FILE WRAPPER HISTORY of a patent application is the complete file starting with the original papers as filed in the Patent Office, and continuing until the application is finally allowed or rejected. These papers are preserved in the Patent Office for twenty years. Changes made in the original application are indicated by pen corrections on the first of the original papers. These corrections are made by the Patent Office, under the authority of each reply from the applicant or his attorney.

If the application becomes abandoned or finally rejected, the papers remain secret unless opened under special conditions. If, however, the patent is allowed, the file wrapper history becomes public, and any one may order a copy of it. The accompanying illustration shows a typical Patent Office action, a reply, and the corrections made on the original specification and claim as the result of these written negotiations.

The contents of a file wrapper cannot be used to test a patent. Its only uses are: (1) to interpret the language of a patent, when that language might have two different, but legitimate meanings; and (2) to prevent a patentee from applying to the claim a meaning inconsistent with its history.

The file wrapper is just as much a matter of public record as the patent, and is as much of a notice and warning to the public as if it were contained in the patent itself.

Mistakes and Corrections

It does not matter that a patentee is mistaken in stating the theory of his invention, if he fully describes the invention itself and its practical results, and gives sufficient directions for putting it into practical use. The law requires nothing more.

In one patent the specification unnecessarily contained a scientific theory concerning the action of aluminum. The inventor thought the aluminum acted to lower the melting point of the mixture and thereby rendered it more fluid. Later, the generally accepted explanation of the phenomenon following the addition of aluminum was that the aluminum acted as a deoxidizing agent. The patent was held valid because the inventor had fully described his invention and the result, and gave directions for putting it into use.

A patent can invoke in support of his invention advantages of which he was not aware, at the time of filing, but the patent must disclose them. As one court decision put it, "The patentee may have builded better than he knew, but he is confined to what he built."

However, if an inventor comes to better understand the principles of his invention while his application for a patent is pending, an amendment of his claim that does not introduce any original matter nor enlarge his invention is within his legal rights.

It is not necessary that the patentee understand or be able to state the scientific principles underlying his invention and "it is immaterial whether he can stand a successful examination as to the speculative ideas involved."

Amendments

Amendments in the description or drawing of a patent application do not invalidate the patent, if they merely amplify and explain what is already reasonably indicated to be within the invention. This rule applies with special force where the in-

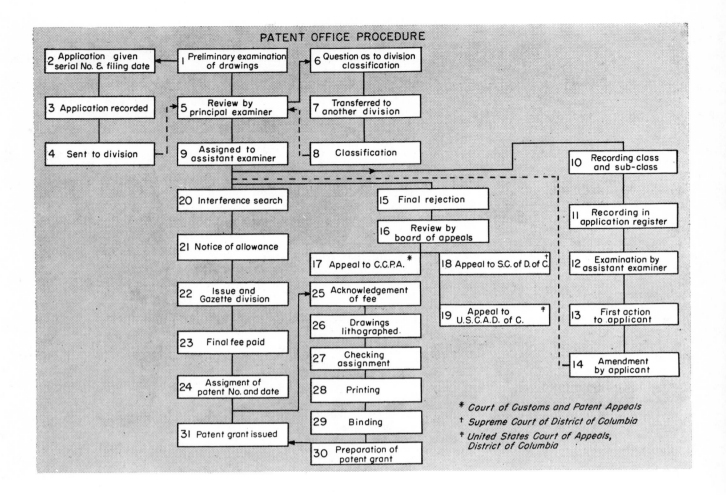

PATENT OFFICE PROCEDURE

2 Application given serial No. & filing date
1 Preliminary examination of drawings
6 Question as to division classification

3 Application recorded
5 Review by principal examiner
7 Transferred to another division

4 Sent to division
9 Assigned to assistant examiner
8 Classification
10 Recording class and sub-class

20 Interference search
15 Final rejection
11 Recording in application register

21 Notice of allowance
16 Review by board of appeals
12 Examination by assistant examiner

17 Appeal to C.C.P.A. *
18 Appeal to S.C. of D. of C. †

22 Issue and Gazette division
25 Acknowledgement of fee
19 Appeal to U.S.C.A.D. of C. ‡
13 First action to applicant

23 Final fee paid
26 Drawings lithographed.
27 Checking assignment
14 Amendment by applicant

24 Assigment of patent No. and date
28 Printing

29 Binding
* Court of Customs and Patent Appeals
† Supreme Court of District of Columbia
‡ United States Court of Appeals, District of Columbia

31 Patent grant issued
30 Preparation of patent grant

sertion is required by the Patent Office.

A patentee who acquiesces in the rejection of his claim and abandons it, based on references cited by the Patent Office, and accepts a patent on an amended claim, cannot maintain that the amended claim covers the combination shown in the references and that it is as broad as the abandoned claim. A patentee who does not abandon, but insists on and sustains his first claim, can later claim all of the benefits of his original specifications, in the courts, if necessary.

The insertion of new claims in a pending application is allowable, provided that general description is included in the original specifications and drawings.

Fraud

When a patent has been obtained by fraud, by mistake or by accident, the United States can bring proceedings against the patentee to have the patent declared void. The suit of the government, if successful, puts an end to all suits which the patentee can bring against anybody. In effect, it

puts the patent at the disposal of the world.

In a suit for infringement of a patent, if the alleged infringer can prove that the patent was obtained through fraud, he will not be held liable for the infringement. Even if there is reasonable doubt as to the actions of the patentee, he will not be excused if he has not previously disclosed all information in his possession relative to the patent.

Test of Invention

An application, even when found allowable, may be placed "in interference" with other applications. It is particularly important that manufacturers and inventors understand what such a procedure means. The interference procedure is a contest heard in the Patent Office to see who was first to make the invention. It then can be appealed to the courts.

The first to think of the invention, reduce it to some practical form and test it to show it is practical, is awarded the patent. Reduction to practice—the manner in which it is to function in use—is the actual test of the invention.

If a person is the first to think of an invention, but the last to reduce it to practical form, then the question is whether he was active and diligent in looking after his rights in a reasonable fashion, from the time his opponent came into the field until his own reduction to practice. If it is found that the inventor was neglectful and "slept" on his rights or that he practiced concealment and secrecy during this period, he can lose his rights even though he was first to think of the invention.

The purpose of this law is to encourage disclosure and filing of patent applications, that the public may have the benefit of them. Hence, one who conceals brings upon himself the suspicion that his experiments were abandoned, or that he did not have the invention at all. There are many other related and complicated rules, but this is the essential one.

Reduction to practice or practical experiment can take the form of making the apparatus, testing it and showing that it is successful; or putting the invention in the form of a patent application and filing the application in the Patent Office. The latter is known as a "constructive" reduction

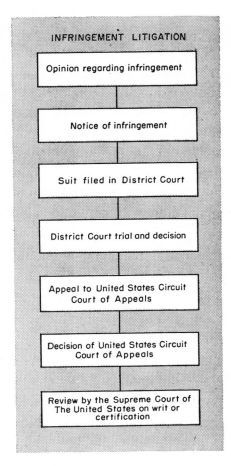

INFRINGEMENT LITIGATION

Opinion regarding infringement

Notice of infringement

Suit filed in District Court

District Court trial and decision

Appeal to United States Circuit Court of Appeals

Decision of United States Circuit Court of Appeals

Review by the Supreme Court of The United States on writ or certification

to practice, and is the best evidence of good intent, in court action.

After a patent is issued, it frequently happens that, through some misunderstanding, it is necessary to have the patent reissued in a revised form to correct errors. This can be done any time within one year of the date of the issuance of the patent. The original drawings and disclosures must not be materially changed; only errors can be corrected, to make the document a perfect disclosure of the inventor's idea.

If, at any time the inventor discovers that he has mistakenly claimed portions of an invention to which he is not entitled, he can file a "disclaimer" on that portion of his patent, thus saving the rest of his patent, and preventing the whole patent from being defeated for lack of prior inventorship. The United States statute on disclaimers includes the following statement:

". . . .Such disclaimer shall be in writing, attested by one or more witnesses, and recorded in the Patent Office; and it shall thereafter be considered as part of the original specification to the extent of the interest possessed by the claimant and by those

claiming under him after the record thereof. But no such disclaimer shall affect any action pending at the time of its being filed, except so far as may relate to the question of unreasonable neglect or delay in filing it."

Infringement

When the patent is issued, others, seeing the value of the invention, sometimes take the invention. This is patent infringement.

The patentee can bring suit for infringement against the offender in the United States courts. The questions before the court are: (1) Whether the defendant has taken the property of the plaintiff patentee, and (2) whether the patent of the plaintiff patentee is valid. Validity of the patent can be rebutted by the defendant introducing prior patents that were not discovered by the Patent Office. Even prior patents discovered in the Patent Office and whose full effect were not realized by Patent Office officials, may be used to defeat the patent. In this respect the court has a sort of reviewing power over the Patent Office. Prior publications can also be used to defeat the patent.

If the invention has been publicly made, used, or sold in the United States two years before the patent application was filed, or before the actual date of invention by the patentee, then proof of such facts beyond reasonable doubt will cause the court to find that the patent is invalid. The court may find that part of the patent is valid and part invalid; and some of the claims may be infringed and some may not be infringed. Each claim stands on its own special merits and is separately treated.

Prior use of the invention in European countries does not defeat the patent. To defeat a patent, a foreign development must be in a publication or in a patent.

Aggregation or Combination?

Many costly law suits have resulted because a designer did not know the legal distinction between an aggregation of elements or parts, which is not invention, and a combination, which is invention if it accomplishes something new and useful.

The Patent Office properly refuses a patent on a design that is merely an aggregation of parts. But the Patent Office sometimes mistakenly issues a patent on something "unpatentable". Later, the owner of the patent sues another for infringement, only to find that his "invention" is not valid and that his patent is void.

A patent was issued to cover a "combination" of elements for the automatic operation of a stoker. It included a stoker, a thermostat to control the stoker and a timing device to start the stoker, so that the fire would not go out for lack of fuel. Later, a competitor put on the market a similar group of devices to accomplish the same purpose. The patent owner sued on the grounds of infringement. He lost, the court holding that his patent was invalid. "The union," said the court, "is a mere aggregation unless the elements, by their united action, perform some function they do not separately discharge." The courts, perhaps unjustly, look upon aggregations as involving no creative intellectual achievement.

Typical of "mere" aggregations is a grease service tank, the patent on which was voided by the court. It included a series of pump or grease-gun supports; a corresponding series of pumps and grease guns; a series of indexes on the rack close to the supports, each mentioning a particular part of the automobile that needed specialized lubrication; a series of identification marks on the pumps; and a corresponding series of identification marks on the racks near the supports for identifying each pump with its support.

The court said about this: "There is no co-action between the support and the pumps, or between the pumps and the legend on the rack. It is the same as a carpenter's cabinet for augur bits, a druggist's cabinet or a hotel-keeper's rack for room keys . . . the old elements are brought together, not in the cooperative union of a true combination, but in the forced relationship of a mere aggregation.

Inventors frequently have the erroneous notion that simplicity or complexity is the test of aggregation or combination. One designer, for instance, worked out an apparatus for mixing and transporting concrete. It consisted of an upright chamber, in the top of which was an opening for introducing the material, equipped with a door to close the opening airtight; a hopper-shaped bottom to the chamber, discharging into a delivery duct; a pipe through which compressed air entered the chamber above the mass of concrete to propel it into the duct; and another pipe delivering compressed air at or near the discharge or lower end of the hopper; and many other elements. However, it was not patentable because it was an aggregation of known devices, each acting in its regular way.

Form I — SUMMARY CARD

ORDER NO..........

Invention or Name of Machine

.... by...

1. Conceived, date of.................................
2. Disclosed, dates of.................................
3. "   To (1)................. How disclosed...............
4.   (2)............. " " ....
5.   (3)............. " " ....
6. Sketches, dates of.................................
7. Written Description, date of.................................
8. Working Drawings (a) Started........day of........19..
9.   (b) Completed....day of........19..
9. ....day of........19..
10. Started Full-Sized Machine..........day of........19..
11. Completed Full-Sized Machine........day of........19..
12. Photographs of:.................................
13. Start of Full-Sized Device, taken......day of......10..
14. Completion of Full-Sized Device, taken....day of....19..
15. Dates Tested:.................................
16. Where Tested:.................................
17. Result of Test:.................................
18. Remarks:.................................
19. ....
20. ....

Form II — PRELIMINARY SKETCH SHEET

Order No.......

1. Subject:
2.

3. Explanation:
....
....
....
....
....
....
4. Sketched by.................. Date.........
5. Witnessed by.................. Date.........
            Date
6. To Whom Explained
     (a).

Form III — RESEARCH RECORD

ORDER NO......

1. Object:
2. ....
3. ....
4. ....
5. Apparatus:
6. ....
7. ....
8. ....
9. Materials:
10. ....
11. ....
12. Method or Process:
13. ....
14. ....
15. ....
16. Result:
17. .... Date.........
18. Experiment by: .... Date.........
19. Witnessed By: .... Date.........
20. Directed By:

Form IV — DRAWING FORM

1.   Supersedes Drawing dated.................
2.   Superseded by Drawing dated.................
3. Name of Job .... 15. Order No. ....
4. Part .... 16. Shop No. ....
5. Tool .... 17. Storeroom No. ....
6. Operation .... 18. Planning Room No. ....
7. Drawn by........12. Traced by......19. Tracing Started by......Date....
8. Drawing Started......13. Tracing Started....20. Tracing Approved by......Date....
9. Drawing Completed...14. Tracing Completed...21. Copies to:
10. Drawing Checked by................Date
11. Drawing Approved by................Date 22. Sheet No........

Form V — MATERIAL PURCHASE RECORD

ORDER NO........

Material	Order Number	Order Date	Invoice Number	Invoice Date	Voucher Number	Voucher Date
1. Steel						
2. Castings						
3. Patterns						
4. Brass						
5. Iron						
6. Aluminum						
7. Alloys						
8. Wire						
9. Chemicals						
10. Paper, etc., etc.						

Records of the Invention Should be Kept

These include factory and laboratory records, preservation of original models, proof and identification of experimental machines, and such records which prove the existence of models or full-sized machines.

A manufacturer of trailers developed a novel trailer truck. He built it immediately and tested it extensively. He took no photographs of the truck. It was built up of parts around the factory, so that there were no drawings. After the tests he decided that he would defer building the apparatus until public taste caught up to the development. Meanwhile, his experimental department, needing the parts for another development, tore down the original truck.

Several years later, after filing a patent application, a Patent Office interference arose. There were no dated records, no drawings, no photographs, no purchase records of material that went into this particular truck—nothing that was definite except the testimony of witnesses, and that was verbal. Although the first to invent and the first to reduce to practice, he failed to make convincing proof to the Patent Office, and lost a very important invention. Thus, a million-dollar business was lost because management did not spend a few dollars on preserving records of the test.

Witnessed Test Runs

The best type of proof of an invention is to actually make the apparatus; or run tests showing what the inventive process is; or produce the product. When this is done, the tests should be witnessed by responsible people who later can testify as witnesses.

Photographs should be taken with these persons included in the pictures, and the negatives should be dated the day they are taken. These negatives should be signed by the inventor and the witnesses. This makes a permanent record, and prints can be used as a basis of making disclosures within the organization and to outsiders. The records of the tests themselves should be carefully kept and dated and signed by those present, including the inventor.

The records covering the making of the test apparatus should also be kept apart from the general commercial records of the corporation, since it is the custom of many corporations to destroy records of this type after several years. All records concerning the invention, including the photographs, should carry the same serial number, which should be carried in a numbered record of inventions.

How to Prove the Date of Invention

Many patent cases have been lost because of inadequate proof of the date of invention. This is often caused by misunderstanding of the patent law covering the case. Inventors may think they have "taken steps" to prove the date of their invention, but they are often wrong.

One form of proof of date of invention, other than filing an application, is some written form of disclosure of the invention—drawings, dated photographs, and written and dated descriptions, signed by the inventor and several witnesses before a notary. This proof should then be mailed to an outsider who can be depended on to testify that he received the disclosure in the ordinary course of business.

Record forms such as these should be kept and used in every department of a manufacturing and research organization. Information should be given in as much detail as possible—a seemingly minor point can later make the differ-

A serious mistake made by many organizations is to have all the proof of the making of an invention and its disclosure limited to persons within the organization, witnessed only by employees and executives of the organization. In a patent office interference case, or in a question of prior use before a court, the other side can claim that the material has been specially fabricated for the occasion.

One of the effective ways to handle this is to provide regular disclosure booklets in which all inventive ideas of the research, engineering and development departments are recorded. These booklets are regularly mailed out from the organization with a statement of the nature of the invention, and whether or not it is to be protected by a patent application.

This proof should include drawings and sketches, dated and signed by the inventor and witnesses. The signatures should be in ink and, if possible, the drawings should be in ink. Either regular disclosure booklets, or a bound disclosure record book should be maintained for this purpose. Such disclosure records should be readily available in every laboratory, on each drafting table and in each experimental shop.

Record Forms

The fundamental purpose of all records of invention is to provide an unquestionable statement of exactly what occurred: Hence, any additional details are always welcome to make clear the record of the events.

Sound proof of this character will prevent litigation, and if litigation does become necessary, it makes success as certain as humanly possible. The accompanying illustrations show suggested patent record forms.

Substitution of Materials

Many designers are under the impression that to substitute one material for another will entitle them to a patent. Usually, it will not; although under certain rare conditions a change of materials has been held to be patentable.

The field for achieving patentability, or avoiding infringement, by substituting one material for another is so narrow that most cases involving this question have been decided in the negative. The substitution of materials can constitute invention when:

1. It creates a new result not usually associated with the material.

2. It involves a new type of construction.

3. It enables new uses to be made of the device.

4. It makes an existing device successful for the first time.

In an electric make-and-break contact, tungsten was substituted for iridium platinum. It was regarded by the trade as cheaper and far superior to the old contact. The court held that it took more than uninventive substitution to make this change and that the invention was therefore patentable.

It was decided by another court that to substitute in a heating device a radiator of copper for one of cast iron or other heavy metal was not patentable, even though the copper radiator was more efficient. It was well known that copper is an efficient heat transmitter, and since there was no change in the function or effectiveness of the combination, there was no invention. However, the court held valid a patent for a water cooler using a coil made of a resilient metal instead of a non-resilient lead or tin pipe. ■

ence between a valid and invalid patent. Sketches and photographs, properly dated and signed, should be attached. If desired, a twelfth form—the patent litigation record—can also be used.

Form VI — CONSTRUCTION RECORD SHEET

Form VII — TEST RECORD SHEET

Form VIII — STATEMENT BY WITNESS OF TEST

Form X — PATENT DEPARTMENT RECORD

Form XI — FOLLOW-UP FORM

Form IX — PHOTOGRAPHIC RECORD FORM

Watch for These Proposed Changes in Patent Law

A recently released report by a President's Commission contains important recommendations for strengthening the U.S. patent system.

HOWARD K. NASON,
President, Monsanto Research Corporation,
St. Louis, Mo.; Public Member of the
President's Commission on the Patent System.

Proposed Changes

Improvement in quality and reliability of issued patents is the objective of proposals to introduce the following features into the system:

1 Inventions to be patentable would have to be novel, useful, and unobvious, as at present. However, under the Commission's proposals, prior publication, public use, or public disclosure anywhere in the world would constitute prior art. Design patents and patents on living plants are considered incapable of meeting the requirements outlined above, or impractical to examine and enforce under these requirements, and other means than the Patent System are suggested for protecting significant and worthwhile contributions in these areas. A modified form of copyright protection might be appropriate. Computer programs also would be excluded as patentable subjects, and copyright protection might be sought for them.

2 The burden of persuasion in the prosecution of an application would rest upon the applicant.

3 Patent Office decision denying a patent claim would be presumed to be correct in judicial reviews.

4 Either the Patent Office or the applicant could appeal to the Court of Appeals for the District of Columbia Circuit for review of decisions from the two courts which now review Patent Office actions.

5 An effective quality control program would be developed and maintained by the Patent Office (hopefully, its own form of a "Zero Defects" program).

6 A Statutory Advisory Council would be established, whose members, appointed by and responsible to the Secretary of Commerce, would maintain continuing surveillance over quality of granted patents (using actions on validity by the courts as one criterion), as well as other key factors such as pendency.

7 The provision for citation by the public of prior art pertinent to the published applications should add substantially to the quality of the examination, thus reducing the number of issued patents invalidated later because of references which were available but not found during the novelty search. More extensive use of all available methods for information retrieval also would contribute to quality of the search.

Incentive to Speed

Reducing pendency, i.e., the length of time required to process an application to final disposition, would, it is proposed, be favored by the following elements of the Commission's plan:

1 Early publication of applications would take much of the incentive out of the "game" of keeping applications in the office as long as possible.

2 The provision that the life of a patent terminate 20 years from the date of the complete application, plus the limited nature of the protection afforded during any interval between publication and issuance, provides

1. filing application

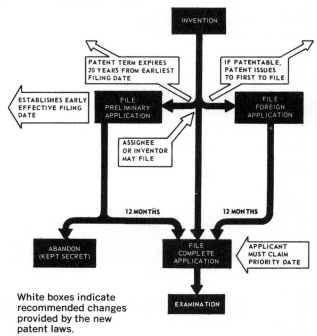

White boxes indicate recommended changes provided by the new patent laws.

2. examination and review

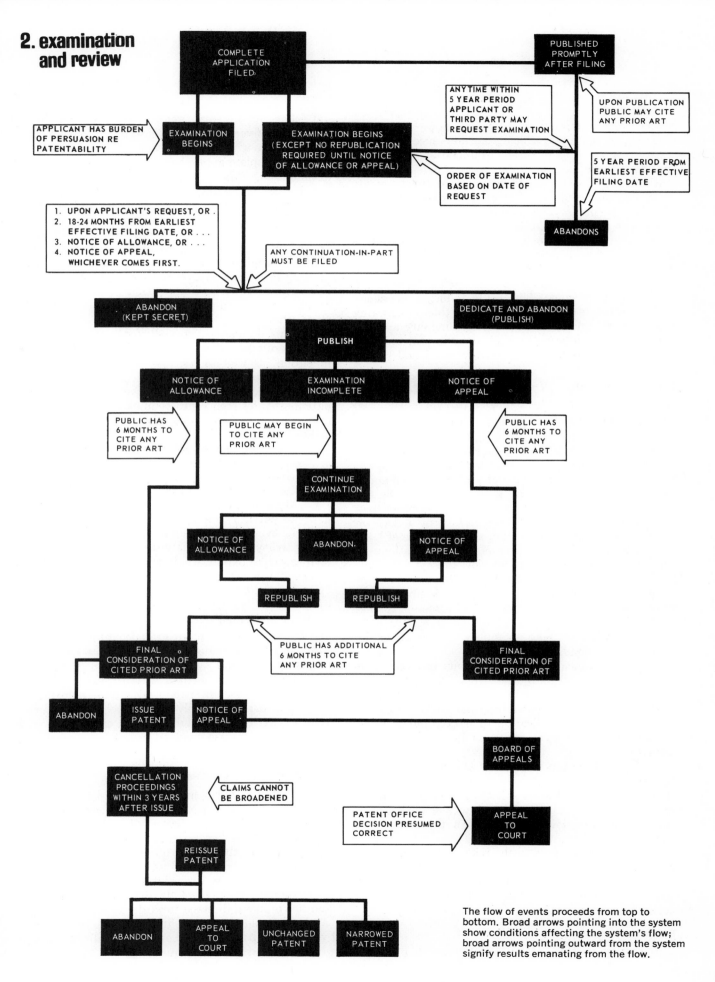

COMPLETE APPLICATION FILED.

PUBLISHED PROMPTLY AFTER FILING

APPLICANT HAS BURDEN OF PERSUASION RE PATENTABILITY

EXAMINATION BEGINS

EXAMINATION BEGINS (EXCEPT NO REPUBLICATION REQUIRED UNTIL NOTICE OF ALLOWANCE OR APPEAL)

ANYTIME WITHIN 5 YEAR PERIOD APPLICANT OR THIRD PARTY MAY REQUEST EXAMINATION

UPON PUBLICATION PUBLIC MAY CITE ANY PRIOR ART

ORDER OF EXAMINATION BASED ON DATE OF REQUEST

5 YEAR PERIOD FROM EARLIEST EFFECTIVE FILING DATE

1. UPON APPLICANT'S REQUEST, OR .
2. 18-24 MONTHS FROM EARLIEST EFFECTIVE FILING DATE, OR . . .
3. NOTICE OF ALLOWANCE, OR . . .
4. NOTICE OF APPEAL, WHICHEVER COMES FIRST.

ANY CONTINUATION-IN-PART MUST BE FILED

ABANDONS

ABANDON (KEPT SECRET)

DEDICATE AND ABANDON (PUBLISH)

PUBLISH

NOTICE OF ALLOWANCE

EXAMINATION INCOMPLETE

NOTICE OF APPEAL

PUBLIC HAS 6 MONTHS TO CITE ANY PRIOR ART

PUBLIC MAY BEGIN TO CITE ANY PRIOR ART

PUBLIC HAS 6 MONTHS TO CITE ANY PRIOR ART

CONTINUE EXAMINATION

NOTICE OF ALLOWANCE

ABANDON.

NOTICE OF APPEAL

REPUBLISH

REPUBLISH

PUBLIC HAS ADDITIONAL 6 MONTHS TO CITE ANY PRIOR ART

FINAL CONSIDERATION OF CITED PRIOR ART

FINAL CONSIDERATION OF CITED PRIOR ART

ABANDON

ISSUE PATENT

NOTICE OF APPEAL

BOARD OF APPEALS

CANCELLATION PROCEEDINGS WITHIN 3 YEARS AFTER ISSUE

CLAIMS CANNOT BE BROADENED

PATENT OFFICE DECISION PRESUMED CORRECT

APPEAL TO COURT

REISSUE PATENT

ABANDON

APPEAL TO COURT

UNCHANGED PATENT

NARROWED PATENT

The flow of events proceeds from top to bottom. Broad arrows pointing into the system show conditions affecting the system's flow; broad arrows pointing outward from the system signify results emanating from the flow.

additional incentive for processing applications as expeditiously as possible.

3 Other incentives are provided for expediting the search and for improving its quality.

4 A provision upon which great difference of opinion exists concerns a deferred examination procedure. Provision has been made for an optional deferred examination system which could be put into effect quickly if needed and could be discontinued when such need clearly was past. The members of the Commission could not reach a majority opinion as to whether deferred examination should be adopted immediately in certain areas on a pilot basis or whether it should be left for future application where, when, and if the need becomes evident.

5 Other provisions which could influence pendency include issuance to the first to file (thus eliminating interferences) and a technique for preliminary applications which would give the applicant one year to determine whether his invention is truly novel and worthwhile.

Speeding Disclosure

Public disclosure of technological advances would be encouraged by the following provisions:

1 The first-to-file concept would encourage the inventor to file at least a preliminary application just as soon as the nature and scope of his invention were apparent to him. The present right to abandon an application in secrecy would be preserved up to the decision point for publication. (However, other features of the system increase the hazard of a decision to retain a patentable invention as a trade secret.)

2 The provision for preliminary applications of simple format substitutes for the present one-year "grace period" in permitting prompt disclosure of science and technology at meetings, in professional and trade publications, and the like. Protection against unauthorized disclosure or usurpation of inventions is provided by the voiding of applications based on information derived from others.

3 Early publication of applications (though hopefully after a first action by the Patent Office, and again with the right to abandon in secrecy protected) should speed disclosure of technical information to the public, minimize needless duplication of effort, and promote additional technological advances based on such information.

4 Creation within the Patent Office of a first rate facility for information handling, including mechanization of the distribution by subscription or sale of documents, would be a powerful aid to the objective of speeding up the flow of information throughout the world.

5 Of special interest to the scientific community is the proposal that the format of a patent include an abstract of technical, rather than legal, content, designed for direct incorporation into modern indexing and information handling systems.

Reducing the Cost

Reduction in the cost of obtaining and litigating patents should result from several recommended features:

1 The preliminary application provision would permit an invention to be protected for one year at little expense while the applicant was deciding whether to file a complete application and thus initiate the full examination. Many applications found lacking in novelty or utility undoubtedly would be abandoned at this stage, thus sparing both applicant and the Patent Office the expense of the complete prosecution.

2 Some of the same economies are claimed by advocates of a system of optional deferred examination. While an applicant could elect to request examination at any time within five years, there undoubtedly would be many cases where examination never would be requested, thus eliminating the additional costs of full prosecution.

3 Some economies, especially for large organizations, would result from the provision that the owner of an invention, as well as the inventor himself, could file the patent application.

4 Adoption of the first-to-file principle would eliminate most interference proceedings, which not only are frequently expensive but also lend themselves to abuses.

5 Major savings would be realized if the objective of a single international novelty search, acceptable in every country where applications are filed on the same invention, could be attained.

6 More desirable still, of course, would be an international patent, obtained on a single application and valid in every country adhering to the necessary enabling treaty. Much greater unification in world law, civil as well as patent, would be required before such an ideal could be achieved.

7 Litigation of an issued patent, which is regarded by many as discriminating against the independent inventor and small entrepreneur because of high cost and of delays which often are encountered, would be speeded up and made less expensive by several proposals. One would be that the office of "Civil Commissioner" would be created to supervise and simplify the pretrial phases of patent litigation, reducing the time and expense involved and helping to correct abuses. An expedited adjudication procedure would cut time and expense involved in settling controversies involving limited damage claims.

Toward the International Patent

International harmonization would be favored by several of the proposals which have been previously discussed, such as the first-to-file concept and the elimination of the "grace period." Progress is already being made by the patent offices of the world in exchanging search data, and continued efforts in this direction, as well as toward the ultimate goal of an international patent, should be pursued diligently. Another proposal directed toward greater international harmony would subject products manufactured abroad by a process patented in the United States to liability when imported into this country. ■

Various indexes provide access to patent information—Table I

Publication	Frequency	Lists Patents by	Subject and Time Coverage	Publisher/Price	Comments
Manual of Classification (with index)	Revised periodically	Lists subclasses: a. By subject matter b. By number	All existing subclasses.	Supt. of Documents, Washington 25, D. C. $8.50, including periodic loose-leaf revisions.	The Manual's index is a readily available means for locating pertinent subclasses.
Annual Index of Patents	Yearly	a. Serial number b. Each inventor c. Assignee d. Title e. Subclass number	All U.S. patents issued during particular year.	Supt. of Documents, Washington 25, D.C. $6.75 for 1962; varies for previous years.	Best way to locate patent if inventor or assignee and approximate year of issue are known. Limited value for general searching.
Official Gazette	Weekly	a. Subclasses b. Inventor c. Assignee d. Title	All U. S. patents issued during week. Gives partial summary and one drawing for each patent.	Supt. of Documents, Washington 25, D. C. $35/yr. domestic; $45/yr. foreign; $1 for single copies.	Useful for updating annual indexes and microfilm subclass lists, and for monitoring newly issued patents.
Official Gazette (microcard edition)	Weekly	a. Subclasses b. Inventor c. Assignee d. Title	Same as Official Gazette. Card sets available from 1950 to present.	Godfrey Memorial Library, Middletown, Conn. $160/yr.	Identical to Official Gazette except printed on microcards.
Lists of Patents in Subclasses	Revised periodically	Contents of current subclasses listed by number only	All U. S. patents. Subclass lists are available separately.	Commissioner of Patents, Washington 25, D. C. 30¢ per page. (Microfilm subclass lists of patents issued prior to 1963 available from Office of Technical Services, Washington 25, D. C., for $70 per set.)	Used for finding numbers of all patents in subclasses of interest. Useful for determining cost of ordering copies of all patents in subclass.
National Index of Patents	Published Oct. 1963	a. Current subclass b. Year c. Subject d. Number	All U. S. chemical patents from 1790 through 1960.	Rowman and Littlefield, 84 Fifth Ave., New York, N. Y. 10011. $300.	Combines listings from government's Annual Index and subclass lists. (Indexes for electrical and mechanical patents available at $250 each.)

How to obtain copies and summaries of U. S. patents—Table II

Publication	Available from	Price	Comments
Individual patents	Commissioner of Patents, Washington 25, D. C.	25¢ per patent.	Order by patent number; convenient coupon books available. Photocopies can also be obtained from patent libraries.
Complete contents of patent subclass	Commissioner of Patents, Washington 25, D. C.	25¢ per patent.	Contents of entire subclass can be ordered by subclass number.
Subscription to patent subclasses	Commissioner of Patents, Washington 25, D. C.	25¢ per patent plus small annual charge.	$25 deposit account must be opened at the Patent Office; previously issued patents in subclass may be ordered. Subscription automatically provides copies of new patents issued in the particular subclass.
Microfiche copies (microfilm cards)	Microcard Editions, Inc. 901 26th St., NW, Washington 7, D. C.	30¢ per fiche (approximately 3.7¢ patent) or $450/yr.	Covers chemical patents only. On negative microfiche in standard 3″ x 5″ AEC and NASA format.
Microfilm copies	Information for Industry, Inc. 1000 Connecticut Ave., NW, Washington 6, D. C.	$275/yr. (about 2.5¢ patent).	Negative or positive 35-mm. microfilm reels cover chemical and related patents.
Official Gazette	Supt. of Documents, Washington 25, D. C.	$35/yr. domestic; $45/yr. foreign; single copies $1.	Issued weekly. Provides partial summary plus one drawing (if any). See Table I for microcard edition.
National Catalogue of Patents	Rowman and Littlefield, Inc. 84 Fifth Ave., New York,	$100 to $150 per year of chemical patents.	Compiles the partial summaries from Official Gazette by subclass for more rapid searching.

What Royalties Should an Outside Inventor Get from a Company?

T. B. HOLLIDAY, Consultant, Elmhurst, Ill

GENERATION of an idea starts with seeing a need. Nine tenths of invention follows or depends on that first step, for any good engineer can produce at least one answer, and usually more, for that need. Despite the great emphasis on group thinking, ideas still come from individuals. Even within the group, the spark that opens a door to further progress comes from one person. The group, which usually represents a great array and diversity of talent, can then improve the idea and add to it.

Often the creative inventor is strongly individualistic and would not be happy working in a group. Anyway, he has an idea, he is not a part of a company, and he wants to see that idea put to work for the benefit of others and himself. At the same time a company wants a new or improved product. How do the two of them get together?

As usual, there are two sides. Both are exaggerated by their proponents, both are hindered too often by greed. Comfortable is he who can see only one side of a question.

The inventor is firmly convinced that his idea is worth a million and often is blissfully unaware of the costs to design, tool, produce, and market a product. His idea is the least costly item in a long chain of necessary events. The inventor is also convinced that everyone is out to steal his idea, or that a company wants to buy it outright for very little, then put it on the shelf.

To protect him, the inventor's attorney urges him to obtain company acceptance of the *confidential disclosure*. This is a device of long history that effectively ties the hands of the company.

The outside inventor faces a serious hurdle, particularly with large companies. It is called the NIH (Not Invented Here) Factor—a built-in resentment of ideas from the outside. All that management needs to ask is, "Why didn't our engineers think of this," for just one case, and from that time forward there will be an invisible but impenetrable wall against inventions from the outside. The in-house engineering staff will tear down the prospects of the idea, show that they have considered something like it, or that it will need improvement and they can do it. Of course an idea can be improved. There has never been an idea that was not subsequently improved by someone else. But the improvement had to follow the idea.

Companies rightfully resent the confidential disclosure, because it ties their hands completely. If the submitted idea parallels the company product line, there is good chance that something similar to the idea is in work at the company—maybe not as good, and maybe better. The disclosure in confidence can prevent a company from bringing out an idea that was generated by one of its own engineers.

As a result, companies have set up policies refusing the disclosure in confidence. One firm advises that it will not pay for that which its competitors or others might do freely. Another states that no confidential relationship will be created or implied by the receipt of an idea for consideration.

Company policies reserve a "reasonable time" in one case, ninety days in another, in which to arrive at a decision. If the company rejects the idea, its reasons for doing so are held in confidence. To the inventor, all of this looks like a one-way street.

There is need for a middle ground where the value of all kinds of ideas can be appraised and improvement brought to the consumer more quickly. A suitable middle ground can be created; the list here is a suggestion to that end. It is based on royalties, because this kind of reward is fairest to both parties. It does not bar cash payments to compensate the inventor for his costs, but it is hoped that cash payments intended for putting the idea on the shelf will be avoided. With royalties, the inventor shares the risk of further development of his idea.

10%—The inventor delivers a final patent, a good design, a working prototype, and engineering drawings in sufficient quality and detail to permit immediate production.

8%—The inventor delivers a patent application, a working prototype, and good engineering drawings. (This would go up to 10% when the final patent is issued.)

7%—The inventor delivers a good final patent, but no engineering.

6%—The inventor delivers a patent application and a working prototype, but no engineering.

5%—The inventor delivers an idea only. The patent will be pursued by the company, and the 5% royalty is paid only after the patent is obtained.

4%—The inventor delivers only an idea.

3%—The inventor's idea is found to be unpatentable, and this royalty holds until competition develops.

2%—A reduction on the royalty for an idea after competition develops.

1%—The inventor delivers what becomes a partial idea in that it is an improvement on something that the company has initiated. It is assumed that the company will open its files to prove that this kind of situation exists.

This table of values is based on the idea of flexibility. A rigid contract would not be drawn, because provision for future contingencies is included. This thought is apparent at the midrange of values. The inventor produces an idea, and the company accepts it at the 4% royalty. If a valid patent is obtained at no further cost to the inventor, his royalty goes up to 5%. On the other hand, should the idea be unpatentable, he will draw the 3% royalty until competition appears, when his royalty drops to 2%. A middle ground could be designed to meet all kinds of situations. It provides ample reward for the inventor, it is not too costly for the company, and a uniform code along these lines will do much to bring ideas to useful products far more quickly. ∎

13.

Market Research, Consultants and Outside Services

motivation research:
What's in it for you?

ANNESTA R. GARDNER

Passing fad? Advertising gimmick? Or a valuable new technique to guide product design? Here are facts to help you make your own decision.

What makes people buy? How can they be encouraged to buy more? Would a new design make the sales curve start climbing?

These are questions every engineer asks. Often, he can answer them too. But in many cases, he'd like more evidence on which to base his decisions. Motivation research, its proponents claim, can give him that aid.

What, then, is motivation research? Basically, it's an extension of market research that tries to uncover the underlying reasons why people like and dislike certain products—reasons which the people themselves may not fully realize.

It is this attempt to find and influence basic attitudes that has earned motivation researchers the title of "hidden persuaders," a title of which they are not entirely fond.

M-R is defined by Lyndon O. Brown, vice-president of Dancer-Fitzgerald-Sample, as "research devoted to getting the best possible answers to the question, 'Why do people behave as they do?'"

The Institute of Motivational Research says the object of M-R is to "define consumer attitudes regarding a product or service . . . and to establish the root causes of such attitudes; to measure their commercial advantages or disadvantages; and to suggest . . . necessary improvements or new departures . . . which will lead to increased sales."

For example, ask most people why they want an automobile, and they'll say "for transportation." If that were so, the vehicle providing most efficient transportation would be the one they would buy. As everyone knows, that isn't exactly the case. Efficiency of operation is only one of many characteristics a prospective car buyer considers, consciously or unconsciously. What, then, are his motivations? A recent study was made by DuPont's Petroleum Chemicals Division of "the emotional factors governing the average motorist's ownership of a car and his choice of a service station." It came up with this answer:

"The average motorist owns and uses an automobile to satisfy one or more of the following needs:

"**The Play Need,** or necessity to relax and amuse himself, and seek diversion and entertainment.

"**The Aggression Need,** defined as the desire to prove one's superiority over another person.

"**The Conservance Need,** involving the need to collect, repair, and preserve things—to take care of the car, and to protect his investment.

"**The Infavoidance Need,** the desire to keep others from thinking that one is inferior in position, qualities, or taste; to void failure, shame, and ridicule." This four-syllable word, coined by DuPont, should not be confused with mere *inferiority complex*. "The motorist doesn't feel precisely inferior; he wants to avoid having others think he is inferior." Infavoidance, DuPont reports, "led all other factors in influencing the motorist's need for auto polish."

SPARK PLUGS VS POLISH

In contrast, spark plug purchases apparently hinge upon satisfaction of the Aggression Need; while Play and Aggression were found to be about equally important in a motorist's choice of gasoline.

These basics may not, however, be the only factors that combine to give a customer his final shove, DuPont notes. They influence his perception and conception of a product. But this perception is, in turn, influenced by such persuaders as previous experience, anxieties about product quality, opinions of family and friends, and advertising and promotion.

Most M-R studies so far have concentrated on the consumer field. But industrial studies are coming along. For instance, a motor manufacturer posed the question, "Why don't more engineers specify dc motors for more products?" There seemed to be many applications in which dc motors could be used—and weren't.

To answer the question, the company first turned to its advertising agency. Here, a market-research study showed that one major reason was the mistaken impression that dc motors could be used satisfactorily only where dc line power was available. But this did not seem to tell the whole story. The agency recommended an M-R investigation, involving "depth interviews" with engineers who weren't specifying dc motors.

This study found a good many engineers associated

do with the past: "It is considered in context with early efforts to produce power." These engineers, then, feel that they will be old-fashioned if they specify dc motors. The M-R group recommended a major campaign to overcome this impression, pointing up the modern characteristics of dc motors by descriptions of new dc products for automation; and showing via case histories that "the new user of dc equipment gains stature by keeping up with industry leaders."

Neither the motor nor the auto study recommended redesigning the product. They were concerned with reasons for buying. But anything which could reinforce the "modern" idea on dc motors (new materials, restyling, and the like) should help broaden their sale; and anything which could help car users satisfy one of their basic needs should be welcome on cars.

HOME AND HARDWARE

As typical of a study that did influence product design, motivation researchers cite this case:

A manufacturer of locks and other building hardware, noting a trend to lighter, slimmer-lined home furnishings, decided to redesign his products. But first he decided to check on the basic factors in home-buying as well as in selection of building hardware. An M-R investigation into home-buying changed his mind. It showed a major factor to be the desire for a solid, substantial base; and substantial-looking hardware played a major role. Changing to a slim design might well have decreased sales—of homes as well as hardware.

Such recommendations seem straightforward enough. But the trouble, to many people, comes when the experts dip into socio-psychological jargon. Maybe this is only a passing phase—a demonstration of "shock treatment" to promote a new idea.

More serious, perhaps, is the matter of the techniques used for motivational research. M-R takes advantage of the usual survey and statistical methods, but it places special emphasis on the "depth interview." Indeed, many consider this a distinguishing characteristic.

This depth interview as its name implies, is an exhaustive investigation of the subject's thoughts, attitudes, and beliefs. It aims at uncovering his "hidden" or subconscious reasons for liking or disliking, wanting or shunning this or that.

PROBE THAT DIGS IN

As might be expected, the psycho-probing is a lengthy process—usually taking an hour or more. So it's likely to be expensive, and even for a major study the number of probes may be held to 50 or less. Even if the interviews are supplemented by a broader survey, the conclusions may still be open to question: Just who are these guinea pigs? How well do they represent the "population" or group from which they are chosen?

Nevertheless, M-R has admittedly come up with useful suggestions—suggestions which might have been "obvious" but which, in fact, had not previously been considered or given sufficient weight.

ONE TECHNIQUE—MANY TECHNICIANS

Where does this leave M-R? It turns out to be an extension of market research, with special emphasis on one technique—the depth interview. It is not a completely new idea, and it does not represent the last word or the final answer on product development.

On the other hand, devotees obviously believe it can provide new directions for product design and promotion. On that basis, at least, it's worth investigating.

The literature on M-R is already reaching staggering proportions. Magazine articles, books, speeches and reports are available in quantity. (The DuPont report mentioned above is obtainable from the Petroleum Chemicals Div., Wilmington 98, Del., and its sales offices across the country.)

Advertising agencies are a primary source of information on M-R. Many of them helped pioneer it.

Finally, as might be expected, there are several consultants who now specialize in motivation research, among them: Institute for Motivational Research; James M. Vicary; and Social Research, Inc. ∎

Buying patterns are influenced by outside factors (to right of large arrow) as well as by basic motivaitons (left). Both groups of factors, Dupont says, contribute to the buyer's perception of a product, and play a role in his final decision.

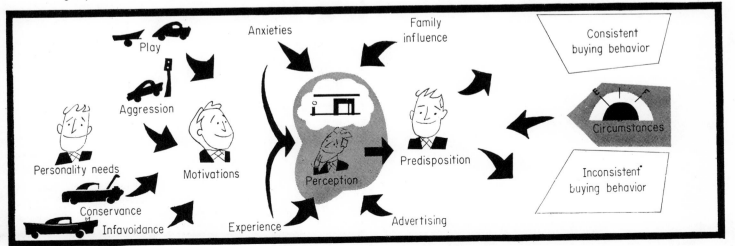

the 1 2 3 4 5 6 7 8 9 10 11 12 13 14 15 16 17 18 19 20 21 22 23 24 25 26 27 28 29 30 31 32 33 34 35 36 37 38 39 40 41 42 43 44 45 46 47 functions of marketing

FENTON B. TURCK, Fellow ASME,
F. B. Turck & Company Inc.,
New York, N. Y.

With the cost of distributing manufactured products totaling $150 billion per year, the functions of marketing become increasingly an important factor. Learn more about these marketing functions, what to do about them.

FIFTEEN years ago, the problem of high marketing costs was great; today, it is even more acute. In 1950, the American consumer paid $90 billion a year through purchases of products to cover the cost of distributing manufactured products. That was a staggering sum; today, the cost is even greater—$150 billion.

Fifteen years ago, the cost of performing the 47 functions of marketing varied widely and ranged from one-half cent of the consumer's dollar to 30 cents. Now the average upper limit has risen to 50 cents of that dollar. Indeed, for some drugs and cosmetics, it is even higher—an almost prohibitive 80 cents.

These facts are well known. What is perhaps not so well known is that the same functions that were required for marketing after World War II are still necessary today. Many years ago, for example, The Great Atlantic & Pacific Tea Company bought its fresh fruits and vegetables from middlemen. The cost to A&P of buying through these produce merchants was

---

the 47 functions of marketing

Market and Marketing Research

*1 Establishment of consumer desires and needs, market actual and total potentials, sales quotas, sales territories, and marketing strategic practices.

Financing

2 Financing wholesalers' inventory of finished products.

3 Financing retailers' inventory.

4 Financing consumer time payments.

Product Design

*5 Industrial and consumer design for style and utility.

Product Testing

*6 Testing of new and modified products for quality, function, and market demand.

Pricing

*7 Manufacturer's cost estimating, and price-discount quoting to wholesaler, retailer, and market demand.

* indicates funtions that have been simplified and improved

about 12 percent of total costs. In order to reduce costs, A&P first tried to educate these merchants in modernization and cost-cutting methods. Failing to get these merchants to improve their warehousing, materials handling, refrigeration, and other procedures, the Company was forced to take over these functions itself. The consequence of A&P's dealing with growers directly, and thus acting as its own middleman, was to reduce these costs to 8 percent. The functions were not abolished—merely shifted to more efficient and lower-cost operation.

In spite of the mountain of paperwork and statistics present today on marketing costs, there still exists a lack of widespread understanding of marketing functions and what to do about them. Part of this problem is due to poor communications between principal department heads, such as the chiefs of manufacturing, finance, and marketing. One department manager doesn't know what another, or others, is doing. Therefore he can't coordinate his activities with others. This is one reason why so little scientific and engineering work and management attention are being applied to this major cost branch of America's great economic life.

In the consumer appliance field, manufacturers such as General Electric and RCA found that many local sales outlets which assumed responsibility for providing servicing actually did not deliver adequate service to the consumer, although they included such functions in their costs. These companies were forced to establish a factory installation to insure that purchasers obtain proper, competent service and to protect the product name. Again, the function itself was not abolished but shifted from the retail outlet back to the manufacturer because of the inability of the retailer to perform the function satisfactorily.

Service Versus Price

As in the past, looking at the price tag of a product certainly does not tell a buyer the entire story regarding whether he is really getting a bargain. By a markdown of a few cents or a few percentage points, the seller is often again, as in the past, able to make the buyer assume the cost of many expensive marketing functions. The buyer still is being deceived, unless he is fully aware that he is not getting his full value in marketing services. The warehousing functions still must be done by and paid for by somebody.

A few cents' difference in a price tag often is not full compensation to the consumer for shifting marketing functions to the consumer from the retailer, from the wholesaler, or even from the manufacturer. In many instances today, as in the past, the marketing functions have really not been eliminated—they merely have been

Packaging

8 Manufacturer's packaging for wholesaler, retailer, and consumer display, utility, handling, and storage.

9 Wholesaler's packaging for wholesaler, retailer, and consumer display, utility, handling, and storage.

10 Retailer's packaging for retailer and consumer display, utility, handling, and storage.

Sales Department Organization & Administration

*11 Manufacturer's coordination of sales activity, budget planning, selection and training of salesmen.

*12 Wholesaler's coordination of sales activity, budget planning, selection and training of salesmen.

*13 Retailer's coordination of sales activity, budget planning, selection and training of salesmen.

Credit Investigation

*14 Credit investigation by manufacturer of wholesalers, retailers, or customers.

*15 Credit investigation by wholesaler of retailer or customers.

*16 Credit investigation by retailer of potential customers.

through the extensive use of computer operations.

Customer Selection

17 Identification and location of potential customers.

Advertising

*18 Manufacturer's advertising to build consumer demand and distributor confidence.

*19 Wholesaler's advertising to promote consumer and retailer interest in wholesaler and product.

*20 Retailer's advertising designed to stimulate consumer to purchase product and trade with retailer.

Sales Promotion

21 Manufacturer's sales promotion aimed at increasing distributor and consumer interest in the product and the manufacturer.

22 Wholesaler's sales promotion to attract and aid the retailer and consumer.

23 Retailer's sales promotion to build local consumer demand for product.

Sales Outlets

24 Manufacturer's selection and appointment of distributing outlets.

25 Wholesaler's selection and appointment of retail outlets.

passed on to the consumer if he has been deceived by looking exclusively at the small reduction in price.

Discount houses are examples of outlets which not only give a reduction in price to the consumer but also which shift marketing functions to the purchaser. E. J. Korvette, Inc., buys at wholesale and sells to the customer at a discounted retail price. The low markup is possible because the ultimate buyer assumes the finance, delivery, and service functions. It is therefore frequently questionable whether the customer gets a bargain even with the low price charged.

A jockeying takes place often to see which marketing channel does what, or to see who can get out of performing a marketing service. The various stages of marketing are shifted to see who is going to perform a function and who is going to get paid for it. The stock is merely available to the customer. Almost everyone in the marketing channel wants to cut his purchase price, or cut out a marketing function, or both.

As labor costs go up, for example, there is a continual attempt to transfer these costs to someone else. Shifting of functions is a competitive factor for the trade, but the 47 functions are irrevocable—they must be done. Many people expect elimination of the cost of these functions, but the marketing system finds out they are not eliminated—merely shifted to someone else in the marketing pipeline. The use of computer-control systems by several in the marketing chain has reduced the price, speeded up the performance, and eliminated some warehouses and duplication of functions, but the 47 functions still must be done.

Even in the supermarket and one-stop shopping center, the functions cannot be eliminated, although some may appear to have been banished. In these outlets, the customer assumes the role of clerk and delivery boy at the customer's own expense in money, time, and misselected merchandise.

Utilizing the Functional Method

By a detailed analysis of marketing into 47 functions, it is contemplated that manufacturers will be able to initiate practical steps to improve their marketing operations. A greater degree of integration among functions, manufacturers, and industries will be possible in the future, however, to avoid duplication of efforts and eliminate unnecessary activity by common consent and agreement among segments of industry. As costs of marketing rise—and in some cases become almost prohibitive—manufacturers, wholesalers, and retailers virtually will be forced to cooperate among themselves for mutual benefit.

Eight recommendations are advanced in order that these much needed reforms may be brought about:

1 The manufacturer should still itemize his marketing operations by functions to the first point of sale, whether this be to the wholesaler or to another manufacturer.

2 Additional marketing functions performed from the manufacturer's point of sale to the ultimate con-

the 47 functions of marketing

Selling

*26 Manufacturer's sales contact, and closing of sales with wholesaler, retailer, or consumer.

27 Wholesaler's sales contact, and closing of sales with retailer or consumer.

28 Retailer's sales contact, and closing of sales with consumer.

Accounting

*29 Manufacturer's cost and sales accounting, budgeting, and expense control.

*30 Wholesaler's cost and sales accounting, budgeting, and expense control.

*31 Retailer's cost and sales accounting, budgeting, and expense control.

Physical Handling

*32 Manufacturer's handling of finished product preparatory to storage or delivery.

33 Wholesaler's handling of product from time of receipt until delivery to retailer or consumer.

34 Retailer's handling of product.

Transportation

35 Manufacturer's delivery of product to wholesaler, retailer, or consumer.

36 Wholesaler's delivery of product to retailer or consumer.

37 Retailer's delivery of product to consumer.

Storage

*38 Manufacturer's warehousing of finished product at factory or in field.

39 Wholesaler's warehousing of inventory in field.

40 Retailer's storage.

sumer should be itemized and realistically evaluated. These functions beyond the manufacturer should be analyzed in terms of the total corporate functions to determine whether these functions are appropriate, adequate, and otherwise satisfactory on an overall basis.

3 Costs of each function per unit of sale should also be determined. Cost trends should be studied and analyzed. Costs which have risen most should be reduced possibly by some new internal or external system.

4 Multiple functions within the marketing system again should be reviewed. Simplification of methods or installation of new systems to coordinate functions and eliminate duplication should be undertaken where necessary.

5 In the case of each marketing function, or group, determination should be made regarding whether present results are adequate in terms of total company operation.

6 Today, manufacturers should consider their marketing policies in the light of actual and potential ultimate markets for their products in relation to other competitive industries as well as to their own industry.

7 Manufacturers still should develop a formal allocation of marketing functions between manufacturer and wholesaler or retailer. But manufacturers should be in close touch with the inventory needs of their outlets so that these needs can be supplied quickly.

8 The various functions required for marketing of new products to different markets also should be itemized and low-cost marketing systems worked out for new products. The expensive trial-and-error search for the development of a profitable market for a brand-new product is no longer necessary, if this function approach is followed.

Marketing Still a Blind Spot

The full importance of marketing is more generally appreciated today than ever before. For this reason, many companies have been collecting mountains of marketing statistics. What to do with them, many companies still don't know, but they now have the means of analyzing them by computer, if more direction can be found for using the figures. Some parts of the $150 billion marketing cost are still almost ignored by marketers and others. Other functions of marketing will be integrated as means are found to quantify these functions properly.

This almost general oversight of marketing operations has been due to a lack of sound basis for coping with company, industry, and national marketing problems. We can now look to the future, however, with more optimism than ever before. In the past, we had a three-legged stool to stand upon. Marketing was defined, measured, and separated into its 47 component elements. We now have the fourth leg of the stool—computerization.

Twenty years ago, management began to apply to all functions of marketing the same standard which had been applied to the functions of production—the standard of productivity per man-hour. This standard is responsible for America's great strides in production over the past 50 years. By this standard of productivity, it has been possible to place exact valuation upon all existing production procedures and to appraise the merits of all proposed improvements. The application of the standard of productivity can do for marketing the same thing that it did for production. Instead of being applied function by function, and department by department, functions and departments may be integrated. For example, the sales effort of one company may be coordinated with the purchasing function of a customer. Little by little, the other functions can be quantified and integrated into the total corporate information system.

We thus have an even more practical way for a company to tackle its marketing problems. This functional approach to marketing, as in the past, can serve the practical purpose of giving individual companies and their customers a step-by-step procedure to improve their marketing operations on an integrated basis. Following the eight modernized recommendations offers a double reward to alert management. One benefit will accrue to profits from operations, another to reduced consumer prices. Action by the individual company and by integrated groups of buyer-seller companies is one key to the total improvement in our marketing system.

This further advancement of our marketing system promises a new and vital economic and social outlook based on continued management-science research and widespread application of industrial engineering procedures. This action by industries will insure the continued advancement and stability of both integrated production and marketing and will build increased purchasing power for the nation. ■

Invoicing

*41 Manufacturer's invoicing to wholesaler, retailer, or consumer.

42 Wholesaler's billing to retailer or consumer.

43 Retailer's cash and invoicing to consumer.

Product Servicing

44 Repair, maintenance, replacement.

Clerical Work

*45 Manufacturer's internal control and record keeping.

*46 Wholesaler's internal control and record keeping.

*47 Retailer's internal control and record keeping.

Why Not Try a "Go-Between" for New Products?

In recent years a number of new firms have sprung up to encourage profitable use of dormant patents

FINDING a backer with capital to develop and market an invention has long been the bane of the engineer working alone. Inventions sometimes pose problems for large companies whose engineers come up with ideas that simply don't fit the product line or promise the volume of business the company requires for a new venture. Inventions from these sources often lie fallow even though there are companies, especially small or medium-size firms, that could develop them profitably.

The inventor's plight has given rise to a new type of firm, the patent development agency, which brings innovator and company together to the benefit of all concerned. For some years now, a few of the large companies have operated affiliates that develop inventions of company employes and outsiders. NAVAN Products, an affiliate of North American Aviation, purchases, licenses, or markets promising new products submitted by individuals. (*PE, Mar 9, '59, p 37*). The products bear the NAVAN trade mark. During a nine-month period ending July 1961, the North American affiliate reviewed some 702 inventions (252 from the outside); expressed interest in 45 (23 from the outside); and will probably develop about 10 of these.

Machine tool line

One of the NAVAN specialties is a line of machine tools that are somewhat simpler and cheaper than many now on the market. One item that will be available soon is a radial drill press with a lightweight head that can be easily positioned. The head arm is a tension design similar to a cantilever bridge in place of the heavy conventional beam. Another invention is a traversing saw that cuts plate 1 in. thick and 4 ft wide. It will sell for $2500.

Recently a number of independents have come on the scene. The Mc-Laughlin Co, a Dallas, Texas consulting firm specializing in product and market research, recently announced that it has added a division known as Patent and Venture Evaluators, which screens new inventions from companies and individuals and circulates the good ones among clients who have subscribed to the PAVE service.

The PAVE contract guarantees each client at least 25 new-product ideas or business opportunities for consideration each year. If the company is interested in one of the ideas, it can then ask PAVE for a detailed study of the required financing and the market potentials. Philip McLaughlin, the company's founder, says six firms are now on contract and another 18 are negotiating with PAVE. He expects to have 25 to 50 participants by next September.

Many new products

The product ideas run the gamut of technology; many are in the mechanics and electronics fields. One product now making the rounds of PAVE clients is a device for use with the National Early Warning System. A compact unit that can be carried in a purse or coat pocket, it is designed to monitor certain predetermined radio frequency bands. If these bands go off the air, the device sounds an alarm.

Other inventions include:

A straddle-seal for introducing fluid pressure into a rotating shaft. The seal allows individual fluid control for various clutches and brakes on the shaft.

A radial-piston type of hydraulic oil motor, which converts reciprocal motion into revolving power through a crankshaft and planetary gearing.

A hydraulic timer actuated by a flexible pressure source metered through an adjustable orifice.

Multiple turbofans powered by a hydraulic drive system having stepless variable speeds and torque equilization.

One well established agency, the National Patent Development Corp, started in New York in 1958 and now has branches in Chicago, Washington, and Zurich. NPDC has some 30 clients, including American Machine & Foundry Co, the Linde Co, Chrysler Corp, and the Armour Research Foundation, all regular sources of inventions for licensing. Other inventions come from individuals and from overseas. The company's president, Jerome I. Feldman, has visited the USSR twice during the past year in search of Soviet developments suitable for cross-licensing.

On the other hand, NPDC has a number of regular clients who want to diversify and retain the patent agency to locate suitable new products. NPDC has also built up an extensive list of American companies that includes considerable information about their diversification intentions. This information, filed on IBM cards, is used as a guide in pinpointing potential licensees.

Screening inventions

When an invention comes its way, NPDC submits it to one of five full-time consultants, each a specialist in some field of engineering. The firm also has ten other consultants available for special problems. The consultants evaluate each invention and suggest that NPDC either drop it, try to license it, or put money into developing it further.

NPDC earns its living by charging a fixed annual fee to companies that retain it as a product scout and taking a percentage of the fees a licensee pays for manufacturing rights to a product. The firm may also market some products it has financed through R & D under its own name.

Feldman estimates his company licensed about 20 patents last year. One of the most recent agreements gave a company rights to manufacture scales based on a new principle that eliminates springs and balance wheels. Another license gave a lighting manufacturer rights to produce a device which warns that an electronic component is going to fail.

Feldman says his company has put its own money into developing a small atomic motor producing about one horsepower. A promising Soviet invention, he says, is equipment for producing very fine glass-insulated copper wire. The wire is only 10 microns in diameter and can be wound around a core of only 1/200-in. diameter. ■

How to select and effectively use a management consultant

Here are several practical guidelines for companies using consulting services

by Henry O. Golightly,

President

Henry Golightly & Company Inc.

YOU CAN GET THE BEST service from a management consultant when you apply a few basic rules that have been tested by time.

Some companies seem instinctive in their ability to select the right management consultant, and then use the service to best advantage. When you examine these situations closely, you discover they have something in common. In every case the company follows five good practices in the **selection** of consultants, and five other good practices in the **use** of consultants.

Here are five rules that experience proves will help you select a management consultant:

1. Don't listen to promises without proof. Each firm you consider will promise some kind of result. Don't let it stop there. Ask for solid evidence that the consultant has performed well in the past, for other firms with needs similar to your own.

Study the way the consultant talks about your needs and about his firm's services. Does he speak in meaningless generalities, or in specifics and with intelligence? Does he suggest only routine solutions to your problems, or does he ask questions that reveal an imaginative approach to your problem?

Ask him to define the objectives of previous work his firm has done, and then to spell out the results of this work.

If he cannot produce real evidence of positive results, continue looking for another consulting firm.

2. Look for the strong men in a consulting firm. Before you retain a consulting firm, meet and get to know the individuals who will work with you. Your opinion of them is more important than your opinion of the man who sold you the service.

The advantage of using a small consulting organisation is that your work is more certain to get the personal attention of a key man. You can get the same kind of service from large or small consulting organizations if you seek out its truly outstanding men. The key is to uncover men of stature and get them assigned to your work, regardless of the size of the consulting firm.

3. Don't consider consultants who are not frank and fearless. One value an outside consultant brings you is his ability to view your needs objectively and critically. But some con-sultants abandon the role of critic and simply try to keep their clients happy. Such consultants destroy the value of the service they sell. Avoid them.

Pick a consultant who demonstrates a deep sense of responsibility even if it means criticizing ideas that are popular in your company. Only by being totally honest and candid can a consultant fulfil his responsibility to your company.

4. Look for experience beyond your own industry. You sometimes get more service from a management consultant firm whose experience comes from fields other than yours alone. The firm may be able to bring you a broader range of possible solutions to your problems. It may give you a competitive advantage by suggesting ideas that have never been tried in your industry before.

On the negative side, when a consultant's experience is limited to your industry, his thinking may be blinded to the same improvement opportunities that you have been overlooking.

5. Look for consultants who will work well with your staff. It is always upsetting to some degree when a consulting firm comes into a company. Ask yourself: Can this consultant operate in a way that will not greatly upset my staff? Success in this regard calls for skill and special qualifications on the part of the consultant.

It also means following certain rules closely. One rule: the consultant should evaluate problems, not people (except, perhaps, psychologists who may be called in specifically to evaluate people). Occasionally a consultant will study a situation and report to his client: "The cause of your problem is Mr. Smith. Replace him and all will be well." This is not responsible consulting. The consultant who operates in this manner loses his effectiveness. In a short time, your staff will not cooperate with him.

The world of the consultant . . .

WHERE DO management consultants come from? How are they recruited and trained? How well are they paid?

In the US, about half the consultants enter the profession from industry. The other half are recruited directly from the university or business school.

Graduates who have become consultants frequently "go back to school," after several years of practice, to take higher courses in business administration.

In Japan, most consultants are university graduates in commerce and economics. Most are under 40.

In Britain, all consultants are recruited from industry. Much the same method applies in the rest of Europe.

All European management associations have a minimum age of at least 25 for admission to membership (in Germany and Switzerland, it is 35).

Most insist on a university education plus from two to ten years (usually five years) experience as a consultant.

In Britain, all new men joining a major consultancy receive from three to six months training, both theoretical and field work.

Staff list—Here is an analysis of the staff of a typical large consultancy, the Dutch firm, Raadgevand Bureau Ir., B.W. Berenschot N.V.

It has 180 fee-earners, of whom 114 have a technical background. Fifty are qualified engineers.

It has 27 university-trained economists and accountants, plus 18 psychologists and sociologists.

The average age of its men is just under 40, with 27 men under 30 and 26 over 50 years of age.

The staff represents about 1,400 man-years of experience as management consultants, composed of 40 men with less than two years experience, 60 men with between two and five years, 30 men with between six and 10 years, 25 men with between 11 and 15 years, and 25 men with more than 15 years.

Good pay—In all countries, time spent on a job is the main basis for the calculation of the fees consultants charge.

Consultants as a whole are well paid, their pay usually consisting of a substantial fixed salary and a profit-sharing or bonus system based on results. Dutch consultants salaries, for example, are "at least equal to the highest salaries paid to other executives in Holland."

Few men working for the big US agencies receive less than $16,000 (£5,700). Some earn three or four times as much.

In Europe, there is little movement of staff from one consultancy to another. Apart from those who retire, six to 10 per cent of consultants leave the profession each year. Three-quarters go into industry, the other quarter into banks.

If a consultant does a good job for you, he is a difficult man to "poach." French consultants' association rules do not permit a member to start working for a client he has already worked for in a consulting capacity. He also cannot work for a competing firm, and he cannot start his own consultancy without the permission of his former employer.

The proper approach is for the consultant to evaluate facts and leave it to the client to determine who, if anyone, is at fault. Select a management consultant who will help you determine what needs to be done, not who is blocking the way.

Once you have selected a management consultant, here are five guides for getting the best service.

1. Define the assignment in precise terms. Sometimes there is a difference between what a company wants from its consultants and what it gets. The cause can be a failure to define the assignment clearly in advance. This can be costly. Give a consultant vague objectives and his results are likely to be vague.

Sometimes the consultant "thinks big" and gets into an area beyond the limited scope of the project you intended. Sometimes he "thinks small" by doing a confined piece of work, when you really intended something broader and more general. This is not to say that an assignment, once defined, should not be changed. Often as the management consultant begins his work, it becomes clear that the assignment—as defined—is not consistent with the real needs of your company. At this point, the scope of the work should be redesigned and agreement reached between your company and the consultant on the job to be done.

Well defined goals are invaluable. When goals are meaningful and specific, they are forerunners of a consulting assignment that can be expected to produce profitable results.

2. Create internal co-operation in advance. Co-operation from your staff can magnify the results of an outside consultant's work. But resistance (including passive resistance) offsets the value of the service.

An outsider can be taken as a threat to your own staff, if his presence is not carefully explained early. The groundwork you lay should be designed to dissolve misunderstandings, jealousies, resistance to change, protective attitudes, and organizational problems. One key point is determining to whom the consultant should report. A good rule: have him report to the man with authority above the man most directly influenced by the consultant's work.

About the author

HENRY O. GOLIGHTLY heads the New York management consulting firm, Henry Golightly & Company Inc. The international arm of this firm, International Management Services Inc., operates from London and Luxembourg.

Mr. Golightly is a graduate of the University of Texas and holds a law degree. Before entering the field of professional consulting, he was vice-president of Rheem Manufacturing Co.

3. Give your time, your support and the facts. Three common mistakes are to retain a management consultant, and then 1) not give him your time and supervision, 2) not give him your demonstrated support, and 3) not give him facts he needs to do his work. One reason you hire a consultant is to get a job done when you lack time to do it yourself. But you may defeat yourself if you fail to invest at least a small portion of the time you save by working with the consultant, both at the start to give him facts, and on a continuing basis to guide what he does.

No one works well in a vacuum. Take time to exchange ideas with the outside specialist, and you will get better service from him. The outsider does not work well with a feeling of insecurity. If a man feels his relationship with you is uncertain, he may lose his willingness to express new opinions. But if he feels he can keep his place of favour even when offering criticism, you will probably develop not only a hard worker, but a faithful supporter. The consultant who can develop this personal involvement in the work is the man who will make your problems his own.

4. Never ask an outsider to break a confidence. Many managers fail to resist the temptation to seek confidential information from a management consultant. Part of the outsider's value to you is that he has or can get information you do not have and cannot get for yourself. Some information may come from other clients. Some may come from persons within your organization who will say things in confidence to a consultant they will not say to you.

If the outsider loses the confidence of the persons from whom he seeks information, his value to you is diminished. Let him use his information to your advantage, but with discretion. That way, you can feel confident he is keeping your confidences too.

5. Use your consultants to help put the recommendations into action. For political, economic or other reasons, compromises are sometimes made in putting into action the programme a consultant recommends. By the time all the compromising is done, the net result is sometimes insignificant compared to what it could be and should be.

The best way to avoid this is to keep the consultant on the job until the changes have been made and the new system is running smoothly. The objectivity a consultant provides in making his study can be equally as effective in putting the programme into action.

The cost of management consultant services can be viewed in two ways. Viewed one way, they are expensive. Viewed the other, they are not.

The fees of a management consultant sometimes seem high because the firm must maintain a staff of highly qualified men who, due to the nature of the work, experience a certain amount of unproductive time that adds to overhead. On the other hand, a well-chosen management consultant provides a service that cannot be performed as well—and perhaps not at all—within your own organization.

It is necessary to have the consultant define the purpose of the study and estimate the fees in advance. This permits the company to budget consulting costs in terms of anticipated results. It also provides good discipline for the consultant. He should live with his estimate, unless unforeseen difficulties arise, changing the scope of the study. If this happens, a new agreement on fees should be reached immediately, consistent with the revised nature of the study.

You can achieve economy in using outside services, not by seeking bargains, but by bringing together the right people with well-planned and well-managed assignments. You must always view the cost in terms of results. ■

The One-Man Engineering Firm

C. J. LYNCH

"There's a race of men that don't fit in," wrote Robert W. Service, the frontier poet and backroom balladeer. And among engineers, independent consultants perhaps belong to this breed. It's more than being a little above average in talent. Their motives are different . . . their attitude is different . . . their goals are different. In these times when most other engineers seek the security and stability of a large corporation, these rebels dodge group creativity, team-oriented business, and a slot in the organization chart. They prefer a basement-size engineering department, independence and the risks of private enterprise.

"I'm a kind of maverick," says one as he tips his chair away from his workbench and clasps his hands behind his head. "I don't work a 9-to-5 day, and of course don't get that regular pay-check at the end of the month. My fringe benefit is the satisfaction of doing the work I want to do, the way I want to do it. It's flattering to think there are companies who will pay me so I can live this way. Some people won't like it. But to me it's exciting—I never know who will call me next or what his problem will be."

The consultant idea, of course, is not a novelty in engineering. Large consulting firms have been around a long time. These are the corporations that supply engineering talent to build bridges and vehicular tunnels, install powerplants and hydro-electric projects. These are consultants in the classical sense—as familiar to the public as they are to the engineering profession.

The engineer's engineer

But in this age of specialties, a new kind of consulting engineer is beginning to emerge. He is the independent who through publicity in engineering journals and society meetings, has acquired a reputation as an expert in a narrow field of engineering—and has capitalized on it. He may rent a room in an office building or he may operate out of his own home; he may make considerable money . . . or he may starve.

Independent consultants can be grouped broadly into two classes. There are those to whom consulting is only a part-time job—perhaps a natural appendage to their work as university professor. They don't rely on it for a livelihood—it's simply a welcome and often challenging source of additional income. They aren't subject to the fluctuating whim of supply and demand—their salaried main job is a hedge against variations in the freelance market.

The other type is an all-out entrepreneur. His sole source of income is the consultant service he can sell. In his firm he is the president, vice-president, sales manager, engineering staff, bookkeeper and shipping clerk.

Sheer engineering competence . . . plus

Versatility, and freedom from confining procedures are the attributes that distinguish him from his fellow engineer. But what other qualities are needed? Engineering competence, of course, is basic. To the independent consultant this means experience, years of it, and a reputation in his established field. For this reason younger engineers have a harder time of it than the older, better established engineer. But a young man with special training is one of the new, fast-growing fields can command respect too.

Salesmanship appears to be the second most desirable quality. "The ability to sell a customer and keep him sold makes the difference in whether the consultant will eat tomorrow," a gear expert explains. Then he adds, "It is also the quality most likely to be lacking in an engineer."

Easy does it

Putting yourself in business isn't nearly as simple as it looks. To hang out your shingle and wait for someone to knock on your door, said one man candidly, "is probably the most certain, and surely the dullest path to bankruptcy you could choose." Advertising is not much good either (aside from the matter of dubious ethics). Most independents don't even bother to list themselves in the yellow pages of the phone book. This field is so small, so new, and so fluctuating that most of the men aren't even listed with their engineering society.

Usually an engineer gets into the consulting business slowly and cautiously—almost accidentally. The first job may come through a friend or business acquaintance and is done on a part-time basis. Then, somewhere during the middle of the second part-time job, he starts feeling that on the strength of his reputation and the broad application of his specialty, the consulting work will support him full-time. (But watch out, warn those who have tried it; the first two years are the hardest and it's best to have some source of independent income.)

After he becomes a little better established, he will probably want to keep several jobs going simultaneously. Contacting new clients may develop into a sizable part of his job. Friends, previous employers, vendors on a previous job, and engineering societies are all good sources. Ringing doorbells of companies that have products related to his specialty is another common technique. Fortified with a scrapbook of published papers and lists of his patents, he hopes to get placed on the list of qualified consultants when a problem in his specialty arises. Some independents send reprints of their by-lined articles to a carefully chosen list of potential clients. One man has an interesting gambit. He scans employment ads for companies trying to hire full-time employes for a job he could do part-time—then sells the company on the idea.

Keeping that wolf from the door

Most well-established one-man consulting firms have at least one or two steady clients who pay them on a retainer basis. A research physicist, for example, is on retainer to two large corporations which he visits perhaps once or twice a year at most. He spends the rest of his time at home, in his laboratory—or at his desk doing undirected research which may or may not lead to something profitable for his two clients. Does he do work for other companies too? "Well," he says, "my clients don't deny me that opportunity, but I don't invite any more work. I can keep busy just working for these two."

Another man, a metallurgist, works for 14 different noncompeting companies which he visits once or twice a month. His office is in the basement of his home located in an attractive suburb. He's been an independent consultant 12 years. In his spare time he teaches, writes books and technical papers. He works hard: lives comfortably.

Why does a company hire an independent consultant? First, and most common reason: a small company requires specialized knowledge to supplement its engineering effort but can't afford to hire a specialist full-time. Even large companies, with many such specialists already on the staff often need an outsider with recognized competence. The consultant offers availability, a fresh viewpoint and sheer engineering competence derived from years of experience with many wide-ranging problems in a narrow specialty.

The other common reason: extra help when the engineering department is overloaded. Most consultants prefer to avoid this type of work—it's too confining, too much of the routine they were trying to avoid when they launched into private practice. But for the employer, they are a good buy in such situations. They involve no overhead, no fringe benefits, and are not a permanent addition to the payroll to be carried when the need is gone. On an hourly-wage basis they are most expensive, but this is not a fair comparison—the full-time staff engineer costs more than twice his base pay in overhead.

Baggy pants no liability

When called in on a job, consultants may be put to work several ways. Those who make regular visits on a retainer usually spend a day talking with the men in charge of various projects. The job of these consultants is to keep efforts on the right track, point in new directions and assure management that money is not being drained away on projects with little merit. Sometimes they are given an office for the day and are visited by people bringing technical problems. "It's a rewarding experience," says a servo-systems expert. "Maybe you were up nearly all night on a previous job. You have a two-day growth of beard, your pants are baggy, shirt open at the neck, but they don't care—you're an expert. They literally line up outside the door. Vice-presidents run to buy your coffee. They pick your brains, you tell them what you know and they are apparently grateful. At least they continue to pay you to come back."

Another common arrangement is to get called in on a particular problem. It may be to design a small gearbox for a particularly ticklish application. In such cases, the consultant usually gets an exploratory contract—this gives him a chance to make some preliminary calculations and estimate what the bill will be. "Performance is what the company wants," consultants stress. "They want that gearbox and they want it within a specified period of time. They don't care where you get the information—books, manufacturer's data, other consultants—it doesn't

matter. Performance is what they want and what they pay for."

Because many clients like to get a production prototype on completion of the job, some men find it convenient to maintain a small machine shop and testing laboratory. And those who have invented a specialized device with a limited market may also have a small production shop. In some cases, the consulting service functions mostly as a sales gimmick. If the application calls for it, he may recommend his patented device and offer to custom-tailor it to the job.

Writing articles for trade publications and technical journals is not a very fat source of income. But the consultants do it—mostly to maintain status in the field. Or, in some cases, the consultant will write an article relating to some specialized work he has done for a company. The article is then published under company auspices, for company publicity; the consultant collects the standard author's fee plus a handsome bonus.

Growing pains for private enterprise

The independents are first to admit that they are not working in utopia. It requires an unusual kind of personality to get into the business and make it pay, they say.

Here are some of the things established consultants list when questioned about factors they underestimated or mistakes they made early in the game:

• It takes time to get established. There will be plenty of rough sledding the first couple of years. It's best to have some money saved up, or some source of independent income to carry you through the slack months.

• Don't forget that expenses are your own. If you take a trip to a society meeting, it comes out of your own pocket. And there will be no group insurance plans or provision for sick leave either.

• A one-man firm has difficulty getting catalogs, company literature, trade magazines. A time-clock man can usually get such things through the regular channels.

• Don't spend so much time on one project that you lose touch with what the rest of industry is doing. The facts a consultant gleans from a wide variety of sources are his stock in trade.

• There are times when you won't get the personal satisfaction of finishing a job you've started. If your recommendations are modified or misinterpreted after the situation has passed out of your control—you are blamed anyway.

• Don't undercharge for your services. Operating costs are greater than they appear at first glance and your workload has cyclical fluctuations. You are a specialist and you should charge accordingly. Fees for consultants vary and are of course, tied to the general economic picture. A daily charge of $150-200 is about average at present.

• Don't overestimate the potential market. One of the first things a company cuts when it begins to get economy-minded is service of this type. During periods of economic stress, the company may want to continue the relationship on a minimum basis but this is not very satisfactory. The consultant may not mind starting on a minimum basis—this is customary. But he anticipates the company will want more of his time when it gets deeper into projects he has suggested. If he is a top-notch man and has done a good selling job, he needn't worry. ∎

the contract engineer

He's a "leased" engineer from a contract firm—rented out for one specific project. He makes a lot of money and also gets a brisk engineering workout. With the job complete, he says goodbye with goodwill all around.

An increasing number of mechanical engineers who used to call a single company home are now leasing their skills to a cross section of American industry.

In the past decade the practice of contract engineering has grown prodigiously, with some 500 contract engineering firms today billing government and private industry more than $400 million a year for the temporary services of engineers and other technical personnel. Mechanical engineers, together with electronics engineers, make up the largest single manpower segment of the industry.

The Deal

What has lured engineers from permanent positions to the peripatetic life? There are several factors.

For some the appeal of more take-home pay has been the deciding factor. The average mechanical engineer working on a contract basis will earn from 20–30 percent more in straight pay than his permanently employed counterpart, or "captive" as he is known in the trade. Working for a firm which requested him in the first place because it was short of personnel, he is also in a good position to pile up plenty of overtime if he wishes. In addition, per diem pay is collected when the engineer is working and living away from home.

However, the contract engineer is not collecting the same degree of benefits as the permanent employee. Although in today's market he is being given several paid holidays, life insurance and health insurance,[3] the contract engineer presently does not receive a pension or any of the other assorted frills offered by most corporations. He realizes this and prefers to use his greater earnings to finance his own retirement plan.[4]

Many Virtues

Other engineers are attracted by the opportunity to

[3] All ASME members can obtain their own health and life insurance under the favorable terms of a Group Plan.

[4] This touches on a subject that is increasingly under discussion— the idea of "portability" of pension credits. Perhaps an engineer should have a pension "policy" that belongs to him, and to which each employer contributes during the period of employment. The U. S. Senate may soon be holding hearings on a bill to establish an employee's "nonforfeitable rights" in private industry's pension plans.

work on a steady progression of state-of-the-art projects. While working for a single corporation, they might find themselves redesigning the same piece of equipment over and over again for slightly different applications. As contract engineers they are being offered positions with corporations that need men for new and crash projects. Rarely does a company pay the additional costs of a contract engineer in order to put him on a routine assignment.

This variety of projects and companies usually asserts its value when a man finally does decide to accept a permanent position. Having been exposed to several top drawer projects and a variety of corporate approaches to working out problems, the contract engineer can usually command a better position and salary than other applicants who have more limited experience.

For many men, the opportunity of working with a company before deciding to accept an offer of permanent employment also has its advantages. Knowing a company's policies and personnel, a man is able to make a more intelligent decision than he could simply on the basis of a recruiter's promises.

For family men, one of the disadvantages of the field has been its migratory nature. It may be fine for the single fellow who elects to work in Florida in the winter and New England in the summer, but the man with a family usually doesn't want to move so often.

Close to Home

Fortunately for these men, the recent growth of the industry has created situations whereby a man can function as a contract engineer and yet return to his home every evening. In such engineering centers as Boston, New York, or Los Angeles, for example, hundreds of firms that employ contract personnel are within commuting distance of residential areas.

Geographical preferences are among the many factors listed when a man submits his résumé to a contract engineering firm. In addition to work and educational backgrounds, résumés include the engineer's preferences regarding wages, hours, types of projects desired, and any other professional and personal factors deemed important. No job assignments are ever made without the mutual agreement of the engineer and the contract

ERNEST J. MILANI[1]
President, Lehigh Design Company,[2]
Waltham, Mass.

[1] Registered Professional Engineer.
[2] Lehigh Design Company, with offices in many cities, is a "contract firm," "renting" engineers. It is a subsidiary of Arcs Industries of New York, N. Y.

firm.

The amount of time a man might expect to stay with a single project varies widely. There are men working for Lehigh Design who have been assigned to the same manufacturer for over seven years. Others have been called in for a week or even a few days. On the average, however, most assignments are for a matter of months. The engineer is usually given a fairly accurate prediction of the duration of his assignment.

In today's market, there is no necessity for an engineer to miss a single day's work between assignments. Major contract firms like Lehigh have consistently had more job requirements than current employment, and the fellow who is terminated from a project on Friday can be at work someplace else on Monday morning, if he wishes. In fact, a mechanical engineer could work 7 days a week, 52 weeks a year, if he so desired. On the other hand, some engineers, bolstered by their extra pay, choose to take frequent vacations or sabbatical leaves.

How It Began

Although it has grown to maturity only recently, contract engineering dates back to the years preceding World War II. It was born primarily as a tooling service for the Detroit auto-makers who needed skilled personnel badly at prescribed intervals but couldn't afford to keep people idle during the long slack periods. During the war, men with a variety of technical skills were recruited by young contract firms which were supplying the needs of manpower-starved manufacturers.

The industry was given another big push by the post-war boom in electronics, and then again in the early 1960's when cost-plus contracts became distasteful to government and corporations could no longer afford to keep idle engineers on the payroll.

Paradoxically, both engineers and corporations are attracted to the contract industry because of its payroll breakdown. Engineers become contract personnel because they will receive more money, and yet corporations hire from contract firms because it is an economy for them.

For a company to hire an engineer by itself for a limited period of time is an expensive proposition. Recruiting costs are high, involving costly advertising and numerous skilled personnel. In addition, costly fringe benefits must be paid a man, even if he will be working for only a few months.

By using a contract engineering firm, a corporation eliminates all recruiting and fringe costs. It pays, in effect, for man-hours of work. The rate per man is higher than on the open market, but compared to total hiring costs, it is an economy.

In addition, most companies find it bad employee relations to hire and fire men at a rapid rate. Contract engineering personnel are taken off the payroll as soon as their work is completed, with never an ill feeling.

Most contract firms and their clients do not actively recruit engineers straight out of college. Experienced men are desired because they can adapt to new problems and new environments more quickly, becoming productive soon after their arrival on a project. The average contract engineer is in his middle 30's and has worked both on a contract basis and "direct."

You Belong to the "Contract Firm"

While working for a client company, the contract engineer is still an employee of the contract firm. He receives his pay and benefits from the contract firm, and in many cases even his supervisors on the job are fellow contract men. In some instances, instead of sending men to a client's facility, Lehigh will form its own technical teams and work on a client's project in its own buildings.

The conditions under which a contract engineer will be requested by a client vary widely. Sometimes one, two, or three engineers will be hired to beef up a priority program. In some cases the hiring is massive. Last year an aircraft manufacturer contracted for approximately 1000 engineers and technical personnel for a high priority project on the East Coast.

In general, a contract firm has a client breakdown of about 50 percent military-government and 50 percent commercial. The commercial segment has been growing rapidly in recent years as corporations have learned about the utilization of this new personnel tool. ■

Working with Engineering "Job Shops"...

Establishing the objectives and defining responsibilities are important preliminaries to getting what you want from

{ # Consulting Development Groups

THE REASONS that a manufacturing concern employs a consultant or development organization depend on such variables as work loads, size of the concern, character of the product, the background of the personnel in the engineering department, and many others. An outside group may be retained to bring fresh ideas to an established product, to provide specific advice on a specialized problem or to relieve the work pressure on the engineering department.

Whatever the reason, optimum results can only be obtained through mutual understanding and cooperation between client and consultants. Suggestions and comments that will help in insuring this goal are discussed in following pages.

ARCHER W. RICHARDS
Executive Vice President
Designers for Industry, Inc.

Establish Objective

The objective should be stated as clearly as possible. Until the consultant or development organization understand the underlying purpose of the project, they cannot proceed intelligently or avoid needless duplication.

For example, suppose the project is to be the redesign of a process machine. The purpose might be to reduce cost, facilitate case of maintenance, speed up production, incorporate more safety features, or increase output of the equipment. If some of the objectives are incompatible, the important ones must be pin pointed.

All data on the product should be made available to the consultant, since before the job is started, he must evaluate the product's limitations and potentialities. He must take into consideration the development history,

conditions of use, performance specifications, user desires, and manufacturing facilities. With this background, both parties can arrive at a mutual understanding not only of what is to be done but how soon, for what fee, and with what facilities.

Expect Contract

The client should expect the consulting organization to have a standard contract form. Normally, this form should contain a complete description of costs and expenses, define patent rights, and outline the confidential nature of the work; concise project work descriptions should be included as a part of the contract (Table I). However, the client should feel free to write his own definitive purchase order in place of the consultants contract if he desires.

The method of basing the project cost will vary with the job. Survey

work—the gathering of field information and preparation of product design specifications—can normally be done for a stated price. Development-design work cannot be set at a fixed price due to inherent "unknowns", but an estimate can be prepared, Table II, and should be expected.

In some instances, where the development is of a highly technical nature, a preliminary authorization of expenditure is the most logical procedure. This authorization covers the preliminary analyses, field investigation, development of specifications and the design approach. The client should expect to get for this preliminary authorization a comprehensive report of findings and recommendations, specifications, and a detailed budget estimate for the following design program.

Whatever plan is followed, this fact should be checked: that the consulting

Table I—Major Points Covered in Contract

COMPENSATION

The Client agrees to pay to the Designer for the services rendered based on the following per hour rates for an eight-hour day or forty-hour week (or for a ten-hour day when men are out of town). Overtime adds $33\frac{1}{3}$ per cent and double time $66\frac{2}{3}$ per cent to the rates, and is performed only upon Client's authorization in writing.

Itemized invoices will be mailed Client on approximately the 1st and 15th of each month, payable net 10 days.

Detail draftsman, laboratory assistant.. —— per hr

For building laboratory or prototype models, samples, pilot production, tools, jigs and fixtures:
Experimental machinist, model builder, technician...................................... —— per hr

For layout drafting, testing, inspection, laboratory work:
Layout man, junior designer, inspector, technical illustrator........................... —— per hr

For product design, field investigation, processing and detail checking:
Project designer, field engineer, production engineer, checker.......................... —— per hr

For preliminary investigations, calculations, creative design, and creative direction:
Project engineer, senior project designer, industrial designer, physicist, market analyst..... —— per hr

For Project formulation, detail planning, and direction of project:
Assistant project manager, senior project engineer, senior industrial designer.............. —— per hr

For consultation, problem analysis, preparation and over-all direction of project reports:
Project Manager .... —— per hr

EXPENSES

The Client further agrees to reimburse the Designer for sums paid for incidental expenses, such as costs of transportation or living expenses, incurred by the Designers, or its employees while traveling in discharge of duties connected with work, costs of reproducing drawings, telegrams, long distance calls, expressage, and for the cost (plus 15 per cent for handling) of materials used.

PATENTS

(a) Designer shall make promptly to Client, and in any event prior to the final settlement under this agreement, a complete disclosure of all inventions made in carrying out any work under this agreement, and Client shall have the right at its own expense, to file, prosecute and act upon applications for patents thereon, and Designer shall secure the execution of the necessary papers and do all things requisite to protect Client's interest in prosecuting such applications to a final issue.

(b) Designer agrees to and hereby does sell, assign, and transfer, or agrees to procure the sale, assignment and transfer unto Client without additional payment by Client, of the whole right, title and interest in and to the said inventions, discoveries, patent applications, letters patent, divisions, continuations and reissues thereof in any country, and including all inventions which for the first time were actually or constructively reduced to practice as a result of any work under this agreement, whether patented or unpatented.

(c) Designer further agrees to procure the appearance of its officials or its employees in any legal proceeding and generally to do everything possible to aid Client, its successors or assigns and nominees to obtain and enforce proper protection of said patent applications, patents and inventions in all countries. Client agrees to pay Designer for the actual time required to perform services requested under this subsection (c) on the basis of rates in effect when services are performed and to reimburse Designer for out-of-pocket expenses incurred in this connection.

(d) Designer agrees to contract with its employees and officers, who are to be connected with the work to be performed hereunder, requiring such employees and officers (1) to assign to Designer or its nominees any such inventions, etc., referred to in this paragraph and (2) to execute and deliver patent applications on such inventions, and (3) to take all other action necessary or desirable to carry out, insofar as they are concerned, the Designer's undertaking contained in this paragraph.

(e) Nothing in this agreement, or any work specified hereunder or in any purchase orders, shall constitute a waiver by Client of any of its rights under any Client's patents.

CONFIDENTIAL NATURE OF WORK

Designer agrees not to disclose to any person, firm, corporation, other than to Client's or Designer's employees or officers directly concerned with work under this agreement, any details or information concerning any design, engineering or development work to be or being performed for Client under this agreement and further agrees not to do for any person, firm or corporation other than Client, any design, engineering or development work on particular subjects or projects concerning which work pursuant to or under this agreement has been, or is being, or is to be undertaken for Client. These restrictions shall continue in effect for six months beyond the completion or termination of this agreement.

MUTUAL CONSIDERATION

The Client and the Designer mutually agree that neither party will employ a member from the other party's staff without the written consent of the parties to this agreement. These restrictions shall continue in effect for six months beyond the completion or termination of this agreement.

organization has clearly defined standard hourly rates for the various types and levels of technical personnel to be employed.

The charges to be paid by the client should be detailed to the nth degree. Itemized invoices should be mailed to the client every two weeks, payable net in ten days. No work should be initiated until after client approval has been obtained. Each client should retain the unquestioned right to end this project at any time, should he so desire. Regular contact with the client should be maintained to make certain that he is satisfied with the results accomplished.

Demand Patent Study

This beginning should be followed by a patent study. This clears the field and establishes what is open country and what is fenced-in territory. This should be coordinated with a detailed analysis of competition, both through literature resources and by contacts with industrial firms.

Expect Cooperation of Entire Organization

The client should rightly expect that, in subjecting the product to an engineering and design analysis, the consultant will enlist the talents of each man on his staff. A design specialist can uncover aspects of the product that may escape the scrutiny of the engineer. A draftsman with a full background in, say, bearings or switches may make suggestions that will improve machine operation. A tool designer can work hand-in-glove with a man deeply versed in process engineering and effect tangible results. An engineer with a wide knowledge of manufacturing methods and machinery can modify the projections of a youthful stylist. Look for an organization with several fields of experience —electronics, electro-mechanical, hydraulic, and mechanical—to be sure that "best ways" will be uncovered.

All in all, the unique faculties of each member of the group should be pooled and applied to the job. This can be done via chatty over-the-board sessions or through formalized, regularly scheduled group conferences. The latter is usually more productive of creative ideas but takes more time.

A consulting organization that does not give its clients this over-all, coordinated service is denying itself a distinguishing asset and depriving its clients of best results.

Insist on Preliminary Design

Once the product has been studied to see what it will and should do, what materials should be used in its development and how much it will cost, the consulting group should produce a preliminary design. This stage of the job is of the highest importance because it is here that points-of-view and approaches first exhibit themselves. Over-insistence on one otherwise desirable element of design may conflict with another. Attempts to adjust the design to fit an unusual field condition may jar with manufacturing requirements. A move to cut manufacturing costs through design simplification may eliminate a feature preferred by users or industrial buyers. Well-reasoned and defensible compromises must be made at this particular time to insure optimum success.

Ask for Laboratory Models

The construction and testing of laboratory models should follow. These should be tested rigorously, both in the laboratory and the field. Products that measure up in the engineering model shop sometimes fail to stand up under the environmental shocks of actual operation. The testing of models and the re-arrangement of designs should continue until both harmonize, and only until it is determined that the performance and product specifications have been met.

Whether these test machines should be constructed by the consultant or the manufacturer is a point that should be determined prior to writing the contract. There are advantages to both approaches.

Manufacture of these test models by the client gives his production engineers the opportunity to evaluate how the design fits in with standard equipment and methods. By the other approach, continuity of the design program and supervision of test construction by the development-design group

places job responsibility where it belongs. In actual practice, the client's engineering department—usually the product engineers who have the responsibility for the designs—work closely with the consulting organization during this stage, so that they are conversant with the problems even if the latter group builds the models. Also, limited initial production runs will overcome any unforseen difficulties.

Let the Consultant Make Drawings

The next step involves the preparation of manufacturing drawings, drawing lists, bills of material, specifications, manuals of operation and maintenance. Some clients believe that an outside firm cannot possibly prepare drawings identical to the ones they use, but this service should be part of the "package" expected from a professional group of independent engineers, Fig. 1. It saves the time of the clients' engineers and allows the consultant to follow through on problems with which he is already familiar. The loan of established standards and a few reference drawings to a consulting organization experienced in working to many different standards practices will insure that the drawings conform to the clients' requirements.

The final step is the manufacture of a prototype. This completed, full sized product should then be tested by part and as a totality. If the tests reveal a need for design modifications, these can be incorporated in the drawings.

This complete follow-through of design gives the final product a thoroughly interwoven identity; each portion of the product is related organically to the whole. This approach also eliminates the manufacturer's having to do a large portion of the work. He is given a design ready for production.

Expect That Work Be Done in Confidence

Besides the points previously discussed, the client should expect that certain ethical standards and procedures will be exercised by the engineering firm.

For example, it is imperative that all work be in complete confidence.

An agreement not to reveal any and all information and data handled by the contracting consultant should be made a part of the contract; any violation should be just cause for an immediate termination. The reasons for this are rather obvious but they bear repeating. The client hires the consultant to serve him, not the industry. He pays good money for this exclusive service. The consultant's innovations and recommendations may create cost savings, better processes and methods, and a superior product. Revealment of any part of these to competitors or anyone else may destroy the client's time advantage.

This area of confidence should embrace all facets of each project. It should include not only patents, copyrights, and trademarks, but all ideas and techniques offered the client during the life of the individual project. The client's name or field of business should not be mentioned when contacting suppliers and other information sources. Normally, the consulting engineer agrees not to re-employ the same technique and methods for a future client until at least six months after the previous project has been ended. The client should be protected patent-wise through an orderly and neat recording of all original and new developments. Each idea or suggestion should be recorded on a special tracing paper, and typewritten reports on all work should be submitted either weekly or semi-weekly. All patentable devices should be assigned to the client at no extra charge whatsoever.

The consultant should agree in writing not to hire the client's personnel during the period of the project and for six months thereafter. This is but common courtesy and yet it is violated almost daily. It goes without saying that a client can hardly feel good about a firm that lures away some of his top engineers. Such practices besmirch the reputation of consulting engineers. In these times of engineer scarcity, it is all the more essential that "pirating" be avoided.

Demand Cooperation but Resist Integration

Client-consultant cooperation is extremely important. The consultant should work with, not outside, the client's organization. Total detachment might result in a product not easily identifiable with other products in a line.

Such procedure also insures client control of the project, and enables the design-development team to coordinate their developments with the particularized character and policies of the manufacturer.

Yet the engineer needs to maintain a clear, undistorted perspective. He should mingle with the client's engineers and designers but never become one of them. If he were to do this, he would soon lose his objective creativeness—the chief quality for which he is being paid. He should avoid using the client's engineering personnel but he ought to use the client's equipment and facilities whenever possible to keep the cost of his services down.

Clients should feel at liberty to visit the consultant's plant or base or operations. A consultant should make no attempt to resist investigation of his abilities and resources. One who does is definitely a bad risk.

While adherence to these principles may not assure a good product—that depends on the consultant—it decreases chances for failure and lessens the possibility of friction. ∎

Table II—Proposal and Cost Estimate

COMPANY
ADDRESS
DESCRIPTION OF WORK
DATE   19

	Project Management	Senior Engineer	Project Engineer	Project Designer	Designer	Draftsman	Checker	Experimental Mgr.
A. PRELIMINARY INVESTIGATIONS — Product: Technology, Function, Structure, Appearance; Products: Competitive; Markets: Demand, Prices; Project Programming								
B. PATENT STUDIES AND EVALUATION								
C. CALCULATIONS AND SPECIFICATIONS — Product Characteristics; Basic Calculations; Design Studies and Specifications; Engineering Conference								
D. REPORT OF INVESTIGATIONS								
E. PRELIMINARY DESIGN — Initial Engineering Layout; Experimental Model Sketches; Function and Appearance Design; Other Industrial Art								
F. PRACTICAL EXPERIMENTATION — Build Experimental Model(s); Test and Modify Model(s); Modify Designs, Calculations and Specifications								
G. CLIENT CONFERENCE: MODIFICATIONS								
H. FINAL DESIGN — Engineering Layouts; Appearance Renderings, Photos, etc.; Finalized Other Technology								
I. CLIENT REPORT: MODIFICATIONS								
J. DESIGN EXECUTION — Detail Drawings; B/Ms, Dwg. Lists, Specs, Prints; Checking								
K. PROTOTYPE(S) BUILD — Test and modifications								
L. PRODUCTION ENGINEERING — Process and Cost Estimating; Special Tool Design and Details								
M. MANUAL OF OPERATION AND MAINTENANCE								
N. FINAL REPORT — Total Services, Hours, Estimated; Service Rate Per Hour, $; Total Services, Amount, Estimated	—	—	—	—	—	—	—	—
TOTAL $								

So You Want To Be A Consultant

Fame and fortune may await the successful consultant, but there are many pitfalls in the process of getting started. Here are hints on what he must know and how to make the plunge.

GUY E. WEISMANTEL, *Western Regional Editor*

Becoming a chemical engineering consultant requires certain experience, interests and aptitudes. These relate to why, how and when someone chooses the consulting profession.

Very few people start out with this goal. The idea may have come to them as they reached the senior year in college. Or, after being with the same industry for a number of years, one might think that he knows a lot about the industry and ought to try to exploit his knowledge.

Still, this is not enough reason to choose a consulting career. Paramount is the innate desire toward proprietorship and strong motivation toward becoming an entrepreneur.

Even then, most engineers do not end up in consulting—for the traits just mentioned can be applied to starting any business. So, rather than consulting, one may find himself owning a company, and selling a product or service.

An analysis of why one individual may choose consulting while another chooses another business enterprise may relate to the former's desire to exploit his technical knowledge, and the latter's wish to use the same but put more emphasis on running a business. The triggers in most cases, however, are the desire to be one's own boss and the personal satisfaction that comes with this responsibility.

Preparation and Requirements

One prerequisite doesn't relate at all to engineering. It is something you definitely cannot have—namely, a wife who insists on living on a monthly paycheck. Seeking low overhead, most consultants who start their own businesses initially work from their homes; so they must be able to get along with the lady of the house all the time. She can be a real asset. Certainly, it is unusual for a man to consider this career without the proper understanding and backing of his wife.

The decision to form one's own consulting company is sometimes quite deliberate, perhaps made several years earlier, sometimes even upon bcoming an engineering graduate. In other cases, a person finally becomes aware of his desire after being faced with, and fed up with, company (or university) status and political problems.

Sometimes an individual's aggressive nature causes him to go on his own. Others, who are sensitive to business and personnel problems, decide to avoid the rat race and do the engineering that they enjoy without the harrassment that accompanies big business. Whereas some people can thrive on the "organization," consulting does offer an alternative.

Quite often, the nature of the consulting business he chooses to enter is not clearly defined until a person reaches a particular point in his career. Then the choice of field is made. From that time, acquiring a background of experience and capabilities becomes a concrete goal.

In other cases, the consultant has, by being associated with a business or industry for years and years, become an expert. (This occurs without one really knowing it is happening.) Then someone or something backs him up against a wall and forces a decision: Are you going to choose consulting and take advantage of the opportunity to be proprietor and manager of your own affairs, or are you going to continue to work for someone else? Witnessing failures of others, an engineer may think about this for years, trying to work up the nerve to quit a job and a paycheck to face the unknown.

CAN YOU live with your wife (and she with you) 24 hr. a day?

The Decision Is Finally Made

Now, it pays to have friends. Every consultant tells you this, and it might be added that it pays to have friends who are aware of, and have confidence in, your abilities. For sure, people who do not know the consultant and people who do not like him won't be giving him business at anytime. But, if an engineer has friends in industry and professional organizations, he is started in the right direction.

Timing is an important consideration when entering the consulting business. Are you ready? Is the economy ready? When all systems are "go", usually the first step is to announce that you are starting on your own by sending a personal letter to all those who know and, even more so, trust you. (For this is a field that requires an ability to keep confidences.)

Your first clients will come from this group, generally by referrals, though there are occasions where a consultant starts with one good customer (in fact, this bird in the hand can be the stimulus that pushes a person into the field). For the business to really succeed, however, one must give it time. Success in the consulting field will not come without hustle, plus knocking on a lot of doors. Even the fully qualified individual with full confidence in his abilities will have to be at least in part a salesman.

An excellent way to get both your name and your abilities on public view is to write articles for technical magazines. In addition to enhancing your professional prestige, the act of organizing an article helps point out gaps in your knowledge. It's difficult to write a good article without learning something in the process.

Is There Opportunity for the Youngster?

The chemical process industries are slow to accept the young genius. Rather, companies tend to seek the advice of the older person with experience and specialized knowledge, plus professional contacts. This may not be right, but it does express the attitudes of the industry. There is a general feeling that whiz kids can consult in the field of electronics, transistors, transducers, etc., where there are few old-timers, but chemical engineering is an area for well-developed, well-seasoned technical know-how. This may indicate that a group of bright young ChEs specializing as CPI computer experts could be highly successful as consultants. We haven't seen this happen—yet. Presently there is some doubt that a man, without having spent the time to acquire experience in his specialized field, can operate successfully as a consultant on his own.

An existing consulting organization is an excellent spot for a young engineer to acquire experience. Here, he can become an authority in his own right.

Are You Old Enough?

Today's ChE consultant may have graduated in 1942 and started his company in 1955; or graduated in 1932 and gone on his own in 1962. Generally, a man younger than 45 has neither the experience nor the gray hairs that will allow him to be accepted.

There is a good basis for a minimum age limit—because consulting calls for much creative thinking, which usually relates to past experiences. The successful consultant has a built-in ability to correlate clients' problems with experience he has had beforehand.

There are glowing horizons for the consulting engineer because there is a shortage of talent, even in the U.S., as verified by the cry heard from industry and government. Possibly, there will be a trend toward "task force consulting" to allow efficient use of what technical talent is available.

The profit motive may force companies to call on the specialist because they just do not have the people themselves.

What Other Preparations Are Necessary?

Most consultants agree that schools do not prepare an engineer for this career. When given a job to "straighten out a plant," one may have to study everything from cooling water to high-speed machinery; it may be necessary to perform a complete plant investigation that the novice just cannot do.

What other preparations are necessary before choosing consulting? Universally, consultants concur that the engineer must have some business background. But this is not enough. He must be versed in marketing and in writing and speaking. To be sure, he must be a good listener.

There are other important factors. One must know how to read a financial statement and an annual report, and be familiar with sales. Prerequisities may be different in each case, so that the degree of emphasis in any one particular area may be different. But there *are* prerequisites. Of these, we must consider:

• Business acumen.

• The ability to sell—both himself and his service, which in consulting amounts to about the same thing.

• Ability to get along with clients and their employees.

• Adequate education—a consultant must be able to prepare reports on technical projects; and he must answer questions of law and business, transportation, market conditions, manufacturing politics, finance,

SELLING HIM-SELF is the beginning consultant's biggest job.

EXPENSES for the first year may total $20,000.

agriculture, economics, all or any one of which may be as important as the technical project itself.

• Professional engineering license in the state where practicing.

• Broad experience in responsible charge of engineering work and projects of the same type and magnitude as those he hopes to obtain from clients.

• Firm belief in his own professionalism and the ability to communicate this to clients.

• Necessary money to live for a 6 to 12-month period during which time his income may not do much more than cover the expenses of setting himself up. One consultant estimates at least $20,000 for the first year's living and business expenses.

Specialization

Small consultants point out that no one can do all jobs efficiently, and to be successful the small consultant should specialize. In the case of a small partnership, all members of the firm need not have all the traits mentioned above, but the firm as a whole must have them. Each individual may have his individual specialty.

Most smaller organizations are specialists in a particular field or related fields. To quote one small consultant, "Offhand, I would say it would be easier to be successful as a specialist, since most of our clients are industrial concerns who have engineering capabilities of their own and only turn to outside firms when they need certain specific knowledge and experience."

Specialization is important because a person may consider serving an industry where there is a limit to the number of consulting jobs available. Alternatively, one might consider specializing in a particular problem area common to all industries in the CPI—e.g., computerization.

One nice thing about specialization is that one can choose his competition, so to speak. For example, in a particular geographical area there may be one consultant who specializes in design of petroleum complexes, another who specializes in inorganic chemistry, and another in chemical marketing. The field might be wide open for a ChE who specializes in personnel relations and communications. This is an area where the chemical engineer can understand the technical mind, and very often this is the thing that a psychologist cannot do because of the inability to talk an engineering language.

Why Are Consultants Used?

Many of the companies that use consultants have a full-time engineering staff, but on occasion a consultant is called in. He can be placed directly on the payroll to handle a particular project, or can be called in on a fee basis. The company itself may seek out the consultant, or perhaps go directly to a college to get the advice of those in academic circles. This is particularly true of R & D projects.

Large companies use consultants to verify internally generated opinions, theories and results. Such corporations may also go to a specialist because not everything in the way of knowledge is "in house." If a firm is expanding into a new geographical area, it may call on a geologist or industrialist for information. Then, too, the company may be interested in a particular problem for only a short time and will then retain a consultant. It may not pay to put on a staff for the period and paperwork involved.

There are companies involved with the CPI that have no chemical engineers on their staffs. A bank, for example, may call on the consultant for something that it is not geared to do itself.

Other businesses may use a consultant to check into acquisitions and merger potentials without revealing themselves. They may also be interested in economic feasibility studies or planning.

Consultants definitely are used for troubleshooting. This is an interesting situation, for the company may not be able to come up with a positive answer to a problem. Plant people may be too tied up to handle the job, and, in this case, a consultant can be hired on an as-needed or one-shot basis.

SPECIALIZATION is the key to success in consulting.

DAILY RATES of $100 and $200 are common; some consultants make as much as $1,000 a day.

What Size Company Uses Consultants

One consultant was really surprised when he hung out his shingle. He had thought that firms too small (and poor) to hire their own engineering staffs would be his best customers, but just the opposite held true. Large firms became his clients because they believe that, even in a large company, staffs can get overworked and will need the talents of people not on the payroll.

Smaller outfits often depend on the equipment and material salesmen to supply the technical know-how that they need. Such firms consider it a waste to have a consulting engineer do a job when supplier firms will do the same job free. But this can really be expensive; the consulting engineer may reveal the problem is not "a better dust collector," but a "change in raw material, and in the process itself."

Consultants are hired because they can do the job quicker, better and cheaper than one who is not familiar with the process or who has no background in the activity.

The Job Itself

Once on the job, the consultant is faced with building a team operation. He is working for and with company employees, and their reactions (particularly if this the consultant's first job with the company) will be varied.

One can run into hostile plant engineers who fear that a consultant may reflect on their own competency. To forestall this, company management should point out that a short-term enlargement of the staff is needed for a specific project.

In general, however, there are not many problems of being accepted by plant personnel because these engineers generally are down-to-earth people who are trying to make a process or plant run for the benefit of the company. Also, it is now so common to call in consultants that no stigma is attached to it.

How Well Does It Pay?

Both the time on the job and the price vary greatly from consultant to consultant and from job to job. For short-term jobs, the consultant usually gets $100 to $200 per day, although some may make as high as $1,000 a day.

A consultant may also work on a retainer basis. This means that he is paid a set amount each month in return for being available for a certain number of hours or days during the month. Often a consultant may be kept on retainer by several firms. This gives him a guaranteed income, but limits the time that he can sell to others since he never has a long period of uninterrupted time available.

One thing of great importance is the setting of a fair fee acceptable to management. On occasion, the exact fee may be flexible, being finally set after the consultant has been on the job a week or two and has analyzed the problem.

Opportunity and Growth

Some consultants prefer not to expand greatly. They find that income may be optimum if the firm has one and a half employees—the engineer and his wife. Whether or not to expand depends mostly on the individual's temperament and economic desires.

Opportunities for the consultant abound. In addition to the many jobs in this country, the whole world beckons. Technical consultants are needed in South America, Asia and Africa. Foreign banks want them, as does foreign industry. For the individual who likes to travel, this field is wide open.

Nevertheless, the average consultant is still a man who works long hours and weekends. Together with the great opportunities come the responsibilities and problems that accompany the privilege of being in business for himself. ∎

Meet the Author

Guy E. Weismantel is CHEMICAL ENGINEERING's Western Regional Editor, based in Los Angeles. He has a B.S. in chemical engineering from the University of Notre Dame. Prior to coming to CE, he worked for the O'Brien Corp., manufacturers of paint and varnish, where he was Western Div. Production Manager and Technical Director.

Don't Let SALESMEN Plan Your Products

IRWIN P. SHARPE, Management Consultant
West Orange, N. J.

A salesman, so the theory goes, is on the firing line —as close to the customer and his needs as it is possible to get. If he is a good salesman he knows his market, he knows his customer, he knows what products and features his customers want—so the theory goes.

Well, it just isn't so. Salesmen are excellent sources of product ideas, but they are emotional, enthusiastic, and their memories are limited to last week's lost sale. Their ideas must be sifted and evaluated. They offer opinion, not facts. And, being good salesmen, they can often sell their opinions, to management's ultimate sorrow.

One manufacturer let his sales department talk him into redesigning his line of industrial temperature controls. A novel method of controlling range settings and a high-fashion instrument case would double sales, they insisted. So a team of crack engineers took two years and $200,000 to develop prototypes.

The prototypes worked, they were beautiful, but when the manufacturer contemplated his tooling cost he got cold feet. He wanted a little objective assurance that remote control and beautiful cases were what the customers wanted—and would pay for.

So, over salesmen's protests the manufacturer set an independent market researcher to work and, just to hedge his bets, set a company group to see what they could find as well.

Both groups made the same report. The customers didn't need, didn't want, and still worse, wouldn't pay for the new features. The reports were so gloomy that the manufacturer decided to shelve the whole project. The executives lost face, the company lost $200,000 and engineering lost two years—all of which might have been avoided with an immediate, and scientific, survey.

The Gang Approach

Often distributors and salesmen lock arms to pressure a manufacturer into putting a new product on the market. The combined attack is pretty nearly irresistable. Distributors, too, are on the firing line. And as far as the manufacturer is concerned, they are his only real customers.

One air-conditioner manufacturer was overwhelmed by his exuberant sales manager and top distributor. The two had carefully "analyzed" their market and, in glowing terms, described the need for a small, central air-conditioning unit for low-priced homes.

The manufacturer underwrote a market study. It showed that while there was a vast latent market for the proposed product, it would be a good long time before customers started beating a path to his door.

Still, the researchers might be wrong. After all, whom can you trust more, your own sales manager or a group of strangers? The manufacturer set his engineering team at work developing the small air conditioner. But, just in case, instead of tooling up to make the new model by the thousands, only a few hundred new models were made. With $150,000 worth of baby air conditioners in his warehouse, the manufacturer sat back and waited for the distributor's carload orders.

He may still be waiting. After two years the distributor had ordered a total of five units. Even at a price far below cost, the inventory barely moved. The sales manager and the distributor sang a familiar tune: "You were too late."

But was he? Certainly the high-fashion market requires split-second timing, but in hard goods "poor timing" is just sales staff cover-up. The real cause of failure was: The market never existed except in the minds of an imaginative salesman.

The salesman is insulated from the customer by a wall of distributors and wholesalers. Distributors and wholesalers are, in turn, screened from customer contact by the retailers. And an insulated salesman or distributor can't tell you what a customer wants. He only knows if the customer likes or dislikes what is offered—and the manufacturer often knows as much about that as he does.

Further, most salesmen have no idea of the technical problems and costs of new-product development. To them, engineers live in a strange world of blueprints, slide rules and drafting boards, and can—with prodding —develop just about anything required. They usually can, but it helps to be sure that the market really requires it. Research time and development costs seem negligible when compared to the pot of gold at the end of a favorite rainbow.

The case against the salesman is summed up by the National Industrial Conference Board: "Because they're anxious to serve their own accounts, salesmen . . . may misjudge the extent of the market for the new product" and "are frequently unaware of the technical problems which must be overcome."

Substitute for Salesmen's Ideas

Begin with market research. Sure get the salesman's opinions, but be absolutely certain you get to the man who makes the buying decision, too. Then, "the research man or engineer will know he is working on a product for which a need has been established. The value of that product provides his incentive. He need never face the frustration and disappointment of having years of effort put on the shelf because his technical success was unfortunately an economic failure. And the fact that fewer research and engineering dollars go down the drain is no small consideration." These are the words of M. E. Mengel, Burroughs vice presdent of product planning.

The moral? Don't let your salesman do your product planning. For that matter, don't let your engineers or executives do it either. If the product is going to be a marketing success, don't let anyone make decisions based on opinion. Get the facts, analyze them carefully, cold-bloodedly. This is what makes new products successful. ■

14.

How to Improve Your Writing, Speaking and Reading Capabilities

Speed-notes for engineers

Specifically designed to work with familiar
engineering and mathematical symbols, this system
will cut your writing time in half.

GEORGE H. LOGAN, Management Consultant

Table I..Basic symbology

$+$ = plus, positive, and	$\log$ = common logarithm
$-$ = minus, negative	$\ln$ = natural logarithm
$\times$ = algebraic x, or multiplied by	ϵ = base of natural logarithms
$\div$ = divided by	π = pi
$\neq$ = does not equal	$\angle$ = angle
$\approx$ = equals approximately, approximates	$\perp$ = perpendicular to
$>$ = greater than, greatly, increased, increasing	$\parallel$ = parallel to
$<$ = less than, reduced, decreasing	$a°$ = a degrees (angle)
$\sim$ = sine curve, cosine curve	a' = a minutes (angle)
$\rightarrow$ = approaches as a limit, approaches	a'' = a seconds (angle)
$\geqq$ = greater than or equal to	$\int$ = integral, integral of, integration
$\leqq$ = less than or equal to	f = frequency
$\equiv$ = identical to	f_n = natural frequency
$\propto$ = varies directly as	cps = cycles per second
$\therefore$ = therefore	m = mass
$(\ )^{1/2}$ = square root	Φ = phase
$(\ )^n$ = nth root	F = force

IN engineering we are obliged almost daily to take technical notes based on verbal communication. Technology's growing complexity thrusts more and more briefings, lectures, conferences, lectures, symposiums, and technical society conventions upon us. By jotting down notes or memorizing, the listener tries to retain the important content of a speech.

But a normal speaking rate is very much faster than a normal writing rate. We have all experienced the feeling that our notes were too frugal —yet we wrote as fast as we could.

Here is a simple system devised by the author for fast engineering notes. Readers should be able to use most of the system immediately. Proficiency will come with practice. Reading speed-notes, even days later when they are cold, is little different from reading any technical article.

Much of this system is based on material familiar to engineers and scientists. The method is a blend of:

1) Word-meanings of conventional engineering symbols. In some instances the usual meanings have been expanded (Table I)

2) A few additional symbols

3) Abbreviations of long words to a few letters which imply their full spelling and meaning

Let us review some conventional engineering symbols and their word meanings:

The plural of a word indicated by any symbol is written with an *s* following the symbol. Thus, *areas* would be □*s; curves* would be ⌒*s; natural frequencies* would be written $f_n s$.

The terms in a formula presented by a speaker are always written exactly as given.

At this point we have covered two of the elements in the system—conventional symbols and coined symbols. We are now ready to discuss phonetic abbreviation of long words and corollary short cuts.

In general, long words are abbreviated by merely omitting vowels. There are two exceptions. When a pronounced vowel is the first or last letter in a word, the vowel is retained, eg, *advnc* = advance. When a word contains a high proportion of vowels, one or more vowels are retained for read-back ease, eg, *reman* = remain.

Actually, the notetaker may retain a vowel whenever he wishes. For him, this may aid clarity. A very important virtue of this system is that there are no inflexible rules on word-shortening. *Ground rules* are presented, true, but variations of these will only slightly decrease the notetaker's speed. There is no dictionary spelling to memorize.

Some additional guidelines:

• The words *a* and *the* are usually omitted.

• Words of one, two, or three letters are spelled in full. Examples: *to, as, I, of, an, at, for, by, or, yes, no, way.*

• The *ing* endings are consistently abbreviated to *g.*

• Borrowing from calculus, a dot above a Speed-Note word designates rate. Thus, *dfln* = deflection and *dfln* = deflection rate.

The Speed-Note version of an excerpt from the article "How To Select Vibration Isolators" is illustrated on the following page. But first some examples of how symbols and abbreviated words are combined:

The natural frequency of the sys-

---

vs = versus, against

$\overline{\underline{}}$ = *ground*

Below are additional coined or adapted symbols and their word-meanings. Observe that the geometry of a symbol connotes the word-meaning.

/ = *ratio, the ratio of*

⊤⊤⊤ = *base, support,*
       mount, foundation

⌒ = *curve, curvilinear*

↔ = *varied, variation*

□ = *area*

↕ = *vibration, motion*

Table II..Typical word abbreviations

anlys	= analysis	*pltg*	= plotting
ampltd	= amplitude	*reman*	= remain
asmg	= assuming	*rsnc*	= resonance
cald	= called	*rltnshp*	= relationship
cnst	= constant	*smpl*	= simple
dmpg	= damping	*smpfd*	= simplified
dmnsls	= dimensionless	*stfns*	= stiffness
dfln	= deflection	*systm*	= system
dfnd	= defined	*sgnft*	= significant
dstrbg	= disturbing	*ths*	= this
eftvns	= effectiveness	*trnsmsblty*	= transmissibility
frdm	= freedom	*thrtly*	= theoretically
frcg	= forcing	*valu*	= value
gvs	= gives	*wth*	= with
hrmc	= harmonic	*whn*	= when
isltr	= isolator	*xprsd*	= expressed
isltn	= isolation		

Original Copy

Analysis of vibration in a system is greatly simplified by assuming: the mass has only one degree of freedom, the resilient support has no damping, and the disturbing motion of the base is simple harmonic, as in Fig. 1. The natural frequency n of the system in cycles per second is

$$n = \frac{1}{2\pi}\sqrt{\frac{k}{m}}$$

where k is the deflection rate or stiffness of support, lb./in., and m is the mass, lb-sec²/in.

If the mass and deflection rate remain constant but the forcing frequency f is varied, the amplitude of the mass varies. The ratio of disturbing amplitude to mass amplitude is called the transmissibility, T, and is defined as

$$T = \frac{1}{1 - (f^2/n^2)}$$

Plotting the transmissibility against the ratio of forcing frequency to natural frequency gives the resonance curve, Fig. 2.

This is a dimensionless relationship, with three significant areas. At frequencies below resonance the motion of the mass is in phase with the disturbing motion and increases as the forcing frequency approaches the natural frequency. At resonance, when the forcing frequency is equal to the natural frequency, the mass is 90 deg out of phase with the support, and the motion, theoretically, is infinite.

With increasing frequency the transmissibility decreases, reaching a value of 1.0 when the disturbing frequency f is 1.4n. At higher disturbing frequencies the transmissibility is less than 1.0. This is the start of the isolation range where the motion of the mass is 180 deg out of phase with the support motion. In this area the effectiveness of an isolator is expressed in percentage of isolation, or $(1-T)100$.

Speed-Notes

Anlys of ↕ in system is > smpfd by asmg: m has only 1° of frdm, rslnt ⊓⊓ has no dmpg, + dstrbg ↕ of ⊓⊓ is smpl hrmc, as in Fig 1. f_n n of systm in cps is

$$n = \frac{1}{2\pi}\sqrt{\frac{k}{m}}$$

whr k is dfln or stfns of ⊓⊓, lb./in., + "m" is m, lb-sec²/in.

If m + dflh reman const but frcg f "f" ↔, ampltd of m ↔. / of dstrbg ampltd to m ampltd is cald trnsmsblty, T, is dfnd as

$$T = \frac{1}{1 - (f^2/n^2)}$$

Pltg trnsmsblty vs / of frcg f to f_n gvs rsnc ⌒ , Fig 2. Ths is dmnsls rltnshp, wth 3 sgnft □s. At fs < rsnc ↕ of m is in Φ wth dstrbg ↕ + > as frcg f → f_n. At rsnc, whn frcg f ═ to f_n, m is 90° out of Φ wth ⊓⊓ + ↕, thrtly, is ∞ .

With > f T <, rchg valu of 1.0 whn dstrbg f "f" is 1.4n. At > dstrbg fs T < 1.0. Ths is strt of isltn rnge whr ↕ of m is 180° out of Φ with ⊓⊓ ↕. In ths □ eftvns of an isltr is xprsd in % of isltn, or (1-T)100.

---

tem = f_n of systm.

The ratio of disturbing amplitude = / of dstrbg ampltd.

Disturbing motion of the base = Dstrbg ↕ of ⊓⊓ .

With three significant areas = Wth 3 sgnft □s.

Ratio, forcing frequency to natural frequency, gives resonance curve = /, frcg f to f_n gvs rsnc ⌒ .

Phase with disturbing motion and increase = Φ wth dstrbg ↕ + >.

The word meanings of the conventional symbols are of course commonly understood by engineers. The coined symbols and abbreviated words quickly register their meaning.

The best way to master this system is to start using it. If you must take notes later today, you'll find that you can at least partially apply this system from just one reading of this article. As you develop skill you'll find that fewer and fewer writing motions will record more and more information.

The foundation is now laid for more complete application. A portion of the article on vibration isolators is reproduced verbatim, with the Speed-Notes version alongside. ∎

TEN RULES FOR THE IDEA MERCHANT

1) Say it, don't write it.

2) Use a blackboard for conceptual work.

3) If you must keep a record, use a machine.

4) If you must say it on paper, use a picture, a handwritten note, a note on a picture.

5) If a typed memo is required, dictate into a machine and have it typed and corrected by someone else.

6) Always include subject, title, data of origination, subject number, and obsolescence date.

7) Accuracy and timeliness are more important than artistry.

8) Use snap-out forms with pre-printed sections for statement and response. Snap-out forms should have the correct number of copies.

9) Procedures usually reflect yesterday's requirements. Question their applicability to today's needs.

10) Work smarter rather than harder. A little thought will save a lot of sweat.

Simple Tricks for Speeding Communications

NORBERT STAHL

Most of an engineer's time and effort is spent writing and talking, yet you have the least amount of training in writing and you probably hate it more than any other assignment.

Needless to say, engineers, playing an important part in a corporation, must communicate. But this does not mean that it must be typed, preserved for posterity, and considered a work of art. It does mean that it should be accurate, on time, and retrievable and have a predetermined obsolescence date.

Although the importance of up-to-date tools is recognized, we seem to shy away from using anything but a pad and pencil for recording verbal information. Yet aid in this area can save more time, money, and frustration than anything an engineer may do.

The recorder helps by overcoming basic stumbling blocks in putting words on paper. Further, it is the rare person who can write as fast as he talks. Your ideas are way ahead of the pencil and you lose the thread of your thought. You start fishing for words to finish a sentence. The sparkle, and the concept, is lost. Dictating them as rapidly as possible seems to retain a ring of naturalness, spontaneity, and originality.

It is also a fact that it is much easier to correct than to originate. Further, it is possible for someone else to do this editorial work so that you, just as in the case of preparing a layout or conceptual sketch, are responsible only for originating information and not for the art work.

The camera breaks down language barriers and transcends educational levels. A photograph makes everyone see the same thing in the same light, and this is the essence of good communication. Take your Polaroid on field trips, to meetings, to the shop—wherever you may be called upon to come away with data.

On a recent international trip, I communicated with a Polaroid camera and a tape recorder alone. It was a highly enlightening experience. Pictures were used for technical data transmission and tape for explanations and notes. Much of the verbal communication needed to be said and heard only once. Consequently, there was no reason to write a memo about it. Many of the pictures served only to clarify a point, after which they had fulfilled their function.

The telephone with a recorder serves the same function as a recorder or camera. The conversation is retained as long as it is needed. If a memo must be created from the conversation, it can be done painlessly, since the facts are before you—not what you remember, but the facts.

The recorder need not be working all the time. That might be embarrassing or inhibiting. Instead you hold the telephone conversation as usual, then before turning on the recorder say, "May we summarize what you and I have said and record it to avoid any misunderstanding?" The little beep, periodically heard over the phone, will tend to keep the conversation factual, but the words will flow and the facts will be down quickly, painlessly, and efficiently.

All three devices—the tape recorder, the camera, and the telephone with the recording device—will not only have the effect of making your work simpler, but will also add (although this is certainly not their primary function) tremendously to your prestige. It is amazing how impressed people are when you appear somewhere with a recorder or camera—or, for that matter, when they hear their telephone conversation is being recorded.

The blackboard takes advantage of the fact that we all like to play teacher. Concepts fall into place, formulas seem to flow more easily, and sentences become shorter. You must have noticed how everyone's attention is focused on the person before the blackboard—and on the facts there. They frequently become the center of the conversation at the meeting.

When you must write, keep these principles (borrowed from simplified drafting) in mind.

Avoid artistry. Cut out elaboration that adds nothing to the message. Assume that the recipient of the message has a smaller vocabulary than you have. Use brief sentences. Express thoughts clearly. More important, before you draw anything, before you write anything, ask yourself why you are doing it, who will receive it, and what purpose it will accomplish. If the idea you create on a piece of paper (such as a memo or basic calculation) will not be instrumental in bringing about an action by someone else, or by yourself, then you have no reason for originating it. If you want to transmit data for informational purposes only, a phone call will do as well.

On filing and unfiling

Basically, you receive information in some form and you transmit it in some form.

1) Do away with all information—in whatever form—if you cannot use it. Although there can be no argument with this basic concept, as days go by you will note that possibly 50% of the material you receive will not instruct you to do things, will not teach you anything. Yet, because you have received it, you file it.

2) File only those papers which require some current or future action.

3) Do not file anything unless you know in advance when you can obsolete it. Every piece of paper should have a purging date. For example, if you receive a directive which tells you to do something for one month, you may want to keep this memo for possibly one year, but when that date arrives it should be destroyed automatically and without hesitation.

4) Keep copies only as working papers. Today's copying equipment is so good that it is sometimes hard to distinguish the copy from the original. This, however, does not alter the fact that an original exists. If you need the information after you have taken the required action, you can always go back to the original. Copies, therefore, should have a short life.

5) Differentiate between filing and stacking. Filing cabinets should contain only originals.

6) Stack chronologically. If you keep only the papers you currently need to do your job, the amount of material you must have at hand will be relatively small. If you further agree to write an obsolescence date on every bit of paper before you stack it away, your pile of papers will not grow in proportion to your tenure at work—it will remain small. Chronological sequence, therefore, is best.

7) Display literature and printed matter in an area accessible to others. For example, if you keep your technical data from a vendor in your desk, your neighbor will also request this information from the vendor. The vendor may make two calls to try to sell his product—he has at least doubled his literature cost. Somebody has to pay. Did both of you really need the duplicate information? ∎

HOW TO "SPREAD THE WORD"..

COURTESY ROCKWELL MFG CO

Systemized methods are required to "spread the word" in any organization, and to that organization's suppliers, customers, employee families and the community in general. Much more attention to "communications" from top to bottom, from bottom to top, and between departments is now the goal of progressive management. The accompanying checklist of what should be done and how it is done, and who gets the information was developed by the Rockwell Mfg Co for its own situation—a multi-plant company operating in several states and making a large number of products for an even larger number of markets. A policy is followed of almost total disclosure of operating information to various levels of management. Most of Rockwell's methods may be used by other companies, but that concern has tailored the methods to the needs of a diversified, decentralized organization. However, this checklist, one of the most thorough analyses that has appeared, can be tailored to your own needs. ■

COMMUNICATIONS CHECKLIST

METHOD	PURPOSE	WHAT IS COMMUNICATED	TO WHOM
President's staff meetings; weekly	To review current operations	Discussion of progress of programs, and matters affecting current status of company, initiation of programs.	Top executives and operating men at headquarters
President's letter; monthly. Prepared by president and his staff.	To keep management informed of current operating status, long- and short-term planning, and the president's thinking on matters affecting company.	Analysis of previous month's operations compared with preceding figures; analysis of inventories and inventory outlook. Matters of current interest: industrial relations, purchasing, public relations, engineering, etc. Personnel changes.	Vice presidents, corporation department heads, plant managers, sales executives
Division vice president's letter; monthly. Prepared by division vice president.	Same as president's letter.	Patterned after president's letter. Provides information pertinent to sales and operations in the division.	Divisional department heads and plant managers, sales managers
Management Newsletter: quarterly. Prepared by president and his staff.	To discuss current and anticipated operations with a wider group throughout the company.	Patterned on president's letter. Analysis of previous quarter's operations; sales forecasts and discussion of changes anticipated to meet new forecasts. Plant budget information, including complete analysis of actual costs compared to budget on such items as shipments, cost of sales, overhead, plant operating profit. Management tips submitted by personnel throughout the company. Subjects of current interest, e.g. training programs, new plant production, product development.	All management personnel from board chairman to foreman.
Activity report; monthly. Prepared by plant manager and his department heads.	To inform headquarters of plant's programs, progress and problems.	Information on production plans, programs in the plant.	President, vice president, staff department heads.

METHOD	PURPOSE	WHAT IS COMMUNICATED	TO WHOM
Annual management meeting; 3-day meeting conducted by president; 3-days by division vice-president.	To inform plant managers and sales organization of company-wide policies and plans for long term, and provide an opportunity to exchange information.	President's review of five years, past and future, including comparison of two year balance sheets. Review of staff operations: industrial engineering, purchasing, advertising, industrial relations, insurance, credit, etc.	Plant managers, corporation staff men, regional sales managers.
Employee meetings; quarterly; conducted by president.	To keep all employees informed of company's status and plans and personnel policies.	Management's thinking on diverse subjects affecting employees, e.g. general business conditions, vacation policies.	All headquarters employees.
Research development report; quarterly.	To keep all divisions informed of all company product developments and plans; standardization program.	News of product developments and central and plant research laboratory projects and divisional engineering departments; news on standardization program.	Management group including department heads.
"HOUR OF ENLIGHTENMENT" meetings; bi-weekly.	To keep executives informed on operations outside their own fields; training in specialties of staff men.	General information on operations e.g. Controller discusses standard cost system.	Non-homogeneous group of middle management line and staff men.
Supervisory conferences; held at department head's discretion.	Seek solutions to operating problems	Discussion of specific operating problems as they arise.	Department supervisors.
Letters to supervisors.	To inform supervisors of specific operating problems as they arise; to pass along worthwhile ideas.	Announcements of new vacation policies, etc.; new procedures e.g. for merit evaluations.	All supervisors at their homes.
Report by president; monthly.	To acquaint general public and business community with company operations.	Informal monthly column including general information on company's philosophy of business and company activities.	An advertisement in business magazines and newspapers circulating to employees, customers, suppliers, stockholders and the business community in general.
Local report by local plant manager.	Same as above report.	Information of interest to the specific community.	Advertisement in local newspapers.
Company-wide house organ	Encourage "community spirit" in the company; provide a media for explaining company policies, attitudes.	News of employees' activities; management's views on general problems affecting operations; features concerning safety, waste, suggestion program, etc.	All employees.
Local house organ	Same as company-wide house organ.	Same as company-wide house organ.	All employees of the particular plant.
Internal publicity releases	Inform key employees of company activities that make the news.	All news bureau releases to general and business publications, plus news releases of internal interest.	Management group, including department heads.
Bulletin boards	Inform employees of matters of general interest.	Information on plant social activities, company-sponsored neighborhood activities, safety information, internal publicity releases.	All employees.
Employee letters	Encourage "community spirit" in the company.	Holiday greetings, notice of community affairs, reminders to vote.	All employees (at their homes)

8 *steps to better engineering writing...*

RICHARD M. KOFF

Lesson.. 1

Vanity and laziness, in that order, are to blame for most bad writing. For some reason, anyone who has learned to read assumes he has learned to write as well. Criticism or revisions are therefore felt to be direct attacks on the author's education or intelligence.

In industry, writing ability is assumed to improve automatically with authority and salary. The president's letters and reports are corrected by no one; the junior engineer's by everyone.

So . . . your first and most important step in learning to write is to swallow some pride. Your golden words will be improved by your boss, by your assistant, even by your secretary. If you really want to learn to write, you must learn to evaluate their criticisms objectively—not react like a wounded bull.

Laziness is a factor, because most people feel that writing a report or a letter is a necessary evil, not an end in itself. Anyone can do it, so it should take no time or effort.

Actually writing is as much thinking work as it is the use of grammar, or spelling, or punctuation. You need imagination (What is my reader interested in? . . . How well does he know the subject?). Logic (What ideas shall I present first? . . . What is the next step?), and perseverance (How can I get my point across faster?). But it is boring to have to go over old territory again, and it can be disconcerting if the mental review reveals gaps in your own knowledge.

So laziness combines with pride to say, "It's enough. It's right. I wrote it and understand it, so will the reader. Thank you, Miss Jones; that will be all."

To break this train of reasoning (or emotion, really) you must recognize that writing is time-consuming, productive work. It is respectable and demanding, and good writing can have almost as much influence on customers, suppliers, associates, and prospects as your company's service or product itself.

HOW TO REVISE

It is usually easier to edit than it is to write; hindsight is better than foresight. In editing you take an involved or complex sentence and reduce it to its bare essentials. You then add complexities, but only if they are necessary to meaning.

In its simplest form, the English sentence consists of subject and predicate; or subject, verb and object. For clarity, positive statements in this form can't be beat. Furthermore, subjects and predicates are nouns and verbs. The English language is so rich that good nouns and verbs need few modifiers. Adjectives and adverbs are often used to make up for poor selection of words in the first place.

Here is an example of a complex sentence and its revision step by step:

> The field of stress analysis is one in which model studies have often been used successfully. (Understandable, but backwards somehow.)

> Models have often been used successfully in the field of stress analysis. (Gets the subject up front. Eliminates "one in which.")

> Models have been used for stress analysis. (Reduced to bare essentials. Are "often" and "successfully" necessary modifiers?)

At this point editing stops. The author must determine his exact shade of meaning. How about:

> Models are useful for stress analysis.

NOW YOU TRY

The following five sentences were written by engineers in letters or reports. Note that you have to read some of them two or three times before you understand what is happening to what. By changing the order of the words or splitting a complex sentence into two or more simple sentences, can you edit them into better writing? Our versions (by no means the only way they could be written) will be found below.

1 .. Familiarity with the method whereby arithmetic operations can be performed is highly desirable.

2 .. The cutting of tubes that will have practically no burr has posed quite a problem to manufacturers for years.

3 .. To obtain the best possible results in the application of induction heating it is sometimes necessary to modify the design of the part to suit the characteristics and practical requirements of this method of heating.

4 .. The choice of the correct alloy is of prime importance and it will be found that a great deal of trouble can be prevented if all details are taken into consideration and if any doubt should arise, one should submit his questions to the Technical Department.

5 .. The base metal of an ornament may very well be an inexpensive imitation even when the surface is highly reflective and of a rich-looking finish.

1 .. Know how to do arithmetic.

2 .. It is difficult to cut tubes without leaving burrs.

3 .. Modify the part for induction heating.

4 .. Alloy choice is critical. When in trouble ask an expert.

5 .. (This is a sleeper.) All that glitters is not gold.

8 *steps to better engineering writing...*

Lesson .. 2

Good writing is rarely achieved in the first draft. This is true for a good business letter or engineering report as much as for a famous play or novel. But, in industry, revision is out of fashion. The current image of a big business executive is a man who can dictate to four secretaries simultaneously and close a couple of million-dollar deals on the telephone between paragraphs.

When executives try to live up to this image, their letters are bad because they are stereotyped, ("We are in receipt of yours of the 10th inst..."), if not rambling and incoherent. An acceptable dictated letter takes careful planning (expert letter writers often make extensive notes before calling for the secretary). You will need a stock of graceful phrases to help tide you over the inevitable awkward places as well.

Our first rule about simple sentences (subject, verb, object) and unadorned nouns and verbs will cover you in most short (one-page) letters. But longer reports and· letters simply cannot be dashed off in this way—not even ·by professionals. When you have to communicate more than just yes or no, or "Why don't we have lunch together some day?", then standard phrases and dictation from notes won't get you off first base. You can dictate the first draft, but that's all it ever will be—a rough draft—needing revision after revision before it will say what you want it to, economically and understandably.

So this is a plea for the brutal art of rewrite. We started last week by editing a few complex, inverted sentences into shorter, more-logical form. Even the best writers produce sentences of that kind in their first drafts. Impatience, laziness, the press of other demands on your time, will tempt you to stop there. The result is poor writing, poor reader impressions, and misunderstanding.

THE SECOND RULE

A close corollary to the "be simple" rule is a second which says, "Be positive, be brave." Sounds like a Middle Ages injunction for knights-errant, doesn't it? But it applies to modern-day writing—particularly to that written by engineers and scientists who, in their written communications, are the worst cowards of our generation. For example:

Under certain conditions of temperature and relative humidity, the moisture content of the air seems to tend to increase the likelihood of oxidation of iron and certain iron compounds when exposed to these atmospheres.
Iron will rust in damp atmospheres.

In an attempt to answer all possible critics the scientific writer modifies his words with "almost, very, maybe, tends to, etc." until the nouns and verbs are covered with a meringue of modifiers.

Nothing in life is absolutely so. You don't have to make this point in every sentence you write. The reader has lived; he knows the risks in crossing busy intersections. Give him your ideas bravely and let later paragraphs, or his own experience, supply the modifiers.

Bravery also implies a positive attitude toward life. Avoid statements which are intended to describe by exclusion or to damn by faint praise. If you wish to damn, damn in so many words. If you think a theory or a person has disadvantages, say so. Don't dwell on the lack of virtue.

Long bearing life cannot be expected in dust-laden environments.
Dust destroys bearings.
Weather predictions are not likely to be as reliable as one might wish.
Weather predictions are unreliable.

Here are five cowardly, negative statements made by engineers. Can you rewrite them in shorter, braver statements without altering the meanings?

1 .. We do not think the proposed gear-tooth design can carry the specified load.

2 .. An inspection of the production run seems to indicate there is a not very careful lathe hand somewhere in the shop.

3 .. We don't have much hope for the mathematical model proposed by Mr Smith.

4 .. The coating can hardly be expected to stand up under salt-water spray.

5 .. No invention resides in adding means to make a device movable when, without such means, the device would not be movable.

1 .. The gear teeth are too weak.
2 .. A sloppy lathe hand is messing up the production run.
3 .. Mr Smith's mathematical model won't work.
4 .. Salt spray will destroy the coating.
5 .. Making an immovable object movable is not invention.

8 *steps to better engineering writing...*

Lesson .. 3

Most of us have been taught in grade school never to begin a paragraph with "I," that it's probably wise never to use that personal pronoun at all. Engineers and scientists have that lesson reinforced in their college years by instruction in the "scientific method" in which objective truth is supposed to be its own best salesman — the colder and harder the better.

Once out of school and faced with some of the market-place atmosphere of industry, we realize that objective truth by itself has only a very small voice to attract the attention of a distracted reader. The argument here is not with "truth," but with excessive objectivity, which freezes all the humanity and interest out of most technical writing.

The man who writes for a larger public, even those who are engineers and scientists, knows better. Thor Heyerdahl, archeologist and explorer, starts his best-selling book:

"I had no *aku-aku.*
"Nor did I know what an *aku-aku* was, so I could hardly have used one if I had had it."

These sentences couldn't be more personal and it's almost impossible to stop reading the book once you start.

They also demonstrate a second, related rule: Be specific. It would be far more logical for Heyerdahl to start with generalities. What were his theories, how were they formed? Instead you are told about an *aku-aku.* No definition of terms, no generalities, but a very specific thing which you are curious to know more about.

To be specific means to talk about trees, not forests; murder and arson and theft, not crime; valves and pumps and reservoirs, not hydraulics; steam and boilers and turbines, not thermodynamics. Steam and turbines make pictures in your reader's mind while thermodynamics is the name of the only course he nearly flunked.

HOW TO BE YOURSELF

At first it will seem difficult, immodest even, to inject yourself into a letter or report. The temptation to generalize (and pontificate) will be almost irresistible. But to the reader the personal note will not seem immodest and the specific reference will add drama. For example, here is a memo written by an engineer to his immediate superior:

This is in reference to Engineering Department equipment and the efficiency thereof. In general, the newest additions have been behaving reasonably well. A ballistics problem awaiting solution for some time has finally been solved. The Structures Department has also been making good use of the equipment. However, there are still certain mechanical and design difficulties to be ironed out. The Human Engineering aspects need some attention to make the unit easier to operate and control. The input-output devices have caused certain delays in handling. Maintenance and repair work will be required ...

But it also could have been written

You asked for my opinions about the new engineering department computer. Well, we've had pretty good results so far. The trajectory integration problem was solved in 15 minutes. The structures men are happy as clams now

that the iterative strut has been programmed. But there are still some bugs. The signal lights occasionally start flashing like a pinball machine, and they really panic you if you've never seen it before. The tape reader jammed last Tuesday and spilled a couple of thousand feet of tape into the control cubby. It took us an hour to clear a path to Sam Jarvis who was running his stress-analysis problem at the time ...

NOW YOU TRY

Here is a paragraph from the introductory chapter of a well-known engineering reference text. Use a little imagination—place yourself in the shoes of the author for a moment—and try writing the paragraph more personally and more specifically to give it some life and interest. Our version (by no means the only one, or the best) appears below.

Before a new idea or process in any branch of engineering or natural science can be utilized, it must be embodied in a suitable physical form. For this reason, a knowledge of the principles of mechanical design is a necessary part of an engineer's training, even though the student may not expect to become a professional designer ...

Engineering is hardware—screws and nuts and bolts, castings and resistors, pilot lights, bearings, gears and IC engines. No matter how theoretical your research, no matter how high up the ivory tower you'd like to work, you must be able to make airplanes out of aerodynamics, radios and TV sets out of solid-state physics.

8 steps to better engineering writing...

Lesson .. 4

Never "tell all."

This simple rule is one of the most difficult for engineers to follow, yet it makes good sense. The reader isn't interested in knowing everything you do about a subject—not by a long shot. Give him what he needs to know; nothing more. It's good psychology, too—you won't have to say "I don't know" to the questions an executive will always ask.

Careful omission of extraneous facts is half the battle. It cuts reports down to manageable size and makes concise writing at least possible. The other half is to omit needless words from the facts you decide are essential. William Strunk Jr., in *The Elements of Style*, wrote:

"Vigorous writing is concise. A sentence should contain no unnecessary words, a paragraph no unnecessary sentences, for the same reason that a drawing should have no unnecessary lines and a machine no unnecessary parts. This requires not that the writer make all his sentences short, or that he avoid all detail and treat his subjects only in outline, but that every word tell."

No one can produce lean writing on the first try. It is difficult enough to get complex thoughts on paper at all. But once you have a sentence before you, it should be relatively simple to weed out the needless words, leaving the thought all by itself and in a form that every reader later will think is the only natural way to express it.

Much of what we have said in previous lessons will result in leaner writing. Be simple, be positive, be brave, be specific—all of these rules will contribute to more concise prose. In addition, there are some standard phrases editors have been trained to blue-pencil almost without thinking:

the fact that (because)	in order to (for, or to)
he is a man who (he is)	check up (check)
in the case of	drop down (drop)
from the point of view of	very
in regard to (about)	at the present time (now)
	this is a picture of (in captions)

And then add to this list those useless modifiers: entirely satisfactory, completely full, slightly pregnant.

At the bottom of this page you will find a letter liberally sprinkled with these phrases and how it might be pared. Is anything lost in the translation?

You respect the shorter-letter writer for several reasons: He writes (and therefore thinks) clearly and concisely. He does not burden the reader with unnecessary information. Also he does not "protest too much." No one could honestly be as apologetic as the first man pretends for three bad castings.

This rule, "don't overstate," means don't sell too hard, don't excuse with more reasons than necessary, don't explain too much. One or two excuses is enough—additional ones cast doubt. When the teacher asked Johnny why he was late for school, he answered, "Mommy's car had a flat tire, the bus didn't stop when I waved, and anyhow I got a splinter in my finger."

The splinter would convince you, the entire story wouldn't.

NOW YOU TRY

The best way to practice concise writing is to read with attention. Look for needless phrases, irrelevant information and overstatements in newspaper reports, technical articles and advertisements. Practice rewriting, mentally, the particularly bad examples. It's not hard, and it can reveal much faulty thinking by the author.

```
Dear Mr ------- :
    It has been brought to our attention that
this company's most recent shipment of
sand cast pump housings was not up to our
usual high standard.  As a matter of fact,
three housings were unsatisfactory by
reason of the fact that dimensions in
more than one case exceeded the allowable
tolerances as given on your blueprints.
    We are very sorry that so unfortunate
and inconvenient an occurrence should
have taken place and are ready and
willing to rectify the situation as
soon as possible.  As in all such cases
we will be happy to replace any and all
such unacceptable castings with new ones.
Please pack them up and ship them to us
so that we can correct our molds and make
new housings according to your drawings.
            Apologetically yours,
```

```
Dear Mr ------- :
        I'm told
  our latest shipment
    of pump housings
        includes
          three
     out-of-tolerance
        housings.

      We're sorry

     this happened

         and if
    you'll return the

    defective housings

  they will be replaced.
        Yours truly,
```

8 *steps to better engineering writing...*

Lesson .. 5

Up to now, we've been studying rules about **what** to write rather than **how.** Vocabulary, grammar, punctuation — these are the mechanics, the tools. And, frankly, you don't have the time or interest to go back and study them in detail.

But you've been speaking, thinking and reading the English language for decades. You can rely on your ear for words and phrases, and with the few hints given below, get away without a review of formal "book learning" in most of your writing.

This means you must rely on what sounds right to YOU—not what you think will sound right to your boss, customer or colleague. Don't try to write "down" to a serviceman in a manual, or "up" to an executive. Anything that sounds unnatural to you—any unfamiliar word, phrase or sentence structure will sound ten times stranger to the man who really knows how to use it.

Most good style manuals or writing texts cover these subjects far better than we can here. The serious student is referred to the bibliography at the end of Lesson 8.

VOCABULARY

Get a good desk dictionary and keep it within reach. If you don't know how to spell a word, look it up. And read the definitions while you're at it—you may be surprised.

To build a bigger vocabulary, read, but a $25 word should not be used if a 10¢ one can be found.

Watch out for: allusion-illusion, being that, between-among, case-instance, comprise, data, different than-from, due to, effect-affect, can't hardly, imply-infer, irregardless, lay and lie, like-as, literally, phase, principle-principal, regard, shall-will, that-which, type, unique, utilize, virtually, very, while, who-whom, you and I.

Here are five examples from the above list. Which are correct usage?

1 .. The higher temperatures will not effect steel hardness.
2 .. Are you inferring that our lathe screws are inaccurate?
3 .. It went together easily like a slip fit should.
4 .. This machine has a fairly unique joy-stick control.
5 .. The tests were virtually finished when we found the trouble.*

GRAMMAR

Again the best bet is to rely on your ear. What sounds right is most likely to be right. Your written English, with proper allowance for more careful phrasing, should be modeled from your spoken style. The most common offenders are:

The split infinitive. An infinitive, for these purposes, is a verb preceded by *to* (to go, to run, to design). The rule is: don't put an adverb modifier after the *to* and before the verb (to quickly go, to breathlessly run, to elegantly design). In each instance the modifier should precede or follow the infinitive. There are exceptions to this rule, but they're rare.

The dangling participle. A present participle (the usual offender) is a verb with an -ing ending. When a participial phrase starts a sentence, you must be very careful that the subject of the phrase is also the subject of the rest of the sentence.

Testing the bearing, race wear appeared at 1000 rpm.
Testing the bearing, I found race wear at 1000 rpm.

Being badly worn, I had the handle replated.
Finding the finish worn, I had the handle replated.

PUNCTUATION

In descending order of difficulty, commas, semicolons and colons cause most punctuation problems. Here's a rundown on these three, plus some comments on hyphens.

All are wrong.

Commas. Parenthetical words and phrases should be separated by commas. (The oldest drill press, shaky and dangerous, was finally replaced.)

Independent clauses joined by a conjunction (and, but, for) should be separated by a comma. (I ordered the replacement parts, but I doubt that they will arrive on time.)

A series of items should be separated by commas. There is a difference in opinion about whether a comma should precede the "and." Decide for yourself and then be consistent. (Lines number one, two, and three will be shut down for repairs.)

For the rest, read a sentence aloud. Place a comma where you pause for emphasis or to make the meaning clear (assuming colons or semicolons do not apply).

Semicolons should separate independent clauses having no conjunction. In other words, two short, complete sentences which you feel belong together may be joined by a semicolon. (Take a short break; that gearbox is heavy.) The semicolon also separates major portions of a series separated internally by commas. (A short, small drill; a heavy, long bushing; . . .)

Colons usually introduce a list, a restatement or an example. (Standard screw threads will be: #4, 6, 8, and 10.)

Hyphens. Look up all compound words unless you are absolutely sure. Most compound modifiers of nouns and verbs take hyphens unless the first modifier ends in -ly. (A four-inch pipe, a fluid-power control, caught red-handed, *but:* an elegantly solved problem).

If you've got the time, dip into H. W. Fowler's *Modern English Usage* now and then. It's not always modern American, but it's a delight to read and includes more examples of good and bad prose than you'll find anywhere else.

8 *steps to better engineering writing...*

Lesson .. 6

How long is a letter, a report, an article? You can count the number of words or pages for an objective total, which might satisfy your engineering instincts—but it will be worthless. The length of a report is measured by your reader's first quick glance. He estimates how long it will take him to read, weighs this against the value or pleasure the subject seems likely to give, and decides whether to read, scan, or ignore.

Good appearance is the best persuader (right after subject matter). Clean typing and well-thought-out illustrations should not need mentioning here, but some common-sense pointers will bear repeating.

TYPED COPY

Only letters should be single spaced. One page of closely typed information, generously bordered in white space, will seem to be only a couple of minutes' reading, and a personally addressed letter is difficult to resist. But be very cautious about running over to a second page. How many such letters have you started to skip through, or hesitated even to start; just because the mass of words was discouraging?

In longer reports, paper economy never justifies single spacing. If the shear weight of a double-spaced report becomes a factor, you've probably written too much. Circulate the conclusions and file the rest.

TABLES

One problem with tables is that they force you to be logical. If you've skimped on an experiment or you don't like the way your product shows up in comparison with the competitor's, it will be difficult to cover up in a table. However, engineers are wild for tables; they collect them the way squirrels save nuts. So it may pay to do a little more research just to have a good table in your report.

Use tables whenever you have four or more sets of data. Even qualitative and descriptive matter can be put in tabular form to advantage.

Use summary tables in the body of a report, details in the appendix.

All tables need title and number (usually roman).

Identify all columns and rows, indicating units where applicable. Note that "inches x 10^{-2}" may be misleading. Should you multiply the listed figure by 10^{-2} or divide? Make sure the reader knows what you mean.

Use the same units for comparable quantities.

Align columns on the decimal point for similar units. Do not align for different units.

Number footnotes across a row, then down and across the next row.

Similar tables should have similar format.

Do not use ditto marks; repeat the figure.

Use a 0 before the decimal point on numbers less than 1 (0.435). Add a comma after the third zero in decimals (0.000,34).

FIGURES

Time and effort spent on good illustrations are as much or more important than time spent on writing. Most people, engineers included, look at the pictures first.

Graphs are better than tables to show trends. The danger here is excessive detail (limit ordinates and abscissas to about half-inch spacing if possible), or too many curves per graph. Curves should be several line weights heavier than the ordinate lines. Use different colors for a one-copy report, different line styles (dashed, dotted, etc.) for reports to be reproduced.

Charts, like bar charts, pie charts and the like, are a bit unsophisticated for an engineer reader, but management and advertising men tend to be impressed. If you must, go whole hog. Use color bars of pressure-sensitive tape or other gimmicks available from your local art-supply store.

Diagrams, cutaways, perspectives, isometrics, even cartoons are all lovely because they transmit a lot of information quickly or a little information powerfully. Keep them simple.

Photographs, the picture-in-a-minute variety particularly, spark up a dull report and make reading a pleasure instead of a chore—if they show something important.

Illustrations must be edited too! The first sketch is just as unsatisfactory as a first draft of a manuscript. Take the time to pare it down to the essentials (retake the picture if necessary). Does the most important information dominate the page?

Any flipping to and from the text should be avoided if possible. Paste the figure right where it belongs in the text or paste it on the right-hand edge so that it can be folded out clear of the report.

Don't get carried away by illustrations. A picture may be worth 1000 words, but 10 pictures are not worth 10,000 words.

CAPTIONS

To be of any use at all, illustrations must be self-explanatory. Captions can do this for you. Here are some pointers:

Never start with "A photograph of . . ." or "A drawing of . . ." The reader can figure that out for himself.

Make the caption something more than a tag or label. Point out what is significant about the figure. Account for every important element, and tell where it is, too (top, right, left).

Be concise. A long caption competes with its illustration, particularly when it repeats the text.

8 steps to better engineering writing...

Lesson .. 7

Who reads engineering reports and letters? Our guess would be:

65% are industrial executives,
15% are engineering colleagues,
15% are students or assistants,
5% are public relations people and the general public.

What is your purpose in writing? A letter may suggest a project and express your interest in doing the R & D. A progress report may show encouraging results but show that costs are over the budget. An article may outline a new design technique developed under your supervision.

In each case your overt purpose is to inform; your ulterior purpose is to influence. You can do neither without the conscious or unconscious cooperation of the reader.

WHERE TO PUT WHAT

Your reader is busy, harried—and lazy. To get his attention, see the suggestions in Lesson 6 about making reports and letters more attractive looking. **To save him from work, predigest the information; put the conclusions up front.**

This is the single most difficult thing to teach engineers. All our training is of the object-procedure-results-conclusions school. We approach the writing task as if it were a problem in geometry: Given . . .

Most of your readers know better than you do what has been "given."

When the doctor returns from the operating room, you ask, "How's my wife? How's the baby? When can I see them?" Sex, weight, time, and blood pressure can wait. Similarly the chief engineer, the research director, the president, want your recommendations first. The why's and wherefore's can come later.

Here's one approach to the technical report based on these principles:

Title page. Make your title short and use an active verb rather than a label. "The proposed 10-gpm pump" becomes, "Will a 10-gpm pump pay its way?"

If necessary, a paragraph of two or three short sentences may amplify the title, but make sure they generate interest rather than destroy it.

"The 5-gpm model is losing sales, but development and tooling costs of a 10-gpm pump will be high. Here are Engineering and Production cost estimates plus a Sales forecast. Net profit should be $20,000 in five years."

The reader *could* stop here, and that's a sign of good report writing, but he's more likely to go on.

Add your name, the date and what other information necessary for the record.

This is enough for the first page of a more-than-10-page report. Shorter reports can combine title with abstract.

Abstract. A much-too-formal word for the most important part of your report. This page (never more than one) has a synopsis of the problem, conclusions (if any), and recommendations. You can give reasons (without proof), tabulate values (without derivations) even photograph a final model (a recommendation in picture form). The combination of title and abstract on one page makes an ideal "short" report.

Contents page. This is really the index. Its primary purpose is for finding specific information. Its secondary purpose: to show the structure of a report, the plan of treatment.

Introduction. Set the stage. Why was the report written? Where did your information come from? How has it been presented?

Body. Here you prove what you said up front. List the "given" and its derivations. The order of presented material should be logical rather than chronological. Make use of subheadings, underlining, capital letters to divide your information into chewable "bites." Leave detail proof for the appendix. Headings must show the structure of the report—they'll be repeated on the contents page.

Conclusions. Recapitulate the reasoning with references to the page where each point is proved.

Appendix. Includes charts, graphs, tabled data, and tangential studies whose conclusions were used in the body of the report.

Bibliography. This may be limited to other reports or it may include technical books, handbooks and the like.

There's nothing sacred in this arrangement. Its greatest value lies in the emphasis placed on the reader—his wandering attention and peculiar interests. Don't be bound by convention or college training. Most likely the ideas that appeal to you will appeal to others. Note carefully the reports you read and admire. What makes them readable? Can you apply the same techniques in your own?

8 steps to better engineering writing...

1 .. VANITY AND LAZINESS, BE SIMPLE
2 .. BE POSITIVE, BE BRAVE
3 .. BE PERSONAL, BE SPECIFIC
4 .. BE CONCISE, DON'T OVERSTATE
5 .. VOCABULARY, GRAMMAR, PUNCTUATION
6 .. TABLES, FIGURES, CAPTIONS
7 .. WHERE TO PUT WHAT
8 .. SIT DOWN AND WRITE

Lesson .. 8

That first sentence is almost impossible to get on paper. You doodle, hem and haw, take a coffee break, look up a reference, and pretty soon it's time for lunch.

You're in good company. There isn't a writer in the world who gets up in the morning eager to rush to work.

The problem is that writing requires a frontal attack—you can't sneak up on it. Engineering problems are surrounded by so many small mechanical tasks—a report to read, a specification to check, availability of components or materials—that you drift deeper and deeper into the heart of a problem by slow stages. By the time you're ready to wrestle with the core, you're saturated with information, the mental engine is all warmed up, and momentum alone can carry you through.

You should try to create the same atmosphere for writing. Reports are based on tremendous amounts of information, most of which must be chewed over several times before a pattern appears. Hurry this chewing process and you'll wind up with poor reasoning, serious gaps, and plain bad writing in the report.

Every report should have a message —one that can be expressed in a sentence or two. What are you really trying to accomplish? What is the best way to set out your ideas and data for this purpose?

The moment of clarity, the perception of a plan or design, finally comes; then the writing can follow your mental design just as an assembly drawing follows a layout.

OUTLINES AND FIRST DRAFTS

Some people can't work without outlines; others can't work with them. Some writers like the erasability of a pencil draft; others can't read their own handwriting. You must choose for yourself. However, a few techniques apply for everyone.

Once started, write the first draft quickly. If you're writing fluently don't let interruptions break the chain of thought. The boss who wants good reports must give you the privacy to write them; don't be afraid to tell him so.

Don't worry too much about grammar, phraseology, or punctuation in the first draft. Get your ideas on paper in logical order and leave the polishing for later drafts.

Opening paragraphs tend to be pretty dull. When you're ready for the first revision, try tearing off the first paragraph or two and begin with paragraph three.

Start unfamiliar ideas well back in familiar territory. The reader is not insulted when he reads what he already knows—he's flattered. This applies only to technical derivations or the explanation of a technical discovery.

Watch for your own boredom. It makes you skip essential links in the chain of reasoning. Writing is slow work and takes more patience than most people believe. Cut off a small slice of subject and give it the works. Continue only if your interest and energy are strong.

It's a rare individual who can write well for more than an hour or two at a time. Take a break, go look out the window, think about something else for a while—and you'll come back refreshed.

When you revise, put off the role of author and imagine yourself in the audience. Each paragraph, each sentence is new. It is clear? What does the author want to say? Could it be said more simply, more directly?

As for the rest, the best teacher of writing is your pencil.

A FINAL TEST

The following paragraphs contain 24 errors. Some are purely mechanical (punctuation, grammar, vocabulary), others are errors in expression. Nine professional editors caught 20 or more of the 24 errors. Can you do as well?

The corrected copy is on the next page.

The four bar linkage has a nearly, but not quite, hypnotic affect on some engineers. Being that the elements are so simple the many different functions they can perform are very surprising. Four bar linkages are utilized in automobiles, folding beds printing presses, and steam engines. They may be designed to closely follow a proscribed path in space to transmit a measured force, or to accurately solve a complex algebraic function.

Four links pivoted at their ends are the principle elements of a four bar linkage. Considering one of the four fixed in space the motions of the others are measured relative to the fixed, unmoving link. Between the changing lengths of the four links an almost infinite number of speeds, and paths are possible for the two moving pivots.

This is the corrected version . . .

of the test on the previous page. Your grammar, vocabulary, and punctuation are above average if you can find 20 of the 24 errors.

The four-bar linkage has ~~a~~ *an almost* ~~nearly, but not quite,~~ hypnotic ~~a~~*e*ffect on some engineers. ~~Being~~ *Since* ~~that~~ the elements are so simple, the many different functions they can perform are ~~very~~ surprising. Four-bar linkages are *used* ~~utilized~~ in automobiles, folding beds, printing presses, and steam engines. They may be designed to |closely follow| a pr~~o~~*e*scribed path in space, to transmit a measured force, or to accu-rately ~~solve~~ a complex algebraic function.

Four links, pivoted at their ends, are the princip~~le~~*al* elements of a four-bar linkage. ~~Consider-ing~~ *is considered* One of the four, fixed in space, *and* the motions of the others are measured relative to the fixed, ~~unmoving~~ link. Changing the lengths of the four links *creates* an ~~almost~~ infinite number of speeds, and paths ~~are possible~~ for the two moving pivots. ∎

Quick check for Writing "Instructions"

HECTOR E. FRENCH
Chief, Engineering Publications Dept.
Sanbcrn Co.
Waltham, Mass.

Sooner or later every engineer has to write complete technical information about some piece of equipment or process—and write it fast. Here's a "prefabricated" outline to help do the job quickly and completely.

Description

—What is this information.
—Purpose of this information.
—How to use this information.
—Other publications required.
—Illustration of equipment.
—Identify manufacturer.
—Equipment name and number.
—Manufacturer's guarantee.
—Relate to other models.
—Relate to associated equipment.
—Modifications available.
—If system, what are units.
—If in larger system, explain.
—What does equipment do?
—What goes in?
—What happens to it?
—What comes out?
—Why do it this way?
—What is equipment used with?
—Where, when, why is it used?
—Who uses it?
—Advantages of the equipment.
—Limitations of the equipment.
—Advertising of product(s).
—Advertising of company.
—Price.
—Reordering.
—Order, shipment, contract numbers.
—Shipping list.
—Shipping damage report.
—Re-shipping requirements.
—Accessories supplied.
—Accessories not supplied.
—Basic principle of operation.
—List characteristics.
—List controls.
—List connectors.
—List cables.
—Power requirements.
—Weight and dimensions.
—Operating supplies required.
—Installation requirements.

Writing "Instructions" (continued)

—Operator requirements.
—Weatherproofing.
—Tropicalization.
—Warnings and precautions.
—If system: repeat for each unit.
—Note patent numbers.
—Give copyright date.
—Notes on Gov't licensing.

Operation

—Repeat from preceding as needed.
—Write to operator's level.
—Operator requirements.
—Illustrations of what operator sees.
—Identify panel controls.
—Unpacking.
—Installation requirements.
—Installation procedures.
—Intercabling drawings, tables, schematics.
—Identify by name and number.
—Tabulate modes of operation.
—When are different modes used?
—How it operates, control-wise.
—Operational block diagrams.
—Enough theory for operator.
—Pre-operational adjustments.
—Turning on the equipment.
—Connecting: inputs, outputs, accessory equip't.
—Standby operation.
—Operating the equipment.
—Emergency operation.
—Turning off the equipment.
—Post-operational adjustments.
—Keeping log of operation.
—Local and remote operation.
—Warnings, precautions.
—Supplies needed.
—Replacing supplies.
—Repeat above for each mode.
—Define unusual expressions.
—Explain unusual procedures.
—Refer to technician's adjustments.
—Operator's tests for operation.
—Operator's maintenance check chart.
—Fuse, tube, vibrator, crystal, indicator and plug-in-unit replacement table.

Theory

—Repeat from preceding as needed.
—Write to reader's level.
—How it works, not why.
—What goes in?
—What happens to it?

—What comes out?
—Compare with familiar equipment.
—Differences between models.
—Diagrams: systems block, unit block, vector, simplified schematic, complete schematic, primary power dist.
—Oscilloscope wave patterns.
—Wave-shape comparison chart.
—Signal-flow analysis.
—System-operation theory.
—Unit-by-unit theory.
—Stage-by-stage theory.
—Theory: by functions performed.
—Theory: output toward input.
—Theory: input toward output.
—Math. basis of operation.
—Theory: each mode of operation.

Preventive Maintenance

—Repeat from preceding as needed.
—Write to technician's level.
—Technician requirements.
—Check-chart for proper operation.
—Maintenance check-chart.

—Lubrication chart.
—Hydraulic maintenance chart.
—Periodical checks (hourly, daily, etc, through annual)
—How gain access for maintenance.
—Periodic overhaul procedures.
—Precautions, warnings.
—Special test circuits.
—Special test setups.
—Re-tropicalization.
—Re-weatherproofing.
—Specify lubricants.
—List special tools.
—List special equip't.
—Tube, fuse, vibrator, indicator, crystal and plug-in-unit locations.
—Pre-maintenance procedures.
—Post-maintenance procedures.
—Cleaning, painting, polishing.
—Corrosion, rust, water, salt-spray, damage, air-filter, cable, connector check.
—Parts-replacement schedule.
—Where to buy replacements parts.
—Supply replacement schedule.
—Where buy supplies.
—Safety precautions.

Corrective Maintenance

—Repeat from preceding as needed.
—Write to technician's level.
—Technician requirements.

—Recommended maintenance approach.
—Illustrations of equipment.
—Component identification charts, drawings and photos.
—Troubleshooting: for system, by unit,
—Signal tracing chart.
—Charts: Oscilloscope wave-form,
—Diagrams: servicing block, simplified schematic, over-all schematic, unit-by-unit schematic, vector, primary power.
—Mechanical exploded views.
—Overhaul procedures.
—Mechanical disassembly dwgs.
—Mechanical reassembly dwgs.
—Accessory equipment required.
—Special tools required.
—List faults and probable causes.
—Special test circuits.
—Illustrations showing adjustments.
—Mechanical, hydraulic, pneumatic, electrical servicing.
—Disassembly, reassembly.
—Emergency repair.
—Voltages on schematic dwgs.
—Wave-shapes on schematic dwgs.
—List of component parts.
—Parts manufacturers.
—Parts ordering.
—Repair: cabinet, corrosion, rust, water damage.

Things to Remember

—Covering letter.
—Get your company's name on it.
—Get your name on it.
—Give date, department.
—Type one side, double spaced.
—Drawings, pics better than words.
—Hold consistent nomenclature.
—Hold consistent technical level.
—Will it be understood?
—Write to reader's level.
—Write to reader's interests.
—Check security clearance.
—Table of contents.
—List of illustrations.
—List of tables.
—Number the pages.
—Use short words.
—Use simple sentences.
—Keep paragraphs brief.
—White space for easy reading.
—Step-by-step procedures best.
—File a reference copy.
—Keep a copy yourself. ■

10 *Steps to better engineering proposals*

Lesson 1...

What is a proposal?

EMERSON CLARKE, Manager, Technical Services, Military Engineering Dept, Zenith Radio Corp

A proposal is an offer to do a job for a potential customer. It tells what will be done, how it will be done, and the terms of performance. The proposed job may be as simple as constructing a small tank, or as complex as designing and installing a space station.

The proposal may be as informal as a verbal statement followed by a handshake, an oral presentation complete with color slides and flip-charts, or it may even be a motion picture. Most commonly it is a written statement varying in length from a single page to a stack of volumes 10 feet high.

As a general rule, an engineering proposal is required only when the item or service is an uncommon one. Only a cost quotation would be required to sell off-the-shelf items. If the items were to be interconnected to make an uncommon system, however, then a proposal might be required by the customer.

Usually, proposals must include: (1) a technical section, (2) a cost quotation, and (3) a statement of the conditions under which the work will be performed and the contract negotiated. The proposal is, therefore, a preliminary to negotiation of a formal contract. It specifies costs and conditions of performance and, in the case of the engineering proposal, it offers a technical description of how the task will be performed and the objectives achieved. Terms of the proposal may become binding upon acceptance by the customer, or they may be offered only as a basis for further negotiation.

The inquiry-proposal system is a time-honored way of doing business.

Each participant strives to protect himself to the full extent of the law, but nevertheless, each depends upon the unwritten factors of goodwill and trust between parties. (This last point is vital in Government R & D contracts where the objectives may be uncertain and the value of the results open to question.)

What do proposals cost?

They are surprisingly expensive because high-priced administrative and technical personnel must be utilized. Here are some ball-park estimates:

● For the brief proposal: $1000 to $5000

● For the medium-sized one: $5000 to $15,000

● For the large (and very large) proposal: up to $250,000 (. . . and some proposals for large systems have cost millions).

Obviously, proposal preparation is not to be undertaken lightly or done carelessly. And the most expensive proposal of all is the one that fails to win the contract.

Engineers prepare most technical proposals. Whatever the size of the proposal, the "proposal project engineer" is the key man, for the success of the proposal depends upon his analysis of the task and his solution to the problems. Cost and other factors excepted, a proposal is only as good as the engineering behind it.

The importance of quality

Essentially, the engineering proposal is a sales package that must *by itself* sell the capability of the company that submits it. Like the sales-man, it represents the company. Obviously, this package should reflect quality. No firm would knowingly send out a sales representative who used bad grammar, who told an incoherent story, or was unkempt. Yet many proposals exhibit these characteristics.

Not that the proposal has to be fancy or obviously expensive, with arty covers and four-color illustrations. Rather, the major quality factors are these (in addition to the prime factor of high-quality engineering, of course):

Contents—
  Compliance with customer requirements
  Clarity and coherence
  Effective illustrations
  Thoroughness

The document—
  Legible type
  Clear reproduction
  Absence of errors
  Neat cover; easy-to-handle binder.

The purpose of quality in a proposal is not to dazzle the customer, but to give him the message with crystal clarity.

Companies that prepare consistently winning proposals are thought to have some magic that brings them the contracts. If there is any special magic, it is the essential magic of good business—

● Have a good product
● Offer it at a fair price
● Sell it effectively.

How to sell it effectively through the medium of the engineering proposal is the theme of these lessons.

Lesson 2...
Your customer

Proposals are written for customers. This may seem to labor the obvious, yet it merits repetition. Too often, proposals are written from the proposer's point of view, with little regard for the customer's desires and needs. Or, the proposer may have only a vague picture of the customer—who he is, what he does, how he operates, and what he really needs. So a principle is established: Know your customer, and know what he wants.

The customer defines his needs by a package of documents called, variously: a *Request for Proposal,* an *Invitation to Bid,* an *Inquiry,* a *Statement of Work,* or a *Bid Request.* Let us call it a bid request, all items to which the engineer must respond being in the statement of work.

Ideally, the bid request is a clear statement of customer requirements that can be answered by a clear proposal. The request sets forth performance specifications, materials, workmanship standards, reporting requirements, schedules, etc. Each of these factors becomes a topic in the proposal, and is answered to the depth necessary to satisfy the customer.

The ideal bid request is no more common than the ideal proposal. If a careful analysis of the request fails to give you a clear understanding of customer needs, the problem may be: (1) the customer has not stated his requirements clearly, or (2) you are out of your technical depth. The answer to the latter is obvious: Don't bid. But if analysis proves (1) to be the problem, then you must go back to the customer for more information

—"hard" information, this time. Usually, a conference or two will dispel the clouds.

But very often the customer cannot clarify his requirements because of the type of job. For example, it's easy to prepare a bid request for a production job where drawings and specifications are available, but not so easy for a research program where all may be conjectural. The bidder responds in a similar vein.

Know your customer

It stands to reason: The more you know about your customer, the better chance your proposal has. This means you must know him in depth, and as far as he permits. Here are some things to know:
- His key people
- How he operates
- His product line
- His strengths and weaknesses
- His facilities and suppliers
- His advance planning
- His "personality."

Thorough customer understanding is particularly important when you submit unsolicited proposals, for then you must know the customer's business and advance planning so well that you can play pitcher on his team.

By law, the Federal Government must obtain most goods and services through competitive bids. Recognizing the importance of the "know your customer" factor, Government agencies strive to tell as much about themselves and their operation as possible, within the limits of security restrictions. Procurement and organizational

guides and advance planning documents are distributed freely to qualified bidders. Also, during the procurement process the Government makes its technical people available for bidder conferences. Conferences are usually called after distribution of bid requests so that bidders have time to come up with pertinent questions.

Actively promote good relations

Make it easy for your customer to evaluate your proposal and to do business with you generally. Here are some ways:
- Assign "customer-compatible people" to the proposal. If you can visualize your proposal writers engaged in a lively discussion with their customer counterparts, chances are they're a good match.
- Make your proposals clear and logical—in other words, write them well. The customer will respond with his business. (See "8 Steps to Better Engineering Writing," page 328.)
- Respect the customer. This is an element often overlooked. (If you don't, your writing will give you away.)
- Sure, it's a hard job writing a winning proposal, but don't be grim about it. Enthusiasm on your part can awaken a like enthusiasm for your product in the customer.
- Be specific and not redundant. Don't wash your customer away in a sea of words.
- Remember that you're writing for technical men; don't take the advertising man's approach. Let hard facts do the hard selling.

Lesson 3...
Now let's organize

A proposal is organized by its outline, and a good outline is vital to its effectiveness. The outline:
- "Builds in" responsiveness by insuring that all customer requirements are answered
- Guides the team that prepares the proposal
- Facilitates the writing.

Outline topics are drawn from two sources. The primary source is, of course, the customer's statement of work. His requirements are slotted into the outline first, insuring that key points will not be overlooked.

The second source of outline topics

is the proposal writer himself, who originates topics that supplement and expand upon those supplied by the customer. At this point, the creative process begins that will culminate in a proposal.

The outline is built by following these steps:
1. Read the statement of work.
2. Set up major sections of the outline.
3. Study the statement of work and make note of all topics to which you must respond.
4. Supplement customer topics with those of your own choosing, selecting

those that explain and justify your approach, and clearly indicate your program.
5. Determine the weight of each topic—whether coordinate (of equal weight) or subordinate, and decide the order or presentation.
6. Assign topic numbers, using the numeration, or decimal, system. For example, a major section might be 3, and its subtopics 3.1 and 3.1.1, and so on.

The outline should mirror the statement of work, and in general, the order of topics should follow the order of the bid request. There is good reason for this in that the customer would like to see his questions answered in the same order he asked them.

While the outlines for solicited and unsolicited proposals are similar, there is a major difference in that the unsolicited proposal must do a double selling job. First, it must convince the potential customer that he really needs the proposed work, and second (like the solicited proposal), it must convince the customer that the proposer can do the job.

So, right up in front of the unsolicited proposal, you must put the topic "Value of the program." (And "value" in proposals always means value to the customer.)

Front matter

The cover should be neat but not gaudy. In design it may reflect the advertising image of the company. Its simple purpose is to announce the contents, identify the sender, and protect the document. Modesty is the keynote, for the value lies in the content of the proposal, and not its trappings.

The title page repeats the cover title, refers to the bid request, recognizes the author(s), and identifies the sender with a complete address. Often, it may have room for approval signatures, and a distribution list (on the reverse side because the front is usually filled up).

The foreword contains information that fits no place else in the proposal, such as acknowledgments, copyright statements, rights in data, and a mention of related documents. *It's not usual in proposals.*

A glossary is also unusual in proposals because the customer is usually an expert in his field. However, a glossary might be needed in an unsolicited proposal where the proposed work and its terminology is unique.

The summary is the keystone of the proposal. It summarizes the content, yes, but does so selectively and with hard facts that back up the sales message. Suppose the customer said: "Tell me in 300 words or less what you have to offer and what's so good about it." Or, as Mark Twain's Jim Smiley put it: "I don't see no p'ints about that frog that's any better'n any other frog." . . . Answer that statement about your product and you'll have a good summary.

The summary can serve other valuable purposes besides its brief appearance in front of the proposal. A copy can be attached to the letter of transmittal as valuable supplementary information. Also, copies can be circulated within the company as general information.

Tables of Contents consist of a list of topics, a list of illustrations, and a list of tables. In the topic list, the breakdown is usually carried to important subtopics, even unto the fourth generation.

Back matter substantiates

Professional papers and other publications referenced in the proposal should be included. Such information is not only substantiative, but also a sterling indicator of capability.

A bibliography is necessary in research projects. Catalog sheets and other technical literature describing a component to be modified or otherwise adapted to meet the requirements of the invitation are valuable.

Detailed résumés of personnel are important in the assessment of capability.

Brochures that describe general facilities may be included on the assumption that they substantiate claims to capability; also, it may be thought that the customer may find something that relates to another, and pending, procurement.

Remember, all information should relate strongly to the requirements of the invitation—anything else clutters. And all material should be listed in the table of contents, otherwise it may never be noticed. Again, the criterion is customer convenience.

Lesson 4 . . .

Introductory: What are you offering?

All writing must have an introduction. It is the means by which you lead your reader into the main body. In brief, it "orients" him.

In proposals, here is what the introduction must do: First, it summarizes general facts about the origin of the task and its scope; second, it comments on the requirements of bid request; and third, it leads into the technical section that tells how you are going to do the job. For unsolicited proposals, there is a fourth requisite: Valid reasons must be offered for doing the proposed work.

Introductory topics

The box on this page contains 24 introductory topics that can be considered typical. Topics marked with an asterisk are often valuable in the unsolicited proposal.

Note that although many topics are presented, only certain ones are applicable to any one proposal. Also, certain topics seem redundant. All possible topics are included, however, because the value of the list lies in the wide choice available to the writer, leaving it to him to select, alter, or change order as he sees fit. The list is essentially a memory-jogger designed to ensure that vital topics are not overlooked.

Depending upon its weight, a topic

Introductory Topic List

1. Purpose of proposal
2. Reference to invitation, or other statement as to origin
3. Scope of proposal
*4. Duration of program
5. Reference to attachments
*6. Purpose of program
*7. Objectives
8. Alternatives and options
*9. Statement of the problem(s)
10. Description of expected end-product, or other result of program
*11. Major design goals or features, of a component, equipment, or system
12. Relation of proposed task to other components, equipments, techniques, or systems
*13. Relation to the state of the art
14. Value of the program: utility, applications, contribution
15. Prediction of performance or other attainment
*16. Estimate of scale of effort
*17. Support required
18. Review of special agreements or arrangements between parties
19. Comments on requirements
20. Statement of feasibility
21. Facilities and personnel available
22. Statement of capability
23. Experience, direct or related
24. Expression of interest

(Topics marked with an asterisk are often valuable in the unsolicated proposal.)

may be allotted a single sentence, one or more paragraphs, or an entire section.

Some general rules

Keep it brief. The length of the introduction should not exceed five pages, and two or three would be better. Although brevity is the keynote, the introduction must not scant essential points, and while generalities are dealt with, these generalities must be fully informative and point the way clearly to what follows.

Avoid "discussions." The discussion section is too often a rambling digression that serves only to confuse. One gets the impression that the writer is gropingly wordily for his theme—a bit of by-play the customer shouldn't be forced to witness.

But again, a discussion that covers background may be necessary in the unsolicited proposal to contribute to problem understanding.

Avoid redundancy. When writing introductions, and indeed, other sections of the proposal as well, there is danger of paraphrasing, or even quoting at length from the customer's statement of work. The result is a watered-down proposal. Words are precious in selling your ideas: Don't squander them on non-essentials, or you'll lose your customer's attention. If this happens, you've lost the contract as well.

Lesson 5...

The technical approach

This is the heart of the proposal—what you are selling. All other information serves only to support this section. It reveals a great deal, too, in that it directly mirrors the competence of the engineering staff and its management. It shows the scope and depth of engineering knowledge, and the awareness of the latest advances in the technology.

In brief, here you win or lose, so make it good.

Let's assume first that your engineering approach is airtight and sure to satisfy the customer. Also, the price is right so competition is clearly outdistanced. Now, the engineering approach must be put into writing.

(It can still be lost, right there. That airtight approach can be so muddied and obscured that the customer can't get the message. Also, key topics can be left out by inexcusable oversight.)

Effective writing is more than word fluency—it's a matter of logical presentation of facts, as well. And in this the unskilled writer can be on a par with the professional—if he knows how to use the outline. The outline ensures that: (1) the engineering approach will be described logically, and (2) no essential topics will be left out.

The box on this page contains a list of special outline topics for the technical section. (The precautions about using such lists, as specified in Lesson 4, apply of course.) The topics are major ones, and each has many subtopics. For example, under Topic 53: "Maintenance," at least two dozen topics can be cited, beginning with:

    a. Access to parts
    b. Chassis design
    c. Fasteners, quick release
    d. Interchangeability (etc).

Thus, if a key topic is maintenance, the engineer can scan the list and be reminded quickly of topics he might otherwise have overlooked.

There is much to be said for the Topic List System. Nearly every engineering and scientific theme covers thousands of topics either immediate to the subject, or related in some way. Of these, perhaps 50 may be vital to the proposal. If the engineer relies solely on memory, he may forget key topics, and the proposal will suffer serious omissions.

The customer didn't forget. Neither did the competitor who ran off with the prize.

Technical Topic List

Preliminary topics
1. Summary of program
2. Phases and tasks
3. Comments on requirements
4. Analysis of major problems
5. Estimate of scale of effort
6. Design study
7. Plan of attack
8. Alternate approaches
9. Literature survey
10. Technical survey
11. Background history and analysis
12. Examination of factors leading to program
13. Relation to state of the art
14. Plan of operation
15. Statement of work
16. Theoretical approach
17. Design approach
18. Technical approach

Detail topics
20. Technical analysis
21. Technical discussion
22. Examination and use of properties, materials, and processes
23. Description of equipment to be supplied
24. Materials, components, or devices to be compounded or fabricated
25. Description of services
26. Relation to existing equipment or system
27. Use of special or unique parts, components, and analysis of same
28. Component selection criteria
29. Special techniques

30. Electrical design
31. Mechanical design
32. Expandability
33. Exceptions to and deviations from specifications
34. Prediction as to success of program
35. Block diagram discussion
36. Description of operation
37. Value prediction
38. Application prediction
39. Analytical methods
40. Experimental methods
41. Point of departure
42. Testing
43. Test instrumentation
44. Tooling
45. Quality control
46. Reliability
47. Producibility
48. Restraints on design
49. Recognized tactical need
50. Value engineering
51. Systems engineering
52. Human factors engineering
53. Maintenance
54. Prototype development
55. Trade-offs in design
56. Cost effectiveness analysis

Concluding topics
57. Statement as to feasibility
58. Support required
59. Customer-furnished equipment required
60. Applications of program
61. Evaluation of program
62. Recapitulation; summary

What plans have you made?

Now that the customer knows *what* you are going to do, his next question is, "How are you going to do it?" Program planning descriptions are particularly important in proposals to the Government. Poor planning and bad management are major causes of program failures under Government contracts. And indeed, this is true of almost any engineering activity.

Major planning topics

For most proposals, planning is embodied in the topics presented in the box.

Program organization. This means facilities and personnel. Middle and top administrative and technical managers are identified, and their function for the program described. Facilities consist of space, matériel, and functional groups. Organization is described, usually with a block diagram. (See "Engineering Organization," *PE* —Apr 9 '59.)

Plan of operation. Detailed planning is usually required for field engineering programs, production projects, service programs, and for systems management. Typical subtopics are contract administration, cost control, customer liaison, subcontracting plans, reports, and testing.

Scheduling. The schedule specifies rate of performance and target dates for all major tasks. It is often displayed as a bar chart, or a **PERT** chart. Accurate scheduling is a puzzling problem to engineers because of the many unknowns, such as:

- Capabilities of personnel: How fast and how well do they work? How quickly can they learn?
- Availability of personnel, facilities, and parts

Program Planning Topic List

1. Program organization
   a. Responsibility assignment
   b. Facilities assignment
   c. Organizational description
2. Plan of operation
3. Scheduling
   a. Origin of schedule
   b. Scheduling factors
   c. Responsibility
4. Facilities to be utilized
   a. Selection factors
   b. Description of facilities
   c. Utilization for program
   d. Status
5. Personnel to be assigned
   a. Identity
   b. Functions
   c. Qualifications

- Overall efficiency of the organization
- Interference from other programs.

Very accurate predictions are nearly impossible, yet a practical level of accuracy must be attained. It's a product of experience, sweat, and guesswork. The schedule is not a bodiless prediction, but a thing that must be lived with if a contract is awarded. Things left to "work themselves out" seldom do.

Facilities. A "facility" can be a piece of equipment, or a functional group such as a model shop. Caution: List and describe only those facilities that are to be used for the program. The temptation to brag is often irresistible, but for the sake of the customer's patience, don't do it.

Personnel to be assigned. List the men and their specific contribution in terms of effort and time. The professional biography or résumé sets forth qualifications.

How much planning information?

Again (and always) the criterion is customer satisfaction. You must provide enough information to convince him you can do the job. Be realistic; otherwise, your too optimistic planning becomes an uneasy fact of life that will have to be lived with upon award of contract.

Are you capable?

Now that you've told your customer *what* you're going to do, you must convince him that you can do the job—that you "have capability." If your company has a good reputation with the customer, you need say very little. But if you are a stranger to him, or if you are bidding on a Government contract, then you'll have to be more explicit.

The major "capability factors" are listed as topics in the box on this page. As with the lists in previous lessons, all topics may not be required —only those that carry maximum conviction to the customer and give him confidence in your ability.

Essentially, your customer wants to know: (a) are your people competent, (b) are your facilities adequate, and (c) what's been your experience with similar jobs? For his own good, the customer wants clear answers, and you must give good evidence.

(Please note the overlap between the planning and capabilities sections in that "personnel" and "facilities" are presented in both. The two topics are compatible, but to avoid cluttering the planning section, "capabilities" is usually broken out as a separate section. However, all capabilities information *can* appear in the planning section if it can be presented with brevity.)

There is a cardinal rule for those who prepare capabilities information, and that is: Know your company. And that means to know it in depth. It's not an easy task, especially in large companies. Much digging may be required. But know it you must, for your company and its products are what you are selling.

Personnel

This capability factor outweighs all others, even the facility factor, for the finest facilities are worthless without qualified people.

The capability of engineers, technicians, and administrators can be set forth in a résumé quite similar to an employment application. The name and title are specified, together with a description of education and experience. And if they carry weight with the customer, professional achievements and society memberships can be included.

It's a good practice to present résumés in two forms, the first as a brief paragraph in the planning section to highlight pertinent experience, and the second in full length (one or more pages) if the customer should want to know more. (In the long form, the résumé belongs in the Appendix.)

Facilities

What your customer wants to know about your facilities is "are they adequate to do my job?" Answering this with regard to space and matériel is easy in that you can cite the square footage and the efficiency of your purchasing system. But for "functional groups" (eg, a model shop), you will have to be more explicit and use some of the capability descriptors listed in the next section.

Capabilities

Six descriptors, with subtopics, can be applied to all companies.

History. Be careful with this one: What you say must relate to customer needs. Stick to historical topics like growth rate, stability, labor relations record, and history of outstanding achievements.

Performance. Again, relate this to

Capabilities Topic List

1. Personnel
   a. Education and training
   b. Experience
   c. Accomplishments
   d. Potential
2. Facilities
   a. Space
   b. Material
   c. Functional groups
3. Capabilities
   a. History
   b. Performance
   c. Reputation
   d. Activities
   e. Interests
   f. Customer understanding
   g. Resources

---

customer interests. Tell about products developed and manufactured, services rendered, and work record. The latter is excellent in proposals to the Government: Contracts can be cited and the work on each summarized in a short paragraph.

Reputation. Companies, like individuals, have reputations. Don't blow the horn too freely. What interests the customer is whether the company delivers on time and without cost overruns, and whether it is a sound and sober member of the business community.

Activities. Dynamic companies are active outside of their regular product line. Advanced developments and research projects sponsored by the company can be cited to show alertness to possible future interests of the customer.

Customer understanding. Customers appreciate it if you know their procedures and requirements and understand their problems. Getting this information takes effort, but the customer will be grateful.

Resources. This refers generally to financial data that proves company stability and soundness. Before he commits himself to a contract, the customer wants to know whether you are going to stay in business.

It's a natural tendency to oversell the customer with capability information—to dig a shovel into the basket of superlatives and really let fly. But do this too often and your customer will come to hate you. Follow the cardinal rule: Tell the customer only what he wants to know!

Lesson 8 . . .

Now let us get organized

It's a fact of engineering life— *proposals* and *pressure* are synonymous. Here's why—
- Proposal-making is a complex coordinated effort of many skills in addition to engineering, such as legal, accounting, purchasing, technical writing, management, and printing.
- It's a task on top of the normal workload.
- — and then there's that deadline!

There will always be pressure: In moderation, it's a fine stimulant to get the job done (and a fine cranium-stimulator, too). But runaway pressure can cause oversights, inconsistencies, and even gross errors. Worse, it can dishearten the proposal team so that ensuing proposals become progressively less effective.

The key to "pressure-relief" is good management of the proposal effort, from start to finish. Here are some ways it can be done:

A Chain of Clearly Defined Events

1. Marketing finds customer; makes contact
2. Bid request received
3. Marketing-engineering analysis: bid/no-bid decision
4. If GO, Proposal Manager is assigned; copies of bid set distributed
5. First general meeting: engineering approach described, brains picked; strategy planned; tasks assigned; management sets up guidelines
6. Technical groups splinter off for separate meetings
7. Proposal is written
8. Manuscript is reviewed by management
9. Manuscript is typed; given final quality control check
10. Proposal is printed and delivered
11. Marketing may request debriefing from customer
12. Proposal is given final analysis by engineering and management; marketing orients it into the overall effort

---

Set up an effective procedure. All proposal-making effort follows a certain sequence, as shown by the box on this page. Set up a standard operating procedure based on this chain of events. Then, all participants will know what must be done, how it will be done, and who will do it.

Make one man responsible. Call him Proposal Manager or Project Engineer, if you like, but make him responsible for the entire proposal effort. Along with the responsibility must go the authority, of course—and he'll need it.

Organize it. Use the basic tool—the outline. Work assignments can be made from it, and all participants will have a map to guide them over the route.

Schedule it. Set up a realistic proposal schedule and adhere to it. It's human nature that some people must fall under the whip of the deadline before they really begin to produce. If they have only the final deadline to contend with, their single tardy burst of energy will be too late, and chaos results. But if management sets up a series of sub-deadlines and enforces adherence, the effort can be paced. Overtime can be predicted and distributed over the entire period, rather than expended round-the-clock just before the deadline.

Also, it's imperative that the schedule allow time for review of the final manuscript; otherwise, some late-sprouting errors may get through to the customer.

(Another comment about the deadline: Cursed as it is, it's the Proposal Manager's best ally, for it forces people to make decisions that otherwise would be put off interminably. Also, the deadline is a must for the unsolicited proposal, which tends to stay around forever unless it is spurred by a deadline.)

Give it top priority. No obstacle must interrupt the chain of events, from inception to printing and binding. Roadblocks often crop up in the strangest places, such as in the company printing plant. Top management must establish a blanket priority.

Use outside help. If your organization is overloaded, a good part of the task can be farmed out to technical writing agencies, engineering service firms, or consultants. And as for actual production of the proposal books, many specialty firms supply expert photography, illustrations, and printing.

If such help is used, their efforts must also be coordinated, for all who work on the proposal are subject to its tyranny.

It's a fact — good management and effective procedures will improve your proposals and enable you to produce more of them. Most important, it will reduce the strain on your engineers, and for this, they will be grateful.

Lesson 9...

Time and money savers

Meetings have been held, tasks assigned, and the proposal course has been charted, you hope through calm waters. Now all hands set to work to produce a manuscript that can be sent to the printer.

How does the manuscript take shape? Around the outline, of course. A good technique is to use an ordinary three-ring notebook, with separators keyed to the major topics of the outline. As inputs are generated, they are slotted into the notebook. Every illustration and exhibit is represented either by the actual item, or by a "voucher" page. This system ensures that nothing is left out. Also, this complete manuscript serves as a guide for the assembly of the printed copies.

Certain proposal inputs, such as résumés, are unchanged from one proposal to the next. Time and money can be saved by printing such material in quantity and storing it for future proposals.

In addition to résumés, other materials can be considered as "stock":

- Brochures
- Catalogs; specification sheets
- Annual reports
- Financial statements
- Professional papers and articles
- Advertising and sales materials.

It's important that stock material not be looked upon as "filler" (or designated by the unfortunate epithet "boilerplate"), for it plays a vital role in the proposal. It must be selected with care and updated frequently to reflect the latest and best information. Most important, and for each proposal, it must be related to the requirements of the bid request. If this is not done, then it deserves the name boilerplate, and its weight can sink the proposal ship.

Proposal reference notebook. Proposals are built one upon another. To take maximum advantage of this fact, extract typical sections from past proposals (summaries, introduction, etc) and store them in a notebook for ready reference. This material is valuable as a writing guide, but it cannot be used unchanged from proposal to proposal.

Checklists. Make up a checklist of the résumés you have stored. The Proposal Manager checks off the names he wants represented in the proposal, and the résumés can be collected and held for assembly.

Checklists can also be made up for the other stock items described in this lesson.

Page numbering. Number pages by section rather than sequentially from first to last. For example, the first page in section 4 is numbered "4-1," etc. By this means, easier sections can be typed ready for the printer undisturbed by the problem sections. Also, if last-minute changes are made and pages added, only one section is affected. This practice applies to illustrations and tables, as well.

Make only one manuscript. Prepare your final manuscript as reproduction copy. Even if changes are necessary, more time is gained than is lost.

Artwork corner-cutters. Use all possible shortcuts such as tapes, pre-printed transparent overlays, shading sheets, etc.

Partial printing. Print or bind only those copies needed for the customer, and hold internal distribution for later.

Set up standards. Standardize formats and procedures so that typing and other processes become automatic.

Set up an expert. Appoint a "proposal specialist" (a technical writer is a good choice) who steeps himself in the art and assumes responsibility for all the mechanics of proposal preparation.

The product for sale is engineering, and it must follow that the proposal will be no better or no worse than the abilities of the contributing engineers. So a direct route to better proposals is to give the engineers maximum assistance.

General efficiency. Set up an efficient system for proposal preparation (Lesson 8). This frees the engineer to concentrate on one task and one deadline—his own.

Provide topic lists. Give him memory-joggers in the form of topic lists, as described in previous lessons.

Give him information. He often needs information, but has no time to dig for it. The company information retrieval system can be invaluable.

Give him clerical support. Take his dictation, type his rough drafts, and do it promptly.

Give him a refuge. Set up a quiet room away from daily districtions, and give him a chance to think.

Keep him up to date. Again, the product for sale is engineering, and the winning idea may come from an engineer who kept abreast of the latest developments. So between proposals, keep his knowledge fresh with a good library system.

The biggest money saver of all lies in the careful selection of programs to bid on. The limited stock of proposal ammunition must be saved for the clearest targets, for it's as much work to prepare a proposal foredoomed to lose as it is to write a sure winner.

Lesson 10 . . .

Now let's get into print

The proposal manuscript has passed reasonably intact through management's final review and approval, so it is now ready to be converted into printed booklets. This process requires preparation of artwork, reproduction typing, printing, collating, and binding.

There are three requirements for the whole process: It must be speedy, it must be economical, it must provide good quality.

The word "quality" with respect to proposals needs defining. Quality doesn't imply elaborate or obviously expensive characteristics that could offend the customer on the ground that he might have to pay for it. (Government bid requests have some pointed words on the subject.) Rather, proposal quality means legible type, crisp artwork, and a book that is bound for easy handling. The goal of the whole process is to provide a message vehicle that the customer can use without eyestrain or other annoyance.

All companies, even the smallest, have facilities adequate to meet the goal of proposal quality. As shown by this lesson, all that is required is standard office equipment and the willingness to use it properly.

In general. Specifications for producing the printed proposals should consider these points:

1. Except for very brief proposals offered in letter form, proposals are usually submitted as bound booklets.

2. Most customers require several copies, and for legal reasons, all copies must be identical. Carbon copies may be unacceptable and erasures disallowed, so some form of reproduction, either by printing press or copy machine, is required.

3. Booklet size is usually $8\frac{1}{2} \times 11$ in. Paper of this size is inexpensive, and copies fit readily into files. Odd-size proposals may attract attention but can be troublesome both to the submitter and the customer.

4. To enhance legibility, proposals are usually typed double-space. Special $1\frac{1}{2}$-line ratchets are available, and conserve space without sacrificing legibility (handy for formulas, too). If single-spacing is used, it's best to double-space between paragraphs.

5. Proposals are usually printed on one side of the page only. This may increase bulk slightly, but it's a big time saver, for otherwise the copy must dry several hours before it can be recycled through the printing press. If the schedule is tight, this delay can be intolerable.

6. How many copies? In addition to those the customer wants, enough extras should be printed for fairly wide distribution within the company. Valuable information can thus be disseminated by merely letting the press run a little longer. By the same token, distribution outside the company should be restricted.

All reproduction copy must be proofread and approved *before* printing. All concerned must understand that no changes can be made in the printed copy. If this rule is not established hard and fast, the writer will have to make changes and to reprint pages right up to the time of delivery. His schedule will become a shambles.

Illustrations. All engineering illustrative techniques—graphs, diagrams, charts, photographs, wash drawings, any visual device that clarifies text—are valuable in proposals. Four restraints apply to proposal artwork, however:

Keep it simple. Elaborate artwork can be costly both in the making and in the reproduction. For example, use four-color printing only when it's absolutely necessary to get the message to the customer.

Restrict detail. Go just deep enough to show the general approach. After all, the customer is supposed to pay for the actual detail design.

Relate it. All illustrations must relate to customer requirements. If the relationship is not obvious, it must be pointed out carefully.

Shortcuts are in order. Use all possible shortcuts; for example, pencil drawings rather than ink. ∎

SHOULD YOU MAKE THAT SPEECH?

*You've been invited to make a public presentation. How do you
evaluate the invitation, for yourself, for your company,
for the profession? Here are guideposts to your answer.*

PAUL R HEINMILLER, Communications consultant

Mfg Engrg Consulting Service, General Electric Company, Schenectady

You have just been invited to make a presentation before an audience. It may be one of many, or an unusual thing for you. It may be an invitation to speak before a "national forum" where you can present broad ideas and company views on significant issues. It may be a talk before a technical-society chapter on some detail of engineering, or it may be for a local high school science club—on careers in engineering.

Guideposts to aid you in accepting, or rejecting, speaking engagements are advisable, for these reasons:

1. To help you use your time more efficiently, and fulfil your job responsibilities more effectively.
2. To gain increased stature and recognition for your company, yourself and for the engineering profession by helping to make sure that qualified individuals fulfil speaking engagements.

There are at least five reasons why you should participate in this type of communications activity:

1. It is your responsibility to let others know your views on technical and nontechnical matters, as a member of a business enterprise.
2. It is an excellent opportunity for your company to gain stature and recognition with audiences important to your corporate welfare.
3. It helps implement your company's communications program by keeping open a key communications channel.
4. It presents an opportunity to project your company's "image" to important audiences.
5. It affords an opportunity for you to gain recognition and stature.

Three kinds of speaking engagements

Significant issues: This is one of the most important, not only for communicating ideas to the immediate audience, but for using speech reprints for planned distribution to important audiences, both inside and outside your company, for source material for further communications activity, and for coverage in popular communications channels. The "multiplier value" often is more important than the value of the information to the immediate audience.

Examples of "Significant Issues" presentations are:

1. Congressional testimony
2. Speeches at national and international conferences
3. Speeches at industry and professional conventions
4. Speeches at leading universities
5. Presentations before government groups
6. Talks to major executive clubs, Chambers of Commerce, etc
7. To state or regional association meetings
8. To local colleges
9. To plant-community audiences
10. Press conferences with national or industry-wide coverage
11. Network radio and TV appearances

Teaching: You undoubtedly spend considerable time "teaching." In general, there is no effort to obtain widespread publicity from these occasions, and the immediate audience *is* important. Examples of teaching engagements are:

1. Management conferences (internal)
2. Conferences of functional or subfunctional managers and functional contributors (internal)
3. Presentations to executive office and board of directors
4. Customer conferences (sponsored by your company)
5. Lectures at colleges, universities, and secondary schools
6. Papers and panel representations before technical, professional, or industry associations

Ceremonial or "business-obligation" appearances: Managers and prominent members of the professional staff are often in demand for situations where a "celebrity" is wanted as a headliner. Many times it is difficult to distinguish between ceremonial appearances and those having real multiplier, or teaching, values. Their prestige and customer-relations values should not be underestimated. Examples of ceremonial or business-obligation appearances are:

1. Local or state Chambers, Rotary, Kiwanis, Lions
2. Dedication speeches, ground breakings, new facilities
3. Graduation ceremonies for training courses (company and noncompany)
4. College and secondary-school commencement exercises
5. Acceptance speeches
6. Company-sponsored conferences

Receiving the invitation

Organizations wanting a speaker approach a company either directly, or through an intermediary, such as a district sales office. A request may be for a "speaker from your company" or a specific person.

If you are asked for by name, you have certain obligations to the sponsoring organization. One obligation is accepting—or rejecting—the offer promptly. If you don't want to fill the engagement, reject it; but at the same time suggest someone else from your organization (with his approval) to handle the assignment. Or, reply that you are willing to suggest someone else from your company. This keeps the ball in your control and prevents competition from getting an edge.

Blind requests, those asking for "a speaker," must be acknowledged promptly. If the accompanying checklist indicates an acceptance is in order, then the most appropriate individual should be selected.

Criteria

Here are some guideposts to help you to accept—or reject—general speaking engagements. To make a decision of this kind usually is more difficult than to decide on an invitation to present a technical paper before, say, a national technical society's semiannual meeting.

1. Is the audience—quality and quantity —worth the time you must invest and the company's money you must spend?
2. Are you being offered a spot on the program worthy of your position and reputation?
3. Can it fit into your busy schedule?
4. Are teaching values or multiplier factors available, such as speech preprints and reprints, plus interviews from press,

radio, TV? Or, is the engagement merely a "ceremonial" (or business-obligation) affair where a "celebrity" is wanted as a headliner?

5. Are you the person best qualified to represent your company? That is, do you have the technical competence and background, position, and over-all company point of view? How well do you speak?
6. Can it be tied in with a business trip?
7. Can other speaking engagements be lined up in the area, or enroute?
8. Is the location accessible, convenient, and served with good transportation facilities? Or will the entire project take more time and trouble than the benefits to be derived?
9. Will it be a presentation of a highly technical nature? If so, do you have the competence?
10. Will it be a survey presentation of general nature? If so, will you be able to fulfil your public-relations responsibilities?
11. Do they really want to hear something, or are they just looking for a speaker to fill a spot?
12. Do you have a presentation available that can be used "as is," or with minor adaptations? Must you develop an entirely new presentation? If so, is it worth it? And can the presentation be used elsewhere in the future?
13. Can the assignment be passed on to a person reporting to you, or two positions removed?
14. If you must decline, can you suggest someone else in your company to handle the assignment?
15. Do you really want to do it?

Should you accept?

If your answers to the above questions fall predominantly in the "Yes" category, you probably should accept the invitation. If the answers run about equally "Yes" and "No," Questions 1 through 5 should be the deciding ones. With "No" for the majority of answers, your best course is to pass it on to someone else in your organization. ∎

How to hold your audience

Know the objective of a speech. Specify
its purpose. Woo the audience as you develop
your theme. Repeat what you have said

by Thomas W. Carlin, Alexander Hamilton Institute, Inc.

THE FIRST JOB in planning any kind of talk is to decide precisely what you want to accomplish. Your objective should be stated in terms of the action you want the listener to take, or the emotion you want him to experience. You can then shape your material around this objective.

Once you have decided what you want to accomplish, you must then turn around and approach your subject from the viewpoint of the listener's own self-interest.

Pride is the root of effective motivation. If you appeal to a person's pride in the right way, he'll react positively and do what you want. Destructive criticism will hurt his pride. The reaction will be negative and it's likely you'll never get what you want.

Marketing specialists have long lists of appeals that motivate people to action. Among them are sex, survival, superiority, approval, comfort, curiosity and so on. Some appeals are logi-cal, some are emotional. Each can be helpful in making an impact.

Here, then, are two basic principles of oral communication — it should have a clearly stated objective and it should be slanted to motivate a specific audience.

The third essential ingredient is a theme. This fulfils two important functions. It determines what material will be used and what will be discarded; also it unites the elements into a coherent whole.

When a speech fails, the most common reason is that the theme was not even clear to the speaker himself.

Organization—Your speaking job is to tell the listener exactly what you are going to say, to say it, and then repeat what you have said. This repetition should not be word-for-word, but should reinforce the basic theme.

The organization of a talk falls into four main departments. There is the introduction, which should catch the listener's attention and set the mood for the rest of the talk; the statement of theme, which should always be stated clearly and precisely—never implied; the body of the talk, containing a distinct number of thoughts; and the conclusion, which should be delivered with power and emotional impact.

The introduction can be effective only if the material used is relevant to the theme. In a good talk, the introduction and statement of theme are usually indistinguishable.

Introductory methods—A good way of catching the attention of an audience is to relate an anecdote. People would rather listen to a pointed anecdote than to a generalization. If the anecdote is told in such a way that the listener can identify with the situation, then the audience will be spellbound.

But an anecdote is not a canned joke. Some speakers can introduce a talk with a joke and make it come off. Too often, however, the joke is old-hat to the audience. This brands the speaker as an amateur.

Another way of grasping the attention of an audience is to pose a problem with which the audience can identify—as long as the speaker intends to offer some solution.

Alternatively you can startle the

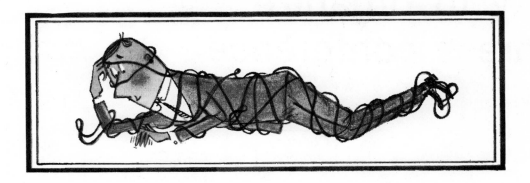

audience. This can be done with a paradoxical statement—"one of the great myths is that mother knows best"; a challenge—"there isn't a man in this room can solve the problem I'm going to describe"; or a pointed statistic—"nine men in this room will be dead of lung cancer in five years".

Distinct thoughts—As a rule, a five-minute talk should contain three thoughts, a ten-minute talk six, and so on. The thoughts should be clearly distinguished from one another and developed in sufficient detail to make their significance to the theme appreciated by the listeners.

The thoughts should be introduced and concluded with transitions that tell the listeners exactly where they are in the development of the talk they are hearing. When possible, the points made in a speech should be introduced in ascending order of importance.

Your speech should build towards a conclusion· that will elicit action. Like the first sentence of a speech, the final sentence is important because of its position.

Vivid and quotable—An effective speaker's language should be vivid and quotable. This means he must walk the line between extremes of being hackneyed on the one hand and overblown on the other.

A talk sounds stilted when the speaker tries to be profound. He uses two-dollar words to express two-bit ideas. He fills his talk with nouns like "implementation" and "utilization", and expressions like "it should be noted that . . ."

Here are a few hints:

1. When you find nouns ending in "-ion", "-ation" and "-osity", change the sentence around to convert the nouns to verbs. For example, "selection of the topic" would be changed to "selecting the topic".

2. Whenever possible, use the active rather than the passive voice. Rather than use "it was observed", say "we noticed".

3. Substitute short words for long ones whenever possible.

4. Remember that a trite vocabulary springs mostly from lazy habits in the use of similies and metaphors that are now cliches. Try to make up your own figures of speech, create your own descriptive style. You may not come up with a literary gem every time, but at least you can be sure your audience hasn't heard it before.

Some of the finest speeches ever delivered have been read. Others have been memorized and delivered verbatim. Still others have been spoken off-the-cuff.

In general, a man must be an accomplished speaker to read a speech and yet make it interesting. Too often, the sheets of paper occupy the speaker to such an extent that he tends to forget the audience.

Memorizing a speech also has it pitfalls. It takes weeks of practice before a memorized speech can ring with sincerity, and there is always the danger of going blank in mid talk and having to grope for a new place at which to continue the delivery. However, most speakers would profit by memorizing at least the main points in the body of their address.

Prepare well—An off-the-cuff address is valuable if it establishes rapport with the listeners, holds their attention and heightens the drama of the occasion. But these things are possible only if the "extemporaneous" talk is carefully prepared.

Most good speakers outline such a talk and practice the speech aloud several times. Then they commit key parts to memory and rely on small cue cards to remind themselves of the basic outline.

Even though he may discover that he is talking to a large audience, the speaker should think of his listeners as individuals. After he has reached the rostrum, he should look slowly over the audience before starting his speech, establishing eye contact with as many individuals as possible. As he talks, he should shift his gaze slowly from one listener to another.

Be natural—The speaker's hands should move naturally except at such times as he is making a gesture for emphasis. The important thing to remember is that hands will make natural movements if you let them. But you must avoid mannerisms and nervous gestures that can be as distracting as the absence of movement.

Naturally, your voice should be loud enough to be heard by everyone and clear enough to be understood. Practicing with a tape recorder can be a big help in correcting faulty speech patterns before they take root.

A conscientious speaker will also, if possible, check the acoustics in the place where he is to speak, having someone listen to him at the farthest corner of the room.

Anyone who follows all these precepts is virtually certain to make an effective speech. ■

How to organize a press conference

by Robert S. Leaf
Vice President, Marsteller International

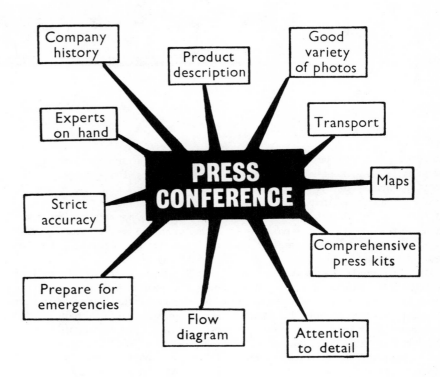

WHEN A COMPANY has a significant announcement to make, it immediately faces a problem. What is the best way to get the news to customers, stockholders, employees and other important audiences?

Often the answer is to hold a press conference. But press conferences must be run well or they will do more harm than good. The impression the press gets of a company will not only affect the coverage of the event itself but also their feelings and writings about the company in the future.

The first rule is simple. Make sure you have something to say. What is highly significant to you is not necessarily so to the press. Editors are busy. The key question should be: "Is a press conference the best way to give the information to the press?" If a detailed news release would serve the purpose just as well, don't have the press conference.

Experts needed—At the conference itself, company experts must be available. If the story is a financial one, make sure the financial expert is on hand. If it is technical, the director of research should be present. See to it that someone from the company attends who can answer any expected question, and answer it authoritatively. Remember, different editors need different information and no press handout can contain it all.

In addition to the basic news story, provide material from which the press can build. If it is a story of a merger, provide a detailed fact sheet on the history of the two companies.

If it is the introduction of a technical product, do not provide only the specifications of the product. Show also how it is significantly different from similar products previously manufactured by the company or other products that serve a similar function. Whenever possible, relate your story to the market place as a whole. But limit yourself to the facts. Don't oversell. If an editor becomes

suspicious that the material is not completely accurate, he might discard the whole story.

Often a story gets major coverage just because of the quality of the photographs. If it is a new process or new product, provide good pictures of the equipment in action. Put people in the pictures. There is nothing more static than a machine by itself. And give editors a variety of pictures so that they can select those of most interest to their readers. If extras such as earnings charts, flow diagrams or other illustrative material help tell the story, put them in the press handout.

Study carefully the list of those who accept your invitation and try to cater to them individually. If you are inviting both the general press and the trade press, make sure your material will satisfy their different needs.

Pity the editor—Regardless of how resourceful an editor is, he works under the handicap of time and a limi-

Organization is essential in dealing with the press. Here are some hints on how to get more publicity from your company announcements

ted knowledge of many specialized fields. The more material you can provide him geared to his particular needs, the greater will be your coverage in his publication.

Give yourself enough time to concentrate on all details. If the press conference will be held at a place that is not well known, provide transportation or easy-to-follow maps. Check facilities to make sure they are adequate for any visual presentations. If your company officials are not accustomed to giving press conferences, you might want to hold a rehearsal to ensure smoothness of the final performance. Make sure there is someone to meet the editors as they arrive.

Try to anticipate every problem. At one press conference featuring a slide demonstration, the projector bulb burned out. The conference was delayed an hour while another bulb was sought.

Your job doesn't end with the conference itself. Talk to editors to see if there is further material they need. Try to develop new angles and make it clear that company personnel will be available for further discussions.

Now that we have looked at the theory of press conferences, let's discuss the practice. Here is what happened when Clark Equipment Ltd., a British manufacturer of earthmoving equipment, held a press conference. This example was chosen because after the conference, Clark sent out questionnaires to editors who attended, asking for their opinions on the conference's strengths and weaknesses.

The conference was scheduled after Clark's management decided their introduction of a new line of rubber-tired tractor shovels would make a legitimate news story. The company also was announcing a major expansion of their manufacturing facilities.

To emphasise the technical aspect of the story, only publications with a strong interest in earthmoving were invited. Others with marginal interest were covered by a mailing that followed the press conference. Thirty-five

publications were invited, and all but five attended.

The day's programme included a welcome by the managing director, an introduction of the new line by the sales manager, a tour of plant facilities, luncheon, a visit to the company's service school and test cell facility, and a demonstration at the testing grounds.

Considerable care was taken to make the editors' job easier. A mock-up of the new line aided understanding. During the factory tour, editors were broken down into groups of four so that detailed questions could be asked. Wherever possible at the lunch, each editor was placed next to the man from the company who could best answer his particular questions.

A nine-page technical release and a specification sheet provided the necessary product background. Additional releases covered the plant expansion and company background.

Attention was paid to possible follow-ups. An editor representing an Irish publication, discovered that Clark's Irish distributor was to be at an exhibition of the equipment the following day. It was arranged for a picture to be taken of the distributor examining the equipment.

The story in print—The press conference achieved its objective. Seventeen features of a page or more appeared in the trade and technical press. Another dozen or so shorter stories also appeared. It was difficult for any customer reading the trade press not to know Clark had introduced a new line.

The questionnaire also indicated the conference's success. The demonstration, the plant tour and the detailed initial briefing all received numerous favourable comments. The editors were especially pleased by the fact that top management was available throughout the day to answer their questions.

For most editors, the demonstration at the testing grounds was the high point of the day. Each piece of equip-

ment was shown operating in normal working conditions. This took the conference out of the conjectural stage and drove home many points that already had been made verbally.

The demonstration also provided another example of how attention to detail can pay off. Because the area was muddy that day, boots were given to the visiting journalists. It was also extremely cold, so a tent was set up where hot coffee and brandy were served. This not only warmed journalists and company officials, it provided a convivial atmosphere in which both groups could review the day's activities.

Many editors went out of their way to praise this thoughtfulness. The moral is clear: always take into account the physical comfort of your guests. Editors expect to work at press conferences. They do not accept invitations with pleasure jaunts in mind. Yet they do appreciate conferences being carried out under as pleasant conditions as possible. The degree to which you show your thoughtfulness can greatly influence the impression they carry away from the conference of your company.

What did Clark do wrong? First, they tried to do too much in one day, the editors said. Most editors felt Clark could have eliminated the visits to the service school and the test cell facilities. While interesting, they did not add to the basic story, and the time spent there could have been added to the plant tour or question period.

The editors were also critical of the photographs that had been taken beforehand. Not dramatic enough they said. Fortunately this had been rectified during the course of the conference. A photographer was on hand all day to take special pictures. When it came time for the demonstration, the photographer took a variety of each piece of equipment in action. The best pictures were selected, printed and mailed the next day to every editor who attended. ∎

If you are a busy executive, you don't have time to read enough. But, paradoxically, your success depends on reading correspondence, memos, notices, business publications, books, journals and newspapers. By reading faster, you can increase your effectiveness and the value of your work

How to read faster

CHECK YOUR READING SPEED

This article contains about 2,600 words. At the average reading speed for business executives—250 words a minute—it will take you 11 minutes to read it. Time yourself. Then read the article again, keeping in mind some of the principles outlined in it. You may be surprised at the results.

HOW MANY PEOPLE these days don't know how to read? Very few, you'll say. Yet many businessmen are now using only 20 per cent of their reading capacities.

They are reading less than 250 words a minute—the average for businessmen generally. This is because they read word by word, at a rate not much faster than they can talk. Trained readers can attain speeds of 1,000 words per minute, and more.

Like swimming, reading is based on habits. The swimmer, when he is not practising a particular stroke, is unconscious of his movements. Most people formed the habit of reading in school, and have made little effort to perfect it to meet the demands of adult life.

Like the swimmer, the reader needs to perfect his skill consciously if he is to survive in his personal sea of business literature, correspond-

ence, newspapers, business publications, etc. He must trade his old bad habits for new good ones.

Outlined below are some fundamental techniques and a Self Improvement Programme that can help you to increase greatly your reading speed with improved comprehension.

Cut your reading time—Skilful reading, like skilful swimming, gives you a good start. It cuts down backlogs of correspondence. It frees you to think and act—or frees time for other duties and pleasures. When you read faster, comprehend and concentrate better, you not only save time, but you also increase the value of your reading. You become a more alert, more responsive reader. You develop your ability to draw more intelligent conclusions from what you read.

Everyone in business and industry can benefit from an easing of his heavy load. You are probably al-

ready giving all the time you can to business reading, and find that the load increases almost every day. Better reading habits—gained through simple practice methods—can cut your reading time in half.

Poor reading results mainly from the tendency of the eye to stop on every word. Your eyes do not simply sweep across the line when you read, but progress in a series of stops and moves, seeing the words only when they stop or fixate. Your reading speed depends largely on the deviations of fixations you make on each line of print.

The following sentence illustrates the eye movements of the untrained reader (each number represents one fixation, or pause of the eye):

1	2	3	4	5	6
If	you	read	word	-by	-word

7	8	9	10	11	12	13
you	spend	needless		time	and	energy

The eye movements of the untrained reader are haphazard, and the slower he reads, the less his mind is held on the subject.

Learning to take bigger visual "bites" of the printed page—reading by **phrases**—is the first and most important step toward better reading.

The skilled reader fixates briefly once on every phrase and absorbs it as a unit.

For his eye movements are rhythmic and efficient. For example, he makes only four fixations compared to the thirteen made by the untrained reader.

1	2
If you read	word-by-word,
3	4
you spend needless	time and energy

Phrase-reading not only increases speed, but it also improves comprehension and concentration by "keeping the mind busy". You can think much faster than you can read, since your mind naturally moves faster than your eye.

If you read slowly, your mind is free to wander. But by reading faster, in phrases, your eyes provide your mind with more absorbing material. You do not have to stop after three or four fixations to assimilate an idea as you do in reading word-by-word. By reading in thought units, you are reading the same way you think, in concepts.

To build an awareness of phrases, try circling them on the printed page. For example, take a pencil and circle each of the meaningful thought units on the exercise paragraph that follows. Read it a second time, taking in each circled phrase. Ten minutes of daily practice will soon have you automatically seeing phrase groups instead of words.

On the Job—The 10-years-after men aren't job-jumpers. Seventy per cent have had either one or two employers, including their present one, since graduation. Only 4% have worked at five or more different jobs. Thirteen per cent are self-employed, and many of the others—especially of the 40% working for firms with fewer than 500 employees—work in family concerns. Middle management men work hard at their jobs. They average 50 hours a week; 15% of them put in 60 hours. Much of their "non-working" time is taken up with business-related activity. Their magazine reading, for instance, is mostly trade or professional journals. In general, they get their deepest satisfaction from their families.

Space-reading — Space-reading—looking at the space just above the line of print, instead of directly at it—is the next step in developing rhythmic eye movements. Even after becoming aware of phrases, you may find it hard to read by phrases. This is because the white spaces between words naturally break the sentence into separate words. Your eye will want to jump from word to word. By focusing on the space above the printed line, you will find

your eye fixations will become smoother, and the phrases will hold together much better.

Once mastered, it will increase your reading speed and lessen the strain on your eyes.

You can also improve phrase-consciousness by letting your eyes move down a column of type with only one fixation per line. At first it will help you to draw a pencil line down the centre of the column, and to follow this with your eyes. Try to see the first and last words of each line of type while looking directly at the centre. Example:

> To write an | article that will interest thousands of top-calibre technical and management men who read today's engineering, business and scientific publications requires a good deal of effort. It isn't easy. But the important thing to remember is: You can write well!

To start, you may find it easier to try the second and next-to-last words of each line of type. Later you may practise this technique on the way to work or during any breaks in the work routine. You will find that it will help greatly to increase your eye span.

Variable-speed reading — This technique will intrigue you. As we're sure you know, you do not read all material at the same speed. You can handle light reading at high speed. Technical material, on the other hand, obviously will slow down any reader because of the greater detail.

Variable-speed reading makes it possible to get a broad picture fast— to go right through the bold-face type and get the whole train of thought. If you want only the highlights you don't have to slow your pace.

However, you can shift speeds as you read . . . if you do want the details. You can go rapidly through the article—with assurance that you will not miss any main point—until you come to a signal about a main point on which you want detail. You can then slow your reading pace to absorb the detail.

Measure your progress — Also helpful is indenting—or not allowing your eyes to read either end of a printed line. When moving down from one line to the next, break away about $\frac{1}{8}$ inch in on the next line. Normally your eye automatically pulls to the white margin on either side and this slows down your

reading speed considerably.

Get in the habit of constantly improving your reading rate by pressing against the very limits of your current capacity for a few minutes every day. Time yourself every now and then to see how you are progressing.

Benefits of pre-reading — Before pre-reading each article, you may think that this process wastes time rather than conserves it. Before long, however, pre-reading (with a little practice) becomes automatic, takes only a minute or two, and you will find that you will:

Save time. Not every article is of equal importance to you. A pre-reading will tell you whether you will profit by a thorough reading of the article at hand. It will tell you if the article is on a subject that will interest you. (Titles and brief descriptions can sometimes be misleading.)

It will tell you if the discussion is too elementary and simply repeats what you already know. Or it will tell you if it is too advanced, if you must get a better background before you tackle the article or book at hand.

If a pre-reading indicates that the article deserves a **thorough reading** then you have also saved time by your preliminary survey. Your advanced sampling of the author's style, your foreknowledge of the major points to be covered and the conclusions to be drawn, all help you to get through the article more quickly.

To pre-read an article, read only the summary of the main points. If the article appears useful to you, read the first two or three paragraphs, which are almost always sure to introduce the subject in a general way. Then quickly continue reading only the first sentences of each paragraph of the article.

Be sure to note subheadings, diagrams, charts, and pictures as you go along. The author will generally summarize his arguments in the last two or three paragraphs. Read them thoroughly. If, after pre-reading, you feel a thorough reading is justified, you are ready to read intelligently and critically, since you already have an idea of what the author is talking about.

Critical reading—Merely understanding what you read is not sufficient; you must evaluate it as well.

Summarizing is an invaluable technique to help comprehension and retention. To collect unrelated facts of varying importance is of no value to you. Therefore, summarizing will help you to organize these facts in order of importance. As you acquire the skill you will be able to summarize mentally, but to start it will be better to write down your summary.

As you read an article, clearly distinguish between main ideas and details. The topic sentence will usually give you the main point of the paragraph and the details will follow in the middle and latter part of the article. Write down the main idea or topic sentence as you read and place the relevant points in order beneath it. This is a simple 1, 2, 3—a, b, c pattern.

Upon finishing, you will have an introduction statement, the main points that are to be retained, and a summary statement. This will provide you with a framework into which more detailed facts can be fitted and thus easily retained.

Best environment — In all your reading, make sure you have a good environment, free from poor lighting and undue distractions. For example, always read in a well-lit room with at least two lights of equal intensity to prevent glare. And remember that excessive comfort will hinder, rather than increase your ability to concentrate.

It is vital to your career that you read with the same professional authority you exercise in all other phases of your job. Not only because it saves time for you. It also pays a bonus in new productive time. How? Because a man's mind moves far faster than he can read.

Thus, as your eye races to catch up with your brain, suddenly you have more time to think. And you think more lucidly. You concentrate easier. Plan more decisively. Move with new confidence. Inspire and impress others.

Thinking and reading can spell the difference between "just doing the job" and real success. ∎

†This article on How to Read Faster was prepared in collaboration with tested procedures developed by The Reading Laboratory, of New York.

15.

Engineering Salaries, Job Satisfaction and Ethics

How engineers' salaries stack up

With the help of surveys, one can now get a pretty good idea of how engineers' salaries vary with management responsibility, type of industry, and number of degrees.

THE engineer has been moving up the professional ladder. Data extrapolated from surveys conducted by the Engineering Manpower Commission of the Engineers Joint Council provide a clear picture of the improved position of engineers when compared with those of other professionals.

The median salary of engineers now exceeds, in all probability, that of psychologists, mathematicians, chemists, meteorologists, and others in the scientific fields. In fact, among technical people, only the physicists come up in salary level to that of engineers (see Table 1). The engineers, however, trail salaried physicians, attorneys, chief accountants, and personnel directors.

Starting salaries of engineers are climbing at a steady rate. Getting a master's degree means about $130 per month higher pay (Fig. 1). This is higher than all other science curricula, but it trails the starting salary of graduates with a master's degree in business administration or industrial management with a technical undergraduate degree. These ambitious scholars were receiving offers of $950 per month back in 1968.

Ph.D. degrees in engineering, which engineers formerly snubbed, now really are worth money—more than $450 per month more than a B.S. in chemical engineering, for example. Starting salaries of Ph.D.s in electrical engineering tend to be higher than those in mechanical engineering.

Engineers in supervisory positions earn substantially higher incomes than those in non-supervisory jobs (Fig. 2). Moreover, the monetary value of higher education is also becoming apparent (Fig. 3). Engineers, however, with supervisory responsibilities, but with only a bachelor's degree, make considerably more than master's-degree engineers who have no management duties. Within each group, however, there can be wide variations in salary. Not shown in the charts are data indicating that the highest median salaries are paid in the Pacific and Middle Atlantic regions, while the lowest salaries are paid in the Mountain states.

Choice of career is another key factor that affects income (Figs. 4 and 5). Working in research and development produces the highest dollar. Engineers in aerospace and defense industries also do well as expected. But it is surprising to note that engineers working for the federal government do better on the average than those in consulting services and in manufacturing and non-manufacturing commercial industries. ∎

Table 1—Engineers' salaries compare well with those of other professions

Profession	Median annual salaries	
	1967	1970*
Medical doctors	$29,000	$35,400
Attorneys	14,800	18,000
Economists	13,100	16,000
Chief accountants	13,100	16,000
Personnel directors	13,000	15,800
Engineers	12,500	15,300
Physicists	12,500	15,300
Chemists	12,000	14,600
Mathematicians	12,000	14,600
Biological scientists	12,000	14,600
Meteorologists	11,700	14,300
Psychologists	11,500	14,000
Anthropologists	11,500	14,000
Earth scientists	11,400	13,900
Sociologists	11,300	13,800
Agricultural scientists	10,000	12,200

*Estimated on the basis of random sampling and projected yearly increase of 7%.

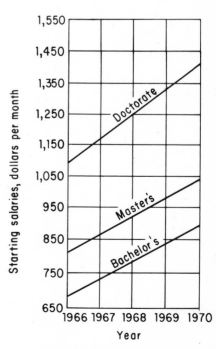

Fig. 1 Starting Salaries are climbing

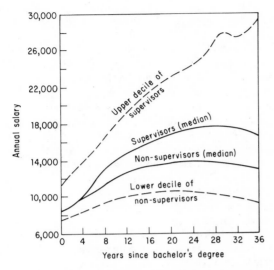

Fig. 2   It pays to be an engineering super-
          visor

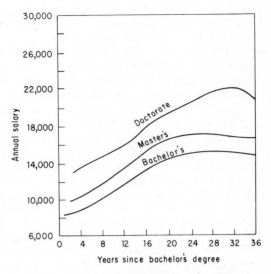

Fig. 3   It pays to get a higher degree

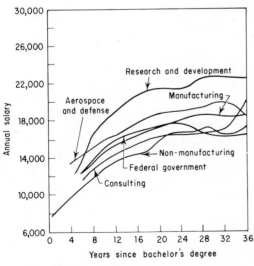

Fig. 4   Career choice affects pay of engi-
          neering supervisors

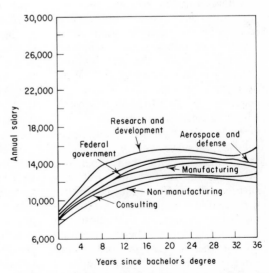

Fig. 5   Career choice also affects pay of
          non-supervisors

Which Personal Traits Lead to High Salaries?

WILLIAM ARNOLD

McGraw-Hill World News

What are the attributes of a successful engineer? What individual characteristics allow some to earn higher salaries than others?

Stanford Research Institute (SRI) of Menlo Park, Calif., claims it is refining a technique that statistically correlates such factors as age, schooling, job experience, and marital status with income level to answer such questions as these.

For the first time, SRI says, employment managers can be made aware of the individual attributes they now are knowingly or unknowingly paying for when they hire an engineer. Engineers, too, will be better able to assess their worth when interviewing.

SRI became involved in salary studies after Congress passed the Salary Reform Act of 1962, aimed at bringing federal pay standards into closer harmony with industry. On contract with the Bureau of the Budget, SRI studied more than 30,000 applications of engineers and scientists employed by 22 aerospace companies.

Characteristics of success. According to Richard P. Howell, project leader, researchers asked themselves: "If salary is an indication of success, what are the attributes of the person making it? What individual characteristics can be successfully related to salary levels?" Their findings show that:

- On the average, engineers' salaries increase yearly until they reach age 48 and then taper off. SRI analysts are not sure, but they surmise that after that age either the capable engineers move into administrative jobs or that these are the engineers who began working during the depression and where salaries have never caught up.
- Engineers who have held four or five jobs earn more money than those who have held three or fewer. However, others are hurt by too much mobility. Those who have held more than five jobs earn less than the others.
- Engineers who remained with their previous employers for five years or more earn more money.

On-the-job experience, measured by the length of time on the job, usually affects salaries favorably.

- Those who left their jobs to return to school full-time but did not obtain a degree earned less money on the average than those who stayed at work. As expected, however, those who got their degree earned more because of the degree's higher "market value."
- Married engineers tend to earn more than those who are unmarried (both those who have never married and those who are divorced).
- Those who attended high-tuition colleges (usually the prestige schools) tend to earn more than those who took their bachelor degrees at low-tuition schools. However, the analysts note that this is only an overall average and there are many exceptions.

With multiple regression techniques, Howell and his associates derived equations that show how some characteristics (age, sex, number of years with previous employer, degrees held, a return to school fulltime, tuition level, major, and number of jobs held) affect salaries.

Case in point. For example, an engineer who is 65 years old, has an MS in engineering, and has had only two employers since his graduation should be making $1600 a month in the Los Angeles area, Howell computes. In the Boston area, he would be making slightly less.

SRI acknowledges that this survey is only the first exploratory step toward a broader, more inclusive technique for understanding salary variations. Ways are needed to evaluate such traits as loyalty, personality, and creativity. More post-hire data and a better understanding of the role of fringe benefits in hiring are also needed.

Ultimately what SRI wants, Howell says, is to enable the employment manager to find that "rare bird" who is the productive, creative engineer. This is a difficult task because productivity varies to such an extent among engineers.

Turnover. Using the same basic employment data, SRI researchers have investigated turnover. Their conclusion is that an engineer applying for a job should be treated like a duck. An employment manager should try to fill a vacancy with an applicant who has already "nested" locally and has his roots down. If no local applicants are available, he should hire those who are following well-established migratory streams of the general population.

A high proportion of engineers hired away from the West Coast—against the migratory stream—return to the West Coast, with consequent high turnover. If a company is hiring in an area outside the path of the migratory stream, it's best to hire a returnee.

Alternatives. Other ways to reduce turnover are:

- Hire a person who is well qualified—but not over-qualified—by educational background for the job.
- Hire an applicant who knows the industry from similar or related experience.
- Hire applicants who manifest ambition, since they tend to be more effective.

Hiring science. Hopefully, the SRI studies will "bridge the communications gap and help managers understand scientific management tools," Howell says. This will enable managers to hire and to manage better the prize engineers.

Howell spiked one widely used management tool—the personality inventory test. "In interviewing a man, you should maintain his privacy as much as possible," he says. "A better tool would be to query his colleagues about him. A sample question might be: 'How does John Doe get along with others? Excellently, very well, average, poorly, not at all?' Anything less than average would rule out the applicant."

Another sidelight of the research, says Howell, is that, contrary to popular belief, defense engineers are more effective than their counterparts elsewhere. Because they work under cost contracts with stringent deadlines, defense engineers are inventive and efficient. ∎

How Engineers Rank Nonfinancial Benefits

ROBERT C. MAY

Automatic Switch Co.

Before accepting your present job you probably weighed many factors—salary, challenging work, opportunity for advancement, security, location. Today you know that the satisfaction you get from your job hinges on other matters as well. The nonfinancial benefits provided by your employer may seem to have only minor importance, but in the aggregate they can make a big difference in your enthusiasm and in your ability to turn out your best work. Which of these job prerequisites do engineers consider most important? To find out, we mailed a questionnaire to several hundred engineers and asked them to indicate which of 18 selected minor benefits were either "important," "nice, but unnecessary" or "not needed." The respondents were most reasonable in their requests. They showed little interest in those factors that make the job seem more important, and concentrated on benefits that assist them in the execution of their duties.

Question sheets were returned by 172. Most respondents were design engineers with titles ranging from Mechanical Designer to Chief Engineer. They covered a broad range of industrial activity and their companies varied in size from the smallest to the largest.

Of all items listed, the need considered most important by all engineers was the opportunity to present ideas to top management and to be advised of company plans.

Less than 4% felt this was not an important factor. Although this does not necessarily indicate that the communication links between middle and top management are weak, it points to a critical area where all companies, particularly large ones, should maintain constant vigilance. Opportunity to mix socially with the top brass, however, was not rated very important. One vice-president summarized it this way, "Those engineers who can make the transition to the executive division are capable of going all the way to the top without a social assist."

Among the tangible benefits a private telephone was voted most important (70%) although one engineer probably voiced the feelings of many when he wrote "I wish I didn't have one." For the most part, respondents felt that a partitioned office, two engineers per room, was most desirable (or perhaps most practical). "More than two per room," commented one, "is intolerable. The phone rings constantly and there is always confusion."

A few items were added to the questionnaire by respondents who felt that the list ignored some important benefits. "Flexible starting and quitting time," was suggested by one, for example, while another pointed to "overtime or extended time policy," and "longer vacations." Environmental factors such as air conditioning, ventilation, low noise level, cleanliness and lighting, were written-in two or three times, as was "adequate space for work, files and meetings." A company library, conference rooms and reserved parking spaces rated mentions by several engineers.

Response to questions relating to need for technicians and secretaries indicates that most engineers are easily satisfied, will settle for only a minimum of supporting personnel. A pool of departmental technicians and departmental secretaries is all that is necessary in most cases. One respondent: "I need a pool of draftsmen and technicians for noncreative work to save my time for design problems."

Except for those benefits that cost nothing to provide (unrestricted flow of information, for example) the large company apparently has some advantages over the smaller firm. A chief engineer from a 250-employe company commented wistfully, "Large companies can afford such niceties. Our graduate engineers have no private offices, no partitions, no secretary (either departmental or private), no titles, no business cards, and none of the other tangible items except opportunity for paid advance study." ∎

HOW ENGINEERS RANK NONFINANCIAL BENEFITS

	Response, percent			
	Import-ant	Nice but unneces-sary	Don't need it	No answer
Intangibles				
Opportunity to present ideas to top management	85	11.5	1	2.5
Being advised of company plans	70	8	2	20
Freedom to attend society meetings on company time	69	27.5	3.5	0
Opportunity to obtain advanced degree	57	31	7.5	4.5
A title	57	17.5	11.5	14
Chance to speak at sales and technical meetings	56	25	14	5
Encouragement in writing articles and papers	49	34	13.5	3.5
Opportunity to mix socially with top brass	17	60	23	0
Tangibles				
Private telephone	70	20	10	0
Business cards	54	27	17	2
Partitioned office	50	28.5	9	12.5
Private office	33.5	44	17.5	5
Key to plant door	29	25.5	42	3.5
Executive-type furniture	11	51	33	5
Personnel Requirements				
Departmental secretaries	69	10.5	8	12.5
Departmental technicians	67	11.5	11	10.5
Personal secretary	22.5	37	29.5	11
Personal technician	17	29.5	33	20.5

Can you afford to pay stay-at-home workers?

Absenteeism is not an incurable problem, but it does present a challenge to managerial ability that is too often shirked, shelved or overlooked

by Auren Uris
Research Institute of America

WANT TO START the yawns coming, at a meeting of managers? Just start talking about absenteeism. To many managers, this is an old problem they have learned to live with. As a result, company money continues to go down the drain.

Although some managers, confused by the contradictions of absenteeism, simply throw up their hands, companies and department heads who have studied the problem and then proceeded in a reasoned and systematic way to minimize it have met with great success. In some cases, absenteeism rates have been cut in half and even diminished to a third.

The first step in understanding the problem is to get away from some of the faulty assumptions—for example:

Absence is a "crime" resulting from wilfulness.

You can pressure people into perfect attendance.

Neither of these ideas is wholly true. Studies of large numbers of absentees generally give this distribution of reasons for absence:

1. Personal illness 55%
2. Personal business 20%
3. Family illness 8%
4. Accidents 5%
5. Transportation 4%
6. Miscellaneous 8%

Statistics like these are interesting though not always helpful. They may hide as much as they reveal.

Intangible factors—One man says he "couldn't come to work because of a headache." A week later, he refuses to go home despite a temperature of 101—"because I've got an important job to finish." What accounts for contradictions of this kind?

Studies by psychologists show that there is an intangible factor causing absenteeism that frequently eludes the statisticians.

A paint company seriously hampered by excessive absenteeism called a top management meeting to consider the problem. The decision was that the company would deal with its problem by finding "a convenient means of getting rid of the worst offenders in the hiring process."

According to this view, absenteeism is a specific ailment like athlete's foot that affects certain individuals. The problem: how to stop it? The company answer: eliminate the "diseased" employees.

The company worked the policy, but in two years no appreciable dent was made in absenteeism. Eventually a consultant discovered that factors within the control of management were a major cause of people staying out. Simply put, managers within the company were creating a climate that encouraged people to stay out for the smallest reason, or none at all.

Case histories—This element, the emotional atmosphere in a department, can be illustrated by two case histories:

John Doe gets up one morning with a headache. The idea of going back to bed has strong appeal. Then he thinks of his job, knowing he'd be leaving his supervisor in a spot. Other people in the department will be inconvenienced.

His own work will fall behind. He goes to work.

Tom Doe also has a headache. Bed feels mighty good. Tom thinks of his supervisor—the old so-and-so. He thinks of the irritations and arguments among the work group. After all, he does have a headache. So he turns over and goes to sleep.

What was missing in the second example was what we may call the 'X' factor—good relations in a work group; rapport between the department head and his subordinates; emphasis on the importance of the work to be done, and the responsibility of the employee to do his part of the job.

How to create 'X'—How do you create a favourable 'X' factor? A study of the relationship between attendance and department size gives one revealing answer:

Number of employees working in a department	Employees having one or more absences per month, per cent
1 to 9	7.9
10 to 19	14.8
20 to 39	24.6
40 or more	20.2

According to these figures, the smaller a work group the better its attendance. Obviously, it's not always practical to reorganize work into five or ten-man departments. People doing the same work must sometimes be located in single large groups. But if a department consists of 20 men, for example, their work areas need not be evenly spaced; they could be arranged in four groups of five.

Measure of effectiveness — Hidden by the all-too-frequent disinterest in absenteeism is an important fact: attendance is one of the few direct measures of managerial effectiveness. This fact, coupled with the more obvious reasons for minimizing absen-

---

Test your awareness of the absentee problem by answering these questions—if you can:

1. Which day shows the highest rate of absence?
2. Which the lowest?
3. What rate of absenteeism is "normal"?
4. Is length of absence more important than frequency?
5. Is the absentee rate higher for women than for men?
6. What is an "excused" absence?
7. Are absenteeism, turnover and injury rates related?
8. Why can't absenteeism be handled by simply cracking down on the offenders?
9. Is management itself responsible for absenteeism?

For the answers, see the next page.

teeism, suggests the need to develop a systematic approach to control of absentees.

You should make an informal study of the conditions in your department. Here are the three steps that can lead to an effective analysis:

1. Get the figures.

Calculating rate of absenteeism is the starting point. The formula is:

$$\text{Absenteeism} = \frac{\text{man days lost}}{\text{man days scheduled}} \times 100$$

Manager 'A' has 20 employees in his department. They are each scheduled for eight hours, 24 days of the month. Checking his monthly records he finds:

No of employees	Days absent	Man-days lost
7	0	0
5	1	5
4	2	8
3	3	9
1	20	20
		Total 42

The total man-days scheduled are 20 (number of people) multiplied by 22 (number of workdays)=440. Manager A's final calculation would be:

$$\text{Absenteeism} = \frac{42}{440} \times 100 = 9.55\%$$

Questions that often come up in figuring this frequency rate are whether excused absences should be included (the answer is "yes") and how about those absences that are unavoidable because of serious illness. These, too, should be included.

2. Evaluate the figures.

In some cases, an absentee rate of 10 per cent may be acceptable while in others 5 per cent would call for action.

If one man is out for 14 days because of serious illness, then you have lost 14 man-days but the loss is unavoidable. Half as many man-days lost in single-day periods by different individuals for trivial reasons, and something is definitely wrong.

Many companies these days are obliged to employ people with outside responsibilities—married women with infants, for example—elderly people, and pin-money earners who don't really need the job.

With such people, absenteeism rises and a perfect attendance record is virtually impossible.

Before accepting your attendance figures as the best attainable, however, be sure that individual reasons for absences are acceptable, that the total absence doesn't interfere with the work, and that there is no sign of "contagion"—absence spreading out of your control.

3. Spotlight the bad factors.

Remember that even where absenteeism appears bad, the great majority of workers have good attendance records. In one such case, it was shown that 76 per cent of the employees averaged less than one absence a month.

The truth is, absenteeism is usually confined to a small percentage of employees, and by using the absentee frequency rate you can spot them.

Make a list of all your people, starting with those who have no absences in a given month and ending with those who are most frequently absent. Then it is easy to keep check on your absentee troublemakers.

Be sure not to assume, however, that these individuals are staying out wilfully. They may have problems that are keeping them out.

Personal interviews—It's good practice to have a returning employee see you personally, before restarting work, to establish the reason for his absence.

If your company has an infirmary, or a doctor is on a retainer for medical services to employees, you can help an individual resolve a doubtful health situation by direct medical advice.

Should the employee have to produce a doctor's certificate or note? In some cases, definitely.

What if you get an obviously phony explanation for an absence from work? There's one thing to make clear: absence does not make the heart grow fonder.

If you appear unconcerned, the employee will adopt a "what's-the-difference?" attitude. Regardless of the reason for the absence, you want the employee to know that he was missed. Then, if he was away for good reason, he'll be pleased to know he's important to the department. If not, he'll recognize the implied rebuke.

"Frankly," said one department head, "I try to make it tough for employees to stay out for doubtful reasons. On the other hand I say: 'If you want to take a day off to go shopping, or visit a relative, I'd much rather you tell me so'."

Four helpful ideas—When an interview uncovers a reason for non-attendance you can do something about, get the employee to agree as to the real cause first. Then, supply a solution.

There are four points to work on:

1. The conditions. Let's say a worker claims he's been forced to stay away because of bad weather and overloaded transportation facilities. You may be able to suggest other ways of making the trip, especially with new employees who aren't familiar with the neighbourhood. Perhaps you can suggest car-pooling for several employees.

2. The work schedule. You may change an employee's hours if some outside situation makes it difficult for him to keep standard hours.

3. The job. In cases where a specific on-the-job condition is at the bottom of the absence, you may be able to remove the obstacle either by reassignment or by modifying the work itself.

4. The employee's attitude. You may find that the cause of absence was the employee's general attitude. Pointing out that other employees have similar or even worse problems may help.

Finally, in extreme cases you must consider stern action. The employee who poses a continual attendance problem may finally have to be firmly and effectively disciplined. ∎

ANSWERS TO THE ABSENTEE QUIZ

1. There's more absenteeism on Monday.

2. Pay day.

3. According to the US Department of Labor: Nobody knows what "normal" absenteeism is.

4. Frequency is generally considered a better measure of the problem.

5. Women present more of an absentee problem. For example, in one departmental study, investigators found that 12.5 per cent of the men had one or more absences against 27.3 per cent for women.

6. "Excused" absence covers the cases where an employee's request for permission to stay out has been okayed by the supervisor.

7. Many companies have found that absenteeism, turnover and injury rates rise and fall together.

8. Attempts to decrease absenteeism by stern discipline occasionally have proved effective. However, resultant grievances and generally low morale often become as bad as the original absenteeism.

9. The answer to this question lies at the very heart of the entire absentee problem. Poor management—more specifically, poor supervision—does cause absenteeism. Good management, and specifically good supervision, reduces absenteeism quite remarkably.

Why do employees resign?

Who are the people leaving your company? Are they mostly misfits encouraged to resign, or are they valued employees whose loss is regretted? Here's how you can organize to forestall the possible loss of good men

by P. W. Maloney
Armour Company

THE COMPANY with a good employment programme will harvest its crop of new employees on a fairly regular basis. But, as you proudly watch the new acquisitions come on board, you had better remember a dismal fact: within five years, it's possible that one-half or more of these people will be working elsewhere.

The termination of professional people in most countries around the world is one of the most serious problems facing business. Unfortunately, it is not a well tended one. Both voluntary and encouraged losses just happen; seldom is there any attempt at programming.

Are you approaching the problem of personnel terminations with the same thoroughness you are probably applying to recruitment and other personnel programmes?

Do you really know what types you are losing? Is it a random slice? Is it only the misfits? Or is your company performing a service for the industry by furnishing postgraduate training, losing (only) your best people to other employers?

Do you know how many people you are losing? Have you ever calculated what proportion of your recruitment programme is necessary just to replace losses? Have you ever estimated how much recruitment expenses can be directly charged to personnel attrition?

Five pointers—There are five ways that management can structure its role in the termination process. None of them calls for excessive expenditures of time or money. When compared with the waste that may have been revealed by the right questions being asked, the investment is small.

1. Keep better records. Retaining data about the people who leave permits a degree of analysis.

2. Conduct termination interviews. This, it is true, will take some time,

but the return may be well rewarding.

3. Do some research. Termination records and interviews must be systematically analyzed, and this should be done periodically.

4. Programme your involuntary losses. A company should co-ordinate what its branches are doing about dismissing inadequate professionals.

5. Plan to prevent the loss of confidential data. There should be clearly defined, rigorously enforced rules that protect your company's proprietary information.

An impending termination should trigger the collecting of data about the employee who is leaving. This should be done by the personnel department.

For research purposes, data should be kept for several years.

First, get the data that will classify the employees who leave. Of all the people that leave, those who resign should be of most concern. They should be carefully separated into four main groups:

1. "Not encouraged, sorry to lose."

2. "Not encouraged, not sorry to lose." Discretion is necessary here. It could be said that some in this group were encouraged to resign; that they are the ones who can be easily replaced with people of more ability. For better or worse this provides an escape for the manager who is leery of indicating too often that he is losing

people he should in fact be retaining.

3. "Encouraged." If anyone is actually discharged, he should be included in this category.

4. "Encouraged, sorry to lose." Although a rarity, it can happen. It describes the capable person who is asked to leave because his particular skill can no longer be used. He should be categorized this way, rather than as an encouraged loss, so that the data on those who are judged unsatisfactory are kept apart.

The file on those who leave you should include background information. This should be written by the employee's immediate superior and should show why a particular resignation was encouraged. The manager should pay particular attention to any of the man's faults that could or should have been identified when he was being hired.

When the loss is not an encouraged one, regardless of whether it is a "sorry" or a "not sorry" loss, the manager should record the reasons the man gives for leaving.

For whatever value it might have, the manager should also indicate what might have been done to prevent the loss from taking place.

Likes and dislikes—The man who is resigning can even be asked to write some of the data. Have him fill out a questionnaire that elicits from him what he liked or disliked about his job and the company.

A termination interview should be a structured approach to learning from a departing employee the facts, attitudes and opinions that are relative to his leaving. And it should be handled by a staff member who has no direct organizational relationship to the person who is leaving.

Is it worthwhile? Will enough be learned, beyond the information that can be supplied by line managers, to justify someone spending an hour or more with the departing employee?

Refer back to your need for getting businesslike about terminations. You will realize that properly satisfying your need for knowledge depends on getting valid information about why people leave.

There are valid reasons for having an independent staff person get these data. First, events leading up to the termination, regardless of who initiated it, are likely to have built barriers that will impede effective communica-

tion between the professional and his superior.

Second, the staff representative is probably closer to the "big picture" than the manager of any department. He can interpret the terminator's comments against a considerably larger frame of reference.

Let's bring out a few cardinal points about termination interviews.

First, the interviewer should have been trained. A session with a person who is resigning will only be valuable if truly basic issues are uncovered and carefully analyzed.

If your organization has systematized its data collection on the people who resign, there is probably a collection of information that the interviewer could, and should, assimilate before he walks into an interview. When the case is unusual or puzzling, he should talk privately with the superior of the person resigning before he starts the interview.

The interview must be structured. A report will lack validity if the interviewer hasn't followed a specific outline from the word go.

You should decide what information you want most, and make sure this is elicited in every interview.

The results of the interview must be written up well. Doing an objective job of this is not easy, and training for the task should be a part of the interviewer's education.

The company that does what has been outlined is well ahead of the game. But it must be sure that effort won't go to waste. Data that fill the personnel department's files won't influence many decisions.

The first "research" job hardly deserves the name: it's simply a matter of reporting the statistics on all the different types of terminations that occur in your company.

When your company first goes into programmed termination planning, it should dig back into its records for a year or two and label earlier terminations. These data will not only be interesting but will also supply a base against which new trends may be compared.

There is one immediate and obvious application for these data: projecting the company's recruiting needs to replace anticipated losses. The recruitment programme based on some foreknowledge of targets is bound to be better than the haphazard recruit-

ment programme of your competitors.

Precise classification—Statistical reports usually arouse management's curiosity about why there are so many losses of each type. The intensity of management's questioning varies exponentially with the closeness of the time when the recruiting budget has to be reviewed.

In such situations, staff units had better be ready with analyses of the termination interviews. When reasonably objective evidence is absent, the void will be filled with defensive arguments about there being plenty of manpower around. However, interview reports can be dangerously misleading when done improperly by unqualified people.

Always remember that when a person leaves your company, specific steps must be taken to prevent proprietary information from being acquired by the company he is joining, deliberately or inadvertently.

First of all, don't assume that a leaving employee is fully aware of his obligation to prevent the transfer of information to his new employer. This must be made clear to him before he leaves.

Second, a person should be asked to sign a statement indicating that he has returned all confidential materials, including handbooks, to his immediate superior. This statement should be obtained by the superior, so that he is personally involved.

Third, your company should routinely write a letter to the man's new employer, advising in what general areas their new employee possesses the kind of information that is of proprietary value.

This puts the new employer on notice, and removes any basis for later claims that the confidential information he may be in a position to acquire was picked up inadvertently.

If the employee has signed an agreement that obligates him even further on security, a copy of this contract should accompany the letter to his new employer.

Businesslike basis—There is a lot of room in most companies for better programming of their termination procedures.

When you estimate what it costs to replace each professional who leaves a company, it seems that the money alone supplies enough incentive for better planning. ■

JOB HUNTING—
FOR
ENGINEERS

PETER L GARRETT
Santa Monica, Calif.

HOW TO

- **bypass Personnel**
- **write impressive resumes**
- **fill out employment forms**
- **get a salary worth working for**

"**S**ystems" is the most popular word in engineering today. Therefore, I shall take the systems approach to job hunting. Just among ourselves, potential job-hunters all, we'll use the three-letter Anglo-Saxon word. Employers, of course, prefer *employment* and *position*.

The systems approach starts with knowing when to quit. If you've been fired or "laid off" (meaning: two or more people fired at the same time), then you have one less problem to solve. Engineers are overhead, and when the Board of Directors (who are the highest overhead of all) want to save money, the first place they look is down. Janitors are good, and so are secretaries; but an engineer is twice as good as either and besides, for a couple of engineers you can sometimes get a secretary thrown in.

And so we formulate the first law: QUIT BEFORE YOU GET FIRED. The first lemma of this law is not to become overconfident because of a recent small raise, sometimes phrased: BE LOYAL BUT DON'T TRUST THEM.

Now comes a psychological point: it's generally later than you think. When you decide to go, go! Don't ooze! The chances are they have seen that shifty look in your eyes and the employment page on your hands.

PERSONNEL DEPARTMENT

The larger a corporation, the slower it moves; and the insensitive skin that covers these mastodons is called Personnel. With forms, the Personnel Department protects itself from contact with the outside world. Any form worth its salt has three distinguished characteristics:

- It takes at least 1½ hours to fill out.

- It is designed to make you look like a slob.
- It asks at least one question that nobody has asked before ("What is the license number of your automobile?")

Personnel managers, of course, know nothing whatever about engineering and very little about the organization of their own Engineering Department. What they use in place of information are special forms, often flatteringly called "Personnel Requisitions." These are somewhat exaggerated job descriptions created by the man Personnel is keeping you from seeing. He exaggerates for two reasons:

- He hopes to imply to you that the job is much more interesting than it is.
- He wants something to show just in case you want more money than the lowest curve of the company's salary formula permits. (By the way, the personnel interviewer may not know Simpson's Rule from Murphy's Law; but he does know when an applicant asks for more money than he himself makes.)

The basic principle of dealing with Personnel people is to avoid them. To do this you need:

1) A resume.
2) Friends.

Take several employment forms and answer the questions that are not on your job history. Put these on page 1 of a vellum. On page 2 and following, put your job history, conspicuously labeled EMPLOYMENT HISTORY. If you are preternaturally honest (or if none of your previous employers has gone out of business), you can use a white-print of this for almost all employment forms and for security questionnaires as well.

WHOM DO YOU KNOW?

Now you are prepared to call your friends. Don't be shy. If you don't know them well enough to ask a favor, then you have nothing to lose by offending them. Let them all know you are available and why. If you have a sensitive conscience or a tendency to be excessively frank, remember this: Why you want to quit is purely subjective and subject to change between telephone calls. While I would not encourage anyone to lie, I should like to point out that there is a hierarchy of values involved. The final evaluation of a "reason for leaving" is, of course, up to the prejudice of the man you're talking to, but some general rules apply.

Boredom is good if you have been there long enough. But be as specific as possible because the new job may also be a bore. If the job were really important, somebody now on the payroll would have had it shoved down his throat. If it were interesting, an insider would have snaffled it. Therefore, do not dwell on boredom in general; be specific. If possible, be specific about something the new outfit doesn't do at all.

No advancement opportunities is another good "reason for leaving" and has the secondary value of pointing out, that money is a consideration.

After landing another job, the reason for leaving should change to *for professional advancement,* freeing *boredom* and *no advancement opportunities* for re-use. *For professional advancement* is a meaningless phrase and therefore does not conjure up unpleasant associations; furthermore, it has a pious sound like the running of water when the bathroom door is closed.

AGENCIES

After you have called your friends, you might as well call one or two of the better employment agencies. But remember; an agency is one more layer between you and the man you want to see. Fill out their form, and stuff the envelope with several of your resumes and a note telling them to MOVE. Now forget about agencies; you won't hear from them until the show is over.

CLASSIFIED ADS

Next consult the classified section of the Sunday paper. Mark the prospects. If you cannot dredge from your memory the name of a single man who works there, call Engineering Personnel and ask them to send you an employment form.

Chances are there is no Engineering Personnel, but this artlessly snobbish approach can save you a lot of time. If you are using your current employer's telephone, it can be important not to waste time with duplicate explanations lest the wrong person walk in on you. In addition you will avoid making out the wrong form. Long before a Personnel Department produces a branch called Engineering Personnel, it produces a bud, "our Mr Jones," and a special form. Mr Jones and his form cannot be avoided if the organization is approached from the bottom. The best you can hope for is to see the right man on the first try.

Four interviews a day is all you can manage; and your average will be more like two or three. You cannot sneak out often enough to do the job. Face up to your responsibilities and get sick for two days. Monday and Tuesday are good, logical days; and Wednesday morning you can complain about spending the long weekend in bed. If you stay up late Tuesday night making out forms, you'll look weary enough to play the part convincingly.

SALARY

When you make out personnel forms in advance, there is generally a blank entitled "salary expected" or "minimum salary." Do not fill these out.

However, the embarrassing question of money has to be discussed. You must grasp the basic fact that your potential employer lives in a dreamworld when it comes to salaries. There may come a time when you will have to pretend to believe his dream. But whether you intend to worship or scoff, it behooves you to learn the score as soon as possible.

You may have noticed articles in engineering magazines from time to time gleefully explaining that job satisfaction of professional employes has been proved, in a recent survey, to be almost independent of pay. In the management type of magazine, the editorial slant differs only slightly. There they catalog all the "inducements" that are rated more important than pay. It is never really clear how the survey was made. But we, as potential members of a representative sample, know that the details of polling do not really matter. We weren't born yesterday. We know what they want to hear; and so did our colleagues who answered those questions.

The first article of management's salary faith is: No really worthwhile *professional* man ranks money first.

The second article of faith is usually phrased, "We pay the man, not the job." Now this statement is less than half true. The company has a top price it is willing to pay for the job to be done. However, it is flexible. It is willing to pay less. How much less depends on the man. It is rude, even foolhardy, to challenge a man's beliefs when they are rooted in necessity.

One of the favorite gambits of personnel interviewers and even of chief engineers is to ask you what you look for in a job. Answer as follows:

1) Challenging work, interesting work, etc.

2) Congenial companions, or anything else you can think of.

3) Money, expressed diffidently, like "And then there's salary, of course."

After you have been put through your paces, perhaps by a team who sweat you in shifts, your turn finally comes. But if you are not sharp, you'll miss it. Your interviewer asks you "what salary you require." In front of him is your resume with your last salary heading the list. *Don't panic!* Refuse to answer. Point out gently that it is not really a question of what you "require" so much as what you have been offered elsewhere. At this point you have broken contact with the salary he sees before him. He is on the defensive. He has no conceivable way of checking on any figure you care to mention. At this point, my friend you're on your own. ■

Personnel offices turn to computers

Computerized personnel files have caught on at last. They are giving a new, higher status to the job of company personnel director

THE JOB of personnel director in a company used to be a stopping off place for a man on the way up or on the way down. Now it is achieving a status comparable with marketing and production.

This assessment by a company executive is justified by the steady, inexorable advance of the computer into corporate personnel offices.

In the early 1950s, companies used card sorters to help speed personnel searches.

By 1960, divisions of several major companies were programming employee data files on computers.

It is only recently, however, that computerized personnel files have really begun to catch on, in industry around the world.

Typically, a computer system is built from existing personnel records—plus a lot of data that management used to disregard because of the difficulty of storing and retrieving information manually.

Basic data can be recorded on tape using 400 to 800 characters, each character representing a different letter or number.

More detailed information, often incorporating some form of skills inventory, can run to 3,000 or 4,000 characters.

Automated programme—Not surprisingly, what is probably the most comprehensive automated personnel programme in the US belongs to IBM. Its Personnel Data System was phased into 28 location systems, including 13 divisional units, and one file maintained at headquarters.

Unifying the system wasn't easy. Most locations had developed their own programmes, which had to be modified to fit the special requirements of the central unit.

At IBM, corporate headquarters keeps less information on rank-and-file than do lower levels within the company. In the field, as many as 4,000 characters of data on the individual are maintained. In corporate-level files, there are as many as 600 to 800 characters.

In effect, the system keeps the bulk of the information where it is most used. When a division has to go outside itself for hard-to-find talent, the headquarters file is employed.

One such search, in the US, aimed at finding a man who could consult with Apollo moon-project engineers on induction motors, uncovered no less than 150 experts, three of whom possessed Ph.Ds.

Computer virtuosity—While placement activity demonstrates a system's flair, it is in the preparation of manpower reports that the system displays its virtuosity.

A typical system turns out dozens of recurring reports at varying intervals, and dozens more on request. Periodic reports often include manpower counts by location, job type, pay, direct or indirect labour, and so forth. Less frequent tallies might project manpower needs by profession.

Special requests cover all manner of topics. Payrolls of whole divisions can be compared, and the job backgrounds of chronic absentees can be studied in detail, leading to possible solutions to the absentee problem.

At Hughes Aircraft Co., one of the simplest reports, a manpower head count by shift, job title, pay, and sex, has become a top management staple.

This is because it provides a key to how well schedules are being met. It shows at a glance the accuracy of manpower forecasts, and signals any abnormally high turnover rate.

"If the report is even a half day late," says personnel director David A. Bowdoin, "our statistics office is swamped with inquiries."

Hughes is now working on a corporate-wide skills inventory. So are many other science-orientated companies.

When Eastman Kodak started to build its information system, it found that some data were duplicated as many as 35 times at different sources for a single employee. Terms were used inconsistently, and information was not available when it was needed. Now Kodak has a centralized computer file of 40,000 employees.

Obtaining information — To get skills information, some companies use an open-ended questionnaire. At Esso, however, information can come to the programmer "on the back of an envelope", as the employee benefits manager puts it.

Standard Oil and its affiliates are cramming their computerized files with perhaps more material than any other company. At Esso Metropolitan Service Corp., for example, the tapes contain a minimum of 4,000 characters on each of the company's 8,000 employees.

Among the items on file are the foreign language skills of each employee, a daily attendance record and even the telephone number of the family doctor.

Advocates of a "fixed vocabulary" survey of skills include McGraw-Hill and IBM. These companies present employees with a long list of all the skills that can be related to the company's business—IBM'S comprehensive survey runs to 46 pages.

Each entry has its own code number, reducing the programming time. But the system is not so adaptable to unforeseen needs.

At RCA, programme designers averted this pitfall but fell into another —by amassing too much information and clogging the system. Subsequently, such items as hobbies and interests were expunged from the record.

At least two companies have attempted to tape applicants as well as employees. IBM's system contains "thousands" of outside people.

Smaller companies, too, are computerizing their personnel departments. Information Science, Inc., a US firm that specializes in data processing in personnel, offers a package programme for companies with 5,000 employees or less.

For the future, personnel men foresee a network of desk-top computers wired to a television screen. These computers will respond instantly to any conceivable manpower problem that a manager might have. ∎

Computer for job hunting...

Computer helps engineers find the "right" job

For the job-hunting engineer and for the engineer-hunting recruiter, the National Manpower Register (MNR) offers a unique combination of "one-stop shopping services." By simply feeding a résumé or a job description into a real-time General Electric computer in Bethesda, Md., NMR is able to match quickly and effortlessly the right engineer with the right job.

"We save the job hunter and the recruiter time when speedy placement is imperative, and we provide the precise job openings or applicants in moments from the central computer file. This means one résumé or job description, submitted to us, is all a job hunter or a recruiter need give out to find all the possibilities available to him immediately," Ed Dear, NMR's executive vice-president comments.

Starting the search. All an engineer has to do is send his résumé to NMR, headquartered in New York City. There, placement counsellors analyze it and code it into the memory of the computer. Once in the system, the résumé is continuously compared with hundreds of job openings. The computer's matches are then examined by the counsellor, and interviews are scheduled between company and applicant.

The service is free to applicants; fees are paid by the employers.

Occasionally, the placement staff, headed by George Sadek who has five years' experience as an industrial engineer, will come across an applicant whose background, they believe, would be particularly suited to a company that may not have any openings at the moment. That company is contacted anyway for as Sadek explains, "There is virtually no company that won't look at (and hire) a good technical applicant, whether or not there is an opening at the time."

Additional exposure. In addition to individual placement, NMR conducts Interview Centers throughout the country. Known as Project Search, these centers bring together companies and job applicants who, because of distance, would not normally have an opportunity to talk with each other. Only last month, Lockheed-Houston traveled to Washington to interview engineers whose résumés matched Lockheed's job specifications and who indicated a willingness to move to another area.

To explore further possibilities, NMR also sends résumés and job specs to 25 affiliated agencies all over the United States.

Problems. Of course, not every engineer can expect to find his "dream job" through NMR. Companies, even though faced with an engineering shortage, are no longer interested in hiring "warm bodies." What they want are applicants who have an up-to-date knowledge of modern technology. Thus, the easiest engineer to place is the recent graduate. Often, companies prefer him to an experienced engineer. Sadek attributes this to today's engineering education.

"Ever since 1960, engineering education from a technical point of view has been far-superior to that of years ago. The education an engineering student received in 1950 was not too different from that of 1930, because the post-war technology had not begun to blossom."

At the other end of the ladder, just about the hardest engineers to place are those over 40 who ended their education the day they graduated and have thereby let themselves become obsolete.

Another difficult applicant is the one who has been caught in what Sadek calls the "wage trap." That is, his salary outstrips his working experience. This is usually the outcome when companies stockpile their engineers.

For example, a firm will hire the ten best graduates of an engineering school. To keep them, they are given continual wage increases. But in actuality, only a few earn their salaries. The others dabble with projects that a fresh-from-classroom engineer could easily do. As a result, when the over-paid, underworked engineer goes job hunting, he finds his background isn't worth his high salary to other companies.

How it began. NMR is the offspring of the now-defunct Engineering Societies Personnel Services, a placement organization that was run jointly by several engineering societies. Two years ago, it began operating as part of Career, Inc. (*PE* — Apr. 11, '66, p.98); last September, it became an independent corporation.

Since then, NMR has placed approximately 750 applicants. The "fall-off" rate (people who remain on their jobs less than 3 months) has been less than 1%.

While most of NMR's clients want jobs close to home, or at least within the boundaries of the U.S., the agency is also able to satisfy those who yearn for more exotic locations. Just recently, NMR helped send two engineers off to an island in the Persian Gulf at $16,000 a year and a $500 monthly allotment to cover living expenses. Prerequisites: engineering experience and a wife.

How secure can you keep your design secrets?

Industrial espionage is big in today's news and is growing. Most dangerous leaks are not through electronic bugs and taps but through open mouths and snoopers

Greatest threat to our national security in these days of cold war and hot technology is not the loss of military secrets but of technical ones. And greatest threat to a company in these days of cold calculation and hot marketing is not the loss of sales plans but of development and technical ones.

The familiar picture of the cloak-and-dagger operator and the current news pictures of the tap and bug artists are both far-fetched in design and engineering espionage. The prosaic fact is that such glamorous methods play a very second fiddle to two others: the blabbermouth (for whatever reason) and the industrial spy who masquerades as a visitor, supplier, or repairman.

The biggest gap in our security—national or proprietary—is the open mouth.

New-style spying. Espionage has been linked by the lay public with intrigue between nations, epitomized by the James Bond series and its imitators. However, even international spying has changed character in recent years. It is now more concerned with industrial processes and products—the missiles, the bombs, the new weapons and methods—

than it is with troop dispositions. It is a form of intellectual, rather than physical thievery. So, too, in industry itself: The pilfering is of ideas, much more important in the continuing healthy growth of a business than physical property.

Thirteen of 15 high-ranking engineers we queried on industrial spying say it is no worse now than formerly. But most of them are in conventional metalworking plants, making traditional products in which model-to-model design advance is not very great. *Harvard Business Review*, a few years back, found that 27% of 200 executives felt that spying and other undercover activities were on the increase in their own industries. Yet 50% admitted they'd pirate a key man to get a competitive secret—and 69% insisted their competitors would.

Marketplace competition seems to have spurred much of the espionage. At least so says Norman Jaspan, who runs a counter-espionage agency employing 500 full-time "management engineers." He estimates that several hundred white-collar thieves are caught stealing company secrets every year, and that five times that number are never tried because of the attendant undesirable publicity. Over 70% of the trade-secret thefts are by supervisors and above, in Jaspan's expert opinion.

Drawing the line. Sen Edward V. Long (D-Mo) and his Senate Judiciary Committee have moved into a full-fledged probe of industrial espionage. It may reveal the need for new legislation, but, said *Business Week:*

"Granted the line is a fine one between what's right and what's wrong in, say, the search for competitive information. But 90 times out of 100, top executives have a pretty good idea of where the line lies. It is their responsibility—as James Roche [president of GM, testifying before the Senate] firmly acknowledged—to stake out standards of ethical conduct and stick to them. Beyond that, it is their responsibility to make sure their subordinates—and their lawyers—understand that they are bound by the same standards."

How secrets slip out of plants

Before World War II, a number of Japanese visited the Zeiss plant in Germany. They were asked to leave their cameras at the door, but it became obvious to the alert guides that several of the visitors were using buttonhole cameras. So when the tour ended, Zeiss officials invited the visitors to watch a new company film in a small projection room. They did—while Zeiss passed X-rays through the room to ruin the film in their concealed cameras.

It is not always possible to detect —or to counter so cleverly—the industrial spy. He may be a supplier, a consultant, a friend, a VIP visitor, a foreign diplomat sponsored by the government. Consider the recent case of Swedish Air Force Col Stig Wennerström, who spied here for the USSR and got many aircraft and missile companies to supply classified data. He said it was easy; companies were almost overeager to do a favor for Sweden. But his ethics were so mixed up that he also gave the USSR something like $300 million worth of Swedish secrets.

Most industrial espionage. is neither that glamorous nor that dangerous, but it is just as easy. It is startling to find how much people will "spill their brains," even without prompting—not only about processes, equipment, and prospects but also about morale, internal conflicts, sales plans, and all the rest. There is something in the human ego that tends to make us talk like a running brook to any admiring stranger . . . and most spies are very personable people.

Easy entree. Getting into a plant is usually very easy. There are occasions that require subterfuge, when a spy must go in under the cover of someone else, but these are relatively rare. In most cases, the spy will get in simply by not advertising his particular interest or connection.

Once in, it takes little to give a spy a lead. A visibly blocked-off area, if inquired about casually, will usually bring some such remark as, "We're developing a new . . . there —very hush-hush." So the spy knows development is under way and in the prototype stage. Occasional references will usually add flesh to this skeleton. Suppliers, subcontractors, and consultants can add more—and often do.

The carelessly exposed prototype

part, the sketch on an engineer's blackboard, the request for data on some unusual subject, the hastily draped sample, the overheard comment or phone conversation, the careful avoidance of certain topics —all these are noted by the skilled.

Loose talk. Where do leaks come from? Disloyal employees. Incautious diemakers. Supply salesmen who didn't or did get the order. Executives who talk too much.

A skilled spy puts bits and pieces together. He may look through windows and fences, or rent a helicopter to verify some of what he's heard, but often he doesn't have to. A consultant said recently that, given the knowledge that somebody has achieved a new idea, he can duplicate it relatively quickly. He would even prefer not to have too many details, because this knowledge might restrict his own solution to the point where it would conflict with the patent the original developer is getting. All he wants is the initial direction; he'll take it from there.

Watching the Fords. Detroit is America's cloak-and-camera capital. On every street corner, most years, are photographers with pictures of next year's models at $25 a print. Actually, the spy system among automotive companies is a tight fraternity. Chrysler has "competitive study engineers" and Ford has "product information specialists," but the industry calls the whole bunch G-2 or G-4 in traditional Army style.

They work from treetops or farmhouses around test tracks, in corner bars and the Detroit Athletic Club, looking less for next year's model ideas as those of two years hence. They haunt tool shops, studios, tire shops, design firms, and component makers. They want to know what's on—or just off—drawing boards, to anticipate weaknesses and strengths for competitive advertising, but more importantly to tell "what not to do," as the retired Ford styling chief, George Walker, puts it. (A few years back, one maker found nine TV cameras behind ventilators in his design room.) They assemble, from bits and pieces of information, mockups of competing cars, making

sure their own planned styling isn't too close.

All of them lock wastebaskets at styling centers, shred waste paper and burn it; all of them require special badges for styling personnel. They destroy mockups and sketches, build walls and screens at exposed points, have police with whistles and 2-way radios. All have guards with telescopes in plant offices. GM Styling Center has an automatic curtain puller triggered by airplane or helicopter sounds.

All have made decoy models that tour their test tracks; all paint new models black to reduce depth perception on telescope-lens cameras. Any amateur attempting to sell one company's data to another would be reported to the police. There is honor, it seems, even among thieves.

Even so, all auto companies have detailed data on each other's models. Ford even had a clay mockup of the Chevelle a year before GM introduced it.

Ethical espionage. This is almost always completely ethical and proper "spying." It shows a lack of originality perhaps, but is entirely accepted in our present business code. As long as no underhanded methods are used, there is no violation of the code—but the borderline is hazy and gray, as in all such instances.

Essentially, in modern business, the most precious commodity is time. So security must consider time primarily. The plans, the projects, the market research—these are most important. The prototype is somewhat less important; it's much farther down the road in time. The test models are still less important. The completed product itself, not important at all—any competitor can lay hands on it if he wants to.

An alert spy is particularly conscious of printed and published material: prints, manuals, booklets, papers, articles, proposals, quotes, annual reports, movies, and all the rest of it. He can literally pick out the sentence in an annual report in which the company president veils a research expenditure in some new area, or the lack of some comment that suggests a new direction in

company thinking. Other published material is much more specific.

Thus far the spy has been doing legitimate information gathering. But on occasion he can beg, borrow, or steal quite specific engineering information—unless everything not in immediate use is under lock and key or is burned. Most organizations simply are unwilling to go to all that trouble, so the information leaks to the spy in waste paper, doodles, printers' proofs, unguarded queries, knowing looks.

Quite literally, the old adage is true: "The best way to keep a secret is by having it known to only one people." The secret of Coca-Cola has been kept this way since 1886. That of Lea & Perrins Worcestershire sauce has been maintained for 125 years; only two company officers know the whole secret at any given time. But most products are much more complex than these, and present methods and formulas must be known to many.

Electronic snooping. The wire tap and the hidden microphone have been extensively publicized in connection with industrial espionage, but their importance is overemphasized. Less commonly talked about are closed-circuit television and automatic cameras, also devices for "surreptitious fact-finding" or "eavesdropping." They have been used, particularly at executive levels, in finance and in the chemical, drug, electronics, and toy industries, but they are not as important as older, more familiar methods.

Senate hearings since 1961 have brought to light the fact that there is even now no adequate penalty for the Peeping Tom who invades your privacy with an electronic device. What's more, the devices themselves, constantly being improved, can be purchased at the nearest radio store, in most cases with no questions asked. Some require no direct connection either to the listener or to a telephone or radio.

Their legitimacy as an aid to law enforcement is still in question, particularly because they lend themselves so well to the obtaining of grounds for divorce and the evidence in bookmaking, the dope traffic, commercial sex, and racketeering. Companies have used them to "monitor" (a high-class word for spying) employees—a highly dubious application. And a number of engineers have been engaged in working out tap and bug detectors and communication devices that are presumably free of danger from either.

Hiding a bug. It is possible to bug a man's office or home with a device hidden in dozens of different ways that will transmit to a tape recorder or broadcast a considerable distance. The notorious transmitter in a martini olive with the antenna disguised as a toothpick, featured in Senate hearings, is matched and surpassed by devices so small that they can be fed to a mouse or strapped on a cockroach.

A telephone can be tapped or bugged easily. One new device makes it possible from any telephone to dial a desired number, except for the last digit, blow a whistle to cut out the central-office ringing impulse, then to dial the last number and be on a direct line to the desired telephone. Some of these devices can be installed in less than 10 minutes, so almost anybody anywhere can be a victim. Any competent electrician can do the job.

Counter measures. As a result, counter-espionage organizations have come into being. They use radio detectors to detect simple clandestine signals, spectrum analyzers and oscilloscopes for more complex ones, digital readout devices to check bugged lines, and so on. But it is still startlingly cheap and easy to bug or tap, expensive and difficult to detect.

California's 1963 law about these devices got its first tryout in March, when San Mateo County authorities caught the president and an ex-convict foreman of one plastics company bugging the office of the president of another. The equipment was a simple microphone at the window, wires through a geranium bed, and a tape recorder. The gardener found the wires—and the police were called. This explained why Bott's Line Inc, Redwood City, was losing contracts to its rival (a recent one was for $11,250, lost by $12.50) for circular traffic-divider disks used on the freeways and called—honest Injun—Bott's Dots.

Dick Cartwright, patternmaker in the employ of James Watt, was imbibing ale one 1780 Saturday night in a pub near London. In his alcoholic enthusiasm, he boasted that Watt was obtaining circular motion from a reciprocating piston. When his companions doubted his word, he chalked a sketch on the bar to prove his point. The sketch was carefully noted by a hanger-on, one James Pickard, Birmingham button manufacturer, who was waiting around in hopes of some such leak. Pickard went to London and patented the crank and connecting rod.

This was certainly not the first instance of idea thievery or of incautious talk by an employee. But the problem was never great until the Industrial Revolution (early 19th Century in England) broke the pattern of small family-owned businesses, multiplying employees and consequent risks of exposure.

Nowadays, with tremendous numbers of employees, disclosure of privy facts is far more prevalent than generally realized. The disclosers are legion: the disaffected employee who wants to get even, the incautious blabbermouth (including particularly the minor executive trying to pose as a big shot among strangers by showing how close he is to decisions), the inventor or originator who has been forced to sign over all rights to his employer or to share credit with an ambitious boss or a committee, the consultant or subcontractor who wants to resell his knowledge, the man tempted by a better job with the competition—or who hopes to be tempted.

This is an extremely difficult set of leaks to stop.

Adopting too many onerous restrictions can tie company operations in knots—as did the old-fashioned small-company practice of requiring all communications to filter through the boss, or the newer one of putting restrictive clauses in employment contracts. The result is that most companies take a calculated risk on everything but key plans and marketing and development data. ∎

How a research pirate operates

Dr Robert Sancier Aries, a brilliant French chemical engineer, taught graduate courses at Brooklyn Polytechnic Institute. He encouraged his students who worked in the labs of large companies to use their everyday work experiences in preparing papers and theses for him. He supplemented this by hiring retired technical personnel and bribing active employees whom he met at scientific meetings.

Thus he built so large a pirating business, with offices here and abroad, that he neglected his classes and Brooklyn Poly dropped him. His "front" was that of a respected consultant, listed in *Who's Who* and serving government and industry.

His undoing began when Merck & Co discovered that he was about to announce a hot new product: a new coccidostat (poultry parasite killer) called mepyrium. A French company that Merck was buying had a license for this product—which turned out to be exactly like the amprolium that Merck has spent $1½ million to develop.

Merck brought suit for piracy, and Aries fled to Europe, where he filed suit against Merck for allegedly buying the French company to get his secrets. He even got a prominent French chemist to backdate his formula five years—but the chemist confessed to the police. And Merck traced its own secret data to Aries through an employee who had been Aries' student and who wrote a peculiar form of ampersand (&). Aries hadn't ever bothered to make a new copy of the stolen flowsheet in his own hand before he passed it out to licensees!

The employee confessed, and a chain of other companies—Rohm & Haas and Sprague Electric among them—found that trusted employees had also passed trade secrets to Aries. The courts awarded judgments of over $21 million in 1964, but Aries is still on the Riviera, claiming that he's been victimized.

What are the rules that engineers live by?

Spying is, of course, essentially a violation of ethics. But no two people agree even on what ethics is. Basically it is following the Golden Rule, which exists in all religions in basically the same form. This is the basis for communal living, but it does not protect the innocent. Just as the careful driver is too often the victim of the careless one, so the ethical engineer is the victim of the unethical one. And each may think the other is at fault.

Engineers are by nature ethical, but business and technology are not. Said J. Lewis Powell: "Technology has no morals; it does not care whether it is used for good or evil. It has no nationality; it does not care whether it is used by friend or foe. It is very efficient, it will eliminate polio or people. It has no feelings; all it cares about is, do you know your mathematics?"

Webster says ethics is "the principles of conduct governing an individual or a profession; standards of behavior."

Professional stance. Every engineering society sooner or later develops a code of ethics, but this guides only the ethical man; it does not stop the unethical one. Professionalism is, unfortunately, not a uniform characteristic, and it is again something that each individual defines differently.

Part of the problem is that a corporation or a company is not and cannot be either professional or ethical; only its members can. And too great concentration on the profit motive at the top will soon permeate the entire structure.

M. A. Fuller of Whirlpool Corp said in an AIEE paper some years back: "As we attempt to satisfy human needs in the context of family living, is it professional to offer to the housewife a gadget to keep the frost off refrigerator evaporator coils that functions every day, frost or no frost, and whose very function hastens the spoiling of meat? Is it professional to offer her new trim on a dishwasher, when what she wants is something that will clean pots and pans? Is it professional to offer her the same old appliance year after year, with the only probability for the future being new trim or production refinements? Rather, is this not the behavior of a technician, who puts on rubber gloves because he has a leaky fountain pen?"

Cue from on high. Fuller could readily have used "ethical" instead of "professional"—because these are basically ethical questions. They exemplify the attitude of too much of industry toward the customer as someone merely to be squeezed. The same attitude often exists within an organization toward men lower down on the totem pole.

Is it any wonder, then, that everyone in the organization becomes unethical, and that unethical attitudes develop toward competitors? There is little difference between cheating a customer and robbing a competitor—which is what spying is. Here are a couple of case studies that illustrate the complication of ethics through the results of a reader survey, taken from a study made by *Chemical Engineering* magazine a couple of years ago:

Case I—The eager applicant. An engineer applicant from a competing company, warming to the interviewer and his subject, discloses trade-secret information. The interviewer files two reports, one detailing the information the interviewee let slip, the other recommending that he not be hired because he talks too much to strangers!

Now for the questions to *Chemical Engineering* readers and their answers: Is it ethical for the interviewer to report information volunteered? 75% of the respondents said yes. If the information resulted from prompting? 78% said no to the question.

Case II—Spy in the sky. A competitor has installed a new process, very sensitive to plant size. You are asked to estimate production costs for your own setup-to-be. You drive by the competitor's plant and can see the new equipment, can even take a photograph. But you can't see the number and size of particular units. Your boss suggests that you rent a helicopter and take a flyover for a closer look.

Again the questions: Is it ethical to take photos through the fence?

77% yes. Is aerial photography ethical? 66% yes. If you believe it unethical, should you reject the boss' idea? 80% yes. If your boss requested aerial photos, would you take them? 72% yes. (Note three things here: that a surprising percentage of engineers think *any* photography is unethical, that aerial photography is much more so, and that most engineers will do what the boss says, even though they believe it to be unethical.)

Raymond C. Baumhart reported in *Harvard Business Review* a study on management that reinforces this point: Most employees take their cues on ethics from their superiors.

Codes of ethics. Thus it behooves the supervisor-engineers to study such codes as that of ASME and the Canons of Ethics for Engineers offered by the Engineers Council for Professional Development. The National Society of Professional Engineers has felt compelled to add 52 rules of professional conduct to the latter—a reminder of the old saw: "God gave Moses 10 commandments 6000 years ago. Since then, man has created over 300,000 laws trying to change them to his way of thinking."

Existing codes are often too broad and "ivory tower." They do not allow for the exigencies of the situation or the engineer's conscience—which are the two major factors in ethical decisions. The very real problem is that the engineer patterns his ethics on those of the business he's in; his connection with a profession, at least in ethics, is rather nebulous. Ethics must, therefore, be taught within the company and in college, so that the individual develops the essential integrity.

The author has at times said: "Morality is should I, or shouldn't I, tell my wife? Ethics is should I, or shouldn't I, tell my partner?"

This is oversimplified, of course, but it illustrates the rather flexible standards we have achieved in business ethics. We differentiate between overhearing a business secret and prying for one, between looking over a competitor's fence and hiring a helicopter to survey his new plant. We damn the Japanese or the Germans or the Russians for copying our ideas while we busily copy those of our competitors. We consider the maiden moral as long as we believe that she yields only to our own blandishments. We believe the other man—particularly a competitor—to be inherently unethical and immoral while we are inherently ethical and moral. And we are curbed in our own flexible interpretations in these matters only when we run afoul of the law. Then we are sincerely surprised.

What we need to curb industrial espionage is perhaps a utopian concept. Management insistence upon completely ethical conduct with respect to customers, employees, and competitors will soon permeate an organization, or many organizations, and these can in time eradicate the evil-doers. But only when the majority declares and observes a clear dividing line in conduct.

"A trade secret may consist of any formula, pattern, device, plan, or compilation that is used in one's business and gives him an opportunity to obtain an advantage over competitors who do not know it or do not use it" (restatement of the Law of Torts, Section 757). Thus almost anything can be designated as a trade secret. So the employee who breaches confidence and the recipient of the confidence can both be disciplined, provided statutes are in existence.

There is no federal statute on trade secrets, however, except 18 USC 1905, which applies to federal government employees who learn trade secrets or other confidential information in the course of their work. The law, on the books for a quarter-century but never invoked, provides for penalties of only $1000 and imprisonment for a year for revealing such secrets to others. John Lindsay, now mayor of New York, tried twice while a Congressman to introduce a broad bill on "Unfair Commercial Activities" (HR5514, 89th Congress, Session I) prepared by bar associations, but it died in committee. The objection was to the phrase "reasonable standards of commercial ethics" in it, which nobody could define accurately. Further, it granted a permanent injunction against use of trade secrets or breaches of confidence, and this is deemed impractical. The increasing frequency of introduction of such bills (another is HR 5578) however, suggests that one may be passed at any time.

A number of the states have statutes, including New York, California, New Jersey, Georgia, Illinois, Pennsylvania, and Nebraska. Others have bills in process. The Federal Trade Commission also has one. Most of these are new laws, so they recognize the trade secret as property. Statutes in other states are limited to theft of physical property, not of ideas or data.

Court protection. Yet the protection of the courts has been invoked on numerous occasions, and sometimes with surprising effectiveness. For example, a company rediscovered an abandoned manufacturing technique, reapplied it, and claimed it as a trade secret of unique value. The court sustained this claim. Again, a high-performance amplifier design was held to be a trade secret even though hundreds had been sold, each complete with a manual showing design and designating all components.

Time-O-Matic Co makes an automatic circuit breaker widely used in display signs. It is not original enough for patent protection but has a mechanism novel enough to be guarded. Recently, two employees decided to go into direct competition. Knowing that copying blueprints is illegal, they set out to memorize every line of the prints, plus essential calculations. This took a year. Then they set up a quickly successful competing company. But the judge stopped them cold, ruling that even carrying mental pictures away from an employer is a violation of confidence.

Paul Steiner made an electric steam iron that was the talk of the trade, but production problems erased his profit. So a big company's offer to take a license attracted him. He asked employees to cooperate with the big company's representatives when they visited for negotiations. They talked freely. Then the big company decided not to take the license—and shortly thereafter came out with a lower-price, more widely distributed competing iron. Steiner sued the giant—and won. ∎

How to plug the leaks

The single best way to plug security leaks is to keep employees contented. Then they won't be tempted to take secrets to other companies—they won't stoop to snoop. Or so executives agreed at an American Management Assn meeting.

This requires a sound and personal personnel policy and high ethics in high places. Norman Jaspan, whose business is gentlemanly counter-espionage, points out that the atmosphere in the executive suite inevitably seeps down into all the other levels. The spectacle of bosses who stab each other in the back (which Jaspan calls "a rite being practiced by thousands of executives in hundreds of businesses"), and who stoop to any trickery to defeat rivals and competitors, will be reflected in loss of ethics all down the line.

Second in importance is to be sure that everyone appreciates the importance of keeping quiet. This requires a firm policy of telling everyone about the areas of secrecy and reminding them continuously of the danger of loose talk.

Defining your terms. Scientists and engineers must be told precisely what trade secrets are. Monsanto, for example, gives each new employee an 18-page security guide and asks him to sign a statement that he will read it. It defines trade secrets, illustrates them, shows their importance and the damage from their loss or disclosure. It attempts to distinguish between professional skills or knowledge and trade secrets, shows the release that the employee must sign when he leaves, covers policy on visitors.

This provides a basis for litigation to protect secrets if necessary, and is an essential factor: The man must have been told, clearly.

Other security steps include the maintenance of effective interaction between employee and supervisor, sensitivity to factors that diminish employee loyalty, and diagnosis of and protection against psychopathic behavior.

Babble. No precautions can really stop the man who discloses vital information unwittingly while still employed. He may do it in conversation—at an engineering meeting, at a cocktail party, or even at home. Unethical companies have in recent years replaced personnel interviewers and others at trade shows and conventions with skilled specialists who consciously try to get men from other companies to "open up."

A room may be bugged or an interview taped, but the commoner device is a talk lubricant, with alcohol as the base. There can be a stimulating modern version of Mata Hari, but much more commonly it's a stimulating conversation about engineering or science—with a few carefully planted questions.

Restrictive clauses. In recent years, the law has been clarified regarding so-called restrictive clauses in employment contracts. Some of the decisions have gone to employees, some to management. The agreement not to compete with a former employer will probably be held invalid by the courts unless it is for a very short time. The courts recognize that a man must work to eat, and the eating is much better if

he works with learned skills.

But a reasonable restrictive clause will be supported, because it is very difficult to differentiate between skill and proprietary knowledge. Say a man has held a key position (defined usually by a substantial salary) in an area involving clearly defined and stated secret processes or special equipment. The court may well enjoin him from even working for a competitor—unless the agreement had no time limit.

The court may also enjoin a man from working for a competitor because he has been privy to "trade secrets" (which can include any formula, pattern, device, or compilation of information like customer lists, sales records, or engineering data) where those "secrets" can be proved vital to the business. What's more, he can be enjoined even if he had no contract, providing he has been told clearly what the company considers to be trade secrets.

Thus when Eugene Mayfield, a former Procter & Gamble junior executive, tried in 1964 to sell the company's 1964-65 marketing plan for Crest toothpaste (considered by P&G as worth a million dollars) to Colgate for $20,000, Colgate informed the authorities, and he was tried and convicted.

In several other recent cases, metalworking companies have been able to prove piracy of ideas or methods by former employees—and those employees have been enjoined from using any even remotely similar data for 10 years, even though they were party to the development.

Patents. Many engineering contracts also include provisions that all patents be assigned to the employer—in some cases even after employment has been terminated. Courts have held that such a clause limited to a year after employment is legal. Other clauses claim patents of employees' immediate relatives as well, and these have been held valid.

So an engineer can be hog-tied by patent restrictions, regardless of what the product is and who pays for the patenting, indicating that the courts recognize the importance of trade secrets. Further, it is easy to prove that development is costly to a company and that secrets are vital; it is difficult to prove the opposite. ∎

INDEX